A
Gui..
to the
Historic
Architecture
of
Piedmont
North
Carolina

The

Richard Hampton

Jenrette *Series*

in Architecture and

the Decorative Arts

A Guide to the Historic Architecture of
Piedmont North Carolina

Catherine W. Bishir *&* **Michael T. Southern**

The

University of

North Carolina

Press

Chapel Hill

& London

Publication of this work has been made possible by a generous grant from the North Carolina Department of Cultural Resources.

© 2003 The University of North Carolina Press
Designed and typeset in Adobe Garamond and
Franklin Gothic by Eric M. Brooks
Manufactured in the United States of America
The paper in this book meets the guidelines for permanence
and durability of the Committee on Production Guidelines for
Book Longevity of the Council on Library Resources.
Library of Congress Cataloging-in-Publication Data
Bishir, Catherine W.
A guide to the historic architecture of Piedmont North
Carolina / Catherine W. Bishir and Michael T. Southern.
    p. cm. — (The Richard Hampton Jenrette series in architecture and
the decorative arts)
Includes bibliographical references and index.
ISBN 0-8078-2772-x (alk. paper) —
ISBN 0-8078-5444-1 (pbk.: alk. paper)
1. Architecture — North Carolina — Guidebooks. I. Southern,
Michael T. II. Title. III. Series: Richard Hampton Jenrette series in
architecture & the decorative arts.
NA730.N8 B492   2003
720'.9756 — dc21   2002015364

cloth   07 06 05 04 03   5 4 3 2 1
paper   07 06 05 04 03   5 4 3 2 1

Page i: *Zimmerman Farm, with family in foreground,
Davidson County (DV9)*
Pages iv–v: *Durham skyline
(Photograph by David Cera and Tom Loter)*

This city . . . is situated in the Old North State, — the happy medium State between North and South, combining the strength of both sections of the country, in the Piedmont district in a climate with air and sunshine resembling that of the famous lake country of north Italy. In this favored section cities are strung all the way down to Charlotte and Gastonia, as pearls upon a connecting thread. The trains are hardly out of sight of the one [town] before the other begins to appear, all busy, prosperous, growing, and likewise interested in higher things as their churches and school buildings and community structures amply show.

Edward Rondthaler, 1923, in
The Memorabilia of Fifty Years,
1877 to 1927 (Winston-Salem, 1928)

Contents

Historical and Geographical Maps

Regional and Site Maps

Preface

This book, a guide to historic architecture in Piedmont North Carolina, is the third in a three-volume series that also includes volumes on Eastern North Carolina (1996) and Western North Carolina (1999). The series is part of the educational and outreach program of the State Historic Preservation Office, North Carolina Division of Archives and History. Each book is intended as a field guide and reference for the traveler, resident, student, and preservationist with an interest in North Carolina's historic architecture. Although too large for a coat pocket, it is meant to fit in a knapsack, glove compartment, or bike basket, for it is intended to accompany the traveler and visitor in the field as well as resting on a bookshelf.

Originally the guide was envisioned as a single volume to cover the entire state, but at the suggestion of the University of North Carolina Press, the three-volume format was adopted as offering a more convenient and portable size for region-by-region use. This approach has also proved to offer a greater opportunity for focusing on the regions that delineate the state's varied landscape and shape its architectural, cultural, economic, and social history. For it is not so much the grandeur or fame of its individual landmarks that defines North Carolina's architectural heritage, but its intensely regional and local character, the sense of place, which captivates the traveler and sustains the residents in this old state. And it is that same sense of localism and regionalism that seems increasingly at risk in the twenty-first century. At a pace and scale unimaginable when we began this series, urban conglomerations are spreading into the traditional small-town and rural landscapes, and familiar patterns of farming, century-old bastions of manufacturing, and customary trading and political centers are vanishing in a blink of the eye. Although both the East and the West are changing fast, the speed and extent of change are most startling in the Piedmont, where population growth and economic transformations have concentrated in the last decades.

The three regional guides follow a familiar division of the state that reflects differences in topography, history, and architectural patterns. North Carolina is a large state, some 500 miles wide. Its three principal regions run roughly parallel to the diagonal line of the coast. The eastern 40 percent of the state is a gently rising, level land of tidewater and coastal plain dominated by sandy or loam soils and predominantly pine forests. This section was the first to be settled by Europeans. Beginning in the late seventeenth century, people of mainly British and African stock developed a maritime commercial agriculture and small port towns. The Piedmont—"foot of the mountain"—is a rolling country across the

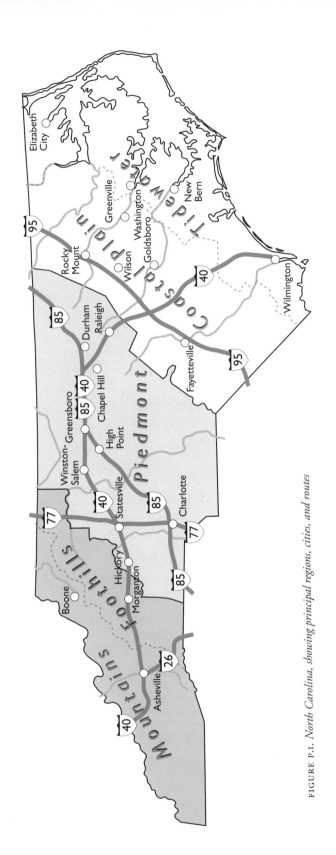

FIGURE P.I. *North Carolina, showing principal regions, cities, and routes*

central portion with chiefly clay soils and mixed hardwood and pine forests. In the mid-eighteenth century a tide of settlers came from the mid-Atlantic area and Virginia and created a society of smaller farms distant from markets, where in the nineteenth century waterpower and railroad networks supported industrial and urban development. In the west the mountains rise against and beyond the Blue Ridge, the Eastern Continental Divide; the timeworn slopes are cloaked in hardwood and evergreen forests. Much of this zone remained the domain of the Cherokees until after the American Revolution. Difficulties of transportation kept the region one of isolated rural communities and small towns until railroads and highways spurred industrial and resort development in the late nineteenth and early twentieth centuries.

North Carolina's topography intensified the economic and cultural differences among the regions. The coastline is a treacherous one, and barrier islands known as the Outer Banks hampered oceangoing trade and prevented the development of a port metropolis. Without a principal city, and with rivers and other natural arteries of trade leading from the backcountry into neighboring states rather than into a North Carolina port, the sections of the state remained distinct and isolated from one another. By 1810 a Raleigh journalist reported that "between the Eastern and Western parts of this State is as great dissimilarity in the face of the country, productions, and means of subsistence as usually exists between different and widely separated nations."

Even after rail networks developed and industrialization worked its changes, the population remained predominantly rural and dispersed, and regional differences persisted. Amid the urban growth of the late nineteenth and early twentieth centuries, little towns and cities combined intense localism with spirited competition for growth. The makeup of the population also strengthened the sense of localism, for the state received scant in-migration after the eighteenth century. While thousands of people left the state, few came in, so that for many years the proportion of native-born residents was among the highest in the nation. The late twentieth century brought a transforming infusion of immigration from other states and countries, a pattern that intensified with the turn of the twenty-first century. Although North Carolina ranks tenth among the states in population, it is still one of the least urbanized. Only toward the end of the twentieth century did a majority of its people live in urban areas. This recent and rapid urbanization, which concentrated in the Piedmont, continued a dispersed pattern among many small towns and cities until the late twentieth century. Toward the end of the century, the trend shifted toward coalescing urban zones of people and wealth around the principal Piedmont cities. Unprecedented immigration and urbanization are blurring old boundaries. Nevertheless, in the Piedmont as well as the coastal and mountain regions, many communities retain their long-standing sense of local and regional identity, including growing respect for the architectural heritage of the distant and not so distant past.

We imagine this guide serving as a friend might when introducing a visitor to the region and its communities: sketching a brief history of the place and outlining the human saga the architecture depicts, then pointing out and relating a story or two about the famous landmarks, strolling through the oldest neighborhoods, and discovering some of the special places that make each community itself. Our purpose is to present examples of common and uncommon architectural traditions, styles, and forms that define the character of each place and that compose broader regional and state patterns. This field guide is meant to complement existing studies. For fuller treatment of localities, the reader is encouraged to refer to the several published local surveys; for analysis of architectural practice and the state's architectural development, the reader may turn to *Architects and Builders in North Carolina, North Carolina Architecture,* and other works cited in the bibliography.

No guidebook can include every important landmark in each community and county. Selection and presentation of entries have followed several rules of thumb. Because the guide is aimed at the traveling public, we have generally selected properties that may be seen reasonably well from a public thoroughfare. In a few instances of exceptionally important buildings, descriptions but no locational information are provided for properties not visible or accessible to the public—chiefly when understanding of the region's architecture would be incomplete without acknowledging these places.

In choosing examples of representative local building types, we have focused on those on readily accessible rather than remote roads and on those that are convenient to other properties mentioned in the text. (The selections are *not* intended to represent a list of properties worthy of preservation, which are far more numerous than can be included here.) We have also given preference to buildings that are occupied and in reasonably good condition. Many important properties have been omitted because they are in ruinous or vulnerable condition, drastic alterations have taken place, or vegetation or distance shields them from public view. Over the period of this project, conditions have changed for many properties. Some originally included have fallen into disuse or decay, while others that were in dire straits have been rescued for new life. In this respect, we have tried to make the book as up to date as possible; however, circumstances are always changing, and we welcome updated information.

Several other factors affected the choice of properties. Different levels of architectural survey fieldwork and research from town to town and county to county are reflected by more or less complete representation and information for various towns and counties. So, too, we chose some individual properties over others when a strong history was available that illustrated trends in the region, or where a good story captured the mood of the time or place. We have also focused attention on those communities and areas with unusually rewarding concentrations of historic architecture accessible to public view.

On the other hand, it has not been feasible to treat some kinds of buildings as fully as they deserve within the entries. Much of the architecture in the Piedmont dates from the second half of the twentieth century; in the last few years architectural historians have just begun to record and analyze the landmarks and general patterns of this era. We have cited only a few outstanding landmarks of the era and hope that future studies will address the heritage of the recent past more broadly. In addition, over the long span of the state's architectural history, its character has been defined by the prevalence of very simple, often rudimentary and short-lived buildings that have stood by the thousands, from the log and earthfast frame houses and barns of the eighteenth and nineteenth centuries to the log and frame tobacco barns, sheds and outbuildings, and modest workers' and tenant houses of the late nineteenth and early twentieth centuries. Today, because of the late twentieth-century revolution in agriculture and the spread of urbanization, coupled with the stunning decline in manufacturing of textiles, tobacco, and other goods, many of these are vanishing; particular examples are too fragile to cite reliably. Hence we have discussed these as important types in the introduction and mentioned their previous or continued presence in the landscape. Travelers who keep an eye open for them will see scores of small farmhouses, barns, and other outbuildings along the back roads—and even in view of interstate highways—and clusters of workers' houses and mills in dozens of towns.

PRIVATE AND PUBLIC PLACES

In using this guide, especially in rural areas, the reader is urged to remember that unless otherwise specified, the properties presented are *private and not open to the public*. Where private properties are easily visible from a public thoroughfare, attention is called to them as parts of the architectural landscape. This does *not* constitute an invitation to visit or trespass! Users of this book are strictly enjoined to respect the privacy of residents and owners—to remain on the public right-of-way, not to set foot or wheel on private property uninvited, and to admire and learn from afar.

Where places are open to the public, this status is indicated. For the most part, detailed descriptions of interior features are restricted to properties that are open to the public in some fashion. As opening hours vary, visitors are advised to contact local chambers of commerce for information on local sites open to the public, bed and breakfast inns, and other businesses operating in historic buildings. The North Carolina Department of Travel and Tourism and state visitors' centers on principal highways offer information about places open to the public. Local and regional guides are also available, and many regions and communities have informative web sites.

ORGANIZATION OF THE GUIDE

The guidebook is organized by regional clusters of counties, an arrangement meant to assist in organizing a visit and in understanding regional architectural patterns. As in most southern states, North Carolina's principal geographical and political unit traditionally has been the county, which encompasses rural as well as urban places. The county unit is the building block for this guide. Map and entry codes (such as AM 1, WK 2, etc.) employ the county code system used for the statewide architectural survey program.

For the Piedmont, the order of county presentation is more complex than in the other two volumes, and it proceeds in a geographical order that necessarily leaps occasionally from one zone to another. It begins with Raleigh, the capital, and ends with Charlotte, the biggest city, with a circuitous path between. This order is meant to accommodate both geographical contiguity and cultural patterns in as balanced a fashion as possible.

Each county unit typically begins with the county seat. Subsequent entries are arranged in geographical order—typically clockwise from the north, thence east, south, and west—around the county, though in some cases geography or history requires a different order. Within towns, the presentation usually begins with the courthouse or the town center, then proceeds around the town core and then outward to outlying properties—in clockwise, linear, or radiating order, depending on the layout of the community. Properties are treated either as individual entries or as components of group entries, according to the density of the area and relationships among buildings in a community or neighborhood. Cross-references to properties treated elsewhere in this volume are denoted with an asterisk; those cited in the Eastern or Western volumes are denoted by a # sign.

MAPS

Simplified county maps are grouped following the introduction; selected town maps appear within the text. These are necessarily much-reduced depictions of complex places, showing only a few of the many roads and streets that weave through the landscape. Four-digit SR numbers indicate secondary roads, which are part of the state-maintained highway system along with North Carolina (NC) and United States (US) highways. These roads have designated names as well as numbers, but for rural roads only the numbers are employed in this guide, for brevity and correlation with standard maps.

Serious travelers in the countryside are encouraged to acquire county-by-county road maps. These are available in commercially published atlases and individually from the Department of Transportation. These complement the official state transportation map from the Department of Transportation. On-going changes in the road system, including new construction and widespread renumbering (and new street numbers to conform to the 911 system), render even the most current maps outdated. We have striven to make the locations clear and accurate, but we expect that readers, like the authors, will sometimes get lost and find something even more interesting down a winding back road.

The county, municipal, and regional maps for the series were planned and designed by Michael Southern using computer graphics software, with guidance from Heidi Perov of the UNC Press. For this volume, Deborah Tharrington prepared the base outline maps with major roads for all counties and many municipalities.

ACKNOWLEDGMENTS

In the early 1980s, the North Carolina State Historic Preservation Office (Division of Archives and History, Department of Cultural Resources) undertook to produce a guide to the historic architecture of the state, based primarily on the existing fieldwork and research in the Survey and Planning Branch of the Historic Preservation Office. The first phase of the project was completed in 1984–85 by the Historic Preservation Office with assistance from a 1983 grant from the National Endowment for the Humanities (RS-20386-83) to the Federation of North Carolina Historical Societies, a nonprofit affiliate organization of the division. During subsequent years, additional fieldwork has been conducted, the format has been modified, and much new information gained from recent county and town surveys and National Register of Historic Places nominations has been incorporated.

The principal source of historical, architectural, and locational information is the extensive collection of survey site files and National Register of Historic Places nomination files, located in the Survey and Planning Branch. These files reflect fieldwork and research conducted since the late 1960s as part of the ongoing statewide architectural survey and National Register of Historic Places programs in North Carolina. Many individuals—too numerous to list in full—have contributed to this growing body of information as staff members and consultants, and their contributions are gratefully acknowledged.

For this volume we have depended on the fieldwork, research, and photographs from many town and county surveys conducted by a variety of architectural historians over the years as part of the statewide survey program. Some of these friends have also assisted by recommending properties for inclusion, drafting initial texts, and reviewing the manuscript. These include the following:

Ann Alexander—Southern Pines;
David and Allison Harris Black—Burlington (Allison), other properties
   and districts;
Kim Withers Brengle—Gaston Co.;
Claudia Roberts Brown—Durham, Eden, Madison;
Marvin Brown—Granville Co., Greensboro, Lincoln Co.;
Patricia Dickinson—Badin, Alamance Co., other properties and districts;
Donna Dodenhoff—Stanly Co.;
Marty Dreyer—Spencer;
Brian Eades—Cleveland Co.;
Linda Edmisten—Raleigh;
Brent Glass—industrial sites;
Heather Hallenburg—Rockingham;
Sidney Halma—Catawba Co.;
Tom Hanchett—Charlotte, Mecklenburg Co.;
Michael and Martha Hartley—Salem, Bethania;
Davyd Foard Hood—Pinehurst, Rowan Co., and other properties and
   districts;
Peter Kaplan—Cabarrus Co.;
Kelly Lally—Wake Co.;
John Larson—Salem (Winston-Salem);
Diane Lea—Durham, Madison;
Mary Ann Lee—Monroe, Raleigh;
Ruth Little—Caswell Co., Durham Co., Eden, Greensboro, Iredell Co.,
   Moore Co., Orange Co., and other properties and districts;
Vickie Mason—Louisburg;
Kirk Mohney—Catawba Co., Davie Co., Yadkin Co.;
Melanie Murphy—Henderson;
Langdon Edmunds Oppermann—Winston-Salem;
Rachel Osborn and Ruth Selden-Sturgill—Chatham Co.;
Dan Pezzoni—Lee Co.;
Laura Phillips—Pinehurst, Hickory, Rockingham Co., Stokes Co., and
   other properties and districts;
Suzanne Pickens—Union Co.;
Helen Ross—Raleigh;

Marjorie Salzman—Anson Co.;

Joe Schuchman—Union Co.;

Linda Simmons-Henry—Raleigh;

H. McKelden Smith—Guilford Co., Warren Co.;

Gwynne Taylor—Forsyth Co. and Winston-Salem;

Paul Touart—Davidson Co.;

Ed Turberg—Richmond Co.;

Bogue Wallin—Catawba Co.;

Mac Whatley—Randolph Co.

The surveys that have been published are cited in the bibliography. Gwynne Taylor, John Larson, Tom Hanchett, and Laura Phillips drafted initial versions of chapters.

Most of the photographs in this volume come from the photographic collection of Archives and History. The majority of these were made over the years by field surveyors and members of the Archives and History staff, including the authors and staff photographers. The excellent work of the staff photographers, including Tony Vaughan, JoAnn Sieburg-Baker, Randall Page, and Bill Garrett, is acknowledged with thanks. Assistance in locating photographs was provided by Steve Massengill, iconographic archivist. Sidney Halma, David Cera, and Tom Lotet took essential photographs. Additional photographs (see Photo Credits) were obtained from the Division of Travel and Tourism, the Duke Special Collections Library, the North Carolina Collection, and the private collections of Sarah Pope and Anne Raines, to whom we are very grateful.

The preparation of this series has relied on the help of innumerable other individuals, organizations, and institutions. The late Robert M. Kelly of Greensboro gave early crucial assistance in coordinating private donations for the project: contributors were Mr. and Mrs. Robert M. Kelly of Greensboro, Boren Clay Products Company of Pleasant Garden (Dean L. Spangler), the Dillard Fund of Greensboro (John H. Dillard), W. L. Burns of Durham, and Mr. and Mrs. A. P. Hubbard of Greensboro in memory of Thomas Turner. These gifts are acknowledged with thanks.

We are deeply grateful to the timely help of Banks Talley and of Dr. Albert J. Michel of Greensboro, whose generosity supported fieldwork and photography for this volume and permitted employment of an intern.

From the beginning, the guidebook project has enjoyed the enthusiastic backing of the Department of Cultural Resources. We are greatly indebted to Betsy Buford, Betty Ray McCain, and Renne Vance, without whose extraordinary support the series as a whole and this volume in particular could not have been completed.

For this volume, present and former staff at Archives and History in Raleigh have provided essential assistance, including earlier fieldwork in the region, technical help, architectural and historical expertise, and moral support. Key among these are David Brook, Claudia Brown, Melinda Coleman, Jeffrey Crow, Linda Edmisten, Paul Fomberg, Renee Gledhill-Earley, Anna Grantham, Katrina Gurley-Chase, Dolores Hall, Al Honeycutt, Davyd Foard Hood, Peter Kaplan, Beth Keane, Ruth Little, Jennifer Martin, Mark Mathis, Linda McRae, April Montgomery, Virginia Oswald, Joy Shattuck, Tim Simmons, McKelden Smith, Greer Suttlemyre, Douglas Swaim, Beth Thomas, Ellen Turco, Sondra Ward, Mitch Wilds, and JoAnn Williford. Nancy Van Dolsen and Ruth Little stepped in at a crucial time to allow the authors to focus on completing this volume.

We thank Chandrea Burch and Bill Garrett for their patience in production of photographs, and Deborah Tharrington for her computer graphics expertise. Susan Myers generously assisted with the index for all three volumes. Christi Dennis assisted in the initial stages and Sondra Ward helped throughout.

We are especially grateful to Claudia Brown, who provided unflagging moral support and leadership; at every stage of this volume and the entire series, and through thick and thin, she has been a source of encouragement and vital help. And to Anne Raines—research, morale, and fieldwork assistant par excellence for this volume—our heartfelt thanks.

For this volume, we have also relied on the knowledge and generous assistance of people familiar with various localities: Frances Alexander, Jean Anderson, Steve Cruse, Tommy and Cindy Edwards, Gayle Fripp, Sidney Halma, Martha and Michael Hartley, Diane Hooper, Richard Hunter, John Hutchinson, John Kennedy, Robbie King, William King, Ted Lawrence, Eric Leland, Ruth Little, Janet Magaldi, Richard Mattson, Ken McFarland, Tina Moon, William Moore, Edwin Patterson, Thilbert Pearce, LeAnn Pegram, Lucy Penegar, Dean Ruedrich, Cynthia Satterfield, John Stevenson, Chris Taggert, Edgar Thorne, Cathleen Turner, James Wall, Helen Walton, Max Way, and many others who provided key information or reviewed various sections. John E. Wells generously made available his research linking buildings with architects. Jack Claiborne and Gary Stanton gave helpful readings of the entire manuscript; Kate Hutchins, Kim Hoagland, and John Bishir helped improve the introduction; and Michael Hill and Ansley Wegner reviewed and offered guidance on the introduction and many county sections. Michelle Michael, Chris Lambert, Laura Capell, and Chris Knodel all aided fieldwork.

Among the many other friends and colleagues who helped this endeavor over the years are John Bishir, Charlotte Brown, Robert Burns, Al Chambers, Ed Chappell, Dan Chartier, Betsy Cromley, Bernard Herman, Myrick Howard, John Larson, Carl Lounsbury, Gray Read, Orlando Ridout, Margaret Supplee Smith, Kathleen Southern, Dell Upton, and Camille Wells. We are especially grateful for the consistent encouragement and expertise of the staff of the University of North Carolina Press, including the editorial, design, and marketing staff who made the series a reality, and particularly David Perry, Heidi Perov, Pamela Upton, and Rich Hendel.

In assembling this guide we have sought to make it as accurate as possible, but inevitably errors have slipped in. Readers are encouraged to provide any corrections, particularly on property locations and factual information, to the authors at the Survey and Planning Branch, Archives and History, Department of Cultural Resources, 4618 Mail Service Center, Raleigh NC 27699-4618. As in the other volumes, and probably even more so because of the selectivity required in the densely populated Piedmont, we know we have left out some wonderful places, some of everyone's—including our own—favorite spots. For this we ask readers' forgiveness. We hope that for every place that does appear in the book, you will visit and delight in many, many more.

Completion of this series, begun in the mid-1980s, embodies the learning and the friendships that have enriched our lives since the early 1970s. It has been an extraordinary privilege to travel the state and meet its history, its buildings and its landscapes, and the people who love them. Thank you all.

Catherine W. Bishir
Michael T. Southern
Raleigh, June 2002

Introduction

PIEDMONT NORTH CAROLINA

LAND & ARCHITECTURE

FIGURE I. *(overleaf) Winston-Salem, from Old Salem: Wachovia Buildings, God's Acre, and Vierling House (Photograph by Catherine W. Bishir)*

We passed through a delicious Country. . . . Here is plenty of good Timber . . . and as there is Stone enough in both [the Haw and Yadkin] Rivers, and the Land is extraordinary rich, no Man that will be content within the Bounds of Reason, can have any grounds to dislike it. And they that are otherwise, are the best Neighbors when farthest off.
—*John Lawson,* A New Voyage to Carolina *(1709)*

The North Carolina Piedmont is a broad and rolling land of red clay hills and lively streams. Part of the piedmont plateau that extends from New York to Alabama, the terrain rises gradually from the fall line to the base of the mountains. The lay of the land and its remoteness from seaports shaped the region's settlement patterns and its identity as part of an upland South different from the Chesapeake, the Deep South, or even coastal North Carolina. As early as 1765 Governor William Tryon reported that in "the Back or Western Counties more industry is observed than to the Eastward." Some have attributed its character to the Scotch-Irish and German settlers, while others believe that the hilly, landlocked zone unsuited to a plantation economy demanded a different ethos. In any case the promising but challenging land and "hard-working, hard-headed" people engendered a practical mindset and distrust of luxury, an emphasis on religion and education, and a spirit of enterprise and "go-aheaditiveness" that made the Piedmont the economic and industrial engine of the New South state.[1]

The early twenty-first-century Piedmont strikes the observer as a fast-paced, urbanizing zone of interstate highways, manufacturing plants and high-tech businesses, suburbs, and strip developments. From Charlotte's metropolitan region of more than 1.5 million people, an urban crescent extends along the interstate highways to meet another million-person zone around the Research Triangle Park, the economic powerhouse begun by mid-twentieth-century Piedmont leaders.

Off the big roads, though, there is a Piedmont heritage with a longer, richer, often quieter story. For many decades after mid-eighteenth-century settlement, this was the "backcountry," a place of mostly small farms, minor industries, and tiny towns separated from seaports by miles of rough land and long rivers full of

1. William Tryon, July 26, 1765, in *Correspondence of William Tryon,* edited by William S. Powell (Raleigh: Division of Archives and History, 1980), 1:136, 139–40; "hard-working, hard-headed" from Jonathan Daniels, "Tar Heels All," in Federal Writers' Project, *North Carolina,* 5; spirit of enterprise and "go-aheaditiveness" from *Raleigh Sentinel,* 24 May 1869, quoted in Murray, *Wake,* 666.

FIGURE 2. *Old St. Paul's Lutheran Church, Catawba Co.* (CT 2)

impediments to navigation. It was a place of varied cultures and persistent traditions, of long efforts to encourage trade and agriculture, and then of rapid industrial and urban growth. Throughout the region, the resident and visitor can trace those stories in the architecture of more than two centuries.

From the eighteenth century, a few buildings recall the diverse settling generation of English and Africans, Scotch-Irish, Germans, and Scots. Most built log houses and barns as they began farming, and a few erected durable stone and half-timbered buildings according to Old World traditions. They founded "dissenting" congregations—Presbyterian, Quaker, Lutheran, Calvinist, Moravian, Baptist, and Methodist—whose churchyards and later generations of meetinghouses dot the landscape. Late eighteenth- and early nineteenth-century buildings display diverse cultural traditions in many areas—in big log barns among German farmers, fine brick buildings in the mid-Atlantic settlement zone, conservatively elegant plantation houses in the northeastern Piedmont, and deep porches easing life near the South Carolina border.

In most sections, nationally popular architectural forms of the nineteenth century recall advances in transportation and trade networks. Some stylish houses and public buildings date from the early national period, but far more numerous are those of the antebellum era, especially in areas boosted by railroad construction from the 1830s onward. Imposing Greek Revival houses, courthouses, and churches, plus a few major national architects' ventures into Gothic

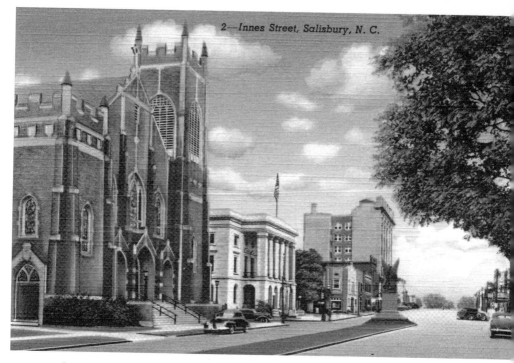

FIGURE 3. *Innes Street, Salisbury* (RW 13–15): *St. John's Lutheran Church, Post Office*

Revival and Italianate modes, show growing participation in the American mainstream.

The Piedmont possesses an extraordinary if dwindling architectural heritage from its industrial transformation in the late nineteenth and early twentieth centuries. Scores of brick textile mills and rows of little mill houses beside streams and railroads, and imposing tobacco factories and warehouses, recall the state's emergence as a regional and national leader in manufacturing.

In towns and cities, a legacy of late and generally dispersed urbanization persists. Many small and medium-sized towns retain classic ensembles: clusters of cottages, bungalows, and towered Queen Anne houses; rows of corbeled brick stores; a few columned banks; and a courthouse with a dome and portico. At the hearts of the spreading metropolises stand vestiges of their early twentieth-century urban blossoming—from emblematic New South skyscrapers to the first generations of professionally planned garden suburbs.

Out in the country, there lies a rolling rural landscape, where families accommodate changing agricultural methods on their red clay land. Cornfields shimmer across rounded hillsides, and old log barns cluster around white-painted farmhouses. Tobacco barns, cotton gins, country stores, and gristmills evoke a not-so-distant past. Country churches of every denomination are well filled, as are churchyards with old markers carefully tended along with new ones. The winding roads cross the streams at concrete bridges instead of fords, and hydroelectric plants direct the energy of the rivers to faraway users; but the quiet and inviting power of the rolling landscape and its quick streams still make the North Carolina Piedmont a "delicious country."

GEOLOGY AND NATURAL RESOURCES

The Piedmont took form millions of years before the seas laid down the sedimentary deposits of the coastal plain. Eons of bubbling, layering, compression, uplift, and erosion produced a complex geology. Hundreds of millions of years ago, the force of one continent crunching up against another raised high mountains. Millennia of erosion wore the land to gentle swells, with occasional ridges and monadnocks of hard rock. Varied formations include granite and gneiss extending north from Raleigh and especially fine granite around Salisbury. Sedimentary brown sandstones occur in present-day Lee and Anson counties, but there is relatively little limestone. Minor deposits of iron and coal near fault lines enticed, then disappointed industrialists, while the southwestern Piedmont became the nation's leading gold producer before the strikes in California.

Many areas have fairly well drained clay and sandy soils atop decaying granites, but in Triassic basins along the eastern edge, sedimentary deposits make farming difficult. Much of the Piedmont carries a heavy cloak of clay, brilliantly red or orange from underlying iron oxides. Forests of mixed hardwoods, chiefly oak and hickory, cover the uplands, but pines prevail on sandier soils, especially in the Sandhills near the southern fall line.

The gently undulating landscape is crisscrossed by abundant streams running with or across the diagonal grain of the land. As they traverse the Piedmont, the streams cut through stone formations to create falls and rapids—good for waterpower, but hard to travel. At the fall line, they tumble down the crystalline rocks, then cross the plain toward the sea. Rivers carried boat traffic from seaports to the fall line but seldom beyond, a situation that persisted despite many projects to improve navigation into the backcountry. The economic potential of the Piedmont's streams lay not in shipping but in waterpower for

FIGURE 4. *(Opposite) River basins in the Piedmont. Two major rivers of the Piedmont, the Yadkin–Pee Dee and the Catawba, spring from the Eastern Continental Divide, then head northeast along the Brevard Fault before encountering stony obstacles and turning south to run through the western Piedmont and South Carolina to the Atlantic. The Dan and the Roanoke begin in western Virginia and join to run east along the border before turning south to enter the Albemarle Sound. Other rivers originate within the Piedmont, including the Tar and the Neuse, which feed Pamlico Sound, and the Deep and the Haw, which join to form the Cape Fear—the only major river with direct access to the Atlantic within N.C.*

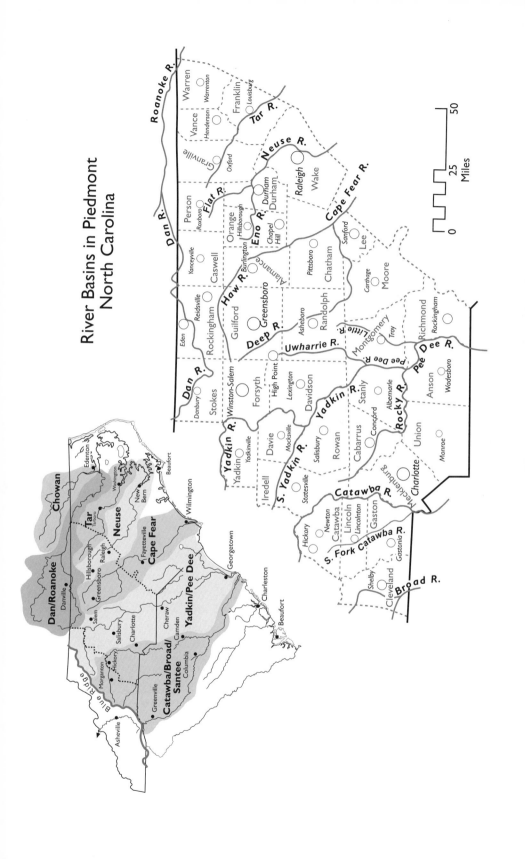

River Basins in Piedmont North Carolina

grist- and sawmills, cotton mills, and the twentieth-century hydroelectric power plants that transformed life in the region.

SETTLEMENT AND DEVELOPMENT
FROM ANCIENT TIMES TO THE CIVIL WAR

Native Peoples

Human habitation in the Piedmont stretches back more than 12,000 years. Distinctive spear points and tools from as early as 8000 B.C. recall ancient peoples' methods of hunting, gathering, and fishing. By about 2000 B.C. the people of the Piedmont were fashioning vessels for agricultural settlements. This way of life developed for several centuries and flowered in villages of the Piedmont (*Town Creek) from about A.D. 1000 to 1650.

When the first Europeans entered the Piedmont, thousands of people in many tribal groups were hunting, fishing, and farming in the region. The Catawbas dominated the western and southern sections, but their numbers dwindled rapidly after contact with disease-bearing Europeans—Hernando DeSoto's party traipsed through in 1540, followed by Juan Pardo's in the 1560s. After devastation by subsequent epidemics, they coalesced toward South Carolina. At the western edge of the Piedmont lived the Catawbas' old rivals, the Cherokee, who moved farther into the highlands as white settlement increased. In 1700–1701 English surveyor John Lawson journeyed from the Catawba River across the Yadkin and the Haw and thence back to the coast via the Neuse, describing the way of life of the Saponi, Occaneechi, Eno, Sissipahaw, Tuscarora, and others. Admiring the fruitfulness and beauty of the high and healthy land and "several creeks, very convenient for Water-Mills," he concluded, "The Savages do, indeed, still possess the Flower of *Carolina*, the *English* [along the coast] enjoying only the Fag-end of that fine Country."[2]

The situation was soon to change. By the 1740s and 1750s, European colonists were settling in substantial numbers in the Piedmont, and within a few years only a few native people remained to perpetuate tribal traditions. Their languages persist in place names: Alamance and Catawba counties, the Waxhaw region and the Uwharrie Mountains, and great rivers, including the Neuse, the Roanoke, and the Dan; the Catawba and the Haw; and the Yadkin and the Pee Dee. The trading paths they had created using the natural advantages of ridges and gaps, valleys, streams, and fording places, shaped the direction of wagon

---

2. John Lawson, *A New Voyage to Carolina* (1709), edited by Hugh Talmage Lefler (Chapel Hill: University of North Carolina Press, 1967), 52, 55, 61. On native people in North Carolina, see Ward and Davis, *Time before History*.

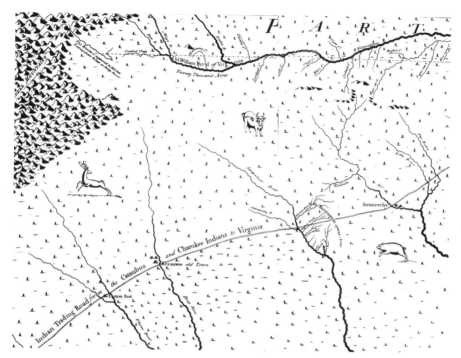

FIGURE 5. *North-central Piedmont, Moseley Map (1733). Until the mid-18th. c. the "backcountry" was peopled chiefly by native groups, with Acconeechy a principal town where the "Indian Trading Road from the Cataubos and Charokee Indians to Virginia" crossed the Eno River.*

roads, railroads, paved roads, and even the interstate highways of the twentieth century, which retrace much of the ancient network.

Frontier Settlement to the American Revolution

European settlement began in earnest in the Piedmont in the 1740s. As thousands of immigrants arrived in other colonies and land grew more expensive, they headed south and west toward available land. Some coastal Carolina residents of English and African descent came upriver into the backcountry, and many Scots traveled up the Cape Fear from Wilmington. But the great immigration came from the north. Thousands traversed the Trading Path from Virginia, through Hillsborough, and across the central Piedmont. Still more trekked down the Great Wagon Road that reached from Philadelphia into the western Piedmont, eventually meeting the Trading Path near Salisbury.

North Carolina's population grew from about 35,000 in 1730, chiefly in the east, to more than 250,000 by the 1770s, with most of the increase in the Piedmont. This growth made North Carolina the fourth largest of the thirteen colonies and radically altered its character. A report of 1753 recalled that only seven years earlier "in the Country that is now Anson, Orange and Rowan

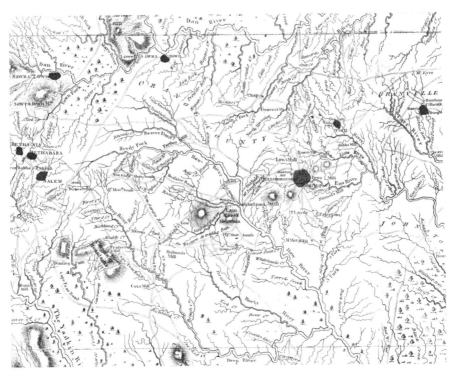

FIGURE 6. *North-central Piedmont, Collet Map (1770). After three decades of rapid immigration Hillsborough occupied the site of Acconeechy, amid a dense network of roads, mills, chapels, meeting-houses, farm sites, and villages.*

Countys, there was not then above one hundred fighting men there is now at least three thousand for the most part Irish Protestants and Germans and dayley increasing." By 1766 Governor Tryon claimed that "this province is settling faster than any on the continent, last autumn and winter, upwards of one thousand passed thro' Salisbury with families from the northward to settle in this province chiefly." The next year a newspaper marveled, "There is scarce any history, either antient or modern, which affords an account of such a rapid and sudden increase of inhabitants in a back frontier country, as that of North Carolina."[3]

The rapidly settled area became embroiled in repeated conflicts. The French and Indian War harried its western frontier from 1755 to 1763, and from the late

3. Matthew Rowan to Board of Trade, June 28, 1753, Colonial Records of N.C., 5:24, quoted in Hugh Talmage Lefler, *North Carolina History Told by Contemporaries* (Chapel Hill: University of North Carolina Press, 1965), 69; William Tryon to Board of Trade, Aug. 2, 1766, Colonial Records of N.C., 7:248, quoted in Lefler, *North Carolina History*, 68; *Connecticut Courant*, Nov. 30, 1767, quoted in Harry Roy Merrens, *Colonial North Carolina in the Eighteenth Century: A Study in Historical Geography* (Chapel Hill: University of North Carolina Press, 1964), 54.

Routes, Rivers, and Early Settlements in Piedmont North Carolina

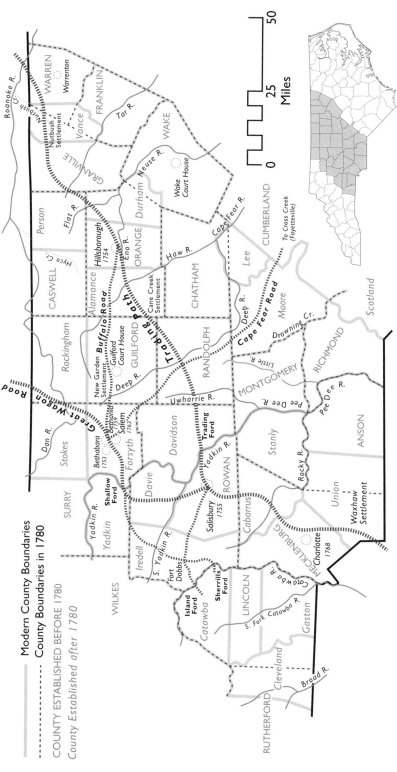

FIGURE 7. *Routes, rivers, and early settlements. The Trading Path led from present-day Petersburg south and west. Today I-85 follows much of its path. The major north-south route was the Great Wagon Road "from Philadelphia to the Catawba Nation," which likewise followed Indian war and trade paths.*

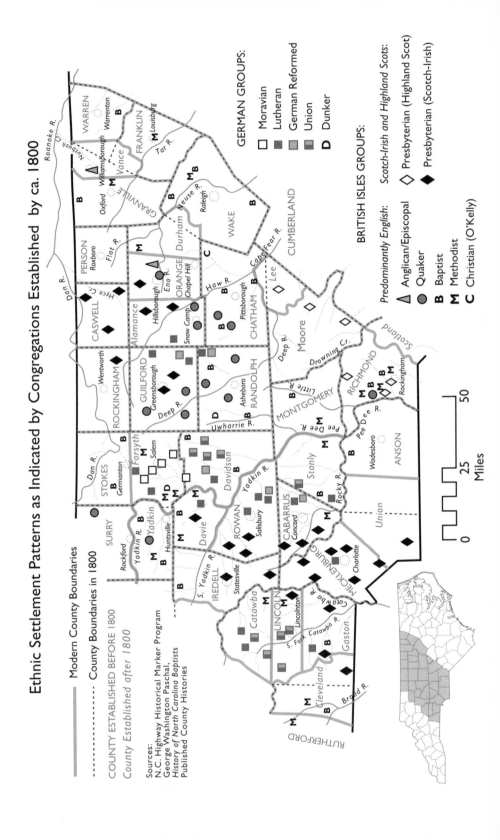

Ethnic Settlement Patterns as Indicated by Congregations Established by ca. 1800

Modern County Boundaries

County Boundaries in 1800

COUNTY ESTABLISHED BEFORE 1800

County Established after 1800

Sources:
N.C. Highway Historical Marker Program
George Washington Paschal,
History of North Carolina Baptists
Published County Histories

GERMAN GROUPS:

☐ Moravian
▨ Lutheran
▨ German Reformed
▨ Union
D Dunker

BRITISH ISLES GROUPS:

Scotch-Irish and Highland Scots:

◇ Presbyterian (Highland Scot)
◆ Presbyterian (Scotch-Irish)

Predominantly English:

△ Anglican/Episcopal
● Quaker
B Baptist
M Methodist
C Christian (O'Kelly)

Miles
0   25   50

1760s to 1771, internal strife between old and new settlements arose as back-country farmers organized the Regulator movement to protest unfair taxation and abuses by court officials. It ended when Governor Tryon led troops from New Bern into the Piedmont and defeated the Regulators at Alamance Battleground. By the eve of the American Revolution, white settlers had staked out most of the land between the fall line and the mountains, and a few had ventured past the Blue Ridge.

Defining the character of the region and state for generations to come, the new North Carolinians arrived in clusters related by ethnic, religious, and family ties. They took up land in a cultural patchwork of relatively small sectors and formed congregations in keeping with their origins. English settlers, who were strongest in the east and central Piedmont, included Quakers and Anglicans, but many were unchurched until Baptist and Methodist missionaries gained converts. Africans, nearly all of whom were enslaved, were most numerous in the northeastern and southern Piedmont plantation sections; they constituted a majority in a few counties and often embraced Baptist and Methodist faiths. In the central and western sectors, the many Germans included Lutherans and Reformed (Calvinist)—who often shared a "union" meetinghouse—a few Dunkards (Baptists), and a large colony of Moravians. The widely dispersed Scotch-Irish or Ulster Scots, who had been transplanted to northern Ireland and then migrated to America via Philadelphia, were typically Presbyterian. They had an especially strong presence in the southwest Piedmont. Colonies of Gaelic-speaking Highland Scots, also Presbyterians, extended from Cross Creek (Fayetteville) on the Cape Fear. Other Scots appeared, especially as merchants, throughout the region. There were also a few Welsh, French Huguenots, and Irish.

Although some settlers came directly from their homelands, many had spent some time—or had been born in—other colonies and then traveled to the Carolina backcountry. Especially in rural areas, some continued to speak German or Gaelic into the nineteenth century, and some Germans, Africans, Scots, and English rendered gravestones, pottery, furniture, or buildings in distinctive ways.

Piedmont settlers spanned the classes. Many had little or no land and

FIGURE 8. *(Opposite) Ethnic settlement patterns as indicated by congregations established by 1800. Beliefs were so diverse in the Piedmont that a frustrated Anglican missionary observed in 1771, "They appear to me like Aesop's crow which feathered itself with other birds' feathers. They have Moravian, Quaker, Separatist, Dunkard principles, know everything and know nothing, look down on others, belong to no one, and spurn others." Early congregations reveal the distribution of settlement as clusters of Germans, English, and Scotch-Irish settlers established farms and communities and founded numerous congregations. Baptists and Methodists grew more numerous through evangelism after 1800.*

FIGURE 9. *Fourth House, Salem* (FY 17). *In the 1760s, Moravian, European-born artisans erected buildings of traditional half-timbered (*fachwerk*) German construction (cf. *Single Brothers House) along with some log structures. These are among the state's chief surviving examples of first-generation European building traditions.*

FIGURE 10. *Allen House, Alamance Co.* (AM 38). *The log house (ca. 1782) with 1 main room and a sleeping loft represents the dwelling of small farmers predominant in the Piedmont during the 18th and early 19th centuries. It was built for John and Rachel Stout Allen on land granted in 1756 to John's father, one of many Quakers who arrived from Pennsylvania.*

FIGURE 11. *St. John's, Williamsboro, Vance Co.* (VN 3). *The substantial frame structure built for an Anglican parish is the only colonial church building in the Piedmont. Whereas in the northeastern Piedmont, as in eastern N.C., the colonial elite affiliated with the official Anglican church—if any— that denomination had scant influence in most of the Piedmont. In many areas Presbyterians figured strongly in local leadership, a position enhanced by their emphasis on education and their prominence during the American Revolution. None of their 18th-c. meetinghouses remain.*

scratched out a slim living by hunting and fishing, running some hogs and a few cows, and raising a little corn. Much of the character of the region, however, was established by middling farmers and tradesmen. Governor Tryon reported that in the Piedmont, "the poorer Settlers coming from the Northward Colonies sat themselves down in the back Counties where the land is best but who have not more than a sufficiency to erect a Log House for their families and procure a few Tools to get a little Corn into the ground. . . . Before they can get into sufficient affluence to buy Negroes, their own Children are often grown to an age to work in the Fields." Thousands of families relied on mixed agriculture and home manufacturing, complemented by hunting and fishing, to meet their own needs and to provide a modest surplus to trade or sell. With settlers' desire for a self-sufficient farming life reinforced by the distance and difficulty of getting goods to and from market, the "yeoman farmer" ideal of plain but plentiful living and an independent mindset took root.[4]

4. William Tryon, July 26, 1765, in Powell, *Correspondence of William Tryon,* 1:17.

FIGURE 12. *House in the Horseshoe, Moore Co.* (MR 6). *From the mid-18th c. through the 19th c., a well-built, 2-story frame house with masonry chimneys was considered a sign of considerable wealth and effort. Probably built shortly before the American Revolution but updated in the early 19th c., the plantation house near the Deep River has the region's characteristic I-house form, shed porch, and brick end chimneys—here with the double shoulders and archaic T-stack form of the 18th c.*

In some sections, a backcountry elite emerged. If few of its members shared the opulent way of life of the eastern gentry, they nevertheless established enduring family positions of power and influence. Some already possessed wealth and status, but many brought only their talents and their ambitions to claim good land and the main chance on the frontier. Thus was formed a permeable elite relatively open to new energy, talent, and money. A plantation culture evolved among tobacco growers in the Dan and Roanoke valleys near the Virginia border and in other areas where smart land purchases laid the groundwork for a plantation slavery economy. Mixed agriculture predominated among large as well as small farmers, who raised corn and wheat and other crops for home use and the market.

Towns in the backcountry were tiny, and some existed in name only. As little towns emerged, lawyers and merchants along with leading farmers dominated local affairs. The principal settlements grew up near the junctions of main trade roads, river fords, and ferry sites. Hillsborough, begun in the 1750s near the old village of Occaneechi where the Trading Path crossed the Eno River, became the political center of the giant mother county of Orange (est. 1752); its neighbor-

FIGURE 13. *Michael Braun Stone House, Rowan Co.* (RW 43). *The house, dated 1766, is one of the few surviving buildings from the first-generation settlers in the Piedmont. Built for German immigrants Michael and Margareta Braun (Brown) near Salisbury and the Great Wagon Road, it reflects traditions also seen in Pennsylvania, western Maryland, and Virginia. See also the *Hezekiah Alexander House* (MK 55) *of similar form for a Scotch-Irish settler from Maryland.*

hood encompassed the Haw Fields area between the Eno and the Haw, admired as some of the finest land in the colony.

As westward settlement filled the Mesopotamia between the Yadkin and the Catawba, the big county of Rowan (1753) was divided from Bladen, with its seat, Salisbury (1755) near the Yadkin River fords and the junction of the Trading Path and the Wagon Road. Other courthouse villages followed as population growth prompted county subdivisions, including Charlotte (Mecklenburg) on the ridge between the rivers and Lincolnton (Lincoln) in the Catawba valley. Some grew informally around a crossroads, but most courthouse towns were laid out as grids with public squares. At the eve of the American Revolution, a typical Piedmont county seat was little more than a village, with a frame or log courthouse and jail accompanied by a tavern and a few houses and stores.

Building on the Frontier

The first generations of Europeans building in the Piedmont shared in the expediency demanded of frontier life. With land to clear, labor in short supply, and manufactured building materials and tools hard to get, most people began with log buildings. These ranged from crude to well-finished meetinghouses and courthouses, houses, and barns. Although no Piedmont buildings are known to survive from the 1740s or 1750s, a few structures, extraordinary in their day, still stand from the period before the American Revolution.

In the eastern Piedmont, a few citizens erected substantial and carefully crafted frame and a few brick buildings in the late colonial period. Most followed forms familiar from the tidewater zone. Typical of planters' and merchants' better houses were 1- or occasionally 2-story frame dwellings with gable or gambrel roofs, neatly finished with brick chimneys, weatherboarded walls, and simple paneling. Some small, late colonial houses survive as wings or cores of later dwellings. In the western Piedmont, a few colonists and communities built exceptionally well. Of several early stone houses built in the region, two remain: the *Michael Braun House near Salisbury and the *Hezekiah Alexander House in Charlotte. The first Moravian buildings in *Old Salem (see Fig. 9) show the congregation's communal accomplishments, as European-trained artisans constructed half-timbered buildings that accommodated Old World traditions to the Piedmont frontier.

A New State, 1780s–1861

During the American Revolution, the Piedmont saw a few major battles at Guilford Courthouse and elsewhere and endured internal conflict and ongoing hardships. When peace came, North Carolina leaders set out to establish the institutions of a new state and stabilize the war-ravaged economy. The eastern counties dominated the government, but because of the greatly increased population in the backcountry, the new state capital and the state university were located on rural Piedmont sites rather than in established coastal towns. In 1792 Raleigh was laid out as the capital with axial streets and squares along the lines of Philadelphia, which was familiar as a national political and trade center. The University of North Carolina (UNC), chartered in 1789, became in 1795 the nation's first state university to open its doors.

Rebuilding the economy was difficult, for the state had little money, and the eastern-dominated legislature resisted paying for costly road and river improvements to benefit western counties. The backcountry towns were villages of no more than a few hundred people each when the first census was made in 1790, and they remained so for decades thereafter. As other states invested in internal improvements, North Carolina's transportation problems grew increasingly troublesome. Piedmont farmers engaged in market production had to haul their wagonloads of corn or wheat to markets in South Carolina and Virginia, roll their hogsheads of tobacco to Virginia towns, or drive their stock and produce to Fayetteville, from which riverboats plied the Cape Fear to Wilmington. Manufactured goods made the reverse journey. Everything from window glass to mill equipment came upriver to Fayetteville or Petersburg, then bumped along

FIGURE 14. *University of North Carolina, Chapel Hill* (OR 45) *(photo ca. 1892). The university was chartered in 1789 and was built on a site southeast of Hillsborough; in 1795 it became the first state university to open its doors. The first building (second from left) was the plain Old East (1793–95; remodeled 1840s) with its pendant, Old West (right) (1822–23, 1840s). South Building (second from right, with cupola) was begun in 1798 but took years to finish due to lack of funds. Among the largest buildings in the state at the time, it followed a simplified Palladian design with a central, pedimented pavilion in a format akin to the State House in Raleigh and to Nassau Hall, the main building at present-day Princeton University. "We imitate Nassau Hall in the conduct of our affairs," wrote one professor.*

in wagons to Piedmont towns and villages. Profits from North Carolina products thus accrued chiefly to merchants and port towns in neighboring states. Moreover, "Agriculture has ceased to yield to the landowner a compensation equivalent to the expense attending the transportation of his surplus to market," stated one report, which predicted that the resultant "tide of emigration" would make the state "the mere nursery for the Western and Southwestern States."[5]

The economy languished. Tobacco cultivation depleted soil fertility and required continual clearing of fresh land, while old fields were left to grow up in weeds. Without replenishment of soils, wheat and corn productivity dropped. Although a few promoted agricultural improvement, most farmers ignored "book" farming and continued old methods. From a burgeoning frontier in the eighteenth century, by the early nineteenth century North Carolina saw immigration taper off and a wave of outmigration begin. Some called it "the Rip van Winkle state" and lamented the departure of thousands—eventually as many as 500,000—including the cream of the younger generations, to new territories.

5. James Seawell, Committee on Internal Improvements report, 1833, in Jack Claiborne and William Price, eds., *Discovering North Carolina: A Tar Heel Reader* (Chapel Hill: University of North Carolina Press, 1990), 24.

Even as many left the region, thousands of self-sustaining small and middling farmers continued to feed their families and produce small surpluses, relying on social networks of exchange for essential goods and services. At the same time, class divisions widened as some Piedmont farmers turned planter by consolidating holdings in land, slaves, and power, while others lost ground. In the tobacco plantation zone, Warren emerged as the wealthiest county in the state, and its planters, along with those in other northeastern counties, owned ever greater numbers of slaves. In southwestern counties, planters and merchants prospered after the discovery of gold in 1799, and Charlotte became the center of the gold rush with a branch of the U.S. Mint. Piedmont planters, lawyers, and leading merchants typically shared values and family connections that separated them from small tradesmen and yeoman farmers and linked them with elite social and political networks statewide.

In the early nineteenth century Piedmont citizens began pressing for reforms to better their own and the state's situation. Some strove for revival of religion and morality. Religious revival movements swept the region as well as much of the nation. Presbyterians, Baptists, and Methodists held revivals at camp meetings and founded new churches, which attracted the formerly unchurched and converts from established denominations. As the antislavery beliefs of Quakers grew increasingly unpopular in the 1830s, many Friends left for free states or changed denominations. By 1860, 80 percent of church members in the state were Baptist or Methodist, with Presbyterians a distant third. Denominations put new emphasis on education, establishing schools and colleges from the early nineteenth century onward.

To awaken the somnolent economy of the Rip van Winkle state, Piedmont reformers such as Hillsborough attorney Archibald deBow Murphey and UNC president Joseph Caldwell called for investment in public education (there was essentially none) and a systematic network of "internal improvements" of river and land routes to ports within the state. A flurry of enthusiasm after the War of 1812 spurred ambitious river navigation projects; but only a few elements were completed, and support waned after the panic of 1819.

In the 1830s, amid the worst era of outmigration, a new spirit emerged. The State House in Raleigh burned in 1831, and in 1833 the state embarked on a monumental rebuilding campaign that, despite cost overruns and a national economic depression, produced a state capitol proudly regarded as evidence that old Rip had awakened at last. In 1835, after mounting demands for adequate legislative representation for the west—and rumblings that "the yeomanry of the West will take the remedy in their own hands"—a new constitution gave greater political power to western counties and thereby boosted state investment in the improvements they sought.

Soon railroads supplanted the canal movement as the hope of opening the

FIGURE 15. *Rock Springs Campground, Lincoln Co.* (LN 11). *A wave of revivalism around 1800 was followed by others throughout the antebellum period. The first flourished among Presbyterians at *Hawfields Church in Alamance Co. and elsewhere but soon spread to Baptists and Methodists. Evangelists appealed to rich and poor, free and slave. Revivals were held in the open air under a tree or arbor, and people camped in the area; in time, permanent framed "arbors" were erected, along with rows of small wooden "tents" for family use during revivals.*

FIGURE 16. *Union Tavern, Milton* (CS 22). *The tavern, adorned in Federal style with delicate fanlights over the entrances, opened in 1819 in Milton, a tobacco trading town near the Dan River—one of several communities "flushed on by the madness of speculation" from early 19th-c. navigation projects. Shallow-draft boats plied sections of various rivers. After the panic of 1819, internal improvements were curtailed, and many promising river ports dwindled or vanished. In the antebellum era the tavern held the workshop of noted free black cabinetmaker Thomas Day.*

David Paton, Architect.   J.Sutcliffe,Litho. Edin

FIGURE 17. *State Capitol, Raleigh* (WK 1). *Lithograph ca. 1840 from drawing attributed to David Paton. Although it took seven years to build and cost more than $500,000, vastly exceeding projections, the capitol, designed by architects William Nichols, Ithiel Town & A. J. Davis, and David Paton, boosted state pride and set a new model for excellence in architecture.*

Piedmont to distant markets. They were supplemented by plank roads that served as feeder routes for farmers and encouraged naval stores production in the Sandhills area. The Raleigh & Gaston Railroad, completed in 1840 along with the State Capitol, tied eastern Piedmont counties to northward lines. Enterprising Charlotte businessmen successfully promoted the Charlotte & South Carolina (1852), thus gaining the first rails into the western Piedmont. Soon afterward the state-sponsored, east-west North Carolina Railroad (NCRR) at last linked the Piedmont to eastern North Carolina ports. As the tracks proceeded, newspapers claimed that prosperity and new buildings went up even before the

FIGURE 18. *(Opposite) Piedmont North Carolina, ca. 1860, showing antebellum railroads, plank roads, navigation improvements, and selected industries. Early 19th-c. efforts to improve roads and river transportation in the Piedmont fell short for lack of funds, but railroads proved more successful. In the 1830s the Raleigh & Gaston and the Wilmington & Weldon linked the capital and the main port, respectively, with northern rails near the falls of the Roanoke. The Charlotte & South Carolina provided a link to Charleston via Columbia. The state-sponsored North Carolina Railroad led from Goldsboro (where it met the Wilmington & Weldon) through Raleigh to Charlotte; topography, proximity to population centers, and politics defined its route, which retraced parts of the Trading Path and shaped future development. The state also began extensions east and west—the Atlantic & North Carolina to the port at New Bern, and part of the Western North Carolina Railroad through the mountains. The longest of several plank roads, called "the Appian Way of North Carolina," was built in 1849–54 from Fayetteville, the head of navigation on the Cape Fear, 129 miles to Bethania near Salem.*

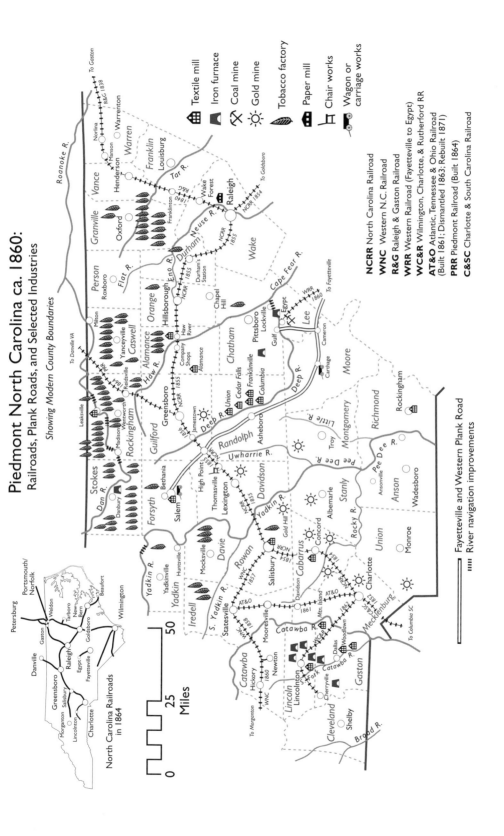

Piedmont North Carolina ca. 1860:
Railroads, Plank Roads, and Selected Industries

Showing Modern County Boundaries

Legend:
- Textile mill
- Iron furnace
- Coal mine
- Gold mine
- Tobacco factory
- Paper mill
- Chair works
- Wagon or carriage works

NCRR North Carolina Railroad
WNC Western N.C. Railroad
R&G Raleigh & Gaston Railroad
WRR Western Railroad (Fayetteville to Egypt)
WC&R Wilmington, Charlotte, & Rutherford RR
AT&O Atlantic, Tennessee & Ohio Railroad (Built 1861; Dismantled 1863; Rebuilt 1871)
PRR Piedmont Railroad (Built 1864)
C&SC Charlotte & South Carolina Railroad

Fayetteville and Western Plank Road
River navigation improvements

North Carolina Railroads in 1864

Miles
0   25   50

rails arrived. Great celebrations took place as the first train steamed into each town, with congratulatory and fund-raising speeches, barbecues, dances, and, in Salisbury, a balloon ascension.[6]

Much of the promise promoted by Piedmont progressives began to take form. Commercial farming and interest in "scientific agriculture" rose as access to market made raising crops more lucrative. Many counties produced wheat and corn at greater profit. Along the South Carolina border and in the upper Cape Fear area, the cotton gin plus plank roads and rails encouraged cotton cultivation. Northern Piedmont counties raised more tobacco and grain, which were still sold mainly in Virginia. Planters and merchants bought more land and slaves and built more elaborate houses and public buildings. If no town in the Piedmont exceeded 5,000 people by 1860, several grew to 1,000 or more and gained banks, fashionable craftsmen and merchants, and other businesses along with schools, churches, and public institutions. Yet these same trends began to marginalize the small farmer and the old subsistence way of life; social and economic distances between town and country and between planter and small farmer grew ever wider.

Industrial production, still a minor adjunct to agriculture, attracted new investors. Many communities had iron foundries, wagonworks, sawmills, tobacco factories, and other small enterprises. Entrepreneurs promoted textile manufacturing to boost agricultural profits and add value to home products within the state, thus spurring local trade and town growth. A few mills began in the 1810s and 1820s, but the industry gained momentum in the 1830s. Some early industries, including the Mount Hecla Mill in Greensboro and the *Salem Cotton Mill, tried steam power but were limited by fuel supplies. Among the pioneers who built mills beside the Piedmont's lively streams—often at old gristmill sites—were the Holt family along the Haw and its tributaries in Alamance Co., Quaker industrialists along the Deep in Randolph Co., John Motley Morehead at the Smith and Dan rivers in Rockingham Co., and the Leaks, Steeles, and others on tributaries of the Yadkin–Pee Dee in Richmond Co. They used northern mechanics and equipment suppliers, and most patterned their operations on New England mills, chiefly the Rhode Island system of many small mills and villages. Some shared knowledge from their trips to northern factories and formed lasting networks of partnerships and marriages. By 1860 many small mills were humming beside the streams of the Piedmont, giving work to white girls and women as well as boys and men and offering farmers a market for greater quantities of cotton.[7]

6. Allen W. Trelease, *The North Carolina Railroad, 1849–1871, and the Modernization of North Carolina* (Chapel Hill: University of North Carolina Press, 1991), 36–37.
7. This discussion draws chiefly on Glass, *Textile Industry in North Carolina*.

FIGURE 19. *Eumenean Hall, Davidson College, Mecklenburg Co.* (MK 61). *One of many denominational academies and colleges for men or women, Davidson was a college for men sponsored by the Presbyterians, a denomination that emphasized education. Sharing many colleges' adoption of classical designs—especially suited to the classical education of the era—is the temple-like form of the debating society hall.*

The state invested for the first time in institutions for the deaf, blind, and insane, facilities regarded as necessary to any civilized state. Reformers at last succeeded in strengthening public education, which they saw as essential to economic improvement and social stability. Aided by federal surplus funds, they established a public school system that briefly in the 1850s was among the nation's best. The state expanded the university, and private sponsors increased the number and quality of denominational academies and colleges, including several for women. By the end of the era, Piedmont leaders saw real accomplishments from their long campaigns. While North Carolina still lagged behind many other states, "improvement" had begun. The state had also begun the shift of economic growth, if not yet political power, from the plantation east to the former "backcountry."

Architecture in the New State

The early national period brought a tremendous rebuilding, followed by a building boom in the late antebellum years. Thousands of citizens replaced crude or worn dwellings with new log, frame, or brick houses; counties erected new courthouses; and congregations built meetinghouses to replace brush arbors or log shelters. Whereas only a few buildings from the colonial period re-

Log House Form and Plan Types

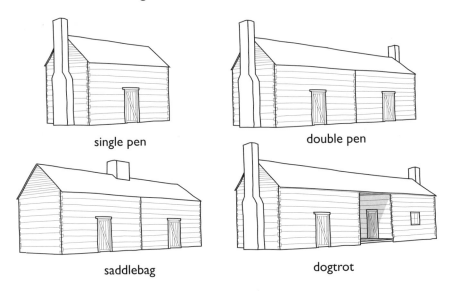

single pen

double pen

saddlebag

dogtrot

Log Notching Types

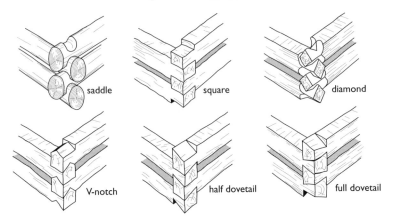

saddle

square

diamond

V-notch

half dovetail

full dovetail

Adapted from Doug Swaim, ed., *Carolina Dwelling*, [1978]

FIGURE 20. *Log house form and plan types and notching types (adapted from Doug Swaim,* Carolina Dwelling *[1978]). By the 19th c., the era from which any quantity of log buildings survives in N.C., most ethnic distinctions in their construction had evidently faded. Most common was the single-pen house, usually with 1 room, sometimes divided by a log or board partition. (A "pen" is a rectangular unit formed by four linked log walls.) Walls were typically 14 to 16 feet long, and few exceeded 18 to 20 feet. Houses of 2 pens might be built all at once or in stages. Some log houses were built with logs exposed and were chinked and daubed between the logs, while others were weatherboarded soon after construction. The Piedmont shows a greater variety of notching types than either the coastal plain or the mountains. Most common are the V-notch and half-dovetail, the latter of which becomes predominant toward the west. The quality of construction ranged from crude cabins, few of which survive, to carefully finished structures of 1 or 2 stories.*

FIGURE 21. *Coble Barn, Guilford Co.* (GF 38). *The double-crib barn has two large log "cribs" sheltered by a gable roof, with a central wagon passage running perpendicular to the roof ridge. Prevalent in the central and western Piedmont areas, this form was built mainly for farmers of German background, but sometimes for their Scotch-Irish and English neighbors as well. For reasons not fully explained, the characteristic Pennsylvania (and Virginia) German "bank" barn set into a hillside seldom appears.*

main in the Piedmont, scores survive from the early national era and hundreds from the antebellum years. Most building was accomplished either by farmers and congregation members themselves or by artisans trained through apprenticeships and experience. Working directly with the owner, the carpenter, the mason, and the joiner erected houses, barns, churches, and public buildings of relatively simple forms, using plans familiar in the locality and finishing them with simple woodwork and hardware.

Log construction continued to predominate, with small, single-pen and occasionally double-pen houses and outbuildings the norm. People of Scotch-Irish, German, English, and African descent all employed log construction. In many rural areas, especially among smaller farmers, log houses continued to be built through the nineteenth century and into the twentieth century. Piedmont farmers of every economic level also constructed their outbuildings of readily accessible logs. Tightly joined logs and planks made smokehouses secure, while wider-spaced logs allowed ventilation into corncribs and haybarns. Log barns became an important building type, especially the double-crib log barns, which were often imposingly large and well crafted.

Frame and brick buildings of the early national era likewise followed traditional forms. Courthouses, meetinghouses, schoolhouses, jailhouses, and mill houses were generally straightforward structures of essentially domestic character, finished according to purpose and budget. Farmers and townspeople built

FIGURE 22. *Person Place, Franklin Co.* (FN 1). *Many of the earliest durable houses that survive, including those built for northeastern Piedmont planters, became part of larger dwellings through a variety of arrangements. The oldest, late 18th-c. section is a typical 1-story gable-roofed house (L). A stylish, pedimented wing was added a few decades later.*

FIGURE 23. *Shaw House, Moore Co.* (MR 10). *Most Piedmont residents, such as the Shaw family in the Sandhills region, built small houses and then added rooms and porches as needed. Small front porch chambers entered only from the porch were often used for guests and called "preacher" or "stranger" rooms.*

FIGURE 24. *Richardson House, Union Co.* (UN 12). *Distinctive along the South Carolina border are houses with broad porches that have the posts set in front of the porch floor. The type spread from Upland South Carolina into other states, and in Alabama it is called a "Carolina porch."*

1- and 1½-story dwellings, and a growing number erected 2-story houses as signs of wealth and status, often as additions to smaller houses. Even the wealthiest typically built according to familiar forms. If few houses were grand or "elegant," many were "neat and workmanlike," as betokened by molded weatherboards and window and door frames, Flemish-bond chimneys, and other marks of quality. With paint, glass, and hardware as well as skilled craftsmen hard to get, such buildings represented substantial investment of time and money.

A few families chose the formality and privacy of a center passage, but until the mid-nineteenth century, many still had the entrance directly into the main room. This pattern occurred in both 1- and 2-story houses of 2, 3, or 4 rooms per floor. Porches and rear shed or ell rooms often extended the space; along the South Carolina border, porches were especially prevalent and sometimes had columns set on bases forward of the porch floor.

The early national period produced the Piedmont's first major brick architecture. Clay was plentiful, but the scarcity of lime limited brick construction. Masonry buildings continued to reflect unusual cost and effort. The Moravians were early builders in brick in the 1780s, and some substantial stone buildings were erected as well. The region's earliest substantial brick buildings of the 1780s and 1790s display a level of skill and elaboration indicative of a fully developed artisan tradition, whether among local or immigrant bricklayers. The state used brick for its public buildings from the 1790s onward, and local governments proudly invested in brick courthouses. By the early nineteenth century the central and western Piedmont boasted a distinctive collection of fine brick houses.

Traditional House Plans of the Piedmont

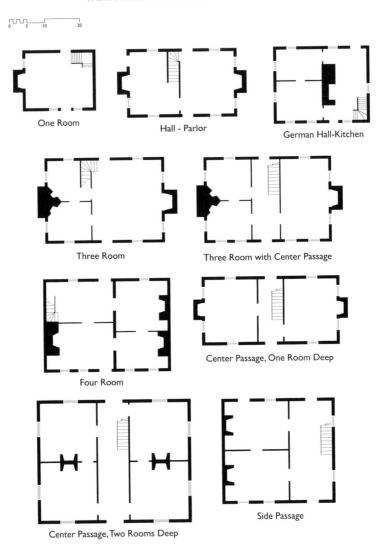

One Room

Hall - Parlor

German Hall-Kitchen

Three Room

Three Room with Center Passage

Four Room

Center Passage, One Room Deep

Center Passage, Two Rooms Deep

Side Passage

Adapted from drawings by Carl Lounsbury and Doug Swaim

FIGURE 25. *Traditional house plans in the Piedmont. A few late 18th- and early 19th-c. houses had center passages, but traditional direct-entry plans persisted into the 19th c. even among large houses. There were many local variations. In the eastern Piedmont, planters built symmetrical 1- and 2-story frame houses; a few had center passages, but many had hall-parlor plans and smaller rear rooms, often containing the stair. In the central and western Piedmont, with its mid-Atlantic influences, hall-parlor plans occurred, but many Quakers and other families preferred a 3-room plan with the entrance into a large room that had 2 smaller rooms beside it. Germans traditionally had the entrance into a large hall-kitchen room; 1 or 2 side chambers were sometimes heated by stoves. Some large late 18th-c. houses had 4 approximately equal rooms without a passage. During the early 19th c., as center passages grew more popular, a common variation bisected the 3-room plan with a passage. After about 1830, symmetrical center-passage plans dominated in substantial houses.*

FIGURE 26. *Davie County Jail, Mocksville.* (DE 1). *In the late 18th and early 19th centuries more communities, such as Mocksville, began building civic and private buildings of masonry. The well-built former jail (and jailer's residence) of brick laid in Flemish bond takes a typically domestic form for its era and occupies a prominent spot near the courthouse.*

FIGURE 27. *Alexander Long House, Rowan Co.* (RW 40). *Distinctive in the Federal period architecture of the western Piedmont is vividly decorative brickwork, with letters and figures formed by glazed headers—here on a double chimney, sometimes on house walls. Such work occurred in the colonial period in English areas of the mid-Atlantic and upper South, but it appeared in the Piedmont from the 1790s into the 1820s. Except for those in Salem, the artisans are generally unidentified.*

FIGURE 28. *Utzman-Chambers House, Salisbury* (RW 21). *During the 1810s and 1820s, the delicate Neoclassicism of the Federal style gained popularity, and some houses began to display exterior as well as interior adornment, such as the pedimented gable ends.*

FIGURE 29. *Utzman-Chambers House, Salisbury* (RW 21). *Fine Federal style interiors akin to other early 19th-c. houses in the western Piedmont include a mantel (left, bottom) with leafy sunburst and small urns and a curved stair with floral bracket (above), showing the influence of Owen Biddle's Young Carpenter's Assistant (1805) from the northeast Piedmont to the southwest.*

FIGURE 30. *Mordecai House, Raleigh* (WK 39). *An early shaper of public taste was English-born William Nichols, who served as state architect in the 1810s and early 1820s. He redesigned the old State House in elegant classical style and planned other buildings in Raleigh, Hillsborough, Lexington, and elsewhere. For the Mordecai family, he retained an old hall-parlor plan plantation house and added a 2-story front section with elegantly simple portico and other early Greek Revival details.*

Many are 2 stories tall with beautifully executed brickwork of Flemish bond enriched with glazed headers, corbeling, or molded brick. Such houses were built for English Quakers, Germans, Scotch-Irish, and a few Huguenots from Guilford to Lincoln and Catawba counties; others appear up the Catawba River in Burke Co.

A Taste for Improvement

Although traditional building forms dominated the region through the nineteenth century, some townspeople and well-connected planters took a growing interest in stylish architecture. "Elegant" and "modern" buildings betokened status for the planter or merchant family and for a community or institution.

The English classicism now known as the Georgian style continued its influence from the 1780s through the 1810s and into the 1820s, while in the latter decades the light Adamesque classicism of the Federal style gained sway. Artisans combined customary forms with national styles to create a dynamic balance of old and new, local and national, producing regionally distinctive clusters of buildings. Planters, especially in the northeastern Piedmont, erected stylish residences incorporating pedimented fronts and porticoes and lavish classical detailing (see Person Place, Fig. 22). Many prospering families, including those

FIGURE 31. *Pine Hall Plantation House, Stokes Co.* (SK 6). *Beginning in the 1830s, but especially in the 1840s and 1850s, planters and townspeople built spacious Greek Revival houses of frame or occasionally brick. Typically these are 2 stories tall beneath a shallow hip or gable roof and have broad, symmetrical facades and large doors and windows framed by wide, classically derived moldings. Most have single or double porticoes with columns or pillars, often in a Doric or Tuscan order, and complementary corner pilasters. Plans typically have a center passage flanked by 1 or 2 pairs of rooms. A popular source was Asher Benjamin's* The Practical House Carpenter *(1830).*

FIGURE 32. *Poplar Tent Presbyterian Church, Cabarrus Co.* (CA 21). *Prospering Piedmont Presbyterians and other congregations built simple but clearly classical pedimented churches, often of brick, with pedimented fronts and pilasters flanking big windows in a temple-like form.*

FIGURE 33. *Blandwood, Greensboro* (GF 11). *New York architect A. J. Davis's designs for the Piedmont progressives constituted a notable chapter in his career and produced some of the state's principal antebellum edifices. (Local builders complained that the state was encouraging the "far-fetched and dear-bought" at the expense of native talent, but the trend continued nonetheless.) Blandwood showed his stylish yet economical Tuscan mode in a trendsetting towered villa for Governor John Motley Morehead, leader of internal improvement and other efforts. A few other Piedmont clients erected Italianate villas (*Montfort Hall; *Cooleemee), but the style did not gain widespread popularity until after the Civil War.*

FIGURE 34. *Christ Church, Raleigh.* (WK 2). *New York architect Richard Upjohn, a leader in the American Gothic Revival, designed Christ Church in his Early English style, with rough stone walls, cruciform plan, and broach spire. The Gothic Revival associated with ancient traditions gained early use among Episcopalians, but by the late 1850s other denominations had adopted the mode.*

FIGURE 35. *Davidson County Courthouse, Lexington* (DV 1). *During the 1840s and especially the 1850s, new courthouses rose that were the pride of their counties and took literally the temple form. Rowan, Davidson, and Guilford counties, their prospects brightened by the NCRR, competed jovially to build the finest "temple of justice." Davidson's was built by George Dudley and William Ashley, who had been involved in NCRR projects.*

of the western Piedmont, adorned buildings of conservative form—but with fashionable mantels, stairs, and other details.

From the 1830s onward, Piedmont leaders adopted national architectural ideals and created some of the most advanced architecture in the state. An unprecedented number of big, elaborate houses rose, while public buildings took

FIGURE 36. *Engleside, Warrenton* (WR 27). *Builders executed some buildings from architects' designs, but more often they planned buildings themselves using traditional knowledge and motifs from popular patternbooks and other examples. The shop of carpenter-contractor Jacob W. Holt in Warrenton was among the largest, and his work, which spanned several counties, combined Greek Revival and Italianate patternbook elements.*

on a grander scale and more stylish character. Most employed the modern classicism of the Greek Revival. The *State Capitol redefined the state's image with one of the finest Greek Revival buildings in the nation (Fig. 17). Where railroads and gold mines raised prosperity, Piedmont planters and townspeople were among the first in the state to adopt the simple, broad forms of the widely popular Greek Revival style. More adventurous were designs in the picturesque mode, as Piedmont clients built some of the state's first Gothic Revival churches and Italianate villas and institutional buildings.

Generally owners and artisans adapted architectural ideas from popular builders' guides, but a few Piedmont clients turned to the founding members of the national architectural profession, most prominently the New York architects Alexander Jackson Davis and Richard Upjohn. The trend grew as railroads and a general "spirit of improvement" expanded in the antebellum era, and other men entered the picture, such as William Percival, who produced vivid Italianate and Gothic Revival designs. At the same time, carpenters and masons drawn to Piedmont railroad towns were among the first in the state to become contractors capable of creating big, stylish buildings from an architect's plans or their own renditions of patternbook designs. Some also operated sash and blind factories and other businesses. John Berry of Hillsborough, Dabney Cosby and Jacob Holt from Virginia, Conrad and Williams of Lexington, and William Murdoch, a Scots stonemason who arrived to work on the State Capitol and then followed railroad building to Salisbury, were but a few of the practical builders kept busy with the "spirit of improvement."

THE NEW SOUTH: CIVIL WAR TO WORLD WAR II

Although the Piedmont was not a battlefield during the Civil War, thousands of its men died or were grievously wounded in military service, and on the home front families suffered from desperate shortages. North Carolina, especially the Piedmont and west, resisted secession until after the firing on Fort Sumter. Internal warfare beset several Piedmont counties, including the old "Quaker belt" where Union sentiment was strong. Lying well behind Confederate lines, Piedmont factories and railroads took on new importance in producing war materials and carrying troops and supplies. Indeed, after the fall of Norfolk in 1862, Charlotte, with its protected rail connections, became the Confederate navy yard. In the last months of the war, Union troops came through the Piedmont, destroying factories and railroad facilities, harrying the citizenry, and stripping farms, but most of the region escaped direct damage. At the close of the conflict, Gen. Joseph E. Johnston and Gen. William T. Sherman met near the railroad village of Durham to settle terms of surrender. Their troops acquired a taste for local tobacco and, after they returned home, sent back for more.

Between the Civil War and the Great Depression, North Carolina experienced an astonishing transformation from the South's poorest state to industrial leader, and from an essentially nonurban state to one characterized by dispersed urbanization. Initially, from 1865 to about 1880, citizens struggled simply to recover from the war and regain momentum. There was tremendous outmigration as both blacks and whites left the state, a trend that continued well into the twentieth century. On the farm, landowners, tenants, and former slaves found new labor arrangements. Towns grew as blacks and whites left the countryside in search of opportunities. The 1880s and 1890s brought a surge of industrial and urban growth that by the early twentieth century had reshaped the contours of the economy, society, landscape, and architecture. For the first time, North Carolina industries and entrepreneurs took leading roles on the national and even international scene.

Several interdependent developments took place: hard times on the farm and increased reliance on cash crops; burgeoning networks of rails and roads; growth of factories employing low-paid native workers to process local cotton, tobacco,

FIGURE 37. *Erwin Mill, Durham* (DH 45). *The New South ethos transformed the Piedmont with railroads and industries, including textile mills, seen as the hope of the region.*

FIGURE 38. *Hickory Depot, Catawba Co.* (CT 18). *Typical of the many depots built from the 1890s into the early 20th c., the station was evidently built by the Elliott firm of Hickory, builders of many depots for Southern Railway, which dominated much of the region from the 1890s on.*

and wood along with development of water, steam, and electric power sources to run them; new investment in public and private education; growing concentration of wealth in towns and cities; and an overall shift of economic strength and urban population from the east to the railroad towns of the Piedmont.

These changes interacted with racial and political developments. Black citizens strove for improved educational and work opportunities and founded fraternal organizations and churches, including Baptist, African Methodist Episcopal, and African Methodist Episcopal Zion, some of which were out-

FIGURE 39. *St. Joseph's A.M.E. Church, Durham* (DH 31). *After Emancipation, black church members established their own congregations. Most met for a time in simple buildings and then constructed substantial brick churches displaying fine masonry work by artisans who were church members. St. Joseph's, designed by Philadelphia architect Samuel Leary, reflects the strength of Durham's black middle class.*

growths of racially mixed antebellum churches. A strong black middle class emerged in several towns. From the 1860s into the 1890s black voters and leaders, usually Republicans, participated in politics. But in 1898 and 1900 the Democrats' "white supremacy crusade," which was supported by many Piedmont business leaders, resulted in disfranchisement of black citizens and hardening of racial segregation laws and practices through more than half of the twentieth century.

Overarching every aspect of change was the deep, broad movement from the small, local, diverse entrepreneurships numerous in the 1870s and 1880s to the big, nationalized, corporate, and standardized systems that emerged by the 1890s and dominated the twentieth century. The latter included the Southern and Seaboard railroads; Duke and Reynolds in tobacco; the Hanes, Cone, Cannon, and Burlington Mills textile empires; regional systems of electric power; and unified state programs of roads and schools. Some of these systems were rooted in New York and other distant capitals, but the state's business elite participated in and even led the process of consolidation. By the 1920s the leadership of the state, often dominated by Piedmont men, took on a character described as "business progressivism" and "progressive conservatism." As North Carolina changed from a backward rural state to one of the most industrialized in the South—called a Progressive Plutocracy and Dixie Dynamo by the mid-twentieth century—the Piedmont led the way.[8]

Hard Times on the Farm

Even with rapid industrialization, for a century after the Civil War, the state remained predominantly rural. As late as 1900 more than 90 percent of its people were country dwellers. In much of the Piedmont, small and middling farmers continued to rely on their own and hired labor to meet their needs and make a small profit from grain, livestock, tobacco or cotton, and fruit. (For several years, trade in dried fruit for urban markets was a mainstay in Winston and Salisbury, while Statesville did a brisk trade in herbs and ginseng for national and international sale.) The big cash crops of tobacco and cotton grew increasingly important, and nearby factories provided a ready market. Extending from the Old Belt along the Virginia border, tobacco cultivation covered new territory when growers found that, if fertilized, the lean, sandy soil of several areas was ideal for the golden, bright leaf manufacturers wanted. At the same time, counties in the eastern and southern Piedmont increased production of cotton for market.

Some farm families regained stability and even prosperity, especially those who could combine limited cash crop production with fairly self-sufficient mixed agriculture, professions, or mercantile businesses. They nourished their land and built or expanded farmhouses and outbuildings. Sawmills enabled farmers to build frame houses more readily than ever before; most followed conservative forms while incorporating new mass-produced materials. If few rivaled the ornateness of town buildings, many farmhouses displayed such novelties as decorated gables and porches, and some of the most prosperous farmers, country doctors, and merchants built stylish residences in Italianate, Queen Anne, Colonial Revival, and Craftsman modes. There were many L- and T-plan farmhouses of 1 or 2 stories; others had 4 rooms under a high hip roof. Typically the farmhouse had a rear ell containing a connected kitchen and perhaps a dining room; these often replaced (or reused) the old freestanding kitchens. In the early 20th c., multitudes of small and middling farmers selected the popular bungalow mode, paralleling trends in towns and across the nation.

8. This section draws on Glass, *Textile Industry*; Hanchett, *Sorting Out the New South City*; and Tilley, *Bright Tobacco Industry*. See also Goldfield, *Cotton Fields and Skyscrapers*; C. Vann Woodward, *Origins of the New South, 1877–1913* (Baton Rouge: Louisiana State University Press, 1951, 1971); and George Brown Tindall, *The Emergence of the New South, 1913–1945* (Baton Rouge: Louisiana State University Press, 1967). See Tindall, *Emergence of the New South*, on North Carolina's "business progressivism" (224) and continuing "conservative progressivism" (645).

FIGURE 40. *Tobacco barns, Carter farm, Rockingham Co., 1985. Cultivation of flue-cured, bright-leaf tobacco originated in the Old Belt along the Virginia border before the Civil War. Production increased rapidly after the war, however, and by the end of the century it had spread into other regions of the state. Tobacco barns were purpose-built to cure the leaf through an exacting sequence of heating over several days. Workers tied "hands" of newly picked leaves onto long sticks, then hung them snugly on "tier poles" in the barns. A flue carried heat from an external furnace into the barn, and once the tobacco was "cured," the farmer removed it from the barn, graded it, and hauled it to market. The labor-intensive but highly profitable crop became the mainstay of many small farmers as well as larger landowners. In the 20th c., production continued to rise, and various improvements were made in barn types and curing methods. Thousands of traditional barns once defined the rural landscape, but they have been made obsolete by automated "bulk" barns and are rapidly vanishing.*

Especially in the western Piedmont, big frame as well as log barns were constructed for hay or livestock. Those who turned to dairy and stock farming, which increased in the early twentieth century, often erected capacious gambrel-roofed barns accompanied by silos for feed. Tobacco curing barns, generally built of log, although some were of frame, proliferated by the thousands as tobacco cultivation expanded into new territory.

At the centers of rural neighborhoods, congregations black and white built neat if not elaborate churches of frame or occasionally brick. Streamside gristmills continued as social and economic focal points; these were soon supplemented by steam-powered roller mills that ground grain faster and finer. General stores proliferated; in addition to providing a wide range of goods and a center of social life, the store often served as a principal source of credit for local farmers.

FIGURE 41. *Carrington House, Granville Co.* (GV 13). *Widely popular in the late 19th and early 20th centuries was the symmetrical 1- or 2-story house, 1 or 2 rooms deep with a center passage, rendered up-to-date with a millwork-adorned porch and often a raised central gable to give a picturesque touch.*

While some farmers maintained their independence, many succumbed to increasingly hard times. The old tobacco and cotton planting counties depended most on farm tenancy and the crop-lien system as successors to the economy of slavery. In other areas, too, dropping crop prices combined with soil depletion and rising fertilizer costs and railroad freight rates drove more and more farm people into debt, trouble, and tenancy. Farmers borrowed at high interest rates against the next year's crop, secured by promises to produce readily marketable cotton or tobacco. Raising these crops, where the big profits were made far from the field, continued an essentially colonial system and kept farm income low. The system also reduced the time farmers could devote to raising their own food crops and livestock, and thus many families became ever more dependent on cash and credit for the necessities of life. Moreover, beginning in the 1870s, fence laws enacted in one county after another reduced the capacity of the small farmer or landless family to raise pigs and cows for their own sustenance. These conditions, "a virtual assault on Piedmont yeoman society," drove thousands into a cycle of poverty and pushed many off the farms and into the factories.[9]

Seeking to better their lot, in the late nineteenth century many farmers organized local granges and joined the Farmers' Alliance, part of a national movement. Gaining strength in the 1880s and early 1890s with the Populist movement, they succeeded in founding the North Carolina College of Agricul-

9. Hall et al., *Like a Family*, 6.

FIGURE 42. *Mt. Ebal Methodist Church, Davidson Co.* (DV 17). *Increased access to sawn lumber and other mass-produced building materials encouraged hundreds of rural congregations to build new churches in the late 19th and early 20th centuries. Many were simple gable-fronted structures such as this one; some were adorned with a touch of millwork, and some had L-plans, towers, or auditorium plan sanctuaries as popularized by denominational publications.*

FIGURE 43. *Murray's Mill, Catawba Co.* (CT 8). *Essential to rural life were grist- and sawmills, from the 18th c. well into the 20th c. They served as centers of social as well as economic activity and were often accompanied by other small industries and a country store.*

tural & Mechanic Arts (present-day North Carolina State University [NCSU]) in Raleigh and won some economic reforms. Agricultural education and extension programs promoted soil and stock improvement and crop diversification, such as peach cultivation, which was introduced in the Sandhills in the 1910s. But while farmers saw demand and prices jump during World War I,

FIGURE 44. *Overby Farm, Stokes Co. (ca. 1900?). Thousands of farmers, landowners or tenants, lived a materially sparse life in plain, even crude farmhouses. Although most have now vanished, rudimentary log and frame farmhouses and outbuildings continued in use well into the 20th c., evidence of the hard times many farm people experienced.*

this was followed by agricultural depressions in the 1920s and then by the Great Depression.

Railroads

At the end of the Civil War, the immediate task was to repair wartime damage to the railroads and then to expand the network. Despite hard times, rail construction had resumed with vigor by the early 1870s. Especially where competing lines kept rates low, inland cities became real trade centers for the first time. Aiming to become "the great central trading place of all this region" and seeing that rails could "equalize the advantages" of inland and coastal locations, Charlotteans generated connections in every direction, including the Midwest and Mississippi River markets, and called their railside cotton sales district "the

FIGURE 45. *(Opposite) Principal railroad construction in Piedmont North Carolina to 1920. The 1880s and 1890s brought rapid rail construction, followed by corporate consolidation at the end of the century: the Southern Railway operated in the Piedmont and west, the Seaboard Air Line skirted it on the east and south, and the Atlantic Coast Line stayed mainly in the plain. All had forebears in the antebellum period (Fig. 18) and incorporated the network of short lines built in the late 19th c. The Piedmont saw relatively little new construction after 1900, chiefly the original Norfolk Southern Railway, completed in the early 20th c. as an alternate Raleigh-to-Charlotte route. Yadkin was the only Piedmont county never to have rail service. By the late 20th c., Seaboard and Atlantic Coastline had joined, then formed CSX Corp. Southern (which had already absorbed the old Norfolk Southern) merged with the Norfolk & Western to create the modern Norfolk Southern. A few branch lines continued or returned to independent local ownership.*

Principal Railroad Construction in Piedmont North Carolina to 1920

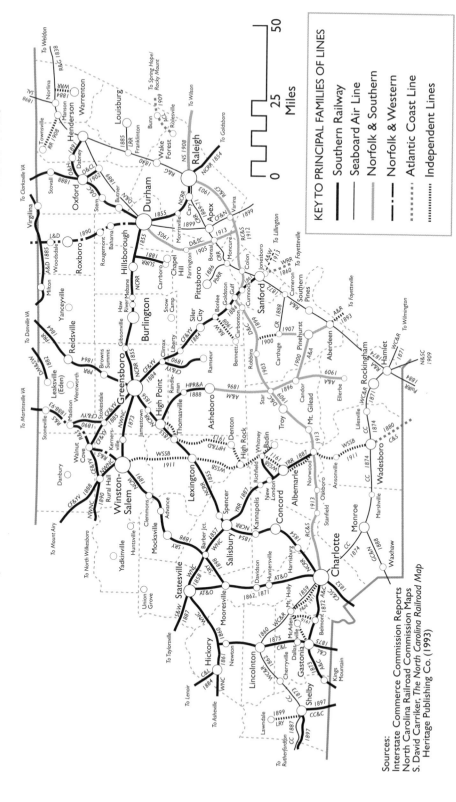

KEY TO PRINCIPAL FAMILIES OF LINES

Southern Railway
Seaboard Air Line
Norfolk & Southern
Norfolk & Western
Atlantic Coast Line
Independent Lines

Sources:
Interstate Commerce Commission Reports
North Carolina Railroad Commission Maps
S. David Carriker, *The North Carolina Railroad Map*
Heritage Publishing Co. (1993)

Wharf." Businessmen in Winston strove mightily to get their first rail link, which was completed in 1873 and opened an era of rapid development. Railroads brought the steam power revolution that transformed the scale of textiles and other industries. They enlarged the potential market enough to justify investment, and they solved the fuel problem by hauling coal from Appalachian mines, thus freeing mills from waterpower sites.[10]

The 1880s and 1890s were the prime period of railroad building, as trackage in the state increased from 1,500 to 4,000 miles. The Western North Carolina Railroad (WNCRR), long-delayed western extension of the NCRR, crossed the mountains and opened the Piedmont to western suppliers and markets, and the Cape Fear & Yadkin Valley Railroad completed tracks from Wilmington to Mount Airy in hopes of creating a trunk line to the midwest. Smaller lines created spurs to previously rail-deprived towns or formed new links between routes. During the 1890s the state's railroads were redefined as part of a nationwide consolidation, wherein national corporations—Southern, Seaboard, and Atlantic Coast Line—divided most of the state's trackage among themselves. The big companies transformed the hard-won east-west routes, built to benefit trade within the state, into links in national north-south corridors.

Industrial Boom

During the 1860s and 1870s, factories were still seen as complements to agriculture, but by 1880 the gospel of the New South proclaimed industrialization

10. "Letter from Charlotte," *North Carolina Weekly Standard*, 20 July 1870, quoted in Janette Thomas Greenwood, *Bittersweet Legacy: The Black and White "Better Classes" in Charlotte, 1850–1910* (Chapel Hill: University of North Carolina Press, 1994), 56; Hanchett, *Sorting Out the New South City*, 32.

FIGURE 46. *(Opposite) Distribution of textile, tobacco, and other industries ca. 1930. The state's industries and industrialists formed a complex network of family and business connections. In textiles the Holts in Alamance Co., the Fries family in Salem, the Moreheads in Rockingham Co., the Leaks and Steeles in Richmond Co., and the Rhynes, Loves, and others in Gaston Co. were among those who built on antebellum foundations. At Concord the Odell family built a textile empire, soon succeeded by the Cannons and their textile city town of Kannapolis. The tobacco business saw dramatic consolidation— a map of ca. 1890 would have shown scores of small, dispersed factories. Tobacco men also reinvested profits in textile expansion. In Winston the Hanes family sold their tobacco business to Reynolds and turned to hosiery and knitwear. Durham tobacco man Julian Carr entered textile production in the 1880s and expanded after his tobacco factory became part of the Dukes' American Tobacco Co. The Dukes, working with William Erwin, a Holt relative and former manager, plowed tobacco profits into textile mills, then turned to electric power production. Many of these industrialists also invested in banking, railroads, and real estate development. Important newcomers were Greensboro's Cone family. In the 1920s, succeeding the Holts in Alamance Co., J. Spencer Love, son of a Gaston Co. textile family, founded Burlington Mills. In the mid- and late 20th c., Cone, Burlington, Cannon, and a few other in-state and outside corporations consolidated ownership.*

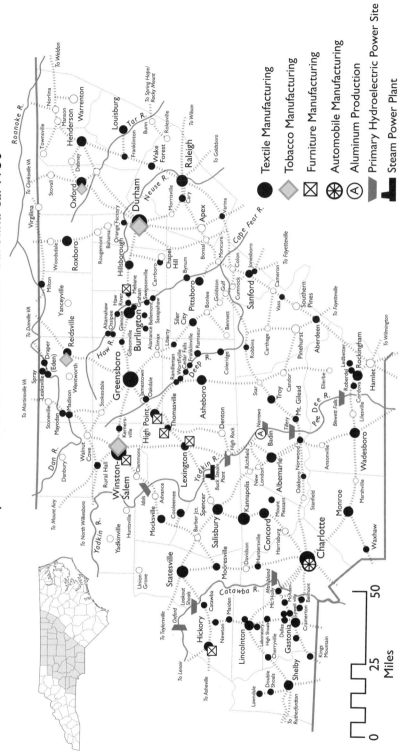

Principal Industries in Piedmont North Carolina ca. 1930

Textile Manufacturing

Tobacco Manufacturing

Furniture Manufacturing

Automobile Manufacturing

Aluminum Production

Primary Hydroelectric Power Site

Steam Power Plant

0 25 50
Miles

as the salvation of the South. The Piedmont moved to the forefront with its regularly touted advantages: proximity to raw materials, including tobacco, cotton, and timber; a moderate climate; railroads and plentiful waterpower; and above all, abundant cheap labor from native men, women, and children streaming off the farms. There were two other key ingredients: state and local governments that favored business and industry, and smart, ambitious, hardworking, and hard-driving entrepreneurs, natives and newcomers, many of whom were strong Methodists, always practical and sometimes visionary, determined to take and make opportunities in the New South.

When the Civil War ended, a few manufacturers were quick to rebuild and expand. Durham became a boomtown spurred by orders from soldiers who enjoyed its tobacco in April 1865, and some cotton manufacturers who operated through the war retooled their mills. Most industrial growth came slowly, however, with improvement of the rail network and the accumulation of capital. By 1880 many tobacco factories and several cotton mills were in operation along with other manufactories, including sash and blind factories, iron foundries, and wagonmakers. The groundwork had been laid for an era of dramatic expansion. In the 1880s the state became the nation's leading maker of tobacco products, and in the early twentieth century it became the top producer of textiles and wooden furniture.

Tobacco

Manufacturing of chewing and smoking tobacco grew rapidly, especially along the northern Old Belt zone, and yielded capital for other enterprises. Scores of tobacco factories appeared in small towns from Oxford to Mocksville. Small or large, initially they needed only hand labor and could be located anywhere convenient to growers and shipping routes. Many stood at the center of town near the depot, accompanied by sales houses and warehouses. In the 1870s, Durham, Winston, and Reidsville emerged as leaders along with Danville, Va. Tobacco businesses traditionally employed both black and white workers, who headed by the thousands to tobacco towns, where they established working-, middle-, and upper-class neighborhoods, businesses, and churches.

Toward the end of the century, a few companies dominated the business. R. J. Reynolds in Winston and the Duke family of Durham, led by James B. Duke, bought up or eliminated competing producers. As national and international leaders, these companies yielded fortunes far beyond anything the state had seen before. The immense profits generated by tobacco manufacturing were often reinvested in textile manufacturing, which boosted that industry, and profits from both went into banking, railroads, and hydroelectric power development, which in turn spurred textile production and other industrial growth.

FIGURE 47. *W. T. Blackwell "Bull Durham" Tobacco Factory, later American Tobacco Co., Durham.* (DH 19). *Built for Durham's pioneering tobacco manufacturer, the big Italianate building presented a grand image and contained multiple operations. It was acquired and expanded by James B. Duke's American Tobacco Co. in the 1890s.*

FIGURE 48. *Reynolds Tobacco Co. Factory, Winston-Salem* (FY 43). *R. J. Reynolds's plug tobacco business was taken into the American Tobacco Co. for a time, but after 1911, when the U.S. Supreme Court ordered ATC's dissolution into Liggett & Myers, American, and R. J. Reynolds, Reynolds soon took the lead in cigarette production with its Camel brand.*

FIGURE 49. *Loray Mill, Gastonia* (GS 5). *The Loray Mill, the biggest under one roof, stands in the dense textile zone around Charlotte that includes Gaston Co., site of more textile mills than any other county in the nation. By the end of the 19th c. most textile (and tobacco) factory owners had adopted industry standards for "slow-burn" or "mill" construction mandated by the northern mill insurance companies that insured many N.C. factories. The standards, designed to slow the progress of a fire and reduce its damage to the building, were developed earlier in New England. Among the key elements were solid brick construction with tapering walls; separation of especially fire-prone stages of production from the rest of the factory; masonry fire walls; heavy timber construction of stout posts and thick plank floors that would char rather than burn quickly; separate stair towers to prevent flames from running up through internal stairs; and a big water tank on top of the tower. Other functional elements included large windows and a maximum depth of the building to assure adequate light on the tasks at the machinery, heavy construction to carry heavy loads and vibration, and often a sufficiently imposing building, especially the tower, to convey the stature and power of the business. The mandated water tower, thick brick walls, and low gable roof, along with the large windows, combined readily with the Italianate style, more or less lavishly adorned with corbeled brickwork.*

Textiles

Cotton factories, which depended on reliable sources of power, developed first at established mill sites on the Deep, Haw, Smith-Dan, and other streams. The Holt family on the Haw was quick to expand, with Thomas M. Holt supposedly the first southern mill man to revisit northern mill suppliers after the war. Industrialists bought old and new mill sites (including, as earlier, former gristmill sites), built and expanded factories, and diversified into finishing and specialty products, thus adding more and more value to their goods. They augmented waterpower with steam in the 1880s and 1890s and then added electric power in the early twentieth century. Prominent mill designers included

Daniel A. Tompkins and Stuart Cramer, active in Charlotte and beyond; Lockwood, Greene & Co. of Boston, which had a Charlotte office; and C. R. Makepeace of Rhode Island, born in *Franklinville.

Freed from the limitations of waterpower, investors erected mills trackside and added capacity at waterpower sites. Between 1880 and 1900, as rail trackage nearly tripled, the proportion of textile mills using steam power rose accordingly. As the number of mills rose from 60 to 318 between 1885 and 1915, capacity soared from 2,500 looms to 67,288, and from 200,000 spindles to 3.8 million. Further growth followed with expansion of the electric power network. Town after town hopped on the cotton mill bandwagon. Some communities added a mill or two, but others mushroomed into textile cities such as Greensboro, Concord, Rockingham, Leakville-Draper-Spray (Eden), Gastonia, and a large area around Charlotte. Largely local ownership of textile factories continued until the mid-twentieth century.

The New South "Cotton Mill Campaign"—"Bring the mills to the cotton"—offered employment to men, women, and children who moved in from the farms to find "public work." Black workers were hired for some tasks, but most millworkers were white. In contrast to other industries, textile manufacturers regularly established mill villages to house their workers. At waterpower sites, which were typically remote from existing towns, mill owners had to build houses in order to attract a workforce. Families coming from the countryside encountered patterns akin to plantation paternalism. They rented their homes from the mill owner, who exerted control over community as well as factory life. The mill stood beside the stream, within sight of the mill owner's or managers' residences above. Up the hillsides rows of dwellings for "operatives" lined narrow streets and lanes.

Mill houses typically repeated forms seen in small farmhouses; some were of log, but most were of frame construction. They stood 1 or 2 stories high, usually with 3 to 5 rooms, depending on the size of the family working at the mill. In *Cotton Mill: Commercial Features* (1899), Charlotte mill promoter and builder Daniel A. Tompkins affirmed the practice of providing spacious lots and rooms for gardens: "The whole matter of providing attractive and comfortable habitations for cotton operatives [is] summarized in the statement that they are essentially a rural people. . . . While their condition is in most cases decidedly bettered by going to the factory, the old instincts cling to them."[11]

Even freed from waterpower sites, industrialists continued to build self-contained mill villages outside town limits. Most laid out grids of streets stretching from the tracks and the mills and built rows of small houses in standard de-

11. Daniel A. Tompkins, *Cotton Mill: Commercial Features* (Charlotte: Observer Printing House, 1899), 145.

FIGURE 50. *Mill houses, Bellemont, Alamance Co.* (AM 37). *In small riverside villages, such as those along the Haw River and its tributaries, rows of millworkers' houses repeat forms akin to small farmhouses. Local millwright Berry Davidson built several mills and villages, including Bellemont and *Glencoe.*

FIGURE 51. *Typical mill house. Daniel A. Tompkins reflected common wisdom in his* Cotton Mill: Commercial Features *(1899) and showed house designs based on those in current use. Many were 1-story, gable-sided houses, sometimes with a rear ell, but there were also L-plan dwellings and other variations.*

signs. Such sites, cheaper than urban land, also abetted the paternalistic control of workers. By the early twentieth century, the southern Piedmont had become "one long mill village," an industrial "state within a state" that reached from the Haw River to the foothills of the Appalachians, with Charlotte as its capital.[12]

Demand for cotton spiked when World War I began in Europe and then zigzagged after the war, and owners strove for greater economies and profits. In the 1920s the state topped Massachusetts as the chief producer of textiles. To at-

12. Glass, *Textile Industry in North Carolina*, 50, 57.

tract and keep workers, some mill owners established model villages with social and recreational facilities and designed by professional landscape designers, notably Earle S. Draper of Charlotte.

While some villages had good housing and working conditions, others were miserable places; child labor and other problems drew growing attention from Progressive Era reformers. As mills grew bigger and managers more remote, the personal quality of paternalism diminished. Demand for higher production by fewer operatives—"the stretch-out" they called it—bred discontent. Workers asserted their independence chiefly by moving from one mill to another for better pay or conditions. Although the native, farm-bred factory hands were less inclined to organize and strike than those in the north, there were intermittent if generally unsuccessful strikes, especially in the 1920s and 1930s. Isolated from city life and increasingly distant from the farm, the mill village developed a separate working-class culture, where residents depended on one another in communities that many described as "like a family."

Wood Products

The third major industry, manufacture of wood products, was stimulated by tobacco and textiles. These industries required wooden hogsheads, wagons, spindles, and bobbins. Winston, Hickory, and Carthage became nationally famous for their wagons and buggies. Some manufacturers soon expanded into furniture production, taking advantage of still-abundant timber and railroad transportation. They were encouraged by the growing regional and national demand for cheap, sturdy home furnishings, which soared in the homebuilding boom after World War I. Thomasville, Hickory, and High Point developed into state and eventually national leaders in the furniture business, and Mebane and other towns also had important furniture factories. High Point became a major national furniture display and sales market, improving prospects for the industry.

Likewise exploiting the forests, the rails, and the steam engine was the proliferation of timbering operations, sawmills, and sash and blind factories and other producers of construction materials. Into the Sandhills' remaining stands of longleaf pines, entrepreneurs built logging railroads and quickly turned the giant trees into lumber to feed town building booms. In nearly every town served by rail, manufacturers founded steam-powered factories to produce newly economical framing lumber, weatherboards, flooring, window sash and doors, and miles of ornamental millwork for local and national markets.

Electric Power

The early twentieth century brought another revolution that sprang in part from the textile industry and that in turn took a vital role in the state's emergence as a national leader: harnessing the immense potential of Piedmont

FIGURE 52. *High Rock Dam and Power Plant, Davidson Co.* (DV 19). *The Yadkin and Catawba rivers, with their great volume and relatively reliable flow originating in the mountains, offered prime sites for hydroelectric power development.*

streams to produce hydroelectric power. In the 1890s industrialists explored power sites on major rivers, where some built mills, while others tried the emerging technology of electric power generation and long-distance transmission to factories. The first successful venture was the 1898 *Idols Power Plant, built on the Yadkin by the Fries family, who transmitted its power to their factories in Salem. The Dukes' exploration of power sites for textile mills (*Cooleemee) spurred their interest in hydroelectric power to boost regional industrial production. About 1900 the Dukes joined South Carolina engineer William S. Lee and others to "electrify" the Catawba River, regarded as the most reliable stream. In 1905 they founded the Southern (Duke) Power Co., which soon became a massive regional utility system.

By the 1920s long-distance transmission of electricity had again transformed industrial production. An observer reported in 1929 that with the state ranking third in the nation in the quantity of developed waterpower, "the recent industrial development of the state has been due more to the development of our water power resources than to any other factor." Electric power enabled the South to outstrip New England in textile production. As much as 80 percent of the state's power came from hydroelectric plants at one time, but the proportion declined as companies added coal-powered electric plants to compensate for floods and droughts. Electric power in textile mills permitted more efficient equipment, better lighting, and air conditioning—the term coined in 1906 by Charlotte mill designer Stuart Cramer for an innovation to benefit the fibers, not the workers. Although rural electrification did not take place until 1935, by the 1920s electricity had already redefined urban life, powering streetcars, electric lights and appliances, and myriad other machines and systems.[13]

Highways

Long regarded as essential to development, highway improvements were slow to come. Although Charlotte-Mecklenburg, Greensboro-Guilford, and Asheville-Buncombe began their own Good Roads programs, few in state or local government were eager to invest in road building until the 1920s, when automobiles and trucks grew too numerous to ignore. The North Carolina Good Roads Association (est. 1902) campaigned long and hard for local and state support for highways and, led by Harriet Morehead Berry of Chapel Hill, the "Mother of Good Roads," finally won passage of the Highway Act of 1921. This, coupled with the 1920 election of Charlotte's Cameron Morrison as the "Good Roads Governor," opened an era of road construction that produced a unified state highway system. Bringing at long last the intrastate and interstate connections that Archibald Murphey and John Motley Morehead had imagined nearly a century before, highways, like railroads, again opened the Piedmont to unprecedented growth. (See map, p. 83.)

Education

For several years after the Civil War, educational advances took a back seat to industrial development. Lack of public interest coupled with industries' reliance on low wages and low crop prices did little to encourage investment. Nonetheless, some progress was made in the late nineteenth century and much more in the twentieth century, with support from Piedmont industrial philanthropists. Sponsors of new private and public colleges, or schools seeking to relocate, often announced their intentions and then selected the community that made the most attractive offers in land and financial support. Competing Piedmont towns hoping to grow or polish their image proved eager bidders.

Among the first new colleges founded after the Civil War were those for

13. Hobbs, *North Carolina: Economic and Social,* 21 (quote); Robert F. Durden, "Electrifying the Piedmont Carolinas: The Beginning of the Duke Power Company, 1904–1925," pts. 1 and 2, *North Carolina Historical Review* 76, no. 4 (Oct. 1999): 410–40, and 77, no. 1 (Jan. 2000): 54–89; Robert F. Durden, *Electrifying the Piedmont Carolinas: The Duke Power Company, 1904–1997* (Durham: Carolina Academic Press, 2001).

FIGURE 53. *Coca-Cola Bottling Plant, Charlotte* (MK 39). *As N.C. transformed itself into the Good Roads State in the 1920s, improved roads reshaped living patterns, including the distribution of goods by truck (including national brands), with Charlotte a regional center. In its most costly undertaking to that time, the state authorized a series of multimillion-dollar bond issues to be repaid by fees and gasoline taxes, and these were complemented by federal funds. By 1929 more than 7,500 miles of highways in the state system and 65,000 miles of county roads had been built or improved. Major routes planned as part of a national system boosted growth in Piedmont cities, including the Central Highway (present-day US 70) retracing much of the NCRR; present-day US 64 from Manteo to Murphy; and US 1 through Raleigh, part of the major route from New York to Florida. Charlotte, a leader in the Good Roads movement, also built the state's first four-lane highway, the 1926 Wilkinson Blvd. from Charlotte to Gastonia.*

FIGURE 54. *Biddle Hall, Johnson C. Smith University, Charlotte* (MK 33). *Colleges established for black students in the 1860s included present-day *Johnson C. Smith University and *Shaw University and *St. Augustine's College in Raleigh. They were followed by *Bennett College in Greensboro, *Livingstone College in Salisbury, and the schools that became present-day *Winston-Salem State University and *North Carolina Central University in Durham, complementing the state-sponsored *A&T in Greensboro.*

FIGURE 55.
Duke Chapel, Durham (DH 49). When *Trinity College in rural Randolph Co. expressed interest in an urban site, Durham Methodists, including tobacco magnates Julian S. Carr and Washington Duke, made sure that Durham's offer won. In the 1920s Trinity's president persuaded James B. Duke to devote millions of dollars to transforming the school, with architectural designs by Julian Abele and Horace Trumbauer of Philadelphia, into *Duke University. The Duke Endowment, supported by the Southern (Duke) Power Co., assisted many black and white colleges in the 20th c. After World War II, the Reynolds tobacco fortune underwrote the move and expansion of *Wake Forest University in Winston-Salem.

black students. Several aimed at training teachers and preachers, others were more technically oriented, and most were denominational institutions aided by northern benefactors and, in time, local industrialists. Established denominational colleges such as *Davidson, *Salem, and *Wake Forest struggled in the postwar years, but many gained new support from Piedmont industrial benefactors and flourished in the early twentieth century. The move and transformation of Trinity College into Duke University in the 1920s was but the most spectacular event in a larger picture of college renewal across the region.

As state as well as private support for higher education grew, Piedmont cities took an early lead. In the 1880s, encouraged by agricultural and educational reformers, the state founded present-day *North Carolina State University as a

FIGURE 56. *Louis Round Wilson Library, Chapel Hill* (OR 45). *In the 1880s and 1890s new state colleges built big main buildings in Romanesque Revival modes. But as construction took off in the early 20th c., regional architects designed buildings in a free classical style applied to relatively economical buff and red brick buildings (*NCSU; *UNC; *East Campus, Duke; *Queens College, Charlotte). By the 1920s a more formal Beaux Arts mode had gained sway. When UNC began its multimillion-dollar transformation into a major university under the aegis of McKim, Mead & White of New York, the extended Beaux Arts quadrangle plan featured consistent "Colonial" architecture in red brick and stone. Other colleges likewise relied on red brick and stone Georgian Revival architecture by regional and national architects to accommodate their growth in the 20th c., with *Salem Academy and College distinguished by a local Moravian Revival mode.*

FIGURE 57. *Gastonia High School, Gastonia* (GS 4). *In the early 20th-c. public education campaign, communities put new emphasis on modern schoolhouses. Most substantial were consolidated and city high schools, which were typically brick buildings of 1 or often 2 or 3 stories, with generous windows, classrooms along double-loaded corridors, and in some cases gymnasium and auditorium facilities; they were more or less elaborately finished in classical or Scholastic Gothic modes. This one, by local architect Hugh White, was among the finest.*

land grant agricultural and technical college for white men. It was followed in the 1890s by present-day *North Carolina Agricultural & Technical State University (A&T), a land grant college for black students, and present-day *University of North Carolina at Greensboro (UNCG), a normal and industrial college for white women; both were authorized by the "farmers' legislature" of 1890, with Greensboro offering the winning bids in land and financial support. In Chapel Hill, UNC slowly recovered from the Civil War and its aftermath, then gained new prominence in advancing education and other progressive causes statewide. In the 1920s, state bond issues supported a multimillion-dollar building campaign, paralleling the highway program, which undergirded the university's transition to a major regional and national institution.

Having essentially collapsed in the post–Civil War era, the public school system had to be rebuilt from scratch. Despite widespread opposition to tax-funded public education, Governor Charles B. Aycock inaugurated the effort in 1900. First came hundreds of small rural and town schoolhouses for graded schools, which were generally segregated by race. Black leaders struggled to obtain adequate funding for schools, with assistance from the Julius Rosenwald Fund augmenting local efforts. Establishment of high schools, along with school consolidation chiefly for white students—facilitated by school buses and better roads—gained importance in the 1910s and 1920s. Leading towns, some counties, and a few mill owners proudly invested in modern school buildings, which were soon considered essential elements in any progressive community.

New South Towns and Cities

Between 1865 and 1930 North Carolina shifted from an almost exclusively rural state to one of dispersed urbanization. Without a metropolis as a focus of power, business, and culture, a series of competing small cities and myriad little towns grew up along the roads and rails. The communities, too, and especially the cities, took dispersed forms, with their growth spread over far-flung mill villages and residential suburbs. The state emerged as the most industrialized but least urbanized in the nation.

As soon as the shooting stopped in 1865, rebuilding began in key towns along the railroad lines. Newspapers touted each factory or store opening or reopening, celebrated the clink of the chisel and the hammer, and described big new houses in admiring detail. In 1880 urban development was still minuscule. Only Wilmington, with 17,000 people, had a population above 10,000, and behind it only Raleigh, Charlotte, and New Bern exceeded 5,000.

Paralleling railroad and industrial growth, the era after 1880 brought marked change. In 1910 town dwellers finally exceeded 10 percent of the total population, and their numbers increased rapidly in following decades. Charlotte (which in 1860 ranked sixth in size with 2,200 people, just behind Salisbury) passed Wilmington as the largest city with 34,000 in 1910. Briefly outstripped by Winston-Salem in the 1920s, it maintained first position thereafter, while the other Piedmont cities jockeyed for growth to 50,000 and 100,000 by midcentury.

Most of the people who filled the towns and cities were native North Carolinians from the countryside or villages. There was relatively little in-migration, and through much of the twentieth century nearly 100 percent of the population had been born in the state. In addition to the small if permeable elite who ran the banks and factories and the thousands of workers who toiled in the mills, a substantial urban middle and working class developed. These citizens worked as railroad conductors and porters, schoolteachers and seamstresses, bricklayers and carpenters and plumbers and electricians, laborers and servants, engineers and salespeople, barbers and druggists, nurses and housekeepers, bank clerks and secretaries, and grocers and cooks. Black and white, they settled in new neighborhoods of small and middle-sized houses, founded churches and schools, and went back to the country for visits to parents and grandparents and church homecomings.

Small towns remained vital to the region. Some old plantation towns dwindled into villages or vanished, to be sure, but most county seats continued in their familiar roles. Some added industrial plants, and most rebuilt their downtowns in brick in the early twentieth century. A few, such as Wentworth and

FIGURE 58. *Downtown Graham, Alamance Co.* (AM 1). *In the early 20th c. many small and medium-sized towns flourished as local centers, and many rebuilt their courthouses and downtown commercial districts. Some such as Graham had the courthouse at the meeting point of axial streets. A few cities, such as Charlotte and Greensboro, moved their courthouses from such positions as traffic and commerce mounted. Harry Barton of Greensboro designed this and many other courthouses, churches, and houses.*

FIGURE 59. *Pinehurst Country Club, Pinehurst, Moore Co.* (MR 15). *In the Sandhills the benefits of temperate climate and pine woods, combined with new rail connections, encouraged health, then recreational resort communities in Southern Pines and Pinehurst, with "cottages," hotels, and country clubs designed by distant urban architects. This Mediterranean design by Boston architects Haven & Hoyt, Lyman Sise overlooks the famous Pinehurst No. 2 Course by Donald Ross.*

FIGURE 60. *Bird's-eye View of Winston-Salem, 1891. At the turn of the century, Piedmont towns mushroomed into cities that transformed themselves within a few decades, rebuilding downtowns and becoming rapidly more suburban and segmented in uses, classes, and races. Here, early in the process, Winston-Salem's grid of mixed uses lies in the distance, and the beginnings of a streetcar suburb curve toward the foreground.*

Dallas, remained tiny places with a courthouse and a handful of other buildings, while others including Warrenton, Hillsborough, Oxford, Pittsboro, Mocksville, and Lincolnton kept much of their antebellum scale and character while accommodating a degree of change. Encouraged by completion of the WNCRR, Salisbury, Statesville, and Hickory built factories and grew steadily. Some communities developed to serve special purposes, most notably Pinehurst, which was laid out by Frederick Law Olmsted as a resort amid the healing pine air of the Sandhills.

The most striking urban growth, however, came in the emergence of the Piedmont cities, an urban boom small by national standards but dramatic for North Carolina. The *Charlotte Observer* marveled in 1902 at its urban scene: "The charm of the view . . . is the picture of moving life, the living current of people and vehicles, the smoke from the factories and the exhaust of the railroad engines on the four sides of the town. . . . A beautiful picture of a busy and thrifty city is framed in the white and black of the steam and smoke of industry." Complementing industrial development, banks and insurance firms played a key role in town growth and prosperity, and new retail enterprises drew shoppers from far and wide.

Each Piedmont city had its own economic niche and distinctive character. Charlotte, with roots in its antebellum gold rush, epitomized New South energy. Claiming "Expenditures Produce Prosperity," native and newcomer entrepreneurs made it a rail and then a highway hub and soon diversified from cotton manufacturing into equipping, financing, and powering the industry regionwide. With its banks forming the "Wall Street of the South," the "Queen City of the Piedmont" was also "the Electric City" and the "Industrial Center of the New South." In Winston-Salem, established Moravian businessmen and newcomers created manufacturing empires in textiles and tobacco, which in the early twentieth century made the city the state's wealthiest by far—the "Town of a Hundred Millionaires." Durham, the upstart tobacco boomtown, grew fast from a railroad stop in 1865 into a national powerhouse, a "Tobacco Capital," and its world-renowned N.C. Mutual Insurance Co. gained Parrish St. the title "Black Wall Street of America." With new rail connections from the 1890s, Greensboro was the "Gate City of the Piedmont" and home to major textile mills, insurance, pharmaceuticals, and other businesses, as well as colleges. High Point, only a few miles away on the NCRR, provided strong competition as a textile and furniture capital. Raleigh, by contrast, had a few manufacturing concerns but remained primarily a government and college town, satisfied with its white-collar tone as the "City of Oaks."

Late Nineteenth-Century Town Plans and Architecture

Despite their varied identities, the cities shared certain patterns of development. In the nineteenth century, each little city clustered around the courthouse or railroad station, and the idea of a "walking city" prevailed. Uses were relatively mixed, with businesses, factories, and houses of different classes and races generally within sight of one another. Principal streets were lined by high-status businesses and fine residences, with lesser houses and enterprises on secondary streets. Beyond the town were a few outlying settlements: mill villages or "suburban" communities established by black residents on former farmland.

Individual city plans differed. Durham is believably described as having grown up around old cowpaths; Raleigh, Charlotte, and Greensboro adhered to formal grids and squares, and Winston extended Salem's grid. Since all the Piedmont towns had remained tiny through the mid-nineteenth century, those that boomed as New South cities began with much the same form as other small towns: Charlotte or Greensboro in 1860 or even 1870 was not much different from Salisbury or Pittsboro. Toward the end of the century, these patterns began to change. While familiar forms persisted in the smaller towns, the fast-growing cities erased the old for the new.

Architecture, whether in small towns or booming cities, combined familiar conservatism with an eager embrace of new styles, forms, and materials that brought an increasingly national rather than regional character. As fast as entrepreneurs erected sash and blind factories and brickmaking plants by the railroad tracks, buildings constructed of newly cheap and available materials went up by the score. Relishing "modern," "tasty," "artistic," and "northern type" modes, builders erected frame and brick buildings in the ornate styles facilitated by

FIGURE 61. *Odell House, Concord* (CA 3). *Builders in the immediate postwar era especially favored the Second Empire style, with its distinctive "French" mansard roof, and the picturesque Gothic cottage, a form seen occasionally before the war and before the Italianate style gained widespread use. Houses took picturesque L- or T-forms or symmetrical forms with central front gables. Porches rich with millwork displayed the products of the sash and blind factories that sprang up beside the railroads.*

FIGURE 62. *Charles T. Holt House, Haw River* (AM 13). *In the 1880s and 1890s the taste for more eclectic and complex architecture found expression in the Queen Anne style. The "ornate," "picturesque," and "modern" national style seen from mansions to cottages featured irregular plans, complex hip and gable rooflines, and varied textures and materials embodying the gusto for new industrial production and wealth. The leading industrialists of the late 19th c. built grand renditions, many from plans by mail-order architect George F. Barber of Knoxville, most of which are gone.*

FIGURE 63. *Womack-Stiers House, Reidsville, Rockingham Co.* (RK 19). *Irregular forms enriched with abundant sawn and turned millwork defined many buildings of the late 19th c.*

mass production. Boldly expressive use of materials—corbeled brickwork, rough stone, and elaborate millwork—enhanced lively and complex forms. The Second Empire and Italianate fashions found widespread use in the 1870s and 1880s, followed by the elaborate and irregular Queen Anne style in the 1880s and 1890s. Industrial barons built big Queen Anne houses downtown in sight of their factories and their workers as public statements of accomplishment and ambition. Among commercial buildings the round-arched Italianate and Romanesque Revival predominated. In the late 1880s and 1890s, new town halls and courthouses, churches, and schools displayed robust versions of Romanesque Revival, Gothic, Italianate, Jacobean, and classical themes. "Substantial," "costly," and "ornate" new buildings, the pride of each community, gave evidence of new hope and wealth. All evoked the New South's diverse energy and frank expression of capital, industrial production, and embrace of change.

Architectural Practice

The late nineteenth-century rebuilding relied on enterprising contractors who often operated sash and blind factories and could plan a building themselves or work from published designs or an architect's drawings. Among these were W. C. Bain of Greensboro, Allison F. Page of Cary, and Fogle Bros. of Winston-Salem. In the masonry trades, blacks were especially prominent, including W. W. Smith of Charlotte and Richard Fitzgerald, leading brickmaker in Durham.

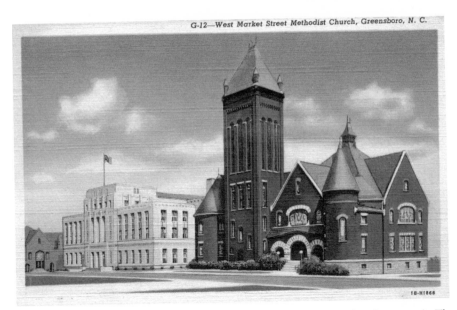

FIGURE 64. *West Market St. Methodist Church and U.S. Post Office, Greensboro* (GF 2, GF 3). *The late 19th c. brought growth in urban congregations, who built large and well chiefly in the Gothic Revival and Romanesque styles. The latter style was well suited to the curved form of the auditorium plan. Many of this type were replaced in the 20th c., but this one, designed by Pennsylvania architect Sidney Foulk, is among the best standing examples. The neighboring U.S. Post Office is among the finest stripped classical designs of the early depression era.*

In contrast to the antebellum era, the prime post–Civil War commissions went to designers of middle rank. Some operated by mail, such as George F. Barber of Knoxville, Tennessee. Many others moved to the state, including Samuel Sloan of Philadelphia and his associate, Adolphus Gustavus Bauer, who planned major state buildings. Other northern architects who came south were G. S. H. Appleget of New Jersey, who turned up from Raleigh to Charlotte; Samuel Leary of Philadelphia, in Durham; and Orlo Epps of Indiana, in Greensboro.

Urban growth and increasing wealth during the twentieth century, coupled with the nationwide expansion of the architectural profession and the popularity of Beaux Arts architectural ideals, made those years a golden era for small architectural firms. As in former times, some Piedmont clients turned to big city practitioners, with Frank Milburn of S.C. and Washington, D.C., and Hobart Upjohn of New York widely popular. A few plum projects went to such prominent designers as Boston's Ralph Adams Cram, Philadelphia's Charles Barton Keen, and New York's Aymar Embury II, McKim, Mead & White, and Shreve & Lamb.

Especially important in the early twentieth century was the emergence of a strong resident architectural profession. As natives and mostly newcomers dis-

FIGURE 65. *Iredell County Courthouse, Statesville* (ID 1). *During the early 20th-c. boom in courthouse rebuilding in classical modes, Charlotte architect Oliver Wheeler's partner Louis Schwend, formerly of Cincinnati, designed the Iredell County Courthouse. It became a prototype for several by Wheeler's firm, which had projects throughout the state.*

persed among the promising little cities, this generation organized the state chapter of the American Institute of Architects in 1913, established a licensing act, and promoted architectural education. Some, such as Hugh White in Gastonia, practiced mainly in a single town. Others used the rails and roads to form overlapping regional webs of practice, such as Greensboro's Harry Barton, Winston-Salem's Northup & O'Brien, and Raleigh's William H. Deitrick, along with Charlotte's Oliver Wheeler, J. M. McMichael, Charles C. Hook, and Louis Asbury, evidently the state's first professionally trained native architect. Most were flexible in their approach. The older men began with the eclectic styles of the late nineteenth century and adapted to the classicism and other revival styles favored in the early twentieth century. The younger generation came up in the Beaux Arts tradition but also accommodated modernist designs from the 1930s onward. Happy to design any type of building, from residence to courthouse or skyscraper, in any style the client desired, they shaped much of the architecture in the newly urbane towns and cities of the Piedmont.[14]

14. See Jackson and Brown, *History of the North Carolina Chapter of the American Institute of Architects,* and Bishir et al., *Architects and Builders in North Carolina.*

G-2—Elm Street, Looking North, Greensboro, N. C.

FIGURE 66. *Elm St., Greensboro* (GF 7). *Rapid early 20th-c. growth redefined the business districts of the leading cities, which became regional retail and financial centers with landmarks such as Greensboro's Kress Store (by Edward Sibbert of New York) and the Jefferson Standard Building skyscraper (by Charles C. Hartmann, who moved from New York). Banking and insurance took on new importance in each growing city. Some major banks sprang from mid-19th-c. roots, including Winston's Wachovia and Charlotte's Commercial National Bank, antecedent of present-day Bank of America. Jefferson Standard merged with others to become a major insurance company, headquartered in Greensboro.*

Early Twentieth-Century Town Planning and Architecture

Beginning around the turn of the twentieth century, the consolidation of business and transportation systems took physical form in both city layouts and architecture. At the heart of the city, the central business district was rebuilt, often repeatedly within a few decades. Industrial wealth went hand in hand with growth in banking, insurance companies, wholesalers and distributors, and retail businesses that included the first generations of regional and national chains and drew shoppers from a broad region. At the same time, a new component of downtown developed: the black main street. With stricter racial segregation after 1900, black businesses that formerly stood alongside white enterprises coalesced in a separate sector of downtown where black entrepreneurs built hotels, shops, theaters, and other accommodations for black customers.

As the entire downtown grew up and out, the mansions that stood on the principal streets near the center of town gave way to commercial buildings or factories. Eager to attain a "city-like" image, and influenced by national models of the Beaux Arts classicism, business and civic leaders commissioned architects

FIGURE 67. *Reynolds Building and Wachovia Building, Winston-Salem* (FY 34, FY 35). *Among the competing cities of the Piedmont, laurels for tallest building shifted back and forth between Charlotte and Winston, briefly resting on Greensboro's Jefferson Standard Building. In 1929 Winston-Salem's *Reynolds Building, by Shreve & Lamb of New York, capped the era and held the title until the neighboring *Wachovia Building was built in 1966 from designs by Albert Cameron of Charlotte. The pair represented the economic engines of the city and region; some called them the Reynolds Building and the box it came in.*

to replace nearly new courthouses and city halls with edifices of restrained classical mien, while churches continued in the Gothic Revival style. Shops or skyscrapers showed Renaissance Revival classical themes redolent of mercantile wealth. For a few businesses, especially those associated with novel uses and national rather than local systems—theaters, gas stations, telephone companies, national chain stores, and a few corporate headquarters—designers used the jazzy geometry of the Art Deco style or the sleek curves of the Art Moderne to give a new and up-to-date image.

The real image-maker for an aspiring city was the new American urban symbol: the skyscraper. Journalist W. J. Cash, probably referring to Charlotte's 12-story Independence Building of 1909, wrote that southern cities had no more need for a skyscraper than "a hog has for a morning coat." But in fact competitive little cities of the Piedmont needed them and built them rapidly. There was a regular "race to the sky" within and among cities, as each new advance in height captured local headlines.

FIGURE 68. *North Elm St., Greensboro. In each city, fine houses in various revival styles lined the streetcar route that made suburbanization feasible. Fairly diverse in house sizes and relatively dense in the first years of the 20th c., in subsequent decades suburbs grew increasingly homogenous and spacious. The early streetcar suburb of Dilworth in Charlotte (1891) followed a grid plan, as did many others, including *Trinity Park (Durham) and *Glenwood (Raleigh) for whites and, for black residents, *Columbian Heights (Winston-Salem); *Lincoln Park and others in Durham; *South Park (Raleigh); and *Washington Heights (Charlotte). Evidently the first curvilinear-plan suburb was Winston-Salem's *West End (1890). Landscape designers used curvilinear layouts for the increasingly exclusive streetcar and automobile suburbs of the 1910s and 1920s, with Charlotte's *Myers Park (1911), by noted urban planners John Nolen and Earle S. Draper, especially influential. Others included an addition to Dilworth; *Fisher Park and *Irving Park (Greensboro); *Emerywood (High Point); *Buena Vista (Winston-Salem); *Forest Hills and *College View (for black residents) (Durham); and *Boylan Heights, *Cameron Park, and *Hayes Barton (Raleigh).*

Suburbs

The great era of city building in the Piedmont meshed with the national movement toward suburbanization. The suburb along with the mill village defined the dispersed and socially segmented character of the early twentieth-century North Carolina city and set a pattern that persists to the present. Cities that had relatively mixed uses, classes, and races in 1880 developed a checkerboard pattern by 1910, which was followed by segregation into ever larger sectors of the expanding city. The central business district, the industrial zone, areas of black and white workers' homes, the residential suburb, and the mill village all gained sharper distinctions as well as greater distance from one another.

National trends, bigger industrial plants, and social attitudes, including stiffer racial segregation, all contributed to the change. What made the spatial revolution possible was the advent of the electric streetcar, which appeared first in Asheville in 1889 and then in Piedmont cities: Winston in 1890, Charlotte

FIGURE 69. *Lee House, Monroe* (UN 2). *Throughout the Piedmont, especially in towns and cities, the Colonial Revival style gained long-lasting popularity. In the 1890s, houses of basically Queen Anne form incorporated classical columns, pediments, and other "Colonial" motifs. The "Southern Colonial" mode, seen here in a design by Oliver Wheeler's firm in Charlotte, appearing ca. 1900, took a more symmetrical form and featured a tall portico, often overlapping a 1-story porch or terrace. In the 1910s and 1920s came the more restrained Georgian and Federal revival styles: red brick architecture with light classical trim defined innumerable houses, churches, school buildings, courthouses, and city halls.*

FIGURE 70. *Culp House, New London, Stanly Co.* (ST 5). *The bungalow was typically 1 or 1½ stories tall, with a broad roof, a low silhouette, a capacious porch, and an informal plan. Combining simple, bold details with economy of construction, the bungalow acquired an aura of progress and domesticity and gained wide popularity in urban and rural N.C. In the May 8, 1911,* Charlotte Observer, *a developer advertised his "Bungalowland" suburb under construction (*Elizabeth): "Out among the pines, the sunshine, the shade, the cool breezes, the pure air—out to the place where nature communes, out to the place where all is homeland, to 'Bungalowland'—that is where you should be. Our 'Bungalowland' means all this and more; it means cozy homes built to look good, last long, and be convenient and comfortable."*

and Raleigh in 1891, and Durham and Greensboro in 1902. Trolleys were often joint projects of electric utility companies and real estate developers. Within a few years, the overwhelming popularity of the automobile intensified the outward and diverging pattern of urban growth.[15]

Most of the first suburbs followed grid plans that extended the existing city plan. They usually had a range of houses from small to large; the latter often faced main thoroughfares. These were soon followed by suburbs aimed at a hierarchy of narrower markets. The top of the line were exclusive garden suburbs, with curvilinear layouts intentionally at odds with the center city grid, deed restrictions that defined minimum house costs and racial exclusivity, and architect-designed residences to attract the elite to "A Country Home on a City Street." Less pretentious suburbs were aimed at the families, black or white, who constituted the fast-growing urban middle classes.

Residential architecture followed national models, whether adapted by builders from popular magazines and builders' guides or designed by architects. Especially popular was the Colonial Revival, from the grandiose Southern Colonial to the more restrained Georgian Revival and its variations. A few clients selected the Tudor Revival or romantic motifs of Mediterranean and French origin. The straightforward practicality of the foursquare house made it popular in town and country, whether in Colonial dress or Craftsman style. But the most ubiquitous house type for rural, small-town, or suburban use was the bungalow, which could be plain and tiny in a mill village or on a farm or could take the form of a large but deceptively low-slung residence in a prestigious suburb. Upper- and middle-class houses of the era displayed new concerns for efficient and convenient use of domestic space. As improved plumbing and electric service became available, sanitation and modern appliances took on greater prominence, and gleaming kitchens and bathrooms became emblems of progress and modernity.

The Great Depression and World War II

The Great Depression, devastating to the state as a whole, had different impacts from one economic sector and locale to another. Farmers, already in trouble with low crop prices and overproduction, were hit hard, and farm tenancy, poverty, and emigration worsened. State and national programs of the New Deal provided important aid to farmers, including price and production stabilization measures for tobacco, extension education to promote "live at home" diversification, and wider electric service through the Rural Electrification Administration (1935), all of which helped stem the tide of out-migration.

15. See Bishir and Earley, *Early Twentieth-Century Suburbs in North Carolina*, and Bishir et al., *Architects and Builders in North Carolina*. On phases of separation, see Hanchett, *Sorting Out the New South City*.

FIGURE 71. *Hanging Rock State Park Bathhouse, Stokes Co.* (SK 4). *Many civic, educational, and recreational facilities were built with assistance from the Works Progress Administration, Civilian Conservation Corps, and other federal programs to alleviate unemployment. As elsewhere in the nation, boldly rustic designs typified CCC work.*

Tobacco manufacturing was essentially "depression-proof" and reaped immense profits from rising cigarette consumption combined with low crop prices. Furniture making, on the other hand, suffered greatly, as did many textile businesses. When mill owners sought to economize with further stretch-outs and reduced pay, workers grew more desperate, and strikes and (usually fruitless) efforts to unionize increased. Many banks collapsed. Construction dropped off so abruptly that many architectural and building firms went out of business. Those who did build—especially in tobacco-rich Durham and Winston-Salem—could afford the best, and their projects offered crucial work for the building trades.

The role of government took on new configurations. To help overextended local governments, the state took over the public school system and the highway system and, to boost efficiency, formed the consolidated university from present-day UNC, NCSU, and UNCG. Federal projects provided jobs and produced U.S. post offices, state and local government and recreational facilities, and school and college buildings. Some construction firms survived the depression only because of government projects. It was World War II, however, that fully reinvigorated the economy, jolting demand for farm products, textiles, and cigarettes and employing thousands of workers in factories, military construction projects, and the armed forces. Despite a hiatus in civilian construction, architects and builders found work again and were poised for growth when the war ended.

During the second half of the twentieth century, the state experienced trans-formations in every aspect of its life and architectural landscape, and the pace and scale of change were most explosive in the Piedmont. Shifts in the economy and population that began in the decades after World War II accelerated throughout the century to create a more populous, urbanized, wealthy, and di-verse region than could have been imagined 50 or 100 years earlier.[16]

Postwar Developments

The years after World War II opened with a clear sense of the state's needs and problems, coupled with a confident determination to improve conditions. Despite the progress of the 1920s, old issues of education, poverty, racial in-equality, and out-migration persisted as they did throughout the South, exacer-bated by the Great Depression. Although some leaders resisted social and eco-nomic changes, others, including governors and legislators who adopted "Go Forward" and "New Day" programs, sought to take North Carolina farther along the road to becoming a progressive American state.

Aided by federal funds, the state spent millions of dollars on roads, including interstate highways. Building on the investments of the 1920s and the efficiencies required in the 1930s, the state gradually pulled public school funding up from the bottom ranks and strengthened public colleges and universities, with the Piedmont's UNC and NCSU attaining national stature. Duke University aimed at becoming the Ivy League school of the South, and in the 1950s Winston-Salem leaders underwrote the move of Wake Forest College to their city and its ex-pansion into a university. Philanthropies funded by Piedmont industrial for-tunes provided essential support to education, the arts, and social programs.

The era also brought strife and some progress toward racial justice, with key leaders striving to avoid the violence that beset some states. Piedmont colleges played a vital role. A&T students' nonviolent sit-ins at the Woolworth store in Greensboro in 1960 were a landmark event in the civil rights movement, which eventually led to desegregation of public schools and greater participation by blacks in the political process.

16. This section draws on Douglas Orr Jr. and Alfred W. Stuart, *The North Carolina Atlas: Portrait for a New Century* (Chapel Hill: University of North Carolina Press, 2000); Hugh Talmage Lefler and Albert Ray Newsome, *North Carolina: The History of a Southern State*, 3d ed. (Chapel Hill: University of North Carolina Press, 1973); Ernest H. Wood III, "The Opportunities Are Unlim-ited: Architects and Builders since 1945," in Bishir et al., *Architects and Builders in North Carolina*; and David R. Black, "Early Modern Architecture in Raleigh Associated with the Faculty of the North Carolina State University School of Design," in National Register of Historic Places Nom-ination Forms (1994).

FIGURE 72. *Dorton Arena, Raleigh* (WK 61). *An early landmark of the state's aim for progress and the talent of the School of Design at NCSU, the boldly conceived design was planned for the state Department of Agriculture by Matthew Nowicki, head of the Department of Architecture, in association with the Raleigh firm of William H. Deitrick. After Nowicki died in a plane crash, the arena was completed by Deitrick, a prominent supporter of the School of Design, whose practice spanned traditional and modernist design.*

In the 1950s, too, the "business progressive" leaders of the state put new emphasis on diversifying the industrial base. A remarkable vision, hatched in 1955 and promoted by a group of business, educational, and government leaders, was the creation of the Research Triangle Park to foster research and high-tech employment and thus new types of jobs in the region. Crucial to the new economy was the postwar proliferation of air conditioning, which undergirded both new technologies and new in-migration.

For many years, to be sure, the region remained relatively rural, its economy still dominated by agriculture along with the "big three" manufacturing categories. In 1950 about two-thirds of the state's 4 million people were rural farm and nonfarm dwellers. Tobacco production continued to rise. In 1970 the state was the nation's leading grower, and the value of the leaf was greater than all its other crops combined. By 1970 rural out-migration was rising and the tenant system was fading as mechanized and chemical processes supplanted traditional hand labor. Still the least urbanized state, North Carolina was the most industrialized, with production rising rapidly. In 1970, with more textile mills and workers than any other state and its industrial workers still among the lowest-paid in the country, North Carolina led the nation in the value of textile, tobacco, and furniture manufactures.

Between 1950 and 1970, as the state's population rose from 4 million to 5 million people, urban dwellers increased from a third to nearly a half of the total. The cities of the Piedmont accounted for much of the change. In 1950 only Charlotte had 100,000 people, but by 1970 that city's population had doubled; Winston-Salem, Greensboro, and Raleigh had more than 100,000, and Durham was close behind. The cities intensified the outward pattern begun by mill villages and suburbs. The day of the mill village was past or passing, as corporations sold off mill houses, but the day of the suburb had dawned with stunning brightness. Throughout the region, developers transformed farmland into housing for the thousands who flocked to town or left the old city center.

Businesses joined the outward flow. In addition to textile mills, all kinds of manufacturing plants, along with shopping centers, banks, churches, schools, and hospitals, moved to the "edge city" near the highways. *Cameron Village, built in the late 1940s in Raleigh, was the first of many regional shopping centers. Because they had been so small for so long, and because their long-standing pattern of dispersion fit readily with national trends, by the 1970s the cities of the Piedmont consisted largely of suburbs that dwarfed their pre-1950 centers.

The postwar era also brought ferment in architecture. Growing national standardization of construction and design ideas shaped much building, in suburban ranch houses and split-level residences, mobile homes, factories, and trucking facilities as well as more imposing schools, banks, and office buildings. As elsewhere in the nation there was a growing gap between the general public's preference for traditional home designs and the architectural profession's promotion of modernist ideals.

It was chiefly in the Piedmont that the mid-twentieth-century architectural debates took their liveliest form and where practitioners of new ideas made their boldest marks. Establishment of the School of Design at NCSU in Raleigh in 1948 reflected state leaders' belief that good modern architecture was essential for a progressive state. Founding dean Henry Kamphoefner recruited a faculty of distinguished designers and trained graduates who promoted the new ideas across the state (see Fig. 72). In Charlotte architect A. G. Odell Jr. and others defined the city as a leader in corporate modernism. Emblematic of the state's rising sense of identity was the selection of nationally famous architect Edward Durell Stone to design the Legislative Building (1962–63) in the "New Formalist" blend of modernism and classicism displayed at his American Embassy in New Delhi. Likewise claiming a new image, business leaders began a new race to the sky, with ever taller modernist skyscrapers of glass, steel, and concrete.

In residential architecture, while a few clients commissioned notable modernist residences, most families who could afford custom-designed residences preferred conservative modes, chiefly the Colonial Revival. With many architects devoted to the modernist idea, and with only a few working in traditional styles, the era of the premier residential avenue or suburb lined with architect-

FIGURE 73. *Charlotte Coliseum, Charlotte* (MK 50). *The large firm of architect A. G. Odell Jr. made Charlotte a center of corporate modernism. His daring, domed coliseum earned his firm, Charlotte, and the state a reputation for progressiveness in the post–World War II South. It was also among the first public buildings in the city to be racially integrated and to be built on a freeway away from the town center.*

designed houses soon ended. Much of the tremendous demand for houses large and small was met by design-build contractors who drew on published sources and their own experience, and house plans grew more and more standardized, aimed chiefly at mass market niches. Suburbs and houses were designed around the automobile. Neighborhoods had broader streets and generously curved corners, and many dispensed with sidewalks. The main approach to the house moved from the sidewalk to the driveway, front porches dwindled, and most houses presented relatively closed street facades and opened chiefly to their backyards.

The New South State at the End of the Twentieth Century

In the last decades of the twentieth century, unexpected events along with hard-won accomplishments combined to transform the social, economic, and architectural landscape. Within a few decades, the ground shifted under the state's traditional economic bases. Rural farm dwellers dropped to less than 3 percent of the population, and the cash value of agricultural products at the farm gate fell to less than 4 percent of the state's economic output. Slowly at first, then with astonishing speed toward the end of the century, the great man-

FIGURE 74. *Burroughs-Wellcome Building (GlaxoSmithKline), Research Triangle Park* (DH 69). *The revolutionary Research Triangle Park was founded on a new site within the triangle of UNC in Chapel Hill, NCSU, and Duke to foster high-tech research and generate investment in higher-paid employment opportunities new to the state. Paul Rudolph's design for the pharmaceutical firm is among the most striking. Research Triangle Park has changed the face and economy of what is now called the Triangle region and far beyond.*

FIGURE 75. *Andrews-Moore House, Franklin Co.* (FN 17). *Piedmont preservation efforts gained strength from the 1970s onward, often in reaction to loss of individual landmarks, then historic downtowns and older neighborhoods. State and local preservation efforts were aided by funds from philanthropic foundations created by Piedmont industrial benefactors. In the countryside, where the Piedmont's fast-changing land uses threaten the rural landscape, preservation accomplishments are made chiefly by individual homeowners and state and local preservation groups. This 18th-c. house, for example, was rescued by the Endangered Properties program of Preservation North Carolina and painstakingly restored by its new owner.*

FIGURE 76. *Brightleaf Square, Durham* (DH 21). *Much preservation activity has been focused on towns and cities, where 19th- and early 20th-c. downtowns and residential sections have gained new appreciation and, spurred by preservation tax credits, many vacated industrial buildings have been renovated for new purposes. Brightleaf Square was a pioneering renovation of a pair of the American Tobacco Co.'s unique, castellated tobacco warehouses. The extensive heritage of textile and tobacco manufacturing architecture presents many preservation challenges and opportunities.*

ufacturing pillars of textiles and tobacco slipped away, as one plant after another closed due to changing markets, automation, corporate mergers, and, especially, the global pursuit of cheaper labor.

At the same time, the Sunbelt boom of the late twentieth century brought new businesses, people, and wealth, which concentrated in the Piedmont and its cities. The familiar advantages of abundant electric power, nonunion workers, good roads, and probusiness governments all encouraged manufacturing, high-tech industries, and financial operations. Net out-migration gave way to in-migration, and the population grew to more than 8 million by 2000—a 20 percent increase in the 1990s alone—as newcomers from other states and nations made the population more diverse than at any time since colonial settlement.

In the 1990s, too, for the first time more than half the state's residents lived in incorporated towns. Dispersed urban patterns shifted to urban consolidation: by 2000 about 40 percent of the people lived in the three largest metropolitan areas, all in the Piedmont. The cities spread out across old farmland and forests at a dizzying pace, adding miles of strip commercial business and far-flung suburbs.

Despite and even because of the pace and scale of change came efforts to maintain a sense of continuity. Spurred by losses of historic landmarks, state and local preservation movements burgeoned. While some small towns withered, others within range of new jobs gained vitality from people who moved there seeking a small-town pace, and in many cities, older urban neighborhoods strengthened their appeal.

As the twenty-first century turned, new changes loomed. With thousands of textile workers laid off and mills closing, the Piedmont saw some of the nation's highest losses in manufacturing jobs. Economic problems hit new as well as traditional sectors. A Raleigh newspaper observed, "Free trade agreements have made it possible for companies to move their production to countries with lower-paid labor and bring back goods they can sell at lower prices, the same way textile companies moved production from New England to the South during the last century"; the editorial reiterated a call to retool education and enterprise to fit the new world economy.[17]

Far more than early nineteenth-century or even mid-twentieth-century reformers could envision, the remoteness of the backcountry has disappeared with global trade, transportation, and information revolutions. Yet, in a landscape of widespread and profound change, there is still great continuity in the Piedmont. The spirit of the region, like its architectural legacy, embodies the long-standing attachment to family and place coupled with hardy individualism, a practical capacity to move and adapt—and the "go-aheaditiveness" and determined resilience of "hard-headed, hard-working" people.

17. "Economy Class," editorial, *Raleigh News & Observer*, June 26, 2001. See also Orr and Stuart, *North Carolina Atlas*, 196.

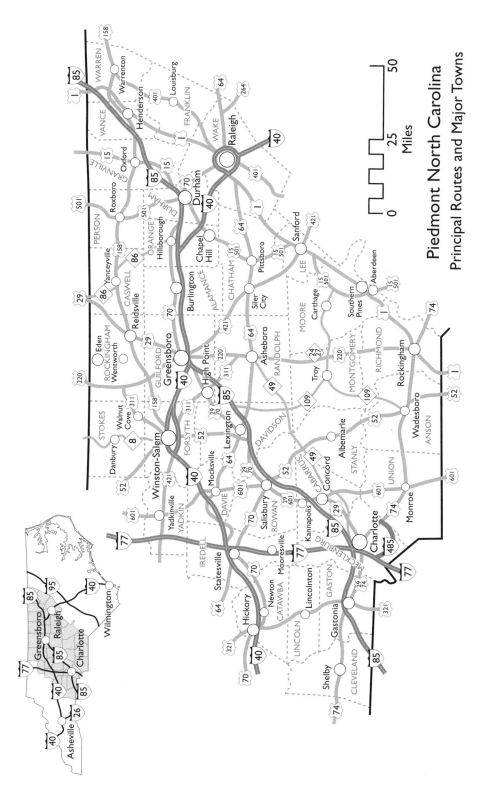

Piedmont North Carolina
Principal Routes and Major Towns

83

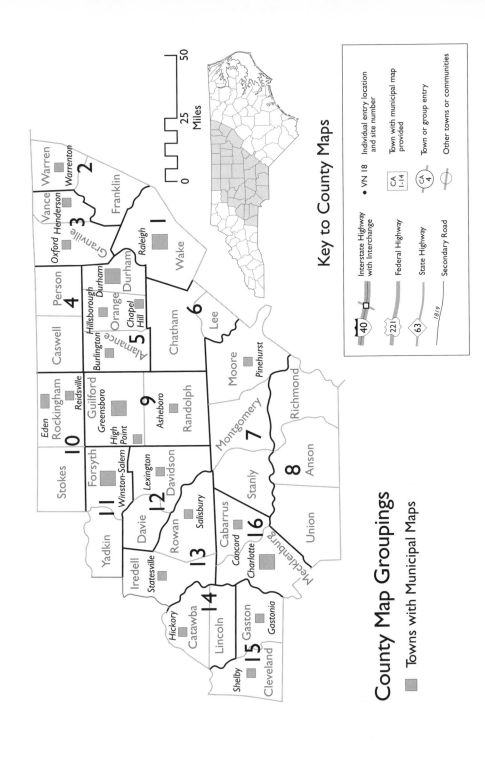

County Map Groupings

■ Towns with Municipal Maps

Key to County Maps

• VN 18	Individual entry location and site number
CA I-14	Town with municipal map provided
CA 4	Town or group entry
◯	Other towns or communities

40 ▭	Interstate Highway with Interchange
221	Federal Highway
63	State Highway
1819	Secondary Road

Miles
0   25   50

Warren — Warrenton 2
Vance / Henderson 3
Granville / Oxford
Franklin 1 Raleigh Wake
Person 4
Caswell
Durham Durham
Hillsborough Orange
Alamance 5 Chapel Hill
Burlington
Chatham
Lee 6
Rockingham Reidsville
Eden
Guilford Greensboro 9
High Point Asheboro Randolph
Stokes 10
Forsyth Winston-Salem 11
Lexington 12 Davidson
Davie Salisbury 16
Yadkin Rowan
Iredell Statesville 13
Hickory Catawba 14
Lincoln Gaston Gastonia 15
Shelby
Cleveland
Moore Pinehurst
Montgomery 7
Stanly
Anson 8
Cabarrus Concord
Charlotte Mecklenburg
Union
Richmond

84

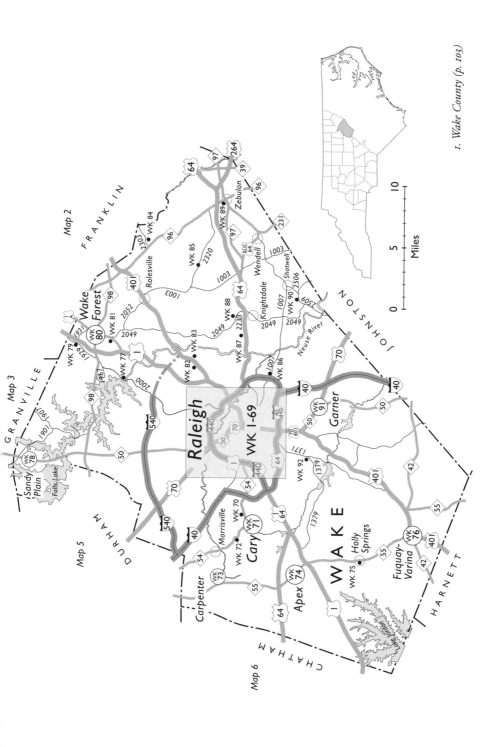

1. Wake County (p. 103)

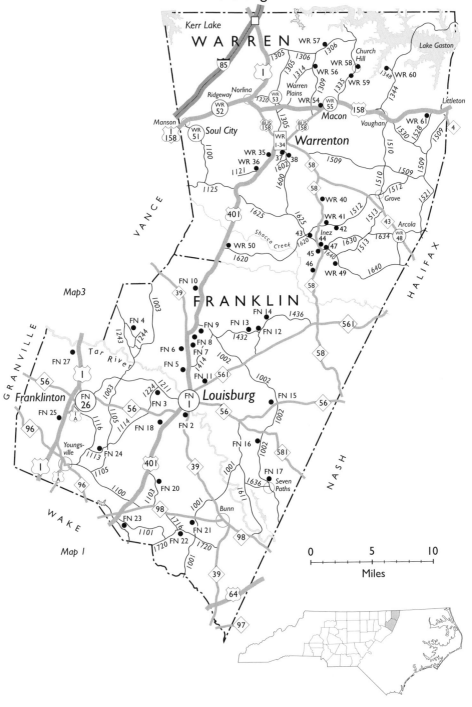

2. Franklin Co. (p. 138) and Warren Co. (p. 146)

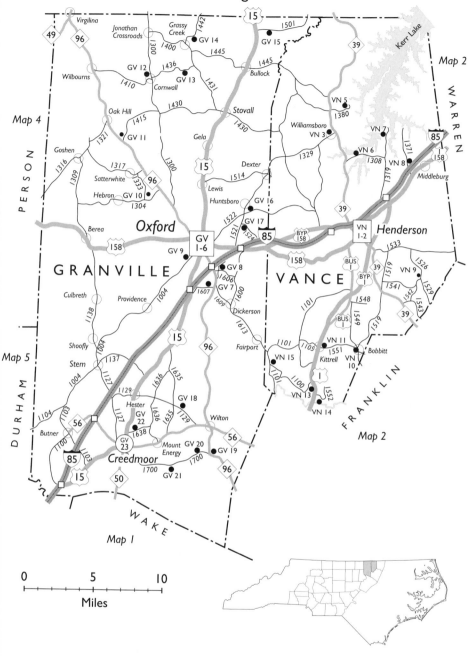

Virginia

Virgilina

Jonathan
Crossroads

Grassy
Creek

GV 14

GV 15

1442

1501

15

39

Kerr Lake

Map 2

GV 12

1436

GV 13

1300

1400

1445

1410

Cornwall

1431

Bullock

1445

VN 5
1380

WARREN

85

Wilbourns

Map 4

Oak Hill

1430

Stovall

Williamsboro

VN 7

1371

158

1415

GV 11

1430

Gela

VN 3

VN 6
1308

Middleburg

1321

PERSON

Goshen

1316

1317

96

1309

1333

Satterwhite

Hebron

GV 10

1304

Berea

Dexter

1514

Lewis

Huntsboro

GV 16

1329

VN 8

1379

158

Oxford

GV
1-6

1522

1521

GV 17

BYP
158

VN
1-2

Henderson

GRANVILLE

158

GV 9

85

158

1533

BUS
1

39

1519

VN 9

1526

1529

GV 8

1606

GV 7

1600

1004

1607

1609

VANCE

1101

BYP
1

1548

1541

1542

1543

Culbreth

Providence

Dickerson

1138

1613

1101

1549

1519

39

Map 5

Shoofly

Stem

1137

1004

15

96

Fairport

1101

1105

BUS
1

VN 11

1551

VN
10

Bobbitt

DURHAM

1127

1129

1636

1635

Hester

GV
22

1638

GV 18

1129

Wilton

56

1100

1
Kittrell

VN 15

552
VN 13

FRANKLIN

1104

1103

56

GV
23

Mount
Energy

GV 20

GV 19

VN 14

Map 2

Butner

1700

85

15

Creedmoor

1700

GV 21

96

50

WAKE

Map 1

0   5   10
Miles

3. Vance Co. (p. 160) and Granville Co. (p. 166)

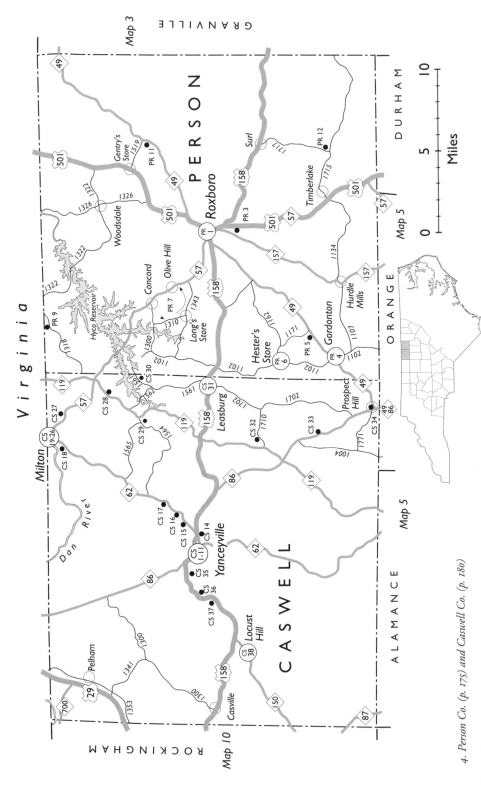

Map content (rotated labels and features):

GRANVILLE — Map 3

PERSON
Roxboro

Surl — PR 12
Timberlake — 1715
158 — 1717
PR 3
501 — 57
157 — 1134
Gordonton
Hurdle Mills
57
49
162 — 1171
Hester's Store — 1107
PR 5 — 1102
PR 6 — PR 4
2011

Olive Hill — Concord
57 — 158
PR 7 — 1343
Long's Store — 1310
1300 — 1102
CS 30
CS 31
Leasburg — 1702
CS 32 — 1710
CS 33
Prospect Hill
49 — 86
CS 34
1771 — 1004

501
1322 — 1326
Woodsdale
Gentry's Store — 1519
PR 11
49

Virginia
1322 — 1318
PR 9
Hyco Reservoir
119
CS 28
1565 — 1562
CS 29 — 1564
1561 — 119 — 158

Milton
CS 27 — 57
CS 19-26
CS 18
Dan River
62
CS 17
CS 16 — CS 15
CS 14
CS 1-11 — Yanceyville
CS 35
CS 36
CS 37
86
62
Locust Hill
CS 38

Pelham
29 — 700
1300 — 1341 — 1353
158
Casville
1300
150

CASWELL

ROCKINGHAM — Map 10
ALAMANCE — 87
ORANGE
DURHAM
Map 5
Map 5

Miles
0 5 10

4. Person Co. (p. 175) and Caswell Co. (p. 180)

88

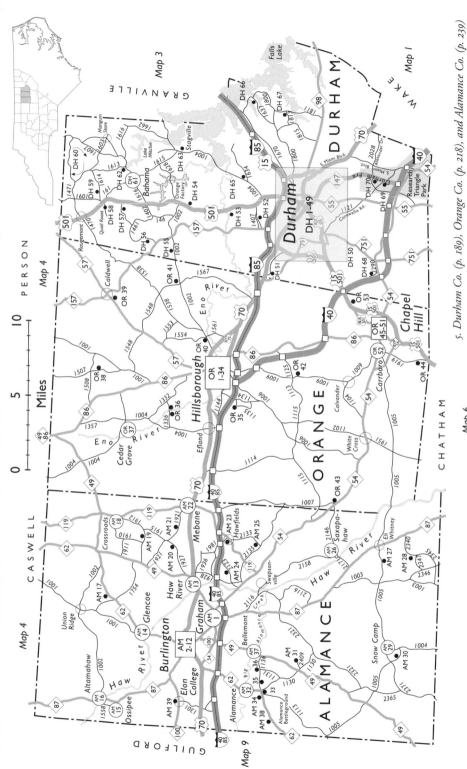

5. *Durham Co. (p. 189), Orange Co. (p. 218), and Alamance Co. (p. 239)*

Map 6

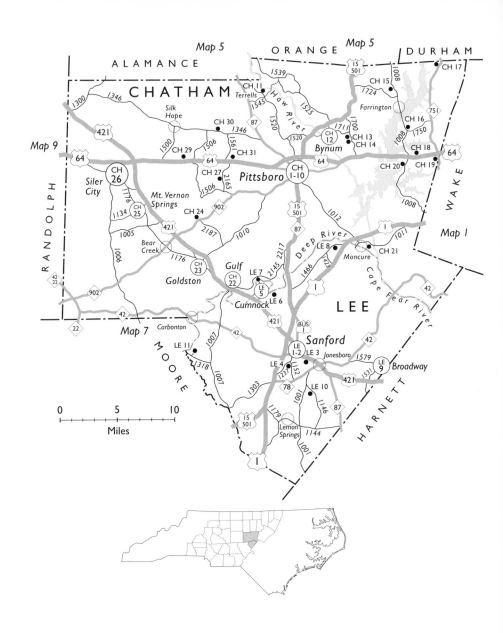

ALAMANCE

ORANGE   Map 5   DURHAM

Map 5

CHATHAM

CH 11
Terrells

1539

Haw River

15
501

CH 15

1724

CH 17

1008

1300

1346

1545

Silk
Hope

CH 30

87

1346

1520

1525

1520

Farrington

1711
1700

751

CH 16

1008

1750

421

1500

CH 29

1506

1561

CH 31

Bynum

CH 12

CH 13
CH 14

Map 9

64

64

CH 27

2165

64

Pittsboro

CH
1-10

64

CH 18

CH 20

CH 19

64

CH
26

1116

Siler
City

1506

Mt. Vernon
Springs

CH
25

CH 24

902

1005

421

2187

1010

1012

15
501

87

1008

1011

Map 1

RANDOLPH

1134

1176

CH
23

Bear
Creek

1176

Gulf

CH
22

LE 7

2145

2217

Deep River

LE 8

1466

1423

Moncure

CH 21

42

Goldston

LE
5

LE 6

Cumnock

421

BUS
1

1

Sanford

Cape Fear River

42
22

902

42

22

Map 7

Carbonton

LE 11

1007

42

1007

1303

LE
1-2

LE 3

123

157

78

Jonesboro

1579

LE 10

1001

1146

421

531

LE
9

Broadway

87

15
501

1179

Lemon
Springs

1144

1001

MOORE

1318

LE 4

LEE

WAKE

HARNETT

0   5   10
Miles

1

0   5   10
Miles

6. Chatham Co. (p. 255) and Lee Co. (p. 263)

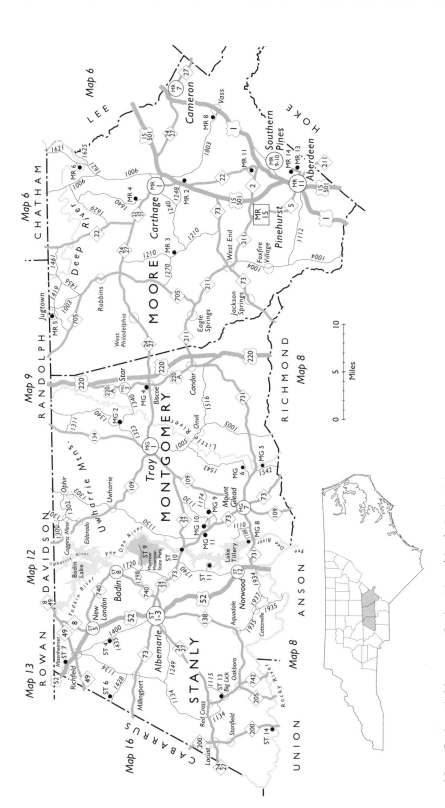

7. *Moore Co. (p. 269), Montgomery Co. (p. 280), and Stanly Co. (p. 283)*

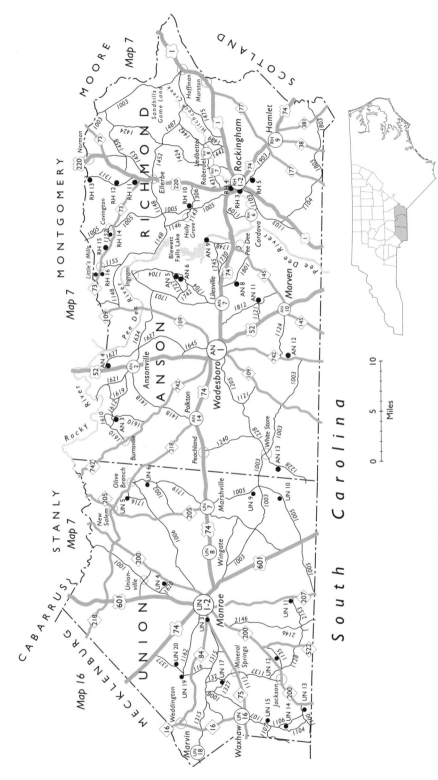

8. *Richmond Co. (p. 290), Anson Co. (p. 298), and Union Co. (p. 304)*

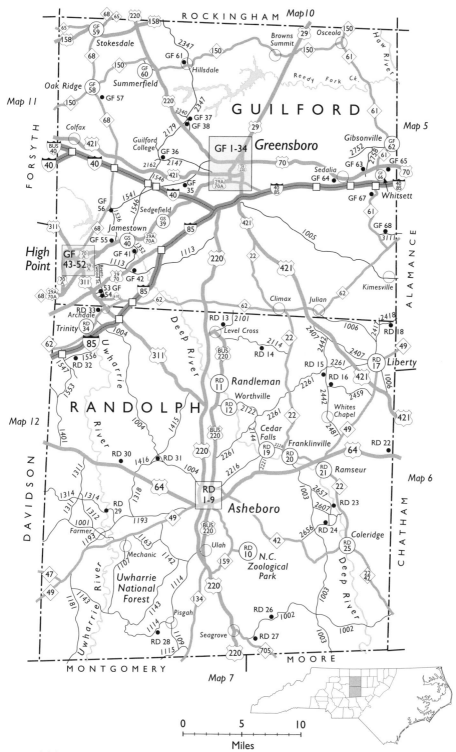

9. Randolph Co. (p. 311) and Guilford Co. (p. 322)

10. *Rockingham Co. (p. 349) and Stokes Co. (p. 361)*

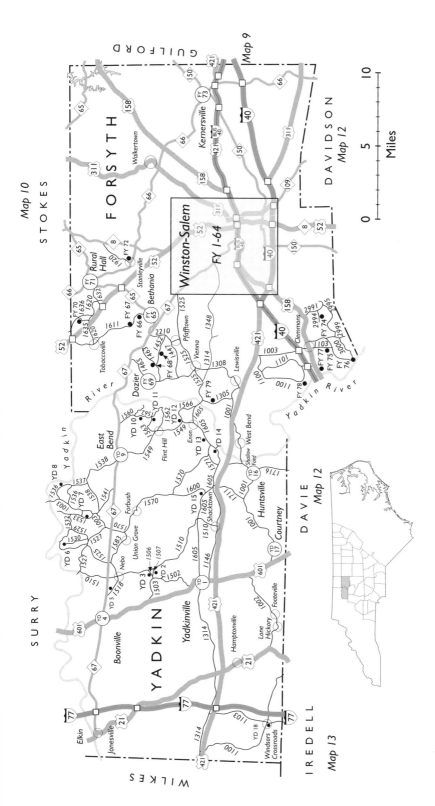

11. *Forsyth Co. (p. 366) and Yadkin Co. (p. 401)*

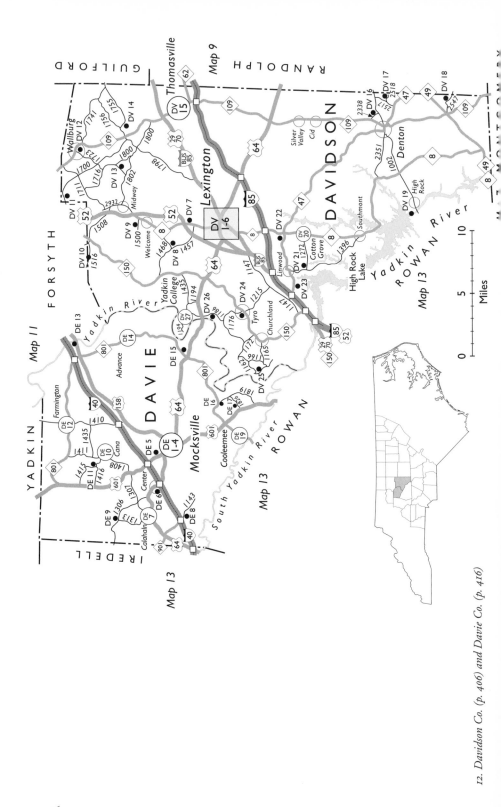

12. *Davidson Co. (p. 406) and Davie Co. (p. 416)*

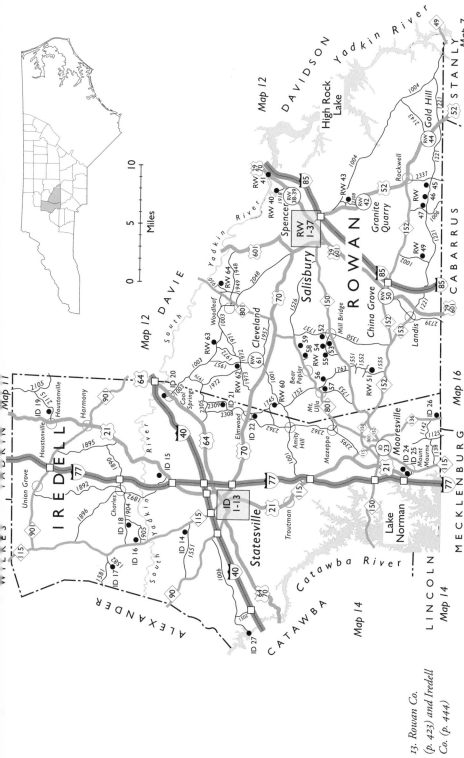

13. Rowan Co.
(p. 423) and Iredell
Co. (p. 444)

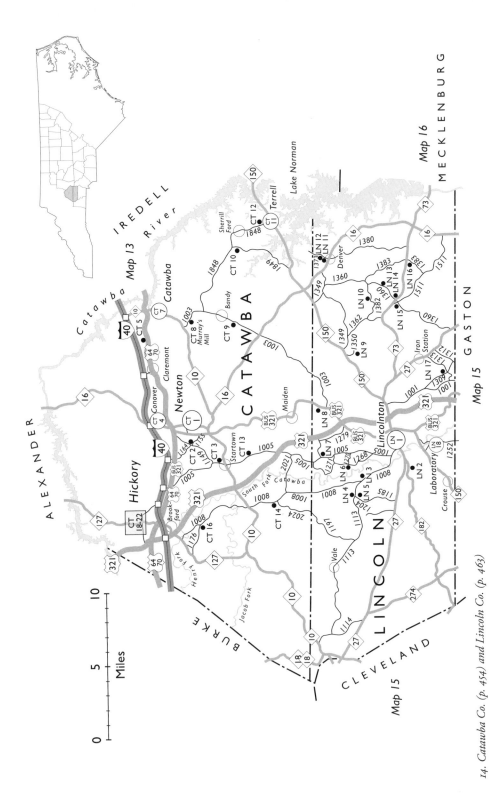

14. *Catawba Co. (p. 454) and Lincoln Co. (p. 463)*

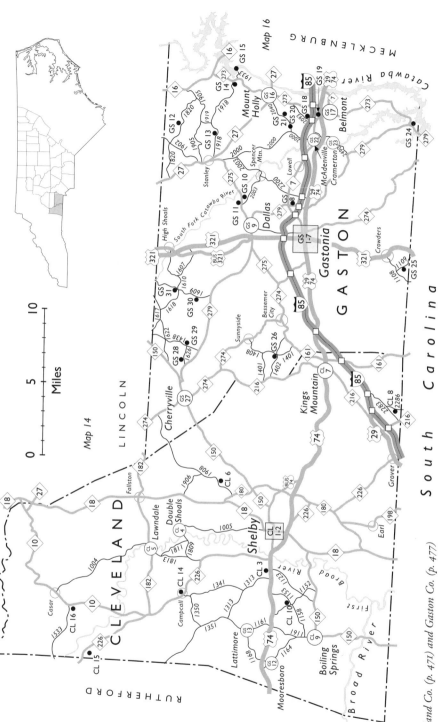

15. Cleveland Co. (p. 471) and Gaston Co. (p. 477)

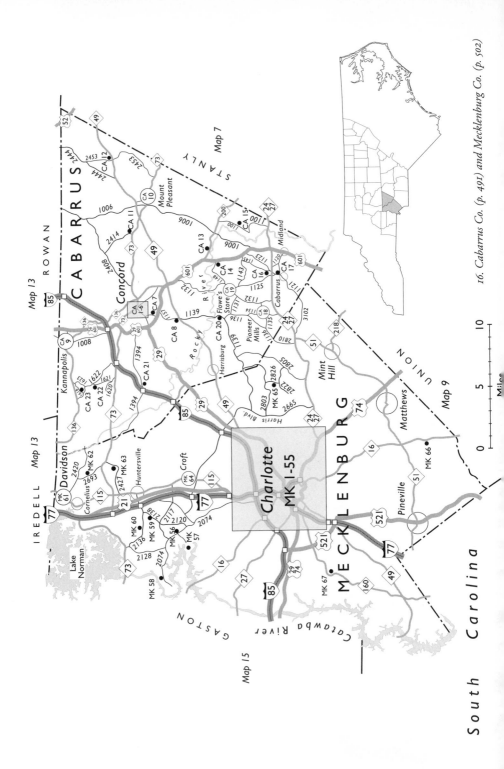

16. Cabarrus Co. (p. 491) and Mecklenburg Co. (p. 502)

Catalog

(Overleaf) Pinehurst Country Club
(Opposite) Streetscape with Administration Building (wᴋ 6), *First Presbyterian Church* (wᴋ 4), *and Raleigh Water Tower* (wᴋ 27)

Wake County (WK)

See Kelly Lally, The Historic Architecture of Wake County, North Carolina *(1994), and Linda L. Harris and Mary Ann Lee,* Raleigh Historic Inventory *(1978).*

Named for Margaret Wake, wife of Governor William Tryon, the county formed in 1771 is unique in thus honoring a woman. Although it was chosen as site of the state capital in 1792, the county remained largely rural until the late 20th c. Spanning the fall line, its territory comprises coastal plain land in the southeast and piedmont terrain north and west. In the 19th c. the Raleigh & Gaston Railroad (R&GRR) and the North Carolina Railroad (NCRR) encouraged commercial agriculture and some manufacturing. Rails were followed by major highways in the 20th c. A leader in cotton, then tobacco cultivation, Wake Co.'s thickly settled rural landscape recalls the prosperity tobacco could bring even small farmers. Numerous small trading towns arose, each with its brick business district and residential areas from the early 20th c. In the late 20th c. the *Research Triangle Park and rapid suburbanization shifted the landscape toward a dispersed urban environment.

Raleigh (WK 1–69)

The planned 18th-c. state capital has an architectural heritage chiefly from the 19th and 20th centuries. In contrast to the commercial and industrial roots of N.C.'s other major cities, Raleigh developed primarily as a government and college town without big factories or big money. For most of its history a genteel distrust of ostentation manifested itself in conservative public buildings and relatively unpretentious residential architecture. The capital was a small place, with 4,700 people in 1860, fewer than 20,000 in 1910, and 47,000 in 1940. Only in the late 20th c. did its borders explode, as the city

grew to 120,000 by 1970 and 270,000 by 2000—bypassing Greensboro and Winston-Salem to rank second to Charlotte.

The original city plan, still legible despite 20th-c. blockage of its axial streets, is the chief vestige of the 18th-c. founding. The young state had no fixed capital until 1792, when commissioners chose a site at *Wakefield, a plantation near the road to Virginia and the Wake Co. courthouse. Named for Sir Walter Raleigh's 1580s "Citie of Ralegh" [*sic*] on Roanoke Island, it was laid out by William Christmas, legislator from Franklin Co. He drew a 400-acre grid with 4 axial streets 99 feet wide, the others 66 feet wide, and 5 public squares, adapted from Philadelphia's plan. Workmen cleared old forests for the city. The central 6½-acre square for the statehouse was named for the Union, and the smaller public squares for Revolutionary War figures: Moore Square on the southeast and Nash on the southwest (both still open) and Burke on the northeast and Caswell on the northwest. The four "main streets"—Fayetteville St. (s), Halifax St. (N), Hillsborough St. (w), and New Bern Ave. (E)—honored court districts in those general directions, and other streets were named for other court districts and for the commissioners and other political leaders. The grid

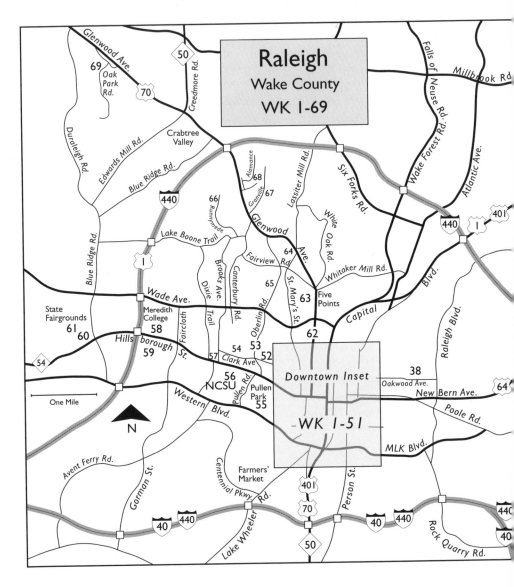

Raleigh
Wake County
WK 1-69

was bounded by North, South, East, and West Sts.

Government and education defined the city. A brick State House was built on Union Square (1792–96) and remodeled in the 1820s. It burned in 1831 and was replaced by the monumental stone *State Capitol (1833–40), completed the same year as the R&GRR, which linked the capital to points north. That route was joined by the NCRR in the 1850s. During the 19th c., state government gradually expanded, and early academies were succeeded by colleges, including de-

nominational schools for white women: *St. Mary's, *Peace, and later *Meredith; co-educational colleges for blacks in the 1860s: *St. Augustine's and *Shaw; and in 1889 the state land-grant college, now *North Carolina State University (NCSU).

Peacefully surrendered in 1865, the capital escaped damage during the Civil War, and an 1879 city directory recalled that as soon as war ended, "handsome stores and dwellings rose rapidly, and enterprise was manifested in many ways." The late 19th c. also brought sash and blind factories, a few

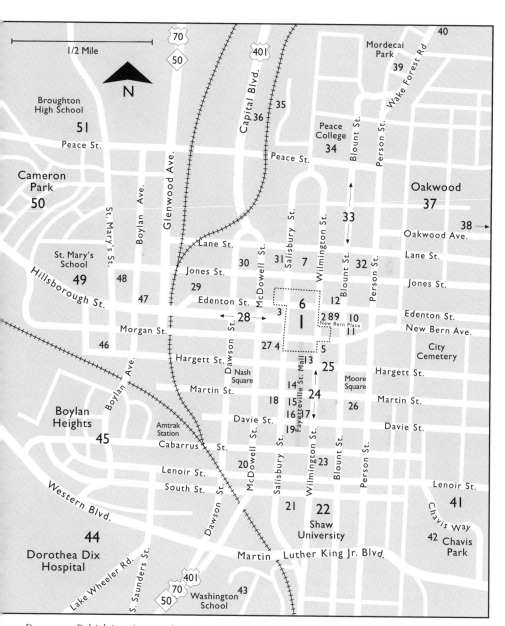

Downtown Raleigh inset (WK 1–51)

cotton mills, and other small manufacturers.

Late 19th- and early 20th-c. growth was accompanied by greater separation of races and classes, though until the mid-20th c., Raleigh retained unusually dispersed patterns. Initially it, like other N.C. cities, had varied uses and large and small residences distributed across the grid. Late in the ante-

bellum era a few citizens erected suburban villas on all sides, and in the late 1860s black citizens established "suburban villages" of *Oberlin and *Method a few miles north and west. With "a growing taste for houses in the suburbs," the first white suburb, *Oakwood, began in the northeast quadrant in the 1870s. Gradually occupation of the old grid shifted, as areas near Shaw (S) and St. Augustine's (NE) colleges drew more black residents, and the north and west attracted whites. Still, a checkerboard of black and white residents persisted well into the 20th c.

With new suburbs made possible by streetcars (from 1891) and automobiles, plus Jim Crow segregation, areas on the south and east became increasingly black and most of the north and west was white. Urban renewal and zoning policies reinforced these trends after World War II. Raleigh's early 20th-c. suburbs trace the transition from grid plan to curvilinear garden suburbs, chiefly along the streetcar routes on Hillsborough St. toward NCSU and along Glenwood Ave. to the streetcar company's Bloomsbury Park. Like others, their developers aimed at the growing urban middle and upper classes with deed restrictions and professionally designed layouts.

Raleigh architecture presents a curious dichotomy: conservative building dominated, but it provided a foil for spectacular exceptions that are among the most adventurous architecture in the state. Most 18th- and 19th-c. buildings were unpretentious 1- and 2-story frame and occasionally brick structures. In the early 19th c., English architect William Nichols introduced a taste for elegant Neoclassicism at the State House and the *Mordecai House, but these were anomalies. In this milieu, construction of major buildings by leading New York architects was all the more remarkable: the State Capitol by Town & Davis, an immense Insane Asylum (*Dix Hospital) by A. J. Davis, and *Christ Church by Richard Upjohn. Some local residents objected to hiring "far fetched and dear bought" architects, but the practice continued nonetheless.

After the Civil War, patronage of major national architects lapsed, but local builders filled demand with mass-produced materials and newly ornate designs. They were influenced by northern architects, including G. S. H. Appleget of New Jersey, Samuel Sloan of Philadelphia and associate Adolphus Gustavus Bauer, and others who provided suitably economical renditions of Second Empire, Italianate, and Queen Anne styles, including Sloan's *Executive Mansion.

These eclectic modes were succeeded by a hearty return to classicism. With few exceptions, 20th-c. Raleigh displayed an undying devotion to the Colonial Revival for residences and Neoclassicism for public buildings. Among the growing architectural profession were builder-architects James A. Davidson and Howard Satterfield (of NCSU) and architects Charles Barrett, H. P. S. Keller, James Salter, James M. Kennedy, Thomas Cooper, and William Henley Deitrick. Especially influential from 1927 to 1959 was Deitrick, who began with revival designs but developed a pioneering modernist firm. A few commissions went to out-of-state architects, including Hobart Upjohn and William Lawrence Bottomley of New York, and others went to N.C. firms such as Northup & O'Brien of Winston-Salem.

A unique chapter opened with the 1948 founding of NCSU's School of Design (SOD), part of a larger progressive impulse to modernize the state's economy and image in the optimistic post–World War II era. Establishing a modernist design school influenced by Frank Lloyd Wright and the European modernism of the Bauhaus, outspoken modernist dean Henry Kamphoefner recruited a constellation of innovative architects, including Matthew Nowicki, Eduardo Catalano, George Matsumoto, James Fitzgibbon, Edward Waugh, and later, Harwell Hamilton Harris; he also invited Wright, Lewis Mumford, and Buckminster Fuller to visit. Although most of the city's architecture continued on its traditionally conservative path, the SOD not only trained new architects but also gave Raleigh a collection of mid-20th-c. modernist designs that gained national and international acclaim. They explored many currents of the era, including structural innovations epitomized by Nowicki's famed *Dorton Arena, modest residences of natural materials in a Wrightian spirit, and geometric compositions in the International style shaped by European émigrés Walter Gropius and Ludwig Mies van der Rohe. A contrasting face of American modernism appeared in the *Legislative Building (1962–63), designed by Edward Durell Stone, leading exponent of the classicized mode known as New Formalism.

The postwar progressive energy also spurred state and private investment in other enterprises, most notably the 1959 establishment of the *Research Triangle Park (Durham Co.) as a pathbreaking research and high-tech center. Its creation opened a stream of new talent and money from other states—an unprecedented trend that transformed the city and region in the late 20th c. This growth has generated an immense ring of suburbs and outlying commercial centers, dwarfing the little pre-1960 city "inside the beltline." Despite many losses, local preservationists have saved key landmarks and neighborhoods in the "City of Oaks."

Downtown Raleigh

Union Square Area

WK 1 State Capitol

1833–40; William Nichols, Ithiel Town, Alexander Jackson Davis, David Paton, consultation by William Strickland; Union Square; National Historic Landmark

The state's chief architectural landmark, the Capitol is one of the nation's finest and best-preserved Greek Revival public buildings. Built of gneiss-type granite quarried 1¼ miles eastward, the cruciform building has a central dome and porticoes at the east and west fronts. The exterior is rendered in a chaste Doric order adopted from that of the Parthenon and displays superbly crafted stonework. Inside, the bright rotunda soars from ground level to a skylit cupola, which illuminates the seated figure of George Washington. The first story contains vaulted passages and flanking offices. The 2-story Senate and House chambers occupy the upper levels; the domed Senate features an Ionic order, and the amphitheatrical House has full-height columns in the Tower of the Winds variation of the Corinthian. In the third story are halls lit by oval domes, plus two Gothic Revival rooms for the Supreme Court and State Library.

Often ascribed solely to Town & Davis, the Capitol is the product of a sequence of accomplished architects. The cruciform plan began when William Nichols remod-

eled the old State House in 1820–24, creating a skylit rotunda as setting for a seated classical figure of George Washington by Italian sculptor Antonio Canova. Much admired, Nichols's edifice burned in 1831, along with the sculpture. After months of indecision over whether to keep Raleigh as capital, commissioners obtained various proposals for designs, including a temple-form scheme from Town & Davis and a cruciform plan from William Nichols Jr. in association with his father, who had left the state for Alabama and Mississippi. Early in 1833 the commissioners chose Nichols's design, a larger version of the State House, hired William Drummond as supervisor, and began construction, using stone carried by an experimental horse-drawn railway from a local quarry.

In mid-1833, however, with the walls already begun, Ithiel Town reentered the project. Working from the cruciform plan, Town and his partner A. J. Davis revised the design in the firm's bold Greek Revival vocabulary to create a complex and original composition, changing arched openings to rectangular ones and adding the massive Doric porticoes on the east and west. Throughout the project, commissioners and architects sought to build "in strict conformity with Grecian rules," adopting orders and moldings from specific Greek models as depicted in Stuart and Revett's widely popular book, *Antiquities of Athens*. Even the dome, Roman in inspiration, was low and simply detailed.

In 1834 Town assigned Scots immigrant architect David Paton as local superintendent, and in 1835 the building committee cut ties with Town and put Paton in charge. Paton brought a sophisticated Neoclassicism from his Edinburgh background and work with architect Sir John Soane in London. Many elements represent Paton's hand. He opened up the rotunda from ground to top to create that bright and soaring space. He also planned the toplit, Soanesque oval domes in the third story and added galleries to the chambers. He drew on Edinburgh precedents for the two curving "pen-check" stairs between the second and third stories: individually shaped stone steps linked by

WK 1 *State Capitol*

special notches form a self-supporting helix contained by the three walls of the stairwell. As work proceeded, Paton and the commissioners occasionally consulted Philadelphia architect William Strickland, who confirmed several of Paton's ideas and also insisted on the honeysuckle cresting atop the dome, instead of a balustrade that he regarded as "Roman" and "inadmissible." The difficult stonework was executed by stonemasons recruited in New York and Philadelphia; many were British immigrants. Most of the marble, hardware, and ornamental plaster molds came from Philadelphia. Exceeding all estimates, the project repeatedly ran out of money, but the commissioners insisted that quality could not be compromised in building "an Edifice designed to last the ages." In the end it took seven years and cost $532,682, not including the stone.

Seen at the time as a nationally important building symbolizing new hope for an economically depressed state, the Capitol has consistently held foremost place among the state's architecture. Having escaped a threatened expansion in the early 20th c., it stands essentially as built. In 1970 a marble replica of the Canova Washington was in-

stalled. In the 1990s original paint colors and granitizing were painstakingly restored, emphasizing the classicism and volume of the interior spaces. Union Square also possesses the state's chief assemblage of public monuments, including a copy of Houdon's George Washington, the state Confederate Memorial (1895), and other memorials to wars and political figures erected through the 20th c.

WK 2 Christ Church

1848–53, 1859–61; Richard Upjohn (New York), architect; James Puttick, Robert Findlater, masons; Justin Martindale, carpenter; steeple, John Whitelaw, mason; parish house, chapel, 1913–14, Hobart Upjohn, architect; H. P. S. Keller, superintending architect; SE corner Wilmington and Edenton Sts.; National Historic Landmark

Designed by the English-born architect who shaped the Gothic Revival in American church architecture, the beautifully executed stone church displays Upjohn's Early English Gothic style in its clean forms and massive walls of rough-hewn stone pierced by simple lancet openings. In 1846 N.C. bishop Levi Silliman Ives, proponent of the High Church Gothic Revival style, wrote to the New York architect on behalf of Christ Church to inquire about a design for "a neat Gothic Church edifice." This was evidently the first of several major southern commissions for Upjohn, who developed an influential long-distance practice by mail. He sent to rector Richard Sharp Mason detailed plans, specifications, and a model showing how to construct the roof, and he ordered fittings from New York suppliers. The contractors for the stone walls and roof had previously worked on the *State Capitol.

Despite financial difficulties, Mason shepherded completion of the cruciform sanctuary (1848–53). The arcaded cloister and corner belltower, part of Upjohn's original design, were built in 1859–61 of brownstone and granite. Atop the tall, superbly crafted broach spire of stone is a locally fabricated gilded rooster weather vane, a traditional English motif; it was cited by legend as "the last chicken left in Raleigh" after Sherman's troops arrived in 1865. The sanctuary has a double-aisle plan (a change from Upjohn's single aisle) with original pews, galleries, and heart pine floors beneath a massive roof truss. A renovation in 2000–2001 exposed the interior construction: framed walls inside the stone walls supported the lathe and plaster and rested on the wooden floor structure. Complementing his grandfather's design, Hobart Upjohn planned the Gothic Revival chapel and parish house (1914) as well as the ornate stone altar and reredos (1915). (See Introduction, Fig. 34.)

WK 3 First Baptist Church

1858–59; William Percival, architect; Thomas Coates, builder; SW corner Salisbury and Edenton Sts.

The symmetrical, stuccoed church with front tower presents a contrasting version of the Gothic Revival style, described when built as a novel example of the "decorated English" style. The congregation of black and white Baptists formed in 1812 and met in the State House before erecting their first

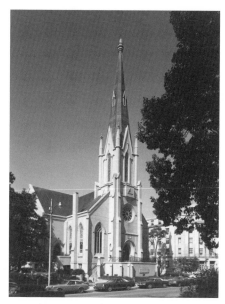

WK 3 *First Baptist Church*

church. After growth during the evangelism of the 1850s, the congregation employed Percival, then in Virginia, to design the large church, his first of several commissions in the state (*Montfort Hall, *New East and New West, *Caswell County Courthouse, #Calvary Church, Tarboro). The church has been expanded over the years.

WK 4 First Presbyterian Church

1897–1900; Charles E. Cassell (Baltimore), architect; Charles Pearson, supervising architect; George W. Waring (Columbia), contractor; SW corner Salisbury and Morgan Sts.

The robustly composed church of dark red brick trimmed in rough stone displays a locally unusual Romanesque Revival style. Dramatizing its corner position, broad gables meet at an angled entrance tower with bold bartizans and open belfry. The congregation was organized in 1816 and met in the State House until completing a small brick church in 1818. Although A. G. Bauer offered a design in the early 1890s, in 1896 the congregation was "considering plans for a new edifice" by Charles E. Cassell, prominent Baltimore architect.

WK 5 First Baptist Church

1904–9; SE corner Wilmington and Morgan Sts.

In 1868 the black members of *First Baptist on Salisbury St., who had been meeting separately since 1865, established the First Colored Baptist Church and built a sanctuary on N. Salisbury St. In 1896 the congregation obtained this property from Raleigh's Catholic parish and soon erected the red brick Gothic Revival structure with buttresses, gables, a corner tower, and stained glass. Reflecting their long heritage, both congregations share the 1812 founding date and the name; the cornerstone here is inscribed, "The First Baptist Church, Organized 1812 . . . 1904."

WK 6 Capitol Square Government Buildings

The Capitol sufficed for state government for nearly a half-century, surrounded by dwellings, hotels, and churches facing the square. In time, government buildings filled the blocks between the churches. A consistent sense of propriety has kept them subservient in scale and style to the Capitol. The oldest is the former **Supreme Court Building** (Labor Building) (1888; William J. Hicks & Adolphus Gustavus Bauer), a 5-story brick structure with corbeling and small mansard tower.

Subsequent buildings returned to the classicism of the Capitol, repeating its rusticated basement, simple pilasters, and clean-cut windows as well as the scale and the light gray stone, each according to its own era and each fully occupying its site. The defining edifice, which initially held the Supreme Court, State Library, and other offices, was the Beaux Arts classical **Administration Building** (Ruffin Building, Court of Appeals) (1913; P. Thornton Marye & Frank B. Simpson; 1 W. Morgan St.), a 4-story palazzo design with rich classical detailing by a prominent Atlanta classicist; he used pilasters, cornices, balconies, and an inset entrance loggia to create a sense of depth on a tight site, and he placed the richly classical (former) Supreme Court chamber in the piano nobile overlooking the capitol.

The **Agriculture Building** (1922–23; G. Murray Nelson & Thomas W. Cooper; 2 W. Edenton St.) was designed by a local firm who set an Ionic colonnade above a striated basement, which extends around the corner to create a dual facade respectful to both Edenton and Halifax Sts. The **N.C. Museum of Natural Sciences** (1999; Robert Winston Carr [Durham], architect), added on the north, is a fresh classical design with a glass-domed corner pavilion.

Stylized classicism with pilasters, raised base, and simplified cornices rendered in warm gray stone also define the **Revenue Building** (1927; Atwood & Nash, architects?; 2 S. Salisbury St.) and the **Education Building** (1938; Northup & O'Brien; 114 W. Edenton St.), which presents an angled entrance bay to the corner in a geometricized Art Deco mode. The **Law and Justice Building** (1939–40; Northup & O'Brien; 2 E. Morgan St.), designed during the Great Depression and built of Mount Airy granite, features tall pilasters and a stylized figure of Justice and a classically detailed Supreme Court chamber. The **Highway Building** (1951; Allen J. Maxwell; 1 S. Wilmington St.) continues the Moderne classical theme with Moderne lobby in terrazzo and green marble.

WK 7 Legislative Building

1962–63; Edward Durell Stone (New York), architect; Holloway & Reeves (Raleigh), superintending architects; Richard C. Bell, landscape architect; 100 block W. Jones St.

Set on axis with the State Capitol, the white marble edifice typifies architect Stone's mid-century work in the classicized modernism called New Formalism. The commission to Stone, one of the most famous American architects of the time, came through his acquaintance with powerful legislator Thomas White (D-Lenoir) and expressed the state's rising sense of its place in postwar America. Its softened modernism suited to its southern setting has weathered changing tastes gracefully.

Sharing the spirit of Stone's famed 1950s American Embassy in New Delhi (another hot capital), with its broad piazza-like colon-

WK 7 *Legislative Building*

WK 8–9 *State Bank and Capital Apartments*

nades, deep roof overhangs, and series of roof pavilions, the building has a pleasantly tropical feeling emphasized by the interplay of indoor and outdoor spaces and the gardens on the terraces, roof, and skylit interior courts. The interior, renowned for the confusing layout of offices on the ground floor, makes beautiful use of natural light, especially where the arcaded roof pavilions rise above the House and Senate Chambers, illuminating the deliberations below, and in the skylit, brass-encircled rotunda, which echoes that of the Capitol. Typical of Stone's Indian-influenced work, delicate geometric motifs of incised marble and filigreed metal screens, as well as the lights, railings, and other fittings, repeat the circular and rectilinear themes established in the larger forms. To keep costs low, he combined marble and brass with more economical materials, including concrete block walls and stock fittings. Built solely for the legislature, it stands astride the former Halifax St. north of Union Square. A daunting state government mall, designed by Odell & Assoc. of Charlotte, extended farther north in the 1970s.

East of Union Square

WK 8 State Bank of North Carolina
1814; Lewis Nicholson, contractor;
123 New Bern Pl.; moved 1 lot east, 1968

Raleigh's only surviving early 19th-c. commercial building, the 2-story Flemish-bond brick structure housed the state bank and the banker's residence. The gable front with bank entrance faces the street, and 2-tier side porticoes served the domestic quarters

above. Rescued and renovated for banking, it has original Federal finish chiefly in the upper stories, including the drawing room across the front.

WK 9 Capital Apartments
1917; C. V. York, builder; 127 New Bern Pl.

The first and finest of several small, high-quality apartment houses downtown, the 5-story tan brick building with Renaissance Revival details frames a bright entrance courtyard and has corners cut out as balconies.

WK 10 Haywood Hall
Ca. 1800 and later; 211 New Bern Pl.;
open limited hours

A simple wooden fence encloses a remarkable survival—a town house, outbuildings, and grounds that once covered the block. Such in-town establishments were typical of N.C. towns in the early 19th c. Built for state treasurer John Haywood, who as a state officer was required to have a Raleigh residence, the 2-story frame house has granite block

WK 10 *Haywood Hall*

foundations, heavy Flemish-bond brick chimneys, and molded weatherboards and window sills. The center-passage plan interior has individualized late Georgian finish including an enclosed stair with Chinese lattice railing and an elaborate mantel by joiner Elhannon Nutt, who advertised work in "a superiour manner to what has been customary in this place" (*Fairntosh, *Ayr Mount). The early smokehouse retains its original finial. After long family ownership, the complex is maintained by the Colonial Dames.

WK 12 *Richard Bennehan Haywood House*

WK 11 White-Holman House
Ca. 1798; 206 New Bern Pl.;
moved from 209 E. Morgan St., 1985

Like *Haywood Hall, the 2-story frame side-passage plan house was built as the requisite Raleigh residence for a state official, Secretary of State William White. Its brick chimneys, stone foundations, modillion cornice, and molded weatherboards and window sills mark it as one of the best local houses of its era, with interiors of late Georgian character. The entrance portico was rebuilt from a photograph. After mid-20th-c. realignment of Morgan St. cut New Bern Ave. into a cul-de-sac, in the 1980s this and other houses were moved here, along with the **Bretsch House** (1890s; 11 S. Blount), a decorated cottage from 105 N. McDowell St.

WK 12 Richard Bennehan Haywood House
Ca. 1854; 127 E. Edenton St.

Planned by Dr. Haywood and his wife Julia Ogden Hicks of New York, the 2-story brick house (in a Flemish variation of common bond) with stone lintels personifies the local Greek Revival: a symmetrical, hip-roofed form with center-passage plan, broad Doric porch, and side bay windows. Family tradition recalls that Haywood, Confederate surgeon, and his former classmate at the University of North Carolina (UNC), occupying Union general Francis Blair, drank a toast here in April 1865 to celebrate the end of the war. The house has been preserved by continuous family stewardship.

South of Union Square

Fayetteville St. Area:
Raleigh's commercial main street reflects at least four chapters of rebuilding, embracing late 19th-c. eclecticism, early 20th-c. classicism including small skyscrapers, mid-20th-c. modernist designs, and a late 20th-c. crop of tall office towers. Until the late 20th c., Fayetteville St. was a lively street lined by theaters, department stores, restaurants, and banks, defined for a time by the classical porticoes of the Capitol at the north and Memorial Auditorium at the south end. In the 1970s a pedestrian mall and a civic center blocked the axial vista, but by the early 21st c. there was talk of reopening the street.

WK 13 Masonic Temple Building
1907; Charles McMillen, architect;
133 Fayetteville St.

In the early 20th c., as Raleigh strove to boost its urban identity, a series of handsome little skyscrapers gave downtown a new aura. Most employed a classically organized and detailed scheme with base, shaft, and capital, as seen in this early example by McMillen, a Minnesota specialist in Masonic buildings (#Masonic Temple, 1898–99, Wilmington). The tan brick 7-story skyscraper is the state's oldest reinforced-steel tall building (Charlotte's 12-story Independence Building of 1906 was razed). Other classically treated skyscrapers of the era include the 8-story **Professional Building** (1925; Milburn & Heister, architects; 123–27 W. Hargett St.); the 11-story

Raleigh Building (1913, 1928; H. A. Underwood; 5 W. Hargett St.), which began with 3
stories, then added 8 more; and the 12-story
Capital Club Building (1929; Frank Simpson or Milburn & Heister, architects; 16 W.
Martin St.).

WK 14 Briggs Hardware Building
1874; 220 Fayetteville St.

The classic Italianate commercial building
retains its 4-story brick facade rich with
metal quoins, window labels, cornices,
brackets, finials, and a parapet proclaiming,
"1874 Briggs Building Hardware." Founded
by builder and manufacturer Thomas
Briggs, the family hardware business used
the building until the mid-1990s; it has been
renovated for offices. Other Italianate commercial facades have been uncovered along
the block, indicative of its late 19th-c. and
early 20th-c. character.

WK 15 U.S. (Century) Post Office
*1874–79, Alfred B. Mullett, supervising
architect of the Treasury; remodeled 1912–13,
Frank B. Simpson; expanded 1938, William
H. Deitrick, architect; 314 Fayetteville St.*

Congress's 1856 appropriation for a Federal
building in Raleigh was shelved with other
southern projects in 1860. Revived in 1874, it
was one of N.C.'s first postwar Federal construction jobs. Built of stone from *Granite
Quarry, N.C., the 3½-story edifice features a
mansard roof, quoined corners, and heavy
bracket cornice; it is the state's sole example
of Mullett's Second Empire mode, epitomized by the Executive Office Building in
Washington, D.C.

WK 16 Insurance Building
(Wake Co. Office Building)
*1940–42; Luther Lashmit
(Northup & O'Brien [Winston-Salem]),
architect; George W. Kane, contractor;
336 Fayetteville St.*

The limestone-clad Art Deco skyscraper, a
restrained 12-story version of the ziggurat
form modeled in the state by the *Reynolds
Building (1929) in Winston-Salem, added a

WK 14 *Briggs Hardware Building*

modernist presence at the end of the Great
Depression. Built for the Durham Life Insurance Co. of Raleigh, the office building
included a major innovation: it was one of
the nation's three first uses of Willis Carrier's
newly perfected (1939) high-velocity air pro-
pulsion system of air conditioning for tall
buildings, the Conduit Weathermaster System. The Art Deco lobby gleams with pink
marble and terrazzo, polished brass, and
mirrors.

WK 17 Former BB&T Building
*1965; Emery Roth & Sons (New York)
with G. Milton Small (Raleigh);
333 Fayetteville St.*

The slim black and silver skyscraper exemplifies the modernist esthetic modeled by
architect Mies van der Rohe. The 16-story
corner building has a 2-story base of black-
granite-sheathed pillars, from which ribbons
of bright aluminum rise against the dark
glass and spandrel grid. Designers Emery
Roth & Sons planned many of New York's

WK 16 *Insurance Building*

glass-and-metal-clad office towers in the 1950s and 1960s. Local associate Small was a student of Mies who had come to work for William Deitrick, then formed his own firm.

WK 18 First Federal Bank
1960; Howard T. Musick (St. Louis), architect; 300 S. Salisbury St.

In the full spirit of the 1950s, the colorful popular rendition of the Miesian mode displays variegated blue glass panels, aluminum mullions, and white marble 5 stories high, complete with the time-weather clock.

WK 19 Sir Walter Hotel
1922–24; William L. Stoddart (New York) and James A. Salter, architects; 400 Fayetteville St.

The straightforward Georgian Revival hotel, 10 stories tall in red brick, has a venerable history as the capital's premier political hotel. During legislative sessions, lawmakers, lobbyists, and others made it their home, and until the *Legislative Building supplied office space in 1962, it was known as the "third house" of the General Assem-

bly. In the 1970s it was converted to housing for senior citizens.

WK 20 Sir Walter Chevrolet Building
1949–50; G. Milton Small/William H. Deitrick, architects; 530 S. McDowell St.

Presaging new trends, the early modernist structure features a state-of-the-art bowstring truss roof curving above broad expanses of glass, the better to display the latest streamlined Chevrolets.

WK 21 Memorial Auditorium
1932; Atwood & Weeks, architects; C. V. York, contractor; 2 E. South St.

The stone edifice with massive Doric portico, built with Works Progress Administration (WPA) aid in memory of war dead, was designed as a complement to the Capitol. The original building is surrounded by late 20th-c. expansions that continue the classical theme.

WK 22 Shaw University
Est. 1865; 118 South St., 700–800 blocks S. Wilmington St.

Founded in 1865 by Union army chaplain Henry Martin Tupper to educate freedmen, the college opened on the former Barringer estate in 1870. Construction by students, faculty, and others was aided by Elijah Shaw of Massachusetts. **Estey Hall** (1874, G. S. H. Appleget; 1907), described as the South's first building for the college education of black women, is a rare survivor of the Italianate school edifices of the immediate postwar era, a 4½-story brick building with arched window labels, quoins, and crossgabled roof with bracketed belvedere.

Leonard Hall (1882; 816 S. Wilmington St.) features Romanesque Revival arched openings and a rounded twin-towered facade. **Tyler Hall** (1910; G. A. Edwards, architect-builder; 814 S. Wilmington St.), in polychromed brick, free classical style, was planned and supervised by faculty member Edwards, who in 1919 was noted in the *National Cyclopedia of the Colored Race* as the "only licensed colored architect in the state."

WK 22 *Estey Hall*

Both were part of the Leonard Medical School, established in 1882 as the nation's first 4-year medical school for black students and one of the first schools, black or white, to have a progressive, graded, 4-year sequence of medical study. From its founding, Shaw served as a cultural and political hub along with educating physicians, ministers, teachers, and civic leaders. Here in 1960 the Student Nonviolent Coordinating Committee began as an outgrowth of the sit-in movement and adopted the anthem, "We Shall Overcome."

WK 23 Pope House

1900; 511 S. Wilmington St.

The 2-story brick residence and office erected for a physician and his family has survived the loss of neighboring houses. Dr. Manassus Pope participated in political affairs despite restrictions of the time. After long family ownership it is under development as a museum.

WK 24 Wilmington St.

Paralleling Fayetteville St. on the east, 2- and 3-story brick buildings, generally with Italianate and Romanesque detail, recall the scale and mixed commercial uses of an earlier day. Among the oldest is the 3-story bracketed **Heilig-Levine Furniture Store** (1870–71; 137 S. Wilmington), which was

erected in the postwar building boom and served as the Carolina Boarding House, a hotel, a grocery, and a furniture store.

WK 25 E. Hargett St.

During the 1920s the first two blocks of E. Hargett St. developed as one of the state's best-known "Black Main Streets," a lively center of commerce, culture, and entertainment, which historian Wilmoth Carter called "the center of everything in the black community in the twenties and thirties." The Mechanics & Farmers Bank (early, late 20th c.; 13 E. Hargett St.) was a financial anchor, while the social centerpiece was the Lightner Arcade (1923; razed), which had one of the few fine hotels for black customers and hosted big bands and other major entertainers. Prominent among surviving buildings is the 3-story **Commercial Building** (1914; 119 E. Hargett St.) of pressed brick with large, arched openings, pilasters, and corbeling, which by the 1930s held the Royal Theatre. The 2-story brick **Delany Building** (1926; 133 E. Hargett St.) had professional offices and organizations. Other 1- to 3-story brick commercial buildings feature corbeled detail and arched windows; some still contain barbershops, shoe repair shops, and a drugstore. At the corner, the big 3-story **Montague Building** (1912; 128 E. Hargett St.) was built just before the emergence of the black main street. The street has been part of the late 20th-c. Moore Square revitalization.

WK 26 City Market

1914; James M. Kennedy (Goldsboro and Raleigh), architect; E. Martin St., Moore Square

Mounting concern for sanitation led the city to replace the odoriferous old city market on Fayetteville St. with a modern facility facing Moore Square. The yellow and red brick building "after the Spanish manner" employed a style at once festive, economical, and functional, with broad tile roofs extending to shelter outdoor produce vendors and farmers; inside were gleaming, sanitary white tile and refrigerated cases for meat and fish.

Discontinued as a municipal market in the 1950s, it had produce vendors until the 1980s brought festive retail development. The nearby blocks long served agricultural suppliers and livery (later automobile) businesses in a functional urban zone complementing Fayetteville St.

West of Union Square

WK 27 Raleigh Water Tower (A.I.A. Tower)

1887; 1938 conversion by William H. Deitrick, architect; 115 W. Morgan St.

The 85-foot water tower of massive stone blocks was built in 1887 to support a 100,000-gallon iron tank for the city's new water system; the gable-fronted brick office was attached in front. The tank was removed and the building abandoned in 1924. In a pioneering historic preservation step, in 1938 Raleigh architect Deitrick rescued the abandoned tower for his firm's offices; in 1963 he conveyed it to the N.C. chapter of the American Institute of Architects (NCAIA). A native of Danville, Va., Deitrick graduated from Wake Forest College and studied at Columbia while working as a draftsman for New York architect Raymond Hood, then began working in 1924 for Raleigh architect James A. Salter. In 1927 he opened his own office. Working in revivalist and modernist modes, his firm was a leader in the state into the postwar era (*Broughton High School, *Dorton Arena).

WK 28 Hillsborough St.

The only original axial street still open from Union Square, Hillsborough St. was once a high-status residential avenue and site of the streetcar line west. A few buildings remain from its prime. The Episcopal **Church of the Good Shepherd and All Saints Chapel** (1875, Rev. Johannes Adam Oertel; 1899–1914, Charles E. Hartge, architect; 125 Hillsborough St.) began with the Carpenter Gothic style, board-and-batten All Saints Chapel (1875) designed by priest and artist Oertel for a congregation formed in 1874 from *Christ Church over the issue of free

pews. In 1899 the German-born architect Hartge planned the Gothic Revival church in rough-cut stone with corner tower and rich interiors. The **Cathedral of the Sacred Heart** (1922–27; Father Michael McInerney [Belmont], architect; 204 Hillsborough St.) shows another face of the Gothic Revival in rough-cut granite with corner tower, designed by the *Belmont Abbey architect of many Roman Catholic buildings. (The city's first Catholic congregation met in the Presbyterian church until its members, including Irish stonecutters at the *State Capitol, erected their first church in 1835.)

Of several fine houses on the street, few remain. The once abundant Southern Colonial Revival style is represented by the **Goodwin House** (1903; William P. Rose [Raleigh and Goldsboro]; 220 Hillsborough St.), an eclectically detailed frame version with tall portico. Of the Victorian mansions, the persistent survivor is the **Dodd-Hinsdale House** (ca. 1879; Thomas H. Briggs, builder [attrib.]; 330 Hillsborough St.), a vivid 2-story house of pressed brick distinguished by its jaunty mansard-topped entrance tower. Longtime home of the Hinsdale family until 1971, it was renovated as a restaurant after decades of uncertainty. Its profile coupled with the towering, circular-plan former **Holiday Inn** (1969–70; 320 Hillsborough St.) created a photogenic contrast.

WK 29 St. Paul's A.M.E. Church

1884–1901, 1910; 402 W. Edenton St.

Intricate brickwork and fine stained glass enrich the imposing Gothic Revival church built for the city's oldest independent black congregation. In the 1840s African American members of Edenton St. Methodist Church began separate services in the church basement. In 1853 they moved to this site the 1829 former Christ Church, a frame building that became known as the African Church. In 1865 the church hosted the state freedmen's convention. Soon the congregation affiliated with the African Methodist Episcopal Church, formally acquired the lot in 1867, and emerged as a center of political as well as religious leadership. Renamed St.

WK 28 *Dodd-Hinsdale House with Holiday Inn*

WK 29 *St. Paul's A.M.E. Church*

Paul's in 1884, the congregation began a brick church supervised by builder, member, and legislator Stewart Ellison. After 25 years of work, the congregation dedicated their large brick church in 1901. In July 1909 a fire gutted the building. With black and white community support, it was rebuilt within the walls by June 1910, including an auditorium sanctuary with dark woodwork, balcony, and stained glass that is among the most impressive in the city.

North of Union Square:
Long a residential area, in the mid-20th c. the northern blocks of the original city became a zone of state government construction.

WK 30 N.C. School for the Blind and Deaf Dormitory
1898; Frank Pierce Milburn, architect; Caswell Square, NE corner W. Jones and Dawson Sts.

Milburn's massive 3½-story brick dormitory —part of a campus that once included antebellum, castellated buildings by builder Dabney Cosby—boasts a prominent dormered and turreted chateauesque roofline.

WK 31 Seaboard (Raleigh & Gaston) Office Building

1861; third story 1891; 300 block N. Salisbury St.; moved from Halifax St., 1977

One of the few antebellum railroad buildings in the state, the Italianate brick building with ornate cast-iron balconies was erected as offices for the R&GRR. It may have been designed by R&GRR architect Thomas J. Holt (*Peace College), who planned the roundhouse that stood nearby.

WK 32 Executive Mansion

1883–91; Samuel Sloan, Adolphus Gustavus Bauer, William J. Hicks; Burke Square, N. Blount St.; open by appointment

Architect Sloan, finding his Philadelphia practice waning after the Civil War, took several southern commissions. Noted as a designer of hospitals for the insane, in 1875 he was hired to plan the #Western N.C. Insane Asylum in Morganton. He won the confidence of Governor Thomas Jarvis, who was campaigning for a new governor's residence; since the early 19th-c. residence at the south end of Fayetteville St. was uninhabitable, the governor was residing at a local hotel. Sloan moved his office to Raleigh, with assistant and draftsman Adolphus Gustavus Bauer. In 1883 the local paper praised

WK 32 *Executive Mansion*

Sloan's "artistic," "ornate" design "in modern style," with "ample porches, hall ways, and windows which every house built in this climate should have." Sloan planned a building of Anson Co. sandstone, but William J. Hicks—builder, architect, and supervisor of Central Prison, which provided workmen and materials—suggested the more economical "penitentiary machine made pressed brick" trimmed in sandstone. After Sloan died in Raleigh in 1884, Bauer and Hicks took over the project, which after funding delays was completed in 1891. The generally symmetrical form and center-passage plan are rendered in the ornate and lively Queen Anne style, with multiple gables and chimneys, floral patterned slate, and a bevy of Eastlake style porches and balconies. The public rooms on the first floor are treated with elaborate woodwork. Family quarters are above. Herringbone brick sidewalks retain signatures of convict brickmakers. Surviving the vagaries of taste, the mansion is Raleigh's chief landmark from the post–Civil War era.

WK 33 North Blount Street Area

Developed as a fashionable address as the city expanded north after the Civil War, the street still has some of its principal Victorian residences, several of which were built for members of Franklin and Warren Co. planter families associated with the R&GRR. In the 20th c. the area declined and houses were razed, but the 1970s brought renovation for state office use and houses from other sites. Notable among the early 20th-c. houses is the **Andrews-London House** (ca. 1916; James A. Salter, architect; 301 N. Blount), a robust Georgian Revival composition in red brick with Doric entrance.

The city's first big house built after the war stunned old Raleigh but set the tone: the towered, 2½-story Second Empire style **Heck-Andrews House** (1869–70; G. S. H. Appleget, architect; John M. Wilson & John A. Waddell [Wilson's Mills] contractors; 309 N. Blount), with mansard entrance tower and ornate millwork supplied by contractors Wilson & Waddell of #Wilson's Mills in

WK 33 *Andrews-London House and Heck-Andrews House*

WK 33 *Hawkins-Hartness House*

Johnston Co. The **Andrews-Duncan House** (ca. 1875; G. S. H. Appleget, Wilson & Waddell?; 407 N. Blount St.) displays similar millwork in a tall, cross-gabled Italianate house built for railroad magnate Alexander Boyd Andrews.

The severely elegant **Hawkins-Hartness House** (early 1880s; 310 N. Blount St.), of crisp pressed brick and asymmetrical, towered form, has fine Eastlake trim on its wraparound porch and within. It was built for Alexander Boyd and Martha Bailey Hawkins; his brother, William J. Hawkins (*Oakley Hall, Warren Co.), former president of the R&GRR, directed construction. The **Lucy Catherine Capehart House** (1897; Adolphus Gustavus Bauer, architect; C. P. Snuggs, builder; 424 N. Blount St.; moved from 403 N. Wilmington St., 1979), a turreted Queen Anne style residence of tan brick, was one of Bauer's last works. The **Lewis-Smith House** (ca. 1854, ca. 1912; 515 N. Blount St.; moved from 515 N. Wilmington St., 1974) is a Greek Revival house with Italianate brackets, an entrance portico of superimposed Doric and Ionic orders, and early 20th-c. additions. The shingled and towered **Leonidas L. Polk House** (ca. 1890; 517 N. Blount St.; moved 2000) was built for the advocate of progressive agriculture and education, a national Populist leader whose likely presidential candidacy ended with his death in 1892. The **Augustus Merrimon House** (1875; 526 N. Wilmington St.), in late Italianate style, has unusual porch trim depicting gears, bolts, and rivets in wood.

WK 34 Peace College Main Building
Ca. 1859–72; Thomas J. Holt, architect; Jacob Holt, contractor; N side Peace St. at Wilmington St.

The 4-story brick building combines the pilasters and heavy portico of many antebellum Greek Revival school buildings (*Louisburg College) with an Italianate bracket cornice. Thomas J. Holt, architect for the R&GRR, provided a design, and his brother, Jacob Holt of Warrenton, contracted to build it. In 1862 the unfinished brick shell was hurriedly enclosed by Raleigh builder Thomas Briggs for service as a Confederate hospital. After housing the Freedmen's Bureau (1865–67), it was completed in 1872 for its intended purpose as a Presbyterian school for women.

WK 34 *Peace College Main Building*

WK 35 Seaboard Railroad Depot (Logan's Garden Center)

1941; 707 Semart Dr.

The red brick, Georgian Revival passenger depot was built to serve Seaboard's travelers on the old R&GRR route. After service ended, it was rescued as Logan's Garden Center, with sales in the waiting rooms and the long passenger shelters shading annuals, perennials, and shrubs trackside, while freight trains rumble by.

WK 36 Raleigh Cotton Mills

1890; C. R. Makepeace [Providence, R.I.], designer; 614 Capital Blvd.

Raleigh joined the textile industry with relatively small mills beside the tracks. The Raleigh Cotton Mills, founded by local investors to card and spin cotton yarn for hosiery, is a long 2- and 3-story building with segmental-arched openings and corner towers. Renovated for residences, it has a strong presence on a busy thoroughfare. Across the tracks, **Pilot Mills** (1892; N. Halifax St.), founded by James N. and W. H. Williamson of the Alamance Co. Holt dynasty to weave cotton plaids and other fabrics, has been essentially rebuilt for new uses.

WK 37 Oakwood

The approximately 20-block neighborhood east and north of the Executive Mansion composes one of N.C.'s most intact Victorian suburbs, a tight grid filled with generally frame versions of Italianate, Second Empire, and Queen Anne modes and slightly later Colonial Revival and bungalow houses. In 1868 R. S. Pullen bought a 29-acre Polk family tract east of Blount St., where he soon began development; this was followed by the Mordecai family's sale of lots east of Peace College. By 1880 a local writer praised the "really wonderful" growth north and east where "bare fields or woods" had given way to "shady streets and rows of elegant houses" — residences for the new urban middle class of office workers, tradesmen, teachers, politicians, and businessmen. Builders included the Thomas Briggs firm in the 19th c.

WK 37 *Heck Houses, Oakwood*

and architect Charles Barrett at the turn of the 20th c.

The **Heck Houses** (1872–75; corner E. Jones and East Sts.), a trio of small, asymmetrical towered Second Empire style dwellings, are attributed to G. S. H. Appleget (*Heck-Andrews House); the design may come from A. J. Bicknell's *Village Builder* (1870). The three brick **Pullen Houses** (1880s; 408–16 Elm St.) were built by developer Pullen in symmetrical forms with center roof gables. The **Stronach House** (ca. 1870, 1886; 414 N. Bloodworth St.) began as an Italianate house and was remodeled in eccentric Queen Anne style with a twin-turreted porch and other lively features. On N. Person St. is the **Murphey School** (1915–16, James M. Kennedy), the oldest of Raleigh's handsome brick schools of the early 20th c. Here in 1960 William Campbell (later mayor of Atlanta) became the first black student to attend a formerly all-white public school in Raleigh. After a mid-20th-c. decline and the threat of an expressway, Oakwood rebounded with one of the state's first locally organized neighborhood revitalizations.

On the east is the picturesque **Oakwood Cemetery** (est. 1869), with fine markers from the late 19th c. onward. In 1866–67 the local Ladies Memorial Association established a Confederate cemetery — one of the first created in the South — on land donated by the Mordecai family, and investors acquired additional Mordecai land for Oakwood Cemetery. Of architectural interest is the little white marble temple designed by architect A. G. Bauer for his wife Rachel (d. 1897); he was buried beside her in 1898.

WK 38 St. Augustine's College
Est. 1867; Oakwood Ave.

Founded by the Protestant Episcopal Church to train black teachers and ministers, the school opened in 1868 in houses on Blount St. and soon acquired land on the east side of Raleigh. Bishop Henry Delany, the first black man to become an Episcopal bishop in the state and the second in the nation, studied theology at the school in the 1880s, then became a faculty member and administrator. In their best-selling memoir *Having Our Say* (1993), his daughters, Sarah (Sadie) and Bessie Delany, described Raleigh at the turn of the 20th c. The oldest building is **St. Augustine's Chapel** (1896), in Gothic style of local stone, built under Delany's guidance by students led by instructor and stonemason George Washington Hayes; transepts and a lych-gate came in the early 20th c. Also of stone are the Romanesque Revival style **Benson Library** (1898) and the large **St. Agnes Hospital** (1909). There are several later 20th-c. brick structures.

Bordering the college is a large neighborhood that developed primarily in the early 20th c. with St. Augustine's as a focal point: **College Park** (E of Tarboro St.) and **Idlewild** (W of Tarboro, between Linden, New Bern, and Glascock Sts.). College faculty and other African American professionals, businessmen, tradespeople, and railroad workers owned their own homes, while some rented dwellings, chiefly 1-story frame houses but also substantial brick foursquares, small bungalows, shotgun houses, and gabled cottages.

WK 39 Mordecai House and Grounds
Ca. 1785; 1826, William Nichols; Mimosa St.; open regular hours

The former plantation house embodies two early construction phases. The rear section of the T-shaped frame house was built as a hall-parlor plan dwelling by planter Joel Lane for his son Henry. Henry's daughter Nancy married Moses Mordecai. After Moses died, Nancy employed William Nichols, the English-born architect who had redesigned the State House, to add the 2-story south (front) section with a central passage and flanking rooms. Nichols's simple but sophisticated design features a 2-tier entrance portico with Ionic over Doric orders, inspired by Stuart and Revett's *Antiquities of Athens*. The restrained Greek Revival woodwork is among the state's earliest examples of the style (#Hayes, Edenton). As the city grew around it, the house tract remained in the family until 1967; in the 1970s it became a civic park, complete with two centuries of Mordecai possessions. Besides the original outbuildings, other small frame buildings have been moved in, including an 1842 **Kitchen** from Anson Co.; the **Badger-Iredell Law Office** (ca. 1810, Raleigh); another Raleigh office building (ca. 1850); **St. Mark's Chapel** (1847, Chatham Co.); and the **Andrew Johnson Birthplace** (ca. 1800, Raleigh), the oft-moved and restored gambrel-roofed building in which the president is said to have been born. The adjoining **Mordecai Neighborhood** was developed in the early 20th c. and contains a representative collection of bungalows, Colonial Revival residences, and Craftsman dwellings in a compact, gently curvilinear streetscape. (See Introduction, Fig. 30.)

WK 40 Norburn Terrace
1898–99; Adolphus Gustavus Bauer (attrib.); 212 Lafayette Rd.

Positioned on a terraced garden, the big T-plan brick house boasts a full complement of late Victorian enrichments, including a central tower, multiple gables, stained glass, and ornate porches.

WK 38 *St. Augustine's Chapel*

WK 41 Southeast Raleigh

Throughout the 19th c., the southeast quadrant of the city contained, like the rest of the grid, a mix of classes, races, and uses. Dating from the antebellum era are the **Jordan Womble House** (ca. 1810–40; 608 E. Hargett St.), a symmetrical Federal–Greek Revival cottage on a high basement of stone blocks; the **Henry Porter House** (ca. 1840s; 555 New Bern Ave.), a 2-story Greek Revival house with 2-story entrance portico; and the **Bagley-Daniels-Pegues House** (ca. 1855; 125 E. South St.), a 2-story Italianate residence, home of publisher Josephus Daniels and, later, Albert Pegues, dean of theology at Shaw.

After the Civil War, black and white developers subdivided lots and built houses in Italianate and Queen Anne styles as well as smaller, simpler dwellings. The **George Lane House** (ca. 1870; 728 E. Davie St.), constructed for a builder and mortician and his wife Adeline shortly after the war, exemplifies the era's 2-story frame houses with center front gable. The **Ligon House** (ca. 1914; 573 E. Lenoir St.) is a 2-story house with Craftsman detail built for educator and Baptist minister John William Ligon and his wife Daisy.

Beyond the original grid, additional residential blocks extended south and southeast, aimed primarily at black families. **South Park**, a "new resident suburb," was developed in 1907 east of Wilmington St. and south of Lenoir, with streetcar service to downtown. On the east, however, as late as the 1920s, **Thompson School** (1923; 567 E. Hargett St.), a brick school with Tudor-inspired detailing, was built for white students. By the mid-20th c. southeast Raleigh had become predominantly black. Late 20th-c. urban renewal destroyed much from the pre–World War II era, but some buildings survive, including elaborately detailed 2-story houses as well as shotgun houses, small bungalows, and L-shaped and front-gabled cottages. The principal streets include E. Hargett, Martin, Davie, Cabarrus, Lenoir, South, and the north-south streets intersecting them.

A social and architectural landmark is the **Masonic Temple Building** (1907; G. A. Ed-

WK 41 *Masonic Temple Building*

wards [Raleigh], architect-builder [attrib.]; 427 S. Blount St.), a 3-story brick structure featuring segmental-arched windows and a corner entrance with fluted iron column. Designed by a professor at *Shaw University, it was erected for Widow's Son Lodge No. 4, established in 1867 by Bishop James W. Hood, a leader in black masonry and the A.M.E. Zion church, and Excelsior Lodge No. 21, formed in 1879. **Tupper Memorial Baptist Church** (ca. 1912, 1957; 501 S. Blount St.) was begun here by the founder of Shaw University as Second Baptist Church in 1866; the two-towered frame church was built in 1912 and brick-veneered in 1957. **Davie Street Presbyterian Church** (est. 1875, rebuilt 1920s; Calvin Lightner; 300 E. Davie St.) was founded by northern missionaries who built a frame church, later reworked by Lightner—builder, civic leader, and church elder—in brick with Gothic Revival style corner tower and ornate corbeling. His son, Clarence Lightner, served as mayor of Raleigh (1973–75), one of the nation's first black mayors elected by a majority white city.

WK 42 Chavis Park and Chavis Heights

Planned to provide "a community for family life in the American way," these were among the state's first New Deal public park and housing undertakings. **Chavis Park** (1935–37; Chavis Way), developed with WPA assistance, opened in 1937 as one of the state's first public parks for black citizens, with a playground, ballfield, swimming pool, and the **Chavis Park Carousel** (ca. 1920, 1937, restored 1982), made by the Allan Herschell Co. of North Tonawanda, N.Y., and moved to the park. The name honored John Chavis, the free black teacher and preacher who taught black and white students at his classical academy in Raleigh (1808–32). In 1938, the year after Congress established the U.S. Housing Authority, Raleigh and Wilmington founded N.C.'s first local housing programs with federal aid, with **Chavis Heights** (1939–41; William H. Deitrick, architect) an early project to provide "modern, healthy homes" to help families leave slums and acquire their own homes. Featured in *Architectural Record* in 1941, the 2-story, 12-unit "house rows" of brick were designed by Deitrick in a "'superblock' plan typical of advanced current practice." (Its demolition is planned as of 2002.) The ensemble also includes **Crosby-Garfield Elementary School** (1938; William H. Deitrick, architect; 568 E. Lenoir St.), one of the first modernist schools in the state, with simple, rectangular forms.

WK 43 Washington School

1924; C. Gadsden Sayre (Anderson, S.C.), architect; 1000 Fayetteville St.

Raleigh's first public high school for black students (now a middle school), the 2½-story brick edifice was designed by school specialist Sayre, with generous banks of windows and elaborate Scholastic Gothic details. It traces back to the Washington School founded in 1866 by the American Missionary Assn. of New York, which stood on South St.

WK 44 Dorothea Dix Hospital

1850–56; Alexander Jackson Davis (New York), architect; Western Blvd.

Davis's magnificent 726-foot-long hospital for the insane, a symmetrical Tuscan composition with arcaded pavilion flanked by long wings with pilasters and tall "Davisean" windows, once dominated the hilltop. The core was razed in the mid-20th c., but the immense wings survived fire and remodelings. Several late 19th- to early 20th-c. buildings dot the sylvan campus overlooking the city.

West Raleigh

WK 45 Boylan Heights

One of the city's first two streetcar suburbs (*Glenwood), Boylan Heights was established in 1907 a few blocks south of the Hillsborough St. route. In the first departure from Raleigh's grid, the Greater Raleigh Land Co. laid out a curving street plan by Kelsey & Guild of Boston. The sweep of Boylan Ave. down the hillside displays the finest houses, while smaller streets and dwellings extend beyond. Large and small Queen Anne, foursquare, Colonial Revival, and bungalow houses were built for a mix of professionals and tradespeople, who were required to spend $2,500 on Boylan Ave. houses, $2,000 on other streets. Like other Raleigh suburbs, the neighborhood took the name of the former owner of the antebellum plantation it occupied: William Montfort Boylan, whose father, William, had acquired Joel Lane's *Wakefield plantation. The younger Boylan's eclectic, Italianate brick mansion, **Montfort Hall** (1858; William Percival, architect; Thomas Briggs & James Dodd, builders; 308 S. Boylan Ave.), symmetrical with center pavilion, arched openings, and cupola (#The Barracks, Tarboro), is the only survivor of Raleigh's antebellum suburban villas. A prime view of downtown Raleigh may be had from the Boylan Ave. railroad bridge.

WK 45 *Montfort Hall*

wk 46 *Wakefield (Joel Lane House)*

WK 46 Wakefield (Joel Lane House)

Ca. 1770, 1790s; 728 W. Hargett St.; moved 1913, restored 1970s; open limited hours

The 1½-story frame dwelling exemplifies the scale of all but the grandest 18th-c. plantation houses. In 1927 it was saved by the Colonial Dames because it was the home of Joel Lane, the planter and political figure who in 1792 sold 1,000 acres to the state for the new capital. After Wake Co. was formed in 1771, commissioners met at Lane's house until a courthouse was built nearby. In the early 19th c. Wakefield was the home of William Boylan, a large landowner and publisher of the Raleigh *Minerva* newspaper. Originally gable roofed, the house attained its gambrel-roofed form with shed dormers in the 1790s. The interior is finished in simple late Georgian style with exposed, beaded ceiling joists. A center passage divides the two front rooms, and a smaller one separates two rear shed rooms. The porch and T-stack brick chimneys date from a 1970s restoration. Interpreted as a freestanding kitchen is a 1-room, heavy timber frame structure (late 18th c.) with unfinished interior; it was built as an Allen family farmhouse north of Raleigh.

WK 47 Elmwood

Ca. 1813; 16 N. Boylan Ave.; private

The handsome side-hall plan frame house, which stood west of town with an unimpeded view of Hillsborough St., was built for John Louis Taylor, chief justice of the state's first supreme court, and his wife Jane Gaston of New Bern. In 1829 Taylor left Elmwood to his wife's brother, Supreme

Court justice William Gaston, who in turn rented it to Chief Justice Thomas Ruffin. It was later home to Romulus Saunders (congressman and minister to Spain) and Samuel A'Court Ashe (newspaper editor and historian), who added the porch and wings.

WK 48 Tucker Carriage House

Ca. 1895; 114 St. Mary's St.

The grand, shingled carriage house–stables was part of the suburban estate of merchant R. S. Tucker, who in the 1850s built an eclectic Italianate villa designed by William Percival. The residence was razed in the mid-20th c., but the later 19th-c. carriage house was renovated in 1988–89 as a community arts center.

WK 49 St. Mary's School

1830s–20th c.; NW corner Hillsborough and St. Mary's Sts.

The shaded campus, once beyond the city, retains a full sequence of architecture from its antebellum founding onward. It began as the Episcopal School for Boys (est. 1832), which erected **East Rock** and **West Rock** (1834, 1835), both 2-story, foursquare structures of stone from the Capitol quarry, and present **Smedes Hall** (1835–37, William Drummond, Thomas Waitt, builders; 1909, Charles Hartge, architect), a 3-story Greek Revival brick edifice on a stone basement. The brick structure was begun by Drummond, a Washington, D.C., builder (#St. John's Episcopal Church, Fayetteville) and briefly superintendent of construction at the *State Capitol (1833–34), and was completed by Waitt, a Massachusetts builder (*Old East, Chapel Hill). The two also built a mansion across Hillsborough St. for banker, planter, and school supporter Duncan Cameron (*Fairntosh). The school closed in 1839, was bought by Cameron, and reopened in 1842 as St. Mary's, an Episcopal school for young women.

St. Mary's Chapel (1855–57; Richard Upjohn [New York], architect) is a prime example of Upjohn's Carpenter Gothic style, with sharp-pitched gable roof, peaked hood at the entrance, slender windows, and

wk 49 *St. Mary's Chapel*

board-and-batten walls intensifying its picturesque verticality. Principal Aldert Smedes chose a design from *Upjohn's Rural Architecture* and requested alterations from the architect (*Christ Church), who produced a custom design and obtained stained glass and other fittings from New York. Harmonizing transepts were added in 1905. The **Language Arts Building** (1887) blends late Gothic Revival and Stick style motifs akin to the *Executive Mansion, while the **Bishop's House** (1904; Charles W. Barrett, architect) is an eclectic brick rendition of the architect's Colonial Revival mode. Charles Hartge, an architect of German background, designed **Eliza Pittman Auditorium** (1906–7) in orange brick with bold free classical details typical of the early Colo-

nial Revival; in 1909 he gave Smedes Hall flanking wings, a parapet, and a towering Colonial Revival portico.

WK 50 Cameron Park

West of *Boylan Heights and adjoining the Hillsborough St. trolley route, the sylvan garden suburb begun in 1910 was platted by engineers Riddick & Mann for Greensboro's N.C. Trust Co. and Southern Real Estate Co.; Raleigh's Parker-Hunter Realty Co. created the marketing scheme aimed "especially to those who wish to buy homes where the best physical and social conditions will be maintained." They used the cachet of the Cameron name as well as part of the estate. To attract upper middle-class buyers, they laid out curving streets and three parks along the ravines, planted trees, built stone retaining walls, and set the minimum house cost at $3,000. As in *Boylan Heights and Glenwood, residences were still closely placed on relatively small lots, creating a neighborly density. A few late Queen Anne–Colonial Revival style houses were built in the first blocks near Hillsborough St., but the predominant architecture from the 1910s and 1920s consists of foursquares, restrained Colonial Revival houses, Dutch Colonial, and bungalows from large to small. Mostly of frame with a few brick houses, they are primarily single-family dwellings, but a few are discreetly arranged as duplexes.

wk 50 *Cameron Park*

WK 51 *Broughton High School*

WK 51 Broughton High School

1927–29; William H. Deitrick, architect;
723 S. Mary's St.

In contrast to the typical Colonial and Tudor Revival vocabulary of 1920s public school architecture, for Raleigh's flagship high school architect Deitrick combined an up-to-date educational program and fireproof construction with campaniles, carved stone, grilled ironwork, and warm-hued local stone in "Lombard Gothic Revival" style. The young architect, establishing his own firm after working with James Salter, won a design competition for the school, which received an NCAIA honor award in 1930 and secured his reputation. Initially called the Raleigh High School, the facility reinforced the northwesterly flow of suburban growth.

WK 52 Cameron Village

1947–50s; Leif Valand, architect;
Clark Ave. at Oberlin Rd.

The South's first regional, planned shopping center and one of the first in the nation, Cameron Village was the brainchild of developer J. W. "Willie" York. In contrast to the small neighborhood shopping centers that complemented downtowns, the new regional type would compete with downtown. York, a builder's son who began constructing veterans' homes after the war, had admired the 158-acre remainder of the Cameron plantation. In 1946 he attended national meetings of the Home Builders Association and the Urban Land Institute, where he met Jesse Clyde Nichols, creator of the famed Country Club Plaza (1920s) suburban shopping center in Kansas City (York named Nichols Dr. in his honor). Thus inspired, in 1947 York and R. A. Bryan optioned the land and launched a combination of a shop-

ping and service center with a multiunit and single-family residential development. York employed Seward Mott, director of the Urban Land Institute, to plan the project and Leif Valand, an architect trained at Pratt Institute, to design the 1-, 2-, and 3-story buildings in a locally congenial blend of modernist and Colonial Revival motifs, red brick and tan stone.

Starting with a "608" housing loan from the Federal Housing Administration, in 1948 York built the simple Colonial Revival style garden apartments with courtyards along "superblock" lines. After securing anchor tenants, in 1949 he started the shopping center blocks in a modernist mode in brick and stone, with outward-facing shops and front parking. In 1950–52 he began the single-family neighborhood, with curving sidewalk-free streets flanked by ranch-style residences in brick, frame, and Valand's favored Tennessee Crab Orchard stone and natural redwood. Cameron Village gained several national awards for planning and neighborhood development. Despite changes, the ensemble is a unique exemplar of American planning ideas of the immediate postwar era.

WK 53 Oberlin

Est. 1860s; Oberlin Rd.,
NW of Cameron Village

Now surrounded by the city, Oberlin is the most intact of N.C. freedpeople's villages established by black citizens on the outskirts of cities. In 1866 black families began to purchase land and build homes about 2 miles west of Raleigh on lots made available by white landowner Lewis Peck and others. First called "Peck's Place," by 1872 the "suburban village" was named Oberlin for the Ohio college attended by many black students. In the 1870s it had a graded school, two churches, and numerous 1- and 2-story houses. Its 750 residents included teachers, doctors, lawyers, brickmasons, seamstresses, and merchants. For a time Rev. M. L. Latta ran the Latta University, with a campus of seven buildings, of which one remains on Parker St. Despite losses since World War II, the village identity persists. The neighborhood retains a range of late 19th- and early 20th-c. houses: 1- and 2-story cross-gabled and L-shaped dwellings, bungalows, and a few Queen Anne style houses. Prominent are the 2-story, multigabled **Graves-Field House** (1880s; 802 Oberlin Rd.); the **Hall House** (ca. 1880s; 814 Oberlin Rd.), an ornate Queen Anne cottage built for the first pastor of the Oberlin Baptist Church; and the **Turner House** (ca. 1900; 1002 Oberlin Rd.), with 2-story portico. **Wilson Temple United Methodist Church** (1910; 1021 Oberlin Rd.), a brick church in Gothic Revival style with a corner entrance tower, was named for Wilson Morgan, African American brickmason and legislator (1870–72), who donated the land. The 2-story, frame **Morgan House** (ca. 1900; 1015 Oberlin Rd.) was built for his son James.

WK 53 *Turner House*

WK 54 Raleigh Little Theatre, Amphitheater, and Rose Garden
1938–40; William H. Deitrick, Thad Hurd, architects; R. J. Pearse, landscape architect; 1988–89, Brian Shawcroft, architect; Pogue St. at Stafford Ave.

With its two clean, rectangular forms exemplifying tenets of the International style, the white-painted brick structure was one of the city's first modernist buildings. Located on the old state fairgrounds (1873–1925), the complex was developed with WPA assistance for a group organized in 1936 with aid from the Federal Theatre Project. Initial designs were donated by Raleigh architect Deitrick, and final plans were made by Thad Hurd of the building committee. In the late 20th c. a series of additions continued the

simple blocky forms in order to serve the needs of the still-active community theater group.

WK 55 Pullen Park Carousel
Early 20th c.; Gustav A. Dentzel Co. (Salvatore Cernigliaro); restored 1978–82; Pullen Rd. at Western Blvd.

The whirling menagerie of more than 50 animals from the celebrated carousel builder Dentzel of Philadelphia displays distinctive forms of chief carver Cernigliaro, who in 1903–9 introduced such characters as the cat with fish, the pig, and the bunny. In 1921 the carousel was moved from Bloomsbury Park (by Carolina Power and Light Co. at the end of the Glenwood Ave. streetcar line) to the civic park named for donor R. S. Pullen, benefactor of North Carolina State University (NCSU).

WK 56 North Carolina State University
Est. 1887; S side Hillsborough St. W of Pullen Rd.

The N.C. College of Agricultural and Mechanical Arts was authorized by the General Assembly in 1887 after a long campaign by Leonidas Polk and other progressive agricultural and industrial leaders. Land was donated by R. S. Pullen. As a land-grant college, the school emphasized agriculture, textile manufacturing, and engineering; its practical character found expression in the sturdy brick architecture of its earliest buildings (1889–1920), which display freely handled Romanesque and classical motifs and bold contrasts of red and cream brick. The original main building, the 3-story **Holladay Hall** (1889; Charles Carson [Baltimore], architect), in Romanesque Revival style with great brick arches and rough-cut stone trim, was built of red "penitentiary brick" manufactured by inmates at nearby Central Prison (*Executive Mansion). **Tompkins Hall** (1901; D. A. Tompkins; burned; rebuilt 1914) was designed by the Charlotte textile mill architect and promoter in a typical mill format for the textile department. Round arches in brick also define the small, towered **Primrose Hall** (1896), the original horticulture

WK 56 *Holladay Hall*

building. In the early 20th c., local architects used brickwork in a robust free classical style, as seen in **Watauga** (1902–3; Barrett & Thompson, architects); **Winston** (1910; Frank Simpson, architect); and **Leazar** (1912; H. P. S. Keller, architect). The **1911 Building** (1909, 1911; H. P. S. Keller, architect), the most distinctive, in red brick with bold white keystones, was named in honor of the class of 1911, which ended hazing of freshmen. Other buildings combine tan brick and stone trim.

A more conventional Neoclassicism appeared in the 1920s work, mostly by New York architect Hobart Upjohn. His **Brooks Hall** (1927; Hobart Upjohn, architect; 1956, 1966, George Matsumoto and F. Carter Williams, additions), built as the library and adapted as the School of Design, is a fine Georgian Revival composition in red brick with overtones of the University of Virginia, featuring a central dome and a stone portico in a Tower of the Winds order. Modernist wings were planned by SOD architects. The **Kamphoefner Building** (1978; Harry Wolf [Charlotte], architect) across the rear courtyard was designed in a direct, red brick modernist form by the leading Charlotte architect. Upjohn continued the red brick Georgian Revival vocabulary in several 1920s dormitories and the **Chancellor's Residence** (1930).

The campus icon is **Memorial Tower** (1921–26, 1935–37; William H. Deacy, W. W. Leland Studios [New York], architect), a belltower of Mount Airy granite dedicated to college alumni and those who served in "the world war." Deacy, of a firm specializing in monuments (*Bennett Place, Durham Co.) described the design as "semi-Romanesque . . . style with Gothic treat-

ment of the vertical lines." Construction was interrupted for lack of donations in 1926, then completed with Federal relief funds. Campus architecture of the later 20th c. explored various trends in modernist design, with the most unusual being the innovative but inconvenient cylindrical **Harrelson Hall** (1961; Edward W. Waugh, Holloway & Reeves, architects).

WK 57 G. Milton Small Office
1966; G. Milton Small & Assoc., architect; 105 Brooks Ave.

Designed by Small for his own firm, the serene little modernist building employs Miesian principles on a tight urban site. Steel columns raise the curtain-walled office story above an open entry and parking area, from which an open stair ascends into the bright offices in the treetops. A similar aesthetic informs Small's suburban residence (1951, 1961; 310 Lake Boone Trail).

WK 58 Meredith College
3800 Hillsborough St.

Opened in 1899 as the Baptist Female Seminary in a great Queen Anne style edifice (A. G. Bauer, architect) on N. Blount St., the women's college was named for Baptist leader Thomas Meredith in 1909 and moved to its spacious campus west of town in 1926. Architects Wilson & Berryman of Columbia, S.C., planned a complete ensemble of red brick Georgian buildings, centered on the **Administration Building** with portico and dome. Subsequent buildings adapted the theme to modernist trends as seen in **Jones Hall** (1938, 1941; William H. Deitrick, architect) and others.

WK 59 Method

The once "suburban" village was begun in 1872 by freedmen Jesse Mason and Isaac O'Kelly near the NCRR 3 miles west of Raleigh. It gained renown from the Berry O'Kelly Training School (est. 1914), which in 1923 became the first accredited 4-year rural high school for African Americans in the state and one of the first in the nation. It closed in 1966 and the ca. 1920 main building is gone, but the simple red brick **Agriculture Building** (1926; 514 Method Rd.) survives. **St. James A.M.E. Church** (1923; 520 Method Rd.) features a corner tower and patterned brickwork; in the churchyard is the grave of school founder Berry O'Kelly.

WK 60 State Fairgrounds Exhibition Buildings

1928; Atwood & Weeks; Hillsborough St. at Blue Ridge Rd.

The colorful and festive concrete structure in Spanish Mission style was built for exhibits when the state agriculture department developed this site as the third state fairgrounds. A red tile roof, towers, twisted columns, and terra-cotta decoration, including bull's head and crop motifs, enliven the long front.

WK 61 J. S. Dorton Arena

1950–52; Matthew Nowicki, William H. Deitrick, architects; Fred Severud (Severud, Elstad & Krueger), engineer; William Muirhead Construction Co. (Durham), contractors; Hillsborough St. National Civil Engineering Landmark

An architectural and engineering accomplishment of international stature, the revolutionary design of Dorton Arena is the first significant application of a tensile suspension or steel-cable supported roof in architecture. It resulted from an extraordinary meeting of progressive minds. Determined to create for the Department of Agriculture a state fair with "the most modern plant in the world," fair manager J. S. Dorton approached the dean of the new SOD. Kamphoefner recommended Nowicki (pronounced Novitsky), the brilliant young Polish architect who had come to New York to assist in planning the United Nations complex and in 1948 became acting head of the Department of Architecture at the SOD. The commission went to Deitrick's firm, with Nowicki consulting architect. George Matsumoto later recalled that the architects had a few ideas before meeting with Dorton, but after comprehending the scope of his vision, they moved quickly toward more daring concepts. "The clients wanted a fair facility to advertise North Carolina as a progressive state and they wanted no copy of anything done before," said Deitrick in a SOD student publication. In 1950 Nowicki produced preliminary drawings for the arena as well as

WK 61 *Dorton Arena (interior)*

sketches for a larger state fair complex. That summer, returning from planning the new Punjab capital at Chandigarh, India, he was killed in a plane crash in Egypt. Deitrick, with the engineering firm Severud, Elstad & Krueger consulting, carried out Nowicki's design for a parabolic suspension structure providing a vast, naturally lighted expanse of uninterrupted space. Funded by a $1.5 million state appropriation, the arena was erected by Muirhead Construction Co. of Durham (who concurrently rebuilt #Tryon Palace in New Bern).

The Livestock Judging Pavilion opened to tremendous acclaim. In 1952 the "eyes of the early fairgoers popped right out," and at the formal dedication in 1953, the governor applauded the vision and foresight of the builders and the people of the state, while the *News & Observer* called it "a great architectural wonder that seems to lasso the sky." National recognitions included the First Honor Award of the American Institute of Architects (1953), the Gold Medal in Engineering of the Architectural League of New York, and others. Worldwide notice came with the exhibition of its model in the Milan International Exposition of Modern Decorative and Industrial Arts and Modern Architecture of 1957 and its widespread publication in Germany as the "Raleigh Arena." Renamed in 1961 to honor Dorton, the arena is used for circuses, horse shows, concerts, sports events, and the state fair. New glass was installed and a coating applied to the concrete in 1976–79. The great swooping concrete frame, vast saddle-shaped roof, and breathtaking interior space make the arena the state's greatest mid-20th-c. architectural landmark. (See Introduction, Fig. 72.)

WK 62 Glenwood Ave. Suburbs

Begun in 1907 by developer James Pou to accommodate the growing urban middle and working class, the pioneering northwest suburb of **Glenwood** (Glenwood Ave. betw. Peace St. and Wade Ave.) flanks Glenwood Ave. along a median that held the trolley line. The tracks led to Bloomsbury Park, created by Carolina Power & Light, which owned the trolley line. Essentially com-

pleted by 1925, the neighborhood contains a grid of streets lined by late Queen Anne houses of classical detail, foursquare houses, and many bungalows, most of frame. The new suburb overlapped the older **Brooklyn**, which was established by 1880 as a racially mixed suburb of railroad workers and tradespeople, of which a portion survives northwest of Peace and Glenwood. In the 1910s and 1920s, development continued along Glenwood past present-day Wade Ave. in a seamless series of neighborhoods concentrated around the intersection known as Five Points, including **Roanoke Park**, **Bloomsbury**, and others.

WK 63 Hayes Barton

Named for Sir Walter Raleigh's home, Hayes Barton was a solidly upper middle-class neighborhood from its inception in 1917. It lay west of the Glenwood Ave. streetcar line, from which a tile-roofed, stone **Passenger Shelter** still stands on Glenwood at Harvey St. Developed by James Pou and E. O. Edgerton, it follows the curvilinear layout of noted planner Earle S. Draper (*Myers Park), with larger lots than its predecessors. Containing Raleigh's best collection of 1920s and 1930s period revival architecture, the suburb includes many carefully detailed Georgian Revival houses as well as Dutch Colonial, Tudor Revival, and English cottage forms, mostly in brick or stone. Refraining from the grandeur of the early 20th-c. elite suburbs in the state's industrial cities, Raleigh's premier neighborhood was distinguished by a harmony of scale and quality of detail that complemented its compact yet spacious plan. The **Josephus Daniels**

WK 63 *Hayes Barton: Carr St.*

House (1923; Howard Satterfield, architect-builder; Caswell St.; National Historic Landmark) is one of the earliest and largest houses, a columned stone residence built for Daniels, secretary of the navy under Woodrow Wilson and publisher of the *News & Observer*. The 1500 block of Carr St. has a cluster of beautifully proportioned and detailed Georgian Revival houses in red brick, the work of William Deitrick and James Davidson. Nearby at 910 Harvey is a towered, fairy-tale French "castle" (1948) of stone and slate, said to have been modeled on an example in *House Beautiful*. The **Alfred Williams House** (1928; 1006 Harvey St.), on a through-block lot, is a striking rendition of Mount Vernon. The few notable exceptions to the revival styles include the symmetrical, modernist **Rothstein House** (1960; G. Milton Small, architect; 912 Williamson Dr.). Unlike its predecessors, Hayes Barton never experienced the slightest diminution of status, but from the 1990s its character has been threatened by giant additions and teardowns for bigger houses.

Adjoining on the northwest, **Country Club Homes** (1938–39, 1949–50; E side Oberlin Rd. N of Fairview Rd.), developed by E. N. Richards, exemplifies the "superblock" residential development of the 1930s and 1940s, with shaded courtyards among multiunit, 1-story brick buildings containing 198 family apartments. The former **Sherwood-Bates Elementary School** (1950; G. Milton Small/William H. Deitrick; 1816 Oberlin Rd.) was one of the first elementary schools in the state to embody new school ideas promoted by the SOD, including large expanses of glass, a flexible floor plan, absence of historicist detailing, and integration into the sloping site.

WK 64 William H. Deitrick House

1936; William H. Deitrick, architect; 2501 Glenwood Ave.

Following Hayes Barton, suburbs continued northwest along Glenwood Ave. in the 1930s and thereafter, with the Colonial Revival the style of choice. A fine and prominent example from the depression years is architect Deitrick's own residence, a beautifully detailed free version of the Georgian Revival in Flemish-bond brick, with Palladian-inspired facade and porch of slim Ionic columns.

WK 65 Tatton Hall

1934–36; William Lawrence Bottomley, architect; John Danielson, contractor; Charles Gillette, landscape design; 1625 Oberlin Rd.; private

In the depths of the Great Depression, Norman and Mishew Rogers Edgerton of Raleigh commissioned a house considered by many the finest Georgian Revival residence in the state. At the recommendation of their landscape designer, Gillette, they contacted the Beaux Arts–trained New York architect Bottomley, known for his Georgian Revival work in Virginia and elsewhere. Displaying his creativity as a revivalist designer, Bottomley planned a symmetrical, Palladian composition with hipped roof, pedimented central pavilion, and extended wings creating a formal facade, but he gave the interior a flowing plan and the garden facade a gently curving arrangement. Economic conditions made the best craftsmanship and materials readily available, including woodwork by Martin Millwork of Raleigh and oversize brick from Virginia.

WK 65 *Tatton Hall*

WK 66 Matsumoto House and Studio

1952–54; George Matsumoto, architect; Frank Walser, builder; 821 Runnymede Rd.

The meticulously proportioned structure—featured on the cover of *Architectural Record Houses*—was designed by an original faculty member of the SOD. Matsumoto, a Californian, explored traditional modular design in Japan and China, studied and worked

WK 66 *Matsumoto House*

with Eliel Saarinen in Michigan, and taught at Oklahoma before coming to Raleigh with Kamphoefner. He specialized in small, geometrically precise houses of economical construction, often including modular, prefabricated elements. He modeled his ideas in his symmetrical, rectangular 1-story house, using cement panels with wooden posts and trim; a private facade addresses the street, while broad windows and a ground story studio overlook the streamside slope.

WK 67 Kamphoefner House and Fadum House
1949–50; Henry Kamphoefner with George Matsumoto, architect; 3060 Granville Dr.; addition, 2002, Robert P. Burns, architect. 1950, James Fitzgibbon, architect; Frank Walser, builder; 3056 Granville Dr.

The immediate impact of the modernist SOD appears in two small but boldly new houses. Considered the first modernist house in Raleigh, founding dean Kamphoefner's 1-story house of brick and wood showed his admiration of Frank Lloyd Wright, for it embodies Wright's Usonian house ideals in a compact, economical, and efficiently planned dwelling of natural materials. With its carport approached by a driveway from a sidewalkless street, and its relatively private street front and openness in back to a golf course, the house showed the suburban reorientation of the era. The Fadum House next door, likewise of Usonian scale and natural wood and glass under a single-slope shed roof, was designed by Fitzgibbon, who came to the SOD from Oklahoma with Kamphoefner. It was featured as "House of the Year" in *Architectural Record* in 1952.

Builder Walser gained renown for the excellent construction of this and subsequent modernist designs.

WK 68 Paschal House
1951; James Fitzgibbon, architect; 3334 Alamance Dr.

Designed for a family with a strong interest in the arts and modern architecture, Fitzgibbon's long, low residence of rough sandstone and natural wood has a warm, naturalistic grace. Adapting Wrightian themes to a suburban southern setting, deep eaves and a front courtyard shelter the flowing plan, while broad expanses of glass open to the hillside in back.

WK 69 St. Giles Presbyterian Church
1968, 1974, 1983; Harwell Hamilton Harris (Raleigh), architect; 5101 Oak Park Rd.

Harris, distinguished exponent of California regionalism in the 1940s and 1950s, taught and practiced in Texas before coming to the SOD in 1962 as an influential teacher and an early voice for contextualism. (His small studio and house of 1961 and 1967 are at 122 Cox Ave. near NCSU.) Harris considered St. Giles his best project in the state. As he intended for the young congregation, the complex has been created one building at a time, linked by covered walkways down the gentle slope to the sanctuary (1983). All have low gable roofs, simple wooden details, and brown shingled walls evocative of summer camps, and the sanctuary features large circular windows framing treetops and sky. Harris saw St. Giles as "a family of buildings for a family of persons." "I like the idea of the church's center as an open space rather than a building," he wrote, with the pines' "discarded needles for a carpet and the sky for a ceiling."

WK 70 WPTF Transmitter Building
1940; William H. Deitrick, architect; N side NC 54 (Chatham/Hillsborough St.), E of Maynard Rd.

The Moderne building with curved corners, bands of windows, and flat roof has a streamlined form evoking the speed and modernity of radio broadcasting—and resembling many radio sets of the day. One of the state's oldest transmitter buildings, it was built for N.C.'s second commercial radio station, founded as WFBQ in 1924 and renamed WPTF (We Protect the Family) by the Durham Life Insurance Co., which acquired it in 1927 (*Insurance Building).

WK 71 Cary

The NCRR depot village, which had but 1,400 people in 1950, mushroomed by the early 21st c. into a Research Triangle city of 100,000. In the late 1860s lumberman Allison F. Page (*Aberdeen) subdivided lots on 300 acres around his lumber mill at the crossing of the NCRR and the Chatham Railroad. He soon erected the **Page-Walker Hotel** (ca. 1868; 119 Ambassador St.), a brick railroad hotel with mansard roof and deep porch overlooking the tracks. When the town was chartered in 1871, temperance advocate Page named it for Ohio prohibitionist Samuel Fenton Cary. (Page's son Walter Hines Page later attained distinction as a journalist and diplomat.) The town grew with the Chatham Railroad and early 20th-c. highways—the Central Highway (US 64) and the future US 1. Recalling a long local tradition of education, the grandly sited former **Cary High School** (1939; S. Academy St.) is a symmetrical Georgian Revival edifice in red brick with central portico; it was built with WPA assistance, successor to a 1907 high school that was one of the first built with state funds. Varied Victorian residences stand on Chatham and Academy

Sts., including the board-and-batten Gothic Cottage style **Ivey-Ellington House** (ca. 1870s; W. Chatham St.), one of many associations of the style with railroads.

WK 72 Nancy Jones House

1803; 837 Durham Rd. (S side NC 54, opp. SR 1785); Cary vic.

The tall frame house displays a regional form: the 2-story front section has a hall-parlor plan, and rear shed rooms flank a porch from which the stair ascends. It was the site of an 1838 meeting at which, the story goes, "the governor of North Carolina said to the governor of South Carolina, 'It's been a damn long time between drinks'"—a cryptic comment that became part of state lore.

WK 73 Carpenter

The once rural crossroad settled in 1865 retains at its center its archetypal frame country stores: **Carpenter's Farm Supply** (1880–90s, 1916), and **Williams's Store** (ca. 1900).

WK 74 Apex

The railroad town was named after its location at the highest point on the survey of the Raleigh & Augusta line. After 1900, as tobacco sales burgeoned, brick buildings replaced frame warehouses, especially along **Salem St.**, which retains a solid row of early 20th-c. commercial buildings. The prime landmark is the **Apex Union Depot** (1914; corner of Center and Salem Sts.), a handsome small-town brick depot of the early 20th c.; it has been restored for community use on its trackside location. A venerable civic building form appears in **Apex Town**

WK 71 *Page-Walker Hotel*

WK 74 *Apex Union Depot*

Hall (1912; N. Salem St.) a classically detailed brick structure that originally had an open market at street level and a public auditorium above.

WK 75 Leslie-Alford-Mims House

1840s–1940s; Church St., Holly Springs

The eccentric, rambling frame house began with a 2-story Greek Revival house built in the 1840s by Scots tailor Archibald Leslie; then it gained a top floor and widow's walk and various wings ca. 1870 for Confederate veteran and merchant G. B. Alford and ca. 1940.

WK 76 Fuquay-Varina

The small railroad town began as Fuquay Springs, developed after 1860 when farmer Stephen Fuquay sold his mineral springs to investors. Trains brought visitors to enjoy the springs. The nearby community of Varina also grew by the tracks, and the two were joined in 1963. In old Fuquay the **Fuquay Mineral Spring** (S. Main St.) still flows in a small park, and a solid Main St. commercial district includes the handsome **Bank of Fuquay** (ca. 1909; S. Main St.) of brick with bracketed cornice and angled corner. There are numerous frame houses in Craftsman, foursquare, and Colonial Revival styles, some of which served as hotels or boardinghouses for visitors to the springs. **Varina Commercial District** (Broad St.) has 2-story Italianate buildings facing the **Varina Union Station** (1910; Broad St.), a frame structure for freight and passengers on the Durham & Southern and Norfolk Southern lines.

WK 77 Falls of the Neuse Mill

1854–55; E side SR 2000 at Neuse River, Falls

Located at the principal falls of the river, the massive antebellum paper mill of granite blocks is a rare N.C. example of early stone industrial architecture. By 1860 it was producing over 500,000 lbs. of paper a year, chiefly for newspapers. In the 1880s it was converted to a textile mill. The old dam site is covered by the Falls Lake dam, but the 3-story mill, measuring 54 by 200 feet, has been preserved. Its coursed ashlar walls, generous windows, shallow gable roof, and heavy timbers and floors have been maintained in a conversion to condominiums.

WK 78 Sandy Plain

The sandy soil of northwestern Wake Co. supported only sparse agriculture until bright-leaf tobacco cultivators learned that it was ideal for their crop if sufficiently fertilized. In the late 19th c. several farmers moved there to escape the tobacco wilt in their native Granville Co. Typically employing 2 to 4 tenant families on farms of a few hundred acres, they cultivated 10 to 30 acres of tobacco, plus other crops. The still-rural settlement includes late 19th- to early 20th-c. farm complexes with substantial frame houses and numerous log and frame tobacco barns and other outbuildings. The **O'Brient House** (ca. 1900; E side NC 50, 0.5 mi. s of SR 1901) is an archetypal 3-bay I-house with ornamented 1-story porch and front roof gable with millwork ornament. The **Cannady-Brogden Farm** (ca. 1904; Edgar Gooch, carpenter; s side SR 1901, 0.3 mi. E of NC 50) presents an ensemble of frame barns, sheds, corncrib, smokehouse, grape arbor, and tobacco barns and packhouses of log and frame. The 2-story house, in symmetrical I-house form with decorated 1-story porch and front and side gables, is credited to local farmer-carpenter Gooch.

WK 79 Wakefields

1770s–1830s; W side SR 1929, opp. SR 1931, W side US 1, Wake Forest; private, visible from road

The classic plantation house, with gable roof, end chimneys, and symmetrical 5-bay facade, has a 2-tier entrance portico with slim Doric columns in a form akin to the *Mordecai House. Greek Revival details come from Asher Benjamin's *Practical House Carpenter* (1830) (*South Brick House, Wake Forest). The site reveals a long sequence of building: the front section is credited to Mourning Person and John Worsham Harris, ca. 1831; the rear ell comprises a 1½-story

WK 79 *Wakefields*

dwelling and kitchen from the 1786–1823 ownership of political leader Ransom Sutherland; and a separate small, gable-roofed frame dwelling, unfinished within, may predate 1779.

WK 80 Wake Forest

The pleasant town grew up around **Wake Forest College**, est. 1834 by the Baptist State Convention. Dr. Calvin Jones had a plantation and post office here in the 1820s and operated an academy in his residence before the Baptists opened the Wake Forest Institute in his house and outbuildings. By 1837 John Berry of Hillsborough had completed the College Building, a 4-story brick structure of simplified Palladian format with pedimented center pavilion akin to *South Building at UNC. Renamed Wake Forest College in 1838, the school developed into a distinguished liberal arts college. It moved to Winston-Salem in 1956 (*Wake Forest University). The campus is now used by the Southeastern Baptist Theological Seminary. The original building established the campus style of red brick with classical detailing. **Lea Laboratory** (1887; John Appleton Wilson [Baltimore], architect) is an unusually early essay in the Colonial Revival in harmonizing Palladian form: the 2-story pedimented center block is flanked by hyphens and 1-story end pavilions, rendered with typical late 19th-c. decorative brickwork. After the College Building burned, alumnus Deitrick evoked its design in its successor, **Stealey Hall** (1933–34, 1935; William H. Deitrick, architect), a 3-story red brick building with pedimented center pavilion

and Georgian Revival details, and the mode continued in other buildings. At the south edge of campus, **Wake Forest Baptist Church** (1913; J. M. McMichael [Charlotte]) has a cruciform plan with central dome and pedimented wings. Nearby, **South Brick House** (1837; John Berry [Hillsborough], builder; SE corner S. Main and E. South Ave.) is the only survivor of Berry's antebellum building campaign, one of two original faculty dwellings. The elegant brick house typifies Berry's work in its fine Flemish-bond brickwork, prompt use of Greek Revival motifs from Benjamin's *Practical House Carpenter* (1830), and Palladian window in the pedimented gable end.

WK 80 *South Brick House*

North Main St. is a fine, shaded residential district with many faculty houses. The 2-story frame **Calvin Jones House** (ca. 1820; 400 block N. Main St.), moved and reworked, is the oldest house and original home of the college. Like others in the area it has a hall-parlor plan plus rear shed rooms. Other houses range from the mid-19th-c. **Brewer House** (229 N. Main), a raised Greek Revival cottage that began as a log dwelling, to several late 19th-c. Italianate and Queen Anne houses to early 20th-c. bungalows and Colonial Revival dwellings. The **W. C. Powell House** (Charles Barrett, architect; 564 N. Main St.) is a symmetrical Colonial Revival residence with high hip roof and wraparound porch, published in the architect's *Colonial Southern Homes*; it was built for a founder of the nearby **Glen Royall Cotton Mill and Village**. The 3-story red brick Mill (1900; C. R. Makepeace, architect; John D. Briggs [Raleigh], builder) is of simplified Italianate style with large segmental-arched windows; the mill housing consists mainly of 1-story duplexes, some with high pyramidal roofs and center chimneys, others with tri-gabled rooflines.

WK 81 Forestville Baptist Church

1859; Jacob Holt, builder (attrib.); W side US 1-A, 0.2 mi. S of SR 2048, Forestville

Located in the former R&GRR depot village, the pediment-fronted church presents an eclectic mix of Gothic trefoils, Italianate brackets, and pilasters suggestive of Warrenton builder Holt, while the interior contains galleries with simple Greek Revival finish.

WK 82 Ivey House

Ca. 1872; W side US 401, 1.0 mi. S of SR 2042

The T-plan Italianate farmhouse of brick is unusual for an era when most farmers built modest wooden structures. Rufus Ivey was a large farmer and part owner of a cotton gin and press and other enterprises.

WK 83 Alpheus Jones House

Ca. 1847; E side US 401, 0.3 mi. S of SR 2042; private, visible from road

The prominent frame plantation house typifies local versions of the Greek Revival style, with broad plain woodwork, center-passage plan, handsome stone block chimneys, and reconstructed 2-tier entrance portico.

WK 84 Green-Hartsfield House

Ca. 1800; SE side SR 2303 N of NC 96

One of several tall, simply finished local plantation houses, the restored 2-story house has the familiar hall-parlor plan with rear shed rooms and original stone block chimney. It was built for William and Sarah Jeffreys Green; their son married neighbor Martha Hartsfield, whose brother Wesley later bought the farm.

WK 85 Riley Hill

Located along SR 2320, the rural community began around a Baptist church established by freedpeople after the Civil War. **Riley Hill Elementary School** (ca. 1927) is a 1-story H-plan brick school described as one of the first brick schools for black students built with aid from the Julius Rosenwald Fund. Among several substantial farmhouses is the **Marriott House** (1920s), a handsomely detailed Craftsman style bungalow with front dormer and broad front porch, built for Charles and Lucy Marriott, community and church leaders whose 855-acre farm was one of the largest black-owned farms in the county at the time. The **Perry House** (early 19th c.), associated with the Perry family (*Cascine) from Franklin Co., is a 2-story frame house with several outbuildings; in 1914 it was bought by Guyon Perry, whose ancestors had been slaves on the farm, and has continued in his family.

WK 86 Oak View

1850s, 1941; 4028 Carya Dr., off Poole Rd. (SR 1007) just E of I-440

Now a civic park interpreting agricultural history, the farmstead centers on a Greek Revival house built for cotton farmer Benton S. D. Williams and remodeled for the Poole family in Colonial Revival style in 1941. Among many outbuildings are barns, a 2-story frame cotton gin, and an unusual dovetailed plank kitchen, which may have served as a dwelling.

WK 87 Midway Plantation

1848; N side US 64, 8 mi. E of Raleigh, Knightdale vic.

The essence of the Greek Revival plantation house, the symmetrical frame house combines a simple Doric entrance portico with generously broad proportions and openings. The center-passage plan is 2 rooms deep on the ground floor, but since the second story is only 1 room deep, it actually echoes an I-house form with rear shed rooms. Built by Charles Hinton, state treasurer, for son David and his bride Mary Carr, sister of Governor Elias Carr, the house and outbuildings have been carefully maintained by the family. The large Hinton family numbered among the most prominent early planters in eastern Wake Co.

WK 88 Beaver Dam
Ca. 1810; N side SR 2049, opp. SR 2233, Knightdale vic.

Built for William Hinton, who owned over 4,000 acres, the 2-story frame plantation house typifies the county in its well-crafted simplicity and hall-parlor plan served by Flemish-bond brick chimneys.

WK 89 Wakelon School
1908–9; Charles E. Hartge [Raleigh], architect; 1001 N. Arendell St., Zebulon

Early in the public school building campaign of the early 20th c., the large brick school was built with ardent local support between the small towns of Zebulon and Wakefield. Hartge's boldly eclectic, red brick edifice features a dominant central entrance tower and pale brick accentuating arched windows.

WK 89 *Wakelon School*

WK 90 Walnut Hill Cotton Gin
1840s; N side SR 2509, 0.2 mi. W of SR 2506, Shotwell

One of the oldest cotton gins in the state, the stout structure was built for Alonzo T. Mial, planter and commission merchant, and operated by the family until the mid-1930s. Here cotton was stored, ginned, and compressed into bales. Approximately 36 by 56 feet, the gabled frame sits on granite piers, between which mules hitched to sweeps turned a central, vertical shaft. After Mial installed a steam engine in 1875, he enclosed the ground story.

WK 92 *Yates Mill*

WK 91 Garner

Named for a local landowner, the town began in the 1870s as Garner's Station on the NCRR. The **Garner Depot** (ca. 1902; 300 block E. Garner Rd.) is a small frame building restored and maintained by the town. Among several frame houses facing the tracks, the **Dr. Braxton Banks House** (ca. 1900; 101 E. Garner Rd.) is a multigabled 2-story frame house with scalloped shingles and sawnwork decoration. The former **Garner High School** (1923–27; 720 W. Garner Rd.), a 2-story brick building with stepped parapets from the era of school consolidation, is preserved as an arts center and housing for the elderly.

WK 92 Yates Mill
18th–19th c.; W side Lake Wheeler Rd. (SR 1371) at Yates Pond

Standing on a mill site in operation since 1761, the frame mill includes several generations of construction from the early 19th c. onward. Restored after long neglect and hurricane damage, it is the only survivor of several 18th-c. mills around Raleigh.

Franklin County (FN)

See T. H. Pearce, Early Architecture of Franklin County (1988).

Settled in the mid-18th c. by immigrants mainly from Virginia and eastern N.C., in 1779 the county was formed from Bute Co., along with Warren Co., and named for Benjamin Franklin. Watered by the Tar River and its tributaries and underlain with granite and gneiss, the land supported mixed agriculture, including tobacco and cotton cash crops. There were a few large planters, but many with plantations of under 1,000 acres. By 1810 the county was one of the few in the Piedmont with a majority black population, which continued until out-migration after Emancipation. Wealth increased after the 1838 discovery of gold—$3 million worth was mined before California beckoned—and construction of the Raleigh & Gaston Railroad (R&GRR) through the county. The county possesses a notable group of late Georgian houses built for the growing planter class of the ca. 1790–1810 era. These are typically 2-story frame houses with Flemish-bond brick chimneys; most show a local preference for the hall-parlor plan, with enclosed stairs rising in rear chambers. These were joined by (or overbuilt into) large Greek Revival and Italianate residences in the antebellum era. Especially in the 19th c., local quarries yielded fine stone block foundations and chimneys. After the Civil War, cash crops of cotton and tobacco increased, along with tenant farming. Despite development from the Research Triangle area and changes in farming, the county maintains an evocative agricultural landscape, with many late 19th- and early 20th-c. farmhouses, tenant houses, tobacco barns, and other outbuildings of log and frame.

FN 1 Louisburg

The county seat and college town on the Tar River was established in 1779 with a grid plan surveyed by William Christmas (*Warrenton, *Raleigh). The Franklin Academy (opened 1805) and its successor *Louisburg College heightened the town's stature and economy. Bypassed by the R&GRR that created Franklinton, Louisburg gained a rail spur in 1885 and grew from a population of about 800 in 1884 to 1,700 in 1910; with about 3,000 people during most of the 20th c., it has maintained its small-town ambience. On the courthouse square, the brick **Franklin County Courthouse** (1850, 1936–37, 1968) evidences a series of 20th-c. remodelings. In front is a 1923 memorial to the first "Stars and Bars" Confederate flag, designed in 1861 by local resident Orren Randolph Smith. Traditional rows of small brick commercial buildings and law offices along Court and other streets face the courthouse square. South of the river are remains of

small industrial and warehouse buildings on the 1885 rail spur. S. Main and Kenmore Sts. include 1- and 2-story dwellings from the late 19th and early 20th centuries.

The prime concentration of 19th and early 20th-c. architecture lies along N. Main St. The massive brick **Louisburg College Main Building** (1857; Albert Gamaliel Jones; N. Main St.) exemplifies the main buildings erected by private colleges in the 1850s. The broad Doric portico and bold Greek Revival details are typical of Warren Co. builder Jones (*Lake o' the Woods, Warren Co.; #The Columns, Murfreesboro). The college traces back to the **Franklin Academy** (chartered 1787 and 1802), which began as a small, 2-story frame building of ca. 1804 (restored, east campus). Enduring hard times after the Civil War, in 1891 the school was acquired by Washington Duke of Durham, whose son Benjamin donated it to the Methodist church in 1907. On N. Main St. at the campus is the **Confederate Monument**.

FN 1 *Louisburg College Main Building*

FN 1 *Williamson House*

Flanking the college, N. Main has brick churches and frame houses from late Georgian to Greek Revival to Queen Anne to Shingle style, some encompassing 18th- or early 19th-c. elements. North of the college, the restored **Person Place** (ca. 1790, ca. 1830; 603 N. Main St.; open limited hours) exemplifies two eras. The south section is a characteristic early house of 1½ stories with compact, steeped-roofed form, hall-parlor plan, and late Georgian finish—Flemish-bond chimney, molded siding, and molded window sills. The north section typifies the late Federal period pediment-fronted houses of Warren and nearby counties. (See Introduction, Fig. 22.)

Several antebellum houses display typically symmetrical forms, broad proportions, shallow hip roofs, and bold but simple Greek Revival details. The **Malone House** (1854–55; Albert Gamaliel Jones, Thomas Raney, builders; remodeled, 1890; 704 N. Main St.) retains Jones's signature Greek Revival trim and spool-molded corner pilasters; client Ellis Malone's letters document Jones's and Raney's work. The **Fuller House** (1857; Albert Gamaliel Jones [attrib.]; 307 N. Main St.), which shares similar elements, was built for Anna Long and Jones Fuller, merchant and cotton broker; son Edwin Wiley Fuller became a novelist and poet. The **Peyton Brown House** (1854; 310 N. Main St.), built for another merchant, is of similar type. The **Williamson House** (1858; 401 Cedar St.) is a 1-story house with center-passage plan and hip roof that gains presence from its large windows and bold Greek Revival pilasters and porch columns. It was built for Temperance Perry William-

son of *Cascine Plantation, who returned home as a widow from Georgia; among the slaves who came with her was John H. Williamson, a legislator and publisher after Emancipation.

Anchoring prominent corners are two asymmetrical brick churches with corbeled brickwork and corner towers: **Louisburg Methodist Church** (1900; Benjamin D. Price [Atlantic Highlands, N.J.]; N. Main at Noble St.), from a widely published church architect, and **Louisburg Baptist Church** (1901–4; Barrett & Thompson [Raleigh]; 302 N. Main St.), featured in architect Charles Barrett's *Colonial Southern Homes*. **First Baptist Church** (1925; 406 Spring St.), with a corner tower and round arches, veneered in brick, was built for an African American congregation independent by 1871. Barrett also designed **St. Paul's Episcopal Church** (1900; Barrett & Thompson; 301 Church St.), a strikingly picturesque Gothic Revival church with rough stonework, shingles, and an open arcade across the front gable. The many late 19th- to early 20th-c. houses include the **Yarborough**

FN 1 *St. Paul's Episcopal Church*

House (1902; M. Frank Houck, builder; 204 N. Main), dramatically asymmetrical with an open dormer-balcony; the Queen Anne style **Bailey-Yarborough House** (1895; 311 N. Main), built for a banker; and the **Bickett House** (1897; 621 N. Main), with a tower and polygonal bay, home of Thomas and Fannie Bickett before he became governor in 1917. The **Joyner Lustron House** (ca. 1949; 604 N. Main St.), with picture windows and enameled steel panel walls, is one of several in small towns that modeled the practicality and modernity of the prefab houses of the postwar era.

FN 2 Green Hill House

Late 18th c.; SR 1760, W side of NC 39, S edge of Louisburg; private, visible from road

A classic early plantation house, the frame dwelling stands 1½ stories above a raised basement and has massive Flemish-bond brick chimneys, narrow dormers, a porch with tapered posts, and a hall-parlor plan plus shed rooms. Green Hill was a Revolutionary era leader and the legislator instrumental in creating Franklin Co. A strong Methodist who often hosted itinerant minister Francis Asbury, in 1785 he held here the first annual conference of the Methodist Episcopal Church.

FN 2 *Green Hill House*

FN 3 Willie Perry House

Early and mid-19th c.; E side SR 1224, just S of SR 1211, Louisburg vic.; private, visible from road

The 2-story, L-shaped frame house combines a Federal era rear dwelling with a Greek Revival front section with central-passage plan. Perry was a physician from a large planter family (*Cascine).

FN 4 Patty Person Taylor House

Late 18th–early 19th c.; NE side SR 1246 betw. SR 1243 and SR 1244, Louisburg vic.; private, visible from road

Among the local late Georgian plantation houses, the 5-bay frame house is one of the few with a center-passage plan, from which extends an original 1-story rear ell. Flemish-bond chimneys and simple exterior detailing contrast with the elaborately finished interior. Taylor, sister of the Revolutionary and anti-Federalist leader Thomas Person (#Person's Ordinary, Halifax Co.), bought 3,190 acres from him in 1783, married in 1785, and probably built the house soon afterward.

FN 5 Battle-Malone-Bass House

Late 18th–early 19th c.; W side US 401, 0.4 mi. S of SR 1414, Louisburg vic.; private, visible from road

The plantation house, 3 bays wide and 2 stories tall with steep gable roof and double-shouldered Flemish-bond chimneys, shares with others of its era a hall-parlor plan and late Georgian finish, with shed rooms to the rear.

FN 6 Wilson Houses

Early, late 19th c.; W side US 401, 1.6 mi. S of US 401/NC 39 jct.; private, visible from road

The pair of 2-story houses reflect a complex history. The southernmost features unusually rich Federal style trim including arched, pedimented central doorways and a classical entablature. The northernmost, once an ell, was a 1½-story dwelling of simple Federal style that gained a second story with center gable and late 19th-c. millwork.

FN 7 Monreath

Late 18th c.; E side US 401, 0.7 mi. S of US 401/NC 39 jct., Ingleside vic.; private, visible from road

Among the oldest houses in the county, the simply finished frame dwelling began as 1½-

story structure and was expanded to 2 stories beneath a hip roof, plus a rear ell, all in restrained late Georgian style. Scotsman James Maxwell, who purchased it in 1807, named it Monreath. In the mid-19th c. it was the summer home of Joseph Blount Cheshire, rector of #Calvary Episcopal Church in Tarboro and a devotee of A. J. Downing's landscape books who planted and grafted rare trees and shrubs.

FN 8 Locust Grove

Ca. 1800; SE side US 401, 0.3 mi. NE of NC 39, Ingleside; private, visible from road

The tall, austerely finished plantation house, one of the county's fine late Georgian frame houses, is 5 bays wide with a hall-parlor plan plus a stair in the rear ell. The three chimneys are of Flemish-bond brick.

FN 9 Foster House

Mid-19th c.; E side US 401, 1 mi. NE of NC 39, Ingleside; private, visible from road

Blending two currents of mid-19th-c. popular architecture, the house takes the form of the Downingesque cottage mode, with raised central roof gable and reduced second story windows, but it is executed in a bold, simple Greek Revival style with hefty corner pilasters, oversize windows, and square-pillared porch.

FN 9 *Foster House*

FN 10 Traveler's Rest

Early 19th c.; W side US 401 at SR 1401, Kearney; private, visible from road

The little frame structure by the road, said to have served as a stop for travelers on the Warrenton-Louisburg stage road, is a neatly

finished 1-room building with a single-shouldered brick chimney. The adjacent Pernell House burned in 1977.

FN 11 Massenburg Plantation (Woodleaf Plantation)

Early 19th c., 1838; N side NC 561, 0.1 mi. W of SR 1418, Louisburg vic.; private, visible from road

The remarkably complete and carefully restored plantation complex includes an antebellum cotton gin, a smokehouse, an office, barns, and a corncrib, along with a house that represents a well-documented transition in construction. Its front section, originally 1½ stories with hall-parlor plan and Federal finish, may have been standing in 1830 when Nicholas Massenburg bought the land, the center of a plantation he expanded to over 2,200 acres. With a growing family, Nicholas and his wife Lucy Davis, sister of Archibald of *Cypress Hall, soon required a larger house. Massenburg's farm journal recorded daily the 1838 addition of a second story and rear wing (in the new Greek Revival style) by white carpenter William Jones, slave stonemasons Washington and Willis, and other slave and free workers. Granite blocks for the chimney and foundations, like those of the pillars of the cotton gin, were quarried nearby.

FN 11 *Massenburg Plantation*

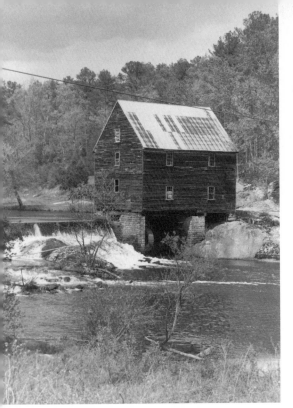

FN 12 Laurel Mill and Col. Jordan Jones House
Mid-19th c.; SR 1432 at SR 1436,
Gupton vic.; private, visible from road

The landmark beside Sandy Creek was the county's last operating gristmill, a plain, 2½-story frame structure combining antebellum and later 19th-c. elements. The turbine-operated gristmill—with an overshot wheel added in a 20th-c. renovation—was operated by Jordan Jones, "the pioneer millman of this section," who also built a sawmill and cotton mill across the creek. Up the hill is an Italianate raised cottage, probably built for Jones in the 1850s.

FN 13 Holly Hill
Early 19th c.; N side SR 1432,
0.9 mi. W of SR 1436, Gupton vic.;
private, visible from road

Of several small early 19th-c. houses in the county, the most intact is this 1½-story frame house with neatly crafted Federal style

details exemplary of the middling planter class. It is described as the home of Jordan Jones of *Laurel Mill before he built a house nearer the mill.

FN 14 Speed Farm
1847 onward; NW side SR 1436, 1.5 mi.
NE of SR 1432; private, visible from road

The prominent farmstead comprises many farm buildings from a long history. Since 1857 it has been the home of the Speed family, who over the years raised grains, tobacco, cotton, and timber. Robert Speed, born at *Rose Hill in Granville Co., bought the 923-acre farm after his marriage to Mary Davis of Franklin Co., and the couple moved into a 1½-story frame dwelling built ca. 1847 for a previous owner. Near the house a milk house, a smokehouse, and a kitchen date from the antebellum era. About 1900 their son Henry Plummer Speed enlarged the house to 2 stories with center front gable and added outbuildings. The farmstead encompasses more than 20 buildings of the 19th and 20th centuries, including an antebellum barn (formerly a cotton gin), sheds, cribs, and a 1-story gable-roofed **Tenant House** (ca. 1935).

FN 15 Dean Farm
1840s; N side NC 56, 0.7 mi. W of SR 1002,
Louisburg vic.; private, visible from road

Standing beside an old road, the farm complex includes a well-detailed Greek Revival house with pedimented ends—an unusual feature in the county—interrupted by fine stone block chimneys. Outbuildings include one of log and one of dovetailed planks.

FN 16 Cypress Hall (Archibald Davis) Plantation
Early 19th c. and later; W side SR 1002,
1.0 mile S of NC 581, Justice vic.; private,
visible from road

With many outbuildings of various eras, the complex exemplifies the "villagelike" plantation character. It was the center of a Davis family plantation of 4,000 acres. The beautifully crafted kitchen is one of only two

FN 14 *Speed Farm*

early stone block structures in the county. The 2-story, 5-bay frame house (ca. 1830, ca. 1900), includes Federal and later eras of building. There is an early 19th-c. frame store or commissary, plus a well house, barns, and tobacco barns. Archibald Davis inherited the land from his father ca. 1821; since the late 19th c. it has been in the Wilson family.

FN 17 Andrews-Moore House
Ca. 1790s, ca. 1830; NE side SR 1002, 0.4 mi. NW of SR 1636, Seven Paths; private, visible from road

The tall frame house displays the best Flemish-bond chimneys in the county—double-shouldered chimneys, beautifully laid with all glazed headers. Standing 2 stories high on a partial basement of English-bond brick, the 3-bay house has a locally unusual 3-room plan with central enclosed stair. The 1½-story rear ell with stone chimney dates from ca. 1830. The house was built for Mary and William Andrews, a planter who owned some 2,400 acres, and descended in the Moore family through their granddaughter. (See Introduction, Fig. 75.)

FN 18 Perry-Timberlake Store
Mid-19th c.; W side US 401, 1.1 mi. S of NC 56, Louisburg vic.; private, visible from road

Standing beside the old road, the gable-fronted frame building with simple Greek

Revival details was part of a plantation complex that included a large frame house and outbuildings.

FN 19 Cascine
Late 18th c.; mid-19th c.; private, no public visibility or access

Unusual continuity of family ownership has preserved the ensemble of two plantation houses, several outbuildings, and some 1,500 acres since Jeremiah Perry took up land grants in 1752 and 1763. The older house, probably built in the 1780s or 1790s, stands 1½ stories tall above a raised partial basement and has a hall-parlor plan, Flemish-bond brick chimneys, and late Georgian details akin to other post-Revolutionary houses in the county; the gable roof extends to shelter small unheated rear rooms flanking a stair passage. The big 2-story frame house

FN 19 *Cascine*

(ca. 1855) is a dynamic blend of Greek Revival and Italianate elements, with a curious combination of 3-bay porch stretched across a broad, asymmetrical 4-bay facade. The 2-room, center-chimney frame office was that of Dr. A. S. Perry, who probably erected the large house. Outbuildings, archaeological remains of slave houses, and scattered tenant houses and log tobacco barns recall a long agricultural history.

FN 20 Clifton House

1850s; E side SR 1103, 0.1 mi. S of SR 1706 (moved); private, visible from road

The symmetrical, generally Greek Revival house features an ornate porch, brackets, and other millwork that suggest an influence from Warrenton builder Jacob Holt. The Clifton family was associated with a nearby mill and mill pond.

FN 21 Freeman House and Cotton Gin

Early to mid-19th c.; W side SR 1001, just S of NC 98, Bunn vic.; private, visible from road

The once typical crossroads pairing includes a simply finished, 2-story frame house with stone chimneys and, across the road, a barn-like, frame cotton gin atop stout piers of stuccoed stone.

FN 22 Baker Farm

Mid- and late 19th c.; S side SR 1720, 0.2 mi. E of SR 1716, Bunn vic.; private, visible from road

Representative of the evolution of many farmhouses, the longtime home of the Baker family includes elements of Federal, Greek Revival, and Victorian construction and features the ubiquitous central front gable of Downing's "rural pointed" style. Frame outbuildings date from the late 19th and early 20th centuries.

FN 23 William A. Jeffreys House

Ca. 1842; S side SR 1101, 0.9 mi. E of US 401, Youngsville vic.; private, visible from road

The unusual house blends a tripartite arrangement with pedimented center block,

typical of the Federal era, with Greek Revival details adapted from Asher Benjamin's *Practical House Carpenter*. It was built for William A. and Martha Hart Jeffreys on a 1,037-acre tract from his father, William M. Jeffreys. William A. died at age 29 in 1845 and was buried in a boulder on his father's land—the "unique tomb" cited by a state highway marker.

FN 24 Robideaux House and Barn

Ca. 1800; N side SR 1113, 0.8 mi. W of SR 1105; private, visible from road

Among the largest of the county's late Georgian plantation houses, the 2-story structure, 3 bays broad with double-shouldered Flemish-bond chimneys, has two large rooms in front, plus unheated rear rooms under the main roof flanking a small stair passage. The big frame barn on a hillside near the house probably dates from the early to mid-19th c.

FN 25 Shemuel Kearney House

Ca. 1760?; W side US 1, 2 mi. S of NC 56, Franklinton vic.; private, barely visible from road

Evidently the oldest house in the county, the small dwelling is unique in its broad gambrel roof and compact 4-room plan with interior end chimneys. It is believed to have been built before the American Revolution for planter Kearney, who called it "the old house" in his will of 1808; his grandson gave the land for Franklinton.

FN 26 Franklinton

Founded as Franklin Depot in 1839 and incorporated as Franklinton in 1842, the community was one of the first towns in the state born of the railroad. Where the R&GRR crossed the Hillsborough Road in 1838–39, landowner Shemuel Kearney deeded the right-of-way plus 10 acres for a depot. Franklinton became an important stop for the area. Near the tracks stands the **Franklinton Depot** (1886; 201 E. Mason St.), built by the R&GRR and moved and preserved by the Franklinton Woman's Club in 1973. The

FN 26 *Franklinton Depot*

little frame building features picturesque kingpost gable ornaments, Italianate door and window frames, and a bay window. The 1886 annual report of the company recorded construction at Wake [Forest], Franklinton, Warren Plains, Macon, and Littleton of "neat and convenient passenger houses, which have added much to the comfort of the traveling public." Only this one survives.

The railroad encouraged modest industrial development, including a tobacco factory, cotton gins, and a sawmill. The largest manufacturing plant in the county was the **Sterling Cotton Mill** (1895 onward; SE corner of Railroad and E. Green Sts.), a complex of brick buildings in typical simplified Italianate mill style. The 2-story "main mill" (1895) has a low-pitched gable roof and arched windows, plus additions of various eras. The cotton yarn mill was founded by local businessman Samuel C. Vann and other family members and grew from 25 to 400 workers before it closed during the Great Depression. It was revitalized by Vann's daughter, Mrs. J. A. Moore, her brother Al, and later her son John (#Roa-

noke Rapids, #Edenton Cotton Mill) and operated until 1991.

The **Vann House** (1917; James Salter [Raleigh], architect; 115 N. Main St.), built for A. H. Vann, son of mill owner Samuel Vann, is an imposing brick residence with tile roof, projecting end bays, and bold Spanish and Renaissance Revival details. The **Methodist Church** (1891–92, 1909; Benjamin D. Price, architect; Main St.), home of the oldest congregation (est. 1844), is an asymmetrical brick building in simple Gothic Revival style, typical of church architect Price. On the east edge of town is the **Dr. J. H. Harris House** (1902–4; J. H. Whitfield; 312 East Mason St.), a striking Queen Anne style house with sweeping porch and half-timbering in the gables.

FN 27 Person-McGhee Farm

Early 19th c., 1890s; W side US 1 S of Tar River, Franklinton vic.; private, visible from road

One of the prettiest sights in the eastern Piedmont, the farmstead in the buxom valley beside the Tar River is a favorite landmark on the main road. The grand Queen Anne style house was erected for Lemuel McGhee, Franklinton merchant, during an era when few N.C. farmers could build such ornate houses. The design may have come from mail-order architect George F. Barber of Knoxville. Attached in back is the Person family's early 19th-c. house. Farm buildings include an early 20th-c. saltbox-form tenant house and several log tobacco barns across a rural landscape maintained by the family.

FN 27 *Person-McGhee Farm*

Warren County (WR)

See Kenneth McFarland, The Architecture of Warren County, North Carolina, 1770s to 1860s *(2001).*

Established in 1779 from the division of Bute Co., Warren was one of the leading plantation counties in the state before the Civil War. Still rural, it possesses an extraordinary collection of plantation era buildings—and many overbuildings—especially many from the years between the 1840 completion of the Raleigh & Gaston Railroad (R&GRR) and the Civil War.

Lying in the Roanoke Valley region but considered healthier than its neighbors eastward, the county was settled chiefly by English and African people who came from Virginia in the early to mid-18th c. By 1790 Warren was one of only three counties in the state with a majority black population (about 4,700 slaves, a few free blacks, and 4,600 whites), and over half the free households owned slaves; by 1860 there were more than 10,000 blacks and 4,900 whites. The county had the highest free per capita wealth in the state. Leading planter families developed a sociable, fashion-conscious way of life that included mineral springs resorts and racetracks. Warrenton became a stylish little town, and depot villages developed along the R&GRR. After the Civil War, as the tenant system took hold, many black and white residents left for better opportunities, a trend that continued through the 20th c. even after Warrenton opened a tobacco market. Despite losses, including the once numerous slave houses and tenant houses, the agrarian landscape and historic architecture of the county and its small county seat gained renewed appreciation in the late 20th c.

Warrenton (WR 1–36)

The small, architecturally rich town of about 1,000 people possesses one of the state's most intact collections of antebellum domestic architecture and illustrates phases of southern small-town development from the early 19th through the early 20th c. The linear plan along Main St. has a compact downtown adjoined by residences, many of which occupy spacious lots. Founded in 1779 and laid out by surveyor William Christmas (*Raleigh), the seat of the new county drew tavern keepers, merchants, artisans, teachers, and lawyers. In 1786 visitor Elkanah Watson found a village "just emerging from the forest," with "a refined neighborhood [and] a salubrious air" that contrasted with the "baneful malaria of the low country." Citizens established academies for young men (1788) and women (1802) and churches in the 1820s, and local lawyers emerged as state political leaders. Warrenton became, as one resident recalled, the "nucleus of the spreading plan-

tations owned by the prosperous, so-called 'aristocratic' class."

Wealth increased in the antebellum era, boosted by construction of the R&GRR in the 1830s—with the nearest stop at *Warren Plains—greater use of fertilizers, and consolidation of land and slave ownership. With about 1,500 people by 1860, Warrenton was famed for its good schools, well-stocked taverns and hotels, stylish buildings, and fashionable artisans and shops. It was said that when Raleigh attorneys went to try cases in Warren Co. court, their wives asked them to bring back hats from Warrenton milliners.

Prosperity and the taste for fashion supported skilled builders whose identities persisted in local memory. Thomas Bragg, who came from New Bern, was an important early 19th-c. carpenter and father of a governor and a general; he and a builder named Burgess are credited with richly finished Federal style buildings, in a style associated with the elaborate plantation house Montmorenci (lost, 1930s). In the 1840s and 1850s

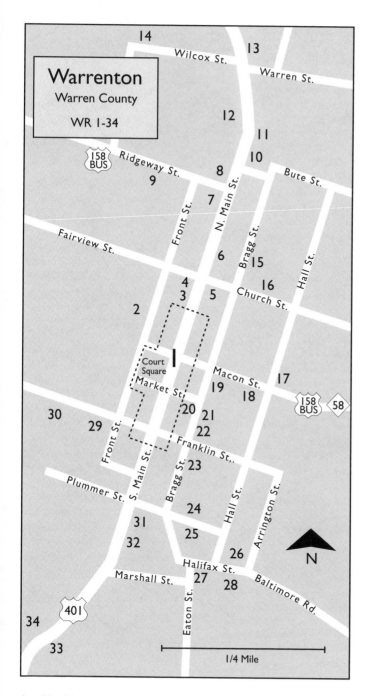

Warrenton
Warren County
WR 1-34

14
Wilcox St.
13
Warren St.
12
11
158 BUS
Ridgeway St.
10
Bute St.
9
8
N. Main St.
7
Front St.
Bragg St.
Fairview St.
6
15
Hall St.
4
3
16
Church St.
2
5
Court Square
1
Macon St.
17
Market St.
19
18
158 BUS
58
20
21
30
22
29
Front St.
S. Main St.
Franklin St.
23
Plummer St.
Bragg St.
24
Hall St.
Arrington St.
31
25
32
26
N
Halifax St.
Marshall St.
27
28
Baltimore Rd.
Eaton St.
401
34
33
1/4 Mile

local builders remade town and plantation architecture in distinctive Greek Revival and Italianate modes. Albert Gamaliel Jones, a native Warren Co. carpenter, executed boldly detailed Greek Revival work here and in other counties. Carpenter Jacob W. Holt moved from Prince Edward Co., Va., to Warrenton in the 1840s with his brother Thomas and brickmasons Edward Rice and Francis Woodson and others. Holt ran one of the largest contracting firms in antebellum N.C., with as many as 60 black and white workers. He built in an eclectic vocabulary drawn from patternbooks by Asher Benjamin, Samuel Sloan, William Ranlett, and others. Although certain design motifs are shared by Bragg-Burgess and Jones and by Jones and Holt, no specific links between them have been documented.

After the Civil War, Warrenton's population dwindled, to 941 by 1870. Although schools and churches were established by freedpeople, and local investors built the Warrenton Railroad spur to the R&GRR plus tobacco warehouses to boost trade, the town never regained its antebellum stature. "Lured by Buck Duke and the promise of wealth into the Yukon of New York City," recalled a resident, promising young men bid their friends "'good-bye . . . we're going to New York by way of Durham.'"

Still, the town maintained a strong sense of pride and identity. An upsurge of civic improvement came in the early 20th c. with new business blocks along Main St., a new courthouse and city hall, a municipal hotel "that no other city of similar size can match," and a modern high school costing over $100,000, plus paved streets and sidewalks, a water and sewage system, and a city ice plant. At the same time came many new residences and churches, chiefly in Colonial Revival styles. The era also brought new interest in colonial and antebellum heritage, and while some landmarks were lost, much remained, and the local architecture gained early attention from historians and preservation leaders.

WR 1 Court Square and Commercial District

Main St. and Court Square

Laid out in the 18th c., the courthouse square is dominated by the 2-story, red brick **Warren County Courthouse** (1906–7; Frank P. Milburn [Washington, D.C.], architect; Phipps & Cooper [Newport News], builders). In 1906 the county considered renovating Holt's temple-form brick courthouse of 1854–57 but instead accepted Milburn's proposal for a new one: a modest Neoclassical design with pilasters and pediment framing the arched entrance, a modillion cornice,

WR 1 *Warren Co. Courthouse*

angled corners, and a large cupola. In front the Confederate Memorial (1913) is an obelisk topped by a soldier.

Framing the square is an unusually complete ensemble of law offices, commercial buildings, and residences. The **T. E. Wilson House** (ca. 1850; Macon St., N of courthouse) is a typical Warrenton type Greek Revival frame house, 2 stories tall, with broad Doric-columned porch, hip roof, hefty corner pilasters, and Doric-columned entrance. It was built for Dr. T. E. Wilson and his wife Janet Mitchel, whose daughter Lizzie Wilson Montgomery wrote an informative local memoir, *Sketches of Old Warrenton* (1924). The **Peter Davis Store** (early 19th c.; 101 Front St., behind courthouse), a 1-story frame building with central chimney, exemplifies the small scale of buildings in early Warrenton. Like others that stood nearby, the little structure provided attorneys with an office in front and a bedroom in back. The **Fain-Hendrick House** (1871; 105 Front St.) is a 2-story frame dwelling with center gable, bracketed cornice, and curly porch brackets suggesting the postwar work of the Holt shop.

Across Main St. from the courthouse, and extending a block north and south, is a solid row of early 20th-c. brick commercial buildings, most postdating an 1881 fire. **Miles Hardware** (ca. 1900; 106 S. Main St.) has an intact pressed-brick facade, painted glass storefronts and long shelves along the walls inside. From before the fire, the 2-story **Brick Store** (1830s; w side Main St. s of courthouse) is one of the oldest commercial buildings in the region; its Flemish-bond brickwork, stepped gables with lunette, and beneath the metal cornice, a plastered coved cornice link it with the 1830s clerks' offices in #Halifax and #Northampton counties, built by brick contractor Abraham Spencer.

WR 2 Somerville-Graham House

Ca. 1850; Jacob W. Holt, builder (attrib.); 107 N. Front St.

The 2-story frame house on a large lot is an elaborate version of the local Greek Revival style, with a fine Doric porch and entrance, triple windows and bay windows, and lavish Greek fret molding. Built for John Somerville and his wife Matilda Kearney—one of several famously beautiful Kearney daughters—it was later home of educator John Graham, who operated a high school here.

WR 2 *Somerville-Graham House*

WR 3 Emmanuel Episcopal Church

1822–24, Thomas Bragg; 1855–57, Jacob W. Holt; 1927, William Lawrence Bottomley (New York), architect; N. Main St.

The picturesque church incorporates three eras of construction. Bragg's simple, gable-fronted frame church was remodeled with a steeple by Holt from a "Village Church" design in Samuel Sloan's *Model Architect* (1852). In 1926 the congregation asked noted Colonial Revival architect Bottomley (*Tatton Hall, Raleigh) to design a new brick church, but economy dictated a "restoration" of the old one. Bottomley kept the basic form and the spire but transformed it in a felicitous Gothic Revival design in Flemish-bond brick. To the rear is a Tudor Revival parish house.

WR 3 *Emmanuel Episcopal Church*

WR 4 U.S. Post Office

1936; Louis A. Simon, supervising architect of the Treasury; 143 N. Main St.

The small red brick post office, typifying the Works Progress Administration (WPA) Colonial Revival style, still serves its purpose and retains a mural (Alice Dinneen, 1938) depicting an idyllic agrarian scene.

WR 5 Warrenton Hotel

1919; 144 N. Main St.

The 3-story, red brick building with Colonial Revival detail was erected during the early 20th-c. civic improvements to provide a good hotel beneficial to town trade and stature. It was renovated in the 1990s as a retirement home.

WR 6 Eaton Place

1843–44; Jacob W. Holt, carpenter; 210 N. Main St.

Long the showplace of Warrenton, the big brick house was built for William Eaton, known as the richest planter in the Roanoke Valley; by 1860 he owned land and slaves valued at over $200,000. He is said to have built it as a summer residence and for his daughter Ella to entertain in during the fall social season. Two stories tall over a high basement, 5 bays wide, and only 1 room deep, the house is built of Flemish-bond brickwork accented with inset plaster panels between the stories—a feature typical of

WR 6 *Eaton Place*

Virginia. Elaborate classical details enrich the large fanlit doorways at both levels, the upper rising into the classical entablature. Traditionally cited to Holt, who came to Warrenton ca. 1844, the house resembles work in his native Prince Edward Co., Va. Interior trim from Asher Benjamin's *Practical House Carpenter* complements a fine curved stair from Owen Biddle's *Young Carpenter's Assistant*. The grounds, which extend through the block, include a heart-shaped boxwood garden and matching brick outbuildings—originally a kitchen and an office.

WR 7 Bobbitt-Pendleton House
Mid-19th, early 20th c.; SW corner N. Main at Ridgeway St.

The frame house was home of 19th-c. carriage maker William Bobbitt and later of local memoirist Victoria Pendleton. Her daughter Katherine Pendleton Arrington, a leader in founding the State Art Society and Museum of Art, added various architectural fragments collected from the county.

WR 8 Former Warrenton (John Graham) High School
1921–22; C. Gadsden Sayre (Anderson, S.C., and Raleigh), architect; NW corner N. Main at Ridgeway St.

Representing a long tradition of education and the civic pride of the early 20th c., the large, handsome $100,000 brick school

with generous windows and classical detailing stands on the site of the 18th-c. Warrenton Male Academy. It now contains county offices.

WR 9 Gloster-Hill-Crossan House
Late 18th c., ca. 1850; 211 Ridgeway St., 1 block W of Main St.

A variation of the local Greek Revival has a side-passage plan, with the pedimented end facing the street enriched with fretwork. Family tradition recalls the brothers Jacob and Thomas Holt as builders, though some details suggest Albert Gamaliel Jones. The south wing began as the small 18th-c. dwelling of physician Thomas Benn Gloster of Ireland; Halifax Co. planter Thomas Blount Hill evidently added the 2-story section ca. 1850 before moving to Hillsborough (#The Hermitage; *Hill-Webb House). In 1858 it became the home of Thomas and Rebecca Brehon Crossan; the former U.S. Navy officer commanded the state's blockade-runner *Advance* during the Civil War.

WR 10 Skelton-Howard-Green House
Ca. 1850; 316 N. Main St.

This restrained rendition of the local Greek Revival, 1 room deep with a small Doric porch, was built for a dentist and was later owned by physicians, who used the little frame office in the side yard.

WR 11 Green-Polk House
Ca. 1850; Jacob W. Holt, Woodson & Rice, builders (attrib.); 326 N. Main St.

Presiding over a curve in Main St., the imposing Greek Revival house is executed in all-stretcher bond brick and finished with oversize (8/8) windows and boldly carved ornament at the entrance. Two stories tall above a raised basement, it is 2 rooms deep at the first story, 1 above. It was built for planter Nathaniel Green, who reportedly moved to town for his children to attend school; his long list of creditors included Holt and Woodson & Rice. Across Main St. is a 2-story frame Greek Revival house, built as Green's guest house.

WR 12 Warrenton Presbyterian Church

1856–57; Jacob W. Holt, Woodson & Rice, builders; 327 N. Main St.

The small, eclectic brick church combines a Greek Revival temple form with portico in antis, Italianate brackets, and (later) Gothic Revival side windows. The congregation (est. 1827) built it with an 1855 bequest of $4,000 for a "neat and suitable Presbyterian Church of brick." The church bell has rung from nearby treetops for more than a century.

WR 13 Mills-Foote-Price House

1840s; Jacob W. Holt, builder (attrib.); 410 N. Main St.

Antebellum artisans, including cabinet-maker Samuel N. Mills, established a neighborhood at the north end of town. The simple Greek Revival finish of the modest 2-story frame house illustrates Holt's work for his artisan associates. In the 20th c. it was the home of the Price family, scene of Warrenton recollections by novelist Reynolds Price. Other small, altered artisan houses stand nearby on Warren St.

WR 14 John W. White House

Mid-19th c.; 312 Wilcox St.

A typical modest house of the mid- and late 19th c., the 1½-story dwelling features a central front gable and millwork indicative of the postwar era. It was the home of longtime clerk of court White.

WR 15 Jones-Cook House

Ca. 1810, ca. 1850; Thomas Bragg, Albert Gamaliel Jones, builders (attrib.); 310 Bragg St.

The 2-story Greek Revival house has the large cornerblocks and Doric-columned porch with paneled railing characteristic of builder Jones. It encloses a Federal period dwelling said to have been built for attorney Robert H. Jones by Bragg as payment of a legal fee.

WR 16 *Boyd-Kerr House*

WR 16 Boyd-Kerr House

1908; Charles Barrett & Frank Thompson, architects; 216 Church St.

Warrenton's prime example of the white-columned Southern Colonial style features a bowed portico in the Corinthian order and elaborate interiors. Built for businessman Walter Boyd, it was later home of political leaders John Kerr Sr. and Jr. and local historian-genealogist Mary Hinton Kerr.

WR 17 Cannon-Davis House

Late 18th–early 19th c.; N side Macon St., W of Hall St.

One of the few remaining small early town houses, the 1-story frame dwelling with attic has a hall-parlor plan and fine double-shouldered chimneys of stone blocks. James Cannon bought the lot in 1792 and sold it to merchant Peter Davis in 1805.

WR 18 Oak Chapel A.M.E. Church

By 1882; Macon St. at Hall St.

Identified as a Methodist Episcopal church on an 1882 map, the frame church is the oldest of several built for Warrenton's newly emancipated black citizens. It combines lancet-arched windows with a bracket cornice and a graceful spire. The congregation was established soon after the Civil War by John Hyman of Warrenton, state senator (1868–74) and the state's first black congressman (1875–77).

WR 19 Warren County Jail
1868–69; 201 Macon St.

In 1868, after a prisoner set fire to the old wooden jail in an escape attempt, the county employed daguerreotypist David Parrish to superintend construction of a fireproof replacement and then to become jailer. The 2-story building, with 2-foot-thick stone walls covered in stucco, is a rare example of mid-19th-c. jail construction. It contained the jailer's residence and cells with fittings from the Paul Jail Building & Mfg. Co. of St. Louis.

WR 20 Warrenton City Hall and Fire Station
Early 20th c.; SW corner Market and Bragg Sts.

The multi-use civic building, erected of red brick with simple classical details during the municipal improvement era, held an opera house, a market, and the fire department as well as city offices.

WR 21 Burroughs House
1846–47, Jacob W. Holt, possible builder; Bragg St.

The plain 2-story frame house may be the dwelling built by Holt for coachmaker Thomas Burrows (Burroughs), from their 1846 contract for a house 28 by 18 feet with "one passage and a room below stairs and 2 rooms up stairs" to cost $386.95. Burroughs would pay Holt with a buggy "like Mrs. Bellamy's," a wagon, a sorrel horse, use of land, and other goods. Several such small 19th-c. houses stood along Bragg St.

WR 22 Jacob W. Holt House
Ca. 1856; Jacob W. Holt, builder; 122 Bragg St.

In an architectural billboard of his up-to-date taste, Holt built "an unusually shaped house for that time," according to a local memoir. In a contrast with more conservative work for his clients, he used A. J. Downing's *Cottage Residences* or Samuel Sloan's *Model Architect* for the picturesque composition with central entry tower, projecting

WR 22 *Jacob Holt House*

gabled wings, and eaves dripping with sawnwork. The unusually light construction may owe to Holt's leasing rather than owning the lot. His large workshop lay to the rear.

WR 23 Plunkett House
Ca. 1817; 204 Bragg St.

Beneath aluminum siding, the Federal period house retains its tripartite form akin to several in the region, as well as original interiors. It was probably built for one John LaTaste and then sold to Caroline and Achilles Plunkett, who ran the academy at the *Fitts-Mordecai-Plummer House.

WR 24 Fitts-Mordecai-Plummer House
Ca. 1805; 210 Plummer St.

The largest early 19th-c. house in town, notable for its full 5-bay width, double-pile plan, and robust Georgian woodwork, was built for Attorney General Oliver D. Fitts. Doric porches were added in the mid-19th c. From 1811 to 1818 it served as the Warrenton Female Academy, operated by merchant-educator Jacob Mordecai (*Mordecai House,

WR 24 *Fitts-Mordecai-Plummer House*

Raleigh) and his family. (Fitts offered the house after their school burned in 1811.) The academy was continued by daughter Caroline and her husband Achilles Plunkett, a French and music teacher from San Domingo. The house later served as the late 19th-c. Shiloh Institute for African American students, a dormitory for John Graham's school, and a residence.

WR 25 Strickland House
1923; 207 Plummer St.

One of several notable early 20th-c. houses in Warrenton, the 2-story, stuccoed dwelling displays an unusual combination of Craftsman and Chalet styles. It is described as an Aladdin precut house, built for Mr. Strickland, a plumber.

WR 26 Arrington-Alston House
1850s; Jacob W. Holt, builder (attrib.); 308 E. Halifax St.

At the bend of Halifax St. are three large, well-preserved 2-story frame houses exemplifying the local Federal, Greek Revival, and Italianate styles. Typical of Holt's format, this big Greek Revival house has a 3-bay, double-pile form with center passage divided by a louvered doorway to accommodate front and rear front stairs. It repeats the local Doric-columned porch and other bold details from Benjamin's *Practical House Carpenter.*

WR 27 Engleside
Ca. 1850; Jacob W. Holt, builder (attrib.); 203 Halifax St.

A house of similar form displays Holt's combination of Italianate motifs from Ranlett's *The Architect*, with arched windows, pendant brackets at the main roof, modillion blocks on the entrance porch, and originally a scalloped balustrade atop the porch. It was built for John White, a Scots-born Warrenton merchant and Confederate commissioner to England. In 1870 he hosted Robert E. Lee during the general's pilgrimage to the grave of his daughter Anne Carter Lee (who died during the war while in Warren Co.), a

visit celebrated in local lore. (See Introduction, Fig. 36.)

WR 28 Coleman-White House
Early 1820s; Mr. Burgess or Thomas Bragg, builder (attrib.); 305 E. Halifax St.

The 2-story Federal style house is one of the few showing the distinctive motifs of the Montmorenci-influenced regional houses, including the Palladian entrance, "spool" moldings, and blind-arched triple windows. The porch replaced a mid-19th-c. Doric one. Built for Dr. Littleton C. Coleman, this was later the home of Scots merchant Thomas White (brother of John, next door) and William J. White, president of the Warrenton Railroad.

WR 29 All Saints Episcopal Church
Ca. 1914; SW corner Front and Franklin Sts.

West of Main St., the church of rock-faced concrete block was constructed by its members in a simple Gothic Revival style on the foundation of a former school. It was the home church of Bravid Harris, the first African American full bishop of the Episcopal Church, who served in Liberia from 1945 to 1963.

WR 30 Sledge-Hayley House
Early 1850s; S side Franklin St. (at Hayley St.)

The big frame house in the local Greek Revival style, with an unusual center-chimney plan, was built for merchant George Sledge and his wife Nancy Fleming. In the early 20th c. it was the home of Nancy S. and Paul F. Hayley, African American educator and legislator, whose daughter Louise married noted physician Dr. Thomas Haywood.

WR 31 Davis-Carr-Jones House
Early 19th c., 1920s; Howard Satterfield (Raleigh), architect-builder; Plummer St. at S. Main St.

The symmetrical, 2-story brick house began as a 1½-story dwelling whose stone chimneys still stand. It was the summer home in the 19th c. of Governor Elias Carr and was enlarged in Georgian Revival fashion by a Raleigh architect-builder.

WR 32 White-Banzet House

1931; Harry J. Simmonds (Greensboro), architect; 312 S. Main St.

One of several fine residences from the early 20th c., the red brick house is a handsomely proportioned and well-detailed rendition of the popular Georgian Revival mode.

WR 33 Alfred Alston Williams House

Ca. 1920; 438 S. Main St.

The large bungalow, clad in brown shingles, with a full complement of Craftsman elements, was built during the early 20th-c. growth era.

WR 34 Norwood-Ellington House

Ca. 1852; 305 S. Main St.

Built for merchant Philip Norwood and his wife Rebecca Turner, daughter of Congressman Daniel Turner, the picturesque raised cottage with cross-gabled roof features the decorative brackets and other hallmarks of the antebellum boom era, plus frilly porch trim.

WR 35 Johnson-Plummer House

Late 18th c.; NW side US 401, 0.25 mi. S of Warrenton; private, visible from road

The 1½-story house with narrow, gabled dormers takes a form favored by 18th-c. planters but often replaced or enlarged in antebellum years. Behind a brick veneer, the L-shaped frame house is intact with its massive stone chimney and simple Georgian finish. Planter William R. Johnson operated a celebrated racetrack here.

WR 36 Watson House

1850s; Jacob W. Holt, builder (attrib.); NW side SR 1121, 0.1 mi. W of US 401, Warrenton vic.; private, visible from road

Like other planters, John Watson expanded his operation in the 1850s (to more than 2,000 acres) and employed Holt's shop to

enlarge a Federal period house in Italianate style. In this case the older house is fronted by an ornate 2-story central block and full-width porch and has flanking 1-story wings.

WR 37 Mansfield Thornton House

Ca. 1885; E side SR 1600, 0.8 mi. N of SR 1602, Warrenton vic.; private, visible from road

The 2-story frame house with hip roof and decorated front porch was built for Mansfield and Mary Christmas Thornton on a farm they acquired in 1884. Son of Alonzo and Martha Thornton, Mansfield Thornton was born a slave but evidently learned to read and write from the daughter of owner William Eaton. Obtaining further schooling after the Civil War, he returned and in 1878 was elected as a Republican to the position of register of deeds, in which he continued until the Democratic sweep of 1900.

WR 38 Shady Oaks

Early 19th c.; E side SR 1600, 0.3 mi. N of SR 1602, Warrenton vic.; private, visible from road

The tripartite house with narrow central block was built for Robert T. and Mary Hinton Alston Cheek, of long-established planter families. By 1812 Cheek owned over 2,400 acres and 20 slaves, plus a tavern and billiard room in Warrenton. The compact T-plan interior shares in a regional school of elaborate, individualized late Federal work cited to Thomas Bragg. The porch and additions date from a late 20th-c. restoration.

WR 39 Elgin

1827–32; Warrenton vic.; private, no public visibility or access

With #Airlie in Halifax Co., Elgin is one of a small group of pediment-fronted plantation houses showing the decorative vocabulary of the Montmorenci school, with hallmark fan-edged triglyphs, spool moldings at the corner posts and the fanlit entrance, and elaborate interiors. It was built for Elizabeth Person and her husband, Scots-born merchant Peter Mitchel, on a plantation from

WR 39 *Elgin*

her father, William. Reversing the usual pattern, a rear addition takes the form of a traditional, dormered 1½-story dwelling.

WR 40 Cheek House
Late 18th–early 19th c.; E side NC 58, 1.3 mi. S of NC 43; private, visible from road

The oldest brick house in the county has a tall, stark form, mixed brickwork including Flemish bond, an arched doorway, and a high stone foundation, evidently from multiple building campaigns. It was the home of James and Emily Cheek, but little is known of its early history.

Inez (The Fork) area:
In the rural neighborhood once called The Fork, several 19th-c. plantation houses stand within a few miles. Regarded as a healthful location, the community was known for its sociability, particularly among the interrelated Alston, Williams, and Davis families. In the Federal period, and again in the late antebellum era, they built and overbuilt fine houses of similar scale and style, including several in Greek Revival and Italianate modes of Albert Gamaliel Jones and the workshop of Jacob W. Holt. Out-migration has altered the landscape, leaving few of the many smaller houses of the slave and tenant families who worked the land.

WR 41 Lake o' the Woods
1852–53; Albert Gamaliel Jones, builder; N side SR 1512, 0.6 mi. E of NC 58; private, visible from road

The complete plantation complex centers on a Greek Revival house preserved by descendants and documented by family papers as the work of Warren Co. carpenter Jones. Planters Edward and Rebecca Pitchford Davis began their married life here in 1829 on property received from his father; they had 6 of their 8 children in a ca. 1790 dwelling (reused as the kitchen) from a nearby site. The 2-story house Jones built features his hallmark large-scale bull's-eye cornerblocks and moldings, spool-beaded corner posts, and geometric tracery at the doorways. The dwelling is surrounded by plantings and a wooden fence with 19th-c. gate; near it stand a kitchen, a smokehouse, and other early outbuildings, plus barns and a stable.

WR 41 *Lake o' the Woods*

WR 42 Pitchford House
Ca. 1810; 1850s, Albert Gamaliel Jones, builder (attrib.); S side SR 1512, 1.7 mi. E of NC 58; private, visible from road

Coeval with Lake o' the Woods, Jones was employed by Rebecca Davis's brother Dr. Thomas Pitchford to enlarge their parents' home into a 2-story T-plan Greek Revival dwelling with signature corner posts, roundel cornerblocks, and triple windows.

WR 43 Shady Grove
Ca. 1830; SE corner jct. SR 1620 and SR 1625, Inez vic.

The unusual pediment-fronted house with 4-bay facade combines details of the Montmorenci school with Greek Revival elements; its 2-room plan and Flemish-bond chimneys at the sides reflect its construction as a front addition to an older dwelling (replaced late 20th c.). The plantation was the home of John A. Williams and his family.

WR 44 Solomon Williams Jr. House
Ca. 1882; NE side NC 58, 0.3 mi. N of SR 1640, Inez; private, visible from road

The 1-story house with hip roof and a decorative front porch continues the symmetry and center-passage plan of its antebellum relatives, but in a smaller version with simpler, mass-produced trim reflecting its post–Civil War date. It was built for Solomon Williams Jr. and Kate White, children of planter families who continued in the community.

WR 45 Cherry Hill
1858; John A. Waddell, builder; W side NC 58, opp. SR 1640, Inez; private, visible from road; open by appointment

The grandly sited hilltop Italianate house presents a graceful exemplar of the Holt school, carefully maintained by descendants. The broad, bracketed porch has slim double posts linked by Tudor-arched sawnwork with budlike motifs. The Tudor arch motif recurs throughout the house, and brackets enrich the bay windows, corner posts, main roofline, and chimney caps. The characteristic center-passage plan, 2 rooms deep, has folding, louvered doors separating front and rear stairs. A row of 19th-c. outbuildings stands to the rear. Successor to "old Cherry Hill," the house was erected for Marina Williams Alston and her three sons after the death of her husband George. Family tradition and an 1859 estate payment of $4,774.69 identify the builder as John A. Waddell, an associate of Jacob W. Holt (*Buxton Place).

WR 45 *Cherry Hill*

WR 46 Buxton Place
1857–61; John A. Waddell, builder; W side NC 58, 0.8 mi. S of SR 1640; private, visible from road

Closely related to Cherry Hill, the imposing Italianate plantation house displays the Holt shop's characteristic bracket cornices and a full-width porch, set on a high basement amid an oak grove and a full complement of farm buildings. It was built for John Buxton Williams and his wife Mary Temperance Hilliard, who by 1860 had over 3,900 acres (800 under cultivation). Williams served as guardian of the Alstons at *Cherry Hill during its construction, and family letters also cite "Mr. Waddell," Holt associate, as builder of Buxton Place beginning in May 1857.

WR 47 Fairmount
1830s–50s; Albert Gamaliel Jones (attrib.); N side SR 1640, 0.4 mi. E of NC 58, Inez vic.; private, visible from road

Displaying Greek Revival elements associated with builder Jones, the 2-story plantation house with pedimented gables and end chimneys was built for Solomon Williams (brother of Marina Williams Alston of *Cherry Hill) and Maria Alston Kearney, who married in 1835. The place remains in the family.

WR 48 Arcola
Jct. NC 43 and SR 1634

The crossroads village served its plantation neighborhood from the mid-19th c. into the mid-20th c. It was established and named for an Italian town by planter Samuel T. Alston of Tusculum plantation, which he named for a Roman town where Cicero and others had their villas. The **Alston-Davis Store** (ca. 1850s and later) at the southwest corner is a 1-story, gable-fronted frame building with simple Greek Revival detail, later operated by the Davis family of *Lake o' the Woods. Southwest is an earlier 19th-c. **Alston Store** moved across the road, and on the northeast corner is the 2-story, gable-fronted **Capps Store** (ca. 1900). Nearby, **Dalkeith** (ca. 1824–25; Thomas Bragg, builder [attrib.]; w side SR 1636, 0.8 mi. s of NC 43; private, visible from road) maintains its pediment-fronted form. Also in the area is **Tusculum** (ca. 1830s; no public access), a tall frame house built for Samuel T. and Ruina Williams Alston, with Federal and Greek Revival elements suggestive of a transition from the Bragg-Burgess school to A. G. Jones.

WR 49 Myrtle Lawn
Early 19th c., ca. 1858; W side SR 1640, 1.4 mi. SE of SR 1630, Inez vic.; private, visible from road

The 2-story frame plantation house, in simplified Italianate style, was built as an enlargement of a Federal period Alston family house for Dr. Robert E. and Valeria Kearney Williams. There are several outbuildings and a cluster of tobacco barns across the road.

WR 50 Heck's Grove School
Early 20th c.; E side US 401, 0.3 mi. N of SR 1620

In Warren Co., local citizens working to build schoolhouses for black students garnered support for nearly 30 schools from the Julius Rosenwald Fund. The school at Heck's Grove, among the largest, is maintained as a community center.

WR 51 Soul City
Est. 1969; SR 1151–1155, S of US 1, Manson vic.

One of several federally supported new towns of its era, Soul City was laid out on farmland near I-85 and the railroad. Led by civil rights attorney Floyd B. McKissick, it was envisioned as "a brand new shining city" of 40,000 to 50,000 people, "without prejudice, without poverty, without slums." De-

velopment was slow, and federal assistance dwindled; but there is a small community with broad, well-lighted streets, public utilities, and several residences. At the center is the **Green Duke House** (late 18th c.; SR 1152 loop), seat of the former plantation of nearly 5,000 acres, a 2-story frame house with hip roof and unusual Georgian interiors.

WR 52 Ridgeway

The community began as a late 18th-c. stage stop, where Marshall's Tavern of ca. 1800 is believed to be the gambrel-roofed rear section of the **Marshall House** (late 18th, late 19th c.; w side SR 1224 at US 1). New life arrived with the R&GRR traversing the ridge for which the post office was named in 1839. The grandest building is **Oakley Hall** (1850s; Jacob W. Holt, builder [attrib.]; SE side SR 1103, just E of US 1), an elaborate Italianate residence built near the tracks for Dr. William J. Hawkins, president of the R&GRR, son of a leading planter family, and a graduate of the University of Pennsylvania medical school. On a tract "near the Ridgeway Depot" he built a small house in 1845, then a big house in the Holt style that shows an ornate blend of Tudor and Gothic arches with Italianate brackets. Son Marmaduke, owner from 1887, called it Oakley Hall; it has been restored after long neglect.

In 1867 Dr. Hawkins, J. M. Heck, Kemp Battle, and others formed the Ridgeway Co., one of several redevelopment schemes in the postwar South, to create a railroad city with northern European workers growing produce for shipment; they commissioned buildings by architect G. S. H. Appleget (*Heck-Andrews House, Raleigh). The vi-

WR 52 *Oakley Hall*

sion was never realized, but some frame houses near US 1 recall the era with touches of Italianate and Gothic Revival styles. The picturesque **Chapel of the Good Shepherd** (1871; E side SR 1107, 0.2 mi. SE of US 1) was funded largely by Dr. Hawkins and aptly praised at completion as "a beautiful chapel of brick, Gothic, measuring 28 × 44, with recess chancel."

German and other northern European immigrants did come later in the 19th c. Their farmhouses repeat standard turn-of-the-century forms, while big barns and well-defined crop fields offer a German-influenced contrast with the rest of the county, such as those along SR 1223, 1224, and 1226. **St. Paul's Lutheran Church** (ca. 1898, rebuilt 1950s; E corner jct. SR 1224 and SR 1226) is a brick church with tower and a churchyard containing many German-language stones.

WR 53 Warren Plains
SR 1322 and SR 1305, 3 miles N of Warrenton

The village began in the 1830s when the R&GRR bypassed Warrenton and made this the Warrenton stop; in 1876 the 3-mile private Warrenton Railroad spur linked the two. The main tracks and all but one of the frame commercial buildings are gone, but the **Warren Plains Depot** (1863–64, Thomas J. Holt, possible architect) stands as one of the finest surviving buildings from the R&GRR. During the Civil War the line transported war supplies and erected several new depots, including this one. It may have been designed by Thomas J. Holt, brother of Jacob and architect for the R&GRR in 1860. The strongly built 1-story frame building has a low hip roof with broad eaves carried by a

WR 53 *Warren Plains Depot*

complex and sturdy truss system. Board-and-batten walls and broad arched and square-headed entrances exemplify the picturesque format of mid-19th-c. depots.

WR 54 Egerton-Brown House
Late 18th–early 19th c.; N side NC 158, at SR 1316, Macon

Close to the road, the small frame house with steep gable roof and double-shouldered chimney of Flemish-bond brick is among the most intact dwellings built by early planters in the county.

WR 55 Macon
US 158

As in many railroad towns where the tracks have been pulled up, the old R&GRR community has several late 19th- to early 20th-c. commercial buildings and houses facing the open track site. The former **Grocery Store** is a 2-story frame building with pedimented front on Main St. (US 158). On Elm St., s of US 158, are small frame houses with big stone or brick chimneys, probably antebellum workers' housing. The **Macon Depot** (mid-to late 19th c.; Elm St.), moved from trackside, has the hip roof, large doorways, and board-and-batten finish typical of the R&GRR. The town was the childhood home of author Reynolds Price; his family's well-remembered **John Rodwell House**, 1½ stories with wraparound porch, still stands on the N side of the track site.

WR 56 Fitts-Perkinson House
Late 18th–early 19th c.; E side SR 1309, 0.2 mi. N of SR 1314, Macon vic.; private, visible from road

The tall, plain frame house, recalling an era before the eclecticism of the mid-19th c., has a big stone chimney serving a side-passage plan, plus rear shed rooms and a 1½-story south wing from the late 18th c. An excellent collection of outbuildings frames the house and forms a courtyard across the road. This was the home of Henry Fitts, a planter, merchant, and Methodist leader who served as minister at *Hebron Methodist Church.

WR 57 Hebron Methodist Church

Ca. 1848–49, 1886, ca. 1910; Jacob W. Holt, builder (attrib.); NW side SR 1306, 0.8 mi. E of SR 1305, Oakville vic.

One of the few country churches from Warren's antebellum era, when Methodism was strong among planter families, the original section was built in simple Greek Revival style, with a gable front and large 12/12 windows lighting the single room. The church was extended to the front in 1886, and in 1910 it gained a narthex and chancel. The congregation traces its origins to 1771, with the biblical place-name Hebron in use by 1810.

WR 58 Gardner Baptist Church

1880s; E side SR 1335 at SR 1337, Church Hill

The frame country church, with Gothic Revival windows and a handsome bracketed entrance tower, may be a late work by the Holt shop. Church history includes the congregation's 18th-c. origins and a reorganization in 1844.

WR 59 Pine Grove Baptist Church and School

Early and mid-20th c.; W and E sides SR 1335, 0.8 mi. S of Church Hill

The small brick-veneered church with corner tower was, according to a plaque, rebuilt 1940–61 for a congregation established in 1873 by African American members of *Gardner Baptist Church. Its form, shingled gables, and belfry remain from ca. 1900. Across the road is a well-preserved frame schoolhouse, which follows Rosenwald school plan no. 20 for a "two teacher community school," with two classrooms flank-

WR 59 *Pine Grove School*

ing the front "industrial room." It was one of nearly 30 schools in the county built with assistance from the Julius Rosenwald Fund (*Heck's Grove).

WR 60 Buck Spring (Nathaniel Macon Plantation)

Late 18th c.; end of SR 1348, Vaughan vic.; open limited hours

Warren planter Nathaniel Macon dominated N.C. politics during his long tenure in the U.S. House of Representatives (1791–1815), where he gained national power as Speaker, and in the U.S. Senate (1815–28). Despite his wealth, after he married Hannah Plummer in 1783 he built only a small, frame dwelling with one room and a loft, to serve until they built a larger house. After her death in 1790 and his election to Congress, he lived frugally in the little house surrounded by many slave houses and other outbuildings. Essentially rebuilt during a 1937 WPA-assisted restoration, it burned in the late 1970s and was rebuilt in the mid-1980s. There are also a frame smokehouse and a substantially reconstructed log corncrib with sheds on all four sides. As Macon wished, at his death in 1837 his grave was marked with a mound of stones placed by his friends.

WR 61 Linden Hall

1841–44; Thomas Bragg, Albert Gamaliel Jones, James Boon, probable builders; NW side SR 1528, 0.25 mi. SW of NC 158, Littleton vic.

The Greek Revival plantation house and matching outbuildings were built for Dr. Charles Skinner and his wife Susan Little on land received from her father, William Person Little, namesake of Littleton. Skinner studied medicine at the University of Pennsylvania and served as a Civil War surgeon. The house follows a T-plan, with a 2-story rear ell with cross stair hall, reminiscent of her father's *Little Manor nearby. Correspondence during construction makes tantalizing mention of Jones (1841), workmen of Mr. Bragg (1843), and "Boon," probably the free black carpenter James Boon.

Vance County (VN)

Named for U.S. senator and former Civil War governor Zebulon B. Vance, the county formed in 1881 from portions of Franklin, Granville, and Warren counties was part of the wealthy 18th- and early 19th-c. plantation zone, settled largely by English and African people from Virginia. Construction of the Raleigh & Gaston Railroad (R&GRR) down the granite formations between the Tar and Neuse rivers increased prosperity and made the depot at Henderson a trading point. The same granite was widely used in chimneys and foundations and was quarried on a large scale at Greystone Quarry and elsewhere. The plantation-era architecture includes notable late Georgian and early Federal plantation houses as well as Greek Revival and Italianate ones, many of which show planters' expansions of older houses.

In the post–Civil War era, farming turned to the tenant system as the Old Belt county became a leading producer of flue-cured tobacco for markets in Henderson and Durham. Agriculture continues with machinery and migrant workers, while residential development extends around Kerr Lake and from the Research Triangle.

Henderson (VN 1–2)

See Melanie Murphy, *An Inventory of Historic Architecture: Henderson, North Carolina* (1979).

In 1838 the R&GRR established a depot near an early 19th-c. stage stop on a main road. The resulting trading town was incorporated in 1841 as Henderson, named for N.C. chief justice Leonard Henderson of a local family. It became the seat of the county formed amid post-Reconstruction politics in 1881. The rail town in the heart of the Old Belt tobacco zone and productive cotton fields grew into a regional marketing and manufacturing center, soon surpassing its parent counties' seats (Oxford, Warrenton, and Louisburg) in size and economic clout. From the 1870s, big tobacco warehouses and a cotton market and gins near the railroad drew crowds of farmers who had previously sent their crops to Petersburg. In 1895 and 1900, leading tobacconists began the Henderson and Harriett cotton mills and villages northeast and southeast of town. Prominent among the local builders and architects of the era was Eric G. Flannagan. Outstripped by Durham, the town remains a local market, with especially strong downtown architecture from the early 20th c.

VN 1 Downtown Henderson

From the heyday as a regional trade center, **Garnett St.** is a long, broad thoroughfare lined by impressive late 19th- and early 20th-c. commercial and public buildings. The chief landmark is the **Henderson Fire Station and Municipal Building** (1908, Robert Bunn; 1928, Eric G. Flannagan; 205 N. Garnett St.), an imposing red brick building of cleanly simplified Italianate character, with campanile-like corner tower—a bell- and clock tower also designed for drying firehoses. Beside it, Italianate **Zollicoffer's Law Office** (ca. 1887; 215 N. Garnett) with decorated porch recalls many freestanding commercial structures now lost. The **Raleigh & Gaston Freight Station** (1870s; 110 N. Garnett) is a small but important bracketed brick building.

Rich and varied storefronts adorn brick commercial buildings from the 1880s–1920s era. Among these are the 3-story Italianate **Davis Building** (1886; 203–5 S. Garnett St.), with its bold, arched window labels; the **Horner Building** (1928; 309–15 S. Garnett St.); and the **Stevenson Building** (1926; 214–16 S. Garnett St.), the latter two of glazed white terra-cotta with polychrome detail. The **P. H. Rose Building** (1929;

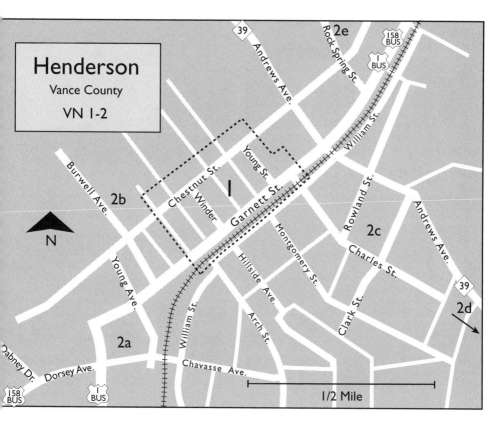

218–20 S. Garnett St.) is brick with polychrome terra-cotta trim featuring rose motifs. The **First National Bank** (1921; 213–15 S. Garnett St.) displays a strong Beaux Arts vault design with Doric columns and entablature. The **O'Neil Building** (1929; 230–34 S. Garnett St.) boasts a Carrera glass storefront. Anchoring the south end of the street is a fine example of Beaux Arts classicism: the former **U.S. Post Office** (County Office Building; 1911; 300 S. Garnett St.). The symmetrical composition in stone has massive corner pilasters and engaged columns framing tall windows beneath bull's-eye windows, and carrying a rich entablature with balustrade.

On Young St., behind the Fire Station, the **Vance County Courthouse** (1884, James R. Thrower, architect; 1908, Milburn & Heister; Young St.) is a pale brick edifice with added portico of Tuscan columns, reflecting Milburn & Heister's pragmatic remodeling of an 1884 building by railroad architect Thrower. The **H. Leslie Perry**

VN 1 *U.S. Post Office*

VN 2 *Mistletoe Villa*

VN 2 *Henderson High School*

Memorial Library (1924; Edward L. Tilton [New York], architect; Young St.) across the street is a broad temple-form building with Doric portico, given to the county by a local family who commissioned the design from the New York library specialist (#Pack Memorial Library, Asheville; *Durham Public Library).

Three conservative Gothic Revival churches mark the edges of downtown. The brick **Holy Innocents Episcopal Church** (1885; H. C. Linthicum [Durham]; 210 S. Chestnut St.) has a gabled facade and corner entrance tower with tall spire; **First Baptist Church** (1912–26; J. M. McMichael [Charlotte], architect?; 205 W. Winder St.), executed in irregular granite, has a buttressed, crenellated entrance tower; and the imposing, granite-faced **First United Methodist Church** (1922–30; E. G. Flannagan, architect; 300 Block N. Garnett St.) features a tall arch in its gable-fronted nave and a buttressed and crenellated corner tower with spire.

VN 2 Residential Areas

The chief residential landmark, located near the railroad, is **Mistletoe Villa** (1885; Samuel Sloan, architect [attrib.]; Young Ave.) (**a**), a resplendent Queen Anne overbuilding of an earlier house, with porches, balconies, dormers, shingles, and bargeboards, repainted in rich dark reds and greens from the original specifications. Credible family tradition attributes the remodeling for Ike Young to the architect of the *Executive Mansion. **Burwell Ave.** (**b**) and adjacent streets off S. Garnett was developed in the late 19th c. with the homes of leading businessmen. Most are traditional cross-gable types with Eastlake or Queen Anne decorative elements, though the **Burgwyn-Lamb House** (1886; 305 Burwell Ave.) is of simplified Italianate villa form.

East of downtown, the residential area around **Charles St.**, **Andrews Ave.**, and **Rowland St.** (**c**) presents varied turn-of-the-century house types, most notably the **Stainback House** (1890s; 222 Charles St.), a fully realized Queen Anne dwelling, and the mansard-roofed **James R. Thrower House** (ca. 1886; 144 Clark St.), built by the railroad architect as his residence. The porticoed, brick **Samuel T. Peace House** (1938; Courtney S. Welton [Norfolk], architect; J. W. York, Raleigh, builder) at 238 Andrews Ave. is the town's major late Colonial Revival residence. **Henderson High School** (1935–36; Eric G. Flannagan; Charles St.) is a large, distinctive school from the Works Progress Administration era, a richly detailed building with Flemish-bond brickwork and cast Tudor trim. Near the southern edge of town is an unexpected **Modernist House** (ca. 1947; w side Andrews Ave.) (**d**), a stuccoed, geometric composition with flat roof and ribbon windows virtually identical to the #Benjamin Mills Jr. House in Weldon and the *Lloyd House in Durham. Their published design source remains unidentified.

North of downtown, the **Henderson Institute Library and Laboratory Building** (1928; Rock Spring St.) (e) is a 2-story brick building with modest Colonial Revival detail, the principal surviving structure of the Henderson Industrial & Normal Institute opened in 1887 by the Freedmen's Mission Board of the United Presbyterian Church, which served as a private, then public school until the early 1970s.

VN 3 St. John's Episcopal Church

1773; John Lynch, builder; N side SR 1329, 0.1 mi. W of NC 39, Williamsboro; open Sunday summer hours

The heart of a wealthy plantation community, Williamsboro was an important inland town during the Colonial and early Federal periods, but it declined after it was bypassed by the R&GRR. The chief landmark is the fine, carefully restored Anglican church. St. John's is one of only three intact colonial church buildings in N.C., the only one in the Piedmont, and the only one of frame construction. The straightforward, gable-fronted structure is covered with molded weatherboards; it has a well-crafted Flemish-bond brick foundation, modillion cornice, and paneled double entrance doors in the west end. The bright interior, typifying the auditory Anglican church model, has an arched ceiling, original gallery with turned posts, and boxed pews; the side pulpit and sounding board date from the 1950s restoration. The specifications and contract (1771) between the vestry and carpenter Lynch survive. (See Introduction, Fig. 11.)

Among the nearby plantation houses, **Sneed's Mansion** (early to mid-19th c.; N side SR 1329, 0.2 mi. W of NC 39), is a Greek Revival frame house that incorporates an earlier dwelling, while the **Fain-Ivey House** (late 18th, mid-19th c.; N side SR 1329, 0.8 mi. W of NC 39) comprises a rear Georgian house and front Greek Revival one, linked by a hyphen.

VN 4 Burnside

Ca. 1800; ca. 1820; Williamsboro vic.; private, no public visibility or access

One of the Piedmont's most elegantly finished Federal period houses, the 2-story, double-pile frame house was evidently built ca. 1800 for planter John Jones and remodeled for Dr. Thomas Hunt with elaborate mantels and molded plaster. Notable is an early smokehouse with hand-riven clapboards.

VN 5 Pool Rock

1820s; ca. 1853, Jacob Holt, builder (attrib.); N side SR 1380, 1.5 mi. E of NC 39, Williamsboro vic.; private, visible from road

In this vivid pairing of eras, two discrete 2-story frame houses stand one in front of the other, joined with a hyphen. The older rear block, built for planter James Taylor, is a gable-roofed house with hall-parlor plan, Flemish-bond brick chimneys, and Federal style finish. In front, the house probably built for Taylor's daughter Mary Elizabeth follows a center-passage plan and has a low hip roof and broad form, with the Holt school's Greek Revival–Italianate signature elements including bracketed cornice and arch-filled windows.

VN 5 *Pool Rock*

VN 6 LaGrange

Early, mid-19th c.; N side SR 1308, 0.8 mi. E of NC 39, Williamsboro vic.; private, visible from road (B&B)

In one of many expansions in the Holt school, the Royster family built the main house with center-passage plan, bracketed cornice, and other eclectic details while making the earlier Robards family house into a rear wing.

VN 7 *Ashland*

VN 7 Ashland

*Late 18th c., early 19th c.; W side SR 1319,
1.7 mi. N of SR 1308, Williamsboro vic.;
private, visible from road*

Among the most famous of the county's
plantation houses, Ashland's two generations of building stand side by side. The
small 18th-c. north section is associated with
Richard Henderson (buried here), the judge
and political leader whose Transylvania Co.
sponsored Daniel Boone's Kentucky explo-
rations. When the large south wing with
side-passage plan was added, the two sections were unified with simplified Greek Revival trim.

VN 8 Pleasant Hill (Rivenoak)

*Late 18th c., ca. 1850s; E side SR 1371,
0.8 mi. N of US 1/158, Middleburg vic.;
private, visible from road*

The tall, imposing, late Georgian house
with double-pile plan is one of the largest of
its era in the region. When it was remodeled
in simple Greek Revival style, the form, proportions, and some original finish (chiefly
the rear facade) remained, including handsome Flemish-bond chimneys with glazed
headers and chevron patterns. The plantation house was built for Revolutionary
leader Philemon Hawkins Jr. and Mary

Davis, who married in 1776. Their son William, probably born here, became governor
(1811–14).

VN 9 Weldon's Mill

*Late 19th c.; W side SR 1526, 0.1 mi. N of
SR 1529; private, visible from road*

One of the few gristmills left in the county,
the 2-story frame mill on Sandy Creek retains its overshot wheel, original stone dam,
and quiet rural setting.

VN 10 Bobbitt Store

*Late 19th c.; SW corner SR 1549 and SR 1519,
Bobbitt; private, visible from road*

The intact and unusually elaborate country
store has paneled shutters protecting the first

VN 8 *Pleasant Hill (Rivenoak)*

floor shop windows. The second story, which contains dwelling space, is covered with weathered wood shingles.

VN 11 St. James Episcopal Church

Ca. 1872; NE corner SR 1551 and SR 1555, Kittrell

The Carpenter Gothic church in board and batten recalls the lasting popularity of Richard Upjohn's *Rural Architecture* among Episcopalians. At its consecration in 1878 the bishop commented, "The addition of a recess chapel, front porch and belltower has greatly improved the building." Kittrell, site of a 19th-c. winter resort and later home to Kittrell College, centered a once wealthy plantation neighborhood.

VN 12 Thomas Capehart House

Late 1860s; Kittrell vic.; no public visibility

The asymmetrical gabled cottage with board-and-batten walls, ornate bargeboards, and pointed-arched windows epitomizes the Downingesque cottage mode that gained popularity in the immediate postwar years. It was built for a Confederate veteran and farmer and may be related to picturesque *St. James Church nearby.

VN 12 *Thomas Capehart House*

VN 15 *Ashburn Hall*

VN 13 Josiah Crudup House

Ca. 1830s, ca. 1900; W side US 1, 1.0 mi. N of SR 1552, Kittrell vic.; private, visible from road

The unusual house began as a Federal period tripartite design, built for a planter, Baptist minister, and legislator. A turn-of-the-century expansion raised the wings to two stories and repeated the Federal motifs.

VN 14 Raleigh & Gaston Railroad Bridge Piers

1839; S side SR 1552, 0.2 mi. E of US 1 at Tar River

The R&GRR was built from north to south and reached Raleigh in 1840. Five wooden bridges carried iron-covered wooden rails across the Roanoke, the Tar, the Neuse, and two creeks; all were Town-truss, covered bridges set on handsome, tapered piers of large granite blocks. At the Tar River, one pier stands clear, and the second protrudes above the earth fill of the most recent bridge. These great granite pylons (and others at Crabtree Creek, Raleigh, and less accessible sites) are evidently the oldest railroad structures in the state (cf. NCRR piers, *Haw River, Alamance Co.).

VN 15 Ashburn Hall

Ca. 1840s; NE corner SR 1101 and SR 1100, Kittrell vic.; private, visible from road

The Greek Revival plantation house was built for the Eaton family and after 1862 was the home of planter Baldy Ashburn Capehart. Unusual features include pedimented bay windows flanking the broad entrance portico and exposed-face interior end chimneys, a type seen chiefly in New Bern. Two 19th-c. frame barns and a meathouse and other outbuildings remain on the well-maintained farm.

Granville County (GV)

See Marvin A. Brown and Andrew J. Carlson, Heritage and Homesteads: The History and Architecture of Granville County, North Carolina *(1988).*

Authorized by the colonial assembly in 1746 as a vast precinct at the western edge of the colony, the county was named for Lord Granville, who retained the proprietary tract that extended across the northern half of N.C. Its progeny included many counties, including Orange (1752) and its offspring and present-day Franklin, Warren, and Vance. Plantations established in the mid-18th c. on the rich clay soils of the northern sector yielded abundant wheat, corn, and tobacco. Located within the Old Belt tobacco zone and oriented to Virginia markets, Granville became the state's top tobacco-producing county, with a large number of slaves raising nearly 4 million pounds of the leaf in 1840 and more than 6 million in 1860.

After the Civil War, tobacco farmers exceeded prewar production levels, and the county became a leader in flue-cured bright-leaf tobacco, which thrived in the "lean," sandy soil of southern Granville. Local tobacconists worked to improve methods of growing, curing, and marketing the leaf and pioneered the crop in eastern N.C. as an alternative to cotton. Ironically, the "New Belt" expansion created such competition that Granville lost its dominance. Despite this and a tobacco disease called the "Granville wilt," the county continues as a major tobacco-producer, with a rural landscape of many farmhouses, barns, and log tobacco barns.

Oxford (GV 1–6)

The town's architectural heritage reflects its development from antebellum county seat to early 20th-c. tobacco sales and manufacturing center. The county seat was established in 1764 on the "Oxford" plantation of Samuel Benton, who donated an acre for the courthouse; in 1811 the county purchased 50 acres for a town from the succeeding landowner, Thomas Blount Littlejohn, and a few houses date from this time. Touted in 1830 as "decidedly the most beautiful village" in the state, Oxford prided itself on its academies and other social and cultural advantages. Its fortunes rose with the tobacco planters' wealth, lapsed after the Civil War, and then rebounded as a tobacco market competing with Virginia.

Especially after the 1880s construction of railroad links to Henderson and Durham, the community blossomed. An 1885 promoter of the "Future Metropolis of the Golden Tobacco Belt" claimed that "Oxford, noted time far back for the excellence of its schools, healthfulness and its cultivated society," had now "added to the advantages a tobacco market that ranks among the most important in North Carolina." With a "continual influx of people," "lofty buildings loom up where it was thought houses would never be built," and many houses were "thoroughly renovated and made to look like new." In the 20th c., however, Durham emerged as the tobacco metropolis, while Oxford remained a primarily local trading center with much of the scale of the 19th and early 20th centuries.

GV 1 Downtown Oxford

The business district radiating along Main, Williamsboro, Hillsboro, and College Sts. retains 2- and 3-story commercial buildings from the 1880–1930 era. The centerpiece and oldest building is the **Granville County Courthouse** (1838–40, John Walthall, builder; 1891 additions, Charles E. Hartge; SE corner Main and Williamsboro Sts.), one of the few antebellum courthouses in the state still

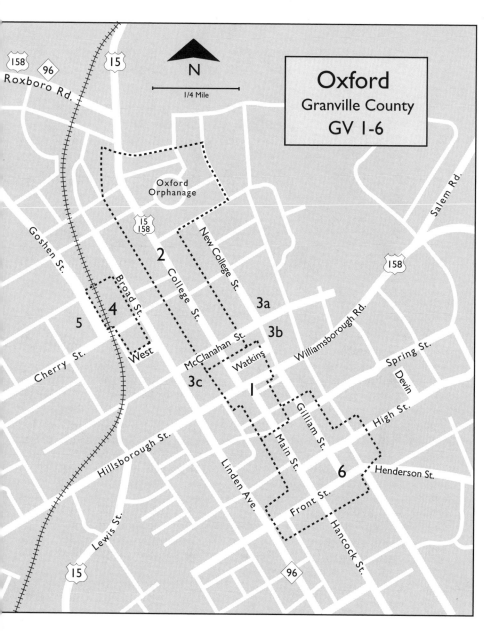

Oxford
Orphanage

Roxboro Rd.

Goshen St.

Broad St.

College St.

New College St.

McClanahan St.

Watkins

Williamsborough Rd.

Salem Rd.

Spring St.

Devin

High St.

West

Cherry St.

Hillsborough St.

Gilliam St.

Main St.

Linden Ave.

Front St.

Henderson St.

Lewis St.

Hancock St.

2

4

5

3a

3b

3c

1

6

serving its original purpose. It is a conservative 2-story building with hip roof and central entrance pavilion, built of brick laid in
Flemish bond and finished with Greek Revival trim and a domed cupola. From the
lobby, 2 curving stairs rise to the courtroom.
The adjoining former **Granville County
Jail** (ca. 1858) is a simple 2-story brick structure serving as a local museum.

Among the notable commercial buildings on Main St. is the **Granville Furniture
Co.** (1885, ca. 1905; 117 Main St.), an ornate
commercial block with arched windows, pilasters, and a corbeled cornice, possibly the
work of architect Charles E. Hartge. The
former **U.S. Post Office** (1913; 145 Main St.)
is a Beaux Arts classical building in red brick
with a dominant Doric portico. **Oxford
Baptist Church** (1928; 147 Main St.) is also
of red brick with a Tuscan portico and tower.

GV 1 *Granville Co. Courthouse and downtown Oxford*

On Williamsboro St. stands a section of the former **National Bank of Granville** (1891; 107 Williamsboro St.), a Richardsonian Romanesque structure in rough-faced stone blocks. The **Orpheum Theatre** (1943; 129 Williamsboro St.) shows a simple Moderne style. Around the corner, the former **Union Bank & Trust Co.** (1913; 108 College St.) takes the characteristic Beaux Arts vault form, with tall pilasters and entablature.

In a small industrial zone northwest of the commercial area, the **R. C. Watkins & Son Barn** (ca. 1910; 108 Watkins St.), a gambrel-roofed brick building, survives from the mule- and horse-trading enterprises once essential to town and country. The nearby **Oxford Buggy Co.** (ca. 1920; 113 Watkins St.), a barnlike frame structure sheathed in brick-patterned metal, housed the blacksmith and woodworking shops of a buggy manufacturer, and after 1935 it was owned by the Watkins family.

GV 2 College Street

The broad, shaded avenue north of downtown ranks among the most beautiful residential thoroughfares in the state. Originally Grassy Creek St., it was renamed for St. John's College (est. 1853). Houses and churches from the 19th and early 20th centuries range from Federal style residences to

Second Empire, Italianate, Queen Anne, and Colonial Revival modes. Built for tobacconists and other industrialists, bankers, lawyers, doctors, and planters, they stand in regular, spacious order beneath great trees.

Anchoring the south end of the avenue, **St. Stephen's Episcopal Church** (1895–1901; Silas McBee [N.Y.], architect; 140 College St.), built to replace an 1833 structure, is an especially fine late 19th-c. Gothic Revival church, a prime work in the state by Silas McBee, a native of Lincolnton who became a noted church architect and editor of the *New York Churchman*. In the spirit of the Early English Gothic parish church, its simple, massive forms are beautifully rendered in rough-tooled blocks of rosy Sanford

GV 2 *College St.*

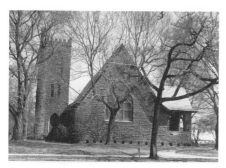

GV 2 *St. Stephen's Episcopal Church*

brownstone, and pointed-arched openings are cut cleanly into the thick walls. The cruciform church presents a broad gable to the street, with an entry porch on the south and a dramatic 3-story tower recessed on the north. The liturgical interior continues the Gothic Revival character in dark wood, with an X truss roof and raised chancel. The intricate Gothic Revival rood screen was carved ca. 1901–3 by rector Robert Bruce Owen from "a design furnished by the architect of the church, Mr. McBee of New York." Over the altar, three beautiful stained glass windows are believably attributed to Tiffany or a follower. Across the street at the **Oxford Methodist Church** (1895–1905; Charles E. Hartge, architect (attrib.); sw corner College and W. McClanahan Sts.), corbeled and molded red brick emphasizes robust and varied forms, especially the 2 entrance towers; the shorter one is polygonal, while the taller one rises from a polygonal base through a cylindrical shaft to a polygonal belfry. The auditorium plan sanctuary retains its original woodwork with incised Eastlake details and a coffered ceiling (#First Methodist Church, Washington, N.C.).

One of the oldest houses in town is the **Taylor-McClanahan-Smith House** (ca. 1817 and later; 203 College St.), which began as a 2-story, side-passage plan dwelling with Flemish-bond chimneys and Federal style finish (including a stair akin to that built by Raleigh carpenter John J. Briggs at *Fairntosh). It was built for William W. Taylor, a physician who served on the *Constitution* during the War of 1812, and his wife Frances Henderson. Later expanded to a symmetrical center-passage form, it eventually gained

a decorated porch. **The Villa** (1889; 208 College St.) is the only Second Empire style house in town, of brick with a central tower. The **C. G. Credle School** (1911; Linthicum & Rose [Durham], architects; 223 College St.) is a symmetrical Colonial Revival composition in brick with an Ionic portico. Among many other renditions of the Colonial Revival is the **C. D. Ray House** (1911; 404 College St.), with full-height Tuscan portico. Queen Anne and Eastlake modes blend in the **Hundley-Cannady House** (1880s; 517 College St.), with geometric boarding and other Eastlake decoration akin to the *Thomas White House. The **Crews-Turner House** (1920s; 709 College St.), a foursquare, brick house with Craftsman porch and porte cochere, was built by local contractor Walter Crews as his own home.

The **Oxford Orphanage** (College St.) traces back to the Masonic-sponsored St. John's College, with its Main Building (1855–58; Jacob W. Holt [Warrenton] and John Berry [Hillsborough], contractors; razed mid-20th c.) of eclectic Gothic Revival style. The school closed during the Civil War, and in 1873 the Masons opened the orphanage. Campus architecture is mainly red brick, simplified Colonial Revival work.

GV 3 Mary Potter School Shop, Shaw House, and Timothy Darling Presbyterian Church

Early 20th c.; E. & W. McClanahan St.

Buildings east and west of College St. recall the accomplishments of educator Dr. George C. Shaw. Born a slave in Louisburg, he attended Lincoln University and Auburn Theological Seminary in Auburn, N.Y., then returned to found an academy and high school named for a Presbyterian donor in N.Y. Until the 1930s it was the county's only high school for blacks. Of the once extensive campus, the chief reminders are the gable-fronted brick **Shop** (201 E. McClanahan St.) (**a**) and the **Dr. George C. and Mary E. Shaw House** (1921; 202 E. McClanahan St.) (**b**), a brick bungalow. West of College St., the **Timothy Darling Presbyterian Church** (1906; se corner W. McClanahan and Broad Sts.) (**c**), a Gothic Revival building with entrance tower, was built in frame, then brick-veneered, for a congregation organized in 1888 by Dr. Shaw and named for a teacher at Auburn.

GV 4 Tobacco Industrial Area

Near the railroad northwest of the business district are the last of Oxford's great tobacco buildings. The **Imperial Tobacco Co. Building** (ca. 1880s; NW corner Broad and West Sts.), an imposing 3½-story brick building with arched doors and windows, was built as a prize house and accompanied by other buildings in the early 20th c. Here Imperial (cf. Durham) redried, packed, and stored tobacco, then loaded it into railcars bound for Norfolk for shipment to Britain. Across the tracks, the **Export Leaf Tobacco Co. Building** (1920s; 220 Cherry St.) is a long, 2-story railside building used for similar purposes. Several blocks of frame houses extend from the industrial sector, with 1- and 2-story dwellings from the late 19th and early 20th centuries.

GV 5 Booth-Bryant-Kingsbury House
Ca. 1817; 417 Goshen St.

The 7-bay, 2-story dwelling has a pedimented center section, like other tripartite houses of the era, and Georgian-Federal detailing akin to *Ayr Mount near Hillsborough. Tradition says it was built for Thomas Booth, who bought it in 1817 from Thomas Littlejohn; an 1817 letter shows Littlejohn employing Raleigh carpenter John J. Briggs (*Ayr Mount, *Fairntosh) for a house in Oxford—perhaps this one. Extensive Colonial Revival changes were made ca. 1910 when the house was moved from its position at the north head of Main St.

GV 6 South Main St.–Front St. Residential Area

Blocks south of downtown present a variety of styles and eras. The **Thomas White Jr. House** (1889; W. C. Bain [Durham and Greensboro], builder; 203 S. Main St.) is an intricately adorned Eastlake–Queen Anne style house by a prolific Piedmont architect-

builder. The Southern Colonial style recurs in the **Hall House** (1913; 221 Main St.), with full-width portico of tall Doric columns; the **Lassiter House** (1908; 221 Gilliam St.), with Ionic portico overlapping a long porch; and the **Royster House** (ca. 1900; Charles Barrett [Raleigh], architect; Raleigh St.), a Queen Anne–Colonial hybrid featured in the architect's *Colonial Southern Homes*. Notable Craftsman style houses include the **Stem House** (ca. 1913; 104 E. Front St.), lifetime home of noted local writer Thad G. Stem Jr. The **Rogers House** (19th c., ca. 1903; Charles E. Hartge, architect; 115 E. Front St.) is one of the few houses credited to Hartge, who remade an earlier house into a bungalow with classical columns. The **Currin House** (ca. 1890s; 213 High St.), in Queen Anne style with orange tile roof, domed tower, and pergola, was built for tobacco buyer James Madison Currin. Originally beyond the town was the **Joseph B. Littlejohn House** (ca. 1819 and later; 219 Devin St. at High St.), which began as a 2-story, side-passage plan house with Flemish-bond chimney and was soon enlarged to a symmetrical, center-passage dwelling; it was evidently built for Joseph Blount Littlejohn and his wife Anne Maria Jones, daughter of political leader Willie Jones of Halifax. Littlejohn, a lawyer from Edenton, bought the property in 1819 from his brother Thomas.

GV 7 Knott's Grove Baptist Church
Dedicated 1867; Jacob Holt school; N side SR 1607, 0.2 mi. W of NC 96, Oxford vic.

Rendered in a local Italianate mode, the gable-fronted frame church was built in town as the Oxford Methodist Church; replaced by 1900, it was moved to serve a new congregation. Like *Salem Methodist Church, it has sawnwork and distinctive acorn-tipped brackets at the cornice, corner pilasters, and inset entrance porch.

GV 8 Central Orphanage
Est. 1882, buildings 1913–30s; SR 1606 at SR 1650, Oxford vic.

Begun by two black Baptist churches as the Colored Orphanage Asylum, the pioneering

GV 8 *Cheatham Building*

the needs, pests, and diseases of tobacco. Expansion in 1938 made it the largest such facility in the nation. The centerpiece **Office and Laboratory** (1939) is a red brick edifice in a Palladian format with elaborate classical detail, curiously suggestive of idealized colonial plantation houses.

institution has provided children with shelter, education, and vocational training for well over a century. Superintendent Robert Shepard, a Baptist minister born a slave, gained support for the institution from churches, fraternal orders, the legislature, and Benjamin Duke of Durham. Notable brick structures date from the early 20th-c. tenure of Shepard's successor Henry Plummer Cheatham, also born in slavery, who served as a U.S. congressman (1889–93). The chief landmark is the **Henry Plummer Cheatham Building** (1915), an imposing brick building with simplified Romanesque motifs and a tall central entrance tower.

GV 9 Oxford Tobacco Research Center
1938, est. 1910; NW side SR 1004, at SR 1195

In 1910 a joint venture of the U.S. and N.C. departments of agriculture established at Oxford a tobacco research center to study

GV 10 Puckett Farm
Ca. 1899–early 20th c.; E side SR 1333, 0.5 mi. N of SR 1304, Satterwhite vic.; private, visible from road

The archetypal small tobacco farmstead has remained in the same family since Joseph and Delia Hobgood Puckett bought the property about 1889 and built the house some ten years later. Typically modest farm buildings constitute the agricultural complex where they raised much of their own food as well as tobacco for the market. The simply finished farmhouse is a small version of the popular I-house with center passage; it has a front porch and rear kitchen-dining ell, which replaced an earlier separate kitchen. Nearby frame and log domestic outbuildings, include a washhouse, a well house, a chicken house, a corncrib, and others; beyond the garden is a frame stable and the privy. Near the road is a stand of four log tobacco barns, of diamond-notched construction, and a similarly built packhouse and striphouse, where the family processed the tobacco after curing.

GV 10 *Puckett Farm*

GV 11 Wilkerson Farm

Early 19th c.; NE side NC 96, 0.4 mi.
NW of SR 1415; private, visible from road

Hard by the road stands a small, sturdily built house typical of the many small and middling farmsteads of the late 18th and early 19th centuries. Evidently built and gradually enlarged for John and Elizabeth Wilkerson, the weatherboarded house has a log core heated by a massive stone chimney, plus front and rear shed rooms beneath a multislope gable roof. Frame and log tobacco barns stand to the south.

GV 12 Adoniram Masonic Lodge

1917; NW corner SR 1410 and SR 1300;
private, visible from road

Built to replace an antebellum lodge (est. 1852) that burned in 1917, the 2-story frame building resembles an I-house form and had schoolrooms below and a lodge above. Along with churches, stores, and mills, such institutions were once centers in rural life.

GV 13 Carrington House

Ca. 1900; S side SR 1436, 1.0 mi. W of
SR 1431, Grassy Creek vic.; private, visible
from road

The classic farmhouse of the late 19th and early 20th centuries is the 2-story frame dwelling 1 room deep, with a wide, decorative front porch, a rear ell or shed, and a gable rising at the center of the front roofline. This handsome version was built for Luther and Elizabeth Watkins Carrington on their middle-sized farm, not far from the old Amis-Dalton Mill on Grassy Creek, which Luther operated with his father. (See Introduction, Fig. 41.)

GV 14 Rose Hill

Ca. 1830s; E side SR 1442, 1.1 mi. N of
SR 1400, Grassy Creek vic.; private, visible
from road

The only antebellum brick house in the county, the Greek Revival plantation dwelling shares the symmetrical, hip-roofed form and broad proportions of local boom-era architecture. Thick walls are laid in 1:5 com-

mon-bond brick, accented by shallow pediments atop the windows. The classical porch dates from the early 20th c. Akin to houses in nearby Virginia, the dwelling was built for John Joseph and Ann Jones Speed from Mecklenburg Co., Va. (*Speed Farm, Franklin Co.).

GV 15 Red Hill

Late 18th–early 19th c.; S side SR 1501,
0.8 mi. E of US 15; private, visible from road

One of the few surviving of northern Granville's early plantation houses, the restored house presents an unusual sequence of three distinct early house types built side by side in telescope fashion. The initial (central) section, with gambrel roof and shed dormers, was evidently built in the 1770s for Jacob Mitchell, a planter from Mecklenburg Co., Va., on his 1,000-acre plantation. Finished in simplified Georgian style, it has 2 rooms, front to back, heated by an interior chimney with corner fireplaces. About 1800 it gained a 1-story wing on the east, and a few years later came the 2-story gable-roofed west section with side-passage plan and Federal style finish.

GV 15 *Red Hill*

GV 16 Salem Methodist Church

1860–61; John Short, builder (attrib.);
school of Jacob W. Holt; NW side SR 1522,
0.2 mi. N of SR 1521, Oxford vic.

The eclectic little frame church combines a Greek Revival style pedimented gable front and corner pilasters; Italianate brackets with acornlike pendants at the cornice, entrance, and pilasters; and Gothic and Greek Revival

GV 16 *Salem Methodist Church*

interior finish—a combination characteristic of Warrenton builder Holt. John Short, enslaved carpenter of a church supporter, is credited as builder.

GV 17 Taylor House
Early 19th c.; S side SR 1524, 0.3 mi. E of SR 1521, Huntsboro vic.; private, visible from road

The county's sole example of the pediment-fronted house was built for Richard and Martha Taylor in Federal–Greek Revival style. It follows the characteristic cross passage plan with two rear parlors. Wings date from various eras. Notable among the outbuildings is a tall frame barn for air-curing tobacco—the method that predated the flue-cured method.

GV 18 Bobbitt-Rogers House
1850s; N side SR 1129, 0.6 mi. E of SR 1635, Wilton vic.; private, visible from road

The 2-story Greek Revival plantation house has typically broad proportions, a hip roof, and a wide porch with slim, cutout pillars, raised on a high basement. It was built for Rufus and Matilda Bobbitt and descended

to daughter Luna and her husband Thomas Rogers.

GV 19 Brassfield Baptist Church
1840s; NE corner NC 96 and SR 1700, Wilton vic.

The oldest church building in the county, home of a congregation formed ca. 1823, is an unpretentious, gable-fronted structure with simple Greek Revival details.

GV 20 Lawrence Farm
Ca. 1840s; NW side SR 1700, 1 mi. W of NC 96; private, visible from road

Typifying the broad proportions and robust Greek Revival detail of antebellum plantation houses, the hip-roofed house follows a T-plan and has a wide 1-story front porch with fluted pillars. Outbuildings include a Greek Revival kitchen and smokehouse, later tobacco barns, and a stable. Center of John and Frances Lawrence's plantation in 1850, the place remained in the family.

GV 21 Allen-Mangum House
1840s (rear), ca. 1880 (front); S side SR 1700, 2.6 mi. W of NC 96, Creedmoor vic.; private, visible from road

The most richly decorated of the many tri-gabled I-houses in the region, the frame farmhouse is a marvel of delicate millwork skillfully applied to emphasize its essential components. Brackets and fancy battens define the gabled roofline, tiny brackets cap the corner pilasters, and the porch is glorified by fleur-de-lis cresting and lacy swags and balustrades. Bearing some resemblance to *Salem and *Knotts Grove churches, it

GV 18 *Bobbitt-Rogers House*

GV 21 *Allen-Mangum House*

was probably built for farmer H. D. Mangum as a front addition to the smaller house of Joseph and Julia Allen.

GV 22 Winston Farm

19th c.; N side SR 1638, 0.8 mi. E of NC 15, Creedmoor vic.; private, visible from road

The farmstead possesses a full complement of farm buildings of types once numerous in the county. The simply detailed, 2-story Greek Revival dwelling was built in two phases by Obediah and Permelia Winston, who owned some 500 acres. Domestic outbuildings include a 19th-c. log kitchen with stone chimney, used before the kitchen ell was added to the house in the early 20th c.;

a frame potato house; a smokehouse; and a stable. There are also a frame packhouse and tobacco barn from the late 19th c., a small tenant house, and various 20th-c. tobacco barns and sheds.

GV 23 Creedmoor

Once famed as the "Mule Capital of N.C.," the little railroad town supplied thousands of mules to pull plows and sleds on local tobacco farms. Begun in the 1880s, it is said to have started as Need More, then toned up its name. With the mule barns gone, the chief landmark of that era is the **First National Bank** (1912; Main St.), a 2-story, tan brick building with round-arched openings.

Person County (PR)

Occupying the hilly divide between the Dan, Neuse, and Tar rivers in an area settled in the mid-18th c. by English and African people and a few Scots, the county formed from eastern Caswell in 1791 was named for Gen. Thomas Person, Revolutionary leader. As part of the Old Belt border area, its farmers have grown tobacco since colonial times. Tobacco plantations prospered, and by 1860 the county was one of four in the Piedmont with over half of its population as slaves. Following long economic stagnation after the Civil War, the late (1890) arrival of the railroad aided access to markets and some industrial growth. It remains an agricultural county, with Roxboro the only incorporated town.

PR 1 Roxboro

Named after Roxburgh County in Scotland, the county seat was established in 1793 at the center of the new county. It was incorporated in 1855 during the bright-leaf tobacco boom. After local entrepreneurs obtained a rail line in 1890—the Lynchburg & Durham Railroad, soon part of the Norfolk & Western—the local paper exulted, "Hurrah for Roxboro, She Is at Last Connected with the Outside World." James Long, a businessman instrumental in getting the rail link, opened a tobacco sales warehouse and a bank within months of the arrival of the first train and led the establishment of the *Roxboro Cotton Mill in 1899. The frame commercial district was rebuilt with brick tobacco warehouses, stores, hotels, and banks; growth continued through the 1920s.

In the business district, buildings of various styles recall the rebuilding era, chiefly the 1920s. The centerpiece is the **Person**

PR 1 *Person Co. Courthouse*

County Courthouse (1930; Charles Hartmann [Greensboro], architect; George W. Kane [Durham], builder; Courthouse Square), which succeeded an initial log structure; a handsome Neoclassical brick building (1824; John Berry [Hillsborough]); and a towered Victorian one (1883; Lyndon Swaim [Greensboro]). Hartmann's design blends familiar classicism with newer modernist trends in a rectangular, blond brick building. A hierarchy of base, pilasters, entablature, and attic, with large windows between paired pilasters, bears stylized classical and Art Deco motifs.

Neoclassical and modernist themes recur in other downtown buildings, along with many 2- and 3-story brick commercial structures of Italianate style. In an unusual variant of bank designs for key corners, the blond brick **First National Bank** (1913; 118 N. Main St.) has a curved corner entrance bay with arched opening framing a curved stair. The **Post Office and Rose's Store** (1911; 200 N. Main St.) at another corner features bold brickwork and classical detailing, repeated in neighboring red brick commercial buildings.

Two modernist buildings suggest the new spirit of the post–World War II era in venturesome form for a small town. The **Roxboro Building** (1949; George W. Kane, builder; 201 N. Main St.), erected as an office for the Roxboro Cotton Mills, has symmetrical, rectilinear massing and horizontal window bands of the International style, well detailed in stone, marble, aluminum,

PR I *First National Bank*

and steel. Next door, the **Kirby Theater** (1949; George W. Kane; 209–17 N. Main St.) presents a Moderne facade with original marquee and ticket booth. The most prominent downtown church is **Long Memorial United Methodist Church** (1920; 226 N. Main St.), a brick, twin-towered church with a fan-shaped auditorium plan.

Main St. has the town's principal concentration of stylish houses from the railroad era, with Italianate, Queen Anne, Colonial Revival, and bungalow stock plus several Craftsman style foursquare houses. The **James A. Long House** (ca. 1900; w side S. Main St. opp. Academy St.) is a big Queen Anne style house with a pair of massive turrets, built for a local farm boy and Civil War veteran, the "builder of modern Roxboro." The **Kitchin House** (1901; w side N. Main at Oak St.), a 2-story frame Colonial Revival house, was the home of Governor William W. Kitchin (1909–13) and houses the local history museum. Moved to the grounds are the **Dr. John H. Merritt Office** (ca. 1906, from Bethel Hill), a small, 4-room frame office with pyramidal roof, outfitted to recall the longtime country doctor's practice, and the frame **Brooks Store** (early 20th c., from Woodsdale).

The Long family brought textile manufacturing to Roxboro, with backing from Durham industrialists and local investors. East of downtown, south of Depot St. is the **Roxboro Cotton Mill and Village**, founded by James A. Long in 1899 and retaining its mill, church, school, and houses, modernized for continued use. The 1-story frame dwellings with pyramidal roofs, many with inset porches, were sold to workers ca. 1960. Success of this mill led to a second one. The **Longhurst Cotton Mill** (1906;

1914; E side US 501, N of downtown Roxboro), first called Jalong (after J. A. Long), is an intact 2-story brick mill by the railroad tracks, but little of its village remains.

Following in his father's footsteps, in 1923 J. A. Long Jr. lured to Roxboro A. T. Baker & Co., manufacturer of velvets and automotive upholstery. It merged with the national firm of Collins & Aikman in 1927, and the mill and village became Ca-Vel for Collins & Aikman Velvets. The **Ca-Vel Mill** (begun 1923; George W. Kane [Durham], builder; w side US 501), cited as the nation's largest maker of velour, was expanded a dozen times by the 1970s. On hillsides south of the mill along Edgewood Dr., Kerr Dr., and connecting streets is the intact **Ca-Vel Village** of the 1920s and 1930s; houses are mainly hip-roofed duplexes with shed porches under the front slope of the roof; others have pyramidal roofs and inset porches like those of *Roxboro Mill Village. North of the mill is the **Ca-Vel Executive Village** (ca. 1934; Executive Dr.), a group of nine 2-story frame, Colonial Revival houses built for office staff; such company-owned housing for white-collar workers is rare. The company sold off all the houses in the 1950s and 1960s. Baseball Hall of Fame legend Enos Slaughter worked at the mill in the 1930s and was playing for the Ca-Vel team when he was scouted by the St. Louis Cardinals.

PR 2 Tobacco Barns

Like its neighbors in the Old Belt, the county has a vanishing wealth of traditional late 19th- and early 20th-c. log tobacco barns. Seen in rows and clusters throughout the county, they follow the form common to the region: tall, windowless buildings typically 16 to 22 feet square. Often they feature one or more pent roofs carried on struts, and many have sheds to shelter workers and equipment. Log notching types include V and saddle notches. Such barns continued to be built into the mid-20th c. A few prominent groups are noted below at Gordonton, Hester's Store, and Olive Hill.

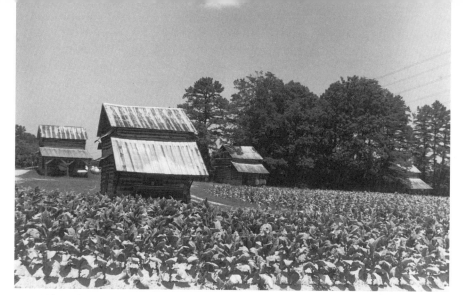

PR 2 *Tobacco barns*

PR 3 Woodsdale Depot
1894; W side NC 501, 2 mi. S of Roxboro

The small, picturesque depot, moved from the Norfolk & Western railroad village of Woodsdale, is a rare example of its type, complete with board-and-batten walls, zig-zag bands of shingles, delicate stick brackets, and openwork gable decorations. It serves as an office alongside a 1905 depot-restaurant from Clarksville, Va.

PR 4 Gordonton
Late 19th c.; jct. NC 49 and SR 1102

The crossroads on a busy road retains characteristic late 19th-c. tobacco-era buildings. The **Cates House** (late 19th c.; E side of NC 49, 0.5 mi. N of SR 1102) and **Baynes House** (S corner of NC 49 and SR 1102) both exemplify a local type, with a familiar 3-bay facade decked with bracketed eaves and other

PR 4 *Baynes House*

turned and sawn trim and, distinctive in the county, a 2-tier porch with a wraparound porch below a central, 1-bay upper porch with eccentric, decorated gable. A 2-story gable-fronted general store stands across the road from the Baynes House. On the west side of NC 49 is a large cluster of log **Tobacco Barns** (ca. 1900) for the Cates farm.

PR 5 Henry-Vernon House
1854, 1896; NW side NC 49, 0.2 mi. SW of SR 1171; private, visible from road in winter

Displaying two eras of construction, the Greek Revival, 3-bay I-house was built by tobacco farmer John H. Henry; after he died in 1895, his niece Corinna and her husband Charles Vernon added the fashionable Queen Anne front ell.

PR 6 Hester's Store Community
Mid- to late 19th c.; SR 1171 and SR 1162, NW of NC 49

Prosperous farmsteads define the rolling agricultural landscape around a crossroads long associated with the Hester family. There are substantial frame farmhouses, smaller tenant houses, and scores of outbuildings, including many log tobacco barns from the late 19th and early 20th centuries. Nicholas Hester settled in the late 18th c. in the area, where his many descendants continued to farm. An especially complete farmstead, still in the family, is the **L. C. Hester Farm** (1844 and later; w side SR 1171, 0.2 mi. S of SR 1162), which centers on a handsome residence with Italianate sawnwork, built for Nicholas's grandson, who served in the Civil War and the legislature. A 2-room kitchen–dining room is among the frame and log outbuildings. One of the log tobacco barns is dated 1891. The **Torrain House** (1822, mid-19th c.; E side SR 1102, 0.7 mi. N of SR 1162) began with a hall-parlor plan, 1½-story dwelling in simple Federal style, including a Flemish-bond brick chimney dated Nov. 27, 1822, then gained a 2-story section in Greek Revival style.

PR 7 Olive Hill–Concord–Long's Store Community

Mid-19th to early 20th centuries; NC 57, SR 1343, 1300, and 1310

The rural neighborhood northwest of Roxboro includes several interrelated farms with characteristic houses and outbuildings. **Concord Methodist Church** (1908; NW corner NC 57 and SR 1300), with entrance towers flanking the gabled facade, retains its basic form and strong presence despite later siding. Well-kept farmsteads are located along NC 57 south of the church. The **Kenneth Clyde Wagstaff House** (1924; E side

NC 57, 0.5 mi. S of SR 1300) is a large, handsome frame bungalow built for Wagstaff and his wife Betty Lou Hester; he raised cotton, tobacco, and grain and ran a cotton gin and a tobacco warehouse in town. The family maintains a nearby cluster of log tobacco barns. Across NC 57 is the **John H. Hester House** (late 19th c.; w side NC 57, 0.7 mi. S of SR 1300), which combines a symmetrical form with ornate millwork on the double porch and bracketed eaves. Numerous outbuildings include log tobacco barns. To the west is the **Charles Winstead House** (1885; N side 1343, 0.8 mi. w of NC 57) in Queen Anne style. At the crossroads village at SR 1343 and SR 1310 **Long's Store** epitomizes a type once central to rural life, a small frame structure with a shed porch, broad shop windows, inset entrance, and tall stepped parapet front. Gathered around the store are representative tenant houses with 1 main room, both 1 and 2 stories tall, some frame but several covered with the stucco seen here and in Caswell Co.; larger farmhouses, some with decorated triple-A rooflines; and log tobacco barns.

PR 8 Burleigh

Mid-19th c.; private, no public visibility

The plantation complex comprises a large frame house with center-passage plan and

PR 7 *Concord Methodist Church*

PR 9 *Waverly*

heavy stone chimneys, and restrained Georgian finish typify 18th-c. plantation houses in the region. It was built for planter John Holloway or his son James on the 500-acre farm that John left to his son in 1799. In 1847 planter and tobacco factory owner Jesse Walker bought the place and soon added a 2-story side-hall plan section with robust Greek Revival finish. In a recent renovation, a small, hall-parlor plan house (early 19th c.) was appended.

bold, simple Greek Revival porches and other elements, plus outbuildings including a very elegant privy with Ionic pilasters. Planter Thomas McGehee had inherited McGehee's Mill and a large plantation on Hyco Creek from his father.

PR 9 Waverly
1825–35; N side SR 1318, S of Va. line; private, visible from road

The finest Federal style house in the county was built for planter and merchant Alexander Cuningham of Virginia. Enriched with elaborate Adamesque detail, the main block follows a side-passage plan, with 2 additional rooms in the 1½-story wing. There are several early outbuildings. Named during the mid-19th-c. interest in Walter Scott's romantic novels, Waverly has descended in the family.

PR 10 Holloway-Walker House
Late 18th–early 19th c., mid-19th c.; private, no public visibility

One of many multistage farmhouses, it began as a 1½-story frame dwelling with 1 main room, plus chambers in the rear shed and upper half-story. The steep gable roof,

PR 11 Street House
Ca. 1848; NW side NC 49, just S of SR 1519; private, visible from road

Overlooking the highway is one of the county's many simple Greek Revival frame plantation houses featuring a pedimented porch with square pilasters. It was built for James H. Street, a tobacco planter with 1,200 acres, a mill, and a store across the road, now a dwelling. There are a well house and a laundry and several farm buildings.

PR 12 Mt. Tirzah
(Stephen Moore House)
Late 18th c., mid- and late 19th c.; E side SR 1717, 0.3 mi. N of SR 1715; private, visible from road

Known for its association with Revolutionary War officer Stephen Moore, the house (with stone dated 1778) was evidently built for Moore and his wife Griselda but evolved over the years to give a predominantly 19th-c. character. The long, L-shaped frame house with deep porches is built around the central stone chimney and stone cellar from the early house. Venerable trees and outbuildings enhance the sense of longevity.

Caswell County (CS)

See Ruth Little-Stokes, An Inventory of Historic Architecture: Caswell County, North Carolina *(1979).*

The green countryside has a distinctive architectural heritage from a long history of tobacco culture. In addition to grand antebellum "bright-leaf boom-era" architecture, Caswell Co. possesses a remarkable collection of small log and frame dwellings, outbuildings, and tobacco barns from the labor-intensive farming of the 18th c. into the mid-20th c. Formed from Orange Co. in 1777, then subdivided to create Person Co. in 1792, Caswell was central to the Old Belt tobacco zone along the Virginia border. Dan River navigation projects boosted trade and the tobacco market town of *Milton.

In Caswell in 1839 Stephen, slave of Abisha Slade, discovered by accident the sequence of heating that cured tobacco to a "bright" golden yellow color, and from Caswell the bright-leaf boom spread. As ownership of land and slaves coalesced and profits rose, grander plantation and town buildings were erected, and old ones were enlarged. Best-known of the county's artisans was Thomas Day, the free black cabinetmaker whose shop in Milton (*Union Tavern) produced architectural woodwork as well as furniture. After the Civil War, without good rail connections, Caswell's tobacco towns were outstripped by Reidsville, Durham, and Winston, but tobacco cultivation continued, as the multitude of late 19th and early 20th c. farmhouses, stores, and log tobacco barns attest.

Yanceyville (CS 1–11)

Established in 1791 as Caswell Court House at the center of the newly partitioned county, the town was dominated by the Graves family but named after local political figure Bartlett Yancey in 1833. It flourished in the antebellum era, with newspapers, cultural societies, hotels and taverns, tobacco factories, and shops and artisans producing fashionable coaches, furniture, hats, and other goods. Local men published articles on improvement of tobacco cultivation and curing. After the Civil War, the town built relatively little until the mid-20th c. Notable 19th-c. architecture concentrates around the courthouse square and along W. Main St.

CS 1 Former Caswell County Courthouse

1858; William Percival, architect; Courthouse Sq.

A grand gesture of county pride on the eve of the Civil War, Percival's exuberant, Ital-

ianate courthouse contrasts with other counties' sober temples of justice. It was erected after fire took its Greek Revival brick predecessor, built 1831–33 by John Berry of Hillsborough. Early in 1858 commissioners chose a plan by John Cosby, son of Raleigh builder Dabney, but by summer Percival had the job. His design won first prize for architectural drawing at the 1858 state fair, and a Raleigh newspaper marveled at "the beauty and magnificence of the new Court House to be erected in Yanceyville." Percival created a lively, three-dimensional composition with domed cupola and with arched central pavilions giving the effect of a villa or palazzo. Pilasters frame the arched windows of the main, upper story and carry an exaggerated corbeled cornice. An arcaded loggia opening from the second-story courtroom features pilasters with a suitably agricultural order of corn and tobacco (*Playmakers Theater, University of North Carolina). The grand courtroom retains its molded plaster ceiling, arched judges' niche, and cast-iron

CS 1 *Former Caswell Co. Courthouse*

brick laid in Flemish bond follows a center-passage plan, 2 rooms deep and features Greek key lintels and an entrance porch with urn-topped balustrade—evidently from Asher Benjamin's *Practical House Carpenter* (1830). Tradition credits Josiah Rucks as builder, though other possibilities include John Berry and Dabney Cosby.

CS 4 Graves Store
1830s; 28 W. Main St.

One of three pediment-fronted brick stores in the county, the building had a store below and living quarters above; it is believed to have been built for Azariah Graves, merchant and tannery owner.

railings. In 1870 the courthouse was the scene of the Klan murder of Republican John W. "Chicken" Stephens, which led Governor William Holden to put the county under military rule. In front stands the Confederate Monument (1921). To the rear is the former **Caswell County Jail** (late 19th c.), a 2-story brick structure with cells from Stewart Jail Works of Cincinnati.

CS 2 Graves-Poteat-Gatewood House
Ca. 1815 and later; North Ave.
at Courthouse Sq.

Growing with the town, the frame house began in the early 19th c. and in the mid-19th c. was the "Village Hotel . . . convenient to the courthouse." In the late 19th c. it gained a central raised gable, bracketed eaves, and decorated porch. In the 20th c. it was the home of the Gatewood family, including artist Maud Gatewood.

CS 3 Clarendon Hall
1842; Josiah Rucks, builder (attrib.);
53 W. Main St.

By 1860 Thomas Johnston, planter, merchant, and president of the Bank of Yanceyville, was the richest man in town, with assets of $161,000. His big 2-story house of

CS 4 *Graves Store*

CS 5 Kerr House
1840s; Josiah Rucks, builder (attrib.);
64 W. Main St.

The large brick house, 2 stories with a center-passage plan and 4 end chimneys, displays a Flemish variation of common bond and simple Greek Revival finish. After serving as an antebellum tavern, it was home of the politically active Kerr family.

CS 6 Martin House
Early 19th c.; 300 block W. Main St.

Typifying many small town houses of its era, the 1-story Federal style house, with Flemish-bond brick walls, has a hall-parlor plan and simple woodwork, plus bold mid-19th-c. elements.

CS 7 Turner-White Apartments

Ca. 1840, ca. 1930; 300 block W. Main St.

In the local tradition of overbuilding, this is unique: a 2-story, brick Greek Revival house transformed ca. 1930 into a white-stuccoed International style apartment house with curved entrance and glass block windows.

CS 8 Thornton House

Early 19th c.; 327 Main St.

The neatly finished frame house is among the oldest of the county's small dwellings. It has a 2-room plan plus additions, with corner fireplaces in a big end chimney and attic chambers beneath a steep gable roof.

CS 9 Dongola

1835–38; 336 W. Main St.

The most monumental house in the county, and one of the grandest in the Piedmont, Dongola was built for tobacco planter Jeremiah Graves and named for a town on the Nile. Architectural historian Thomas Waterman cited a kinship with houses in Virginia (cf. *High Rock, Rockingham Co.), but the builder is unidentified. The 2-story, L-shaped brick house features a tall portico of four unfluted Doric columns of stuccoed brick, an order favored by Asher Benjamin. Facades show an unusual hierarchy of treatments: broad triple windows, arched in the first story, define the front, while simpler openings occur elsewhere. Front and side walls are laid in Flemish bond, and the rear

is in common bond. The Doric cornice carries around only the front and street side.

CS 10 Yanceyville Presbyterian Church

1850; Alfred A. Mitchell, builder; Union and Harvey Sts.

The simple Greek Revival brick church has a crossetted entrance beneath a plastered pediment and two big windows on each side, which light a sanctuary with galleries on Doric columns. According to the minister's diary, the plan was drawn by Dr. Nathaniel Roan, local physician, and construction was done by Alfred A. Mitchell.

CS 11 Dr. Nathaniel Roan House

Ca. 1838, ca. 1850; N. 3rd at E. Main St.

The unusual 1½-story brick house combines Greek Revival elements with a picturesque gabled pavilion with bracketed porch and curvaceous bargeboards.

CS 12 Tobacco Barns

Ca. 1870–ca. 1940s

As part of the Old Belt tobacco-growing counties, Caswell has some of the state's oldest tobacco barns. They are generally of log construction and square in plan, often measuring about 16 by 16 feet, with diamond, square, half-dovetailed, saddle, or V notches. Pent roofs—sometimes as many as three tiers—supported by struts protect the walls and shelter storage and work areas. The now obsolete barns of Caswell and nearby counties form an extraordinary, fast-shrinking collection of flue-cure log tobacco barns

cs 9 *Dongola*

cs 12 *Tobacco barn*

from the late 19th c. onward. Prominent clusters are near NC 62, NC 119, and elsewhere. With their weathered logs and the clay daubing sharing the hue of the earth, these structures built to supply international corporations harmonize paradoxically with the natural landscape.

CS 13 Small Houses

Caswell's thickly settled rural landscape retains a remarkable number of small houses, from the 19th c. into the early 20th c. Especially numerous is the single-cell, 1/1 house—typically with 1 main room with a sleeping loft, though a few have a second story, plus rear shed rooms and an end chimney. Facade arrangements vary from a door alone to a door plus 1 or 2 windows. This form also appears in Rockingham and other Virginia border counties, in towns as well as on farms. They are built of frame or log, sometimes weatherboarded. Some were covered in tan stucco, probably in the 20th c., when an unidentified but enterprising stuccoist made his way through the area.

CS 13 *Typical small houses*

CS 14 Graves House

Late 18th c.; S side NC 62 (E. Main St.) at US 158/NC 86 E of Yanceyville; private, visible from road

The county's only intact tripartite house is rendered in severely plain Georgian style, with a 2-story front-gabled central block between 1-story wings. The property was owned in the 18th c. by planter Solomon Graves, who moved to Georgia ca. 1819 and sold the place to nephew Azariah, whose grave lies nearby.

CS 15 Poteat House

1855–56, 1928–29; N side NC 62, 1.2 mi. NE of NC 86; private, visible from road

Characteristic of the local Greek Revival, the 2-story frame house has a low hip roof, broad door and window openings, and a 2-story Doric entrance portico. It was built for planter James Poteat, whose children became prominent educators, including William L. Poteat, president of Wake Forest College and proponent of academic freedom. The house was restored and enlarged in the 1920s.

CS 16 Melrose

Early, mid-19th c.; NW side NC 62, 2.3 mi. NE of NC 86; private, visible from road

The pair of 2-story frame houses links two eras of family building. The plantation was established by James Williamson, sheriff and legislator in the late 18th c.; son George, also sheriff and legislator, became one of the county's largest planters. The rear hall-parlor plan section exemplifies the Federal style, while the ca. 1840 front part repeats its proportions in a Greek Revival mode. The Doric entrance portico was rebuilt in the 1930s.

CS 17 Johnston House

Early 19th c.; W side NC 62, 1.2 mi. S of SR 1597; private, visible from road

Moved and restored, the little frame house with steep roof, stone chimneys, and hall-parlor plan conveys the scale of homes of middling planters. It was built for John and Frances Donoho Johnston, who owned a few hundred acres; son Thomas became the richest man in Yanceyville (*Clarendon Hall).

CS 18 Longwood

Late 18th–early 19th c., 1850s; NW side NC 62, 0.8 mi. SW of NC 57, Milton vic.; private, visible from road

Like many others, the plantation house grew in stages. The 2-story, L-shaped form encompasses a small early dwelling, a 2-story Federal period house, and a Greek Revival expansion with pedimented porticoes. The farm complex also comprises a frame kitchen, a log corn crib, a log tenant house, and a log tobacco barn. Located near the line between the Donoho and Saunders lands, the house may have been home briefly to Romulus Saunders, congressman, judge, and minister to Spain.

Milton (CS 19–26)

The linear village has an evocative air of faded urbanity unmatched by any other N.C. community, with substantial and stylish 19th-c. buildings lining Broad and flanking streets. Located on a promontory overlooking Country Line Creek, the Dan River, and the Virginia line, Milton was founded in 1796 as a tobacco and flour inspection town to compete with Virginia. When early 19th-c. projects promised to open navigation to the Roanoke River and Albemarle Sound, a land boom was "flushed on by the madness of speculation." With warehouses, tobacco factories, a textile mill, and other industries, along with banks, schools, and artisans, Milton became a center for Dan River planters. It flourished through Caswell's tobacco heyday, but despite late 19th-c. rail links, it fell behind as new tobacco towns gained strength; its population dropped from 1,200 in 1860 to 235 in 1970.

CS 19 Clay-Irvine House
1820; NE corner Broad and Academy Sts.

Built for land speculator Henry M. Clay and later home of tobacco merchant Samuel Irvine, the big Federal style house stands on a large lot where a stone retaining wall encompasses an old boxwood garden.

CS 20 Milton Presbyterian Church
1837; N. Broad St.

The temple-form brick church opens to the street but accommodates the steep slope to the rear. The portico, among the earliest examples of the Greek Revival in the county, complements the Flemish-bond brickwork and fanlit entrance; it is tempting to credit John Berry, who built the 1831–33 court-

house and whose *Orange County Courthouse (1845) combines similar elements. The fine pews with curved arms were made by cabinetmaker Thomas Day, who with his wife Aquilla became a member in 1841.

CS 21 Winstead House
Ca. 1830; N side Broad St.

Another of Milton's impressive town houses follows a double-pile plan in brick laid in Flemish bond. An original brick kitchen stands in the yard.

CS 22 Union Tavern
Ca. 1818; S side Broad., between Lee St. and Farmer's Alley

Famed for its association with cabinetmaker Thomas Day, the 2-story brick building was built as a tavern during Milton's early heyday. It is rendered in elegant Federal style, with Flemish-bond facade and common bond elsewhere, a Doric cornice along the 6-bay front, and 3 fanlit entrances. The tavern run "in a genteel and comfortable manner" had a center passage dividing two large rooms, where arches supported partitions of the multichambered second floor. A 1989 fire gutted the building, which is under restoration. From 1848 to 1859 it was the residence and workshop of Thomas Day, freeborn black cabinetmaker from Virginia; his large shop of free and slave workers earned a regional reputation for fine work in an individualized Empire style. In addition to furniture for the region's elite, he produced distinctive curvilinear stair newels, mantels, and other elements for houses in the area. (See Introduction Fig. 16.)

CS 23 Milton State Bank
1859–63; N side Broad St.

Built as a branch bank of the State Bank of N.C., the building combined banking rooms (and a vault) entered from the street and the banker's residence served by a side porch. It continues the local preference for Flemish-bond brickwork with fashionable Italianate brackets. An original brick kitchen and other outbuildings stand to the rear.

CS 23 *Milton State Bank*

After the state bank closed in 1865, it housed other banks and is now a residence.

CS 24 Milton Commercial Buildings
Ca. 1880; N side Broad St.

The intact row of Victorian commercial buildings, with corbeled brickwork and arched openings, retains its shop windows and porches sheltering the sidewalk, evoking an earlier era of business.

CS 25 Milton Baptist Church
Ca. 1840; E side Bridge St., N of Broad St.

The gable-fronted Greek Revival church features Flemish-bond brickwork on the main facade and 1:5 common bond on sides and rear. Paired doors appear on the pedimented front, with Greek key lintels akin to those at *Clarendon Hall. The plastered panels on the sides are a feature seen more often in Virginia than in N.C.

CS 25 *Milton Baptist Church*

CS 26 Bridge St. Houses
Ca. 1840–50; N. and S. Bridge (Warehouse) St.

Three 1-story Greek Revival style houses, built on high basements with Italianate porches, recall riverport merchants and tradesmen. Most visible is the small **Oliver House** (NE corner Bridge and Broad Sts.); the **Gordon House** (E side of N. Bridge St.) was built for saloon operator Field Gordon; and the similar **Wooding House** (E side of S. Bridge St.), along with several outbuildings, was built for brickyard operator John Wooding.

CS 27 Woodside
Mid-19th c.; Thomas Day (attrib.); N side NC 57, 2 mi. E of Milton

The symmetrical Greek Revival house typifies the boom era, with low hip roof, entrance portico, and center-passage plan 1 room deep. The interior features woodwork in the style of Milton cabinetmaker Thomas Day: a spiral newel adorning the stair and a parlor mantel with curved frieze and engaged Ionic columns, flanked by arched niches. The house was built for Caleb Hazard Richmond and his wife Mary Dodson, who married in 1838; a native of Rhode Island, he ran a foundry, sawmill, and plow manufactory as well as a plantation.

CS 27 *Woodside*

CS 28 Red House Presbyterian Church
1913; SE side NC 119, 0.9 mi. S of NC 57

The eclectic Neoclassical Revival brick church, with stout columned portico, tile roof, and stained glass, was built for one of

CS 28 *Red House Presbyterian Church*

the county's oldest congregations, which began with the mid-18th-c. Hyco Presbyterian Church. Pioneering minister Hugh McAden, who served as pastor before the American Revolution, is buried here (cf. *McAdenville).

CS 29 Monroe Long House

1895; S side SR 1564 at SR 1565, Long's Mill

The large, stylish frame house is among the best-preserved Victorian houses from the post–Civil War era. It presents an L-plan form with ornate inset porch and bay window to the road, plus an equally elaborate front with center gable and porch. The farm is part of a rural community around Long's Mill, which extends along NC 119 and SR 1564 and 1565 and includes farmhouses of many eras, with log and frame agricultural buildings.

CS 30 Garland-Buford House

Ca. 1860; Thomas Day (attrib.); SE side SR 1561, 0.7 mi. NE of SR 1562

Epitome of antebellum exuberance, the 2-story frame plantation house is decked in

CS 30 *Garland-Buford House*

sawnwork, with bracketed roofline and entrance portico and bevies of scallops, even on the window muntins. Tradition says it was built for Milton physician John T. Garland, who left it unfinished when his wedding plans were canceled. The work has been attributed to Thomas Day.

CS 31 Leasburg

US 158, at SR 1702 and SR 1561

Once a political, trade, and educational center, the linear village along US 158 was settled in the mid-18th c. by the Lea family from Virginia and served as county seat from 1777 until the division of the county in 1792. Called "Sweet Leasburg" by the late 19th c., the pretty village then had 18 white frame houses, 4 stores, picket fences, and boxwood-bordered walks. It still recalls earlier times, with large and small frame houses facing the (widened) road, showing one or more phases of Federal, Greek Revival, Italianate, and Queen Anne modes. Unusual is the little **Drummer's House** (ca. 1860, s side 158) built for traveling salesmen. The **Solomon Lea House** (early 19th c., w side SR 1561, N of US 158), a small dwelling with Greek Revival doorway, was the home of a 19th-c. Methodist minister and educator who was first president of *Greensboro Female College and founded Leasburg's Somerville Female Institute. Just N of town the **Lea-Newman House** (ca. 1838; E side SR 1561, 0.2 mi. N of US 158) is a well-preserved Federal–Greek Revival style 1½-story house with early outbuildings.

CS 32 Grier's Presbyterian Church

1856; N side SR 1710, 0.6 mi. E of NC 119, Frogsboro

Serene in its oak grove, the quintessential frame country church has a single entrance in the gable front, with two tall, broad 12/12 windows on each side, adorned only with crossetted Greek Revival moldings (*Yanceyville Presbyterian Church). The congregation, oldest in the county, traces back to the 1753 Upper Hyco Meeting, where Hugh McAden served later in the 18th c.

cs 33 *Shangri-La*

cs 34 *Warren House*

CS 33 Shangri-La

1965–78; Henry Warren, builder; E side NC 86, 3.8 mi. N of Prospect Hill; private, visible from road

This wonderful miniature village, 3 to 4 feet in height, was created of white quartzite or flint rock by Henry Warren after he retired from farming and running his gas station. The intricately and often humorously rendered village contains a church, a mill, a theater, a silo, a house and garage, rock retaining walls, and extensive landscaping. Topical buildings such as the Watergate Hotel are featured. Warren created his village in the yard of his stone bungalow near his stone gas station on NC 86, and his neighbor Junius Pennix worked with him. Warren welcomed everyone during his lifetime; his motto appears on a plaque: "Let me live in a house by the side of the road and be a friend to man."

CS 34 Warren House and Store (Prospect Hill)

Ca. 1858; jct. NC 49, NC 86, and SR 1771; private, visible from road

A classic pair of antebellum buildings marks the prominent crossroads. The brick temple-form store with 2-story pedimented porch — one of the state's few surviving antebellum country stores — was built by Franklin Link Warren and served travelers on the Hillsborough-to-Milton stage road. Its brick walls are laid in 1:3 brick bond with Flemish variation. The intact interior in-

cludes a post office in the rear and an oval, balustraded opening between stories for hoisting merchandise. Across the road Warren's well-preserved, 2-story, frame plantation house continues the Greek Revival style enriched with delicate latticed porches facing both roads.

CS 35 Bartlett Yancey House

Ca. 1810, 1856 (date brick); S side US 158, 0.6 mi. W of NC 86, Yanceyville vic.; private, visible from road

The 1½-story, hall-parlor plan rear section of the plantation house was built for congressman and legislator Bartlett Yancey and his wife Ann Graves. After their deaths, daughter Ann and her husband Thomas Womack added the 2-story Greek Revival front section. Yancey's law office, a log barn, and the family cemetery complete the complex.

CS 36 Shelton House

1843; S side US 158, 2.0 mi. W of NC 86; private, visible from road

The small brick house, 1½ stories tall with traditional 2-door, 2-room plan, features a Doric entrance porch and other Greek Revival detail, complemented by a frame barn and log kitchen.

CS 37 Holderness House

Ca. 1851; W side US 158, 2.8 mi. W of NC 86; private, visible from road

Bold and simple forms of the local Greek Revival define the prominent house with low hip roof and a 1-story, pedimented entrance portico with Doric columns. Unusual are the 1-story wings, each with a matching portico. To the rear is a saddlebag log outbuilding.

cs 38 *Brown's Store*

CS 38 Locust Hill

The crossroads on the stage road, the longtime home of the prominent Brown family, was called Brown's Store until the 1840s. The **Brown-Graves House** (late 18th c.; s side of NC 150, 1.3 mi. sw of US 158; private, visible from road) offers a rare N.C. example of a formal Georgian style plantation house: 2 stories tall and 5 bays wide with a double-pile plan and a high hip roof underlined by a modillion cornice. (The portico is late 20th c.) It was built by John Brown or his son Jethro, who operated a tavern and a 1,700- to 2,000-acre plantation. There are several 19th-c. outbuildings. Calvin Graves, owner from 1843 to 1877, built the Greek Revival law office in the front yard. As speaker of the state senate in 1848–49 he cast a tie-breaking vote that favored the N.C. Railroad over a route through Caswell—a local political suicide to benefit the state as a whole. Across the road is **Brown's Store** (late 18th–early 19th c.), one of the oldest store buildings in the state—a timber-framed structure with a heavy stone and brick chimney and a fieldstone basement—which also served as a stage stop and post office. The Greek Revival style **Neal House** (1855–57; N side NC 150, opp. SR 1128) was built for Stephen Neal, who acquired the store tract in 1843. Northeast is **Rose Hill** (ca. 1802 and later; no public visibility), a 2-story frame house with hall-parlor plan, where Jethro Brown kept a tavern and hosted a society "constituted for intellectual improvement." In 1817 Jethro deeded the place to son Bedford Brown, legislator and U.S. senator, who added a wing containing a Federal style parlor.

Durham County (DH)

See Claudia P. Roberts (Brown) and Diane Lea, The Durham Architectural and Historic Inventory *(1982).*

Durham (DH 1–49)

Born of the railroad and tobacco manufacturing, Durham moved rapidly through phases of urban development—from a raw whistlestop village of 250 people to a bustling New South boomtown to a city of substantial institutions and elegant architecture by the early 20th c. It had 18,000 people in 1910 and 52,000 by 1930, ranking third after Charlotte and Winston-Salem. As early as 1881 its leaders had sufficient clout to establish a hard-won new county with Durham as its seat. The city has a few landmarks from the 19th c., but its strength is in the rich ensemble of early 20th-c. architecture in its downtown and neighborhoods, the fine Beaux Arts Gothic Revival campus of *Duke University, and the state's prime collection of tobacco manufacturing architecture.

The village of Durhamville Station grew up in the 1850s around a stop on the North Carolina Railroad (NCRR) and was named for landowner Bartlett Durham. By the onset of the Civil War it had a depot, frame houses and stores, and a small tobacco fac-

tory. Its saga of phenomenal growth began when soldiers plundered the factory's smoking tobacco at the end of the war and found it so tasty that upon returning to their homes throughout the nation, they flooded manufacturer John R. Green with orders for "that good Durham tobacco," which was later patented as Bull Durham. Well located on the railroad adjoining the northern Piedmont's Old Belt bright-leaf tobacco zone, Durham soon led the nation in production of smoking tobacco. Industrialists strengthened their position with additional rail connections in 1873 and 1890, and tobacco factories and sales and storage warehouses, which employed black as well as white men and women, made Durham an employment magnet. "Come on, we have room for all who come," trumpeted the local *Tobacco Plant* in 1881.

Thousands of people arrived to find work and opportunity. Ambitious men arrived from the countryside and smaller towns to create businesses, and some became wealthy and powerful at a startling pace. The fast-growing city supported an increas-

Five Points, downtown Durham, mid-20th c.

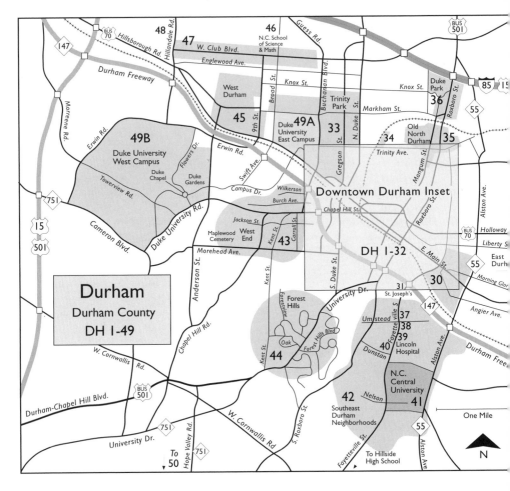

Durham
Durham County
DH 1-49

One Mile

N

ingly stratified but remarkably diverse and flexible social fabric. Not only did a new white elite emerge, but the city gained fame for its strong black middle and upper class, as businessmen, physicians, manufacturers, and artisans established businesses, schools, and, especially important, financial institutions. Durham was also a social mecca, especially during tobacco sales, and in the 20th c. it developed a nationally renowned blues tradition.

From many competing tobacco manufacturers, two giants emerged. W. T. Blackwell & Co., founded in 1870 as an outgrowth of Green's firm and led by Blackwell and Julian S. Carr, made Bull Durham smoking tobacco the top seller in the nation. W. Duke, Sons, & Co. was formed in 1878 by former tobacco farmer Washington Duke

(*Duke Homestead); his sons Brodie, Benjamin N., and James Buchanan Duke; and George W. Watts of Baltimore. (Watts, like Carr, brought essential and timely capital as well as talent, for their fathers purchased interests in the emerging firms to launch them in business.)

To outstrip "the Bull," which dominated smoking tobacco, in 1881 Duke turned to cigarette production, and in 1884 James B. Duke revolutionized the business by replacing hand rolling with the Bonsack cigarette machine. The company skyrocketed. In 1890 James B. Duke formed the American Tobacco Co. (ATC) and took over competitors in every area of production except cigars, eventually including Carr's firm. With offices in New York, where J. B. Duke moved in 1884, the ATC developed into a

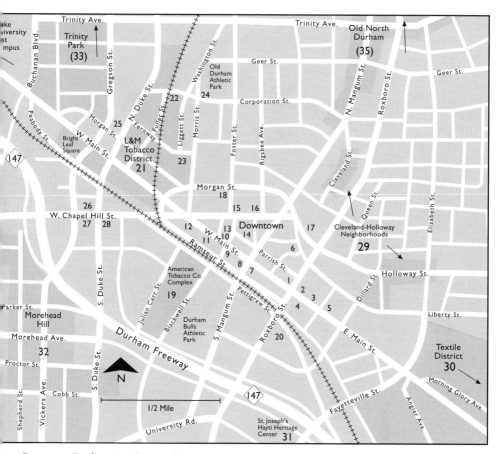

Downtown Durham inset (DH 1–32)

giant trust before it was broken up in 1911. Durham thereafter jockeyed with Winston-Salem for primacy, with Liggett & Myers and the ATC's brands, including Chesterfield and Lucky Strike, competing with Camel, Winston, and Salem. In the mid-20th c. Durham manufactured about a quarter of the cigarettes made in the country.

Tobacco industrialists spun off their immense profits into a host of other industries and businesses. Both Carr and the Dukes turned to major textile production in Durham and beyond. (Generally, the Dukes and associates focused in north and west Durham, while Carr invested east and south.) The Dukes also moved into hydroelectric power production, founding the Southern (Duke) Power Co. in 1905, headquartered in Charlotte. The industrialists and others also

established banks, real estate firms, and insurance companies that expanded their wealth and the city's growth.

Vital to the city's identity was the N.C. Mutual Insurance Co. (est. 1898) and its affiliate, Mechanics & Farmers Bank (est. 1907). Led by John Merrick, Aaron Moore, and Charles C. Spaulding, by the early 20th c. the insurance company was the largest black-owned business in the nation. With the bank it made Parrish St. famous as the "Black Wall Street of America." The business provided a unique base for black leadership and institutions and undergirded Durham's reputation as the "Capital of the Black Middle Class."

Durham's captains of industry also invested in the city's educational and social institutions. In 1892 the Dukes and Carr, strong Methodists, joined others in providing land and money to bring *Trinity College to Durham and support its growth. They and others aided many black and white schools, hospitals, libraries, and churches. Present-day *North Carolina Central University (NCCU), est. 1909, grew into a state college with support from black and white benefactors. And in 1924, encouraged by Trinity's president, James B. Duke donated millions to transform Trinity College into Duke University.

As it grew, the city shared in national patterns, shifting from the mix of housing and industry around the depot to separate industrial, commercial, and residential sectors, especially after the creation of an efficient streetcar system in 1902. Although James B. and Benjamin Duke and other top executives had mansions on 5th Ave. or in New York suburbs, other magnates built fine residences in Durham—first within sight of the factories, then on elevated suburban sites in all directions. Southeast of downtown, the black community known as Hayti developed by the 1870s, and by the early 20th c. it was famed for its vibrant main street and commercial center. The black elite built mansions on Fayetteville St. and nearby, and to the south, middle-class neighborhoods concentrated around *NCCU and Lincoln Hospital. West and north of downtown, Trinity College and *Watts Hospital became centers of white middle-class suburbs. East and West Durham emerged as separate communities around their textile mills. In contrast to many N.C. cities, Durham has continued a checkerboard pattern of neighborhoods, with the elevation of the terrain a defining element between neighborhoods of different races and economic levels.

Architectural patterns encapsulated the city's rapid development. Plain and expedient buildings around the depot were soon succeeded by ambitious Italianate houses and factories (*W. T. Blackwell, *W. Duke Sons & Co.) and ebulliently eclectic Queen Anne and Romanesque Revival edifices. The early 20th c. remade much of downtown in a more restrained, generally classical mode evoking a "citylike" image of sophistication and culture. Charlotte architect Charles C.

Hook and Southern Railway architect Frank Milburn produced buildings in classical, Spanish, and Chateauesque designs. A few clients employed such distant architects as Boston's Ralph Adams Cram and Kendall & Taylor and Philadelphia's Horace Trumbauer and Julian Abele (*Duke University). Local firms included Thomas Atwood and his partners Arthur C. Nash and Raymond Weeks, and Durhamite George Watts Carr. These men worked generally within the Beaux Arts revivalist tradition, with occasional ventures into the Art Deco and Moderne styles. Builders as well as architects planned the hundreds of bungalows large and small, Craftsman foursquares, and varied Colonial Revival houses that filled the neighborhoods.

In the mid-20th c., Durham, like Winston-Salem, saw tobacco sales rise during the Great Depression and through World War II and several years thereafter. Later in the century, however, its tobacco and textile economy began to lose ground. Outward movement from the center city was accompanied by urban renewal and freeway construction, which in the 1960s and 1970s destroyed many landmarks and essentially leveled Hayti and other African American neighborhoods. In the late 20th c., shifts in manufacturing, corporate structures, and the tobacco market, coupled with the growth of Duke University and its medical center, changed Durham's image from the "City of Tobacco" to the "City of Medicine." The last tobacco factory closed in 2000. At the same time, Duke and Durham became part of the revolutionary Research Triangle enterprise. The state's fourth largest city at the turn of the 21st c., Durham is the most diverse of the Triangle cities. Its legacy of industry and education creates a lively social and political mix and a body of architecture expressive of the vitality of the town tobacco built.

Downtown Durham:
Durham grew steadily in all directions from the 1854 depot at the corner of E. Peabody and Corcoran, with a succession of frame, then masonry business buildings, churches, and houses. The business district on Main and nearby streets reflects the early 20th-c. rebuilding from

the eclectic frame and red brick boomtown into a predominantly Neoclassical urban setting in stone and pale brick.

DH 1 Durham County Courthouse
1916; Milburn & Heister (Washington, D.C.), architects; George A. Fuller Co., builder; 208 E. Main St.

Erected on the site of its brick, Romanesque predecessor, the 4-story building faced with Indiana limestone accommodates Beaux Arts classicism to a compact site. Pilasters rise from a basement story to a heavy entablature. The ornate Corinthian order enriches the recessed entrance front, and the simpler Doric order carries around the building.

DH 1 *Durham Co. Courthouse*

East of courthouse

DH 2 First Presbyterian Church
1916; Milburn & Heister, architects; 305 E. Main St.

Here the architects of the courthouse used a dynamic and colorful Gothic Revival design, with contrasting brick and stone accentuating projecting and receding forms. The congregation (est. 1871) had built a frame church in 1875 and a brick one in 1890.

DH 3 Former Durham County Public Library
1921; Edward L. Tilton (New York), architect; 311 E. Main St.

Sponsors employed New York library specialist Tilton (#Pack Library, Asheville) to

DH 3 *Former Durham Co. Public Library*

replace the original Queen Anne style library of 1897. Funded in part by the Carnegie Foundation, the Neoclassical design is rendered in sandstone-colored brick with a wooden portico with Ionic columns.

DH 4 Johnson Motor Co. Building
Early 1920s; George Watts Carr, architect; 326 E. Main St.

The best-preserved of several glamorous showrooms of the early automobile age features a limestone facade, festooned with garlands and set off by tooled copper window frames and green onyx marble trim. The company began in the 1910s and operated here until the 1970s. The **Alexander Motor Co. Building** (1923; Milburn & Heister, architects; 330 E. Main St.) has a somewhat altered classical facade.

DH 5 St. Philip's Episcopal Church
1907; Ralph Adams Cram (Boston), architect; Parish House, 1940, George Watts Carr, architect; 403 E. Main St.

The small but powerfully composed church exemplifies the sophisticated medievalism of

DH 5 *St. Philip's Episcopal Church*

ecclesiastical architect Cram. In the spirit of English parish churches, the simple form with gabled nave and heavy front entrance tower is distinguished by ruddy, irregular stonework, accented by pale, smooth stone. It replaced a frame church of 1880.

DH 6 Trinity United Methodist Church
1924; Ralph Adams Cram (Cram, Goodhue & Ferguson [Boston]), architects; head of Church St.

When their brick, Gothic Revival church burned in 1922, the congregation turned to a national firm specializing in church architecture. Cram, devoted to the revival of authentic medieval forms, designed numerous churches, mostly Episcopal, in American industrial cities (*St. Philip's; *St. Paul's, Winston-Salem; #Trinity, Asheville). The stone-faced, cruciform structure displays a panoply of High Gothic Revival decoration, with a central entrance tower, capped by a spire (1985), and a dramatic sanctuary with truss ceiling. The congregation began in the country in 1830 and moved to town in 1860.

West of courthouse

DH 7 Citizens National Bank Building
Early 1910s; Rose & Rose (Durham), architects (attrib.); 102 E. Main St.

The white-marble-faced bank, in the popular temple form with Ionic columns flanking the entry, was built for a firm founded in 1905 with Benjamin N. Duke as president.

DH 8 Kress Building
1933; Edward F. Sibbert (New York), architect; 101 W. Main St.

Faced with colorful glazed terra-cotta foliate ornament, this and the *Kress Building in Greensboro are the state's prime examples of the distinctive Art Deco designs created by company architect Sibbert across the nation, when chain stores were new to most communities. Nearby, at **111 W. Main St.** (1893), a narrow section of a building with arched windows and corbeled cornice survives from the 19th c.

DH 9 First National Bank Building
1913–15; Milburn & Heister, architects; 123 W. Main St.

For many years the tallest building in town, the 8-story bank at a prime corner has classical ornament in Indiana limestone defining the base and intermediate stories of tan brick; the top story is richly finished as a classical frieze in limestone. It replaced a red brick bank (1887) founded by Julian Carr and others.

DH 10 Trust Building
Ca. 1905; Charles C. Hook (Charlotte), architect; 212 W. Main St.

With its curved corner accentuated by striated brickwork and classical details, the 5½ story building of buff brick was considered the city's first skyscraper and was one of the first Neoclassical designs downtown. Named for the Durham Loan & Trust Co. (est. 1904 by George W. Watts and the Dukes), it also housed Fidelity Bank (est. 1888 by Benjamin N. Duke) and the Home Savings Bank (est. 1904 by George W. Watts with son-in-law John Sprunt Hill [*Hill House]). The nearby **Temple Building** (1909; 302 W. Main St.), with stuccoed walls and tile roof in a Spanish Revival mode, was reportedly built with materials left over from *Watts Hospital.

DH 11 Old Hill Building
1925; Atwood & Nash (Durham), architects; 309 W. Main St.

The classical facade in stone has brass-framed arched windows rising through the upper 3 stories, cartouches with the monogram of client John Sprunt Hill, and a full entablature and balustrade at the roofline. Thomas Atwood and Arthur C. Nash had a successful, primarily Beaux-Arts practice (*University of North Carolina [UNC], Chapel Hill).

DH 12 Snow Building
*1933; Northup & O'Brien
(Winston-Salem), George Watts Carr,
architects; 333 W. Main St.*

This beautifully detailed building and the
#S&W Cafeteria in Asheville are the state's
finest small commercial buildings in the Art
Deco style. The 6- and 7-story stone facade
has a stylized Gothic Revival verticality, with
pilasters rising to a spiky roofline, and a recessed entry in a luxuriant Deco-Gothic
frame. The design was from Northup &
O'Brien, whose Durham office during the
1920s was staffed by George Watts Carr of
Durham. After the office closed in 1929,
Carr completed the building and opened his
own practice.

DH 12 *Snow Building*

DH 13 Hill Building (CCB Building)
*1935–37; George Watts Carr and Shreve,
Lamb & Harmon (New York), architects;
George Kane, contractor; 111 Corcoran St.*

Its dramatic stepped-back silhouette still
commanding the skyline newcomers, the 17-
story Moderne skyscraper was designed by
Carr in association with the New York designers of the Empire State Building and the
*Reynolds Building (1927–29) in Winston-
Salem. Though taking a more conservative
form, the limestone-faced skyscraper shares
their ziggurat motif and spirit of modernity
and features restrained Art Deco detail in
marble and aluminum. Built for John
Sprunt Hill as headquarters for the Home
Savings & Trust Co. (*Trust Building), the

DH 13 *Hill Building (CCB Building)*

depression-era project provided welcome
employment for construction workers and
suppliers. In the mid-20th c., mergers resulted in Central Carolina Bank & Trust
Co., with John's son, George Watts Hill Sr.,
as chairman.

DH 14 Mechanics & Farmers Bank (North Carolina Mutual Life Insurance Co.)
*1921; Rose & Rose, architects; 116 W. Parrish
St.; National Historic Landmark*

The centerpiece of Durham's renowned
"Black Wall Street of America," the 6-story
tan brick building with Neoclassical limestone detail was built as the headquarters of
the company that became the N.C. Mutual
Life Insurance Co. It began in 1898 as the
N.C. Mutual & Provident Association,
founded by John Merrick and Dr. Aaron
Moore and others. Merrick, a former brick-

DH 14 *Mechanics & Farmers Bank*

story brick building at **106 W. Parrish St.** was erected in 1909 for additional offices, and the company also acquired the 2-story, brick **Clements Building** (1908; 104 W. Parrish St.) on the corner. After the company moved to their 1966 *N.C. Mutual Building, the Parrish St. building continued as the bank.

DH 15 Home Federal Savings Bank
Ca. 1960; 315 E. Chapel Hill St.

Capturing the verve of popular commercial architecture of the 1950s and 1960s, the golden-finned building with rounded corner contains a curving mezzanine overlooking large expanses of glass. The design is attributed to an unknown St. Louis architect (cf. *First Federal Bank, Raleigh), but its footprint recalls that of the Center Theater that preceded it on the site.

DH 16 U.S. Post Office
1934; Atwood & Weeks, architects; 323 E. Chapel Hill St.

The Beaux Arts classical building has pilasters and a portico in antis rendered in an unfluted Doric order. Brass, copper, and marble enrich the elliptically vaulted lobby.

DH 17 First Baptist Church
1927; Reuben Harrison Hunt (Chattanooga), architect; 414 Cleveland St.

With its broad Ionic portico facing downtown, the massive limestone-faced church dramatizes the axis of Chapel Hill St. The congregation, begun as a country church in 1845, moved to Durham in 1850 as the first in town. It occupied various sites before commissioning Chattanooga church specialist Hunt to design the present church (#Central Methodist Church, Asheville).

DH 18 Durham Auditorium (Carolina Theater)
1926; Milburn & Heister, architects; 211 Roney St.

Central to the civic transformation of the 1920s, the municipal auditorium was de-

layer born a slave in Sampson Co., moved to Durham in 1880, established relationships with white leaders, including Washington Duke, and became a successful businessman. Moore, a native of Columbus Co., trained at *Shaw University and in 1888 became Durham's first black physician. The firm struggled at first, but in 1900 Moore's nephew, Charles Clinton Spaulding, became general manager and invigorated the company. In 1906 the company erected its headquarters on this site and soon formed Mechanics & Farmers Bank, which shared the building. Modeling Booker T. Washington's ethic of black self-help and enterprise, by 1910 the firm claimed to be "the world's largest Negro business," and its leaders—"the triumvirate"—took prominent roles in philanthropy, education, politics, and society.

Renamed N.C. Mutual in 1919, the company had local architects Rose & Rose design the 6-story headquarters with the bank at street level and insurance offices above. Spaulding, who became president in 1923, gained state and national stature in political, educational, and business circles. The 3-

signed for vaudeville and live theater, then converted to a movie palace in the 1930s. The festive Beaux Arts facade incorporates Corinthian pilasters, an entablature with floral decoration, and lunettes with cornucopias of fruit and flowers. It was restored and expanded in the late 20th c.

Tobacco District:
Radiating from the railroad tracks, mainly west and south of the Central Business District, the development patterns of the tobacco buildings are best understood from a train or an airplane or tall building. The zone was filled with frame, then brick, factories and warehouses that made it a hive of activity, often jammed by farmers' wagons and hundreds of workers. Reflecting growth and changes in production and management, the tobacco industrial architecture includes a few late 19th-c. buildings and more from the early 20th c. Most of the sales warehouses are gone. In the late 20th c., drastic shifts in the tobacco business emptied the warehouses and factories, and many have been converted to new uses.

These factories and warehouses compose an extraordinary collection of tobacco industrial architecture. They have thick, tapered brick walls and heavy timbers of slow-burn construction, similar to textile factory architecture; in fact, the New England Mutual insurance companies insured and influenced the construction of both textile and tobacco buildings. Generally Italianate stylistic motifs prevailed in the factories until streamlined forms took over. By contrast, the storage warehouses, where heavy casks of tobacco were aged, include not only plain and utilitarian buildings but also a magnificent series of castellated marvels of the mason's art; their dramatic rooflines combine ventilator shafts and fire walls with exuberant medievalism.

South of Central Business District

DH 19 American Tobacco Co. Complex
Est. 1874; bounded by W. Pettigrew, Blackwell, and Carr Sts. and Jackie Robinson Blvd.; National Historic Landmark

A landmark in industrial history extends south from the railroad tracks. Built for the firms that dominated Durham and the nation in tobacco, the long, highly visible complex represents the multiphase evolution of tobacco manufacturing architecture. The operation began with W. T. Blackwell and Co., which built the distinctive, 4-story Italianate style **Bull Durham Tobacco Factory** (1874) at the northeast corner of the block; its size and substantial brick walls, granite trim, and lavish Italianate details proclaimed the company's success and ambitions. (See Introduction, Fig. 47.)

The firm began with Durham, when Robert Morris opened the first tobacco factory near the depot in the 1850s. By 1864 John Ruffin Green, a Person Co. farmer, was sole owner, and it was his tobacco that was stolen by soldiers in 1865 and for which they soon sent orders. In 1866 he patented the Bull Durham name and image, reportedly inspired by the bull's head on a jar of Coleman's Durham brand mustard. In 1869, shortly before his death, Green took as partners William T. Blackwell and James R. Day, also Person Co. boys; in 1870 young Julian S. Carr of Chapel Hill joined the firm when his father bought a third interest in it. By 1872 the local *Tobacco Plant* claimed Bull Durham was the nation's most popular brand of smoking tobacco.

Specializing in top quality "bright" tobacco grown by farmers in the adjoining Old Belt zone, the company grew from a dozen employees in 1869 to hundreds of factory workers in 1883. Blackwell had a huge image of the trademark bull painted on the building, accompanied by a steam-powered calliope. A Greensboro newspaper reported in 1876 that it "imitates the bellowing of the bull with all its variations to a dot. It can be heard for miles. . . . The effect on strangers who are not aware of the existence of an artificial bellower is remarkable." By 1880 the firm had built the west wing, the first of several additions. Introducing mechanized production and soon processing 5 million pounds a year, the plant was described as the world's largest smoking tobacco factory. In 1883 Julian S. Carr and others bought Blackwell's interests and, competing against Duke and others, expanded advertising dramatically, as artist Jule Korner (*Korner's Folly,

Kernersville) had giant images of the trademark bull painted across the nation.

Resisting acquisition by the Dukes' ATC (est. 1890), in 1898 Carr sold to Union Tobacco; but in 1899 American bought Union, and the Bull Durham factory was thus sold to its old rival. American added four big warehouses and factories with the ornate medieval character that projected the company's image. After the trust was dissolved in 1911, the reorganized company added over the years three austere factories at the southeast end toward the present-day freeway. Here Bull Durham smoking tobacco and Lucky Strike cigarettes were manufactured for much of the 20th c.—as many as 20 million cigarettes per hour in the mid-1950s. As late as the 1930s the "hoarse bellow of the bull whistle" terminated the workday. Seen from the freeway, the complex presents a linear sequence of factory development running back from the mid-20th c. to the 1870s, encapsulating the history of the industry. After a period of disuse, a large redevelopment was planned in 2001–2.

DH 20 Venable Tobacco Co. Warehouse
1905, 1910s; 302–4 E. Pettigrew St.

The only intact example of the many independent tobacco warehouses of the late 19th and early 20th centuries, the plain brick building of slow-burn construction consists of 3 units fronted by a stepped-gable facade. The firm purchased tobacco in local sales houses, redried it, and shipped it all over the world.

West of Central Business District

DH 21 Liggett & Myers Tobacco Co. (American Tobacco Co.) Tobacco Buildings
1880s–1940s; blocks N of Southern Railway's main Durham line and W of the Norfolk & Western spur track at the W edge of the Downtown Loop

The immense industrial complex encompasses many stages of growth in the tobacco empire created by W. Duke & Sons. The company was formed in 1878 by Washington Duke; his sons Brodie, Benjamin N., and James Buchanan; and partner George W. Watts. The Duke family (*Duke Homestead) had begun manufacturing tobacco on their farm, "drummed" it across the state and nation, and then moved to town by 1874. In 1880 Washington Duke sold his interest to Franklin Co. native Richard Wright. Rather than competing with "the Bull" in smoking tobacco, in 1881 the Dukes turned to cigarettes, popular in Europe but new in America and ideal for the local bright tobacco. Initially the company hired about 100 skilled Russian and Polish Jewish immigrants, followed by local white girls and women, to roll the cigarettes by hand. The company opened factories in 1884 in Durham and New York. In 1884 James B. Duke gambled on investment in the Bonsack rolling machine, which as perfected by mechanic William T. O'Brien (*O'Brien House) automated the process and placed the company at the forefront of the industry.

Beside the tracks, still recognizable, stands the big, red brick **W. Duke Sons & Co. Cigarette Factory** (1884; William H. Linthicum; 600 W. Peabody St.), a clear statement of the company's ambitions. Here the Dukes shifted from hand rolling to the Bonsack machine. The U-shaped Italianate building once stood 4 stories tall but was reduced to 2; it is best seen in relationship to other industrial landmarks from the railroad side.

The **American Tobacco Co. and Liggett and Myers Warehouses** on nearby streets are some of the most spectacular monuments of tobacco architecture in the state. Seven cluster on Duke, Main, and Gregson Sts. Erected by the ATC in a medieval revival style, the massive red brick buildings feature dramatic rooflines and elaborate ornamental brickwork. After James B. Duke formed the ATC in 1890, the giant firm began to buy tobacco directly from farmers—"Sooold American!" resounded at tobacco sales—rather than from middlemen. This helped control prices, supply, and processing of the leaf. Beginning in 1897, the ATC built warehouses designed to store and age 1,000-pound hogsheads of tobacco for 3 to 5 years. The slow-burn construction, thick brick

DH 21 *Hicks and Toms warehouses*

walls, fire walls and fireproof metal shutters, strong interior supports and floors, and complex system of ventilation through chutes and stacks were essential to security and the aging process, while the ornate, castellated character complemented the functional demands and reinforced the aura of wealth and power.

Built year after year as needed, the warehouses are dated on cornerstones and named for company employees and associates: **Walker** (1897; 601 W. Main St.); **O'Brien** (1899; 610 W. Main St.); **Hicks** (1900; 208 N. Fuller St.); **Toms** (1903; 206 N. Fuller St.); and **Watts and Yuille** (1904; 904 W. Main St.). (See Introduction, Fig. 76.) Later streamlined versions were built by Liggett & Myers after the ATC trust was dissolved in 1911: **Flowers** (1916; 610 Morgan St.); **Carmichael** (1926; 400 N. Duke St.); **White** (1926; 600 N. Duke St.); and **Bullington** (1927; 500 N. Duke St.). Following changes in the industry, Watts and Yuille became Brightleaf Square shopping center in 1981, a pioneering renovation project, where the sturdy interior construction is readily visible. Other former warehouses contain offices, housing, and other functions. Nearby is the large, brick **Power Plant** (1926, 1938; NE corner N. Fuller St. and Fernway), with prominent pilasters and big, 2-story arched windows.

The **Chesterfield Building** (1948; 705 W. Main St.) is an immense 7-story brick building reflecting the mid-20th-c. growth of cigarette production. Located on the site of Washington Duke's mansion, its sheer brick walls clothe a fireproof steel and concrete structure, with small windows cut cleanly into contrasting dark gray bands of brick and a black marble-framed Moderne entrance. Across the street the **Liggett & Myers Research Laboratories and Offices** (late 1940s) feature Moderne entrances.

DH 22 Brodie L. Duke Warehouse
Ca. 1878; SW corner of Corporation and Liggett Sts.

The plain, hip-roofed, rectilinear brick building in 1:5 bond is Durham's oldest surviving warehouse. Brodie Duke, older half-brother of James and Benjamin, established his industrial and real estate operations on the north side of town and built this warehouse about the same time he became a partner in the family firm.

DH 23 Imperial Tobacco Co.
1916; 215 Morris St.

The big Romanesque Revival style brick factory rivals the nearby ATC buildings in its scale and ornamental brickwork, curved and gabled parapets, and white stone accents. The British company was formed in 1901 to compete with Duke's European market expansion and later entered the U.S. market and built plants in Virginia and the Carolinas in similarly ornate style.

DH 23 *Imperial Tobacco Co.*

DH 24 Durham Athletic Park

1939; George Watts Carr, architect; 500 Washington St.

Long home of the Durham Bulls, the classic American ballfield gained fame as the setting for the movie *Bull Durham* (1988). When the old El Toro ballfield burned in the 1930s, financier John Sprunt Hill donated a new one. Designed by Durham architect Carr, its most distinctive feature is its cylindrical, spired ticket office. Echoing Blackwell's factory calliope, a mechanized bull bellowed and emitted smoke to celebrate home runs. Minor league baseball flourished here into the 1990s, when the Bulls moved to a new ballpark (complete with bull) by the freeway. The DAP serves many community purposes.

DH 25 Julian S. Carr Junior High School and Durham High School

1922–26, George Watts Carr; 1923, Milburn & Heister; 1930, Raymond Weeks, architects; Morgan and N. Duke Sts.

The imposing public school complex from the city's Neoclassical rebuilding includes harmonizing red brick buildings of Georgian Revival style, originally Central Junior and Senior High. The smaller junior high was designed by Carr during his association with Northup & O'Brien. The senior high was designed by Milburn & Heister, with a 3½-story central block with pilasters, arched windows, and a stone balcony, topped by a baroque cupola. The auditorium, gym, and music wing came ca. 1930, and other additions followed.

DH 26 Duke Memorial United Methodist Church

1907–12; George Washington Kramer, architect; Norman Underwood, contractor; 504 W. Chapel Hill St.

With its dramatic pair of belltowers flanking a broad gable, the big tan brick and granite building accents the skyline. Church specialist Kramer of Ohio and New York, author of *The What, How, and Why of Church Building* (1901), freely combined Romanesque and Gothic motifs and created a fine auditorium. The congregation originated as a Sunday school class begun by devoted Methodist Washington Duke, whose family supported the 1907 edifice in his honor. It stands on the site of William T. Blackwell's residence.

DH 26 *Duke Memorial United Methodist Church*

DH 27 Home Security Life Insurance Building

1958; Raymond & Rado (New York), architects; G. Milton Small & Joseph N. Boaz (Raleigh), supervising architects; SW corner W. Chapel Hill St. at Duke St.

Simple forms and beautifully handled proportions and details define the office building as a fine and early exemplar of the modernist tradition of Mies van der Rohe. The 5-story, T-plan structure is constructed with steel columns that make the upper 4 stories appear to float above the base. Slender ribbon pilasters of dark, polished stone frame a light and open grid of glass and metal. Arthur Clark and George Watts Hill Jr., officers of the firm founded by John Sprunt Hill, sought a first-class modernist design. Working with Henry Kamphoefner, dean of the School of Design in Raleigh, they considered several national firms and selected Antonin Raymond and Ladislav Rado, a New York team of international reputation, and employed as local architect Milton Small, a former student of Mies in Chicago before coming to Raleigh in 1948. (The elder Hill preferred a Georgian building but agreed to the modern design.) The prize-winning office building, apparently the state's first in the Miesian mode (*North Carolina National Bank, 1959–61, Charlotte), is well maintained for civic use.

DH 28 North Carolina Mutual Life Insurance Headquarters

1966; Welton Becket & Assoc., architects; SE corner W. Chapel Hill St. at Duke St.

Featured in *Fortune* magazine's list of America's ten outstanding buildings of the 1960s, the 10-story office building on its ridge-crest—site of Benjamin Duke's estate "Four Acres"—is a commanding presence in the skyline. The structure is built of precast concrete and steel in an unusual engineering system, wherein the floors are cantilevered out from the central service and structural core. (Several years after construction, it became necessary to reinforce the corners.) As headquarters of the internationally known

DH 28 *N.C. Mutual Life Insurance Headquarters*

insurance company (*Mechanics and Farmers Bank) begun in Durham in 1898, it continues as a major presence in the economic and community life of the city and the state.

East of Central Business District

DH 29 Holloway-Dillard-Cleveland St. Area

In the late 19th c., the residential area west of downtown was a fashionable section, with a "Mansion Row" of industrialists' Queen Anne style houses soon joined by Colonial Revival residences. Rejuvenated after many losses, the neighborhood includes Holloway, Dillard, Cleveland, and nearby streets. The **Leary-Coletta House** (1891; Samuel L. Leary, architect; 809 Cleveland St.), a dramatic, asymmetrical Shingle style–Queen Anne house, was the home of the Philadelphia architect responsible for the first main building at Trinity College and *St. Joseph's A.M.E. Church.

DH 30 Eastern Durham Textile Manufacturing Area

In the early 1880s, tobacco magnate Julian S. Carr began manufacturing cloth bags for smoking tobacco, then expanded into other textile production, especially after he sold his tobacco business in 1898. His textile investments spurred development in eastern Durham. The prime landmark is the **Durham Hosiery Mills** (1902; 803 Angier Ave.). The big, magnificently detailed mill by the tracks is dominated by a 6-story Romanesque Revival style tower with elaborate corbeled bands, arches, and panels; the 4-story factory itself features characteristic broad, tall arched windows and a low gabled roof. Powered by steam and electricity, Mill No. 1 was the pilot mill of a company established in 1898 by Carr (*Carr Mill) that grew to include 16 factories. It was later used for storage, then converted to housing.

Nearby is the immense castle-like complex of the **Golden Belt Mfg. Co.** (1900–1930s; jct. Morning Glory Ave. and Norfolk & Western RR), with the brick factories of ca. 1900 bedecked with frontispieces and

DH 30 *Durham Hosiery Mills*

towers, pilasters and corbeled cornices; "G B M CO" emblazons the towering smokestack. Established by Carr as a cotton mill and tobacco bag factory, the operation grew to employ some 700 women and girls in the factory, while hundreds more worked at home finishing and tagging the little bags. The **Village** has several blocks of 1- and 2-story frame houses, from plain, small, gabled dwellings to stylish bungalows.

Farther east, **East Durham** was the site of Carr's Durham Cotton Mfg. Co. (1884), the city's first; from that mill there survive only a few early 20th-c. brick additions and scattered 1½-story, board-and-batten mill houses flanking the freeway. In the early 20th c., S. Driver and nearby streets developed into a large neighborhood with Queen Anne houses, cottages, and bungalows and substantial churches, schools, and a small business district at Driver and Angier Sts. near the railroad.

DH 31 St. Joseph's A.M.E. Church
Begun 1891; Samuel L. Leary (Philadelphia), architect; 800 Fayetteville St.

A lone landmark of old Hayti, the monumental brick church was built for a congregation founded in 1869 by Rev. Edian D. Markham. The members worshiped first in a brush arbor, then in a log building that doubled as a school. Known as Union Bethel for the original A.M.E. church founded in Philadelphia in 1787, the congregation began a campaign for a large brick church in 1890, with their own funds and gifts from Julian Carr and Washington Duke. The cornerstone was laid in 1891 for the church named St. Joseph's. Leary, architect of the original Main Building at Trinity College (*Duke University), designed a powerful asymmetrical composition, blending Romanesque and Gothic Revival motifs and placing a soaring tower alongside a broad gable front. The sanctuary has a radiating plan, a polychromed ceiling of pressed metal, and a front oculus depicting benefactor Washington Duke. The church served as a center for the civil rights movement of the mid-20th c. and is part of a community arts and heritage facility. (See Introduction, Fig. 39.)

DH 32 Morehead Hill

Although the 19th-c. industrialists' mansions along Chapel Hill St. have vanished, Morehead Hill possesses the prime examples of the next generation of residential splendor. **Greystone** (1911; Charles C. Hook [Charlotte], architect; Irving & Casson [Boston], interiors; 618 Morehead Ave.) is a Chateauesque residence of light brick and Vance Co. granite, built for James and Mary

Lyon Stagg. James was the son of NCRR officer Francis Stagg (*Stagg House, Burlington) and Sarah Durham, sister of Bartlett Durham. He entered railroading, quarried granite at Greystone in Vance Co., became Benjamin Duke's executive secretary in 1893, and married Duke's niece, Mary Lyon, in 1897. After living in New York, the Staggs and B. N. Duke returned to Durham and had houses designed by Hook, architect to many industrialists of the era (*Duke University; *Hambley-Wallace House, Salisbury).

The Spanish Revival style **Hill House** (1910; Kendall & Taylor [Boston], architects; Irving & Casson [Boston], interiors; Thomas Meehan [Germantown, Pa.], landscape design; 900 S. Duke St.) is Durham's most opulent period revival mansion. It was erected for John Sprunt Hill and his wife Annie Louise Watts, only daughter of Duke associate George Watts (*Watts Hospital).

DH 32 *Hill House*

Hill, a native of Duplin Co. and a UNC alumnus, became a leading financier and philanthropist. The large, stuccoed house features baroque ornament in cast stone, a red tile roof, and luxuriously appointed interiors, restored as a meeting place.

In addition to these status-defining mansions, the neighborhood includes a range of houses from architect-designed residences to simple builders' houses on Vickers Ave., S. Duke St. and others, with the Colonial Revival predominating. An especially fine English Tudor design is the **Budd House** (late 1920s; G. Murray Nelson [Raleigh], architect; 903 S. Duke St.), with multiple gables and rich brick, stone, and half-timbered detail.

DH 33 Trinity Park and Trinity Heights

The neighborhoods north and east of the Trinity College campus (*East Duke) constitute one of Durham's oldest suburbs. With the advent of an efficient trolley line, businesspeople as well as college faculty built stylish residences in the new Trinity Park and Trinity Heights. As in other turn-of-the-century suburbs, there is a compact grid plan and a spectrum from imposing residences—Colonial Revival, Queen Anne, and Spanish Revival—to cottages and bungalows. Predating the suburb are the picturesque Queen Anne style cottages erected

DH 33 *Watts St., Trinity Park*

on the Trinity campus for faculty, then moved into the neighborhood in the 1910s. They include the **Crowell House** (1891; 504 Watts St.), with half-timbering and a peaked corner tower, first occupied by John Franklin Crowell, president of Trinity during the move from Randolph Co.; the cross-gabled **Pegram House** (1891; 1019 Minerva Ave.), home of physics and chemistry professor W. H. Pegram; and the **Bassett House** (1891; 1017 W. Trinity Ave.), 2 stories with shingled, cross-gambrel roof; its first resident was history professor John Spencer Bassett, remembered for the controversy over his 1903 essay on racial issues. Trinity's trustees upheld academic freedom despite strong pressures.

DH 34 Pearl Cotton Mill Village

Est. 1892, ca. 1905, 1924; 900 blocks Washington and Orient Sts.

The island of small frame houses survives from the textile operation founded in 1892 by Brodie Duke and named for his daughter Pearl, and later part of *Erwin Mills. Set apart by its topography, the neighborhood contains two basic house types: 1890s 2-story houses for duplex or single-family residences—914 and 918 Orient are especially intact—and 1920s 1-story bungalows. From the nearby apartment complex at Trinity Ave. and Duke St. rise Pearl Cotton Mill's 4-story mansard-roofed tower and smokestack; the factory was razed in 1971.

DH 34 *Pearl Cotton Mill Village*

North Durham:
North of downtown, suburbs developed from the 1890s onward, including property of Brodie Duke on the north. Neighborhoods from working class to middle and upper class include most popular house types of the first half of the 20th c., chiefly simplified Queen Anne, Colonial Revival, and bungalows, with a few exotic revival themes.

DH 35 Old North Durham

The suburb began in the 1880s when printer Henry Seeman and attorney James S. Manning built frame, Queen Anne houses out in the country (112 W. Seeman St., 1911 N. Mangum St.); the **Manning House**, one of the finest Queen Anne style houses in town, was featured in the movie *Bull Durham*. Growth intensified in the early 20th c. with streetcar service and Brodie Duke's sale of lots. Especially notable is a row of five stylistically diverse 1920s bungalows at 111–21 W. Seeman St. Many substantial foursquares, such as the **Mangum House** (1111 N. Mangum St.) and the **Umstead-Rollins House** (1101 N. Mangum St.), blend Colonial Revival and Craftsman detail.

DH 36 Duke Park

1400 block N. Mangum St.,
1700 block N. Roxboro St., and vic.

The suburb just south of the city park by the same name emerged in the 1910s and 1920s with period revival houses and bungalows, many designed by local architects Rose & Rose and George Watts Carr. In the 1930s the park was developed with rustic structures built by the Civilian Conservation Corps (CCC). The **Richard H. Wright II House** (1920s; George Watts Carr, architect; 1429 N. Mangum St.), with Mount Vernon inspired portico overlooking the park, is one of the city's grandest Colonial Revival residences. Evidently the state's earliest house in the International style is the **Gamble House** (1935; Greene & Rogers [Asheville], architects; 1307 N. Mangum St.), designed by Asheville architects to express Mr. and Mrs. Howard Gamble's interest in modern arts and architecture. Built of stuccoed, poured

DH 36 *Gamble House*

concrete, sleek rectangular blocks form an asymmetrical composition accentuated by bands of windows that turn the sharp corners. The innovative house was featured in national magazines and among Durham's "points of interest."

Southeast Durham:
Extending south from E. Pettigrew St. through the traditionally black neighborhoods known as Southeast Durham, Fayetteville St. long served as "Durham's Black Main Street." The area known as Hayti developed south of the railroad as early as the 1870s. By the early 20th c. the area encompassed several neighborhoods. The finest houses stood along the ridges, especially Fayetteville St., and smaller ones filled the lower terrain. The N.C. Mutual Life Insurance Co. and the associated Merrick-Moore-Spaulding Land Co. (est. 1910) were active in developing the area and erecting houses for workers in tobacco and other industries. Durham's leading African Americans maintained strong ties with white leaders, gained support for substantial public schools, and established illustrious social and cultural institutions in the area. One of these, located in the 1400 block of Fayetteville St., was the Algonquin Tennis Club, which included many N.C. Mutual employees and was described by historian Walter Weare as "a new aristocracy . . . whose impulse for reform came . . . from a sense of racial duty and noblesse oblige."
Hayti, which encompassed fashionable early 20th-c. houses, brick commercial buildings, churches, and theaters, was heralded as one of the most progressive black neighborhoods of the New South. In 1939 the area was reported as having 12,000 residents; in 1955, 27,000. Virtually all of Hayti proper was destroyed in the

1960s and 1970s by urban renewal and clearance for the Durham Freeway. South of the freeway, much of the post-1910 development survives, highlighted by *NCCU and the residential neighborhoods built for black merchants, tradespeople, and professionals.

DH 37 Stanford L. Warren Library
1940; Robert Markley, architect;
1201 Fayetteville St.

Erected for one of the state's oldest libraries for blacks, the Neoclassical Revival style brick building has a pedimented frontispiece framing the entrance, flanked by tall round-arched windows. The classicism continues within, including classical figures in artistic and literary pursuits. The library, which originated in 1913 with a Sunday school library begun by Dr. Aaron Moore, is named for library leader Dr. Warren, donor of the site.

DH 37 *Stanford L. Warren Library*

DH 38 Dr. Joseph Napoleon Mills House
1910s; 1211 Fayetteville St.

Standing on a large corner lot, the house combines late Queen Anne massing and classical detail, including a deep wraparound porch with cut granite pillars. It exemplifies the substantial and stylish residences, most of which have been lost, built for Durham's

DH 38 *Dr. Joseph Napoleon Mills House*

black professional and business leaders. Dr. Mills, on staff at Lincoln Hospital, also served the N.C. Mutual Life Insurance Co. and in other business and civic roles.

DH 39 Pearson House

1921; 1215 Fayetteville St.

The Craftsman bungalow, one of several built from a Sears, Roebuck design, was the home of John Pearson, owner of a pharmacy in Hayti, and his wife, known as "Miss Dyer," one of the first licensed female pharmacists in the state.

DH 40 J. C. Scarborough House

1916; 1406 Fayetteville St.

The big frame house with imposing portico of Southern Colonial style was built for businessman Scarborough, founder of a leading funeral home. Like many houses in Durham, it incorporated materials from razed buildings, including ornate mantels from Julian Carr's mansion. Scarborough supervised construction.

DH 41 North Carolina Central University

1925–present; Atwood & Nash, Atwood & Weeks (Durham), architects; Lawson St.

More than a dozen Georgian Revival style red brick buildings at the west end of campus represent the two decades of growth after the school became the N.C. College for Negroes in 1925. In 1909 Dr. James E. Shepard founded the nonsectarian National Religious Training School and Chautauqua for the Colored Race. In 1923 it became a state normal school; in 1925, the nation's first state-supported, 4-year, liberal arts college for black students. The architects, also active at *UNC in Chapel Hill, provided designs in their favored Georgian Revival mode. The **Clyde R. Hoey Administration Building** (1929), the centerpiece of the older section of campus, is a symmetrical composition with an enriched entrance pavilion. In front is a statue of Dr. Shepard, founder and long-time president. The architects supplied related designs for the **Alexander Dunn Hall**

DH 41 *Clyde R. Hoey Administration Building*

(1930) and **Annie Day Shepard Hall** (1930), the latter named for Dr. Shepard's wife, the granddaughter of Caswell Co. cabinetmaker Thomas Day (*Union Tavern). Buildings erected under the auspices of the Public Works Administration continue the architectural theme.

DH 42 Southeast Durham Neighborhoods

The large residential area flanking Fayetteville St. comprises one of the state's most intact examples of the early 20th-c. suburban neighborhoods developed by and for upper and middle-class black citizens. On the east side of Fayetteville St., the **Lincoln Hospital** neighborhood developed around the hospital founded through the efforts of Dr. Aaron Moore, John Merrick, and Dr. Stanford L. Warren, with support from the Duke and later the Hill family. A late 20th-c. hospital replaced the original, but the residential section of stylish bungalows, foursquares, and other houses erected for physicians and other professional and business people continues along Lincoln, Dunbar, Merrick, and nearby streets.

West of Fayetteville St., the **St. Theresa** and **Dunstan** neighborhoods developed south of Hayti. Large and small houses of the early 20th c. range from the big, columned residence at 1311 Fargo St. to the row of simple frame duplexes (ca. 1930) that march down the hill in the 100 block of Dunstan St. **J. A. Whitted Elementary School** (1922; 200 E. Umstead St.) is a red brick edifice with simplified classical motifs, originally built as Hillside High School. In

1950 Hillside High moved into a larger building on Concord St. (razed, 2003).

The most architecturally diverse neighborhood is **College View**, which developed south and west of the college flanking Fayetteville St. and grew in response to NCCU becoming a state-supported college in 1925. Streets that curve with the terrain are lined by handsomely detailed bungalows and Spanish Mission, English Cottage, and Colonial Revival dwellings. Some of the best examples stand along Formosa and Pekoe streets. Unusual is the **Lloyd House** (1950s; Clyde Lloyd, builder; 126 Nelson St.), built by the owner from plans he admired in a magazine (as yet unidentified). A World War II veteran, Lloyd worked as a chauffeur and butler but took a bricklaying course that enabled him to construct the house over four years. With its asymmetrical composition of flat-roofed forms, curved corner glass block at the entrance, and corner windows, it shares a still-unknown source with a few other modernist houses built for black and white N.C. families. "I came across this house that just hit me. There is a house I'd like to build for this gal of mine," recalled Lloyd in 1998.

DH 43 West End

As in much of the city, the irregular terrain delineated economic and social strata in the residential sector west of the industrial district. Along the ridges, prosperous black and white citizens built their imposing residences. Tobacco magnates W. T. Blackwell and Benjamin Duke erected mansions on W. Chapel Hill St. that are long gone, and Richard Fitzgerald, the black businessman and the city's leading brickmaker, had his brickyard on present-day Kent St. and his big Queen Anne style house, "The Maples," on Gattis St. In lower-lying areas, rental and owner-occupied housing developed for black and white occupants. A number of modest, single-family and duplex houses still stand, such as those in the 1300 block of Morehead Ave.

Richard Fitzgerald gave the land and built **Emmanuel A.M.E. Church** (1888; 710 Kent St.), the oldest church building in Durham; the gable-fronted, brick structure in Gothic Revival style has stained glass windows and a 2-story belltower and was subsequently stuccoed. The **Fitzgerald House** (1890s; 906 Carroll St.), an unpretentious, 2-story frame dwelling with end chimneys and broad porch, was built for Cornelia and Robert Fitzgerald (Richard's brother) as their "Homestead on the Hill." Granddaughter Pauli Murray, noted civil rights attorney and Episcopal priest, spent childhood years here and related the family saga in *Proud Shoes.*

The **O'Brien House** (ca. 1892; 820 Wilkerson Ave.), a 2-story, Queen Anne style frame house, typical of the late 19th-c. city, was built for master mechanic William Thomas O'Brien. When James B. Duke bought two of Virginia inventor James Bonsack's new automatic cigarette rolling machines, Bonsack sent mechanic O'Brien to install them. Duke promptly hired him to perfect the machine, which revolutionized the industry.

DH 44 Forest Hills

Durham's first true automobile suburb, Forest Hills emerged in the early 1920s when New Hope Realty Co. responded to the growing demand for spacious residences in a pastoral setting. On rural land southwest of town, the developers commissioned planner Earle Sumner Draper (*Myers Park, Charlotte) to lay out curvilinear streets around a 9-hole golf course. To design houses, the firm employed Northup & O'Brien, who in turn hired young Durham architect George Watts Carr. The developers built a few "seed" houses from stock plans modified by Carr. Despite the company's demise after 1929, development continued in the 1930s, with predominantly Colonial Revival houses designed by Carr, H. Raymond Weeks, and others. A notable series of Georgian Revival residences designed by Carr lines **Oak St.** A modernist exception is the **Evans House** (1950; 1401 Forestview), with a low profile and broad expanses of glass, built for Durham mayor Eli N. Evans. Most imposing is **Pinecrest** (1920s; George Watts Carr, architect; 1050 W. Forest Hills Blvd.), a multiga-

bled English cottage residence built on a prime hilltop for neighborhood developer James O. Cobb; it was later home of Mary Duke Biddle.

DH 45 Old West Durham

Originally called Pin Hook, West Durham opened with a few residences in the 1880s, and rapid development commenced when the Duke interests began Erwin Mills in 1892; for many years it was an unincorporated community. The centerpiece and raison d'être is **Erwin Cotton Mills No. 1** (1892–1909; 2000–2400 W. Main St.). The "Old" and "New" mills of the 1890s are long, handsome, 2-story red brick buildings, attached end to end. Both are lighted by tall, segmental-arched windows and accented with decorative brickwork. The mill was elongated as the operation grew and marked by short towers at intervals. The **Mill Office** takes a gabled domestic form, with corbeled

brickwork and a wraparound porch. These buildings were renovated in the late 20th c. as offices and housing, while other parts of the mill were razed.

The founding of Erwin Cotton Mills in 1892 heralded the Dukes' entry into the textile industry. Their old competitor Julian Carr had already begun textile manufacturing, and the Dukes and partner George Watts wanted to diversify their investments. Benjamin N. Duke and Watts recruited as manager and partner young William Allen Erwin. A native of Burke Co. (#Bellevue, Burke Co.), Erwin was a great-nephew of Alamance Co. textile pioneer E. M. Holt and in 1874 joined the Holts in expanding their operations. The story goes that the Dukes named the new mill for Erwin at their attorney's suggestion, so its failure or glory would fall upon him.

Under Erwin's management, by the mid-1890s Erwin Mills had become one of the state's largest mills, with 1,000 workers and 25,000 spindles and 1,000 looms, and more soon to come. The firm opened other mills in Durham, took over operation of *Pearl Cotton Mill, and built mills at #Erwin and *Cooleemee on the South Yadkin River. Initially making muslin for tobacco pouches, the company soon moved into denim, and by the 1920s it was the largest manufacturer of denim in the world.

As the mill grew, the adjoining **West Durham** expanded with shops, churches, fashionable houses for mill management, hundreds of houses for millworkers, and its

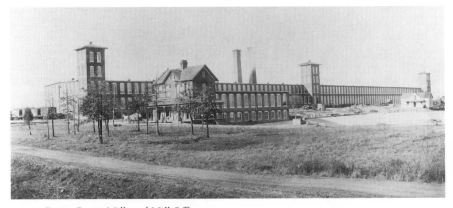

DH 45 *Erwin Cotton Mills and Mill Office*

DH 46 *Watts Hospital*

own business district, with 1- and 2-story commercial buildings lining **9th St.** across from the mill. Although much of the mill-workers' housing has been lost, several blocks of the **Erwin Mills Village** remain relatively intact, including the pyramidal-roofed, 1-story frame duplexes on Edith, Knox, Virgie, and Carolina Sts. **St. Joseph's Episcopal Church** (ca. 1905; 1902 W. Main St.) evolved from the West Durham Episcopal mission founded for employees in 1894 by Erwin, a strong Episcopalian. He and his siblings donated funds for the small granite church, built in the Gothic parish church tradition in memory of their parents, Joseph and Elvira Holt Erwin (*The Homestead, Lexington). Across the railroad tracks, the large frame Colonial Revival style **E. K. Powe House** (ca. 1900; 112 Swift Ave.), built for the Erwin Mill production manager and Erwin's brother-in-law, is one of the few textile executives' residences left in West Durham. Moved to the same location is **Sunnyside** (ca. 1904; Hill C. Linthicum, architect), the Colonial Revival home of mill executive, brother Jesse Harper Erwin.

DH 46 Watts Hospital (N.C. School of Science and Mathematics)

1908–10, Kendall & Taylor (Boston), architects; 1926, Arthur C. Nash, architect; 1950s; 1912 W. Club Blvd.

The ensemble of handsome stuccoed buildings on a 27-acre campus was a philanthropy of Duke associate and banker George W. Watts. Boston architect Bertrand Taylor (designer of the predecessor Watts Hospital of 1895) planned the first seven buildings ac-

cording to the latest theories of medicine and in a "modified Spanish mission type" with Renaissance Revival details. At a time when the public had only begun to consider hospitals for healing as well as dying, the architecture offered an aura of sunny and cheerful places and a warm welcome, with stuccoed walls, red tile roofs, and classical ornament at the entrances. The 3-story **Administration Building** is the most elaborate, with arcaded loggia and wrought iron balconies. Emphasis on fresh air and sunlight defines the open campus, the large windows and many balconies, and the long, narrow **Pavilions** with their semicircular sunporches topped with curved roofs above Tuscan colonnades. As a model medical facility, Watts set Durham on its course as the "City of Medicine." Succeeded in 1976 by Durham Co. General Hospital, the campus was renovated in the 1980s as a school.

DH 47 Club Boulevard
W. Club Blvd. betw. Broad St. and Hillandale Rd.

West of Watts Hospital, development of the tree-canopied boulevard began with houses near the hospital for staff, including large foursquare residences in the 2000 and 2100 blocks. Extension of the streetcar line and establishment of a golf course encouraged construction, which continued through the 1930s. Especially fine bungalows and foursquare types were built in good numbers, along with Tudor Revival and other cottage styles, some from published designs.

DH 48 Durham Water Works

1917–50; W. M. Piatt & Co., engineers;
1405 Hillandale Rd.

The 10-acre lake and waterworks were established in 1917 and expanded in the 1920s. The initial buildings are 1- and 2-story Italianate brick structures with arched openings and corbeled cornices; streamlined concrete additions were made after World War II.

DH 49 Duke University

Along with the tobacco and textile industries, one of the principal building blocks of Durham is Duke University. Its predecessor, Trinity College, began in the 1830s as a rural subscription school in Randolph Co. and was transformed under Braxton Craven into the liberal arts, Methodist-affiliated Trinity College by 1859. When it became known that Trinity College wished to move to a city, local Methodist ministers persuaded Washington Duke, Julian S. Carr, and others to offer substantial funding and land in 1890, and the college moved to Durham in 1892. Washington Duke gave $100,000 in 1896 on condition that the school admit women students, and like amounts in subsequent years were forthcoming. Under college presidents John F. Crowell, John C. Kilgo, and William P. Few, and with continued support from the Dukes, the college developed as a respected institution known for its support of academic freedom.

In the 1920s, under President Few's leadership, Trinity became a major beneficiary of James B. Duke and the Duke Endowment he created. As the family fortunes soared with electric power production, James B. Duke carried the family tradition of philanthropy to education and Methodist charities to an unprecedented scale. At Few's urging he donated millions to transform the college into a university named for his father, Washington Duke. In 1924 he established the Duke Endowment, with beneficiaries that included the new university and other colleges (*Davidson College, *Johnson C. Smith University), hospitals, Methodist churches, and charities in the Carolinas. Duke died unexpectedly in 1925

and thus never saw the campuses he envisioned.

Before his death, however, Duke had taken a strong role in planning the new campuses. He selected the Philadelphia architectural firm of Horace Trumbauer to plan the 1925–27 reworking of the former Trinity College at the East Campus, followed by the new West Campus. East became the Woman's College, and West included the men's Trinity College and the graduate school, main library, medical and law schools, and Duke Hospital (opened 1930). Both were planned by Julian Abele, the African American architect who was chief designer in Trumbauer's firm.

DH 49-A Duke University: East Campus

1890; 1900–1920, Charles C. Hook; 1925–27,
Julian Abele, Horace Trumbauer

The East Campus occupies the 62-acre site donated to Trinity College in 1890. Several buildings were erected in the 1890s, including the big Romanesque Revival Washington Duke Building designed by Samuel L. Leary, but only three survive: the 3-story frame **Ark** (1898), built as a gym; **Epworth Inn** (1892–93, 1914), a deep-gabled, stuccoed building altered from the larger, Shingle style College Inn; and **Crowell Science Building** (1892), a 3-story brick building with pilasters and segmental-arched windows. During the first two decades of the 20th c., Charlotte architect Charles C. Hook designed numerous buildings, of which the principal surviving landmarks are the pair of tan brick, classically detailed **East Duke Building** and **West Duke Building**, which flank the entrance drive and the seated statue of Washington Duke.

The centerpiece of the campus is the serenely symmetrical quadrangle. For East, the women's campus, architect Julian Abele adopted a somewhat domestic architectural vocabulary inspired by the University of Virginia, traditional red brick and white trim in a blend of Georgian Revival and Jeffersonian classicism. Subtly varied brick buildings line the long green that culminates at **Baldwin Auditorium** (1925–27), a domed composition with Ionic portico adapted from mod-

DH 49A *Baldwin Auditorium*

DH 49B *Dormitory quadrangle, West Campus*

els at the University of Virginia. It was named for Mary Alice Baldwin, Duke's first female faculty member and dean of the Woman's College.

DH 49-B Duke University: West Campus
1927–32, 1938–39; Julian Abele,
Horace Trumbauer

For the West Campus on a large rural site, James B. Duke and President Few took active roles in early planning, including the choice of the Collegiate Gothic style after Few visited Princeton and the University of Chicago, positioning of buildings on the site, and selection of the local stone. Architect Abele combined a generally symmetrical, hierarchically arranged Beaux Arts campus plan with a rich and sophisticated Gothic Revival architectural vocabulary. Beyond the central campus are later buildings in modernist and Gothic Revival modes.

Approached by the long axis leading to the towering chapel, the campus features a series of quadrangles enframed by classroom and dormitory buildings. Their irregular forms and artful details often conceal their bulk and seldom suggest the utilitarian spaces within. Motifs from many periods of Gothic architecture combine with contemporary touches, including symbols of activities and departments within, from theology to science to movies. Unifying the ensemble is the warm-hued, highly variegated gray to orange stone from an Orange Co. quarry, set off by carved limestone and slate roofs.

Presiding over the campus, as James B. Duke intended, is **Duke Chapel** (1930–32),

the state's premier monument of the late Gothic Revival style. (See Introduction, Fig. 55.) Its 210-foot-tall entrance tower is based on the Bell Harry Tower of Canterbury Cathedral. It opens into the high, vaulted sanctuary, a magnificent space in the full spirit of English Gothic. A rich program of Gothic Revival detail defines the cathedral-like chapel inside and out. Built during the Great Depression, it employed first-rate craftsmen from far and wide: stone carving was done by John Donnelly of New York; woodwork by Irving & Casson–A. H. Davenport of Boston; ironwork by William H. Jackson Co., New York; stained glass by G. Owen Bonawit, Inc., of New York; and tiled vaults by Rafael Guastavino Jr. Adding individuality are the Duke family members' recumbent statues on their sarcophagi (carved by Charles Keck of New York) in a chapel beside the chancel and the statues of church reformers and southern heroes flanking the main portal. A statue of James B. Duke stands on the green in front.

Adjoining the campus is the beautiful 60-acre **Sarah P. Duke Memorial Gardens** (Ellen Biddle Shipman, designer), begun in 1932 as a gift to the university from Mary Duke Biddle to honor her mother. Landscape architect Shipman designed the terraced section of the gardens, which shows her fondness of Italian themes in uniting stonework and plantings. Shipman had a long and distinguished career, with most of her work in the north, but late in life she designed a few gardens in N.C.; this is believed to be her only surviving public garden.

DH 50 Hope Valley

Begun in the late 1920s, Hope Valley was Durham's first full-fledged country club suburb, located several miles from downtown, with large wooded lots fronting an 18-hole golf course planned by the famed Donald Ross (*Pinehurst). Developed as select homesites for physicians and administrators at the new Duke University Medical School and Hospital, the suburb has architect-designed houses in period revival styles. The Norman Revival style **Clubhouse** (1928; Milburn & Heister, architects) commands a ridge overlooking the golf course. By the late 1930s, more than 40 houses were concentrated on Chelsea, Dover, and Devon roads, including 11 "seed" cottages primarily in the Tudor Revival and English Cottage styles. Some of these employ stone from the same quarry as Duke's West Campus.

DH 51 Bennett Place
State Historic Site

Memorial, 1923; farmstead reconstructed, 1961; SW corner SR 1313 and 1314

The farmhouse of James and Nancy Bennett (Bennitt), a yeoman farming family, became by chance the site of the largest surrender of troops in the Civil War. Here, after more than a week of intermittent negotiations, on April 26, 1865, Gen. Joseph Johnston surrendered to Gen. William T. Sherman all the Confederate troops in the Carolinas, Georgia, and Florida. In the early 20th c., the Durham Chamber of Commerce and others decided to erect a memorial at the site. The old house burned in 1921, but the state funded the **Bennett Place Monument** (1921–23; W. H. Deacy [W. W. Leland Studios, New York], architect), with two Corinthian columns symbolizing North and South and an entablature inscribed "Unity." Although some objected to memorializing a site of surrender, Confederate veterans leader Julian Carr and others dedicated the monument to national reconciliation and the origins of Durham's prosperity. In 1960–61 two local log houses that resembled the Bennetts' were moved to the site and restored.

DH 52 Duke Homestead
State Historic Site

Ca. 1852; 2828 Homestead Rd.

The restored farmstead built by tobacco pioneer Washington Duke typifies small Piedmont N.C. farms of the mid-19th c. Here Duke began as a small tobacco farmer, but after serving in the Confederate army, he turned to manufacturing "Pro Bono Publico" smoking tobacco, with his own labor and that of his three sons, Brodie, Benjamin, and James Buchanan Duke. They processed the leaf by hand and "drummed" it on the road. In 1869 Brodie moved to Durham and began a small factory, and by 1874 Washington had moved his family and factory there as well. The modest 2-story, 1-room-deep house with rear ell has a shallow gable roof with wide eaves and a double door framed by sidelights and a transom. Hand-planed pine boards sheathe the interior. The farm buildings include a 1930s reconstruction of the small, barnlike factory (ca. 1870). A flue-cure tobacco barn, typical of thousands, is part of the complex, and the visitor center depicts tobacco cultivation and production.

DH 52 *Duke Homestead*

DH 53 West Point on the Eno

W side Roxboro Rd., S bank of Eno River

The 40-acre park, comprising the West Point community that grew up around a late 18th-c. gristmill, includes accessible examples of typical 19th-c. rural architecture. The **McCown-Mangum House** (ca. 1843) is a simple, 2-story house with a hip roof, center-passage plan 1 room deep, and rear ell. It has plain Greek Revival finish, with 2-panel doors and simple mantels with pilasters; walls are plastered in the parlor and sheathed with pine elsewhere. The house was probably built for John Cabe McCown, who ran the mill in the mid-19th c.; in 1893 Presley J. Mangum, a Durham businessman, moved here with his family, including son Hugh, who became a prolific photographer of the South and had his darkroom in the board-and-batten **Pack House** (ca. 1880). A typical log **Tobacco Barn**, about 17½ feet square, dates from the early 20th c. Near the archaeological remains of the early mill complex are reconstructions of the gristmill and a blacksmith shop.

DH 54 Cox-Pope-Tippett House

1880s; E side NC 501 N,
3.3 mi. N of Eno River

The picturesque house was built for A. G. Cox, superintendent at Orange Factory, an antebellum cotton mill and village that stood nearby until the late 20th c. The frame dwelling exemplifies a popular form, 2 stories tall with center-passage plan beneath a tri-gabled roof, plus lavish sawn bargeboards and eave trim and a decorated wraparound porch. Later generations built matching additions. The farm includes barns and a well house.

DH 55 Hardscrabble

Late 18th and early 19th c.;
N side SR 1002, 1.2 mi. W of
SR 1003; visible at a distance
from road

The 2-part plantation house comprises two 2-story frame dwellings, each typical of its era: in front is a late Georgian style house with a 3-room plan and double-shouldered chimneys of Flemish-bond brick; at the rear is a house of similar form with early Federal finish, a hall-parlor plan, and single-shoulder chimneys in 1:3 bond. A Cain family plantation from 1779, it was named Hardscrabble during lean times in the 19th c. The farm is now a residential development.

DH 56 John McMannen House

Ca. 1840; W side SR 1461, 1.7 mi. N of
NC 157, South Lowell vic.

The 2-story frame house with center-passage plan exemplifies the dwellings of middling farmers. Touches of Greek Revival include pedimented gable ends and simple trim. McMannen, a Methodist leader involved in running an academy here, established industrial enterprises in the community known as South Lowell. In 1855 he bought land at Durham's station on the "great North Carolina railroad," laid off a town, and advertised lots for sale.

DH 57 Roberts-Crabtree Farm

19th c., 1918; S side SR 1464, 0.8 mi.
W of US 501, South Lowell vic.

Overlooking a broad valley, the farmstead lies in one of the county's finest rural landscapes. In 1918 Charles Crabtree built the 2-story frame farmhouse with hip roof, front central gable, and wraparound porch. Some of the outbuildings, including a log kitchen and a smokehouse, date from the earlier 19th-c. Roberts farm here.

DH 58 Quail Roost

1939; E. Bradford Tazwell (Norfolk, Va.),
architect; W side NC 501 at SR 1468

The site was developed in 1875 as a shooting club for Durham business leaders and associates from New York and Baltimore. George Watts Hill later acquired it and established a model dairy farm. Visible from

DH 58 *Quail Roost*

the road are the impressive gambrel-roofed dairy barns and terra-cotta tile silos of Hill's nationally acclaimed model Golden Guernsey farm of the 1930s and 1940s. His Georgian Revival residence is secluded in the woods.

DH 59 Hill Forest Camp
1930–34; E of US 501, off SR 1601,
1 mi. down SR 1614

The trio of well-preserved rustic log buildings exemplifies many such projects undertaken by the Works Progress Administration and the CCC. In 1929 George Watts Hill donated 400 acres to present-day North Carolina State University (NCSU), which made it an outdoor laboratory for its new School of Forestry. The first building, ca. 1930, is the large, 2-story meeting facility built of round logs, with upward tapering corners. Stair and balcony railings are made of peeled branches. The smaller residential buildings have logs in decorative patterns and fieldstone chimneys.

DH 59 *Hill Forest Camp*

DH 60 Northeast Durham Co. Tobacco Farms

Much of this corner of the county is still rural, with many medium-sized farms evoking the tobacco economy and architecture of the early 20th c. The numerous frame farmhouses include small dwellings of 1 to 3 main rooms and 2-story houses usually with center-passage plans 1 room deep plus ells or sheds in back. Many feature front center roof gables and decorated porches. Frame sheds, barns, garages, and other outbuildings abound. Log tobacco barns still stand, comparable to those in Person, Caswell, and

Granville counties, as well as ordering houses and grading houses, though their numbers are diminishing rapidly.

DH 61 Bahama
Late 19th–early 20th c.;
jct. SR 1615 and SR 1616

The settlement begun ca. 1880 had a post-office named Hunkadora. The new name (Ba-HAY-ma), adopted in 1891 when a railroad depot was built, came from the local BAll, HArris, and MAngum families. The crossroads village includes a cluster of frame stores, a Masonic lodge, and modest churches and dwellings, including 1- and 2-story residences, bungalows, and foursquares.

DH 62 Spruce Pine Lodge
1930s; N side SR 1616, 0.2 mi. W of SR 1613;
open limited hours

The rambling lodge overlooking Lake Michie is a fine and accessible rendition of the Arts and Crafts–derived rustic style popular in parks and resorts throughout America. Walls are of peeled logs, decorative half-logs adorn the gables, and rustic lattices of peeled branches frame the lake view from the porch. It was built for Mary Lyon Stagg (*Greystone) for summer use; she later gave the property to the city.

DH 63 Stagville State Historic Site
1799–1860; E side SR 1004, 1.4 mi. S of
SR 1615

Until the late 20th c., a vast expanse of northern Durham Co. remained in agricultural use, the legacy of the Bennehan and Cameron families who owned large plantations here (see Jean Anderson, *Piedmont Plantation*). Two of the plantation centers, **Stagville** and **Horton Grove**, are preserved to depict antebellum agriculture and architecture.

The conservatively finished frame house at **Stagville** epitomizes plantation residences of the era. It was built for Richard Bennehan and his wife Mary Amis. Bennehan, a native of Virginia, worked initially for Orange Co. merchant William Johnston. In 1776 he

DH 63 *Stagville Plantation House*   DH 63 *Horton Grove Slave Houses*

married the heiress of an eastern N.C. planter family and soon purchased the first of many tracts that made him a leading planter and merchant. After acquiring the old Stagg family farm beside the Trading Path from Petersburg, he opened a store by the road in 1787 and then constructed the residence nearby. The initial phase (ca. 1790) is a small, frame, hall-parlor plan house of 1½ stories, probably erected by local builder Martin Palmer. In 1799 Bennehan—by this time owner of nearly 4,000 acres and 42 adult slaves—added a surprisingly modest 2-story section with a formal parlor and side passage. Both sections feature robust late Georgian finish and first-quality carpentry, including fine molded window and door sills. The Bennehans' daughter Rebecca married Duncan Cameron (*Fairntosh), while son Thomas remained at Stagville until his death in 1847. Stagville and Fairntosh were inherited by Rebecca's son Paul Carrington Cameron, who was probably the richest man in the state before and after the Civil War.

Horton Grove was one of several plantation centers on the Bennehan-Cameron lands. From an earlier farm here is the **Horton House** (late 18th–early 19th c.), built of dovetailed planks with a 1-room plan, corner stair, and balancing front porch and rear shed. A devotee of scientific agriculture, Paul Cameron built the row of four unusually well-constructed 2-story **Slave Houses** (1860), with timber frames infilled with brick and covered with board and batten. There are 2 rooms per floor, divided by a stair; some have a single front entrance, while others have two. It is not certain how many slaves occupied the houses. After the Civil War, some freedpeople continued to

live here and in other slave and tenant houses on the plantations, now lost.

In Sept. 1860, Paul reported completion of the "'best stables' ever built in Orange (at Stagville) 135 feet long"—the imposing **Stable and Barn**. With its complex roof truss and heavy frame presenting a tour de force of traditional carpentry, the frame barn covered with board and batten incorporates spaces for livestock and storage of hay. Also at Horton Grove are a later, typical log **Tobacco Barn** and sites of other structures. The plantations remained in the hands of descendants until the mid-20th c. and were largely rural until the late 20th-c. residential and industrial development of Treyburn.

DH 64 Fairntosh
1810–23; William, John, and Elias Fort, carpenters; John J. Briggs, carpenter; William Collier, brickmason; Henry Gorman, plasterer; Elhannon Nutt, joiner; no public access or visibility

The house and outbuildings erected for Duncan and Rebecca Bennehan Cameron compose a remarkable ensemble from one of the largest plantations in the state. Duncan, a lawyer from Virginia, came to Hillsborough and soon married the daughter of Richard Bennehan, who gave them a large tract of land. Duncan's detailed records provide unusual documentation of the artisans' work on the large and handsome frame house (1810–13) in elaborate late Georgian–early Federal style (*Ayr Mount), rear addition (1818–21), and Neoclassical piazza (1827). Outbuildings include a front row of schoolhouse, office, and schoolteacher's house and a rear line with 2-story kitchen,

DH 64 *Fairntosh*

dairy, smokehouse, and commissary. After Duncan became a bank president and moved to Raleigh in 1836, Paul Cameron made his home at Fairntosh, as did his son Bennehan after him.

DH 65 Catsburg Store
1920s; NW corner SR 1004
and SR 1634, Weaver

The country store at a prominent intersection was built by Sheriff E. G. "Cat" Belvin —so called "because of his small size and easy moves." A friend suggested naming the settlement Catsburg and painting a big cat on the front parapet of the typical frame store.

DH 66 Holloway House
1880s; SW corner of SR 1637
and SR 1800, Redwood

The I-house with typical front roof gable has peaked window surrounds, bracketed and paneled cornice, and decorated porch— elaboration seen more often in town than in the country.

DH 67 Nichols House
Ca. 1812; N side SR 1813,
0.2 mi. W of SR 1811

One of the few small early houses left in the county, the 1½-story frame house has stout chimneys of Flemish-bond brick and a steep, dormered gable roof sheltering a hall-parlor plan. The roof extends over balancing rear shed rooms and engaged front porch, which has an enclosed porch chamber.

DH 68 Leigh Farm
Ca. 1835; end of SR 2290; limited public access

Just beyond the path of I-40, the farmstead is a rare survivor of its era. Richard Stanford Leigh and Nancy Ann Carlton married in 1834 and probably built the house soon afterward on a 500-acre tract they received from his father. The couple had 15 children, and their farm grew to nearly 1,000 acres by 1860, with 200 acres improved. With 16 slaves they raised wheat, corn, cotton, and vegetables. Exemplifying the modesty of all but the largest planters' dwellings, their house is a 1½-story frame structure with 4-room plan and plain, well-crafted trim and pine sheathing. The outbuildings, which epitomize the small size, specialized forms, and varied construction methods of the 19th c., include a tiny, cupboard-sized frame dairy set on legs and insulated with sawdust, a log smokehouse with half-dovetailed notching, a V-notched corncrib, and a square-notched tobacco barn. A restored diamond-notched log dwelling said to have been a slave house has one of the state's few surviving log chimneys, with V-notched base and wooden stack.

DH 68 *Leigh Farm*

Research Triangle Park

Opened in 1959, the pathbreaking Research Triangle Park (RTP) of more than 5,000 acres was planned to bring higher-paying jobs to the area and encourage economic development. To a greater extent than could have been imagined at the time, its establishment and growth have taken a crucial role in transforming the region. The park lies within and is named for a triangle formed by three research universities: Duke University

DH 70 *National Humanities Center*

in Durham, UNC in Chapel Hill, and NCSU in Raleigh. The concept and reality of RTP developed through cooperation among government, industrial, academic, and nonprofit bodies. Industries and governmental agencies established national research headquarters with emphasis in computer and internet development, electronics, pharmaceuticals, toxicology, telecommunications, and biotechnology, including IBM, Northern Telecom, Glaxo, Burroughs-Wellcome, Becton Dickinson, Chemstrand, and the Environmental Protection Agency. The nonprofit Research Triangle Foundation oversees development and planning guidelines that assure low density and a "campus-like appearance." Some 45,000 workers stream daily to the park from Raleigh, Durham, Chapel Hill, Cary, and beyond. The best view of its scale and complexity is from an airplane approaching the nearby Raleigh-Durham International Airport.

DH 69 Burroughs-Wellcome Building (GlaxoSmithKline)
1970; Paul Rudolph (Florida and New York), architect; Cornwallis Rd., Research Triangle Park; visible from road; not open to public

Designed as the American research headquarters for the British pharmaceutical company, this complex housing laboratories, offices, cafeteria, auditorium, and testing facilities was one of the first buildings in the Research Triangle to attract national attention for its design. Architect Rudolph cited the topography as inspiration for its form and siting (*Architectural Record*, Nov. 1970). The hexagon-shaped steel module that dominates the design is fitted on and into the monumental A-frame of the building. Stone aggregate covered panels form a lively surface. Inside, the light-filled lobby soars to the top of the great A-frame. Windows in the downface of the hexagon provide light and a view along with privacy and shade in the east-facing building. A substantial addition in harmonizing design stands to the west. (See Introduction, Fig. 74.)

DH 70 National Humanities Center
1978; Hartman-Cox, architects; Alexander Dr., Research Triangle Park

Described in the *AIA Journal* of May 1979 as a "Monastic Retreat for Secular Scholarship," the 30,000 square foot building is designed to allow both privacy and fellowship for the lucky scholars who study and write there each year. The building has an almost domestic modesty of scale, complemented by simplicity of materials—primarily white-painted brick. It couples individual offices with a bright commons room where the scholars for join for lunch and other informal meetings. Windows and skylights wash the interior with light and open the spaces to the sylvan surroundings.

Orange County (OR)

Founded in 1752 as a great mother county of the backcountry, Orange was traversed by the Trading Path from present-day Petersburg, Va., which crossed the Eno River near the ancient town of Occaneechi and the site of present-day Hillsborough. Early 18th-c. explorers John Lawson and William Byrd marveled at the fine land between the Eno and the Haw rivers, and settlers chiefly from Virginia and Pennsylvania soon established farms. Hillsborough was seat of the immense county, though its role shrank as Orange was divided into other counties in the 18th and 19th centuries. After the University of North Carolina (UNC) was sited in southern Orange Co. in 1792, the college town of Chapel Hill grew around it, followed by Carrboro on a late 19th-c. rail spur.

Although the county had a few large planters, most farmers owned small to medium-sized tracts, and nearly all raised grains, tobacco, livestock, and food crops; tobacco increased in the late 19th c. and dairying in the early 20th c. Despite late 20th-c. development, much of the county remains rural, especially in the north and west, with fields, pastures, and stands of oaks and hardwoods defining an agrarian landscape of unpretentious frame and log houses, barns, sheds, and tobacco barns.

Hillsborough (OR 1–34)

The small county seat possesses a unique identity that traces from its origins as colonial center of the backcountry and a prestigious little 19th-c. town where powerful people built simply. Hillsborough's special character arises not only from its important collection of 18th- and 19th-c. architecture but also from the retention of its spacious and informal urban landscape. Laid out in 1754 by surveyor William Churton, the 18th-c. grid plan still possesses many of the qualities—large semirural lots abutting a compact downtown, abundant plantings, outbuildings, and a mix of large and small houses—that once characterized many of the state's leading towns.

Initially called Orange, the town was renamed Corbinton, then Childsburg, for land agents of Lord Granville, then Hillsborough in 1766 for an English official. As seat of a vast western county, the village became the "political, social, and economic center of the whole backcountry" and a magnet for ambitious lawyers, merchants, and others. In the 1760s Hillsborough became a focus for the Regulator movement protesting colonial officials' abuse of power.

The movement ended in violence in 1771 when Governor William Tryon's troops defeated a band of Regulators outside Hillsborough (*Allen House) and hanged six of them. During the American Revolution, Hillsborough residents took important roles, including Thomas Burke, who was governor (1781–82), and Francis Nash, brigadier general under George Washington. Signer of the Declaration of Independence William Hooper moved here from Wilmington in 1782. The legislature met in Hillsborough during the war (1778, 1782–84), and the town hosted the Constitutional Convention of 1788.

During the 19th c. Hillsborough men continued to distinguish themselves in state forums: state supreme court chief justices Thomas Ruffin and Frederick Nash; banker and judge Duncan Cameron; internal improvement and education advocate Archibald D. Murphey; governor, senator, and secretary of the navy William A. Graham; publisher Dennis Heartt; and Reconstruction governor William Holden. The healthy location of the town also drew Wilmingtonians and other eastern Carolinians for summer stays and encouraged the establishment of several academies. In the 18th c. and most

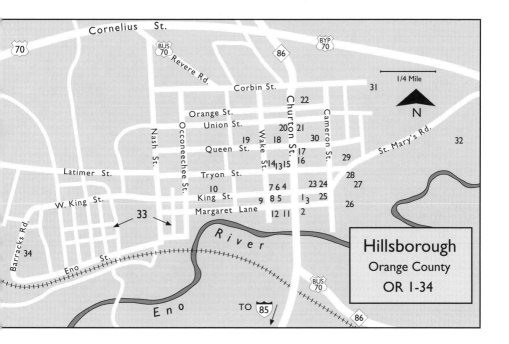

Hillsborough
Orange County
OR 1-34

of the 19th c., residents of every class and race, slave and free, lived in intermingled patterns, with small dwellings and slave houses interspersed among large houses. In 1833 a visitor from Connecticut found the town more to his liking than other small southern towns. Praising the "several beautiful residences" with "large gardens, full of flowers and fruit trees," he commented, "If the houses had a new covering of paint—and the yards were a little more neat . . . you might suppose you were in a New England village."

Despite the arrival of the North Carolina Railroad (NCRR) in the 1850s, Hillsborough grew slowly thereafter. Post–Civil War industrial growth in Durham prompted a (strongly resisted) division of the county to form Durham Co. Although local men founded small textile mills near the NCRR, industrialization was relatively modest. When the downtown was rebuilt in the early 20th c. and a new courthouse was erected behind the antebellum one in the mid-20th c., the new buildings continued a familiar scale.

Hillsborough's architecture is generally conservative and well crafted, chiefly the work of regional artisans. From the 18th c.

onward, most citizens built relatively unpretentious architecture with only occasional gestures at grandeur or fashion. From the 18th c. a few small wooden structures, some built to "save" lots, survive as cores of later houses.

A remarkable collection of architecture from the early 19th c. includes 1½-story Tidewater type dwellings and 2-story frame houses with stout brick chimneys, finished with restrained Georgian or Federal woodwork. A few clients and builders, however, responded to fashionable trends. In addition to those following customary hall-parlor, side-passage, 3-room, and center-passage plans, a number of houses—most built for clients from other regions—feature cross passages across the front and variations on the Palladian-influenced tripartite scheme with a center block plus flanking wings. In the 1820s, English architect William Nichols, active in Raleigh and at UNC, evidently planned *Eagle Lodge and *St. Matthews Church with early classical and Gothic motifs and may have had a hand in other local work.

Probably influenced in those projects by Nichols, Hillsborough master brick builder John Berry adapted late Federal and Greek

Revival elements from his own architectural books and became a leading regional builder, erecting the *Orange County Courthouse and building *Smith Hall at UNC from designs by New York architect Alexander Jackson Davis. For former governor William A. Graham, Davis drew up schemes in 1853 to remodel his Hillsborough home into an Italianate or Gothic residence, but Graham decided on a simpler plan in keeping with the "exceeding plainness of the buildings of our town."

Late 19th- and early 20th-c. building continued the prevailing conservatism, chiefly in simple Queen Anne, bungalow, and Colonial Revival styles. Steeped in tradition, the community celebrates its history through a local museum and a good crop of commemorative markers, and despite surrounding development pressures, it maintains a small-town scale and ambience that make it a rewarding place to escape the pace of the urban Triangle region.

OR 1 *Old Orange Co. Courthouse*

OR 1 Old Orange County Courthouse

1845; John Berry, designer and builder; 106 E. King St.

The architectural centerpiece of Hillsborough, the courthouse is among the finest in the state. The masterwork of brick builder John Berry, it combines beautiful craftsmanship with the straightforward dignity of a Greek Revival "temple of justice." Berry drew upon his collection of architectural books by Minard Lafever and Asher Benjamin for the Doric portico and 2-stage domed clock tower on a rusticated wooden base. The stair in the vestibule hall shows his favored use of a stair bracket from Owen Biddle's *Young Carpenter's Assistant.* Walls of fine Flemish bond have pilasters dividing the bays and flat arches above large 12/12 sash windows. Rising directly from the ground, the portico offers unimpeded access to the building. First-floor offices flanking a center passage retain simple Greek Revival finish, and the courtroom above has been returned to court use.

OR 2 Orange County Courthouse

1953; Archie Royall Davis (Chapel Hill), architect; 106 E. Margaret Ln.

Designed by a leading mid-20th-c. practitioner of the Colonial Revival, the red brick courthouse harmonizes with its predecessor but features Georgian Revival details and a pedimented pavilion of Palladian inspiration.

OR 3 Cadwalader Jones Law Office

Early 19th c.; 131 Court St.

The small but prominent red brick structure, with its gable front facing the courthouse, exemplifies the small law offices once characteristic of county seats. Their size had no relation to the status or influence of their occupants, a situation that continues in the unpretentious offices of many small-town law firms.

OR 4 Eagle Lodge

1823; William Nichols; John Berry & Samuel Hancock, builders (attrib.); 142 W. King St.

The elegantly austere cube with a small Ionic portico is credibly attributed to En-

OR 4 *Eagle Lodge*

glish architect Nichols. The lodge (chartered 1791, reorganized 1819) built the hall in 1823 and still occupies it. The 2-story hip-roofed building of Flemish-bond brick contains a front cross hall and a large meeting room. Evidently an early project of Berry when he was working with master bricklayer Hancock, it exposed him to Nichols's sophisticated taste.

OR 5 Colonial Inn
1838 and later; 153 W. King St.

Serving as the Orange Hotel, Occaneechee Hotel, Corbinton Inn, and Colonial Inn, the picturesque and rambling frame building shows several phases of 19th- and 20th-c. expansion. The 2-tier porch 9 bays long extends out so that the sidewalk passes through it—an element once common in N.C. towns. A few doors east, the old "Cedar Walk" path between streets evokes a quieter time.

OR 6 Samuel Gattis House
Ca. 1909; 158 W. King St.

The large frame house on its spacious lot is one of many that blend the asymmetrical massing of the Queen Anne style with Colonial Revival details. A picturesque well house stands atop a well dug in the 18th c.

OR 7 Twin Chimneys
18th, 19th c.; 168 W. King St.

The 2-story frame house, traditionally dated ca. 1770, attained its present form in the 19th c. Pairs of chimneys in Flemish-bond

brick flank a double-pile plan. The tall, arched front windows with Italianate frames are a type popular throughout town, attributed to decorator Jule Korner of *Kernersville, who worked for Julian Carr in advertising Bull Durham tobacco and remodeled a house near town for Carr in similar fashion.

OR 8 Parks-Richmond House
18th, late 19th c.; 175 W. King St.; B&B

Expanded in the late 19th c. and for a time part of the Occaneechee Hotel, the big frame house with Italianate bracketed eaves and front center gable is one of many local residences enclosing an 18th-c. core.

OR 9 First Baptist Church
1860–70; William Percival, architect; D. Kistler, John Berry, builders; 100 block S. Wake St. at W. King St.

The modest early venture in the Romanesque Revival style was designed by eclectic architect Percival on the eve of his departure from the state (*New East, New West, Chapel Hill). Construction was begun by builder Kistler, halted by the Civil War, and completed by Berry, with corbeled brick panels and cornices and round arches enlivening the gable-fronted sanctuary and recessed corner tower.

OR 10 Ruffin-Snipes House
Ca. 1800; 1840s, John Berry, builder (attrib.); 320 W. King St.

The handsome 2-story frame house has a front section of late Georgian character and was remodeled with rear rooms and Greek Revival front porch probably by John Berry.

OR 11 Cameron-Nash Law Office
Early 19th c.; 143 W. Margaret Ln.

The little law office, with steep gable roof and a door flanked by windows, is neatly finished with wainscot and Federal style fluted mantel. It was built either for young attorney Duncan Cameron (*Fairntosh), who owned the property from 1801 to 1807, or for

Frederick Nash, N.C. Supreme Court chief justice, who owned the property, which included a house and other outbuildings, from 1807 until 1858. After Nash died, his daughters Sally and Maria Nash and their cousin Sarah Kollock operated the Nash and Kollock "school for young ladies," using the office for music classes and adding a west wing.

OR 12 Walker-Palmer House
Early 19th c.; 173 W. Margaret Ln.

The 1½ story frame house, set on a raised basement and with narrow, gabled dormers, shares something of the form of the *Ruffin-Roulhac House but has an unusual transverse-passage plan with end chambers and two large rear rooms, suggestive of *Ayr Mount. Federal woodwork is of conservative Hillsborough cast. The house was evidently built for Caroline Mary Mallett Walker, wife of Carleton Walker of the Cape Fear area, during her ownership from 1823 to 1846.

OR 13 Nash-Hooper-Graham House
1772 and later; 118 W. Tryon St.

The 2-story frame house began as the home of Gen. Francis Nash, who was killed in battle in 1777. William Hooper, a signer of the Declaration of Independence whose home near Wilmington was destroyed by the British, bought the Nash property in 1782 and lived here until his death in 1790. The house was substantially rebuilt in the 19th c. and was later the home of Governor William A. Graham (1869–75).

OR 14 Methodist Church
Ca. 1859–60; John Berry, builder; 100 block W. Tryon St.

The simple gable-fronted Greek Revival church of brick typifies Berry's good craftsmanship and conservative stylistic touches. The entrance tower dominates a pedimented, windowless gabled facade, and large side windows of 16/16 sash brighten the sanctuary.

OR 15 Presbyterian Church and Cemetery
1815–16, ca. 1892; John Berry & Samuel Hancock, builders; NW corner Churton and W. Tryon Sts.

The congregation organized ca. 1816 and served by noted minister John Knox Witherspoon was an important influence in Hillsborough. The simple brick church, an early work by Berry and Hancock, has been continuously used, with changes as needed, including a ca. 1892 remodeling. The churchyard contains many old graves and markers. Nearby on Churton St. is the early 20th-c. **Museum** of local varicolored stone like that used at *Duke University.

OR 16 Robertson-Cheek House
Ca. 1846, 1870s; 219 N. Churton St.

Set far back from the street, the 2-story frame house epitomizes the center-gabled Italianate bracketed form popular throughout the state in the late 19th c. It is believed to have been remodeled from an antebellum dwelling.

OR 17 Dickerson's Chapel A.M.E. Church
Ca. 1790, 1891, 1947; SE corner Queen and Churton Sts.

The long history of the gable-fronted building began as the ca. 1790 courthouse, the county's third, which was moved to this site when its 1845 successor was erected. It was used as the First Baptist Church, then as a Quaker school for black children in the 1860s. After becoming Dickerson's Chapel A.M.E. Church, it was remodeled in 1891 in Gothic Revival style, then brick-veneered in 1947.

OR 18 Hasell-Nash House
Ca. 1820; 116 W. Queen St.

Although most of the tripartite villa residences in the state were built for eastern planters, Hillsborough had its share, including *Moorefields and *Ayr Mount. Built for Eliza Hasell of Wilmington, who owned the lot from 1819 to 1828, this version has a ped-

OR 18 *Hasell-Nash House*

imented 2-story center block fronted by a porch of Ionic columns and flanked by matching 1-story pedimented wings, with Gothic-arched vents in the tympana. Rather than a transverse-hall plan, the center section has a side-passage plan; much original Federal finish survives. Its stylish format has suggested an influence from William Nichols.

OR 19 Berry House

1814; Samuel Hancock, probable builder; 208 W. Queen St.

The 1½-story brick residence of Rhoda Berry and her son John was probably built by Samuel Hancock, brickmason and mentor of master builder John. The plain little building, with a 3-room plan with center passage, is important as the home of the noted builder and as a rare example of housing of the middling and artisan class.

OR 20 Burwell School

Early 19th c., 1848–49; John Berry, builder; 319 N. Churton St.; open limited hours

The complex, originally the Presbyterian manse, housed the Burwell School, a noted Presbyterian academy for girls. From 1837 to 1857 it was run by Anna Burwell until she and her husband, Presbyterian minister Robert Burwell, left for an academy in Charlotte. During their tenure the old 2-story hall-parlor plan house was enlarged by builder John Berry to create a center-passage plan. Restoration of the school returned the exterior to its mid-19th-c. appearance and preserved interior features of various periods. Outbuildings include a brick classroom of two rooms and a necessary house.

OR 21 Shepperd Strudwick House

Ca. 1903; Ralph Adams Cram (Boston), architect; 318 N. Churton St.

The graceful composition in a Southern Colonial style reminiscent of the Deep South was designed by the Boston architect best known for his Gothic Revival work, including N.C. churches. A 2-tier portico with full-height columns stretches across the front, sheltering French doors. Shepperd Strudwick, of a local family, became a broker in Richmond, Va., and married Susan Nash Read, sister-in-law of the architect.

OR 22 Ruffin-Roulhac House

Ca. 1820; Martin Hanks, carpenter (attrib.); ca. 1830s; 101 E. Orange St.; open business hours

Center of a complex that once occupied the whole block, the 1½-story dwelling evidently began with a side-passage plan 2 rooms deep, then gained 2 rooms on the east to produce a center-passage plan. Interiors include a fine Federal style stair in the Owen Biddle mode favored by John Berry and openings framed by early Greek Revival moldings with roundel cornerblocks. The front porch is probably 20th c., while the 19th-c. back porch has columns of wedge-shaped bricks (*Bingham School). Outbuildings include a former law office. Prominent residents included Francis L. Hawks (Episcopal cleric and grandson of #Tryon Palace architect John Hawks) in the 1820s; Frances Blount Hill, who enlarged the house ca. 1830; Anne and Thomas Ruffin (chief justice of the N.C. Supreme Court) after the Civil War; and the Roulhac family. The

OR 22 *Ruffin-Roulhac House*

property was rescued and converted to a town hall in 1972.

OR 23 Yellow House
(William Courtney House)
Late 18th c.; 141 E. King St.

The tall 2-story frame house high above the street is among the oldest dwellings in town. It was known as the Yellow House by 1801. Set on a basement of irregular stone, it has a severely plain facade, narrow windows, and double-shouldered chimney of Flemish-bond brick with glazed headers; it retains some early features, including a fully paneled wall inside. William Courtney, a Quaker, acquired the property in 1777—perhaps with the house—and evidently ran a tavern there.

OR 24 Seven Hearths
Late 18th–early 19th c.;
157 E. King St.; private

Cited as an early 19th-c. tavern, the rambling 2-story house on its well-planted corner lot typifies the substantial houses of the Piedmont in its gable-roofed form and end chimneys. Set high on its basement, it contains locally characteristic Federal-era reeded mantels, plus early wings and ells.

OR 25 Alexander Dickson
House and Office
Late 18th c.; 150 E. King St.; moved 1983;
open as visitors center

The compact 2-story frame house with 1-story ell exhibits elements of the earliest architecture of the Piedmont: vertical proportions, brick-nogged framing covered by molded weatherboards, simple Georgian finish, and a brick chimney with an unusual combination of an English-bond face and Flemish-bond sides. The original 3-room plan interior was updated with a center passage and Federal trim in the early 19th c. The 1-room freestanding office is mid-19th c. Both buildings stood on the southwest edge of Hillsborough, near the present-day I-40/85 corridor, and are cited as headquarters for Gen. Joseph E. Johnston during his ne-gotiations with Gen. William T. Sherman at *Bennett Place.

OR 26 Burnside
1834–35; Jack, John Berry, builders; opp. E end of Margaret Ln.; limited public visibility

The large, simply finished frame house was built for Anne Ruffin and Paul Cameron. Paul practiced law briefly in Hillsborough before returning to *Fairntosh, plantation of his father, Duncan, as an agriculturist. The property was from Anne's father, Thomas Ruffin, state supreme court chief justice, whose frame **Law Office** remains along with other outbuildings. Carpentry was directed by Jack, a slave carpenter, and brickwork was by John Berry.

OR 27 Hughes Academy
Ca. 1864; on grounds of Orange Co. Board of Education, E end of King St.

Moved to this site for preservation in the 1990s, the 1-story, 2-room frame building with central chimney served an influential rural school established by Dr. Samuel Hughes near *Cedar Grove in 1845 that operated into the late 19th c. The interior retains ghost marks of desks faced to the wall in 19th-c. fashion. Nearby is the restoration of the **Cameron Ice House** (1850s), a brick-lined octagonal pit 17 feet in diameter with octagonal roof that served the residents of *Burnside; it is the largest structure of its type known in the state.

OR 28 St. Matthews Episcopal Church
1826; William Nichols, architect; St. Mary's Rd.

Seeking to revitalize the denomination that lapsed after the American Revolution, N.C. Episcopalians erected a few early 19th-c. churches that were traditional in form and Gothic chiefly in their pointed-arched doors and windows. A parishioner's letter notes architect Nichols's role in planning St. Matthews. Built on land given by Thomas Ruffin, the little church on a hill began as a simple gable-fronted structure of Flemish-bond brick with pointed openings. It later

gained more elaborate Gothic Revival elements, including the entrance tower (1830, rebuilt 1850) and spire (1875); the gallery (1835); and exposed beam ceiling and chancel extension (1868). The churchyard contains graves of Hillsborough leaders and eastern N.C. sojourners.

OR 29 Hill-Webb House

Ca. 1800, mid-1850s; E. Tryon St. at St. Mary's Rd.; B&B

One of the most stylish mid-19th-c. houses in town, the towered Italianate villa was probably inspired by A. J. Downing's *Cottage Residences*. It was created for planter Thomas Blount Hill of the #Hermitage Plantation in Halifax Co., recently of Warrenton, and his wife, Maria Simpson of New

OR 29 *Hill-Webb House*

Bern, who had spent summers in Hillsborough as a girl. After acquiring the property in 1853, they transformed an earlier house (ca. 1800) into a fashion plate akin in form to the *Jacob Holt House in Warrenton. A 2-story brick kitchen and other outbuildings remain.

OR 30 Heartsease

Late 18th c., early and mid-19th c.; 113 E. Queen St.

The modest frame house embodies several phases: the small 3-bay core probably dates from the late 18th c.; the 1½-story east wing and dormers were added in the early 19th c.; and the 2-story west wing came later in the 19th c., followed by the shed porch. This was the home of Dennis Heartt, a native of Connecticut who from 1820 to 1869 edited and published the influential *Hillsborough Recorder*. His apprentices are said to have occupied the gabled attic; they included William W. Holden, later newspaper editor and Reconstruction-era governor.

OR 30 *Heartsease*

OR 31 Sans Souci

Early 19th c.; 237 E. Corbin St.

The 2-story frame dwelling with side-passage plan was probably built for Dr. William Cain and Mary Ruffin, who married in 1819. She was the sister of jurist Thomas Ruffin; physician and planter William was the son of planter William Cain (*Hardscrabble). Slightly later wings created a tripartite scheme, and the porch dates from the late 19th c. Outbuildings include a former slave quarters and a carriage house.

OR 32 Ayr Mount

1814–16; William Collier, brickmason; John J. Briggs, carpenter; Elhannon Nutt, joiner (attrib.); open by appointment

William Kirkland, a native of Ayr, Scotland, became a merchant in Warrenton, married his partner's sister, Margaret Scott, and moved to Hillsborough in 1793. As his business and family grew, he acquired a plantation overlooking the Eno River, and about 1814 he began construction of a house that he named for his birthplace. The state's chief tripartite-plan house in brick, it comprises a 2-story, 40-by-40-foot main block and flanking 1-story wings, all with side gables. Set high on its foundation, the tall house has walls laid in Flemish bond, molded water tables, modillion cornices, and on the main facade, stone lintels. The small portico was reconstructed in a late 20th-c. restoration. The plan has a transverse front passage opening to the wing rooms and two unequal rear rooms in the main block. Elaborate interiors, akin to *Fairntosh, present a distinctive blend of late Georgian and early Federal elements, including ornate mantels probably by Elhannon Nutt, who advertised his capacity to work in a "superiour manner" (*Haywood Hall, Raleigh). See Jean Anderson, *The Kirklands of Ayr Mount.*

OR 33 West Hillsborough Mill Villages

Despite the proximity of the NCRR, Hillsborough never shifted its focus toward the tracks, and industrial development remained minor. By the late 19th c. there were a few tobacco factories, a carriage factory, and other small operations in the south and west sectors near the railroad and the river. The freight and passenger depots (lost) stood at the foot of Nash St. Around the turn of the century, local investors climbed on the textile manufacturing bandwagon: Allen Ruffin and James Webb founded the Eno Cotton Mill (1896) near the depot, and Shepperd Strudwick and others started the Bellevue Mfg. Co. (1904) on Nash St. north of the tracks. The companies erected several blocks of mill housing on both sides of the Eno River, chiefly 1-story gable-sided frame dwellings. Most intact are the **Bellevue Mill** and its village near the southwest corner of Nash and W. King Sts., part of an extensive community known as West Hillsborough.

OR 34 Commandant's House

1859–60; John A. Kay (Columbia, S.C.); John Berry & Henry Richards, builders; Barracks Rd., Hillsborough vic.

When Charles C. Tew of S.C. began a military academy at Hillsborough, he had archi-

OR 32 *Ayr Mount*

tect Kay design castellated brick buildings akin to those of his alma mater, the Citadel. Although Tew left when the Civil War began and was killed at Sharpsburg, the academy continued to provide the Confederacy with young officers. The campus housed a military school after the war, then became the headquarters of the Farmers' Alliance (1895–1920). The big academy building was razed in 1938, but the Commandant's House survives as a private residence. It is the only intact N.C. example of the romantic military mode.

OR 35 Moorefields

Late 18th c.; NW outer corner SR 1135, 0.1 mi. W of SR 1134, Hillsborough vic.; private, not visible from road; visitation by appointment

One of the prominent men of the Cape Fear who came to Hillsborough was planter and Revolutionary officer Alfred Moore. After the war, he turned to law, becoming state attorney general, justice of the N.C. superior court, and in 1799 justice of the U.S. Supreme Court. Said to have been Moore's summer home, Moorefields is a small but stylish tripartite-form dwelling, possibly updated by Alfred Jr., who inherited the property in 1818. It has a narrow, gable-sided central section, which contains a side passage and a single large parlor, flanked by 1-story wings, each two rooms deep. The interior is notable for the Chinese lattice stair railing and a reeded mantel with overmantel. (One of the major 18th-c. plantation houses outside Wilmington, John Burgwin's "Hermitage" [lost] was an early model of the tripartite form.)

OR 35 *Moorefields*

OR 36 Faucette and Ellis Houses
Early–mid 19th c.; S side SR 1336, both sides SR 1337 at Eno River

The Faucette (Faucett) family settled along the Eno in the late 18th c. and continued into the late 20th c. (An early 19th-c. Faucett house, known as Chatwood and said to have served as an inn beside an old ford, is located on a private road a few miles south near Faucett Mill.) This **Faucette House** (w side Eno River) is a 2-story frame house with modest Federal and Greek Revival detail, a hall-parlor plan, and brick end chimneys; it is said to have been built for David and Elizabeth or their son Joseph and his wife Polly Tinnen, who married in 1822. East of the river is the **Ellis House, "Little Ayr Mount,"** so called for its brick construction and tripartite form. It is plainly finished, with 1:4 bond brick and simple flat arches over openings in the 2-story center block and flanking 1-story wings. It was evidently built in the early to mid-19th c. for Ira Ellis, a Methodist minister who rented David Faucette's mill and in 1860 offered for sale his 6-room "good brick house" and a "first rate threshing machine. . . . Owner too old to work it."

OR 37 Cedar Grove
Intersection of SRs 1004, 1352, and 1357

The village began in the early 19th c. where the Hillsborough-Milton road crossed the road to Greensboro. It had a post office by 1828 and soon acquired an academy, a church, a tanner, a coachmaker, a physician, a blacksmith, and stores. Still standing are two 2-story frame country stores with front porches, the **Allison-Oliver-Pender Store** (1880s; NW corner) and the **Ellis Store** (est. 1923; SW corner). To the north beside a large cemetery the **Cedar Grove Methodist Church** (1939) was a Gothic Revival sanctuary built of local stone for a congregation est. 1832; the congregation plans to rebuild on the old walls following a fire. **Eno Presbyterian Church** farther north was built in the 1890s and later brick-veneered for a congregation established in the 18th c. Around the crossroads, especially along SR 1004 leading west, are farmsteads with simple 19th-c. houses, Colonial Revival residences, and bungalows.

OR 38 Walter Hawkins Farmstead

Mid-19th c. onward; W side SR 1507, 1 mi. S of SR 1508; private, visible from road

The representative farmstead beside the road has simple frame and log buildings from a long continuum of farming. The original farmhouse, thought to date from the 1840s, is a typically small, 1-story frame house with a large stone end chimney. Walter Hawkins, who bought the place in 1900, built a frame I-house, which gained various wings and porches. The informal assemblage of over a dozen outbuildings includes a garage and a privy near the house; a log smokehouse, a frame corncrib, and a large frame barn; and down the farm path, a stand of log and stuccoed tobacco barns.

OR 39 Jordan House

Ca. 1875; SE side NC 57, 0.2 mi. S of NC 157, Caldwell vic.; B&B; private, visible from road

One of many substantial farmhouses in northern Orange Co., the prominent frame house is an especially ornate Italianate rendition of the I-house form, with gabled entrance pavilion and decorated porch. It was built by Dr. Archibald Jordan, physician, teacher at the local Caldwell Institute, operator of Jordan Brothers general store and pharmacy nearby, and elder at Little River Presbyterian Church.

OR 40 Sunnyside

Early 19th c., 1840s; John Berry, builder; NW corner SR 1002 and SR 1554; private, visible from road

Despite 20th-c. alterations, the big frame house is important as the home of John Berry, a local brickmason who became a regional contractor of unusual stature. He amassed property, served in the state legislature, and was regularly appointed arbiter in building disputes. Acquired and reworked by Berry in the 1840s, the place was the childhood home of Berry's granddaughter Harriet Morehead Berry, "Mother of Good Roads" in the early 20th c.

OR 41 St. Mary's Episcopal Church

1858–59; NE corner jct. SR 1002 and SR 1548, Caldwell vic.

Established in the 1750s, St. Mary's parish was reinvigorated in the 19th c. Possibly the work of John Berry, the small Gothic Revival brick church has buttresses flanking lancet openings and a simple interior. An 18th-c. graveyard lies nearby. Nearby is the early 20th-c. brick **St. Mary's School**. St. Mary's Rd. was an important early route and still traverses a rural landscape.

OR 42 Neville House

19th c.; E side SR 1009, 0.2 mi. S of SR 1113; private, visible from road

The 1-room log house beside the road typifies innumerable small log houses in the county, many of which are remote from view. Measuring about 18 by 20 feet, the 1-story house is built of hewn logs with half-dovetailed notching and contains a single room with enclosed corner stair. The Neville family, who have owned the farm for at least three generations, have preserved it near their newer residence.

OR 42 *Neville House*

OR 43 Bingham School

1845–64; NE corner NC 54 and SR 1007, Oaks vic.; private; B&B

The complex served from 1845 to 1864 as the home and school of William J. Bingham and his sons, who operated a series of re-

spected schools in the Piedmont and western parts of the state. (Descendants published the *Courier-Journal* in Louisville, Ky.) A small house of log and brick-nogged timber frame, which stood when Bingham obtained the property, became a rear ell when he added the large 2-story Greek Revival style dwelling. A colonnaded porch of rounded brick columns creates a rear courtyard, and there are several 19th-c. outbuildings.

OR 44 Smith-Cole House

Early 19th c.; W side SR 1919,
0.3 mi. N of US 15/501, Carrboro vic.;
private, visible from road

The prominently sited plantation house is among the oldest and largest in the county, 2 stories tall with a 5-bay double-pile plan and pairs of tall brick end chimneys. It was the longtime home of the Smith family, whose lives and those of their slaves are depicted in descendant Pauli Murray's *Proud Shoes*. From the 1880s the place was owned by the Cole family.

Chapel Hill (OR 45–51)

The state's first university town has a special character acknowledged in its nickname, "the southern part of heaven." The village developed along with the university founded in 1792, and their identities are so closely bound that students traditionally identify themselves simply as studying at "Chapel Hill" (see book spine). Despite explosive late

20th-c. growth of town and university, thus far their historic cores have been preserved by community and institutional efforts. Along Franklin St., meeting place of town and gown, the 19th- and early 20th-c. campus stretches south, and adjoining residential streets maintain the informal paths, low stone walls, big trees, and relatively unpretentious houses from quieter village days. Beyond the center extend miles of new campus and town development.

OR 45 University of North Carolina at Chapel Hill (a–p)

See John V. Allcott, *The Campus at Chapel Hill: Two Hundred Years of Architecture* (1986).

Throughout its history, the university has occupied a unique place in the state's heart, engendering immense pride in its academic or athletic excellence, occasional resentment of its liberal or elitist elements, and shared nostalgia and power networks that link the state's communities, generations, and leaders. "Groved with magnificent ancient trees," as Thomas Wolfe wrote, the old campus centers on two quadrangles south of Franklin St. and retains nearly all of the university's principal buildings from the 18th c. onward. This rich history of collegiate architecture in its sylvan oasis encapsulates the architectural history of the state and represents the work of generations of local builders and architects and of leading designers in the state and the nation.

The university was chartered in 1789 by the General Assembly, which specified a healthful location at least 5 miles from any courthouse or capital. In 1792, after considering local offers of land and support, commissioners selected rural Piedmont sites for the university and the capital. William R. Davie, leading advocate for the school, praised the chosen site "on the summit of a very high ridge" as "excelled by few places in the world, either for beauty or situation or salubrity of air." Like many American colleges, it was well removed from urban influences—"inaccessible to vice"—and its open mall plan allowed for expansion. The first building, *Old East, was ready for classes to

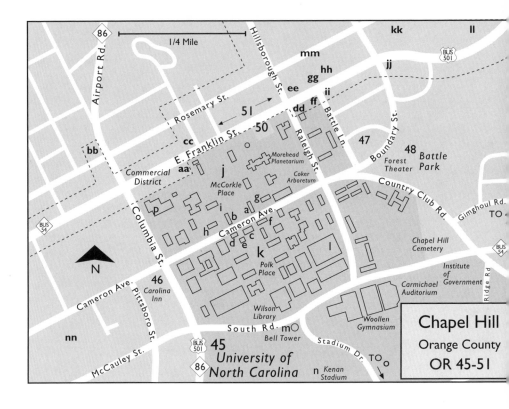

Chapel Hill
Orange County
OR 45-51

begin on January 15, 1795. UNC thus became the first state university in the nation to open its doors.

Led by men trained at the College of New Jersey (now Princeton), including President Joseph Caldwell, proponent of internal improvements and public education, the classically oriented school for men grew slowly to over 100 students by 1820. Continually hampered by lack of funds, the campus gained a sequence of hard-won, conservative brick and frame buildings.

In the 1840s, however, president and former governor David L. Swain inaugurated a building campaign. In 1843 he consulted alumnus Robert Donaldson of New York for advice on a designer for campus improvements. Donaldson suggested his friend Alexander Jackson Davis and advised the architect to plan simple, economical buildings of stuccoed brick. This was the first of several N.C. projects for the noted New York architect after dissolution of the Town & Davis firm (*State Capitol). After a visit in 1844 (*Blandwood, Greensboro), Davis provided designs for stylish landscaping and architecture in Tuscan and classical modes. He was followed in the late 1850s by architect William Percival. Unified by a warm-colored wash or stucco applied to old and new buildings, these landmarks of the small antebellum university cluster around E. Cameron Ave. at the head of the north quad, their orientations recalling changing campus layouts of the early years.

Operating through the Civil War only to close during Reconstruction in 1871, the university reopened in 1875 after long campaigning. The story is told of how Chapel Hill citizen Cornelia Phillips Spencer, leader in the campaign, upon receiving news of passage of a bill to allow reopening, climbed to the top of South Building to "ring the bell" and announce the news. During hard times in the late 19th c., the principal construction project was Memorial Auditorium, designed by Philadelphia architect Samuel Sloan as a spectacular venture into late 19th-c. eclecticism; it was razed in 1930 by devotees of the Colonial Revival.

The early 20th c. brought extraordinary development toward a new vision of a major university. First came Neoclassical and collegiate Tudor style buildings extending the original campus. Most were designed by Frank P. Milburn, who accommodated dignity and economy as required in an era when the president and alumni had to raise private funds for each building. After 1920, in response to soaring attendance after World War I, a master plan for growth and a successful campaign for a multimillion-dollar state bond issue undergirded an immense construction program, centered on a second quadrangle to the south. Most of the old buildings were reworked inside. Architects included William Kendall of McKim, Mead & White of New York as consulting architects and Arthur Nash, who came to Chapel Hill in 1922, formed with Thomas Atwood the firm of Atwood & Nash, and promoted the Beaux Arts, Colonial Revival vocabulary that infused campus and town for a half-century. The decades after World War II saw rapid growth to a university of more than 25,000 students and an extensive campus with diverse architecture, including some of the state's earliest Postmodernist designs.

a, b. Old East and Old West

Old East, 1793–95, James Patterson, builder; Old West, 1822–23, William Nichols, architect; 1844–45, Alexander Jackson Davis (New York), architect; Dabney Cosby, Collier & Waitt, builders; 1924

Old East, the university's initial main building, is the oldest state university building in the nation. Its cornerstone was laid October 12, 1793, in a ceremony led by William R. Davie, "Father of the University" and Grand Master of Masons. It was dedicated in January 1795 in time for the state university to become the first in the nation to open its doors. Detailed specifications and plan and elevation drawings of 1793 and a 1797 student sketch depict the plain 2-story brick building, which was intended as a wing of a larger building. Constructed of brick laid in Flemish bond, it was similar to dormitories at Yale and elsewhere and took the form essentially of an adjoining pair of gable-sided

houses, each with a center doorway and flanking windows. The third story was added in 1822 by William Nichols, state architect (*Mordecai House, Raleigh), who also built the matching Old West across the quad.

In the 1840s, architect A. J. Davis planned additions to accommodate the student debating societies, Philanthropic and Dialectic. He extended both buildings to the north and gave them dramatic Tuscan facades, each with a pediment above tall pilasters flanking a full-height opening. Bracketed eaves unified old and new. The society halls were elegantly fitted out by Milton free black cabinetmaker Thomas Day but remodeled in the 1920s for dorm rooms. In the late 20th c. the buildings were restored, including re-creation of 19th-c. cupolas. Old East is a National Historic Landmark.

c. South Building

1798–1814; Samuel Hopkins, initial builder; 1927

Planned since 1792 as the Main Building, the big brick structure was begun in 1798, but after money ran out in 1801, it stood unfinished for years, with students essentially camping inside. Only after long campaigning by President Caldwell were funds raised for its completion in 1814. Modeled generally on Nassau Hall at Princeton, the austere Palladian design is traditionally credited to trustee Richard Dobbs Spaight of

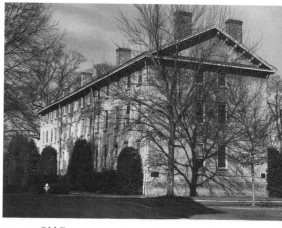

OR 45a *Old East*

OR 45c *South Building with Old Well*

New Bern. It was modified over the years: a belfry was removed 1822, then replaced in 1860; in 1897 President Edwin A. Alderman installed a Georgian Revival surround at the north entrance, copied from Westover in Virginia; and in the 1920s Arthur Nash added the south portico and lowered the roof pitch.

d. Gerrard Hall
1822–37; William Nichols, architect

The 2-story gable-roofed brick building 7 bays wide was designed as the "New Chapel" by state architect Nichols. It originally had an impressive Ionic portico on the south, reflecting a short-lived south-facing campus plan of the 1820s.

e. YMCA
1907; Frank P. Milburn, architect

Longtime hub of student activities, the Y was designed in a modified Tudor Revival style by Milburn, architect of most of the campus buildings from 1898 to 1920.

f. Smith Hall (Playmakers Theater)
1849–52; Alexander Jackson Davis (New York), architect; John Berry (Hillsborough), builder

The small but monumental temple-form building is one of Davis's principal surviving works in N.C. To accommodate a "Library and Assembly Room" for receptions and the annual commencement ball, Davis combined his pilastered Tuscan mode with a more ornate Corinthian-derived portico adjudged suitably "elegant" for the festive purpose. He consulted frequently with President Swain and builder John Berry and commissioned a New York firm to carve the column capitals, in which classical acanthus leaves were replaced by corn and wheat—a motif Davis had seen at architect Benjamin Henry Latrobe's U.S. Capitol. The exterior is largely intact, while the interior has been reworked as bath house, law school, and Playmakers Theater, whose stars included Paul Green, Andy Griffith, and Thomas Wolfe. National Historic Landmark.

g, h. New East and New West
1859; William Percival, architect; Thomas Coats, builder; 1925, Atwood & Nash

The striking pair of stuccoed brick Italianate dormitories flanking Old East and Old West were planned by William Percival, who made a brief appearance in the state in the late 1850s and probably won the commission over Davis because of proximity. In contrast to his more exuberant designs (*Caswell Co. Courthouse), he used a restrained Tuscan

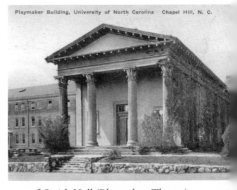

OR 45f *Smith Hall (Playmakers Theater)*

style to harmonize with Davis's buildings. He set the pair at right angles with Old East and Old West and gave each a raised center pavilion and a belvedere. To create a level cornice line across the sloping terrain, however, he made New East four stories tall and New West three. Although their window proportions were disturbed in a 1920s remodeling, the tripartite compositions survive.

i. Person Hall

1795–98; Samuel Hopkins, Philemon Hodges, builders; 1886, 1894, 1936

The second oldest state university building in the nation, originally the university chapel and meeting room, is of brick laid in Flemish bond. Round-arched windows suited to a chapel are accentuated by fine, rubbed brick and keystones. After *Gerrard Hall succeeded it as chapel, it was used and expanded for various purposes.

j. McCorkle Place

Extending from Franklin St. to Cameron Ave., the beautiful old north quadrangle is named for early educator and Presbyterian minister Samuel Eusebius McCorkle (*Thyatira Presbyterian Church, Rowan Co.). An icon of the school, the **Old Well** (1955; Eggers & Higgins [New York], architects) began as a crude structure atop the water supply for the 18th-c. university. In 1897 President Edwin Alderman, seeking modest beautifications to the campus, installed the "Westover" door at nearby South Building and covered the well with a domed, columned temple after the Temple of Love at Versailles. It was rebuilt on stone in 1955. The leaning, cabled **Davie Poplar** is revered as the tree under which William R. Davie determined the site of the university. (The nearby "Davie Poplar Jr." was judiciously planted in 1918 from a graft.) The simple obelisk of the **Caldwell Monument** (1847; Struthers [Philadelphia], maker) memorializes Joseph Caldwell, "the first president of this university" and "an early, conspicuous, and devoted advocate of Common Schools and Internal improvements." The **Confed-**erate Monument** (1913), honoring students and alumni who served in the "war of 1861–65," has a relief panel showing a student dropping his books to answer the call to arms and is topped by a figure of a soldier known as "Silent Sam."

Lining the quad are key buildings from the early 20th-c. expansion. On the east is one of the first and grandest: **Alumni Building** (1898–1901; Frank P. Milburn, architect), of tan brick and stone with arcaded walls, arched windows, and a Corinthian portico, returned to symmetrical, classically inspired forms and was praised as "modeled after the Boston Public Library, with the addition of a very beautiful classic portico." The **Morehead Planetarium** (1949; Eggers & Higgins [New York], architects) continued the red brick Georgian Revival mode begun in the 1920s, in a domed design that refers to the University of Virginia. It was donated by alumnus John Motley Morehead III, who made his fortune as a chemist with Union Carbide (*Spray, Eden) and in 1945 created a foundation to fund the planetarium and the prestigious Morehead Scholarship program at the university.

OR 45j *Alumni Building*

West of the quad, the Tudoresque **Battle-Vance-Pettigrew Building** (1912; Milburn & Heister, architects) was built as a dormitory; its most famous student resident was novelist Thomas Wolfe. The Neoclassical Revival style **Hill Hall** (1907, Frank P. Milburn, architect; 1930, Atwood & Nash, architects) was built as a Carnegie library, then gained an auditorium for a music center funded by the John Sprunt Hill family of Durham. Other notable eclectic and classical buildings of the era stand outside the quad and along Cameron Ave.

k. Polk Place

1921 and later; John Nolen, landscape designer; McKim, Mead & White, consulting architects; Thomas C. Atwood, supervising engineer; H. P. Alan Montgomery, Arthur C. Nash & H. R. Weeks, architects; T. C. Thompson & Bros., principal contractors

Stretching down the slope south from South Building to Wilson Library, the grand Beaux Arts quadrangle was created as part of the building surge of the 1920s. Initially called "South Quadrangle," it is named for alumnus James K. Polk, 11th president of the United States. The campus expansion, to accommodate the post–World War I leap in the student population, followed a campaign waged by alumni, faculty, students, and others that in 1921 secured legislative approval of the first multimillion-dollar bond issue.

Before World War I, urban planner John Nolen (*Myers Park, Charlotte) had suggested a southward doubling of the quadrangle as a concept for campus growth, an idea that was further developed in the 1920s plan. For the immense and complex project, the university employed as consulting architects McKim, Mead & White of New York, the nationally renowned firm then headed by architect William Kendall. Engineer Thomas C. Atwood was chief supervisor, with specific buildings designed by architect H. Alan Montgomery and, after 1922, by Arthur C. Nash of New York, who moved to Chapel Hill and entered partnership with Atwood; associate H. R. Weeks succeeded Nash as partner in 1930. Construction began with four dorms in 1921 and proceeded southward as funds were made available; other dorms in similar style were erected elsewhere on campus.

Working with Kendall, Nash used Beaux Arts principles to integrate the new quadrangle with the old. A key element was creation of a new south facade for *South Building with a towering Ionic portico (1927) facing the new quadrangle. Standing at the crest of the hill, the venerable landmark became a fulcrum of the campus design. Along the south quad, secondary axes on east and west are headed by buildings with Ionic porticoes. The consistent Georgian Revival vocabulary of classically detailed red brick buildings defined an official "Colonial" campus style, from the richly detailed **Manning Hall** (1923), with stately Ionic portico and cupola, and the twin 1922 structures, **Saunders Hall** and **Murphey Hall**, to simplified work of the 1930s through the 1950s.

At the south terminus, a spot set apart for an "extra-ordinarily important" edifice, the 1920s work culminated in the **Louis Round Wilson Library** (1929; William Kendall [McKim, Mead & White] and Arthur C. Nash, architects). Forming a powerful complement to the Ionic portico of *South Building, the great domed library with Corinthian portico embodied the university's claim to national stature in its kinship to McKim, Mead & White's Low Library at Columbia University. Faced in pale limestone to contrast with the predominant red brick, its symmetrical 3-story composition with piano nobile expresses the spaces within. It now holds the Southern Historical Collection, Rare Book Collection, and N.C. Collection, including early N.C. period rooms. (See Introduction, Fig. 56.)

l. Walter Royal Davis Library

1983; Mitchell/Giurgola (Philadelphia), architects, with Leslie N. Boney Jr. (Wilmington)

One of the state's first major Postmodernist designs, the library is among the most distinguished late 20th-c. buildings on campus, planned by the internationally renowned architectural firm of Mitchell/Giurgola; a key early work was the #Wright Brothers National Memorial Visitors' Center (National Historic Landmark) at Kitty Hawk. Reiterating the customary red brick and classically derived detailing, the architects "tamed the library's daunting bulk" by breaking up the mass with a clerestoried gallery and a series of study towers. A spectacular space is the 2-story, light-filled reading room on the north. As Allcott explains, its double-vaulted ceiling recalls great libraries in the classical tradition, but it is hung from the gable roof rather than carried on piers; light replaces traditional structural elements, and at the ends, nonstructural arches with spaces instead of keystones form an intriguing visual frame.

m. Morehead-Patterson Bell Tower
1930–31; McKim, Mead & White (William Kendall)

Continuing the axis across South Rd., the Venetian-inspired belltower was the last major project at the university before a hiatus in the Great Depression. Benefactor John Motley Morehead III (*Morehead Planetarium) proposed a gift of chimes for South Building and renaming it Morehead, but this offer was rejected; a joint offer with his cousin and fellow alumnus Rufus Lenoir Patterson to build a memorial carillon tower was accepted—supposedly when librarian Louis Round Wilson was out of town. Designed by Kendall, the 167-foot tower is of red brick and Indiana limestone, with arcaded ceiling of Guastavino tile.

n. Kenan Stadium
1927–28; Atwood & Nash, architects; T. C. Thompson & Co., contractors

The home of Tar Heel football was funded by William Rand Kenan Jr. (the UNC graduate who discovered calcium carbide) as a memorial to his parents. The stadium originally seating 24,000 was described in the dedication pamphlet as planned to fit into a "natural amphitheatre" in a flat-floored valley cut by streams at a spot called the Meeting of the Waters. To "adapt the structure to the natural forest and stream beauty of the location," the stadium was hollowed into the hillsides and the surrounding forest preserved, with winding access paths through the trees.

o. Chase Cafeteria
1965; Milton Small & Assoc. (Raleigh), architects; Manning Dr. at Skipper Bowles Dr.

The first building on the central campus to embody the post-1960 shift away from the "Colonial" norm was the clean-lined cruci-

form building in the International style. Floating above its recessed base, it combines dark glass with white piers, slim mullions, and broad, horizontal roof slab. Small was among the state's leading architects in the spare, geometric mode of Mies van der Rohe, with whom he had studied in Chicago. It is currently endangered.

p. Ackland Museum and Hanes Art Center
1958, Eggers & Higgins, Atwood & Weeks; 1983, Gerald Li, Clark, Harris, Tribble & Li (Charlotte), architects; S. Columbia St.

The art museum marking a transition from campus to town continued the Georgian Revival style that dominated both after World War II. The adjoining classroom and studio, repeating red brick and stone, was one of the state's first essays in the Postmodernist aesthetic, with plays on classical themes that won the 1984 design award of the South Atlantic Council of the American Institute of Architects.

OR 46 Carolina Inn
1924, Arthur C. Nash; 1939, Atwood & Weeks; SW corner Columbia St. and Cameron Ave.

The capacious red brick inn for alumni and other guests, a project of financier-alumnus John Sprunt Hill, was built at the edge of campus in "the Southern colonial style" with a portico of Mount Vernon type. Donated to the university in 1935, it was expanded by Atwood & Weeks, followed by later 20th-c. renovations. Memorials and historical images evoke a continuity of spirit in the state and university establishment.

OR 47 Senlac
Ca. 1843, 1876; 203 Battle Ln.

On the site of an old grammar school near campus, Judge William Horn Battle, founder of the UNC law school, built a 2-story frame house, which was enlarged by his son Kemp, a history professor who worked to reopen the university and became its longtime president. He named it Senlac after the hill on which King Harold of England stood against his foes at the Battle of Hastings.

OR 48 Battle Park and Forest Theater
Off Country Club Rd. E of campus

The rugged, forested park of some 60 acres is a unique vestige of the natural landscape that once framed the university. Memoirist William Meade Prince recalled that it seemed "a perfect and well-balanced combination of the Garden of Eden, the Forest Primeval, and the Happy Hunting Ground." In a vale at its edge is the Forest Theater, an amphitheater of local stone, which was begun in 1919 and remodeled in 1940 with Works Progress Administration (WPA) funds.

OR 49 Gimghoul Castle
1924–26; N. C. Curtis and Waldensian stonemasons; E end Gimghoul Rd.

The collegiate romantic conceit of stone towers, crenellations, and turrets was built for a secret college society called the Gimghouls, established in 1889. They bought a forested promontory on which they had UNC graduate and architect Curtis design a club building suitably "medieval and mysterious looking." It was built of local fieldstone by Waldensian artisans from #Valdese.

OR 49 *Gimghoul Castle*

OR 50 Chapel of the Cross
1844–48, Thomas U. Walter (Philadelphia), architect; 1925, Hobart Upjohn (New York), architect; 304 E. Franklin St.

The small Gothic Revival church was built in brick from a design provided by Philadel-

phia architect Walter: its crenellated entrance tower, buttresses, and lancet arches create a much simplified version of his #St. James Episcopal Church in Wilmington. University chaplain William Mercer Green propelled construction, even supplying brick fired in a kiln on his property. Hobart Upjohn's imposing stone church next door shows his elaborated Gothic Revival style in an edifice supported by Episcopalian industrialist William A. Erwin (*Erwin Mills, Durham).

OR 50 *Chapel of the Cross*

OR 51 E. Franklin Street Area (aa–nn)

Franklin St. encompasses a lively college-town commercial district to the west and a carefully maintained historic residential avenue bending around toward the east. The **Commercial District** reflects efforts to retain a village aura and the influence of architect Arthur C. Nash's 20th-c. red brick "Colonial" vocabulary and the "Williamsburg" facelift of the 1940s and 1950s. Especially fine is **University Methodist Church** (1926; James Gamble Rogers [New York], architect; 150 E. Franklin St.) (**aa**), designed by a leading New York revivalist architect with a classical portico and soaring Wren-type spire; the large and beautiful sanctuary has galleries around 3 sides and tall, arched, clear glass windows. The **Chapel Hill Town Hall** (1938–41; Atwood & Weeks, architects; NW corner Rosemary and Columbia Sts.) (**bb**), built with WPA assistance, is a municipal building and fire station wrapped in an elegant Georgian Revival skin, with pedimented facade, sunbursts over the fire engine bays, and a cupola. The former **Chapel Hill Post Office** (1937; Louis A. Simon, supervising architect of the Treasury; 179 E. Franklin St.) (**cc**) repeats the red brick and portico and contains a mural depicting the cornerstone laying of Old East.

The eastern blocks of **E. Franklin St.** and other nearby streets are tree-shaded avenues where informal walkways (unpaved until the late 20th c.) and picturesque stone walls, introduced by New England professors in the early 19th c., define an area of unusual charm. The earliest houses are generally traditional 2-story frame dwellings with large, informal yards. Large and small houses of university people recall the economically and stylistically conservative flavor of earlier days in Chapel Hill. In the late 20th c., several previously modest houses gained large additions.

Near the campus stands the **President's House** (1907; Frank Milburn; 402 E. Franklin St.) (**dd**) in Southern Colonial style with Corinthian portico and flanking wraparound porches. Across the street is the **Old Law Office** (1840s; Dabney Cosby, builder [attrib.]; 401 E. Franklin St.) (**ee**), a small, stuccoed Italianate structure built for Samuel F. Phillips, who used it as a schoolhouse and law office, later shared with Judge William Horn Battle; it was the birthplace of the UNC law school. The **Love-Spencer House** (1887; 410 E. Franklin St.) (**ff**), a multigabled 1-story frame house with wraparound porch, was built for math professor James Lee Love, who later moved to Harvard with his wife June Spencer; their son, J. Spencer Love, founded Burlington Mills and Burlington Industries. June's mother, Cornelia Phillips Spencer, who lived in the house for several years, led in the campaign to reopen the university; it is said that when someone declared her to be the smartest woman in N.C., Governor Zebulon Vance responded, "And the smartest man, too."

The **Widow Puckett House** (1817–20, 501 E. Franklin St.) (**gg**) is a conservative 2-story frame house, 3 bays wide with a pair of brick chimneys. It was probably built for Jane Puckett, a postmaster's widow who ran a boardinghouse. Sold in 1820 to Denison

OR 51 *Widow Puckett House*

Olmstead, a chemistry professor from Yale, it was later home of Dr. James Phillips, math professor, whose children Samuel and Cornelia grew up here. The **Presbyterian Manse** (mid-19th c.; 513 E. Franklin St.) (**hh**) was built for the chaplain William Mercer Green (*Chapel of the Cross); it was later owned by Charles Phillips, professor of engineering and mathematics, and then by the Presbyterian church. The **Hooper-Kyser House** (1814; 504 E. Franklin St.) (**ii**), another simply finished 2-story frame house, was built for professor of ancient languages William Hooper (grandson of the signer of the Declaration of Independence); in the 20th c. it was the home of famed band leader Kay Kyser.

Among numerous turn-of-the-century residences, the **Lawson House** (early 20th c.; 604 E. Franklin St.) (**jj**) is a capacious Shingle style bungalow form with great sweeping gables. Locally celebrated is the **Horace Williams House** (1852; 611 E. Franklin St.; open limited hours) (**kk**), an irregular dwelling that resulted from 1-story additions to an original hexagonal nucleus, built for chemistry professor B. S. Hedrick reportedly to emulate the structure of bee cells; it is now an arts center. The **Henderson House** (1900–1910; 721 E. Franklin St.) (**ll**) is a handsome early Colonial Revival house, built for poet Barbara Bynum Henderson and her husband Archibald Henderson, noted historian and mathematician. Flanking Franklin St. and extending beyond the campus are several residential neighborhoods notable for their sylvan character and houses ranging from plain 19th-c. frame dwellings to more or less elaborate Queen Anne, Colonial Revival, and bungalow houses. **Rosemary St. (mm)**, parallel to Franklin St. on the north, and several streets leading from it have an especially fine series of residences of every era. The **Cameron-McCauley Neighborhood (nn)** south and west of the old campus likewise contains a representative range of 19th- and early 20th-c. houses, as do other sections with curving roads and generously planted lots.

OR 52 Carrboro

A village called West End grew up around the Chapel Hill Station on an 1882 rail spur from University Station. Located near Hillsborough, University Station was the nearest stop on the NCRR and 10 miles from Chapel Hill. A little train called the "Whooper" brought passengers to the Chapel Hill station, from which jitneys carried them to the university. The railroad community developed as a center of commerce and industry, and in 1913 it was named for mill owner Julian S. Carr. The centerpiece is the **Alberta Mill** (Carr Mill) (1899, 1912, 1918, 1976; Weaver and N. Greensboro Sts.), which was begun as a small steam-powered railside operation by Thomas F. Lloyd, a farmer who also ran a gristmill and a cotton gin. The typical 2-story Italianate brick mill displays slow-burn construction with heavy timber posts and thick plank floors. In 1909 Lloyd sold the mill to Durham tobacco-textile tycoon Carr. He made it Durham Hosiery Mills No. 4 and nearly doubled the mill in 1912 and 1918. Operating intermittently, the mill was vacant for years before its renovation as an early project of the Tax Reform Act of 1976.

Nearby, the **Carrboro Station** (1913; 201 E. Main St.) is a characteristic frame building, 1 story beneath a broad hip roof with deep overhangs on brackets. The former **Lloyd Grist Mill** (ca. 1916–21; 101 B St.) retains a 2-story brick building with arched windows, rebuilt in the early 20th c. after a fire. The early 20th-c. **Commercial District** concentrates on E. Main St. and has rows of 1- and 2-story brick buildings with modest corbeled detail. The oldest residential areas, including Shelton, Weaver, Carr, Oak, and

OR 53 *Blue Cross Blue Shield Service Center*

Maple Sts., contain modest houses built for tradespeople, artisans, and millworkers. Some built by Lloyd and others for millworkers are 1-story gable-sided dwellings with center chimneys, front porches, and rear ells. Others for varied occupants are similar in form but somewhat larger, often with decorative front gables. Several have notable stone walls or columns, the craftsmanship of local black masons, including the Strayhorn family. Even after becoming contiguous with Chapel Hill, Carrboro maintains a separate identity, whimsically calling itself "the Paris of the Piedmont."

OR 53 Blue Cross Blue Shield Service Center

1973; A. G. Odell Assoc. (Charles McMurray) (Charlotte), architects; S side NC 15/501 (Durham–Chapel Hill Blvd.)

The great glass structure is as eye-catching at the turn of the 21st c. as it was when it dazzled viewers in the early 1970s. The 4-story building, 400 feet long and 100 feet wide, is a clean rhomboid form with its 3-story glass walls set at 45 degrees. The upper 3 stories are elevated on stout columns and shelter a recessed glass-enclosed lobby at the ground level. The client wanted a glass building but realized the problems of such a building in the hot, sunny climate. The architect designed the outward-sloping south and west walls to mitigate the summer sun, as does the tinted, sky-reflecting glass.

Alamance County (AM)

See Carl R. Lounsbury, Alamance County Architectural Heritage (1980).

The county offers a microcosm of Piedmont history, with traditional log and frame farmsteads, the 19th-c. shops of the North Carolina Railroad (NCRR), and pioneering textile mills and villages. Long home of the Sissipahaw (Saxapahaw) people, the area along the Haw River and Alamonsy (Alamance) Creek had by 1728 the "reputation of containing the most fertile high land in this part of the World." Settlers arriving from the mid-18th c. onward included Scotch-Irish Presbyterians mainly in the east, English (and a few Irish) Quakers in the south, and Germans to the west. The county was formed in 1849 from Orange and named for the Battle of Alamance that ended the Regulator movement in 1771 (*Allen House).

Beginning in the 1830s, local men, including Edwin M. Holt, founded cotton mills, often at old gristmill sites, along the Haw River and its tributaries. Although the modest waterpower limited the scale of individual mills, cumulatively they constituted a major early operation. In the 1850s the NCRR extended across the county and located its central repair shops at Company Shops, now *Burlington. The Holt mills did well during the Civil War and quickly retooled for growth and expansion into increasingly finished products. Edwin handed over management to his sons, Thomas (who became governor), James H., William, L. Banks, and Lawrence Holt, and sons-in-law James White and James Williamson. The Holts also founded Commercial National Bank in Charlotte (1874), ancestor of present-day Bank of America. The family built 9 major mills in the 1880s alone; several were the work of local millwright Berry Davidson. In 1892 the Raleigh News & Observer, urging that "mills must be brought to the cotton fields," proclaimed, "We wish every county in the State was an Alamance." By about 1900, 23 of the county's 27 mills were controlled by the Holt dynasty, and a local historian exclaimed, "What the Flemish have been to England, what the Venetians have been to southern Europe, that are the Holts to Alamance and to North Carolina." By the 1920s, however, following strikes and various economic changes, the Holt family had turned to other interests, and the local industry was eclipsed by growth elsewhere. In the mid-1920s, business was transformed by J. Spencer Love, who formed Burlington Mills and built it into Burlington Industries, the world's largest textile company in the mid-20th c.

AM 1 Graham

The new county's seat was laid out in 1850 and named for Governor William A. Graham of Hillsborough. When the NCRR was routed through the county, Graham refused to allow tracks or repair shops in town, but it became the home of leading industrialists and eventually a few factories. The Lancaster square plan, with its courthouse at the meeting of two axial streets (Main and Elm) and the corners notched out, emphasizes the

handsome **Alamance County Courthouse** (1924; Harry Barton [Greensboro], architect). Showing architect Barton's skill in adapting Beaux Arts principles to tight budgets and settings, the stone-faced edifice has full-height porticoes in a Tower of the Winds order facing N. and S. Main. The Confederate Monument (N) dates from 1914. (See Introduction, Fig. 58.)

Small-scale brick commercial buildings frame the square and extend along Main and Elm. The oldest is the **Nicks Store** (ca. 1850;

AM 1 *Alamance Co. Courthouse*

SE corner), with a canopy over the sidewalk in typical 19th-c. fashion and interior cast-iron columns with lotus capitals (*Hawfields Presbyterian Church). The **Vestal Hotel** (ca. 1912; 14–22 Court Sq.), an elaborately corbeled brick building, accentuates the northeast square.

Two houses recall the textile mansions that once distinguished Graham and Burlington. **Elmhurst** (1869; 141 S. Main St.) was built by E. M. Holt for daughter Mary Elizabeth and her husband James Williamson of Caswell Co., founder of *Ossipee Mill and others. Built in front of a Greek Revival dwelling, the asymmetrical house features a mansard-roofed entrance tower and ornate Italianate millwork, plus a matching drive-through for the bank that rescued the house in 1994. The **White House** (1871; 213 S. Main St.; open regular hours), built or remodeled for Emma Holt

AM 1 *Elmhurst*

and husband James White, is a symmetrical Italianate design with central entrance pavilion and decorative millwork suggestive of the patternbooks of A. J. Bicknell (*L. Banks Holt House, *Lawrence Holt House).

West of the courthouse, the **Graham Presbyterian Church** (1856; 1897–1908, Charles Reade [Richmond, Va.], architect; 200 W. Harden St.), a remaking of an older church, is a robust form in rich red brick, with arched windows and a stout corner tower by an architect known for his work at Union Seminary. Construction was aided by members of the Holt family who converted from their father's Lutheran faith. Only a corner turret remains visible of the large **Oneida Cotton Mill** (1882, 1887; 219 W. Harden St.), founded by local merchants as the town's first mill and bought by L. Banks Holt in 1887. The **Scott-Mebane Mfg. Co.** (1898; 220 W. Harden St.), a small 2-story brick building with segmental-arched windows and a stepped gable, was built for L. B.'s sons-in-law H. W. Scott and J. K. Mebane. N. Main and flanking streets have the principal concentration of late 19th- and early 20th-c. houses, in Italianate, Queen Anne, Colonial Revival, and Craftsman modes. In the early 20th c. an electric interurban streetcar line—the Burgrahaw Traction Co.—ran up N. Main and linked Graham with Burlington and Haw River.

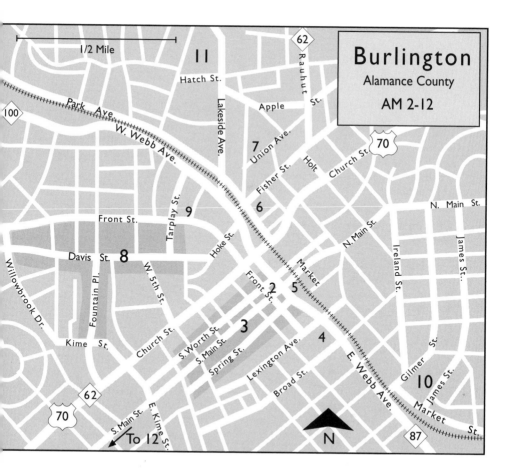

Burlington (AM 2–12)

See Allison Harris Black, *An Architectural History of Burlington, North Carolina* (1987).

Burlington's grid-plan business district is ringed by diverse residential neighborhoods, textile mills, and their villages. Although the grandest Queen Anne style textile mansions are gone, other 19th-c. buildings survive along with those of the early 20th c., including Moderne work of the Burlington Mills era. The town began as a railroad village and flourished as a 20th-c. textile center. In the 1850s the NCRR, rebuffed by Graham, acquired land 2 miles west for Company Shops, with repair shops, a railroad hotel, houses, and churches. It was the center of NCRR operations through the Civil War and beyond. In 1871 the NCRR was leased to the Richmond & Danville Railroad (R&DRR), which in 1886 moved its shops to Virginia.

The next year, civic leaders renamed the town Burlington, after rejecting Holtsville and Carolinadelphia. The R&DRR became part of Southern Railway, which built the immense *Spencer Shops near Salisbury.

Compensating for the loss of the shops, from the 1880s onward, the Holts and others built steam-powered factories by the tracks. In the early 1920s, however, a slump hit the textile industry, and Holt family interests shifted elsewhere. A new era began when local businessmen recruited J. Spencer Love. The young, Harvard-trained veteran was working in his family's textile business in Gastonia when he accepted an offer from civic leaders eager for a "Bigger Better Burlington." To begin Burlington Mills, he and local investors built new mills and updated old ones, modernized production methods, diversified into rayon and other synthetics, and expanded rapidly. In 1935 Love moved the headquarters to Greensboro. With 14 plants in that year, the company continued through the Great Depression and World War II. After the war, Love transformed the industry by creating a vertically integrated corporate structure, producing everything from raw materials to finished consumer goods. Reorganized in 1955 as Burlington Industries, by 1980 it had become the world's largest textile company; with global changes it declared bankruptcy in 2001 but continued production.

AM 2 *Burlington Passenger Station*

AM 2 Burlington Passenger Station

1892; Front St. at S. Main St.

The brick depot, built by the NCRR (R&DRR) shortly before the line was leased to Southern, has a characteristic hip roof, octagonal tower, and half-timbered detail. Moved from trackside, it serves as a community center.

AM 3 Downtown Burlington

Extending from the tracks, the central blocks of S. Main, S. Spring, E. Davis, and E. Front Sts. have predominantly 2- and 3-story brick buildings postdating an 1884 fire, many with restored storefronts. The tallest is the **Atlantic Bank & Trust Co. Building** (1928–29; Charles C. Hartmann [Greensboro], architect; 358 S. Main St.), a 9-story skyscraper for "Bigger Better Burlington" by the architect of Greensboro's famed *Jefferson Standard Building (1923). Hartmann rendered the classical base, shaft, and capital composition in Art Deco style, cited by the local newspaper as "an art work" showing "advanced ideas in this type architecture." The **Alamance Hotel** (1923–25; Charles C. Hartmann, architect; J. R. Beamon [Raleigh], contractor; 514 S. Main St.), 7 stories in red brick, was built by local investors to provide the requisite first-class businessmen's hotel. The nearby **May Hosiery Mill** (early 20th c.; 534 S. Main St.) is a large brick factory complex expanded over the years by the local family whose name is emblazoned on the tall smokestack.

Among many other commercial buildings are the restored **Paramount Theater**

AM 3 *Atlantic Bank & Trust Co. Building*

(1928; 128 E. Front St.), which combines classical and Art Deco motifs, and **Efird's** (early 20th c.; 133 E. Davis St.), with a 3-story terra-cotta facade blending Gothic and Art Deco themes. The 400 block of Spring St. includes simplified Art Deco and Moderne designs of the 1930s. The former **U.S. Post Office** (1936; Louis A. Simon, supervising architect of the Treasury; 430 S. Spring St.) is a modest Moderne-classical building in red brick, with murals (1940) depicting an antebellum local depot scene and workers in a modern textile mill.

Just beyond the center, the **Burlington**

Chevrolet Dealership (1948–49; 508 Church St.) features a sleek Moderne showroom with curved corners and enameled-panel walls—which showcased the new 1950 model cars—plus a rear service facility. The **First Christian Church** (1920; 415 S. Church St.), a large, red brick sanctuary with Tuscan portico and dome, punctuates the northwest end of downtown. On the southeast end the **First Baptist Church** (1922–23; Herbert B. Hunter [High Point], architect; 400 S. Broad St.) in pale yellow brick presents an imposing Ionic portico.

AM 4 St. Athanasius Episcopal Church and the Church of the Holy Comforter

1879–80, Rev. J. A. Oertel, John Coble, builder; 1908–11, Hobart Upjohn (N.Y.), architect; 300 E. Webb Ave., 320 E. Davis St.

Dating from the Company Shops era, St. Athanasius is a simple board-and-batten structure built on land given by the NCRR. Oertel, an artist and Episcopal priest in Morganton, provided a design influenced by Richard Upjohn's *Rural Architecture*. A chief sponsor was Holt cousin and associate William A. Erwin—an Episcopalian from Burke Co. who operated a mercantile business in Company Shops, then became an officer of the Holt mill operations and in 1892 moved to Durham (*Erwin Mills)—his sister Margaret, and her husband Lawrence Holt. In 1908 the parish employed New York architect Hobart Upjohn (grandson of Richard Upjohn) to plan a larger church, endowed by Margaret and Lawrence Holt in memory of their daughter. The imposing, cruciform Gothic Revival church, built of rock-faced Mount Airy granite with a tall

AM 4 *St. Athanasius Episcopal Church*

corner tower, was among the architect's first commissions in N.C.

AM 5 North Carolina Railroad Co. Foundry and Engine House

Mid-19th c.; NE side Webb Ave. at N. Main St.

Across the tracks from downtown, two 1-story brick structures survive from the once extensive Company Shops repair facility. Most visible is the 17-bay-long **Engine House** (1870; 101 N. Main St. by tracks), with pilasters flanking arched openings beneath a corbeled cornice. It sheltered 15 engines on 3 tracks running through it. The 1-story brick **Foundry** (1858; Walter Gwynne, engineer-designer; Huston & McKnight [Greensboro], builders; betw. 100 blocks of N. Main and N. Springs Sts.), with pilasters and corbeling, is the last of the original 1850s NCRR repair buildings.

AM 5 *North Carolina Railroad Co. Engine House*

AM 6 Francis Stagg House

1850s or 1860s; 317 N. Park Ave.

The frame house recalls the association of the picturesque mode with railroad progress. Perhaps adapted from a "small villa" design published by Samuel Sloan or A. J. Downing, the 2-story, T-plan, gable-fronted center section features simple brackets and bargeboards at the shallow gable roof. It was the longtime home of Francis Asbury Stagg, NCRR secretary and leader in the 1860s and 1870s.

AM 7 Holt-Frost House

Ca. 1889; 130 Union Ave.

One of the few full-blown Queen Anne style houses standing in the city has a high roof, a deep porch, and a wealth of balconies, gables, and fancy millwork. It was built for Ella and James G. Holt, employee of the R&DRR.

AM 8 Fountain Place and W. Davis St. area

The prime concentration of late 19th- and early 20th-c. residential architecture lies west of the commercial district. Reflecting Burlington's continuing prosperity into the 1930s, the shaded neighborhoods include frame cottages and bungalows along with imposing Queen Anne, Colonial Revival, and Tudor Revival residences. **Fountain Place** (1917–40) is a small, planned development with entrance gateposts, a landscaped median (with fountain), and solid but unpretentious houses in the Tudor cottage, bungalow, Colonial Revival, and Dutch Colonial modes epitomizing the domestic ideal presented in national magazines. **W. Davis St.** shows a sequence of eras as it extends westward. Edwin C. Holt, grandson of E. M., built the striking **Cheatham House** (1925; 1007 W. Davis St.), an H-plan composition with modernist flat-roofed forms, for his daughter Dolores and her husband W. T. Cheatham. Edwin's own Georgian Revival style **Holt-McEwen House** (1925; 1011 W. Davis St.) was acquired in 1929 by hosiery manufacturer James McEwen. Among the fine Tudor Revival houses is the **Allen Gant House** (1929; 1022 W. Davis St.), a half-timbered and stone mansion built for the son of John Q. Gant (*Altamahaw Mill). The **Benjamin May House** (1930–31; Oscar Hokanson [Philadelphia], architect; 1211 May Ct.) is a sophisticated stone house of English character with irregular plan and craggy slate and stonework, built for a founder of *May Hosiery Mills.

AM 9 First (German) Reformed United Church of Christ

1940–41; Charles C. Benton & Sons (Wilson), architects; 513 S. Front St.

The Romanesque Revival church, with campanile-like belltower, displays the robust forms and vivid red brick and white palette of many Lutheran and Reformed churches from the late 19th c. onward.

Textile Mills and Villages:
*Several late 19th- and early 20th-c. mills and their villages stand just beyond the town center, near the railroad tracks. Most have been altered repeatedly. *Lakeside (N) and *Windsor-Aurora (SE) are representative, with the largest collection of mill housing around the latter. Various house forms appear, some of types seen in D. A. Tompkins's Cotton Mill: Commercial Features (1899). Many from ca. 1900 are 1-story, side-gable dwellings with center front gables, some with center chimneys; others take an L-plan form. From the 1910s and 1920s onward they are gable-fronted, in blocks or mixed with other types.*

AM 10 Aurora (Lafayette) and Windsor Mills and Villages
Gilmer St. and James St. N of E. Webb Ave.

Lafayette Mill (E. Webb Ave. betw. Gilmer and Flanner Sts.) was founded in 1882 by Lafayette Holt as the first mill in town and included an innovative steam plant. A cousin of the E. M. Holt family, Lafayette had studied cotton manufacturing in Lowell, Mass., and designed several local mills. In 1885 Lawrence Holt acquired and expanded the plant, which he renamed Aurora; it was later sold after Laurence resisted son Eugene's idea of switching to rayon. Although the main mill (N side Webb Ave.) is covered, a section known as **Pickett Hosiery Mill** (1904–8; s side E. Webb Ave. at Everett St.) is intact, with segmental-arched windows, parapet, and monitor roof.

Established by Robert and James H. Holt Jr. and also designed by cousin Lafayette Holt, **Windsor Mill** began as a yarn spinning factory, expanded to cotton fabrics, and was sold in 1903 to the Southern Textile Co. of New Jersey. The plant includes the initial 2-story mill and 3-story tower in simple Italianate style, plus a smokestack and various additions of the 20th c. The original **Office** (1890; Gilmer St. at Market St.) is a 2-story building with corbeled cornice, arched windows, and 1-story porch.

Flanking Webb Ave. and the railroad extends a large, nearly seamless expanse of Aurora and Windsor mill housing from the 1880s into the 1920s. Scores of 1-story mill houses offer a textbook sampling of Tompkins's models, plus slightly later gable-fronted bungalows. The 900 block of E. Davis has a strong grouping associated with Aurora. Larger houses for upper-level employees stand on Mebane St. and Webb Ave. The **Ireland House** (late 19th c.; 520 S. Ireland St.), a decorated, picturesque cottage with front roof gable in the spirit of A. J. Downing's designs, was probably standing when the Holts bought the land from J. R. Ireland (1895).

AM 11 Lakeside Mills

400 blocks of Lakeside Ave.,
Hatch St., and Kent Ave.

The last and most intact of five cotton mills established in Burlington by the Holt family between 1883 and 1893, Lakeside was founded by James H. Holt and sons and designed by cousin Lafayette Holt. Modest growth kept the factory and village nearly as built. The 1-story brick **Mill** (1892–93; 423 Lakeside Ave.) has a clerestory and segmental-arched windows; the superintendent's office, store, and storage buildings stand nearby. The small village maintains its semirural character, with 1½-story, center-chimney houses of the 1890s and front-gabled dwellings of the early 20th c.

AM 12 Menagerie Carousel

Ca. 1912–17, 1948; Daniel Carl Muller,
carver (Dentzel Co., Germantown, Pa.);
Burlington City Park, S. Main St.

After a long search, in 1948 Burlington found an old carousel in Genoa, Ohio, for its civic park. Its 46 animals—standers and jumpers including horses, cats, pigs, a lion, an ostrich, and a giraffe—are attributed to master carver Muller of the famed Dentzel carousel manufactory. This and Raleigh's *Pullen Park Carousel are among about 20 operating Dentzel carousels in the country.

AM 13 Haw River

Jct. US 70-A and NC 49 at Haw River

The riverside village retains key elements from its days as a much larger manufacturing center. Of the first five cotton mills in Alamance Co., only Haw River's **Granite Mill** (1844) stands relatively intact. (Little remains from the early mills at High Falls [Hopedale], est. 1832; Cane Creek, est. 1836; *Alamance, est. 1837; or *Saxapahaw, est. 1844.) It was established by Benjamin Trollinger and his father, John, near the old Trollinger's Ford on the Haw. John had founded the county's first cotton mill (High Falls, 1832), and his German grandfather, Adam, had an 18th-c. gristmill. Benjamin, a contractor for the NCRR who facilitated acquisition of land for Company Shops, got the railroad to cross the Haw at his cotton mill, built the bridge to carry it, and opened a short-lived railroad hotel. His **Haw River NCRR Bridge Piers** (1851) beside the present-day bridge show the fine, rough-cut stonework and tapered form characteristic of antebellum bridges; they are among the principal vestiges of the original NCRR.

Trollinger's hotel and business failed after a hotel was built in Company Shops, and in 1858 E. M. Holt and son Thomas bought the well-located property. After the Civil War, Thomas promptly updated and expanded—"as fast as I made money, I invested it in machinery"—and added weaving and dyeing. Beginning in 1880, he and son Charles rebuilt the dam, introduced steam power, and expanded Granite into the largest mill in the county; it peaked ca. 1912 with 3,000 workers and about 23,000 spindles. The family sold it in 1928.

On its namesake stone outcropping, much survives of Trollinger's antebellum **Granite Cotton Mill** (1844 and later; E side of Haw River; visible in winter), a gable-roofed, 4-story building of 1:3 bond brick, with large 12/12 windows in arched openings and heavy chamfered posts and joists within. The 1886 **Finishing Plant** is a 2- and 3-story 1:5 brick structure with pilasters and tapered buttresses at alternate bays. Across the road the **Thomas M. Holt Mfg. Co. Complex** (1880s, Lafayette Holt, designer; 1890s, C. R.

Makepeace & Co. [Providence, R.I.]; sw corner US 70-A and SR 1935) is a large brick factory that was steam-powered from the outset. The initial 1-story section is of standard mill construction. The 2-story section, which features a stylized Romanesque Revival tower, shows an unusual construction type: as reported in the *Manufacturer's Record* of Apr. 29, 1898, the mill featured "V-shaped" or "zigzag walls built for light and strength" designed by Makepeace, a son of Randolph Co. who became a major national mill architect. This form, patented in 1894 by Rhode Island mill engineer Charles Praray, had columns carrying the floor and roof loads, permitting windows to fill the V-plan bays and increase natural light in the mill. Soon rendered obsolete by electric lights, only 5 such mills were built, here and in Georgia and Alabama. Sections of the zigzag wall are still visible though bricked in. (Endangered, 2002.)

AM 13 *Thomas M. Holt Manufacturing Co.*

The community also encompasses a cluster of corbeled brick stores near the mills. On nearby streets, the 1- and 2-story mill houses, mainly from the 1890s, include several 1-story dwellings with off-center chimney and central front gable, resembling the "Four-room Gable House" in Tompkins's *Cotton Mill: Commercial Features*. Across the

AM 13 *Haw River mill houses*

river from Granite Mill (on Oakwood, Elk, Short, River, and Lang Sts.) is a grouping of 19th-c. workers' houses—2 stories beneath a shallow gable roof, unusually tall and narrow with interior chimneys in the rear slope of the roof. Above the mills on N. Main are residences for upper-level employees, merchants, and others, including decorated Queen Anne style houses. On a nearby hill **Haw River Methodist Church** is a simple Gothic Revival building with a shingled belfry tower and a cemetery with markers to Adam Trollinger and to Artelia Roney Duke, known as "the prettiest woman in Alamance" and the second wife of Washington Duke of Durham; her sons Benjamin and James Buchanan Duke erected the granite wall in her memory.

Overlooking the village from across the river is the large frame **Charles T. Holt House** (1897; George F. Barber [Knoxville], architect; James R. Montgomery, builder; 228 Holt St.; private, visible from road in winter), one of the best surviving examples of the Queen Anne mansions designed for N.C. industrialists by mail-order architect Barber. It exemplifies Barber's ebullient, asymmetrical compositions, with complex roof, tower, dormers, and broad wraparound porch, enriched with new "Colonial" classical motifs. (See Introduction, Fig. 62.)

AM 14 Glencoe
SR 1598, SR 1600, W of NC 62 at Haw River

One of the most intact small mill villages in the state, Glencoe epitomizes the scale and rural setting of 19th-c. streamside textile mills. The 1880–83 waterpowered mill was one of the last established in the county (*Ossipee, *Altamahaw). Upstream from their Carolina Mill (1869) on the Haw, E. M. Holt and sons James and William acquired the grist- and sawmill site in 1878. The sons, Presbyterian converts, gave the mill a Scottish name, and in 1880–83 the brothers extended the millrace, erected a mill and village, and installed machinery from Baltimore and Lowell, Mass., with much of the work done by millwright Berry Davidson. By 1890 the mill employed 40 men, 57 women, 20 boys, and 16 girls. Initially they produced plaid, checked, and striped cotton fabric, but after James's son Robert assumed direction, he enlarged the factory to add napped outing for blankets and nightgowns. The mill was later run by the related Green family until it closed in 1954.

Nearly all the key buildings survive except the frame church, lost in the late 20th c. The 3-story **Glencoe Mill** by the river has thick brick walls and heavy timber construction, rendered in Italianate style with quoined corners, arched windows with keystones, and a fine stair tower with corbeled cornice. The 1-story brick **Company Store and Office** above the mill repeats the arched windows and corbeled work. Lining the two streets uphill from the mill are about 35 **Workers' Houses**, which in their traditional forms and generous spacing exemplify the accommodation of rural habits in industrial housing. The 2-story frame houses have 2-room plans and originally had separate kitchens, though in the early 20th c. kitchens were attached as ells. Some of the houses have brick nogging in the hand-sawn framing. Roofed in tin, they sit on brick piers and have front porches. After a period of disuse, renewal of the village is a model project

AM 14 *Glencoe mill village*

of Preservation North Carolina. Nearby, the **Robert Holt House** (late 19th c.; w side NC 62, N of Haw River) was built for the bachelor son of James Holt who managed Glencoe and had a stock farm here. The 2-story frame house with bracket cornice, center bay, and wraparound porch is surrounded by landscaping and outbuildings.

AM 15 Ossipee
SR 1558 at Haw River and Reedy Creek

Established in 1882 by E. M. Holt's son-in-law James Williamson to manufacture cotton plaids, Ossipee was the dynasty's last new waterpowered mill. The 2-story brick **Ossipee Mill** has typical corbeling, arched windows, and two 3-story towers, served by a stone millrace. When built, the mill had the latest in automatic sprinklers, fire hydrants, and running water. The village includes both 1- and 2-story dwellings, some quite small, with center and end chimneys.

AM 16 Altamahaw
NC 87 at Haw River

The **Altamahaw Cotton Mill** (1880–81) was established by John Q. Gant and millwright Berry Davidson on the latter's land. Gant, a friend and associate of the Holts, was also related to the family by marriage. Davidson, who had just built the Holts' mill at *Bellemont, completed the Altamahaw mill in 1881 and in 1882 sold his interest to L. Banks and Lawrence Holt. First producing cotton yarn, the mill soon added woven fabric. The Gants continued in textiles, and the much-expanded brick mill is still part of the family's Glen Raven Mills. Several streets of late 19th–early 20th c. **Workers' Housing** include 1- and 2-story dwellings with end or center chimneys. The 2-story brick **Store** (ca. 1896) has metal trim from the George L. Mesker Co. Probably the state's most distinctive mill office is the **Altamahaw Mill Office** (ca. 1890; s side SR 1002, at SR 1567), built in Queen Anne style and houselike form, with multicolor brickwork, touches of half-timbering, and a belt course with OFFICE in projecting bricks. John Q. Gant

AM 16 *Altamahaw Mill Office*

had his office here and slept in the upstairs bedchamber when work kept him late.

AM 17 McCray School
1915–16; Andrew Nash, carpenter; NW side NC 62, 0.5 mi. N of SR 1754, Burlington vic.

The 1-room, gable-fronted frame schoolhouse, built by residents for black children in the rural neighborhood, was adapted from "Design No. 1" in *Plans for Public Schoolhouses* (1911) by Raleigh architects Charles Barrett and Frank Thompson, distributed by the state board of education. Closed in 1951, the restored school is used as an educational site for elementary school students.

AM 17 *McCray School*

AM 18 Crossroads Community
Jct. SR 1912 and NC 119

The aptly named village focuses on the essential church and store. **Cross Roads Presbyterian Church** (ca. 1876) was established ca. 1770 by a Scotch-Irish congregation, which later replaced a frame meetinghouse with the gable-fronted brick building with

segmental-arched windows. Some say the timbers of the old church were reused in the gable-fronted, frame **Stainback Store**. The nearby **John W. Stainback House** (ca. 1880; N side SR 1910, 0.1 mi. w of NC 119), a 2-story farmhouse with center-gabled roofline, brackets, and a decorated porch, is one of several in the neighborhood.

AM 19 Dickey Mill
Ca. 1880; N side SR 1912 betw. SR 1910 and SR 1915, on Quaker Creek

Of the many gristmills that once served the county, one of the few still standing is the tall, frame mill house with monitor-like roof built by brothers Jim and Allen Dickey, of an established local family. The stone dam was rebuilt ca. 1900 after a flood. The site once included a general store, a cotton gin, and a sawmill along with the gristmill, which operated until 1940.

AM 20 Griffis-Patton House
1839–40; W side SR 1927, 0.4 mi. S of SR 1921, Mebane vic.; private, visible from road

The 2-story brick house, 5 bays wide with Greek Revival detail, is among the most ambitious antebellum residences in a county of simple log and frame architecture. It was built for Mary and William Griffis on a plantation assembled by his father.

AM 21 Woodlawn School
1911–13; N side SR 1921, 1.5 mi. E of SR 1927, Mebane vic.

The 2-room frame school with belfry was built for white students from a design in

AM 21 *Woodlawn School*

Barrett and Thompson's *Plans for Public Schoolhouses* (*McCray School). As the booklet suggested, it was built in stages: it was first a complete 1-room school, then an additional classroom was added on the left.

AM 22 Mebane

The large plant of the **White Furniture Co.** (est. 1881, 1924; NE corner E. Center and N. 5th Sts.) housed one of the longest-operating manufacturing firms in the state. The company began producing window sash and doors in 1881, then expanded in 1896 to make bedroom and, soon, dining room furniture. Growing as N.C. became the nation's leading furniture manufacturing state, the family-owned company supplied furniture to the Panama Canal housing and the #Grove Park Inn in Asheville. Rebuilt after a fire, the 1924 main factory and other brick buildings line the tracks. The book and photography exhibit *Closing* (1998) recorded the last days of its operation in 1993.

AM 22 *White Furniture Co.*

AM 23 *Hawfields Presbyterian Church*

In the brick business district beside the tracks is the **U.S. Post Office** (1939; Louis A. Simon, supervising architect of the Treasury; Center St.), a 1-story red brick Colonial Revival building with a mural depicting tobacco cultivation (1965). Residential areas north and south of the railroad include churches as well as houses mainly from the early 20th c. The **B. Frank Mebane House** (ca. 1855; down drive, E side 200 block S. 5th St.), a 2-story frame house with hip roof and bracket cornice, was the home of the producer of a popular patent medicine whose son, B. F. Jr., became a textile magnate (*Leaksville). Outstanding among many bungalows is the **Warren House** (ca. 1920; 301 S. 5th St.), of stone with stout, stuccoed porch pillars and a matching 2-car garage.

AM 23 Hawfields Presbyterian Church
1852–55; W corner NC 119 and SR 1981, N and S sides, Mebane vic.

Home of a venerable congregation, the Greek Revival brick church is preserved amid additions. The "Haw old fields" with its "extraordinary rich land" attracted Scotch-Irish and English settlers from the

1740s onward, and when Presbyterian minister Hugh McAden preached at "the Haw Fields" in 1755, he found "a considerable congregation, chiefly Presbyterians." A mother church in the area, Hawfields hosted the first meeting (1770) of the Presbytery of Orange and a great revival in 1801 that sparked the movement in the region. Another spurt of revivalism supported construction of the brick church in the 1850s. Its simple pedimented form and fine Flemish-bond brickwork make it a prime example of the Greek Revival country church. The sanctuary has two aisles and a gallery carried on slender metal columns with lotus capitals (*Nicks Store, Graham).

AM 24 Kerr Scott Farm
1919–50s; NW side SR 2123, 1.5 mi. NE of NC 54; private, visible from road

The dairy farm recalls the progressive agriculture promoted by state farm leader and governor Kerr Scott. After studying agriculture at present-day *North Carolina State University, he returned home to farm, and before his 1919 marriage to Mary E. White he remodeled a small antebellum farmhouse into an up-to-date bungalow. Scott became a farm agent, administrator of agricultural programs during the New Deal, state agriculture commissioner (1936), and governor of the state (1948), always maintaining the farm and his identity as the "Squire of Haw River," one of the "Branchhead Boys." His son Robert also served as governor. The farmstead includes gabled and gambrel-roofed dairy barns (1910, 1929, 1941), a milking parlor, a silo, and other structures.

AM 25 S. W. Patton House
Ca. 1810, ca. 1830; NW side SR 2133, 2.3 mi. S of SR 2135

The prominent frame house began as a 2-story brick-nogged dwelling (ca. 1810) with side-passage plan and 1:3 brick end chimney, then gained a 1-story wing (ca. 1830) with stout fieldstone chimneys. Later 19th-c. outbuildings include a salt house, an outhouse, and a well house.

AM 26 Saxapahaw
SR 2146 and SR 2158 at Haw River

Named after the Sissipahaw (Saxapahaw) people who had a village here by the 16th c., the present village began with a cotton mill established in 1844–48 by John Newlin and sons, of the Snow Camp Quakers, using waterpower from a mile-long millrace from the Haw. They also had a saw- and gristmill, the latter rebuilt by Berry Davidson in 1866. In 1873 E. M. Holt bought the Newlin mill and operated it with sons-in-law James Williamson and James White, who rebuilt the mill in 1880 and erected new sections in the early 20th c. Closed in 1924, the plant was bought in 1927 by C. V. Sellars, who with nephew B. Everett Jordan—later U.S. congressman—modernized the facility. The oldest section of the mill, the **Spinning Mill** (1906–17), is a 3-story brick structure with broad windows, a low gable roof with clerestory, and slow-burn construction. Across the road stand the brick **Company Store and Office**, with corbeled and pressed metal trim, and the **B. Everett Jordan House**, a frame bungalow. Along the hillside behind the store and across the river are mill houses of varied types, including one small log house on Church St. The Jordan family has renovated the buildings for new uses.

AM 27 Spring Friends Meeting House
1907; S side SR 1005, 1.0 mi. W of NC 87, Eli Whitney vic.

Named for the nearby spring, the meeting was organized in 1751 and established in 1773 as the center of an early Quaker settlement. An earlier meetinghouse had two entrances into rooms for men's and women's business meetings. The present modest frame meetinghouse, with a entrance in the gable front and pointed windows lighting the center-aisled meeting room, was built soon after the Society of Friends adopted the Uniform Discipline (1902), which marked a transition to the gable-fronted form akin to that of other denominations.

AM 28 West Grove Friends Meeting House
1915; W side SR 2340, 0.2 mi. N of SR 2347

The small frame building in its grove shows the continuation of the old meetinghouse form. When this "conservative" meeting was established in 1915, other meetings, such as *Spring Friends, were erecting buildings like those of mainstream Protestant denominations. A few groups such as West Grove split off and repeated the traditional, symmetrical plan with two entrances in the long side opening into men's and women's meeting rooms separated by sliding panels.

AM 28 *West Grove Friends Meeting House*

AM 29 Snow Camp

An early center of Quaker settlement founded by the Dixon family and others, the rural community extends from the crossroads near Cane Creek. Among the oldest houses is the **Allen House** (1852; Berry Davidson, builder; NW side SR 1005 at SR 1004), a conservative frame dwelling attributed to regional builder and millwright Davidson, who apprenticed under miller Solomon Dixon. The tall, narrow house has a traditional hall-parlor plan and a chimney of 1:4 bond with double, stepped shoulders—a form akin to Davidson's later millworkers' houses. The **Snow Camp Dam** (ca. 1780; W side SR 1004 at Cane Creek) is a fieldstone dam built by the Dixon family in the 18th c.; Quaker miller Simon Dixon is said to have brought his millstone with him from Pennsylvania. The **Snow Camp Telephone Exchange** (1915; W side SR 1004, 0.2 mi. S of SR 1005), a little 2-story frame building with pyramidal roof, was built by a local telephone company. Just south of it is one of the more visible of the county's many log houses, the **Dixon-Coble House** (early 19th c.; W side SR 1004, 0.3 mi. S of SR 1005), a 2-story, V-notched log dwelling with irregularly placed windows and a stone chimney with brick stack; built for the Dixon family, it was moved here by Randolph Coble, who married into the family.

A short distance west is **Cane Creek Meeting House** (est. 1751, 1942; NW corner SR 1005 and 2371), a venerable and still-active Quaker site. The simple Colonial Revival brick meetinghouse was built as successor to meetinghouses that burned in 1873 and 1942. A marker recalls that Cane Creek's "first monthly mtg was held by women Friends 10 Mo. 7 1751," and their representatives attended quarterly meetings in Perquimans Co. The large graveyard has markers from the 18th c. onward.

AM 30 Sword of Peace
Historical Drama Site
SR 2407, SE of SR 1005; Snow Camp

Near Cane Creek Meeting, the outdoor drama commemorates the local Quaker heritage with buildings moved to the site. Early log buildings include 1- and 2-room structures of V-notched logs, with the **Teague House** (late 18th c.?) especially well crafted with chamfered ceiling joists and pegged rafters. Three meetinghouse plans are represented. A small, 1-room log building of old materials depicts the original Cane Creek Meeting House. The frame **New Hope Meeting House** (1904; moved from Sophia, Randolph Co.) was built for a conservative group who separated from Marlboro Meeting in 1904 and built a traditional form with gabled sides and 2 entrances on the long front, opening into rooms for women's (L) and men's (R) business meetings, with movable partitions between. The frame **Chatham Friends Meeting House** has an entrance in the gable front and windows along the sides and was moved after the Chatham Meeting (est. 1824; SR 2340) built a brick meetinghouse in 1978.

AM 31 Cedarock Park
N and S sides of SR 2409, just E of NC 49

Now part of a county park, the **Garrett Farmstead** was settled in the 1750s by the Albright family. About 1830 Polly Albright married John Garrett, and they built a small, V-notched log house; they later added a 2-story frame house with hall-parlor plan and simple Greek Revival detail and made the log house into a kitchen. Around these the family erected a smokehouse of plank construction and a corncrib, a post office, and a barn of frame. By 1850 the Garrett family had 5 children and owned 5 slaves and 115 acres (85 improved and 30 unimproved), raising livestock and producing butter, wool, corn, wheat, and food crops. Also in the park is the **Curtis House** of similar form and plan; its residents are said to have operated a small cotton mill on nearby Rock Creek.

AM 32 Alamance
Est. 1837; NC 62 at Big Alamance Creek

Late 19th-c. and early 20th-c. mill houses line the road running up from the site of E. M. Holt's pioneer cotton mill—birthplace of a manufacturing empire. Inspired by Henry Humphries's steam-powered Mount Hecla cotton mill in Greensboro, in 1837 Holt and partner William Carrigan erected a waterpowered cotton mill at the Holt family gristmill site on Big Alamance Creek. Working on credit and aided by Thomas Ruffin (*Hillsborough), Holt bought machinery from Paterson, N.J., erected a frame mill, and employed a northern machinist to teach the making of cotton yarn. A visitor of 1849 found "quite a village," with "neat log houses, occupied by operatives," and "intelligent white females" at work at 12 looms and 1,350 spindles. After Carrigan left in 1851, Edwin took his son Thomas (later governor) and other sons into the business. From a traveling French dyer Thomas learned the art of dying yarn before weaving it and developed the famous "Alamance Plaid"—the first factory-dyed cotton cloth in the South. Running profitably through the Civil War, the Holts emerged ready to retool and expand while others struggled to recover. The frame mill burned in 1871 but was rebuilt by Berry Davidson and stood until the 1940s. The Holts replaced the log houses with 1- and 2-story frame dwellings ca. 1850–1900. These include 2-story, 3-bay houses with end chimneys akin to those at *Bellemont, *Glencoe, and elsewhere.

AM 33 *Edwin M. Holt House (Locust Grove)*

AM 33 Edwin M. Holt House (Locust Grove)

1849; Alexander Jackson Davis (New York), architect; Eli Denny, builder; S side NC 62, 0.2 mi. E of SR 1113, Alamance vic.; private, visible from road

The little frame villa is among the few houses in the state built from a design by architect Davis. On March 2, 1849, E. M. Holt wrote to the architect that he had seen his design—a "Small Classical Villa"—in the January *Horticulturalist* magazine: "Though that design does not suit me, yet a friend insists on my calling on you for a design." Holt and his wife Emily Farish and several of their 10 children were living in an early 19th-c. house, which he had hired local builder Eli Denny to expand. The pioneer industrialist Holt (*Alamance) kept up with na-

tional advances in the industry along with his friends John Motley Morehead of Greensboro and Francis Fries of Salem. It was probably Morehead, for whom Davis had designed *Blandwood, who encouraged Holt's interest. Holt asked Davis to adapt the plan to the South, where "the Kitchen is always in a separate building" and "sleeping apartments more roomy & better ventilated than the North." Denny began the house on March 19 and finished it by summer, thriftily retaining the old house in back. Though modest, the cross-plan villa, with 2-story gable-fronted center section and flanking 1-story wings, represented a clear departure from local building traditions. Holt lived here the rest of his life; at his death in 1884 he was one of the richest men in the state. He was a member and benefactor of nearby St. Paul's Lutheran Church, where the old churchyard has several German-language stones.

AM 34 L. Banks Holt House (Oak Grove)

Late 18th–early 19th c., ca. 1875; N side NC 62 opp. SR 1113, Alamance vic.; open regular hours

The farmhouse, seat of the Holt dynasty, stands on the farm established ca. 1760 by Michael Holt II (son of Michael I, a German who arrived 1740). He or his son Michael III built a modest dwelling, which in the early 19th c. was the home of Michael III and his wife Rachel Rainey and their 6 children, including planter and physician William Rainey Holt (*The Homestead, Davidson Co.) and Alamance textile pioneer Edwin M. Holt. In the mid-19th c. Edwin's son

AM 34 *L. Banks Holt House*

Lynn Banks Holt and his wife Mary Catherine Mebane of Caswell Co. transformed the dwelling into an L-shaped Italianate house with ornate millwork like his brother's *Sunny Side. Outbuildings include a carriage house, a corncrib, and a 2-story granary built in 1872. L. Banks Holt was a leader in the postwar expansion of the family textile business. Restored and furnished with family pieces, the house contains the Alamance Co. Historical Museum.

AM 35 Lawrence Holt House (Sunny Side)

1871–75; S side NC 1136, 0.3 mi. E of NC 62, Bellemont vic.

The stylish, T-plan Italianate house, built for Lawrence S. Holt at his marriage to Margaret Erwin of Burke Co., shares several motifs with other Holt family houses, possibly inspired by the patternbooks of A. J. Bicknell, including the bracket cornice, ornate porch, and crenellated chimneys. Youngest son of E. M. Holt, Lawrence worked for a time in Charlotte and persuaded family members to join him in founding Commercial National Bank (*Bank of America) there in 1874. He entered the family textile business in the early 1870s, founded several mills with various kinsmen, and moved to Burlington.

AM 36 Kernodle-Pickett House

1895–96; N side NC 1123, opp. SR 1131, Bellemont vic.

The farmhouse beside the road is an unusually full-blown rural version of the Queen Anne style, complete with bay windows,

gable ornament, and wraparound porch. Like some other especially elaborate farmhouses, it was built for a country doctor, in this case Dr. Loften Kernodle; after 1900 it was the longtime home of Dr. John A. Pickett.

AM 37 Bellemont

Est. 1879; NC 49 at Big Alamance Creek

The prototypical mill village downstream from *Alamance was established in 1879 by E. M. Holt's sons Lawrence and L. Banks. It was constructed largely by local contractor and millwright Berry Davidson using timbers cut with a circular saw—then a local novelty. Wagons hauled northern-made looms and other machinery to the site in 1880, 1881, and 1882. The 3-story brick mill beside the creek is in ruins, but the village is generally intact. Lining the road that rises south of the mill are evenly spaced, 2-story **Workers' Houses** (ca. 1880) with deep back gardens; like many in the county they are essentially identical frame dwellings, 3 bays wide with end chimneys, hall-parlor plans, rear ells, and front porches. There are also a few 1-story houses with interior chimneys. In 1880 the *Alamance Gleaner* praised Bellemont as "the neatest, prettiest factory in the county," where the mill, "the store, the tenant houses, and all the surroundings are neat as a pin and are pleasing to look upon." (See Introduction, Fig. 50.)

AM 38 Allen House

Ca. 1782; Alamance Battleground State Historic Site, N side NC 62, 3.0 mi. SW of Alamance; open regular hours

The house, moved and restored, offers access to a well-crafted late-18th-c. log dwelling. Built for John and Rachel Stout Allen, who married in 1779, and traditionally dated 1782, it originally stood near *Snow Camp on land granted in 1756 to John's father, one of the Pennsylvania Quakers of *Cane Creek Friends Meeting. Raising a family of 12 children, John worked as a farmer, teacher, carpenter, and storekeeper, and Rachel served the community with her medical skills. Family papers record the exchange of work and goods among neighbors that made up the rural "social economy." In 1967 the house was moved here to recall the back-country farmers involved in the Regulator movement, including the Allens' relatives. Measuring 17½ by 25 feet, the 1-room, V-notched log house is heated by an interior stone chimney, a contrast with more usual exterior chimneys. Logs are hewed only on the sides and infilled with clay, twigs, and straw. Cantilevered logs support the porch roof. The neatly crafted interior carpentry includes sheathing and batten doors, smoothly hewn ceiling joists, half-lapped common rafters with feet mortised and pegged into the top plates, and attic floor-boards pegged to the joists. (See Introduction, Fig. 10.)

Across NC 62, two **Markers** commemorate the 1771 Battle of Alamance here in which Governor William Tryon's troops defeated the protesting Regulators, ending the Regulator movement and forcing many to leave N.C. An obelisk was erected nearby in 1880, and another memorial, depicting a Regulator hanged, was moved from *Guilford Battleground.

AM 39 Elon University
1907; 1920s; Herbert B. Hunter (High Point), architect; Elon

Begun in 1889 as Graham College and sponsored by the Church of Christ, the school was located at the Mill Point railroad stop. **West Dormitory** (1907), the oldest campus building, exemplifies the eclectic red brick classicism of the turn of the century. After the 1890 administration building burned in 1923, the Holts and the Dukes underwrote 5 new buildings "all of colonial architecture," including the **Administration Building** and **Carlton Library** in red brick Georgian Revival style.

Chatham County (CH)

See Rachel Osborn and Ruth Selden-Sturgill, The Architectural Heritage of Chatham County, North Carolina *(1991).*

Despite growing development pressures, the county maintains its rural landscape of small and middle-sized farms. It was settled in the 18th c. by Scots coming up the Cape Fear River and English (including many Quakers) and Scotch-Irish migrating south from Pennsylvania. Partitioned from Orange in 1771, the county and its seat were named for William Pitt, Earl of Chatham, a friend of the American colonies in Parliament. Farmers raised wheat, corn, livestock, and food crops, and a few eastern planters arrived to escape summer heat and threats of war. In the early 20th c., farmers added truck and dairy farming and big gambrel and gabled barns and silos.

The Haw and Deep rivers traverse the county to form the Cape Fear. Their proximity to coal and iron deposits in southern Chatham (including present-day Lee Co.) spurred many 19th-c. navigation projects to bypass the rapids and create a "Pittsburgh of the South." None succeeded, and mining and manufacturing remained small in scale, as did towns that rose and fell. By 1896 it was reported that despite "meagre facilities for navigation . . . this defect is supplied by the railroad." The Raleigh & Augusta (R&ARR) had a branch to Pittsboro, and the Cape Fear & Yadkin Valley (CF&YVRR) of 1884 brought trade to Gulf, Goldston, and Siler City, "all of which have become centers of industrial pursuits." US 64 along an old route sparked growth in the 20th c., and proximity to the University of North Carolina in Chapel Hill and the Research Triangle Park brought further development.

Pittsboro (CH 1–10)

Established in 1787 as county seat, Pittsboro developed into a stylish little town known for its hostelries and academies and its planters, doctors, and lawyers. Besides accommodating regular visitors to court sessions, the town welcomed Wilmington and New Bern families who regularly summered here and occasionally stayed. The Lancaster square grid plan of half-acre lots centers on the courthouse square at the meeting of four axial streets, with the corners notched out of adjacent blocks. Its buildings encompass gradual town growth from Georgian and Federal styles of the late 18th and early 19th c. to various early 20th-c. modes. Long bypassed, the town gained a branch from the R&ARR in 1886.

CH 1 Chatham County Courthouse
1881; Alvis J. Bynum & William Lord London, builders; US 64 BUS (East and West Sts.) and US 15-501 (Hillsborough St.)

Its commanding presence in the traffic circle and square at the geographic center of the state made the courthouse a landmark on the 550-mile "Manteo to Murphy" US 64, which now bypasses the town. The design recalls a composition popularized in Asher Benjamin's *American Builder's Companion*, with a piano nobile containing the courtroom accentuated by pilasters, a portico, and a 3-stage cupola. Remodeled in 1959 and restored in 1986–90, the courthouse gained a clock in its cupola in 1999. The Confederate Monument on the north was erected in 1907. Among the notable commercial buildings framing the square are the **Blair Hotel** (1917; 105–21 Hillsborough St.), a Mission style brick building on the site of the old Central Hotel, and the **Justice Motor Co.**

CH 1–3 *Chatham Co. Courthouse, Pittsboro Presbyterian Church, and Pittsboro Masonic Lodge*

(1949; George F. Hackney [Durham]; 103 West St.), a Moderne auto dealership designed by a cousin of Chevrolet dealer Fred C. Justice.

CH 2 Pittsboro Presbyterian Church
1850, ca. 1875; 95 East St.

The church began in 1850 as a simple brick gable-end building with square central tower; renovation after an 1875 storm probably added the Gothic Revival belfry. After a 1920s remodeling, the church was restored in 1971 to its 1875 appearance.

CH 3 Pittsboro Masonic Lodge (Columbus Lodge No. 102)
1838–40, 1849; Martin Hanks, carpenter; East St.

Built for a lodge chartered in 1837, the temple-form frame building began as a 2-story structure of domestic form and finish. The Greek Revival portico extension came in 1849, after lodge minutes recorded discussion over fluted vs. square columns. The lower floor has served various community functions, and the lodge is still active. To the rear is the small, frame **Charles Manly Law Office** (ca. 1842; George Ellington, carpenter), built for attorney and governor Manly near the corner of Hillsboro and Salisbury Sts. and moved here in 1970.

CH 4 Hall-London House
Ca. 1836; 206 Hillsborough St.

The transitional Federal–Greek Revival style house was built for Dr. Isaac Hall, who came to Pittsboro from Scotland Neck ca. 1836. It evidently gained the picturesque Gothic Revival latticework porch about the time of his daughter's 1856 marriage. From 1880 to 1918 this was home of journalist and lawyer Henry Armand London.

CH 5 The Yellow House (Patrick St. Lawrence House)
Ca. 1787; 203 South St.

The oldest building in town and probably the county, the 2-story frame house was built by Lawrence, an original town commissioner and multifaceted entrepreneur, as his residence and inn at the public square.

CH 5 *The Yellow House*

(It has been moved twice.) Covered in beaded weatherboard and well finished throughout, as early as 1798 it was known for its yellow paint. The center-passage plan features a paneled partition that slides up to the ceiling to open passage and room into one large space, one of a variety of arrangements by which innkeepers accommodated their buildings' semipublic purpose (*Union Tavern, *Tyro Tavern, *Brummel's Inn, *Wright Tavern).

CH 6 Lewis Freeman House
Ca. 1815, late 19th c.; 205 W. Salisbury St.

At the core of the small house is the 1-room frame residence of Freeman, Pittsboro's most successful antebellum free black resident and owner of 6 town lots. A rare survival of the neatly finished 1-room houses once common in N.C. towns, it was expanded over the years, including a porch credited to local contractor Bennet Nooe Jr.

CH 7 Henry Adolphus London II House
Ca. 1895; Bennet Nooe Jr., builder;
440 W. Salisbury St.

Alternating bands of diamond- and square-cut wood shingles on the front bay and gable distinguish the Queen Anne cottage as the work of local builder Bennet Nooe Jr. Built for a member of a leading Pittsboro business family (grandson and namesake of the builder of the *London Cottage), the house occupies a spacious lot with a tree-lined drive that was part of the old road to Hillsborough.

CH 7 *Henry Adolphus London II House*

CH 8 Lustron Houses: Clark House, McCallum House
1950; 505 Credle St.; 707 West St.

Two similar houses exemplify the manufactured dwellings designed by architect Carl Koch, made in Columbus, Ohio, and delivered on tractor-trailers. Made for economy, efficiency, and easy cleaning, both exemplify the 2-bedroom model: 1,080 square feet, about 12½ tons, base price $9,000. They are built with 20-foot wall sections of enameled steel in 2-by-2-foot panels, with metal tile roofs. The low-maintenance interiors are finished in gray and yellow, including rubber baseboards.

CH 9 A. P. Terry House
Ca. 1900; Bennet Nooe Jr., builder;
465 Pittsboro Elementary School Rd.

Saloon-keeper Terry's Queen Anne residence exemplifies the work of local lumberman, contractor, and longtime mayor Nooe, who is said to have built as many as 1,000 houses and stores in Pittsboro, Raleigh, Durham, Lexington, and Chapel Hill between 1893 and 1904.

CH 10 London Cottage
Ca. 1861; E side SR 1516, 0.4 mi. N of SR 87;
private, visible from road

Built by businessman Henry Adolphus London and called "the cottage" by the family, the house exemplifies the picturesque mode promoted by Downing's *Cottage Residences* and other works: a 1½-story board-and-batten dwelling with an irregular plan, bracketed cornice, bay window, and peaked window hoods.

CH 11 Baldwin's Mill
Ca. 1807?; NE side SR 1520,
0.6 mi. N of SR 1545, Terrells;
private, visible from road in winter

By 1807 Samuel Baldwin, a farmer and Baptist minister, ran a mill on Terrell's Creek; along with a sawmill, a cotton gin, a blacksmith shop, and a general store, the mill served the rural community through much of the 19th c. The large frame mill house, of

Baldwin's era or later, stands on a fine dry-laid stone foundation near a dam of similar stonework and was privately restored in 1941.

CH 12 Bynum

The small mill village of the county's first major textile enterprise began in the 1870s when brothers Carney and Luther Bynum founded the **Bynum Mfg. Co.** on the Haw River near the family flour mill (1860); mill-wright Berry Davidson, who had built the flour mill, installed the machinery in the cotton mill in 1874. In 1886 the Bynums sold the mill to industrialist J. M. Odell of Concord. The factory burned in the late 20th c., but the village retains blocks of millworkers' houses up the hill north of the mill. The 14 original houses are 1½ stories tall, each with 2 main rooms; later ones are 1 story with 2 main rooms and an ell. The founding brothers built their own houses about 1880 facing each other from separate hills: the **Luther Bynum House**, an I-house with an ornate sawnwork porch, and the **Carney Bynum House** (ca. 1880), a larger, cross-gable, double-pile house. **Farrell's Store** (ca. 1910) is a well-preserved frame country store with stepped parapet front and intact storefront, still busy as the Bynum General Store. The village has been enriched in the late 20th c. with the art of local sculptor Clyde Jones.

CH 12 *Farrell's Store*

CH 13 Hackney-Hudson House
Ca. 1840; W side SR 1700, 2.4 mi. N of US 64, Bynum vic.

With its array of 20th-c. outbuildings, the big 2-story frame house typifies the relatively plain plantation houses of the region. It has an asymmetrical facade and simple Federal and Greek Revival detail.

CH 14 Mount Gilead Baptist Church
Ca. 1900; W side SR 1700, 1.1 mi. N of US 64, Bynum vic.

The frame country church with 3-stage entrance tower, built for a congregation est. 1824, presides from a hilltop.

CH 15 Merritt Farm
Early 19th c., ca. 1880s; W side SR 1008, 0.8 mi. N of SR 1717; private, visible from road

The well-preserved farmstead centers on a typical late 19th-c. farmhouse, 2 stories tall with center front gable and a delicately adorned porch. Log outbuildings, some predating the house, include tobacco barns, a smokehouse, storage houses, and a kitchen, built with square and half-dovetailed notching.

CH 16 Joseph B. Stone House
Late 18th–early 19th c.; E side SR 1008, 1.5 mi. S of SR 1752, Farrington vic.; private, visible from road

Combining late Georgian and Federal elements, the 2-story plantation house has an unusual front entrance: a double door opens into the center passage, and an adjacent single door opens into the north parlor. The house was occupied by the Stone family from the antebellum era until the mid-20th c. and was subsequently restored.

CH 17 O'Kelly's Chapel
Ca. 1900; W side NC 751, at Durham Co. line, Farrington vic.

The 1-room, gable-end frame chapel exemplifies the simple country church, with a touch of the Gothic Revival in its arched entrance. Its simplicity belies its importance in church history: as a historical marker notes, it was here that the first Christian Church in the South was established by James O'Kelly, a former Methodist preacher who in 1794 founded a movement that became known as the Christian Church. The chapel is the fourth on the site.

CH 18 Beckwith-Goodwin Farm
Ca. 1819, ca. 1839; N side US 64, 0.9 mi. E of SR 1008; private, visible from road

The farmstead maintained by continuous family ownership epitomizes the small scale of buildings of N.C.'s yeoman farmers. The initial single-pen log house with massive stone chimney (and later porch) was probably built for Wiley Holland, who bought 50 acres in 1819. In 1839 his daughter Matilda married Silas Beckwith, and the couple is believed to have built the slightly larger house with hall-parlor plan, making the older house their kitchen. Log and frame outbuildings include a barn, a potato house, and cribs.

CH 18 *Beckwith-Goodwin Farm*

CH 19 J. B. Mills House
Early, late 19th c.; SW corner US 64 and NC 751; private, visible from road

Standing beside the highway, the Queen Anne style farmhouse, with multiple gables, broad porch, and fancy millwork, was built in front of an earlier 1-room dwelling with Flemish-bond brick chimney.

CH 20 Ebenezer Methodist Church
Ca. 1890; W side SR 1008, 0.7 mi. S of US 64

The Gothic Revival country church was moved from the B. Everett Jordan Dam area

in the 1970s. The congregation (est. 1827) had previously worshiped in a small log church with log chimney, which survived into the 1970s.

CH 21 Haywood Presbyterian Church
1859; S side SR 1011, Haywood (Moncure vic.)

The pedimented, Greek Revival frame church is the chief vestige of the short-lived riverport town of Haywood, founded by 1800 where the Deep and Haw rivers form the Cape Fear, which is navigable below Fayetteville. After thriving modestly in the antebellum era, Haywood faded into a small rural community after the Civil War.

Upstream at the falls of the Deep River is the site of **Lockville** (no public access). From the Cape Fear Co. of 1791, efforts to build canals, locks, and dams to the iron and coal fields all failed for lack of money (*Cumnock, *Endor Iron Furnace, Lee Co.). Portions of the canal system remain, as well as a 1922 powerhouse from a hydroelectric plant.

CH 21 *Haywood Presbyterian Church*

CH 22 Gulf

The little community grew up on the Cameron-Gulf plank road, a spur of the "Appian Way of N.C." from Fayetteville to Bethania. The 2-story, Greek Revival style **Haughton-McIver House** (ca. 1853, ca. 1870s) was probably built as a plank road hotel for Lawrence Haughton, an incorporator of the Gulf-Graham plank road spur to Alamance Co. The simple Gothic Revival **Gulf Presbyterian Church** (1882) and the Queen Anne style **Dr. Robert Palmer House** (ca. 1903) recall continuing growth, especially after the cf&yvrr arrived in the 1880s. The **Marion Jasper Jordan House** (1893; s side sr 2145, 0.7 mi. e of Gulf), a big foursquare frame house with 2-tier porch lavished with sawn and turned ornament, was built for a lumberman.

CH 23 Goldston

The cf&yvrr from Wilmington to Mount Airy spawned new trade centers such as Goldston, with classic frame stores beside the tracks. The **Farmers' Union Store** (1899), with high parapeted front, bracket cornice, and intact interior began as the Bynum & Paschal Store, then became the Farmers' Union store in 1910, a cooperative store where farmers could buy, sell, and barter for goods. To the south is the earlier **Farmers' Union Store** (ca. 1908), built on land acquired in 1894 by the predecessor Farmers' Alliance, part of an organization that gained political power in the state in the early 1890s. Several late 19th–early 20th-c. frame houses also face the railroad, including the Italianate style **Paschal-Womble House** (1889; 421 Main St.) built for merchant L. F. Paschal.

CH 23 *Farmers' Union Stores*

CH 24 Meroney's Methodist Church
Ca. 1900; NW side NC 902, opposite SR 2187, Goldston vic.

The typical frame country church, third building of a congregation est. 1808, features a shingled 3-stage entrance tower and lancet arched windows.

CH 24 *Meroney's Methodist Church*

CH 25 Mount Vernon Springs

The community settled by Quakers grew up around a mineral spring known as Indian Springs and Quaker Springs, then named in the 1850s for George Washington's home. A resort hotel flourished with the railroad in the late 19th c., and a railroad village east of the springs (begun as Ore Hill for an 18th-c. iron furnace operated by John Willcox) changed its name to Mount Vernon Springs in 1926. Amid the frame houses along the road, the chief landmark is **Mount Vernon Springs Presbyterian Church** (1885), built in simplified Gothic Revival style on land donated by the hotel owner.

CH 26 Siler City

The town at the junction of the old Raleigh-Salisbury and Fayetteville-Greensboro roads began as the 19th-c. stagecoach stop of Matthews Crossroads. Briefly called Energy, it was named in 1886 for Samuel Siler, descendant of an early German family, who donated the land for the depot of the new cf&yvrr. Soon factories near the tracks were making wood products—washboards, chairs, sash and doors, etc.—as well as textiles and feed. In the central business district along N. Chatham and other streets, the most notable of the brick commercial buildings is the **Hotel Hadley** (1908; 103 N.

Chatham St.), an ebulliently ornate hotel built by businessman F. M. Hadley with all conveniences, including running water and gas lighting, and an arcaded second-story loggia of turned spindlework.

Several streets of early 20th-c. residential architecture include E. Raleigh St. and N. 3rd Ave. Most striking is the small but flamboyant and remarkably intact **Gregson-Hadley House** (1903; W. H. Tippett, architect; 322 E. Raleigh St.), of brick in Queen Anne style with turret and wraparound porch. It was built for J. C. Gregson, a founder of the Hadley-Peoples Mfg. Co. who with the Hadleys (later owners) led the local textile industry.

CH 26 *Gregson-Hadley House*

Other downtown landmarks include **First Baptist Church** (1927; Harry Barton [Greensboro]; 314 N. 2nd Ave.), a large brick building with Romanesque and Moorish-inspired motifs, and the **U.S. Post Office** (1940; 116 E. Raleigh St.), a Works Progress Administration (WPA) Colonial Revival design in Mount Airy granite; its mural depicts farm life and the early 19th-c. John Siler House (razed for the post office). The **City Hall** (1939–40: R. R. Markley [Durham], architect; Carl Phillips, builder; 311 N. 2nd Ave.) is a Colonial Revival WPA building of Randolph Co. granite. **Siler City High School** (Paul Braxton School; 1923; Charles Coker Wilson [Columbia, S.C.], architect; 119 S. 3rd Ave.) is a red brick building with Art Moderne highlights in white stucco.

CH 27 William P. Hadley House and Gristmill

1850s, 1885; W side SR 2165, 2.0 mi. S of US 64, Pittsboro vic.; private, visible from road

Set amidst some of the county's prettiest farmland, the complex characterizes the diversified interests of 19th-c. farmers. Descended from Quaker settlers, farmer and miller Hadley was a community leader and co-owner of a toll bridge over the Deep River at Egypt (*Cumnock) and had landholdings of 600 acres. The 2-story, center-passage frame house blends Greek Revival details with Italianate bracket cornice. His frame gristmill, on a site used by 1838, operated until the 1930s.

CH 28 Aspen Hall and Alston-DeGraffenreidt House

Ca. 1810, ca. 1820s; private, no public access or visibility

Two fine plantation houses atypical of the predominantly yeoman farming county stand north of the old stage road (US 64) west of Pittsboro. **Aspen Hall** was built for Joseph John "Chatham Jack" Alston, of a large eastern Carolina family. He settled in the county in the 1790s and built a 2-story frame house, which became a rear ell to his subsequent 2-story, 5-bay residence of Federal–Greek Revival style, attributed to local carpenter Martin Hanks. A mile away, Alston is said to have built the **Alston-De-Graffenreidt House** for son John Jones Alston ca. 1810 as a 2-room dwelling, which was soon enlarged into a 5-bay, double-pile house with raised basement and hip roof

CH 28 *Alston-DeGraffenreidt House*

and an elaborately finished parlor. It was inherited by John's daughter Delia Alston DeGraffenreidt ca. 1870.

CH 29 Alston-Dark House

Ca. 1840, 1919; N side US 64, 1.0 mi.
W of SR 1506, Siler City vic.; private,
visible from road

The 2-story, late Federal style dwelling was built for Phillip K. D. Alston, tenth child of Chatham Jack (*Aspen Hall). Merchant C. C. Cheek purchased the property in 1898, and in 1919 his daughter and son-in-law Newby Dark made the house a lodge for a hunting club, adding a big 2-tier porch and various barns and outbuildings.

CH 30 DeGraffenreidt-Johnson House

Ca. 1850; N side SR 1346, 1.0 mi.
W of SR 1561, Silk Hope vic.; private,
visible from road

The well-sited, 2-story frame house, a blend of Greek Revival and Italianate features (*Hadley House and Mill), was built for planter John Baker DeGraffenreidt, who married Delia Alston, daughter of John Jones Alston (*Alston-DeGraffenreidt House). Outbuildings date from the early 20th c.

CH 31 Wade Hampton Ferguson House

1915; N side US 64, 0.1 mi. E of jct.
w/SR 1561; open as county arts center

This highly visible farmhouse, facing west across its broad fields, illustrates a popular late 19th-c. and early 20th-c. form: the 2-story house with front-facing roof gable. A simply detailed porch reaches across the front, and a rear ell takes a similar form. Built for Ferguson on a 240-acre grain and cotton farm, from the 1920s it was the center of a dairy farm that included a dairy barn and granary. The landmark on US 64 has been preserved as an arts center.

Lee County (LE)

See J. Daniel Pezzoni, The History and Architecture of Lee County, North Carolina *(1995).*

The county, formed from Moore and Chatham in 1907 and named for Robert E. Lee, lies at the northernmost edge of Highland Scots immigration into N.C. (*Buffalo, *Euphronia Presbyterian churches). The geologically complex area has had a long role in the state's extractive industries. The sandhills pine forests of the south and east supplied naval stores and timber. From iron and coal mines near the Deep River, entrepreneurs supplied iron during the American Revolution and provided the Confederacy with iron and coal, but the quantity and quality of deposits thwarted hopes of making this the "Pittsburgh of the South." In the late 19th c., fine brownstone was quarried around Sanford for fashionable builders in northern cities, and as tastes changed, brickmakers used the shales and clays of northern Lee to make the county the state's chief brick producer. Subsistence farms predominated through the 19th c., but as timbering and naval stores production cleared away the pine forests, farmers turned to cash crops of cotton and tobacco. An unusual in-state migration from the Old Bright Belt counties of Surry and Yadkin introduced flue-cured tobacco in the early 20th c., and Sanford became a Middle Belt market town in 1915.

Sanford (LE 1–2)

The railroad era brought the first incorporated towns in present-day Lee Co. Jonesboro, for which a major geological fault is named, was settled ca. 1869 on the old Western Railroad from Fayetteville to Egypt (*Cumnock). In 1872 the Raleigh & Augusta Railroad from Raleigh to Hamlet crossed the Western 2 miles north of Jonesboro, and the town of Sanford, named for a construction engineer, arose at the junction. Jonesboro was annexed to Sanford in 1947. Sanford's economy was bolstered with the brownstone and brickmaking industries. Tobacco warehousing, a textile mill, and other factories diversified the economy and produced a substantial commercial district and handsome early 20th-c. neighborhoods. Architects from several N.C. cities designed key buildings, as did local architect L. M. Thompson and builders Joe W. Stout and Lincoln Boykin.

LE 1 Downtown Sanford

The business district beside the rail junction is a showplace for the local brick industry, with early 20th-c. buildings displaying varied brickwork techniques enriched by brownstone or terra-cotta trim. The former **Sanford Town Hall** (1909–10; Joe W. Stout, builder; 143 Charlotte Ave.) announces its public status with a massive 3-story central tower, its convex roof capped by a domed and columned lantern. Decorative brickwork includes corbeling, horizontal banding, and flat, segmental, and round-arched openings. Next door, the **Coca-Cola Bottling Co. Building** (1907, 1931; 131 Charlotte Ave.), displaying a company design, has a jazzy Art Deco facade of blond brick with a frieze of tiny Coke bottles and stepped terra-cotta panels above the second-story windows, three with Coke bottles in relief and the fourth with the name in script.

LE 1 *Coca Cola Building and Sanford Town Hall*

The **Railroad House** (1872–73, moved 1962; 110 Charlotte Ave.; open as museum limited hours) recalls Sanford's birth as a railroad town. The Gothic Revival cottage was built by the Western Railroad as a dwelling for W. T. Tucker, the depot agent and first mayor, and his wife, Inder, who operated the Sanford Institute academy here. The crisply detailed board-and-batten house —complete with spiky king posts in its many steep gables—is one of the state's prime examples of the picturesque cottage mode, a type often associated with railroads. Endangered in 1962, it was moved and restored by the Railroad House Historical Association. Behind it is the former **Sanford Passenger Depot** (ca. 1910), a brick depot typical of the Seaboard line, with flared eaves carried by large wooden brackets with onion-shaped pendants. On the south is the **Seaboard Freight Depot** (ca. 1926), a long gabled building covered in board and batten, where a steam locomotive (1911, Baldwin Locomotive Works) sits on a stretch of track.

The 1920s brought a downtown con-

LE 1 *Railroad House*

struction boom. The **Carolina Hotel** (1926–27; L. M. Thompson, architect; 102 Carthage St.) is a 4-story building featuring a round arch of decorative brickwork above the central entry. Built as a vaudeville and cinema house, the **Temple Theater** (1924–25; Eric G. Flannagan [Henderson], architect; Joe W. Stout, builder; 120 Carthage St.) shows architect Flannagan's favored blend of Colonial Revival and Art Deco. The interior, with colorful proscenium arch and embossed metal ceiling, was restored in the 1980s as a performing arts center.

The **Bowen Motor Co. Building** (1925; James M. Workman [Greensboro], architect; Jewell-Riddle Co., builders; 234 Carthage St.), built as a Ford showroom and garage, exhibits the flair of many early automobile dealerships, here with a Spanish Mission facade with decorative parapets, terra-cotta medallions, and arcades. The most distinctive storefront is the **Stroud-Hubbard Building** (1928; L. M. Thompson, architect; Joe W. Stout, builder; 112 South Steele St.), 2 stories with Tudor Revival–influenced terra-cotta detail. The **Wilrik Hotel** (1925; C. Gadsden Sayre [S.C.], architect; Joe W. Stout, builder; 200 Wicker St.), with 2 lower stories in white brick and limestone and red brick above, is the town's tallest building at 6 stories; the local paper predicted that its "first sky scraper" would "put Sanford on the map."

LE 1 *Wilrik Hotel*

South of downtown are two key buildings associated with local African American institutions. Built for a congregation founded by freedpeople in 1868, **Fair Promise A.M.E. Zion Church** (1926; A. Lincoln Boykin, builder; 712 Wall St.) is a brick sanctuary with corner entry tower and smaller secondary tower on the west side. Builder "Link" Boykin adapted the design from a plan published by Benjamin D. and Max C. Price of Philadelphia. Boykin also built the **W. B. Wicker School** (1927 and later; A. Lincoln Boykin, builder; 806 S. Vance St.), a utilitarian brick building that began as the Lee Co. Training School and was later named for a black educator.

LE 2 Sanford Residential Areas

From the 1870s the principal residential sections radiated north from downtown along Hawkins Ave., Steele St., and Horner Blvd. (Endor St. before 1960). Architecture from the 1880s through the mid-20th c. includes Queen Anne, Craftsman Bungalow, Colonial Revival, and Tudor Revival—the last frequently the work of Sanford architect L. M. Thompson. Most houses, even those of business leaders, are of relatively modest scale.

Oldest is the **John D. McIver House** (ca. 1885; 309 Hawkins Ave.), a frame I-house with 2-tier porch, built for a farmer who wanted to live closer to his business interests in the new town; he returned to his farm after a year to escape the busy pace of town life. Next door, the **Duncan and Kate McIver House** (1893; 315 Hawkins Ave.) is a modest Queen Anne cottage that belies its owner's position as a leading businessman and mayor. The **Gavin House** (1922; John B. Matthews Jr., builder; 305 Hawkins Ave.) is Sanford's most imposing early 20th-c. residence, a frame Southern Colonial house with monumental Ionic portico.

Key institutional buildings are **First Presbyterian Church** (1928; L. M. Thompson, architect; Joe W. Stout, builder; 205 Hawkins Ave.), a Gothic Revival edifice with unequal towers and a rose window over an arcaded front entrance; **St. Thomas's Episcopal Church** (1928–31; L. M. Thompson, architect; O. Z. Barber, builder; 312 N. Steele St.), Gothic Revival in dark red brick with a truncated corner entry tower; and **Sanford High School** (1924–25; George Berryman [Columbia, S.C.], architect; 507 N. Steele St.), a 2-story brick school with Neoclassical details by a leading practitioner in modern school planning.

Two planned neighborhoods appeared west of N. Horner Blvd. **Rosemount** was laid out about 1910 in a grid bounded by Horner Blvd. and Gulf St. between Gordon St. and Weatherspoon St. Southwest of it, **McIver Park**, developed by Kate McIver after the death of her husband Duncan, followed in the 1920s with two curvilinear streets, Sunset and Summit. Prominent residences by L. M. Thompson include the **Makepeace House** (ca. 1920; 304 Summit Dr.), a Craftsman bungalow with Palladian gable windows; the **Isenhour House** (1929; 318 Summit Dr.), of multigabled form with faux half-timbering in the gables; and the **Heins House** (1929; 410 N. Gulf St.), a Tudor Revival house Thompson adapted from a brick manufacturers' association patternbook. The **Casey House** (1926; 205 N. Gulf St.) is a low-profile brick bungalow built from a published plan by Atlanta architect Leila Ross Wilburn.

LE 3 Lee County Courthouse

1908; Charles McMillen (Wilmington), architect; S side Horner Blvd. at McIntosh St.

When the county was formed in 1907, Sanford and Jonesboro vied for county seat; as a compromise the courthouse was built midway between the two. For years the state's only courthouse with an RFD address, it is surrounded by strip development. The straightforward Neoclassical Revival edifice of red pressed brick—even to the columns of its Ionic portico—evokes the county's brick industry; but in fact the building predates the birth of that industry here, and its bricks came from South Carolina. Brownstone column bases and Ionic capitals are one of the few local uses of that material, which was quarried in Sanford but shipped elsewhere.

LE 3 *Lee Co. Courthouse*

LE 4 Buffalo Presbyterian Church

1880; John Masemore, builder; S corner SR 1237 (Carthage St. ext.) and SR 1152, Sanford vic.

Sited in a grove of oaks, the frame church exhibits the classic pedimented form with

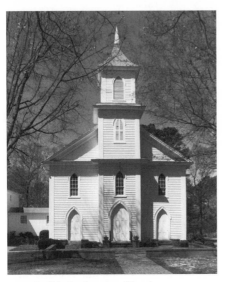

LE 4 *Buffalo Presbyterian Church*

front entry tower and Gothic Revival touches in the lancet-arched windows. It was built for the county's oldest congregation, which began in 1797 with the regular preaching of Rev. William D. Paisley in a log chapel near this site. The cemetery includes notable brownstone memorials fashioned by French stonecutters who came to the county in the 1890s to work the local quarries.

LE 5 Cumnock (Egypt)

The Deep River community was first called Egypt because the bountiful corn crops of Peter Evans's plantation attracted buyers during a drought, as in the biblical story of Joseph. Located in the state's only significant coalfield, which flanks the river for several miles, the state's largest and longest-operating coal mine was at Egypt. Some coal was mined from the 18th c., but major commercial mining began with the 1854 opening of the Egypt Coal Mine by New York financier Thomas Andrews. Hope mounted as the state geologist predicted on the Deep River "a CITY greater than Lowell." During the Civil War the mine supplied fuel for the Confederate navy and blockade-runners. The coal, along with pig iron from nearby *Endor Furnace, was hauled by the Western

Railroad, completed in 1863, from Egypt to Fayetteville and thence by Cape Fear River barges to Wilmington.

The mine closed in the 1870s, but enthusiasm returned in 1888 when northern investors purchased it and 2,400 acres of coal and timberland, planned a city, and built a Queen Anne style hotel, the Egyptian Inn. The Western Railroad was completed to Wilmington as the Cape Fear & Yadkin Valley Railroad, and by 1900 over 200 miners were at work. In 1895 the place was renamed Cumnock for a mining village in Scotland. After a series of mine explosions and financial reversals, the mine closed permanently ca. 1930. Nothing may be seen of the mine, and its 400-foot shaft is sealed. Of the once busy village, the chief landmark is **Cumnock Methodist Church** (ca. 1890; 5513 Cumnock Rd.), a small gable-fronted frame church with entry tower, built for a Congregational Christian group following the resumption of mining in the 1880s; it later served Quakers and Methodists.

LE 6 Endor Iron Furnace
Ca. 1862; Cumnock vic.; site under development as public park

The Deep River valley harbors iron ore as well as coal, which was mined from the 18th c. This furnace may have been built ca. 1860 by Wilmington investors including Donald MacRae, who owned land on the Deep River, but by 1862 it was operated by the Endor Iron Co. to supply iron to the Confederacy. (Endor was the biblical home of a conjuress consulted by King Saul.) The trapezoidal stone furnace, evidently the largest in the state, stands 35 feet tall and 32 feet square. It is well constructed of rough brownstone blocks, with an inner conical bosh (shaft) and handsomely worked arched openings on all four sides. Like others of its type (*Moratock Furnace), it stands by a bluff to enable workmen to trundle material across a bridge from the hill to charge the furnace from the top. A charcoal blast was used to smelt pig iron. After the war, Delaware manufacturer George Lobdell converted the furnace to a hot blast process; but

LE 6 *Endor Iron Furnace*

his ambitious industrial schemes failed, and the furnace was shut down by 1876. Most above-ground evidence of the complex operation has vanished, but the furnace is part of a planned civic park.

LE 7 Deep River Camelback Truss Bridge (Bridge #155)

Ca. 1908, Cambria Works (Johnstown, Pa.); 1932; SR 1400 (Chatham Co. SR 2153) over Deep River, Cumnock vic.

The 160-foot camelback truss occupies a bridge site used since the 1830s near the coal and iron mines of the Deep River. This bridge, which originally spanned Neals Creek near Lillington, was reassembled here in 1932 to succeed a wooden bridge, from which the stone pier at the north end remains. The metallic geometry gracefully spans the river between forested banks, a once common sight on country roads, now vanishing as truss bridges are replaced. When a new concrete bridge was built adjacent in the 1990s, this bridge was saved in place by a local group for pedestrian use in a riverside park.

LE 8 Farrish-Lambeth House

1852 (date brick); S side SR 1466, 1.2 mi. NE of SR 1423; private, visible from road

One of the county's most intact antebellum buildings, the I-house has an unusual asymmetrical 4-bay front that reflects its off-center-passage plan. Greek Revival finish includes a modillion cornice, paneled corner

posts, and symmetrically molded door and window surrounds with cornerblocks.

LE 9 Broadway

A marker in the archetypal railroad village declares that it was settled in 1870, incorporated in 1907, and named for a broad, level opening in the pine forests. It grew with the grandly named Atlantic & Western Railroad, completed from Sanford to Lillington in 1905. Among the 1-story brick commercial buildings, the **Bank of Broadway** (1909; 231 N. Main St.) is a handsome little structure with houndstooth courses and arched openings. North is the **Stevens Milling Co.** (1934, 1945; N. Main St.), a towering complex with a 3-story brick building housing a roller mill, plus silos and elevators for feed made from local grain. South is the **Stevens House** (ca. 1906, 1928; 310 S. Main St.), a 2-story brick-veneered Southern Colonial house with portico, the home of mill owner Samuel Stevens. The **Chandler House** (1907; ca. 1925, Leslie P. Cox, builder; S. Main St.) is a foursquare frame house remodeled in the 1920s in Craftsman style, home of George Chandler, merchant, lumberman, and a founder of the Bank of Broadway.

LE 9 *Stevens Milling Co.*

LE 10 Leslie-Winstead House

1870s; W side SR 1146, 0.7 mi. S of SR 1001; private, visible from road

The well-preserved farmhouse, which may incorporate an antebellum dwelling, com-bines a traditional form with turned and sawn finery, including a curious gambrel-roofed porch topped by a gabled balcony. Outbuildings include 19th-c. log structures from the area.

LE 11 Euphronia Presbyterian Church

1885–86; Daniel C. Campbell, builder; end of SR 1393, N side SR 1318, 1.8 mi. W of SR 1007

Standing in a remote and tranquil setting, the simple but elegant frame country church follows a traditional gable-fronted form, with tall, shuttered windows on the sides, a polygonal apse, and a wood-shingled turret with wooden finial spike on its 3-stage bel-fry. The Highland Scots congregation (est. by 1814) was founded in association with the Euphronian Academy by Rev. Murdock McMillan. The name is from the Greek "of good mind."

Moore County (MR)

Formed from Cumberland Co. in 1784, Moore Co. was named for Revolutionary War officer Alfred Moore (*Moorefields, Orange Co.). Its varied topography encompasses rolling clay land in the north, which supported farming and pottery making, and barren sandhills in the south, where old-growth longleaf pines supplied turpentine and timber industries. The northern part was settled by Piedmont Scotch-Irish, some Scots, and English, including some Quakers, while the south was home to Highland Scots from the Cape Fear zone. Trade was boosted by the 1850s Fayetteville to Salem plank road across the county. Late 19th-c. railroads brought industrial logging, followed by the winter resorts of *Pinehurst and *Southern Pines, which capitalized on the dry, temperate winter climate created by deep deposits of sand from ancient seas. The climate and railroads also encouraged early 20th-c. fruit cultivation, including famed sandhills peaches. Much of the county's architectural heritage is remote from view, including early 19th-c. farm and plantation houses, early 20th-c. "peach mansions," and remnants of the piney woods tradition of simple log and frame dwellings, some with wooden chimneys and lightwood block piers. Local historical organizations—beginning with the Moore Co. Historical Association founded in 1946, and early preservation leaders, including "Buffie" Stevenson Ives, sister of Adlai Stevenson—have preserved key examples of vernacular building.

MR 1 Carthage

Named for the ancient city in northern Africa, the county seat was established in 1796 on a ridge between the upland and sandhills sections of the county. In the 1850s the Fayetteville & Western Plank Road through town spurred business, with the Tyson & Kelly Buggy Co. becoming the county's largest manufacturer. In 1885–88 local leaders built the Carthage Railroad to tap the Raleigh & Augusta Railroad (R&ARR) at Cameron. The buggy company expanded as Tyson & Jones, with sales throughout the South. New houses and churches rose, and businesses burgeoned. In the 20th c., however, Carthage's growth slowed as Lee Co. was divided from Moore, other towns increased, and the buggy factory reduced production and then closed in the 1920s. The town of about 1,000 people retains notable architecture from its turn-of-the-century heyday.

At the apex of the ridge, the **Moore County Courthouse** (1922; Christopher Gadsen Sayre [Anderson, S.C., and Ra-

leigh], architect) is a conservative Renaissance Revival building, 3 stories tall in limestone with engaged Ionic columns at the east and west fronts. Southwest of the courthouse stood the **Tyson & Jones Buggy Co.** (106 Ray St., s of McReynolds St.), manufacturer of carriages from the plank road era into the automobile age. Its complex of brick buildings (ca. 1898–1906) burned in 1976, except for the 1-story company office with arched windows and ornate corbeling.

As in many towns, main roads were also premier residential streets. McReynolds St. (NC 24/27) west of the courthouse has the chief concentration of fine houses and was embowered by great trees until it was widened in the 1960s. The **W. T. Jones House** (1897; Charles Pearson [Raleigh], architect; 301 McReynolds St.), a towered frame Queen Anne house rich with sawn, turned, and shingled ornament, was built for the carriage painter from New Bern who was recruited by Tyson in the 1850s and became a partner and later president of Tyson & Jones. **Carthage Methodist Church** (1897–98; A. C. Campbell [Aberdeen], con-

MR 1 *Carthage Methodist Church and Charles T. Sinclair House*

tractor; 401 McReynolds St.), one of the state's largest frame churches, maintains its imposing character despite later siding; the Gothic Revival church features a 4-story corner tower with open belfry and a large, hooded arched window on the long street facade. Next door, the grandest of several Colonial Revival houses built for leading merchants is the **Charles T. Sinclair House** (1914; Frank Simpson [Raleigh], architect; Joe Stout [Sanford], builder; 403 McReynolds St.), a massive yellow brick house in Southern Colonial Revival style with curved portico.

East of the courthouse, the **John Sinclair House** (early 20th c.; 208 Monroe St.)., built for Charles's brother and business partner, has an Ionic portico engaged under a big hip roof. From antebellum years, the restored **Bruce-Dowd-Kennedy House** (1850s; SE corner Monroe and Rockingham Sts.; open limited hours) is a Greek Revival cottage with hip roof, set on sandstone piers, with a matching rear wing. It was evidently built by physician Samuel Bruce for his daughter Lydia and her husband Clement Dowd, who moved to Charlotte, where Dowd flourished in politics and banking. Shaded residential side streets have Queen Anne, Colonial Revival, and bungalow styles. The **George Calvin Graves House** (1882, 1897; 202 Barrett St.) was built for a merchant, livery stable operator, and pharmacist who created an eclectic concoction of towers, turrets, bays, porches, and wings

with Second Empire, Queen Anne, and Colonial Revival elements. The **Carthage Town Hall** (1939–40; Herbert Phillips, McDowell Co., supervising stonemason; 203 Barrett St.), a 1-story stone building with Craftsman and Colonial Revival details, was built by National Youth Administration workers as a community house; Eleanor Roosevelt came to the dedication.

MR 2 Thomas School and Bellview School

1860s; early 20th c.; E side US 15/501/NC 22, 0.2 mi. N of S fork of NC 15/501 and NC 22, grounds of Moore Co. School Offices, Carthage vic.

Two early county schoolhouses have been moved and preserved to depict past eras of education. The **Thomas School** in the woods is a 1-room, V-notched log building with fieldstone chimney, typical of many 19th-c. schoolhouses. It served the Samarcand community ca. 1860s–75. The **Bellview School** is a classic 1-room country schoolhouse reflecting early 20th-c. improvements, built of frame with a recessed entry in the gable front, neatly finished and topped with a belfry. It has windows along one side in a practice of the time.

MR 2 *Bellview School*

MR 3 James Bryant House and McLendon House

Early 19th c., late 18th c.; E side SR 1210, 1.4 mi. N of SR 1240; open limited hours

Located near a tributary of the Deep River, the restored houses illustrate important building traditions in the southern Pied-

MR 3 *McLendon House*

mont. The 1-room plank kitchen is described as the house built for Joel McLendon, farmer and gristmill owner, before 1779. It is built of precisely hewn heart pine planks, joined with half-dovetailed notches so tight that no chinking is needed. Planks rather than framing fill the gables, and pole roof purlins are set into them, a seldom surviving form sometimes termed a "cabin" roof. The interior has exposed ceiling joists and log walls; the stone chimney was rebuilt. By the early 19th c. the farm was home to James and Ann Bryant, who raised corn and livestock on 400 acres, 135 improved. They built a simply finished 2-story frame house with hall-parlor plan and front shed porch and rear shed rooms. Its height, Flemish-bond brick chimney, and neat Federal style detailing made it one of the best houses of its time and place. The site is maintained by a local organization.

MR 4 Kelly House

*1842; NE side SR 1640, 0.6 mi.
N of NC 22/24/27, Carthage vic.;
private, visible from road*

Once center of a 3,000-acre plantation, the big frame house is the most imposing of its era in the county. The Kelly family also founded the buggy factory in Carthage. Conservative in its transitional Federal–Greek Revival finish, the double-pile plan house with hip roof has a pedimented entrance porch, a fanlit entrance, 9/9 windows, and molded siding and trim.

MR 5 Jugtown Pottery Complex

*1920s and later; Henry Scott and sons,
builders; W side SR 1420, 0.2 mi. N of
SR 1419, Seagrove vic.*

The clay-rich area around the Deep River near the confluence of Moore, Randolph, and Chatham counties supports a long tradition of pottery making that began in the early 19th c. Prominent among many operations is Jugtown Pottery, with log buildings of the 1920s that, like the pots themselves, reflect the conscious blending of traditional and arts and crafts concepts of the era. The complex was established ca. 1921 by an enterprising and artistically inclined couple, Jacques and Juliana Busbee (born James Busbee and Julia Royster of prominent Raleigh families). Devotees of the Arts and Crafts movement, the Busbees collected N.C. pottery and in 1917 established the pottery in Moore Co. to produce wares for sale at Juliana's tearoom in Greenwich Village. They employed local potters and introduced Asian design elements into traditional forms. Ben Owen, of a local family, emerged as Jugtown's reputation-making master potter. Other potters in the state had also added "art pottery" elements into customary utilitarian ware to expand their market. Like other crafts promoters of the era (#The Spinning Wheel, Asheville), the Busbees erected rustic log buildings as a setting for their enterprise. Of traditional V-notched construction by local builders, these include the ca. 1921 salesroom and turning room with pug mill and the Busbees' log dwelling of ca. 1924. Other buildings in harmonious character have been built over the years; since 1983 the Owens branch of the family has continued the operation. Potters in the Seagrove area and elsewhere make the state one of the nation's principal centers of the living tradition.

MR 6 House in the Horseshoe State Historic Site

Ca. 1772; end of SR 1624

Located on a plantation in a horseshoe bend of the Deep River, the 2-story frame house is one of the few 18th-c. buildings in the southern Piedmont and among the most ambitious. Built for Philip Alston, a troublesome member of a widespread eastern N.C. planter family, it was the scene of a 1781 skirmish between Whigs (including Alston) and Tories; bullet holes and other battle scars are part of the tour. In 1798 the 2,500-acre plantation was purchased by Benjamin Williams, twice governor, who became in 1801 an early planter of cotton in the area. The large, well-finished house features double-shouldered Flemish-bond end chimneys with unusual T-plan stacks of a type characteristic of northeastern N.C. and Virginia. Entered from a full-width shed porch, the interior is finished with flush-boarded walls. Williams added early 19th-c. wings (since removed), a center-passage plan, and architectural embellishments, including an ornate mantel and enriched entrance suggestive of joiner Elhannon Nutt (*Haywood Hall, *Ayr Mount, *Fairntosh). (See Introduction, Fig. 12.)

MR 7 Cameron

The pleasant village near US 1 was incorporated in 1876 with the arrival of the R&ARR and was supposedly named for railroad official Paul Cameron (*Fairntosh). It began as a turpentine market, but local entrepreneurs made it "the dewberry capital of the world" when the cultivated form of the blackberry was introduced in the 1890s. Farmers consigned as many as 90,000 crates a year to dealers who packed them and sent them off by rail.

In the linear town along Carthage St., verdant lots and neat picket fences set off modest, picturesque frame houses, which are well garnished by decorative millwork. Cottages of 1½ stories are especially numerous, though there are several 2-story houses, with styles ranging from Italianate to Queen Anne and Colonial Revival. Some, such as the **Turner-McPherson House** (1867, 1910; Barrett & Thompson [Raleigh], architects), combine picturesque gables and millwork with columned Colonial Revival porches. Punctuating the streetscape are small frame churches, the **Cameron Presbyterian Church** (ca. 1879), gable fronted with a bel-

MR 7 *Turner-McPherson House*

fry and arched windows, and the **Cameron Methodist Church** (ca. 1886; Duncan & Alex Campbell, builders [attrib.]), of similar form with narrow proportions and steep pediments, vestibule, and tower. At the base of the hill near the railroad, a cluster of brick and frame commercial buildings recalls the golden age of the dewberry. In recent years the community has become an antique shop mecca.

MR 8 Taylor House
1879; Mr. Allen (Raleigh), builder; N side SR 1803, 0.9 mi. W of US 1, Vass vic.; private, visible from road

The unusually elaborate farmhouse combines Gothic and Queen Anne–inspired form and ornament—a steep cross gable with bargeboards, projecting bays and balconies, and a bracketed porch—with a conservative 2-story form. Outbuildings match the house, and nearby are a fine gambrel-roofed barn and other farm buildings, all carefully maintained. The house was built for Dr. Leslie Taylor and continued in the family.

MR 9 Southern Pines

Soon after the R&ARR traversed the sandhills in 1877, developer John T. Patrick of Wadesboro visited the area, heard about consumptives cured by the dry and temperate climate and pine air, and recognized the potential for a health resort at the elevated tract known as Shaw's Ridge. He bought 675 acres of cheap land and planned a town grid with wide streets and hollow blocks with building lots around open courtyards with pedestrian walkways. He advertised "Southern Pines, the Ideal Place for Consumptives"; offered lots to physicians; courted the press and railroads; and named streets for northern states to attract purchasers. Development was slow at first but increased from the 1890s onward. The concurrent growth of Pinehurst encouraged Southern Pines to shift its focus from healing to recreation. It drew wealthy northerners and emerged as a winter resort with a busy social season, equestrian sports, and golfing. Shingled bungalows and big hotels and boardinghouses with broad porches multiplied, and the downtown filled in with shops, a theater, and other facilities. During the 1920s, residents commissioned designs from Aymar Embury II, a New York architect known for his country houses. Like others of his generation, he combined flexible Beaux Arts plans suited to modern living with colonial and other Neoclassical details, often in a red brick Georgian Revival mode. The tidy community continues as a mecca for golfers, equestrians, retirees, and other year-round residents.

MR 9 *Weymouth*

Patrick's town plan creates an unusual central business district, with a dense and orderly layout of large hollow blocks with buildings lining the street and occasional passages into interior courtyards that allow for parking. The predominantly red brick Colonial Revival commercial architecture was largely rebuilt after a 1921 fire, with several designs by architect Embury. The **Southern Pines Depot** (ca. 1900; S. T. Moffett [Southern Pines], builder [attrib.]; 215 N.W. Broad St.), a 1-story frame building with German siding and a hip roof with flared eaves, was evidently erected by Seaboard soon after the firm took over the R&ARR and other routes.

Residential streets meander beneath the tall pines and among lush evergreen plantings. There are a few late 19th- to early 20th-c. frame cottages, decorative Queen Anne style dwellings, and frame bungalows. The predominant residential architecture embodies the 1920s preference for Colonial and Tudor Revival styles. Among the most visible Embury houses is **Weymouth** (1922; Aymar Embury II [New York], architect; SE corner Ridge Rd. and Connecticut Ave.;

limited public access), a Georgian Revival residence in red brick and frame built for novelist James Boyd. The estate was begun in 1904 by his grandfather, also James Boyd, a Pennsylvania industrialist. Embury kept the older house as a section of a linear, asymmetrical Beaux Arts plan with wings for guests and entertaining, offices, and servants. Here Boyd wrote *Drums, Marching On*, and other works and entertained a social circle that included Thomas Wolfe, Sherwood Anderson, John Galsworthy, and Paul Green. The estate is now a writing center, begun by state poet laureate Sam Ragan and others.

Loblolly (1918, 1928; Aymar Embury II, architect; 140 S. Valley Rd.), a luxurious residence of English and French inspiration, with steep roofs and gables, arched openings, and varied stucco and brick surfaces, was built for James Boyd's aunt, Mrs. A. P. L. Dull, then expanded by Embury for the Vale family after a 1926 fire. One of many smaller but equally picturesque designs appears in the **A. B. Yeomans House** (1923; 380 E. Pennsylvania Ave.) with tiled gambrel roofs and stuccoed walls typical of work by its owner, a Chicago landscape architect and relative of the Boyd family, who moved to Southern Pines and designed buildings as well as landscapes. **Mayfair Apartments**

(mid-20th c.; 165 N. May St.), a modernist contrast, is a remarkably intact cluster of Moderne style apartments and single-family dwellings grouped around courtyards, all 1-story high with flat roofs with white stuccoed walls, curved corners, and corner windows.

MR 10 Shaw House

Early, mid-19th c.; 780 SW. Broad St.; open limited hours

A representative and accessible example of the small but well-finished farmhouses of the 19th c., the 1-story frame dwelling shows a traditional sequence of growth. The farm was established by Charles Cornelius and Mary Ray Shaw, of Scots descent, who arrived in the 1820s from Cumberland Co. Charles served as postmaster, engaged in mixed farming, and acquired extensive pineland for naval stores. At the joining of two main roads at "Shaw's Ridge" they built their house, which they enlarged as they raised 12 children. At the core is an early 19th-c. house, finished with lapped and flush boarding and richly carved Federal style mantels. (Related local mantels and furniture are attributed to an unidentified itinerant craftsman.) It was expanded with rear shed rooms and an engaged front porch with "stranger" rooms—entered only from the porch—to produce a characteristic "coastal cottage" form. "Stranger" or "preacher" rooms on the porch, offering hospitality but separation from the family rooms, were a frequent feature in the southern and eastern N.C. Big chimneys of sandstone and brick rise at the ends; one is dated 1842. Lightwood blocks—an element seen often in the sandhills pine country—remain under part of the house. The family added a rear kitchen and dining ell later in the 19th c. After the railroad crossed the Shaw property, Southern Pines developed on part of their land and has grown up around the house. Rescued in 1946 by the Moore Co. Historical Association, it is accompanied by two small log houses and a dovetailed log corncrib moved from the county. (See Introduction, Fig. 23.)

MR 11 *Pine Needles Inn (St. Joseph's Hospital)*

MR 11 Knollwood Heights

Among the developments of the 1920s were Knollwood and Knollwood Heights, located toward Pinehurst. A centerpiece was **Pine Needles Inn** (St. Joseph's Hospital) (1927; Lyman Sise [Boston], architect; E side NC 22 [Central Dr.] N of NC 2), an immense resort hotel 5 stories tall with multiple towers, rendered in red brick and cast stone in a Jacobean Revival style. It became a hospital in 1948. The **Donald Ross House** (ca. 1928; 415 Fairway Dr. betw. NC 2 and NC 22), a 2-story brick house of restrained English cottage cast, was home of the famed golf course designer.

MR 12 Aberdeen

The small town has notable railroad-related architecture from its turn-of-the-century growth as a manufacturing and shipping point for timber and turpentine. Named Aberdeen in 1887 for the local Scots heritage, it began as Blue's Crossing after the R&ARR was extended from Sanford to Hamlet in the 1870s. In the late 1870s lumberman Allison Francis Page (founder of Cary in Wake Co.) bought over 14,000 acres of pinelands, built rail spurs and sawmills deep in the woods, and established a huge lumber mill at Blue's Crossing. By the 1880s, it was reported, "The large circular saws almost rush through these giants of the pine forests," and Page was supplying lumber to build "more houses than any other firm" in central N.C., feeding building booms in Durham, Raleigh, and elsewhere. He established the Aberdeen & West End Railroad, which became the Aberdeen & Asheboro Railroad. Turpentine distiller John Blue came from Cumberland Co. and invested in various enterprises, then founded the 1892 Aberdeen & Rockfish Railroad (which still operates), linking up with the Atlantic Coast Line south of Fayetteville. In 1901 Seaboard Air Line took over the R&ARR and with the Aberdeen & Asheboro built a depot as Aberdeen's "gateway to Pinehurst."

Their **Aberdeen Union Station** (1905–6; T. B. Creel, builder; s side Main St. at Sycamore St. betw. RR tracks) was erected by leading local builder Creel, who came from Cary with Page. In a standard Seaboard design, the handsome red and tan brick depot is 1 story tall beneath a deep hip roof with wide eaves. It houses the Carolina Dinner Train and a railroad museum. Northeast, the **Aberdeen & Rockfish Railroad Office Building** (1904; T. B. Creel, architect and builder; NE corner E. Main St. and RR tracks) is a 2-story brick building with hip roof, which overlooks the tracks of its line. Next door is the **Bank of Aberdeen** (1906; T. B. Creel, builder; 107 E. Main St.), a modest brick building with Romanesque Revival arched openings and metal cornice. The 100 block of W. Main St. has several 2-story brick structures erected by local builder Creel, including the **Aberdeen & Asheboro Railroad Building** (ca. 1906; 117 W. Main St.), in tan brick with red brick trim. The **Page Memorial Methodist Church** (1913; J. M. McMichael [Charlotte], architect; T. B. Creel, builder; 119 W. Main St.), in red brick with an Ionic portico and central dome, was built in memory of A. F. Page and his wife Catherine. The **Page Memorial Library** (1907; 102 S. Poplar St.) is a diminutive structure of rock-faced concrete block with a concrete Tuscan-columned entrance announcing its purpose.

Among many frame houses in late Victorian, Colonial Revival, and bungalow modes, the oldest is the **Malcolm J. Blue House** (ca. 1880; 312 S. Pine St.), a 2-story frame house with simple Greek Revival detail, built for the local turpentine distiller who became the first postmaster at "Blue's Crossing." The big Southern Colonial style **John Blue House** (ca. 1888, 1903; Charles C. Hook [Charlotte], architect [attrib.]; 200 Blue St.) was built and remodeled for the founder of the Aberdeen & Rockfish Railroad. The nearby **Faith Presbyterian Church** (ca. 1890; 513 Bethesda Ave.) is a modest, gable-fronted frame structure built for a congregation formed in 1867 and one of the most prominent landmarks of African American history in the county.

MR 13 Bethesda Presbyterian Church
1860; Archie McLeod & Norman McCaskill, builders; SE side NC 5 and SR 2042, 0.2 mi. NE of SR 2063

Set in a quiet, naturally landscaped setting among old graves, the severely simple church is one of the most evocative of the state's Scots Presbyterian churches. It was built on land donated by Malcolm M. Blue for a congregation founded in the 18th c. Specifications for the 2-story, 35-by-45-foot building describe each element from the heart pine frame and rock pillars to the carefully measured placement of doors, windows, and seating along the two aisles and in

MR 12 *Aberdeen Union Station*

MR 13 *Bethesda Presbyterian Church*

the galleries. Little altered except for the late 19th-c. vestibule with steeple, the church is maintained as a historic shrine along with the burial ground.

MR 14 Malcolm Blue Farm

Early to mid-19th c.; SW corner SR 2042 and Ernest L. Ives Dr., Aberdeen vic.; open limited hours

The small frame house exemplifies a regional form, with front porch and rear shed rooms sheltered by the deep gable roof, which extends at the ends to protect the brick chimneys. It is finished with simple late Federal and Greek Revival details and interior walls in planed sheathing. In time, the family partitioned the hall-parlor plan to form a center passage and attached a rear kitchen-dining ell. Malcolm McMillan Blue was part of a large Highland Scots family engaged in farming and naval stores production. Owner of more than 5,000 acres in 1860, he gave the land for *Bethesda Church. His son Malcolm J. was active in Aberdeen, while son Neil continued to farm into the early 20th c., erecting frame barns and other agricultural buildings. The complex has been restored as a museum of rural life.

MR 14 *Malcolm Blue farm*

MR 15 Pinehurst

National Historic Landmark District

The model resort village, designed for James W. Tufts of Boston by Frederick Law Olmsted and Warren Manning, is an extraordinary and carefully tended oasis of luxuriant year-round greenery, leisurely curving streets, and intentionally informal architecture from the 1890s onward. In 1895 Tufts, a philanthropic pharmacist and patenter of soda fountain equipment, established Pinehurst as a "health resort for the weary and overworked" northern working people, especially those whose lungs needed the "curative virtues in the aromatic breath of the pine." Rail connections could be made at Aberdeen or Southern Pines. Tufts bought over 5,000 acres of timbered land from the Page family and others and commissioned his friend Olmsted to design the 100-acre winter resort village.

Then at the end of his long career as the dean of American landscape design, Olmsted faced at Pinehurst as at #Biltmore the challenge of creating a beautiful and naturalistic landscape from a cutover site. He planned a curvilinear layout around an oval village green. His associate Warren H. Manning took charge and continued after establishing his own firm in 1896. To transform a scene of dead pines and bare sand into "an attractive evergreen landscape . . . during the winter, and an abundance of flowers during the early spring," he used primarily native pines, hollies, and other plants. Planning every detail down to the shrubbery beds beside the roadways, he had more than 200,000 plants set out immediately, a nursery begun, and precedents established that have continued to the present.

Construction began in the summer of 1895, and the resort opened in February 1896 with the *Holly Inn, some boardinghouses, and a few cottages. By the next winter, "A New England Village in the South" opened the first full season of 1896–97. In 1897, after learning more about the transmission of tuberculosis, Tufts excluded consumptives and invited prosperous northerners to "the most popular and complete winter resort in the sunny South." He employed the Boston firm of Kendall, Taylor & Stevens to design the *Carolina Hotel and other buildings. The relatively informal frame buildings—hotel, store, boardinghouse, or cottage—had broad porches and Victorian and Colonial Revival detailing, the latter predominating in the 20th c. In 1897–98 Tufts installed the first golf course, modeled on the famed St. Andrews course in Scotland. Enjoying a lively

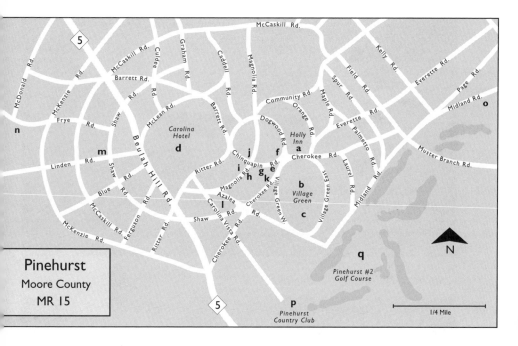

Pinehurst

Moore County

MR 15

social season from November through April, many northerners made Pinehurst their winter home. Scots-born golfer Donald Ross came to Pinehurst in the 1900–1901 season, became the golf professional, and began his long career designing some of the nation's finest golf courses.

After James Tufts died in 1902, his son Leonard and other family members maintained ownership and control of the village while selling lots to private owners, with covenants to protect the ambience. They added a racetrack and improved the golf facilities, attracting a "vast army of golfers which constitute the cosmopolitan assembly gathered here" and made the village "complete, perfect, and unique." Growth in the 1920s as a year-round community brought more stylistically diverse architecture from designers such as New York country house designer Aymar Embury II. Development slowed in the 1930s, but in 1936 the PGA National Championship was played at Pinehurst and brought national attention to *Pinehurst No. 2 Course, which Donald Ross had just redesigned. In 1970 the Tufts family's Pinehurst, Inc., was sold to the Diamondhead Corp., which made major changes before it went bankrupt. Since 1984,

when the Club Corp. of America acquired the property, Pinehurst has restored much of the earlier character of its hotels, golf courses, and cottages within a growing community. The winding roads, mature plantings, and manicured but informal open spaces create an atmosphere of "secluded peacefulness" in accord with Olmsted's and Manning's designs.

The restored **Holly Inn** (1895; Burr & Sise [Boston], architects; Cherokee Rd. opp. Village Green) (a) was the first hotel in Pinehurst, a 2-story frame building in Colonial Revival style with hipped and gambrel roofs and dormers; a portico replaced a center tower in the early 20th c. It has been enlarged regularly over the years. In front of the inn the oval **Village Green** (b) remains the central open space. At its south end rises the **Village Chapel** (1924; Hobart Upjohn [New York], architect) (c), a Colonial Revival design in red brick with Tuscan portico and tall spire, built for the interdenominational Pinehurst Religious Association; it won Upjohn an international Diploma of Merit at Turin.

The other landmark hotel, the big 4-story white frame **Carolina Hotel** (1899–1900; Kendall, Taylor & Stevens [Boston];

MR 15 *Carolina Hotel*

MR 15 *Pinehurst streetscape*

W. C. Bain [Greensboro], builder) (**d**), greatly expanded and restored, features Colonial Revival details and a distinctive cupola. In 1899 the *Manufacturer's Record* noted that builder Bain of Greensboro was to erect Tufts's 350-room hotel for $100,000. In 1915 Annie Oakley came to the community, and with her husband Frank Butler she lived at the Carolina Hotel from November to May until 1922, giving shooting demonstrations and teaching skeet shooting.

Other buildings from the early years stand at the heart of the village. The 2-story **Pinehurst Department Store** (1897; Rand & Taylor, Kendall & Stevens [Boston], architects; Cherokee and Chinquapin Rds.) (**e**), covered in German siding and shingles, with ells linked by a porch, displays the comfortable style similar to other initial buildings, including the **Casino** (1896; 5 Chinquapin Rd.) (**f**), 2 stories in frame with porches. The **Village Court** (ca. 1930; William C. Holeyman [Greensboro], architect; 40–48 Chinquapin Rd.) (**g**) is a block of stores subtly rendered in varied Colonial Revival forms to create a village scale. In the original village, picket fences complement many gardens and houses. **The Nest** (1896; 60 Magnolia Rd.) and **Hawthorne** (1896; 50 Magnolia Rd.) (**h**), both multigabled frame houses with decorative porches and millwork, were among the cottages built by James W. Tufts for Pinehurst's second season; in 1919 Donald Ross bought Hawthorne and lived there for several years. **Magnolia** (ca. 1904, 1914; 65 Magnolia Rd.; B&B) (**i**) began as a multigabled Queen Anne style house but was tamed to a sedate Colonial Revival building with columned porch in 1914. The first home of Leonard Tufts in town was the 2-story shingled house with dormers and wraparound porch known as **Mystic** (1899–1900; Kendall, Taylor & Stevens [Boston], architects; 105 Magnolia Rd.) (**j**), "a very elaborate cottage" with "all the modern improvements." A contrast appears in the Byzantine design of **Carolina Theater** (1922; Aymar Embury II [New York], architect; 90 Cherokee Rd.) (**k**), a hexagonal brick building with green tile roof, for movies and live theater.

Beneath tall pines throughout the curving maze of streets there are many shingled bungalows, rustic log dwellings, and English manor and cottage types. **Log Cabin** (1908; W. W. Dinsmore [Boston], architect; Azalea Rd. at Shaw Rd.) (**l**) is a rambling log house

that began as a bungalow. The **Marr House** (1921–22; Kelly & Graves [Boston], architects; 60 Linden Rd.) (**m**) has brick and half-timbered walls and a corner turret of "old English half timber design." **Shadowlawn** (1929; A. B. Yeomans [Southern Pines], architect; 128 Frye Rd.) (**n**) is a luxurious Tudor Revival house with stone, stucco, and half-timbering. **Dornoch Cottage** (1925; 120 Midland Rd.) (**o**), brick with a slate roof, was the winter home of Donald Ross after 1925.

On the southwest side of the original village is the **Pinehurst Country Club** (1922; Haven & Hoyt, Lyman Sise [Boston], architects; s end Carolina Vista Rd.) (**p**) in a picturesque Mediterranean mode in concrete and tile with arcaded porches overlooking the perfectly tended golf courses. (See Introduction, Fig. 59.) The pièce de résistance of Pinehurst is **Pinehurst No. 2 Course** (1901, 1935; Donald J. Ross, designer) (**q**), a mecca for golfers worldwide. Ross designed it early in his career in 1901, and in 1935 redesigned it with grass instead of sand greens before the PGA tournament. He considered it the best "test of championship golf I have ever designed," and it earned a reputation as one of the finest in the nation. Its challenging and subtle design takes advantage of the natural sand and grass features and offers the skilled golfer a variety of ways to play each segment. Altered in the 1970s, it was restored to Ross's design and in 1999 hosted the U.S. Open Championship, which is scheduled to return in 2005. Ross designed many courses, including several in N.C., but this is the gem.

Montgomery County (MG)

The county formed in 1779 from Anson Co. was named for Gen. Richard Montgomery, who died early in the American Revolution. In 1841 the county was divided forn Stanly. In the northern half of the mostly rural county rise the Uwharrie Mountains, an ancient and isolated range with hardwood forests; to the south the land levels into pine forests, with the southeastern corner extending into the sandhills. The Uwharries had some of the state's most productive 19th-c. gold mines, remembered in community names such as Eldorado and Ophir. Cotton was a key crop in the southern section, supplanted in the 20th c. by peaches and other crops. Railroads were late to come, but the original Norfolk Southern Railway traversed the county in the early 20th c. on its route between Raleigh and Charlotte, boosting industries in small towns along the way.

MG 1 Troy

The county seat on the edge of the Uwharries was laid out in 1843 for the newly divided county and named for the ancient city, a parallel to Carthage in neighboring Moore Co. The **Montgomery County Courthouse** (1921; Benton & Benton [Wilson], architects; SE corner E. Main St. (NC 24/27) and S. Main St.) is a dignified Neoclassical Revival building of tan brick and cast stone with monumental Doric portico. Along Main St. north of the courthouse, the most prominent residences are the **Wade House** (mid-, late 19th c.; 214 N. Main St.), a tur-

MG 1 *Montgomery Co. Courthouse*

reted Queen Anne style overbuilding of an earlier house, and the **Blair House** (ca. 1900, ca. 1920; N. Main St. at Blair St.) in Southern Colonial Revival style. The **Hotel Troy** (early 20th c.; 401–7 N. Main St.) is a 3-story brick structure with original storefronts and cast-stone classical detail. Early industries are recalled by the **Troy Milling Co.** (1917; 611 N. Main St.), a 3-story brick structure with stepped gables and segmental-arched windows, and the 2-story brick **Capel Rug Mill** (ca. 1917; N. Main at Ophir St.), the town's best-known industry. Built for a congregation founded in the early 19th c., **Shiloh Methodist Church** (1883; W side N. Main St.) is a simple frame church of traditional gable-fronted form with double entrance doors and a small belfry; it is maintained for reunions.

MG 2 Forks of Little River Baptist Church
1930s; E side SR 1340, just S of SR 1323, Okeewemee

Founded as Little River Church ca. 1758 through the evangelism of Shubal Stearns of *Sandy Creek Church in Randolph Co., this is one of the oldest Baptist congregations in the state. Camp meeting revivals were held here in the early 19th c., and the congregation was mother church to others in the region. The present gable-fronted frame structure with porch stands beside its old cemetery in a rural Uwharrie setting.

MG 3 Star

The little towns of Star, Biscoe, and Candor grew up in the late 19th c. along logging railroads that were eventually absorbed into the original Norfolk Southern Railway. Star, the smallest, retains its commercial row (US 220A/Main St.), including the **Bank of Star** (ca. 1910), a small but stellar 2-story brick building with exaggerated corbeling, quoins, and hoodmolds over round-arched windows. The **Magnolia Inn** (N. Main St.), a rambling late Queen Anne frame house with wraparound porch, served as a railroad hotel, and the little board-and-batten **Angus Leach House** nearby is restored at the spot where merchant and postmaster Leach established and named the community in 1875. The early 20th-c. frame **Star Depot** stands at its post by the tracks.

MG 3 *Bank of Star*

MG 4 Biscoe School

1908, 1920s; W side Main St. (US 220A), N of NC 24/27, Biscoe

Set in a broad lawn, the 2-story brick building is one of the state's largest and best-preserved schools from the first years of the early 20th-c. school building campaign. The T-plan building, which housed all grades through high school, features arched openings and wide corner pilasters. In the late 20th c. it was rescued for community use.

MG 5 Town Creek Indian Mound State Historic Site

Ca. 1450–1550 or earlier; 1950s reconstruction; E side SR 1542, S of NC 731, Mount Gilead vic.; open regular hours; National Historic Landmark

The mound and associated site by the Little River comprise the state's principal reconstruction of ancient Native American architecture. Some authorities believe that around A.D. 1450 people of Mississippian culture related to the Creek Indians entered the Pee Dee valley (supplanting Siouan groups who had lived in the region for about 1,000 years) and left after a century. Others suggest a different process, wherein from ca. A.D. 1200 onward, native Siouan people gradually adopted cultural practices from tribes to the South. The ceremonial mound at Town Creek, a center of religious and community life, is the northernmost temple mound built by Mississippian-influenced peoples on the East Coast (mounds in western N.C. were built as town houses, whereas this was a temple mound). Following archaeological investigations begun in the 1930s, the 12-foot-high mound was restored in the 1950s under Dr. Joffrey Coe (UNC). Two buildings and a log palisade have been reconstructed.

MG 5 *Town Creek*

MG 6 Haywood House

Mid-19th c., early 20th c.; N side SR 1543, 1.5 mi. NE of NC 731, Mount Gilead vic.; private, visible from road

The county's most imposing farmhouse—a 5-bay, frame I-house with 2-story Ionic portico—stands on fertile Little River land owned by six generations of the Haywood

MG 7 *Mount Gilead commercial district*

MG 10 *Zion Methodist Church*

family. Family tradition holds that part of the house was the home of Byrd Haywood, who settled here ca. 1780, though its present appearance reflects an early 20th-c. remodeling by Dr. Oscar Haywood.

MG 7 Mount Gilead

Settled by 1830, the cotton trading center later became a depot on the original Norfolk Southern Railway. **Main St.** is lined by 2-story commercial buildings with decorative brickwork. **First Methodist Church** (1910), the most prominent building, is a robust Gothic Revival brick church with unequal corner towers; **First Baptist Church** (1919) is a smaller version. The **James A. McAuley House** (1885, early 20th c.; 202 W. Allenton St.; open limited hours) is a 2-story frame Colonial Revival house, now the Mount Gilead Museum.

MG 8 Lake Tillery Dam
*1928; Electric Bond & Share Co.;
end of SR 1188, Hydro*

One of several dams built to harness the Yadkin–Pee Dee system, the 1,200-foot-long structure is of concrete gravity construction, 86 feet high with 18 floodgates. The power plant is an "umbrella" or outdoor plant, with steel covers protecting the generators.

MG 9 Edmund DeBerry House
*1820s; W side SR 1174, 0.8 mi. N of SR 1130,
Mount Gilead vic.; private, visible from road*

The county's best-preserved early 19th-c. structure is a 2-story, 5-bay frame house with

Flemish-bond brick chimneys, home of planter, mining promoter, and congressman DeBerry. According to legend, here he unwittingly hosted the infamous land pirate of the 1830s, John Murrell, who was posing as a preacher. The story goes that Murrell held crowds spellbound at a camp meeting at nearby *Zion Methodist Church while his cohorts looted the worshipers' unprotected farms.

MG 10 Zion Methodist Church
*1854; N side SR 1112, 0.4 mi. E of NC 73,
Mount Gilead vic.*

The large frame country church of traditional gable-fronted form has strong proportions and a commanding hilltop presence. In recent years the twin entrances for men and women were changed to a single central entrance, and a small steeple was added. One of the oldest Methodist congregations in the state, it was founded in 1786 as Scarborough's Meeting House by Rev. Hope Hull.

MG 11 Dr. John Henry Montgomery House
*Ca. 1850; SW side NC 73, 0.6 mi.
N of SR 1112, Mount Gilead vic.;
private, visible from road*

Former seat of a cotton plantation and one of the county's few vestiges of the antebellum era, the Greek Revival house has a double-pile plan under a hip roof, wide corner pilasters, and entrances with sidelights and transoms.

Stanly County (ST)

See Donna Dodenhoff, Stanly County: The Architectural Legacy of a Rural North Carolina County (1992).

The pleasant county retains many unspoiled rural areas with unpretentious farmhouses and agricultural buildings of many eras, as well as small towns recalling early 20th-c. growth. The land on the west bank of the Yadkin River attracted settlers of English descent in the 18th c., while Germans from Cabarrus and Rowan counties gathered farther west and Scotch-Irish from South Carolina and the mid-Atlantic took up lands throughout the area. In 1841 Stanly Co. was formed from the portion of Montgomery Co. west of the river and named for New Bern politician John Stanly; it is one of several Piedmont counties strategically named for easterners. There were a few plantations along the Yadkin and Rocky rivers, but small farms predominated, long famed for good wheat and other grains. In the 19th c., gold mining enriched the area, with 11 mines in the county at one time. Potential river trade with South Carolina was impeded by the Narrows of the Yadkin, a rapids-filled gorge in the Uwharrie Mountains, and recurrent typhoid epidemics dashed several attempts at port towns below it. Town growth finally began with the late 19th-c. railroads that encouraged textile, timber, and building supply industries. In the early 20th c., a major hydroelectric dam spanned the Narrows, and the aluminum-producing town of *Badin was established.

Albemarle (ST 1–3)

The county seat and main town is an archetypal early 20th-c. railroad and textile community. The well-kept architecture presents a representative picture of mainstream trends and types of the era, creating an ambience of unassuming but comfortable prosperity. When a post office village known as Smith's Store was chosen as seat of the new county in 1841, it was renamed for one of the 17th-c. Lords Proprietors of Carolina. It remained a village until the Yadkin Railroad arrived in 1890 from Salisbury to Norwood, prompting construction of textile factories. The town grew from 300 in 1897 to 3,000 in 1905 and redoubled its industries and size after the 1911 Winston-Salem Southbound Railway (wssb) improved north-south connections.

ST 1 Downtown Albemarle

The hilltop commercial district centers on the courthouse at Main and 2nd Sts. The courthouse dates from the 1970s, but many

early 20th-c. corbeled brick storefronts still mark those and neighboring streets. An evocative civic amenity from the turn of the century is the **Albemarle Opera House–Starnes Jewelers Building** (1907; L. A. Moody, builder; 127–33 W. Main St.), which housed shops below and a theater above; it hosted traveling performances for only a few years before conversion to other uses, but a

ST 1 *Albemarle Opera House*

late 20th-c. restoration uncovered the second-story row of 5 round-arched windows
topped by circular windows to light the theater and balcony. The Moderne storefront in
black Carrara glass dates from 1939. A similar spirit informs the **Albemarle City Hall**
(1938; Northup & O'Brien [Winston-
Salem], architects; J. D. Harwood & Son,
builders; N. 2nd St.), a 3-part brick building
that combines Moderne and classical elements typical of the 1930s. The major
Protestant denominations built prominent
brick churches in and near downtown, most
before 1925 in Gothic and Neoclassical Revival styles.

Close to the business district are two
buildings from early Albemarle. The **Marks
House** (ca. 1847; N. 3rd St.; open regular
hours) is a 1-story, hall-parlor frame house
with conservatively late Federal style trim.
Built as a dwelling for merchant Daniel
Freeman, it was acquired by the Marks family in 1884. Serving various purposes, enlarged, and moved, it has been restored to
its earliest appearance. The nearby **Suggs
House** (ca. 1841, ca. 1874; N. 3rd St.; open
regular hours) began as a 1-story log dwelling, evidently from the county seat's founding; Confederate veteran Isaiah W. Suggs's
frame additions produced the center-passage
I-house with broad front porch, rear ell, and
simple Victorian finish.

ST 2 Railroad Industrial Corridor

West of downtown and down the hill, a linear industrial district extends north-south
along the parallel tracks of the WSSB and the
old Yadkin Railroad. One of the last surviving depots on the 90-mile WSSB from Win-

ST 1 *Marks House*

ST 2 *Albemarle Depot and All Star Mills*

ston to Wadesboro, the **Winston-Salem
Southbound Depot** (ca. 1912; W. Main and
Railroad Sts.) is a long frame building with
freight and passenger functions under the
hip roof and a gabled stationmaster's bay
trackside. Dominating the skyline, the towering row of concrete silos of the **All Star
Flour Mills** (early 20th c.; RR at W. Main
St.), capped with frame watchmen's shelters,
soars 70 feet above the tracks. Northward
along the rails are the town's two largest textile mills and associated villages. **Efird Mfg.
Co.** (est. 1896; N. Depot St.) was the first
mill in the county, founded by textile industry titan James W. Cannon, local businessman Ireneus Polycarp Efird, and his son
John, who managed the plant until 1927.
Cannon also held controlling interest in
Wiscasset Mills Co. (est. 1898 and later; N.
Depot St. betw. 3rd and 4th Sts.) to the
north. Both plants grew over the decades,
with numerous 2- and 3-story brick buildings in varying degrees of alteration. The
surrounding early 20th-c. **Mill Villages**
flank the railroad and Town Creek. West of
the creek and US 52 stand 1-story frame
houses on "Mill Hill" described in 1905 as
having "good gardens and modern com-
forts"; on the east side along N. Depot St.
are 2-story houses for larger families.

ST 3 Northeastern Residential Areas

Middle-class residential districts east and
north of downtown comprise block after
block of modest, handsomely detailed, and
neatly kept bungalows and period revival
houses. The leafy canopies of E. Main St.,
Pee Dee Ave., and E. North St. shade a mix

ST 3 *Dr. Charles I. Miller House*

of styles from the 1910s to the 1930s, including exceptionally fine bungalows. The **Dr. Charles I. Miller House** (1925; 931 E. Main St.) is an "airplane" bungalow with a small 2-story central block rising above a strong horizontal composition of low gables and stout porch posts expressing the Arts and Crafts ideal of shelter. On N. 2nd and N. 3rd Sts. several of the town's wealthiest families built conservative, Colonial Revival style brick houses, such as the **Dr. Julius Clay Hall House** (1912; Louis Asbury [Charlotte], architect; 224 N. 2nd St.) and others.

ST 4 Kendall Baptist Church

1904-5; Ruben Rogers & Doc Ritchie, carpenters; W corner SR 1435 and SR 1400, Austin Mills vic.

The big frame country church with lancet windows and towering steeple, third at the site, has a commanding presence in the countryside above Town Creek. The congregation held brush arbor services here for several years, officially organizing in 1830 and erecting a log meetinghouse on land belonging to Sam Kendall.

ST 5 New London

A post office village called Bilesville on the old Salisbury Road began to grow when William Parker's nearby gold mine, operated since 1859, was purchased in the 1870s by an English firm, the New London Estate Co., which introduced advanced equipment and made it the county's most successful mine; production continued under various owners into the 1930s. In 1891 the town gained a depot on the new Yadkin Railroad from Salisbury and was incorporated as New London. Within a decade the Yadkin Railroad built a spur south to the Whitney project on the river (*Badin), which made New London a busy junction with several small industries. The era supported substantial 2-story frame houses along Main St. and side streets. Notable is the **Henry W. Culp Sr. House** (1922; S. Main St.), a lumber company owner's unusually sophisticated bungalow, with dormered hip roof sheltering a deep porch; a foundation of fine rusticated, cream-colored granite carries an openwork porch balustrade of granite bricks—perhaps from the famous Rowan Co. quarries that supplied the Yadkin dam construction (*Granite Quarry). (See Introduction, Fig. 70.)

ST 6 Bethel Bear Creek Reformed Church and Community

1928; Louis Asbury (Charlotte), architect; N side SR 1428, 0.3 mi. E of Cabarrus Co. line

Flowing south through western Stanly into the Rocky River, Big Bear Creek drains the rolling farmland settled in the late 18th and early 19th centuries by German families coming east from Cabarrus Co. Among these were members of the old Dutch Buffalo Creek Union Church, who in 1806 established a log meetinghouse here, continuing the shared accommodation of Lutheran and Reformed services. About 1875 the Lutherans built a church elsewhere, and the Reformed congregation built a frame church in 1879. In the 1920s the congregation was sufficiently prosperous to hire Charlotte architect Asbury to plan the unusually imposing country church, a large brick Gothic Revival building with parapets, buttresses, and granite trim. The old cemetery lies to the west. It became part of the United Church of Christ with the national union of Reformed and Congregational churches in 1957.

The church centers a community of German-descended farmers long admired for thrift, order, and wise land management. In 1888 a visitor from Newton praised the "well tilled and productive farms" with "large barns" and "elegant houses" for "a most delightful and inspiring state of progress and prosperity." Under the example of Levi Lipe, the county agent for farm demonstration programs, in the 1920s the area gained renewed acclaim for progressive farm practices, still evidenced by its neatly kept traditional and bungalow farmhouses, windmills to pump water, and large tin-clad gambrel-roofed barns and other outbuildings on well-tended farms averaging only 100 acres. The **Levi and Jane Lipe House** (ca. 1920; corner SR 1428 and SR 1451) is a big frame bungalow with bracketed eaves, front gabled dormer, and stout porch posts, aptly modeling the progressive farm dwelling of the times.

ST 7 Pfeiffer University

1925–48; Odis Clay Poundstone (Atlanta), architect; US 52, 1.0 mi. NW of NC 49, Misenheimer

The orderly campus of red brick Colonial Revival buildings by a rural highway was built for a Methodist college that traces back to the work of educator and missionary Emily C. Prudden of Connecticut, who came south in 1883 at age 50. Of the 15 rural mission schools she founded during more than 20 years in the Carolinas—an accomplishment especially remarkable for her having been deaf since age 17—the most successful and longest lasting was Oberlin Home and School begun in Caldwell Co. in 1885. Later renamed Mitchell School, in 1910 it acquired this railside location, became a junior college, and in the 1930s was renamed for supporters Henry and Annie Merner Pfeiffer of New York. Mrs. Pfeiffer, also a benefactor of *Bennett College in Greensboro, probably recommended Atlanta architect Poundstone, who remade both campuses in restrained Georgian Revival style. He remodeled the 1925 Administration Building (1925) and designed ten new buildings. The school grew into a 4-year college, then a university.

ST 8 Badin

See Brent D. Glass and Pat Dickinson, *Badin: A Town at the Narrows* (1982).

The "Town at the Narrows," site of a major Alcoa aluminum-processing plant, was one of the last company towns created in N.C., and one of the most unusual. Its unique history stretches back to earlier efforts to harness the great river. The Narrows was a gorge in the Uwharrie Mountains about 2 miles long and as little as 80 feet wide, through which the Yadkin "pours with great violence," as the river drops over 200 feet in 10 miles. Many saw its potential as a power source: in 1796 a visitor declared, "Perhaps there is not in the United States a more eligible situation for a large manufacturing town." Tindalsville was sited below the Narrows, where the Yadkin and Uwharrie form the Pee Dee, and where early promoters of internal improvements envisioned a great inland port. But necessary improvements never came, and after typhoid struck the town, in 1835 Dr. Francis Kron found "at the landing . . . the ruined frames of those houses which twenty years back formed the bulk of Tindalsville."

The Narrows site itself, unsuited to waterside factories, drew new interest with the late 19th-c. advent of long-distance transmission of electric power to railside sites, which encouraged industrial development. In the 1890s English-born mining engineer Egbert Barry Cornwall Hambley (*Hambley-Wallace House, Salisbury; *Granite Quarry) spearheaded a vast regional development plan for manufacturing, mining, real estate, and utilities, centered on a hydroelectric dam on the Yadkin just above the Narrows—"a giant scheme to grapple with and subdue elemental nature," a Lexington newspaper claimed. Hambley secured support from Pittsburgh financier George I. Whitney (an associate of industrialist Andrew Mellon). The Whitney Development Co. thus formed soon acquired nearly 30,000 acres in 5 counties, operated mines and quarries, began the 1,100-foot dam, and laid out the adjacent town of Whitney. But within a decade misfortunes defeated the enterprise. The recurrent typhoid depleted the work force at the dam, and Hambley died of the fever in 1906 at age 44. The Whitney Co. went bankrupt in 1910, leaving Whitney only a place-name by the river. The

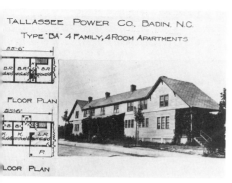

TALLASSEE POWER CO. BADIN. N.C.
TYPE "BA" 4 FAMILY, 4 ROOM APARTMENTS

FLOOR PLAN

LOOR PLAN

ST 8 *Plan for Quadraplex, Badin*

granite abutments of the unfinished dam may be seen when waters of Badin Lake are low.

After this failure came the hard-won success of *Badin. Planned and begun in the 1910s by a French aluminum company and completed by an American one, it provided a higher quality of residential and institutional buildings than most company towns and was one of few to provide housing and cultural facilities for black workers. In 1912, seeking a source for electricity for production of aluminum, the Southern Aluminum Co., a subsidiary of L'Aluminum Française, purchased the Whitney property on the Yadkin. The company abandoned the incomplete dam to build one right at the Narrows a few miles downstream. French engineers laid out a town (named for company president Adrien Badin), erected workers' housing, and began construction of the dam and aluminum plant. In 1915 war in Europe forced the company to give up the project, which it sold at a loss to the Aluminum Co. of America—controlled by none other than George Whitney's former associate Andrew Mellon. Alcoa and the affiliated Tallassee Power Co. continued to build on the existing town plan but redesigned the dam and aluminum works, beginning production in 1917.

Streets are laid out in irregular patterns following the gentle contours of the land, with spacious lots and generous greenery. South of Falls Rd. along Boyden St. and flanking streets are the most distinctive vestiges of the French presence and influence: numerous 2-story **Quadraplexes**—4-unit

apartment buildings—built for workers' housing. Designed by the New York firm of Pierson & Goodrich, the long, narrow frame buildings are said to have been based on a form popular in France at the time and feature complex rooflines of intersecting gables, sheds, and engaged porches. After Alcoa began to sell the units to workers in the 1930s, owners personalized the apartments, sometimes with four different wall materials, colors, and window treatments on a single quadraplex. The company also built 1½-story duplexes and single-family houses for superintendents along Henderson St. On an elevated site above the village is the chief landmark of the French period, the **Badin Clubhouse** (1912–14) (Stanly Co. Country Club), a graceful 2½-story frame building with angled wings and enveloping 1-story porch. Alcoa's housing north of Falls Rd. consists primarily of 4- and 5-room hip-roofed bungalows with engaged porches. Gable-fronted bungalows and duplexes were erected for black workers in **West Badin**. Lining Falls Road is a commercial district of 2-story brick stores. In the 1910s and 1920s the company also built brick churches and schools for whites and blacks and a community hospital.

When completed in 1917, the **Narrows Dam** (James W. Rickey, Alcoa chief hydraulic engineer) was the world's highest overflow type dam: 216 feet high and 1,650 long, creating a head of 187 feet—higher than Niagara Falls, marveled local guides. The reservoir of over 5,300 acres submerges the once formidable Narrows. The power plant, which provides electricity to Alcoa's Badin Works 1½ miles west, has had continuous expansion and modernization. Alcoa announced the closing of the aluminum plant in 2002.

ST 9 Morrow Mountain State Park

Est. 1935; Thomas W. Morse, landscape architect; Civilian Conservation Corps (CCC) and Works Progress Administration (WPA), builders; open regular hours

The state park beside the Yadkin River resulted from the private efforts of local businessmen and donors, a state government designer, and Federal work programs. Located in the Uwharrie Mountains, an ancient range that rose 400 million years ago out of a shallow inland sea, the large park was named for James M. Morrow, a principal land donor. State landscape architect Thomas Morse followed Federal park design precedents, employing rustic forms and local materials. CCC workers cleared and graded the land, and the WPA erected lodge buildings, picnic shelters, a bathhouse, and a pool—distinctive structures of horizontal blocks of light gray slate quarried in the park, laid in a random ashlar pattern.

Within the park stands the **Dr. Francis J. Kron House** (ca. 1830; reconstructed 1961), home to a physician, horticulturist, and civic leader widely respected in the Uwharries. Born in Prussia and educated in France, Kron arrived in 1823 with his French wife, Catherine, whose uncle owned land in the area. In 1834 they bought from William McGregor a 1-story frame dwelling with hall-parlor plan, engaged porch and rear shed rooms, and slate chimneys. Ruinous by 1961, it was rebuilt from physical evidence, along with the doctor's clinic, medicinal root cellar, and other structures. Kron's 1835 journal is a rare depiction of the then-remote area, where local roads were "the Devils race-path," and at the Yadkin, "For ten cents the ferry man sets you over and tells you besides funny tales on his neighbors."

ST 10 Swift Island Ferry Bridge
1927; NC 24/27/73 over Pee Dee River

The reinforced concrete, rib-arched, open spandrel bridge is the second longest of its type remaining on the state highway system. Eight spans stretch 1,060 feet, 99 feet above the stream bed. It was built by Carolina Power & Light Co. (CP&L) under supervision of the state highway commission to replace a bridge built just 5 years earlier, which was to be flooded by CP&L's Lake Tillery Dam. The 1922 structure was destroyed in a celebrated test of aerial bombing during Christmas week of 1927.

ST 11 Randle (Randall) House
Late 18th–mid 19th c.?; S side SR 1807, opp. SR 1743, Norwood vic.; private, visible from road

By the early 19th c. a community of substantial planters flourished in "the Fork" near the confluence of the Pee Dee and Rocky rivers. One of the few remaining plantation houses is the 2-story frame homeplace of the Randle family. Tradition holds that it was built by 1800 for John Randle, planter and mill owner who acquired the land in 1778, or by 1824 by his nephew, also John Randle; its Federal–Greek Revival character suggests a slightly later construction or major remodeling. The elder Randle was one of a group of early Methodists from Virginia who settled here and hosted itinerant ministers Francis Asbury and Jesse Lee. Across the road, **Randall's Methodist Church**, founded ca. 1785 as one of the region's oldest Methodist congregations, occupies a 1974 building surrounded by an old cemetery.

ST 11 *Randle (Randall) House*

ST 12 Norwood

The town in "the Fork" traces back to Allenton, a late 18th-c. village on the Pee Dee, but in 1810 a typhoid epidemic drove the residents to higher ground, where the transplanted community was later named for a postmaster. In 1891 it became the southeastern terminus of the Yadkin Railroad, built from Salisbury to tap timber, mining, and farm resources, then a rail hub with the arrival of the north-south WSSB in 1911 and the east-west Norfolk Southern Railway in 1912. The largest enterprise was the **Norwood Mfg. Co.** (1890s and later; W side N. Main St.), a textile factory and mill village remodeled and expanded in the 1940s by the Collins & Aikman Co.; as at their *Ca-Vel plant at Roxboro, the firm erected Colonial Revival frame houses for executives (McCullough Place). The Main St. commercial district retains early 20th-c. 1- and 2-story brick storefronts, some with corbeled brickwork and bracket cornices; the classically detailed metal front of the **Hathcock Building** (ca. 1900; N. Main St.) is credited to Mesker Bros. of St. Louis. **First Presbyterian Church** (1924; E side S. Main at Turner St.), in rich red brick, features finely crafted Gothic Revival detail and matching corner towers. Houses span the town's history, including I-houses and Craftsman bungalows along **Allenton St.**, which leads down to the Pee Dee and recalls the old town. Among the oldest houses is the **Palmer-Lisk House** (ca. 1885; B. F. Ivey, builder; S. Main St.), a 1-story frame Italianate style dwelling with front porch engaged under a broad-gabled attic room and brackets in vine patterns with drop pendants.

ST 13 Cagle House

1886–1901; N corner NC 205 and SR 1115, Big Lick; private, visible from road

A multitude of bracketed gables and a decorated wraparound porch make the 1-story frame house a fine representative of the late 19th-c. picturesque mode. It was built in 3 stages for Billie and Mary Jane Cagle; a farmer and merchant, he served as mayor

ST 13 *Cagle House*

and postmaster of Big Lick (named for a salt lick frequented by deer) when it was a thriving crossroads village with an academy, stores, and industries. The Norfolk Southern Railway crossed southern Stanly Co. in 1913, and all the businesses moved 2 miles south to the new depot at Oakboro.

ST 14 Morgan Memorial Church

1884; W side NC 200, just N of Union Co. line, Stanfield vic.

The utterly plain, unmarked, white clapboard church was built by descendants of Drury Morgan, a Union Co. merchant and planter, and over time it has served Lutheran, Baptist, and Presbyterian congregations. In a common arrangement, the gable front has separate entrances for men and women. Four windows on each side light the sanctuary with its slatted board pews and iron stove. It is maintained by a family association for annual reunions.

Richmond County (RH)

"No county presents more striking contrasts in its soils, timbers, and productions. . . . The streams which originate in the pine lands and tend towards the Pee Dee river, at Rockingham encounter a sudden and violent change of geological formation—encounter ledges of rock, precipitate themselves below in lofty cascades, and give that commanding water-power which has concentrated at Rockingham six large cotton factories." Thus did an 1896 report on the state's resources describe Richmond Co.'s natural potential. Straddling an ancient coastline, the county encompasses in its western portion fingers of the ancient Uwharrie Mountains and hilly, clay Piedmont farmland with mixed hardwoods, while sandhills and pine forests cover the flatter eastern zone. The area was settled chiefly by English and Scotch-Irish people coming south along the Yadkin–Pee Dee River from the upper Piedmont, Scots moving westward from the Cape Fear valley, and some arriving from South Carolina. The county was established in 1779 from Anson, with the Pee Dee the dividing line, and until 1899 encompassed present-day Scotland Co. To augment naval stores production and cotton cultivation, in the 1830s local leaders founded one of the state's first cotton mills, near Rockingham. Encouraged by the 1869 arrival of the Wilmington, Charlotte & Rutherford Railroad (WC&RRR), these men and connected families established a textile empire with Rockingham as the business center. After capturing the southbound route of the Raleigh & Augusta Railroad (R&ARR) in 1877, the depot town of Hamlet 6 miles east of Rockingham developed as a rail hub. In the late 20th c., changes in the textile industry depleted the textile manufacturing base and the mill villages, of which the most intact examples are cited below.

Rockingham (RH 1–2)

Manufacturing and agriculture of the 19th and early 20th centuries made Rockingham a prosperous community, as reflected in its downtown architecture and the residential section flanking Fayetteville Rd. It was founded in 1784 as the seat of Richmond Co.; both were named for Englishmen who supported the American colonies. Located on high ground between Hitchcock and Falling creeks on an ancient ridge of Uwharrie stone, it served as a trade center for local cotton farmers and naval stores producers. Taking advantage of the topography, members of the Leak, Steele, and Cole families established the antebellum Richmond Mfg. Co. (*Great Falls Mill) on Falling Creek.

After the Civil War and the arrival of the WC&RRR, seeking to create "the Lowell of North Carolina," they established other mills on Hitchcock Creek, beginning with

*Pee Dee Mill #1 in 1876. Robert L. Steele Sr. took a lead role, but the interwoven textile elite also included other Steeles, Leaks, Coles, Walls, Covingtons, and Ledbetters, many of long-standing planter families. William Entwistle, an English weaver who began at Great Falls in 1871, became superintendent at Pee Dee in 1878 and established and operated other mills. In time they introduced steam power at *Pee Dee #2, *Hannah Pickett, and others, and the hydroelectric power plant at *Blewett Falls (1911–12) on the Pee Dee added capacity.

By the early 20th c., surrounded by 11 mills and villages, Rockingham thrived as the management, retail, and banking center and home to owners and managers. In the 1940s, however, family connections with the business dwindled; strikes closed factories for weeks at a time; and nearly all the mills were sold to outside corporations, which updated and expanded several plants. Textile production remained high for a few more decades, then dwindled with broader shifts in the industry, requiring town and county to diversify the local economy.

RH 1 Downtown Rockingham

An imposing survival from the early 20th c., the **Richmond County Courthouse** (1922–23; Charles C. Hook [Charlotte], architect; J. P. Little & Son [Charlotte], builder; Franklin St.) is a Neoclassical composition veneered in pale stone, with recessed, columned entrances facing in three directions. The former **U.S. Post Office and Federal Building** (1934–36; Louis A. Simon, supervising architect of the Treasury; 125 S. Hancock St.) in orange brick displays a contrasting Art Deco character with simple cubical forms and stylized classical and geometric motifs. The lobby mural, *Human Aspects of the Postal Service* (1937), was painted by Edward Lanning.

(1904–5; 201 E. Washington St.) was home of the town's first bank, founded in 1891 by leading industrialists with Thomas C. Leak Sr. as president. The 2-story brick building combines corbeled brickwork and segmental-arched windows with a pedimented facade. The **Rockingham Depot** (1910; Caroline St.), a 1-story red brick station typical of Seaboard, is slated to be moved to a new site downtown.

RH 2 Fayetteville Rd. Residential Area

Along the premier residential avenue of Fayetteville Rd., the lineup of substantial, stylish houses evokes the tight family and business network that dominated town and county for more than a century. Especially popular was the Italianate mode, alone or combined with Greek Revival elements. The **Steele-Fisher House** (ca. 1845 and later; 613 Fayetteville Rd.), a 2-story frame dwelling with Italianate brackets and central roof

RH 1 *Richmond Co. Courthouse*

RH 2 *Fayetteville Rd. streetscape*

The **Manufacturers Building** (ca. 1904; 220 E. Washington St.), a straightforward commercial building of cream-colored brick with hip roof and modest classical details, housed the administrative offices of five textile companies. Robert L. Steele Jr. led in construction of the facility where policies and prices were established. The various corporations had individual offices but shared chambers for board and stockholder meetings. In 1925 on the sidewalk in front of the building, mill owner W. B. Cole shot to death his daughter's lover; he was acquitted after a sensational trial (*Sikes House, Monroe). The **Bank of Pee Dee Building**

gable, was built for Robert J. Steele, a founder of the Richmond Mill, and his wife and cousin, Elizabeth Steele; it is cited as headquarters of Union general Judson Kilpatrick when his troops stopped in Rockingham in 1865. Most striking is the big, elaborate **Robert L. Steele Sr. House** (ca. 1850; 705 Fayetteville Rd.), a mix of Greek Revival and Italianate elements built for Steele, leader in the postwar textile industry, and his wife Hannah Pickett Leak. The broadly proportioned frame house features hefty corner pilasters, a bracketed cornice, and a 1-story porch adapted from the Doric order, plus a belvedere commanding a panoramic

RH 2 *Robert L. Steele Sr. House*

view of town and mills. The **Leak-Scales House** (ca. 1860, 1899; 706 Fayetteville Rd.), a 2-story, L-plan Italianate house was built on E. Washington St. for Walter F. Leak, "kingpin" and founder of Richmond Mfg. Co.; in 1899 grandson Walter Leak Scales moved it here.

Farther out, the **Ledbetter-Leath House** (1888; 804 Fayetteville Rd.), an ornate, late Italianate house, was built for John Ledbetter, founder of the *Ledbetter Mill. Oldest in town is evidently the **Steele-Johnson-Cole House** (ca. 1838; 816 Fayetteville Rd.), a 2-story house of 1:5 bond brick in simple Federal–Greek Revival style with Italianate additions, said to have been built for Robert J. Steele Jr. to woo Judith Mosely Leak Steele, his brother Thomas's widow; they wed in 1840. The **Entwistle House** (1938; E. W. Renicke [Southern Pines], builder; 916 Fayetteville Rd.), built for William H. Entwistle, grandson of a company founder, follows a Palladian format with pedimented central pavilion.

On a nearby street is the **Leak-Wall House** (ca. 1853; 405 E. Washington St.; open limited hours), a Greek Revival and Italianate combination with high, bracketed roof, built for W. C.'s brother John Wall Leak and his wife Ann Cole Leak. President of the antebellum mill, he rebuilt his fortune and the *Great Falls Mill after the war. Early 20th-c. descendants added Colonial Revival elements and a formal garden by Charlotte's Earle S. Draper. It houses the county historical society and arts council. In the yard is an immense Cedar of Lebanon dated to 1850. **First Methodist Church** (1899; 410 E. Washington St.) is a substantial Romanesque Revival edifice in red brick with stone trim, built

for a congregation established in the early 1830s; the auditorium plan sanctuary has fine stained glass windows in Tiffany style.

RH 3 Great Falls Mill Ruin

1869–70; burned 1972; S side US 74, 0.2 mi. W of US 220, Rockingham

A dramatic architectural ruin beside the highway, the craggy 4-story brick walls and great tower rise from the kudzu-draped site beside the "great falls" of Falling Creek. The original cotton mill here, one of the earliest in the state, began operation in 1837 as the Richmond Mill. Located on an old gristmill waterpower site, it was erected for the Richmond Mfg. Co., organized in 1833 by Walter F. Leak along with William L. Cole, Francis T. Leak, Robert J. Steele, and Alfred Dockery, who went to Falls River, Mass., to obtain the machinery; Walter Leak's nephew and son-in-law, John Wall Leak, became president in 1854. John Shortridge, who came from Rhode Island in 1846 to work at the mill, later developed other factories and the town of *Hamlet. Operating through the war, the mill was burned in 1865 by Union soldiers. In 1869–70 Walter F. and John Wall Leak and Robert Leak Steele (Robert J.'s nephew) organized the Great Falls Mfg. Co. and rebuilt the mill by 1870 on a much larger scale. It inaugurated Rockingham's postwar textile growth and epitomized the Italianate industrial architecture of the era. It closed during the Great Depression and burned in 1972.

RH 3 *Great Falls Mill ruin*

RH 4 Pee Dee Mill
No. 1 and No. 2 Mill Villages
Late 19th–early 20th c.; US 220 near
N. Lee St., NW of central Rockingham

Two eras of mill development flank the road north of town. Organized soon after the *Great Falls Mill was rebuilt, **Pee Dee Mill No. 1** (Steele St. at Aslington St.) was founded in 1874 by John Wall Leak and Robert L. Steele Sr. Located in the valley beside Hitchcock Creek, the complex includes several buildings of various dates. Most prominent is an imposing 3-story mill built in 2 stages, with broad windows filling the bays between tall pilasters. Numerous 1-story frame operatives' houses overlook the curving road above the mill. In 1898–1900 **Pee Dee Mill No. 2** was completed under Robert L. Steele Jr. as the first in the county powered by steam. The brick factory has been reworked, but the grid-plan **Village** is fairly intact. Pee Dee 2nd Ave., Pee Dee 3rd Ave., and Pee Dee 4th Ave. on a terraced hillside are lined by small frame workers' houses, typically 1 story with gable roofs, center chimneys, and decorated entrance porches. There are also two brick **Stores** near the former mill and the frame **Pee Dee Methodist Church** (early 20th c.; Pee Dee 2nd Ave.).

RH 5 Hannah Pickett Mill No. 1
(Safie Mill)

Ca. 1908; 300 Mill Rd. (SR 1903),
East Rockingham

Incorporated by W. B. Cole. and his uncle Robert L. Steele Jr., the factory was named for a relative who reinforced Cole's place in the corporate family tree: his grandmother Hannah Pickett Leak, wife of Robert L. Steele Sr. "With such a saintly name," said Cole, "the plant cannot fail." The factory began as a hosiery yarn mill in 1908 and then expanded into cloth production. It was sold to Safie Bros. in 1944 and later closed. The dominant element is the original 2-story main building, of stylized Italianate character in rock-faced concrete block, unusual for mill construction. A dramatic campanile-like stair tower in block and brick features narrow arched windows and corbeled brick-

RH 5 *Hannah Pickett Mill No. 1*

work. Additional brick buildings with generous, arched windows date from the 1920s, when the mill grew into the largest in the county. It is part of East Rockingham, a large industrial sector with several railside mills and continuous villages. Workers' housing comprises sections of streets numerically named for the mills, such as Hannah Pickett 2, 3, 4, and others. The early 20th-c. houses include 1-story, side-gabled dwellings, typically with center chimneys, and pyramidal-roofed bungalows with inset corner porches.

RH 6 Cordova
SR 1109, 0.3 mi. S of SR 1117
on Hitchcock Creek

One of the county's largest mill villages, Cordova has seen continued change since it was founded by Robert L. Steele Sr. and sons and completed by Robert Jr. The **Steele Mfg. Co.** (1895–98 and later), located in the steep valley where Hitchcock Creek nears the Pee Dee, began as a 2-story brick mill and was greatly expanded. The village above has 1-story side-gabled workers' houses and larger ones for upper employees, plus stores and churches. The factory was sold to Burlington Mills in 1946 but after 1984 housed a paper company.

RH 7 Roberdel
SR 1424 on Hitchcock Creek

The mill village was established in the early 1880s by Robert L. Steele Sr. at a site where he and brother Thomas had a grist- and sawmill (1860–80). The name is said to come from a silver baby cup Steele gave to Robert Steele Leak inscribed, "From Old Robert L. to Young Roberdel." Sold in 1929 to the Entwistle firm, the mill burned in 1970, but much of the village remains, including well-kept 1-story workers' houses with center chimneys and side-gable roofs. The **Company Store** (ca. 1884) beside the mill pond is a long 1-story brick building with a gabled front.

RH 8 Ledbetter
SR 1442 on Hitchcock Creek

The classic 3-story brick mill was built for the **Ledbetter Mfg. Co.**, founded in 1882 for Thomas Ledbetter and nephew John Steele Ledbetter. They invested turpentine profits to start a yarn mill—originally called South Union—near the site of an 18th-c. gristmill and John Shortridge's woolen mill. Picturesquely sited by its mill pond, the factory has broad segmental-arched windows and a low gable roof. Run by three generations of Ledbetters, it was the county's last family-owned mill to be sold (late 20th c.) and has been renovated for new use.

RH 9 Hamlet

Incorporated in the late 19th c. when its size suited its name, Hamlet developed into one of N.C.'s major railroad interchanges and hub of the Seaboard Air Line system in the 20th c. It began as Sand Hill on the WC&RRR (Central Carolina Railroad [CCRR]), where in the early 1870s John Shortridge built a woolen mill producing "Hamlet Woolen Tweeds." A native of England, he moved as a child to Rhode Island and learned the textile business, came to

work at the Richmond Mill, and in 1850 with Robert J. Steele founded a woolen mill on Hitchcock Creek (*Ledbetter), which was burned during the Civil War. In 1876, learning that the north-south R&ARR was coming through the county, he got the line routed to intersect the CCRR near his mill rather than through Rockingham. The resulting rail center gained importance after Seaboard, which absorbed the R&ARR and the CCRR, was incorporated in 1900. The principal architecture of the early 20th-c. railroad heyday concentrates in the business districts near the tracks and nearby neighborhoods.

The centerpiece of town, one of the state's finest turn-of-the-century passenger stations, was built at the crossing to serve both routes. The **Hamlet Passenger Depot** (1900; betw. Main St. and Hamlet Ave.; to be moved across the tracks for restoration) displays characteristic elements of small-town train stations—splayed eaves, pent roofs, brackets, and projecting bays—adapted to serve the juncture of two main lines. Two long perpendicular wings join at a great circular pavilion that provides views in all four directions. Its broad conical roof merges with those of the wings, with deep, splayed eaves carried by chamfered triangular brackets. Below, a second broader pent roof sweeps around the building to shelter the passenger platform. Well into the 20th c. the station was a major stop on the route between the Northeast and the Deep South. Charlotte journalist Jack Claiborne recalls the excitement of the era when the "Silver Meteor" arrived on its run from New York to Florida: "The unmistakable, steam-engine smell of that station, the bustle of activity around it, the mystique of all those trains (both passenger and freight) arriving from glamorous places, the old-time porters and their high, four-wheel baggage carriages, the conductors and station agents in their stiff caps, blue suits and vests, and pocket watches—ah, that was an age that has really passed."

Two commercial districts flank the railroad. The largest, on Main St., retains its rows of 1- and 2-story early 20th-c. brick storefronts, some with corbeling and metal

RH 9 *Hamlet Passenger Depot*

cornices. Defining the corner of Main and the tracks is the large **Terminal Hotel** (ca. 1912; 3 Main St.), a social and architectural linchpin of the railroad town. The long 2-story brick building has a corner tower and shaped parapets, plus a porch added for the movie *Billy Bathgate*, filmed here in 1991. Also part of the classic ensemble of downtown institutions are the former **Hamlet Opera House** (1916; E. A. Lackey, builder; ca. 1927; 46 Main St.), which gained an Art Deco facade in the 1920s; the temple-fronted **Bank of Hamlet** (ca. 1912; E. A. Lackey, builder; 55 Main St.); and the **Hamlet Post Office** (1940–41; Louis A. Simon, supervising architect of the Treasury; 105 Main at Lackey St.) in orange brick trimmed in limestone.

Prime residential areas of the early 20th c. adjoin downtown on the northwest and include substantial brick churches and a range of popular house styles. Some houses appear to derive from Aladdin, Sears & Roebuck, and other catalog sources. Well represented are the foursquare type, simplified Tudor Revival and Colonial Revival modes, and especially bungalows, ranging from rustic to Oriental to Craftsman styles. Notable examples include **612 Rice St.**, with deep porches in a California bungalow flavor, and **538 Main St.**, a striking Craftsman style

house of broad wingspread and unusually bold detailing.

RH 10 Alfred Dockery House
Early–mid 19th c.; E side SR 1005, 0.1 mi. S of SR 1143; private, visible from road

Built for Alfred and Sarah Dockery, who married in 1823 and had ten children, the plantation house is the finest in the county—a symmetrical brick dwelling, 5 bays wide beneath a hip roof, with a Doric entablature and other Greek Revival trim. Unusual is the center-passage plan 1 room deep plus two original 1-story rear ells. An advocate of internal improvements, Dockery assembled a 3,200-acre plantation and invested in the Richmond Mill. In a long and distinguished political career, the independent-minded Dockery served as state legislator and U.S. congressman, Whig candidate for governor in 1854, and a founder of the state Republican Party in 1867. He was a longtime president of the Baptist State Convention. Nearby is **Cartledge Creek Baptist Church** (est. 1774, 1869, and later; w side SR 1005, 0.2 mi. N of SR 1143), a small frame church that Alfred Dockery helped rebuild. Begun as Dockery's Meeting House in the 18th c. with leadership from his grandfather Thomas, in 1833 the congrega-

RH 10 *Alfred Dockery House*

RH 11 *Ellerbe Springs Hotel*

tion hosted the meeting of the Baptist State Convention that led to founding of Wake Forest College.

RH 11 Ellerbe Springs Hotel
1905–6 and later; Henry E. Bonitz (Wilmington), architect; W side US 220/ NC 73, 0.2 mi. N of US 220/NC 73 fork, Ellerbe vic.; open as B&B, restaurant

Evoking the days when the sociable as well as the sick traveled to "the springs," the rambling frame hotel is among the last of the small 19th-c. mineral springs resorts that dotted the Piedmont. In the 18th c. the site gained popularity for its healthful air and the healing attributes of the springs. Highland Scots named the area "Fairgrounds" in 1793 after the regular Scottish Fair held here until 1840. In 1871 the Ellerbe Springs tract, named for an early 19th-c. owner, was sold to Rockingham investors, and in 1905 Thomas C. Leak (*Bank of Pee Dee) developed it with a 30-room hotel—"perhaps the noblest and tastiest summer hotel in N.C.," said the local paper—plus a springhouse–dance pavilion, cottages, and a lake: "One had not lived until he had a vacation at Ellerbe Springs." Closed in the 1920s, it served various purposes before reopening in the late 20th c. The 2-story frame hotel has simple Colonial Revival finish and generous porches on the main section and recessed wings. The nearby town of **Ellerbe**, an early 20th-c. railroad village and trade center for lumber, peach packing, and tobacco, has 1- and 2-story commercial buildings with corbeled decoration.

RH 12 Bostick School
Ca. 1880; E side SR 1317, 2.2 mi. N of US 220, Ellerbe vic.

The utterly plain gable-fronted frame school typifies the many country schools of the late 19th c., when local residents joined to build schoolhouses for their children. It has been restored in its rural crossroads setting.

RH 13 Mount Carmel Presbyterian Church
Mid-19th c.; W side SR 1317 at Montgomery Co. line, Norman vic.

On a quiet rural site near its 20th-c. brick church, the congregation established in the 18th c. has kept its early frame meetinghouse and tended the graves of the largely Scots congregation. Many are marked by uncut rocks or simple circular- or triangular-headed stones. The little meetinghouse captures the essence of early worship spaces, with two doors in the gable front and two windows on each side, plain boarded walls, and slatted benches facing the pulpit.

RH 14 Covington Rosenwald School
Ca. 1920; S side SR 1152 betw. NC 73 and SR 1005, Covington vic.

The neatly finished, 2-teacher frame school is one of hundreds built in the state with aid from the Julius Rosenwald Fund, which helped black citizens construct good quality schoolhouses. It has been restored as a community center.

RH 15 Powellton

1850s; N side NC 73, 0.5 mi. W of SR 1152, Little's Mills vic.; private, visible from road

The Greek Revival plantation house, located in the cotton-producing Pee Dee River valley of northwest Richmond Co., displays the characteristic 2-story block with low hip roof and center-passage plan 2 rooms deep, with the facade emphasized by 3-part front windows and central doorways at both stories. A kitchen is linked at the side by a breezeway. Nearby but distant from the road is the similar **John P. Little House.**

RH 16 Stanback and Little Houses

Ca. 1880; both sides NC 73 at SR 1161, Little's Mills vic.; private, visible from road

Two large Italianate houses of similar finish face each other across the road; both have broad cross gables with bracketed eaves, projecting bays, and 1-story porches trimmed in sawnwork. Recalling the cotton wealth of northwestern Richmond Co., both houses were built for families who settled the area in the colonial period, and they may incorporate antebellum elements.

RH 17 Watson Farm

19th c.; Hoffman vic.; no public visibility

Located in the sparsely settled sandhills, the well-maintained farmstead is a remarkable survival of a once prevalent way of building. Home of a family who arrived in the 18th c., the weatherboarded log house has a stone and mud chimney with timber bracing, protected by the roof overhang; cypress foundation blocks; batten doors with strap hinges and an unglazed window with batten shutter; and smooth-boarded interiors. Outbuildings include a log smokehouse, a corn and hay barn, and others.

Anson County (AN)

Long home of the Catawbas and the Waxhaws, the land between the Pee Dee and Rocky rivers was colonized in the mid-18th c. by intersecting streams of Scotch, English, Scotch-Irish, and African people coming up the Pee Dee and the Cape Fear valleys and southwest from Pennsylvania and Virginia. It was part of the original Anson Co. (est. 1750), an immense mother county that was partitioned into Rowan, Mecklenburg, and others. Agriculture, especially cotton production, dominated until the mid-20th c., as represented by scattered plantation houses, tenant houses, and small farmsteads. Local quarries yielded brownstone (sandstone) widely popular in the 19th c. (*Executive Mansion, Raleigh). Despite efforts to improve river navigation and a plank road from Cheraw to Salisbury in the 1850s, transportation was difficult until 1874, when the Carolina Central Railroad (CCRR) crossed the county. Urban and industrial growth remained small while nearby Charlotte boomed, a pattern that continued even after construction of the Winston-Salem Southbound Railway (1911) and better roads. The county produced progressive agricultural leaders, including Farmers' Alliance leader L. L. Polk (*Polkton) and Hugh Bennett, founding director of the U.S. Soil Conservation Service, who emphasized education, soil conservation, and diversification beyond cotton. In the mid-20th c., extension agents encouraged farmers to plant peach orchards on old cotton fields. Dotted with former railroad and farming villages that waxed and waned with changing times, the county remains rural. The principal products are gravel and timber, with much of the dramatic topography of ridges and rivers covered in forests.

AN 1 Wadesboro

The hilltop county seat was chartered as New Town in 1783 to replace an earlier one near the river. It was established by Revolutionary patriots Thomas Wade and Patrick Boggan and was renamed for Wade after his death in 1787. Except for the *Boggan-Hammond House and the *Burns Inn from the antebellum era, most of the architecture dates from the late 19th and especially the early 20th c., when railroads encouraged trade and factories, including the Wadesboro Cotton Mill (1890), a cotton oil factory, and a silk mill. The CCRR linked Wadesboro to Wilmington and Charlotte; in 1880 the Cheraw to Salisbury railroad got as far as Wadesboro; and in 1911 the Winston-Salem Southbound arrived from the north. The population grew from 800 in 1880 to 1,500 in 1900 and 4,500 in 1910.

The centerpiece is the **Anson County Courthouse** (1914; Wheeler & Stern [Charlotte]; Courthouse Square), a Beaux Arts classical edifice in tan brick. The main (w) front has a Doric order portico recessed in antis, and pedimented porticoes mark entrances on the north and south. Its design differs from the prolific firm's standard dome-and-portico formula. On the courthouse square are a Confederate Monument (1906), a memorial to the women of the South (1934), monuments to the World Wars, and a gazebo-like Revolutionary War memorial (Daughters of the American Revolution, 1921) with pillars of local brownstone and a tile roof. In the adjoining business district, the 2-story frame **Burns Inn** (1846; 104 W. Martin St.), 8 bays wide with a deep porch, is a rare survival of the frame hotels and stores once common in courthouse towns. Designed to complement the courthouse, the **U.S. Post Office** (1932–33; James A. Wetmore, acting supervising architect of the Treasury; 105–11 Martin St.) is a symmetrical 2-story building in cream brick with pilasters, arched openings, and a balustraded roof. The predominant building

298 ANSON COUNTY

AN 1 *Anson Co. Courthouse*

stock consists of 1- and 2-story brick commercial structures, many with ornamental corbeling in their upper stories; especially intact rows appear on Greene, Rutherford, and Wade Sts. Most display versions of Romanesque and classical designs, such as the imposing **H. W. Little & Co. Building** (1906; 109 S. Greene), a hardware store in continuous operation, 2½ stories with arched windows and name parapet. A contrast appears in the linear Art Deco facade (ca. 1930) at 116 W. Wade St.

Adjoining the commercial district are residential streets with houses and churches contemporary with downtown. The chief reminder of early Wadesboro is the **Boggan-Hammond House** and the **Alexander Little Wing** (late 18th–early 19th c.; 210 Wade St.; open limited hours) just east of downtown. Preserved as a local museum, the simple 1-story, brick-nogged frame dwelling (at the rear) has a hall-parlor plan and restrained Georgian-Federal woodwork. It is believed to have been built in the late 18th c. by Patrick Boggan, town founder and Revolutionary figure, probably for his daughter Eleanor and her husband Wade Hammond. After 1839 the house was owned by jurist Alexander Little, who evidently added the 2-story, side-passage plan wing of late Federal style. The two were separated in the 20th c. and restored in the 1960s.

Brick churches occupy prime corners. Especially striking is **Calvary Episcopal Church** (1892–93; Silas McBee, possible architect; 308 E. Wade St.), built for a congregation est. 1820. The elegant little church in Early English Gothic Revival style takes an asymmetrically picturesque form with buttressed red brick walls, transepts with rose

AN 1 *W. Wade St. commercial buildings*

AN 1 *Boggan-Hammond House*

windows, a semicircular apse, and a prominent corner entrance tower. Church history recalls that a parishioner patterned it after churches in his native England. Silas McBee, noted church architect and editor of *The New York Churchman*, is credited with making the altar and may also have supplied the architectural design (*St. Stephen's Episcopal Church, Oxford).

Well-kept and shaded residential streets of the same era extend south, east, and west from downtown, including Brent, Leak, Morgan, Wade, West, and other streets. Aligned along ridges that extend fingerlike above intervening ravines, they contain a representative mix of late Queen Anne, Colonial Revival, and bungalow styles.

AN 2 Ansonville

The village was founded as "College" about 1844 by Pee Dee planters attracted to its high and healthy site. They built fine houses and established the Carolina Female College, which drew students from several southern states from 1850 to 1867. (The 3-story brick school, razed in the 20th c., was one of the state's largest antebellum buildings.) Located on a plank road route, a few buildings remain from the mid-19th-c., generally Greek Revival with local brownstone foundations, outbuildings, and garden walls. At the north end the **President's House** (ca. 1850; w side SR 1621 [Plank Road], 0.1 mi. N of US 52), surviving from the college, is a conservative 2-story, 5-bay frame house with simple Greek Revival detail and a 2-tier portico. **All Souls Episcopal Church** (ca. 1880; E side US 52, just S of SR 1418) is a modest stone building with a stout entrance tower at the gable front.

On a knoll behind a fine brownstone wall, the most imposing landmark is the **William Smith House** (ca. 1845, Mr. Hatchett [attrib.]; ca. 1880s; E side US 52, 0.25 mi. S of SR 1418). It began as a 2-story, double-pile Greek Revival dwelling under a shallow hip roof; its tall portico and 1-story wings were late 19th-c. additions. Formally arranged outbuildings include a kitchen and others contemporary with the house and a late 19th-c. frame barn with Gothic arcade of stuccoed stone. The complex was begun by William Gaston Smith, planter, merchant, and leader at the college, and renovated for his son William A. Smith, Confederate veterans' leader active in textiles, banking, and education. Tradition cites this house and others, along with the college, to a Mr. Hatchett of Philadelphia; he could be William Hatchell, a mechanic from Virginia, listed in Anson in the 1850 census with

AN 2 *William Smith House*

3 other mechanics in his household. Across the road is the **Major S. W. Cole House** (1840s; Mr. Hatchett [attrib.]; w side US 52, 0.25 mi. S of SR 1418), a 2-story, hip-roofed Greek Revival house of brick; its fine ironwork porch was taken to Charlotte. The **William Little House** (ca. 1840s, early 20th c.; w side US 52, 0.3 mi. S of SR 1418), a 2-story Greek Revival house of frame, received a large portico and flanking porches in the early 20th c.; it retains several outbuildings.

AN 3 Rocky River Baptist Church
Late 19th c.; S side SR 1612, 0.1 mi. W of SR 1610, Burnsville vic.

The beautifully simple frame church, poised on a knoll above a bend in the road, has a symmetrical gable front topped by an open belfry with bell. The Missionary Baptist congregation was begun by 1772 and organized in 1776, making it one of the earliest of its denomination in the region. The noted free black preacher Ralf Freeman was minister here in the late 18th and early 19th centuries; his grave is in Ansonville.

AN 4 Cedar Hill Methodist Church
1888; S side SR 1627, 0.1 mi. E of US 52, Cedar Hill vic.

The plain, gable-fronted frame church, little changed since its construction, rests on solid brownstone piers, a distinctive local feature. The newly founded congregation erected the church for $700 and dedicated it in 1889.

North Pee Dee:
Overlooking the winding Pee Dee River, SR 1703 and SR 1704 run along ridges through a long-settled agricultural area, where plantation houses may be glimpsed at a distance and modest churches and farmhouses still stand near the road. Others lie beyond public view or in disrepair.

AN 5 Savannah Methodist Church
1887; SW corner SR 1704 and SR 1727

The modest, gable-fronted frame church with central entrance was built in 1887 for a congregation established before 1819. Methodists took early hold in the county, along with Baptists, but most of the congregations occupy new churches.

AN 6 Benjamin Ingram House

Ca. 1840; W side SR 1704, 1.0 mi. S of SR 1727; private, visible from road

High on a ridge overlooking the broad Pee Dee valley, the 2-story frame house typifies middling planters of the mid-19th c. It is symmetrically composed with a hip roof and exterior end chimneys, a 1-story full-width porch, and a center-passage plan with Federal–Greek Revival finish. The 1-story rear ell is an older house; several 19th-c. outbuildings remain.

AN 7 Lilesville

Vestiges remain of the cotton-trading town that began by 1828 and flourished with the CCRR. The **Nelson P. Liles House** (ca. 1850; N side of Wall St., W of commercial district), built for a merchant and town namesake, is one of the largest Greek Revival houses in the county, 2 stories tall with a center-passage plan, hip roof, and robust Greek Revival doorways at both levels. The small **Commercial District** on Wall St. retains corbeled brick stores built after a 1910 fire. Near the railroad on Cowan St. is a **Store and Post Office** (19th c.?), a long, 1-story board-and-batten building with heavily nailed chevron-boarded doors.

AN 8 Solomon Jones House

Ca. 1860; Solomon Jones, carpenter; W side SR 1801, 1.5 mi. S of US 74, Gravelton vic.; private, visible from road

The hip-roofed frame house with side-passage plan and side wing presents a porch treatment characteristic of the South Carolina border area: engaged beneath the main hip roof, the main posts of the 2-story porch stand on bases forward of the porch floor, while a 2-tier porch with decorative millwork stands behind it. Jones, carpenter and farmer, probably built the house about the time he bought the 300-acre tract in 1860.

AN 9 Blewett Falls Dam and Power Station

1912 and later; Pee Dee River, end of SR 1748

In 1905 Hugh MacRae of Wilmington, a businessman active in developments from Wilmington to Linville, organized the Rockingham Power Co. to build a dam and hydroelectric power plant on the Pee Dee, for which textile mills in Wadesboro and Richmond Co. provided a market. It was named for an 18th-c. landowner and ferry operator. After financial problems and a flood closed MacRae's firm, the Yadkin River Power Co. was formed in 1911 and opened the plant by June 1912. It merged with Carolina Power & Light in 1926. A concrete gravity-type dam some 1,600 feet long and 50 feet high spans the river (visible from the Richmond Co. side), and a canal directs water past an island to the power plant, where it flows through steel penstocks to the turbine. Stepping down the slope, the power plant is a 2-, 3-, and 4-story industrial brick structure with low-pitched roofs and segmental-arched openings. An adjoining recreation area offers views of the plant with its great arched openings at the mouths of the penstocks.

AN 10 Morven

The most evocative of the county's old railroad villages, Morven was founded ca. 1823 by Hugh McKenzie, postmaster, who

AN 9 *Blewett Falls Power Station*

named it for his mother's home in Scotland. Originally Morven lay on the Cheraw-Salisbury plank road, but with construction of the 1880 Cheraw-Salisbury Railroad, it moved west to the tracks, was incorporated in 1883, and became a center of cotton trade and culture. Unique among the cluster of 1-story brick and frame stores is the **Set-Back Room**, a 1-room gable-fronted frame building where local men gather for afternoon card games; a spade symbol is painted above the door. The bracketed, board-and-batten **Morven Depot** (1900; W side US 52, 0.1 mi. S of NC 145) stands beside the track bed. The **Thomas V. Hardison House** (1910; NW corner US 52 and NC 145), built for a businessman instrumental in moving Morven, is a Queen Anne style house tempered by Colonial Revival elements and enhanced by an ornate iron fence. Next door, the **Morven Presbyterian Church** (1916), brick with a Doric-columned portico, was built for a Scots Presbyterian congregation, described as the first in the county, which began in the 18th c. and moved to Morven in the 1880s. Next door is the **Morven School**, a substantial early 20th-c. brick school with arched windows and front stair tower. East on Main St. stand the **Morven Baptist** and **Morven Methodist** churches, Gothic Revival red brick buildings. Three miles SE of Morven (off SR 1829 from US 52) is the site of **Sneedsborough**, laid out in 1795 and promoted by Archibald DeBow Murphey and others as an inland port on the Pee Dee; one scheme proposed a canal linking it to the Cape Fear River and Wilmington. By the mid-19th c. its fortunes had declined, and it eventually vanished.

AN 11 Bennett-Dunlap House

Ca. 1835; E side SR 1812 opp. SR 1121, Morven vic.; private, visible from road

The double-pile Greek Revival house with 2-story porch is the most visible of several mid-19th-c. plantation houses in southeastern Anson. The story goes that James C. Bennett remained loyal to the Union through the Civil War, only to be shot dead on his porch by Sherman's men near the end of the conflict. Used as a location in *The Color Purple*, filmed in the area in 1985, the house has since lost its back porch and ell but retains its prominence in the landscape.

AN 12 Ratliff House

Ca. 1852; E side NC 742, 0.7 mi. S of SR 1124; private, visible from road

Exemplifying an important regional form, the 2-story main block, with hall-parlor plan and 2 front doors, is expanded by shed porches front and rear with porch chambers enclosed at the ends. One front porch chamber is accessible from within, the other only from the porch — a "preacher room" balancing hospitality and security. The plantation house was built for John and Susan Ratliff and descended in the family until 1990.

AN 13 Chambers-Morgan House

Mid-19th c.; W side SR 1228, 2.2 mi. S of SR 1003, White Store vic.; private, visible from road

The 2-story plantation house is dominated by a broad 2-tier porch engaged under the main roof, which stretches across the 5-bay front and shelters the 3 front doors. Paneled

AN 10 *Thomas V. Hardison House*

AN 13 *Chambers-Morgan House*

pillars and other elements are finished in simple Greek Revival style. Part of a large cotton plantation neighborhood in the Waxhaw area, about 1940 the farm was enrolled in the Brown Creek Soil Conservation District, the nation's first.

AN 14 Polkton

When the CCRR was routed through the county in the early 1870s, Leonidas L. Polk laid out a village on his trackside land. Member of a local farming family, Polk became a state agricultural and educational leader—a founder of North Carolina State University, publisher of *Progressive Farmer*, president of the National Farmers' Alliance, and probable Populist candidate for the presidency but for his unexpected death in 1892 (*L. L. Polk House, Raleigh). The **Polk House** (ca. 1830; S side SR 1419, just E of NC 218), his birthplace and family home, is a 2-story frame house of simple Federal character, with end chimneys and a shed porch with enclosed porch room; here he published the *Ansonian*. The **Polkton Depot** (ca. 1900; W side NC 218, N of tracks), a gabled building with German siding, has been saved on a nearby site. There are a small commercial district and numerous turn-of-the-century frame houses.

Union County (UN)

See Suzanne S. Pickens, Sweet Union: An Architectural and Historical Survey of Union County, North Carolina *(1990).*

Formed in 1842 from Anson and Mecklenburg, the county was named Union to resolve a dispute between Whig and Democrat factions who wanted Clay or Jackson. Like neighboring counties, it was settled by Scotch-Irish and other largely self-sufficient farmers, with cotton gaining importance in the 19th c. Links with neighboring South Carolina were strong. Several houses have porches with the pillars freestanding in front of the porch floor, a feature seen in N.C. chiefly along the South Carolina border.

Economic troubles after the Civil War, coupled with the arrival of railroads—the Central Carolina (CCRR) in 1874 from Wilmington to Charlotte and the Georgia, Carolina & Northern (GC&N), 1888–92—increased reliance on cotton and on the crop-lien and tenant systems. Many farmers, however, thrived sufficiently to build unusually stylish farmhouses in the late 19th and early 20th centuries. Little railroad towns sprang up, and the county seat of Monroe flourished into a cotton market and manufacturing town. In the late 20th c., as farming diminished, the eastern section of the county remained relatively rural, while the west saw rapid suburbanization from Charlotte.

Monroe (UN 1–2)

See Mary Ann Lee, *An Inventory of Historic Architecture: Monroe, North Carolina* (1978).

Laid out as seat of the new county in 1843, Monroe remained small until the CCRR put it on a main east-west line in 1874 and the GC&N linked it to Atlanta in 1892, making it a regional rail hub. Ambitious men came from farms and villages to become cotton brokers, general merchants, bankers, and manufacturers. From the 1870s through the 1920s, its streets filled with wagonloads of cotton and its neighborhoods with increasingly impressive houses. These include numerous Southern Colonial residences with big porticoes overlapping 1-story porches—a form reminiscent of the region's tradition of freestanding porch columns. There are also portions of mill villages for Iceman and Icemorelee mills (altered) in the north and west.

UN 1 Downtown Monroe

Presiding over the town from its elevated central square, the **Former Union County**

Courthouse (1885–88; Thomas J. Holt [Raleigh], chief architect; J. T. Hart, contractor; 1926, Charles C. Hook [Charlotte], architect; Courthouse Sq.) is the chief landmark of town and county. Among the state's finest surviving Victorian public buildings (*Cabarrus County Courthouse), the boldly composed 2-story brick edifice presents an eclectic blend of classical, Italianate, Second Empire, and Eastlake motifs. The opposing fronts are equally elaborate, with tall, arched windows lighting the second story, a pro-

UN 1 *Former Union Co. Courthouse*

jecting entrance pavilion, and an ornate mansard-roofed porch with iron cresting. A tall cupola with pilasters, brackets, pediments, urns, and four clockfaces rises to a dome. Supervising architect and presumably designer was Thomas J. Holt (brother of builder Jacob W. Holt of *Warrenton), formerly architect for the Raleigh & Gaston Railroad. In 1926 Charles C. Hook designed the complementary 2-story wings. On a facing corner is the former **Union County Jail–Monroe City Hall** (1847–48; 102 W. Jefferson St.), a much simpler building of Flemish-bond brick, unusually formal for an antebellum jail, with corbeled pediments at the 1-bay entrance pavilion and gable ends. A jail until 1893, it served as city hall until 1972.

Rows of brick and stone-fronted commercial buildings, generally of 2 and 3 stories, face the square and nearby streets. A rounded corner entrance tower emphasizes the prominent **Bank of Union Building** (1905–6; 100 E. Franklin St.), 3 stories tall in yellow brick with red mortar and trimmed in stone, including marble Ionic columns at the corner entry. It was constructed for J. R. Shute & Sons and contained the bank, their grocery, and on the upper floors, the local Jackson Club. The **Monroe Hardware Co. Warehouse** (1924; G. Marion Tucker [Monroe], contractor; 109 N. Hayne St.) is a massive brick building built for a major local firm, 3 stories tall and 16 bays long, rendered in tapestry brick with steel windows and stylized classical details in concrete. Among the many corbeled brick commercial buildings are the **Belk Buildings** (ca. 1901–5; 209–11 N. Main St.), which by the 1920s were part of the Belk Brothers store, begun in Monroe by William Henry Belk in 1888 as "the New York Racket"—"Belk Sells It for Less." William and his brother John soon developed the regional department store chain that still continues. The former **Monroe Post Office** (1913; Oscar Wenderoth, supervising architect of the Treasury; 407 N. Main St.), located near the late 20th-c. high-rise courthouse, has a strong Neoclassical presence in red brick, with portico in a Tower of the Winds order and large, round-arched entrance and windows. The **Monroe**

Passenger Depot (1906; 100 Smith St.), 1 story in brick with tall hip roof and flaring eaves, typifies the depots built by Seaboard, which took over the CCRR and others.

UN 2 Residential Areas

The residential sections southeast, south, and west of the business district represent the full range of domestic styles from the prime cotton era. Many are unusually substantial and stylish for a town of modest size, including several by Charlotte architects. The **Gaston Meares House** (ca. 1898; George F. Barber [Knoxville] [attrib.]; 110 S. College St.), built for a railroad engineer, is among the most exuberant of many town and county versions of the Queen Anne cottage. The early 20th c. produced a multitude of bungalows and, especially prominent, grand columned residences in the Southern Colonial style. The most spectacular is the big, frame **Dr. John M. Belk House** (1903; 401 S. Hayne St.), erected for the South Car-

UN 2 *Dr. John M. Belk House*

UN 2 *Gaston Meares House*

olina–born physician who with his brother William created the Belk department store chain. After William moved to Charlotte (*William Henry Belk House), John remained in Monroe. His house epitomizes the Southern Colonial style with its colossal portico of Composite order columns engaged beneath the main hip roof and sheltering a balustraded, 1-story wraparound porch with Ionic columns.

The **James H. Lee House** (1912–14; Wheeler & Stern [Charlotte], architects; William Ervin Wallace, carpenter; 501 S. Church St.) is a restrained Southern Colonial Revival house, with Ionic entrance portico overlapping a 1-story wraparound porch; it was built for a businessman who moved from Marshville, established a drugstore and then a dry goods store, and became a bank president and industrialist. (See Introduction, Fig. 69.) The **Houston-Redfearn House** (1870s and later; 506 S. Church St.) evidently began as an Italianate residence and gained a full-height Corinthian portico ca. 1905. The **Heath-Williamson House** (ca. 1874; 601 S. Church St.) typifies Italianate residences of the early railroad days, with narrow, gabled entrance pavilion and bracket cornices.

Franklin St. was a main thoroughfare and prime residential avenue. Many fine houses remain on W. Franklin, such as the **Shannon House** (1901; 406 W. Franklin St.) in Queen Anne style with classical details; the **Iceman House** (1911; G. Marion Tucker, contractor; 900 W. Franklin St.), a graceful rendition of the Southern Colonial Revival with Corinthian portico and flanking wings, built for the founder of local cotton mills; and the **Stack House** (ca. 1916; 1002 W. Franklin St.), an especially fine Craftsman bungalow, asymmetrical with shingles and rough stonework, built for a bank cashier. Notable on E. Franklin is the **Blakeney House** (1903; Charles C. Hook [Charlotte], architect; John Wallace [Monroe], builder; 418 E. Franklin St.), designed for a bank president from South Carolina by Hook in ornate Colonial Revival style. Farther east, a member of the same firm planned the **Sikes House** (1926–27; Louis D. Sutherland [Charlotte], architect; G. Marion Tucker

[Monroe], contractor; 1301 E. Franklin St.), a large and opulent residence of yellow brick with green tile roof and classical detailing, built for attorney John Sikes the year after he successfully defended millionaire industrialist W. B. Cole in a sensational murder trial (*Manufacturer's Building, Rockingham).

UN 3 Waxhaw-Weddington Roads District
Ca. 1900; jct. NC 75 and NC 84

At a once rural crossroads west of town, local businessmen originally from the countryside constructed a cluster of stylish residences on semirural estates, where they enjoyed farming as a diversion from industry, banking, or law. These include the Queen Anne style **Heath House** (1897) in the fork of the road; the symmetrical, red brick **Redwine House** (1908; G. Marion Tucker, contractor) south of the fork; and on the north, the Queen Anne style **"Crow's Nest"** (ca. 1905) and the Prairie-style-influenced **Edward Crow House** (1916). There are numerous farm outbuildings.

UN 4 Union Springs Arbor and A.M.E. Zion Church
Ca. 1877, 1921; NW side NC 200, 0.2 mi. NE of SR 1620, Monroe vic.

The arbor named for a nearby spring is believed to have been constructed ca. 1877, the year the 2-acre site was bought for $7 as "a place of Divine Worship for the use and membership of the African Methodist Episcopal Church in America." Antebellum Methodists, black and white, worshiped together in churches and camp meetings, but after the Civil War they established separate churches and meeting grounds. The arbor is a gable-roofed structure of mortise and tenon construction, with a shed roof extending on all sides. Pews and benches sit on an earthen floor, facing the pulpit. Adjacent is the simple, gable-fronted frame church with triangular-headed windows.

UN 5 John Simpson House

*Ca. 1878; NW side SR 1716, 0.5 mi.
SW of NC 218, Olive Branch vic.;
private, visible from road*

Lavished with fancy millwork representative of the county's unusually decorative farmhouses, the symmetrical frame house features a 2-story entrance porch with bracketed cornices, chamfered posts, and intricately sawn balustrades. Several 20th-c. frame outbuildings remain.

UN 5 *John Simpson House*

UN 6 Ross House

*Early 20th c.; W side SR 1719, 0.9 mi.
N of SR 1002, Olive Branch vic.; private,
visible from road*

The rambling 1½-story farmhouse is one of several in the locale that show unusually fullblown versions of the hybrid Queen Anne–Colonial Revival mode. They combine the complex massing of the former with classically inspired porch columns and details of the latter. The house was built ca. 1906 for Joseph and Lila Ross and enlarged ca. 1916.

UN 7 Marshville

The railroad village, settled in 1874 as Beaver Dam on the new CCRR and renamed for a local family in 1897, has a cluster of brick stores near the tracks and an irregular grid with frame houses from Queen Anne cottages to bungalows. The **Marshville Town Hall** (1914; 201 N. Elm St.) is a small, bold design in brick, with big windows and recessed classical entrance, built for a bank

that closed in 1930. The **Marsh-McBride House** (1914–17; 207 S. Elm St.) was built for merchant Edward Marsh as a brick Southern Colonial residence with Corinthian portico. North of town is the **Marshville Cemetery and Gazebo** (E side NC 205), given by the Marsh family and notable for the large gateway gazebo (1901; Atlas Redwine Edwards, carpenter) of octagonal form with latticed sides and arched drive-through openings.

UN 8 Wingate

The community grew up around the Baptist college that began as a high school in 1895, became a college in 1923, and is now Wingate University. A small central quadrangle retains the oldest buildings, all of red brick with cast-stone trim in a hearty blend of classical and Tudoresque elements: **Burris Building** (1933), **Efird Memorial Library** (1946), and **Alumni Hall** (1946). Nearby are the red brick **Wingate Baptist Church** (1922; 108 E. Elm St.), with a dome and portico; the **Stewart House** (1912; 102 E. Elm St.), in Queen Anne–Colonial Revival style, where students once boarded; and other early 20th-c. houses.

UN 9 Ashcraft House

*Ca. 1854; SW side SR 1005, 1.1 mi. NW of
SR 1003; private, visible from road*

The handsome 1-story Greek Revival farmhouse raised on brick piers has a center-passage plan 2 rooms deep. Broad proportions are emphasized by the wide pedimented end gables and front porch and immense 16/16 windows.

UN 10 Morgan House

*Ca. 1850?; NW side SR 1005, 2.1 mi. S of
SR 1003; private, visible from road*

Combining key regional construction traditions, the simply finished 2-story frame farmhouse, 1 room deep with a center passage, is greatly enlarged by porches and chambers. The hip-roofed front porch has enclosed porch rooms flanking a broad open bay, with freestanding posts in front of a re-

UN 10 *Morgan House*

cessed, balustraded inner porch. There are several outbuildings.

UN 11 Trinity United Methodist Church
1905; NW side SR 2153, 0.1 mi. SW of NC 207

The county's best-preserved frame country church features intersecting gable wings with Gothic pointed windows and touches of decorative millwork. In the elbow rises a tapered belltower with spire.

UN 12 Richardson House
1865–69; N side SR 1135, 1.0 mi. NE of SR 1128, Jackson vic.; private, visible from road

Following the regional form, the 1-story frame house is raised on a high basement and features balancing rear shed rooms and engaged front porch. The porch roof is carried on posts that stand in front of the balustraded porch floor. Two entrances open into a hall-parlor plan. Family tradition reports that Eli Richardson began the house in 1865, using his own timber and brick and working on it when farming demands permitted. It stands on land in the Richardson family since the mid-18th c. (See Introduction, Fig. 24.)

UN 13 Tirzah Presbyterian Church Session House
Early 19th c.; SE side SR 1100, 1.0 mi. SW of NC 200, Jackson vic.

The congregation, founded in 1804 from Old Waxhaw Church in South Carolina and given the Hebrew name for "delightful," is one of the oldest in the county. At the edge of the churchyard (behind the 1955 church), the frame session house is a simple, 1-room building for church leaders' meetings typical of the denomination.

UN 14 William Walkup House
Completed 1869; W side SR 1106, 1.0 mi. S of SR 1104, Waxhaw vic.; private, visible from road

The massive frame farmhouse, once famed as the largest in the county, is said by tradition to have been built by Col. William Walkup to replace his (possibly similar) house that burned on "Windy Friday," March 9, 1855, when windswept fires destroyed many buildings and forests. The hip-roofed main block, 5 bays wide and 2 rooms deep, adjoins a 2-story rear ell. Especially notable, the tall, pedimented front portico has plain, full-height columns that, in keeping with regional tradition, stand on their own bases and overlap a 1-story porch with upper balustrade serving entrances at both levels. (This form may anticipate the overlapping portico-porch schemes of the Southern Colonial mode seen in the *J. W. Belk House and others.) The engaged 2-tier porch along the rear ell repeats the post arrangement. A 1941 marker placed by the Daughters of the American Revolution (DAR) commemorates the 1780 Battle of the Waxhaws on the plantation.

UN 15 Rehobeth Presbyterian Church
1911; SE side SR 1107, 0.5 mi. NE of SR 1106, Waxhaw vic.

A portico of hefty Doric columns gives monumentality to the small brick country church. Its classical design may reflect South Carolina precedents. The congregation organized in 1911 revived the name of an antebellum congregation.

UN 16 Waxhaw

Facing the tracks that gave it life, Waxhaw boasts a strong collection of brick commercial buildings from its railroad heyday. It is part of an area known as the Waxhaws for the native people who lived here before

Scotch-Irish settlers arrived to establish a dispersed agricultural settlement straddling the line between North and South Carolina. The village gained energy from the GC&N in 1888, and frame, then brick business houses were erected on East South Main St., West North Main St., etc., flanking the tracks. Among the corbeled brick buildings are the **R. J. Belk Store** (ca. 1894; 200 E. S. Main St.), built for a branch of the Monroe Belk Brothers' stores and operated by cousin Ralph, and the **A. W. Heath Co. Buildings** (1898 and later; 103–9 W. S. Main St.), home of a general store, including an especially handsome 2-story brick building in round-arched style. In back is a plain, frame structure built as a corn and wheat mill ca. 1905. There are numerous 1- and 2-story Queen Anne style houses and other frame dwellings and brick churches, including the classical temple-form **Waxhaw Presbyterian Church** (1929; 416 W. N. Main St.) and the Gothic Revival **Waxhaw Methodist Church** (1923–28; 200 McDonald St.). A few miles south, near the state line, is the **Andrew Jackson Birthplace Marker** (1910; end of SR 1105, off SR 1107), a granite marker with a log cabin in high relief, erected by the DAR; future president Jackson was born in the Waxhaw settlement to parents who lived on the South Carolina side, but one tradition claims that his mother came to her sister's home here to give birth.

UN 17 Pleasant Grove Camp Meeting Ground
Est. 1830; NW corner SR 1327 and SR 1329, Waxhaw vic.

The aptly named complex is one of the largest and most evocative of the Piedmont's campgrounds that began with the Great Revival of the late 18th and early 19th centuries. It was established by Methodists in 1830 as an outgrowth of the ca. 1787 McWhirter Camp Ground, which lacked a good water supply. A contract for $125 to build the central arbor was let to John C. Rape, and members and neighbors lent a hand. Heavy hand-hewn and chamfered framing forms the large, rugged structure composed of a gable-roofed core surrounded by a broad hip-roofed pent; tradition recalls that carpenter George Winchester was the only man around who could construct the complex roof form. By 1860 rows of more than 200 "tents"—small frame or log cabins—formed two squares around the arbor. Later in the century a small frame church was built, predecessor to the present-day 1895 gable-fronted frame church. Its location within the meeting ground precinct is unusual.

After use declined, the campground was closed in 1902, and all but 1 tent were removed. Renewed interest in the 1930s led to the rebuilding of 71 tents by 1935, and more were added over the years. Rows of small frame tents, along with the surviving early

UN 17 *Pleasant Grove Camp Meeting Ground: central arbor*

log one, form a large square around the arbor amid the grove. The campground remains in active late-summer use.

UN 18 Marvin

In the linear village along an old road, large trees shade modest frame houses of popular turn-of-the-century styles, along with neatly kept churches: the original **Banks Presbyterian Church** (1881; NE side SR 1315, just N of SR 1307), a little gable-fronted frame building later used as a store and dwelling; present-day **Banks Presbyterian Church** (1911; Charles C. Hook & Willard G. Rogers [Charlotte], architects) immediately north, slightly more elaborate with a corner tower and Gothic Revival openings; and the **Marvin Methodist Church** (1870s, 1920s; NE side SR 1315, 0.2 mi. NW of SR 1307), in brick with corbeled panels emphasizing the center gable and corner entrance tower.

UN 19 William Houston House
Early 19th c.; N side SR 1162, 0.8 mi.
N of NC 84; private, visible from road

The severely simple frame dwelling, one of the oldest in the county, recalls many others now lost or changed. Standing 2 stories tall beneath a gable roof, with a low upper story, it has a hall-parlor plan plus rear shed rooms and rear ell. A regional feature appears in the posts that carry the shed porch and stand well forward of the porch floor. It was built for William and Elizabeth Grey Houston, who married in 1809 and farmed here until his death in 1870.

UN 20 Hawfield House
1906; E side SR 1377, 1.1 mi. N of SR 1162;
private, visible from road

Among the best-preserved of several Queen Anne–Colonial Revival farmhouses in western Union Co., the 2-story frame house centers on an unusual polygonal entrance bay echoed by the 1-story porch. It was built for community leaders William D. and Julia Houston Hawfield as one of the finest houses in the neighborhood.

Randolph County (RD)

See Lowell M. Whatley Jr., The Architectural History of Randolph County, North Carolina (1985).

The county in the heart of the Piedmont offers views of the Uwharrie Mountains in the southern section that make "every road a scenic highway." Mid-18th-c. settlement created an especially diverse pattern of dissenting religious groups with ties to New England as well as the mid-Atlantic region, which shaped the county's social, economic, and political life. In the 1750s Baptists arrived and founded *Sandy Creek Baptist Church, a mother church of the faith across the South, and Quakers established early meetings as part of the central Piedmont "Quaker belt." (The county now has more Quaker meetings than any other N.C. county, all with 20th-c. meetinghouses.) Germans, including Dunkers (Baptists) in the northwest and Lutheran and Reformed groups in the northeast, were part of the larger settlement in eastern Guilford and western Alamance counties.

The county was formed from Guilford in 1779 and named for Peyton Randolph, president of the Continental Congress. Dominated by small farmsteads and with Quakers and others who opposed slavery and favored manumission, the county had relatively few slaves or slave owners. Abolitionist and Unionist beliefs gained strength during the Civil War, and Governor Vance sent troops to quell anti-Confederate disturbances. As in some mountain counties, after the war Republicans were numerous, a tradition that persisted in the 20th c.

Bisected by the Deep River, the county was home to a pioneering textile industry with Quaker entrepreneurs among the founders. The first mill was built at *Cedar Falls in 1837, followed by *Franklinville (1838), Island Ford (1845), Union Factory (1848), and Allen's Fall (at *Ramseur, 1850). Along with the Haw River mills of Alamance Co., these constitute the state's chief examples of rural, waterpowered mill villages.

Asheboro (RD 1–9)

The county seat and small industrial city, with notable buildings from its early 20th-c. growth era, began in 1793 as a grid-plan village and was incorporated and named for Governor Samuel Ashe in 1796. Of its village days—with but 200 people as late as 1876—only the *Asheboro Female Academy remains. Bypassed by mid-19th-c. rails, Asheboro welcomed the 1889 High Point, Randleman, Asheboro & Southern Railroad, which made "a village into a thriving town." Wood processing factories came first, and elaborate houses adorned with millwork sprang up, followed by substantial brick commercial, industrial, and public buildings. After the first hosiery factory (*Acme-

McCrary) opened in 1909, textiles became the main industry. Early 20th-c. neighborhoods retain strong groupings of bungalows, Colonial Revival houses, and later styles. Public and private clients commissioned designs from Charlotte and Greensboro architects, and in the mid-20th c. Eric G. Flannagan of Henderson and then native J. Hyatt Hammond designed an unusual number of modernist buildings for a relatively small community.

RD 1 Randolph County Courthouse
1908–9; Wheeler, Runge & Dickey (Charlotte), architects; 145 Worth St.

One of eight similar N.C. courthouses (six survive) planned by architect Wheeler and

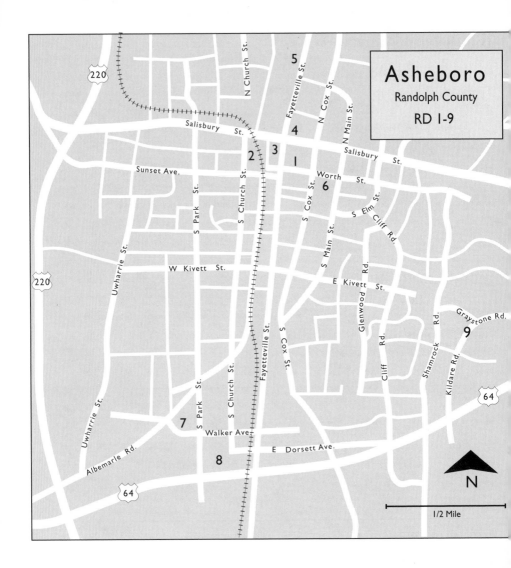

associates, the Neoclassical design follows
the prototype *Iredell County Courthouse
of 1899. This economical rendition in yellow
brick with tile and sandstone trim cost only
$34,000 but repeats the robust and lively
form with portico and mansardlike dome.
The **Randolph County Jail** (1914; 149
Worth St.) features castellated and corbeled
detail typical of prison architecture of its era.
Lawyer's Row (1909; 125 Worth St.), a 1-
and 2-story brick building with corbeled,
arched openings, was built by local attorneys
for offices convenient to the courthouse.

RD 1 *Randolph Co. Courthouse*

RD 2 Asheboro City Hall

1938; Albert C. Woodruff, architect;
146 N. Church St.

The sleek limestone-faced structure displays the simplified Art Deco mode disseminated to small towns in many such public buildings assisted by the Works Progress Administration. Smooth planar surfaces recede from a central entrance pavilion, and pierced geometric stone panels light the stairs within. The "Municipal Building" held a library, a fire department, and a courtroom as well as city offices and has a fine Art Deco council chamber.

RD 2 *Asheboro City Hall*

RD 3 Acme-McCrary Hosiery Mills

1909, 1915–24; North St. between Sunset
and Salisbury Sts.

The county's first hosiery mill, a steam-powered knitting plant, began in 1909 in the 2-story Italianate style brick building (sw corner Salisbury and North Sts.). Expansions over the years produced a large, multibuilding plant modernized for continued use. The **Acme-McCrary Recreation Building** (1948; Eric G. Flannagan, architect; 148 North St.), a handsome structure of simple modernist character, held a gym, a cafeteria, a swimming pool, and a bowling alley.

RD 4 First Methodist Church and Parsonage

1924, ca. 1934; Harry Barton (Greensboro),
architect; 224 N. Fayetteville St.

The prominent complex includes a church in bold Romanesque Revival style, plus campanile and parsonage—all in dark red brick set off by green tile roofs (*First Baptist Church, Siler City).

RD 5 Randolph Hospital

1931–32, 1946–76; Eric G. Flannagan
(Henderson), architect; 373 N. Fayetteville St.

In his first and most impressive Asheboro project, architect Flannagan planned a civic hospital funded by the recently established Duke Endowment. In the first unit, he established a restrained Art Deco style that he repeated in subsequent expansions. When the entrance facade was replaced in 1951, the stone cornice with the hospital name was reused.

RD 6 McCrary Houses

Worth Street; private

At the entrance to a large residential section, three fine early 20th-c. residences of a leading business family illustrate popular revivalist styles. The **D. B. McCrary House** (1905; 212 Worth St.), an opulent Southern Colonial house with tall Ionic portico, bowed entrance pavilion, and flanking 1-story porches, was built for a hardware merchant and founder of *Acme-McCrary Mill. His sons followed suit in the Tudor Revival **J. F. McCrary House** (ca. 1933; W. C. Holeyman [Greensboro], architect; 232 Worth St.) and the Georgian Revival **C. W. McCrary House** (ca. 1930; Harry Barton [Greensboro], architect; 240 Worth St.).

RD 7 Asheboro Female Academy

1839; W. Walker Ave.; open limited hours

The last vestige of early Asheboro is a 1-story, 5-bay frame building with gable-end chimneys, home to a private academy chartered in 1839 and operated until about 1892. In 1970 it was moved here from downtown and restored as a museum.

RD 8 Asheboro High School

1949–50, 1952–53; Eric G. Flannagan,
architect; later expansions; 1221 S. Park St.
at US 64

Facing the street across a broad lawn, the large facility with flanking auditorium and gymnasium continues the Moderne vocabulary of architect Flannagan's *Randolph Hospital, with buff brick, some set diago-

nally in broad panels, and geometric limestone trim. Allegorical carvings over the entrance depict science, sports, drama, music,
and the lamp of knowledge. A 1980 arena in
front of the original gymnasium alters the
balance of the facade.

RD 9 Kildare Road Houses
1950s; Kildare Rd.

A cluster of modest but venturesome houses
shows the modernist work of early graduates
of the North Carolina State University
School of Design who founded practices in
the 1950s. J. Hyatt Hammond, a 1953 graduate inspired by Eduardo Catalano and Frank
Lloyd Wright, returned to his native county
and began practice in Asheboro. The houses
built by Hammond and associate Clyde
Dorsett and carefully integrated into the
landscape were considered quite radical at
the time. The 2-story **Clyde Dorsett House**
(1956; Clyde Dorsett; 741 Kildare Rd.) displays a Bauhaus influence, while the low-
lying, elongated **J. Hyatt Hammond House**
(1958; 801 Kildare Rd.) embodies Wrightian
themes. Across the street is a "straightforward little contemporary house" built about
the same time for a client: the **Earl Pleas-
ants House** (NW corner Greystone and Kildare Rds.). On the northwest side of town,
the **James O. Trogdon House** (1968; Arthur
Cogswell [Chapel Hill]; Neely Drive) reflects a Wrightian modernism.

RD 9 *J. Hyatt Hammond House*

RD 10 N.C. Zoological Park
*1980s–90s; NC 159 spur, 5 mi. S of
US 64, Asheboro vic.*

The 300-acre state zoo, famed for spacious,
natural habitats created for various species,

includes two notable buildings for that purpose. The **R. J. Reynolds Forest Aviary**
(1982; O'Brien/Atkins Associates [Chapel
Hill]) is a plexiglass geodesic dome that encloses an unbroken space, 55 feet high and
140 feet in diameter, where birds fly freely
and build their nests in the trees high above
visitors looking up from the winding paths.
The **African Pavilion** (1984; Hayes, Howell
& Assoc. [Southern Pines]) is a swooping
white tentlike structure of Teflon-coated
fiberglass, 350 feet long and 90 feet high.
The upper section contains a dark, humid
evocation of tropical rain forests, and the
lower portion is arid and open, with the
flora and fauna of savannahs and grasslands.

RD 10 *African Pavilion, N.C. Zoological Park*

RD 11 Randleman

Textile manufacturing here began in 1849
when 12 Quaker stockholders organized the
Union Mfg. Co. and built a 50-by-120-foot
mill, the largest in the antebellum county,
using advanced slow-burn mill construction. John B. Randleman and John H. Ferree bought the mill in 1868 and renamed
mill and town, centered on the **Randleman
Mfg. Co.** (est. 1849, 1880s and later; NW corner of High Point and Main Sts.). The old
mill burned in 1885 and was rebuilt on the
remaining walls and stone foundation; warehouses and other buildings also stand at the
site. The 2-story frame **John Randleman
House** (1849, 1870s; 215 Commonwealth
St.) began as a "manager's house," which
Randleman acquired and expanded into a
T-plan house with picturesque millwork.

Several other bracketed and decorated frame houses of mill owners and superintendents stand along **High Point St.**, as well as smaller houses for workers on High Point and nearby streets. A town landmark is **St. Paul's Methodist Episcopal Church** (1879; Peter Clark, brickmason; Allen Redding, carpenter; Jule Korner, decorator; sw corner High Point and Stout Sts.), donated by Randleman and Ferree as the first brick church in the county. It retains portions of an elaborate interior paint scheme of trompe l'oeil marble in Gothic themes, executed by "Reuben Rink"—Jule Korner of Kernersville, decorator for the Piedmont industrialists (*Korner's Folly). After Randleman's

RD 11 *St. Paul's Methodist Episcopal Church*

death in 1879 (and burial at St. Paul's), Ferree and other associates added 2-story mills of standard brick mill construction, including **Plaidville Mfg. Co.** (1886; Poplar St.) and **Mary Antoinette Mill** (1895; Plaid St.). Downstream, **Naomi Falls Mfg. Co.** (1879–80 and later; E. Naomi St.) was begun by Randleman and Ferree and completed by the latter at Naomi Falls of the Deep River, named for Naomi Wise, who drowned nearby in 1808 (*Providence Friends Meeting); the altered mill and scattered 2-story millworkers' houses and other buildings remain.

RD 12 Worthville
1880s; SR 2122 on Deep River

In a village that remained independent until 1986, the **John M. Worth Mfg. Co. Mill** by

the Deep River illustrates the continuous growth of 19th-c. mills, with a series of sections in brick, Italianate style. The adjoining village, still a distinct community, includes millworkers' houses of two main types: 2-story, center-hall plan dwellings with kitchen wings, similar to those at Naomi, and more numerous 1-story versions.

RD 13 Lee and Elizabeth Petty House and Richard Petty Museum
Early 20th c.; N side SR 2101, 0.4 mi. E of US 220 BUS, Level Cross; house private, museum open to public

Set under big shade trees, the frame bungalow typifies thousands of modest early 20th-c. farmhouses, but this one has a special place in NASCAR racing history as home to the sport's most famous family and a testament to the rural roots of stock car racing. The house was built by the parents of Elizabeth Toomes Petty, whose husband Lee joined the racing circuit in 1948. By the end of the century four generations of Pettys collected over 270 wins, with their son "King" Richard Petty's 200 victories making him NASCAR's most successful driver. The museum in the converted garage contains race cars and Petty family and NASCAR memorabilia. The museum may be moved to Randleman.

RD 14 Providence Friends Meeting
Est. 1760s; 1929; S side SR 2114, 1.1 mi. E of SR 2106, Level Cross vic.

Part of the crescent of Quaker settlement reaching across northern Randolph from Guilford to Chatham and Alamance counties, Providence is one of several early meetings that continue in 20th-c. brick buildings, in this case a simple Gothic Revival style structure with tower and steeple. Friends in Providence community met from 1762 and built a meetinghouse in 1769. In the cemetery across the road is the grave of Naomi Wise (d. 1807), heroine of the state's oldest known ballad, "Little Omi," recorded by Doc Watson and others. Naomi died in the Deep River when her lover Jonathan Lewis "kissed her and hugged her and turned her around, and threw her in deep waters where she might drown."

RD 15 Melancthon Lutheran Church

1902; SW corner SR 2442 and SR 2261, Liberty vic.

Formed from *Richland Lutheran Church after a doctrinal split among N.C. Lutherans in 1820, the congregation built its first church here in 1849, naming it for Philip Melancthon, associate of Martin Luther. The frame country church with entrance tower, along with its sheltered outdoor tables for covered-dish dinners and its adjacent cemetery, are carefully tended and used for reunions.

RD 16 Sandy Creek Baptist Meeting House

1820s; NE corner SR 2459 and SR 2442, Liberty vic.

The little building is a landmark in Baptist history and one of N.C.'s best examples of the simple meetinghouse form. The church was founded in 1755 by Shubal Stearns, a charismatic Separate Baptist minister from Boston whose "tones were . . . captivating, and his eyes seemed to have had almost magical power over those upon whom they were fixed." By 1772 Sandy Creek had become "mother, grandmother, and great grandmother to 42 churches" from the Chesapeake to the Mississippi. In 1830 the Sandy Creek Association took part in founding the Southern Baptist Convention. According to tradition this little 20-by-25-foot log structure—the third built for the

RD 16 *Sandy Creek Baptist Meeting House*

congregation—was erected in 1822 or 1826; it was weatherboarded in 1870 and later covered with asphalt sheathing. In 1836 the congregation split, with the Sandy Creek Primitive Baptist congregation keeping the old church but now worshiping in a nearby ca. 1940 frame building.

RD 17 Liberty

The archetypal turn-of-the-century railroad town focuses on the **Liberty Depot** (ca. 1905; 156 W. Swannanoa St.), the only remaining depot of the Cape Fear & Yadkin Valley Railroad's route across northeast Randolph Co. The line organized in 1879 had origins in antebellum efforts to link the Yadkin and Cape Fear rivers. The first section, built in 1884 from Fayetteville to Greensboro, brought rail service to Randolph Co. and a vital outlet for textile products; in 1888 it was completed from Mount Airy to Wilmington. The depot has a characteristic deep roof with braces supporting broad eaves and a turret atop the trackside observation bay. Likewise typical of the 1880s–1920s rail era, the commercial district on Swannanoa St. retains original brick and pressed-metal storefronts, and more than a dozen substantial frame houses with wide, decorated porches line up overlooking the tracks on Asheboro St. The **Dr. A. J. Patterson House** (ca. 1884; S. Patterson St.) is a simple 2-room dwelling from the early days restored as a local museum.

RD 18 Richland Lutheran Church (Richland Gospel Church)

1849; S side SR 2418, 1.2 mi. E of SR 2417, Liberty vic.

At the southern edge of the extended German settlement between the Haw and Deep rivers (*Old Brick Church, Guilford Co.), in 1760 Lutheran and Reformed Germans began a union church called Barton's Meeting House. In the 1790s the Lutherans built their own meetinghouse at this site, and in 1849 they voted to erect a new one, apparently the present-day austere gable-fronted frame structure with small belfry.

RD 19 Cedar Falls

Est. 1836; SR 2226 and SR 2144 at Deep River

The picturesque valley illustrates the development of the region's isolated waterpowered mill villages. Here in 1836 members of the Elliott and Horney families established the county's first mill, the **Cedar Falls Mfg. Co.** (1846 and later; SR 2144), which opened in a frame mill in 1837. In 1846 the company replaced it with a 3-story brick mill 50 by 100 feet, the largest in the county. Some of its 1:3 bond brick walls survive within 1950s expansions, plus portions of the dam and millrace. The most prominent antebellum building is the **Lawrence-Wrenn House** (ca. 1850; N side SR 2226, 0.7 mi. E of SR 2141), a frame 2-story Greek Revival house unusually stylish for the county, featuring pedimented ends, a central-passage plan, and details from Asher Benjamin's *Practical House Carpenter*. Showing a direct New England influence, it was built for Austin Lawrence, a New Hampshire manufacturer who bought property here in 1848 and in 1852 advertised for sale his new house "finished in the latest style," with linked kitchen and other outbuildings, "in a romantic part of the village."

In 1895 a second mill was built to the east, under superintendent Orlando R. Cox: the **Sapona Mfg. Co.** (SR 2226), a 1-story brick structure later expanded and given a bracketed, domed entrance tower. The **Cox House** (ca. 1895; SR 2221), built on a hilltop for the superintendent, is a big, rambling, frame Queen Anne style dwelling with wraparound porch. The former **Cedar Falls**

Post Office (ca. 1890; SR 2226) is a small frame building with parapet false front built against a steep hillside. Other 19th-c. houses, warehouses, and Baptist and Methodist churches complete the village.

RD 20 Franklinville

The small town along the hills overlooking the Deep River encompasses two antebellum textile mills established by Quaker entrepreneurs: Franklinsville (original spelling) and Island Ford, each with its own village. Despite losses and changes, the town has the chief grouping of antebellum mill architecture—over 2 dozen structures—in the state. At the west end the **Franklinville Mfg. Co.** or "Upper Mill" retains portions of the original 1838–40 stone and brick mill—an 80-by-40-foot, 3-story "factory house" burned and rebuilt in 1850s—amid later 19th-c. expansions. Elisha Coffin, descendant of Quakers from Nantucket and owner of a gristmill on the property from 1821, was a founder of the mill. Only the dam and race survive at the site of the Island Ford or "Lower Mill" (1846, rebuilt 1895; NC 22 at Academy St.), begun in 1846 by Elisha Coffin, George Makepeace, Thomas Rice, and others. For these Quaker industrialists, Moses Brown, Quaker founder of Slater Mill in Rhode Island, was a heroic model.

Many elements of the antebellum and later 19th-c. mill villages flank NC 22 (Main St.). A rare survival of a once numerous breed are four small hall-plan frame mill houses of ca. 1838–40—**"Cotton Row"**—on W. Main St. Also on the west, near the

RD 19 *Lawrence-Wrenn House*

RD 20 *Coffin-Makepeace House*

Upper Mill are 2-story, antebellum frame houses built for mill owners and managers and expanded and adorned for their successors; late 19th-c. porch trim came from the local Bush Creek Lumber Co., est. ca. 1872. The oldest is the **Julian House**, a late Federal period house, with flush sheathing across the facade behind a late 19th-c. porch. The **Curtis-Blue House** was greatly expanded about 1880.

On a hill above the village, the **Coffin-Makepeace House** was built ca. 1840 for founder Elisha Coffin with details from Asher Benjamin's patternbook; after conflicts over the issue of slavery, he moved to *New Garden in Guilford Co. near other family members. The house was occupied after 1850 by mill engineer George Makepeace, whose son George Henry added the broad, ornate 2-tier porch. Grandson Charles R. Makepeace, born here, became a nationally leading mill designer headquartered in Providence, R.I., who designed several N.C. mills.

At the town center stands **Hank's Lodge** (1850; Spencer M. Dorsett & Thomas W. Allred, builders), a rare example of an antebellum fraternal lodge for an industrial community; the 40-by-20-foot temple-form structure was built in simplified Greek Revival style by local carpenters on a contract of $1,350. The brick **Methodist Church**

(1912; J. H. Burrow, brickmason; D. A. Curtis, carpenter; Main St.) features a corner tower entering an auditorium plan sanctuary with adjoining Akron-plan Sunday school. At the east end at Academy St., and up the hill to the north of Main St., along Rose and Weatherly Sts. are 19th-c. millworkers' houses and those of various local entrepreneurs.

RD 21 Ramseur

Located south of US 64 is an especially well-preserved mill village, informally arranged on the hillside down to the Deep River. The raison d'être is the **Deep River–Columbia Mfg. Co.** (1850–1963; SE side Main St., SR 2615 at Deep River). Here at Allen's Fall the Deep River Mfg. Co. began by 1850 and within a decade had 20 looms and 1,056 spindles operated by 9 men and 42 women. Reorganized after the Civil War by W. H. Watkins as the Columbia Mfg. Co., it grew to 300 looms and 10,000 spindles by 1900 and closed in 1963. The riverside complex offers a microcosm of mill development. The 1850 **Deep River Mill** is among the most intact antebellum mills in N.C.: a simple rectangular building, 2 stories tall, of 1:3 common-bond brick with rectangular sash windows and heavy tapering wooden support columns. A third story and 3-story ad-

RD 21 *Deep River–Columbia Mfg. Co. Mill*

dition from ca. 1880 are distinguished by 1:6 bond brickwork and segmental-arched windows. The engine house and picker house were built before 1885; the 4-story stair tower, ca. 1885–88. There are also warehouses, a superintendent's office, and a pump house.

In the town—named by mill owner Watkins in honor of his friend Confederate officer Stephen Ramseur (d. 1864)—the commercial district on Main St. includes the **Company Store** and other brick and frame structures of the late 19th and early 20th centuries. **Jordan Memorial Methodist Church** (1896–97) is a handsome Gothic Revival frame church with a prominent corner tower. A local museum occupies the tiny frame **Post Office** (ca. 1880) behind the public library. On streets that fan out from the mill stands an excellent collection of houses from the 1880s onward, including the dwellings of millworkers, managers, owners, and local merchants. Workers' houses are generally 2-story frame dwellings with center passages, while managers' and owners' houses are often L- and T-shaped, 2-story houses in Italianate and Queen Anne styles, as seen on Main, Coleridge, Liberty, and Oliver Sts. The **W. H. Watkins House** (ca. 1885; 901 Main St.) has been altered as part of a funeral home.

RD 22 Marley House

Ca. 1816, mid-19th c., ca. 1920; N side US 64, just W of Chatham Co. line; private, visible from road

Located on the old stage road from Raleigh to Charlotte, the unpretentious farmhouse is a landmark on US 64, which runs past scores of typical Piedmont farmsteads. In a familiar story of gradual expansion, the house was begun ca. 1816 when Thomas Marley, an enterprising young farmer and miller, built a 1-room, V-notched log dwelling on a 211-acre tract inherited from his father. He soon doubled his acreage, raising livestock, grains, and some tobacco and cotton; he also ran a stagecoach stop, a post office, and a store at "Marleys Mills." He accordingly expanded the house into a 2-story frame dwelling by the 1840s and added the rear ell. His son, who was born here in 1862 and lived here

until his death in 1944, added the porch ca. 1920. Among the outbuildings are two early 19th-c. log structures from Chatham Co.

RD 23 Beane-Cox Mill

Early 20th c.; E side SR 2657, 2.5 mi. SE of SR 1003; private, visible from road

Built by Allison Beane and later run by Raymond Cox, the gristmill operated into the 1980s. The tall, stark frame structure typifies mills abundant in the Piedmont from the 18th through the early 20th c. Until 1945 it was powered by an iron overshot Fitch waterwheel made in Hanover, Pa., which remains in place.

RD 24 Hinshaw Farm

Ca. 1885; N side SR 2656, 1.2 mi. E of SR 1003; private, visible from road

The farmstead in the heart of a rural Quaker settlement centers on a substantial frame house with tri-gabled roofline and fine sawnwork porch and bracketed roofline. Twin front doors open into two equal rooms, a contrast to the usual center-passage plan. A small antebellum house stands to the rear. Across the road is a massive barn with unusual wagon ramp rising to the second story, a scheme unique in the region and attributed to ideas Thomas Hinshaw, a Quaker, brought back from Indiana after refugeeing there during the Civil War along with other local Quakers. In 1866 he do-

RD 24 *Hinshaw Farm*

nated a site for the small, 1-story frame **Evergreen Academy** (1867), established with support of the Baltimore Association of Friends as part of their efforts to aid the war-torn South (*Model Farm, Guilford Co.). The school operated for some 40 years.

RD 25 Coleridge
Est. 1882; NC 42 and NC 22 at Deep River

The quiet community is a nearly complete survival of a small late 19th-c. riverside textile mill village. Near the old Foust's Mill site, the **Enterprise Mfg. Co.** was established here in 1882, and its village was named for mill founder James Cole. Beginning with a 2-story frame structure and 26 workers, the plant expanded gradually, especially after Dr. Robert Caveness purchased majority interest from his father-in-law Cole. Most of the principal buildings, built in brick in Romanesque industrial style, date from the early 20th c. From the Caveness era are the large brick mill (NC 42), company store, office, bank, warehouse, and pump and power houses. North on SR 2652 is the frame **Concord Methodist Episcopal Church** (early 20th c.), with towers opening into an auditorium plan sanctuary and Akron-plan Sunday school, home of a congregation established at Foust's Mill in 1825. Mill houses, concentrated near the church and east of the mill along SR 1005, take varied forms, adorned with sawn and turned work. Dr. Caveness and his brother, a vice-president at the mill, built big Queen Anne style frame residences lavishly finished with brackets and other ornate millwork, of which the brother's **John Caveness House** (SE corner NC 22/902 and SR 1005) is the more visible.

RD 26 Yow's Mill
Early 20th c.; N side SR 1002 at Fork Creek, 3.0 mi. E of NC 705, Seagrove vic.; private, visible from road

The frame gristmill is well maintained and picturesquely sited beside its stone dam, where the first mill began in 1820. It now houses a pottery.

RD 27 Fair Grove Methodist Church
1900; S side SR 1002, 0.1 mi. E of NC 705, Seagrove vic.

Epitomizing the frame country church with its simple pointed windows and entrance giving a Gothic Revival touch, this is the third church on the site, where the early 20th-c. Why Not Academy and Business Institute operated in a schoolhouse on the grounds.

RD 28 Pisgah Covered Bridge
Ca. 1910; J. J. Welch, builder; S side SR 1114, 1.6 mi. W of SR 1109, Pisgah; private, visible from road

The 40-foot bridge is one of only two covered bridges left of hundreds that once stood in the state (*Bunker Hill Bridge, Catawba Co.). Evidently privately built, it has 4 dry-wall stone piers supporting the bridge, a modified queen-post truss system, and braces sheathed to form small buttresslike supports.

RD 29 Parker's Mill Bridge
1924; Grady L. Bain, consulting engineer; Steel and Lebby (Knoxville, Tenn.), contractors; SR 1314 over Uwharrie River

The double-span concrete spandrel-arch bridge characterizes the handsome bridges of the 1920s "Good Roads" era that transformed the state.

RD 30 Jess Robbins Farm and William Kearns Farm
19th–early 20th c.; N side US 64, 1.0 mi. W of SR 1318; private, visible from road

Set against Mt. Shepherd, the tallest peak in the Uwharrie chain, are two especially fine farmsteads with rolling fields and extensive collections of outbuildings from mixed agriculture, including a large gambrel-roofed barn and a slatted corncrib. The farmhouses exemplify a form popular among substantial farmers: the 2-story frame dwelling with a raised central gable and a wide porch adorned with sawn and turned millwork. The Kearns House (E) includes a small, ca. 1845 hall-parlor plan dwelling and a 2-story section of ca. 1890. The Robbins house (w) is a T-shaped residence built ca. 1900.

RD 31 Dr. A. C. Bulla House

1844; NW corner SR 1004 and SR 1416, Asheboro vic.; private, visible from road

In 1844 physician Bulla built his 2-story, 3-room plan house, with an engaged porch of a type more common in the coastal plain than the Piedmont. Like many country doctors, he built a small frame office but raised it about 4 feet off the ground, supposedly to protect patients' privacy.

RD 32 Harper House

Ca. 1815, ca. 1830; S side SR 1556, 1.1 mi. E of SR 1547, Archdale vic.; private, visible from road

The 2-story frame Federal style plantation house was built in two stages for Jeduthan Harper or his son Jesse, large landowners active in local politics.

RD 33 Moses Hammond House

Ca. 1880; N side NC 62 just W of US 311, Archdale; open as bank

One of the last 19th-c. survivors of the old Quaker community of Archdale, now remade by highways, the elaborate Italianate house with projecting central bay and flanking porches was built for the manager of

W. C. Petty & Co. The regionally important sash and blind factory was begun in 1866 by Hammond and his Petty brothers-in-law, who had manufactured shoe pegs for Confederate soldiers during the war. The house presents a catalog of the firm's products: tapered porch posts, brackets with drop pendants, pedimented window frames, moldings, mantels, and staircase. Hammond headed the state temperance union and was a prohibitionist candidate for lieutenant governor in 1888.

RD 34 Trinity

The town was the site of the forerunner of Duke University. The school was founded in 1838 as Union Institute, a rural subscription school, and by the 1850s flourished as Trinity College under the leadership of president Braxton Craven. Drawn by donations of land and money by Washington Duke, Julian Carr, and others, the college relocated to Durham in 1892 and evolved into Duke University. None of the academic buildings survives, but several late 19th-c. frame dwellings housed faculty. The **Stephen B. Weeks House** (ca. 1870; E side NC 62), a 2-story L-plan house with inset porch, was briefly home to the eminent N.C. historian who taught at Trinity before moving with the school to Durham.

Guilford County (GF)

See Marvin A. Brown, Greensboro: An Architectural Record *(1995); Ruth Little-Stokes,* An Inventory of Historic Architecture: Greensboro, North Carolina *(1976); and H. McKelden Smith,* Architectural Resources: An Inventory of Historic Architecture *(1979).*

Established in 1771 from parts of Orange and Rowan counties, Guilford Co. is watered by tributaries of the Deep and Haw rivers and crossed by ancient trails that became the routes of intersecting railroads and highways. Beginning in the 1740s its farmland attracted clusters of European settlers, who soon built their first churches: German Reformed and Lutherans in the east, British Quakers in the south and west, and Scotch-Irish Presbyterians in the central portion and beyond. They established a strong tradition of log construction and in the early 19th c. erected substantial brick houses, typically with 2- or 3-room plans and fine brickwork. The first Guilford Courthouse was in the western section, but after Randolph (1779) and Rockingham (1785) counties were partitioned off, a more "suitable and centrical" seat was located at Greensboro in 1808. After the North Carolina Railroad (NCRR) crossed the county (1851–56), Greensboro grew into a major rail and industrial center, and High Point emerged as a competitive textile and furniture manufacturing city. Some areas remain rural, with small farms and country stores and churches, but major highways and suburban growth altered much of the county in the late 20th c.

Greensboro (GF 1–34)

Greensboro was a small county seat and trading town from 1808 until the end of the 19th c., when "the Gate City to the Piedmont" took off as a regional focus of manufacturing, commerce, and higher education. It grew from 3,000 people in 1890 to 16,000 in 1910 and 53,000 by 1930, exceeded only by Winston-Salem and Charlotte. The city's identity reflected both the energy and power of its businesses and the cultural and reform influences of its educational and religious institutions. A few landmarks remain from the small antebellum town, but the city's architectural strength is in the imposing downtown buildings, diverse suburbs, and large textile mill villages from the late 19th and especially the early 20th c.

Named for Gen. Nathanael Greene, hero of the nearby Battle of Guilford Courthouse (1781), the town at the crossing of several coach and wagon roads drew pioneering industrialists and educators as well as the usual lawyers and tradespeople. In 1828 Henry Humphreys founded the Mount Hecla mill,

the state's first steam-powered cotton mill, which inspired other Piedmont industrialists, such as E. M. Holt (*Alamance). Quakers began *Guilford College west of town in 1834, and Methodists founded a female academy in 1833 and *Greensboro College for women in 1838. In 1851 ground was broken in Greensboro for the NCRR, which was routed through town thanks in part to resident John Motley Morehead, NCRR president, former governor, and industrialist (*Leaksville, *Spray). The first trains met near Jamestown in 1856, setting the stage for industrial and commercial growth. For years the town remained a village with two principal streets lined by trees and widely spaced wooden houses.

During the 1880s, as the state's rail network thickened, Greensboro became a hub. Three lines intersected on S. Elm St.: the NCRR, the Cape Fear & Yadkin Valley Railroad (1888), and the Richmond & Danville Railroad; the city was also served by the Piedmont Railroad (1864) and the Northwestern N.C. Railroad (1890). As in Charlotte, multiple rail connections offering

GF 7 *Elm Street*

competitive rates to bring in coal and take out goods attracted manufacturers and merchants of textiles and tobacco, brick and tile, furniture, textile mill bobbins, flour, and myriad other goods.

The 1890s expanded the scale of transportation, business, and education. In 1895 the railroad lines were consolidated into Southern Railway, which made Greensboro a major stop and transfer center. In 1893 Baltimore merchants Moses and Ceasar Cone opened a local branch of their New York cotton marketing firm and soon founded the first of their large textile mills, which with their villages formed a separate city northeast of town. Other textile and clothing manufacturers soon followed, and in 1935 J. Spencer Love (*Burlington) moved the headquarters of Burlington Mills to Greensboro. The 1890s also brought to town pharmacist Lunsford Richardson (#Selma, N.C.), whose cold salve, Vick's VapoRub, began the Vick Chemical Co. In the 1890s, too, the first major insurance companies started in Greensboro, which by the 1910s was a capital of southern insurance companies, including the Dixie Fire, Pilot Life, and Jefferson Standard firms. Thousands of workers flocked to town, expanding the city and its industrial character.

In addition to Greensboro College, Bennett Seminary for black women was established in 1873 and became *Bennett College in 1926. In the 1890s, when the state legislature authorized a normal school for white women and a land grant school for black students, Greensboro won both: *University of North Carolina at Greensboro (UNCG) and *North Carolina Agricultural & Technical State University (A&T). "Progressive Greensboro" was often cited as one of a dynamic Piedmont triad: Greensboro for textiles, High Point for furniture, and Winston-Salem for tobacco. In the mid-20th c. its strong black and white schools and congregations made it important in the Civil Rights movement as site of the successful, nonviolent 1960 sit-ins at the *Woolworth's lunch counter.

From the little antebellum town only a few buildings remain (*Blandwood). The architectural heritage from the post-1880 growth years, mainly the 1910s and 1920s, displays popular national styles in works chiefly by resident architects. As the old pattern of mixed uses, races, and classes began

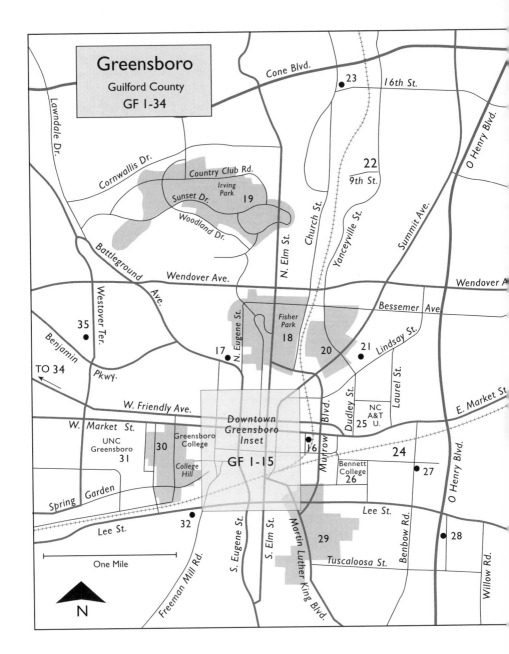

Greensboro
Guilford County
GF 1-34

Lawndale Dr.

Cone Blvd.

• 23   16th St.

O. Henry Blvd.

Cornwallis Dr.

Country Club Rd.

Irving Park

Sunset Dr.   19

Woodland Dr.

22
9th St.

Church St.

Yanceyville St.

Summit Ave.

N. Elm St.

Battleground Ave.

Wendover Ave.

Wendover A

Bessemer Ave.

Westover Ter.

35 •

Fisher Park
18

Benjamin Pkwy.

TO 34

17 • N. Eugene St.

20   21 • Lindsay St.

Laurel St.

W. Friendly Ave.

Downtown Greensboro Inset

GF 1-15

Dudley St.

NC A&T U.
25 •

E. Market St.

W. Market St.

UNC Greensboro
31

30

Greensboro College

College Hill

16

Murrow Blvd.

24

O Henry Blvd.

Bennett College
26

• 27

Spring Garden

32 •

Lee St.

29

Lee St.

Benbow Rd.

• 28

Willow Rd.

One Mile

S. Eugene St.

S. Elm St.

Martin Luther King Blvd.

Tuscaloosa St.

Freeman Mill Rd.

N

to break up in the late 19th c., suburbs developed. Several neighborhoods focused around schools, including *College Hill near *Greensboro College and UNCG on the west, and Dudley St., Nocho Park, and others near *Bennett College and A&T on the east. Beginning in 1902, electric streetcar lines led from downtown to white suburbs to the south, north, and west, and garden

suburbs of increasing opulence (*Fisher Park, *Irving Park) reached north and west. Workers' housing along the railroads included *Pomona on the west and the Cone-Sternberger textile empire on the northeast.

The city gained a few buildings from distant urban design firms—Hobart Upjohn of New York, Sidney W. Foulk of New Castle, Pa., Charles Barton Keen of Philadelphia,

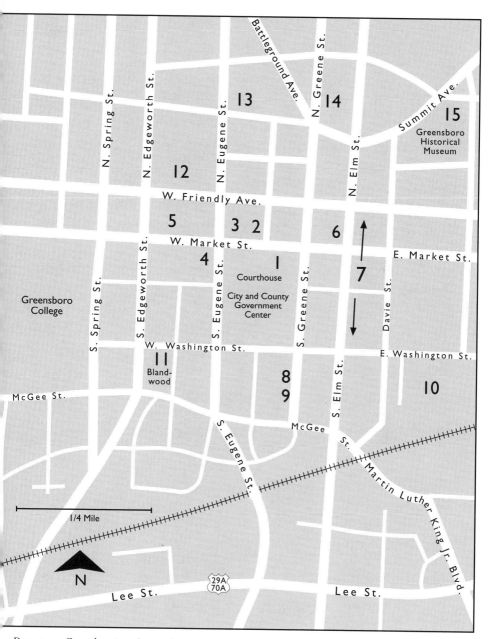

Downtown Greensboro inset (GF 1–15)

and later, Eduardo Catalano of Cambridge —but most Greensboro clients relied on local firms founded by architects who had moved from other cities. Prominent in the boom years were W. C. Bain, a builder-architect and manufacturer also active in Durham and elsewhere; Orlo Epps, an Indiana architect trained at Cornell, who arrived ca. 1890; and architect Frank A. Weston, who came from Denver ca. 1904. The 1910s and 1920s attracted Harry Barton of Philadelphia and Charles C. Hartmann of New York, both trained in the Beaux Arts tradition.

Weathering changes in the textile business and shifts in its economic base, Greensboro ranked among the state's largest cities from 1930 onward, and as of 2000 its population of nearly 224,000 placed it third in size. In the late 20th c., Greensboro saw its share of losses to freeways and urban renewal, but local preservationists have also saved and rejuvenated key elements of its 19th- and early 20th-c. urban heritage.

Downtown Greensboro

GF 1 Guilford County Courthouse and Guilford County–Greensboro Government Center

Courthouse, 1918–20; Harry Barton, architect; William P. Rose, builder; Government Center, 1969–73; Eduardo Catalano and Peter Sugar (Cambridge, Mass.), with McMinn, Norfleet & Wicker (Greensboro), architects; W. Market St.

The first courthouses stood at Market and Elm Sts., until Jefferson Standard bought the site and a new location was selected on W. Market St. Harry Barton, a native of Philadelphia who had worked in the office of the supervising architect of the Treasury, saw Greensboro as "a city with a future" and moved there in 1912, working first with Frank Weston, then establishing his own firm that produced many courthouses, schools, churches, and residences. He gave his adopted county a Beaux Arts edifice in keeping with Greensboro's emerging stature: a 3½-story stone-clad building with Ionic porticoes front and back and pilasters carrying an enriched entablature beneath a balustraded attic story. In the mid-20th c. a city-county government facility was designed to fill the block, while Barton's courthouse was

GF 1 *Guilford Co. Courthouse*

retained. Noted modernist architect Eduardo Catalano, a native of Argentina who had taught at the North Carolina State University (NCSU) School of Design, planned the large-scale complex of cast-in-place concrete, with bold, stepped-back masses and flexible interior spaces, arranged around the old courthouse and an open plaza.

GF 2 West Market St. Methodist Church

Begun 1893; Sidney W. Foulk (New Castle, Pa.), architect; 302 W. Market St.

Although many 19th-c. urban congregations erected big Romanesque Revival churches, most have been lost, leaving this imposing building as one of the state's prime examples. Architect Foulk designed church and college buildings in Virginia and the Carolinas as well as Pennsylvania. Built of dark red brick and trimmed in rough granite in a somewhat Germanic Romanesque mode, it has broad gables alternating with swelling curves of the corner towers and round-arched entry. The massive tower and high roof feature copper cupolas and gable ornaments. The classic auditorium-Akron plan combines a curved and sloped sanctuary with a Sunday school with small classrooms around a central space. Partitions open to form a "vast auditorium to seat 2,000"—for a city of about 10,000. The $52,000 project in the depressed mid-1890s benefited workers and suppliers: woodwork from the Bain Building Co., brick from the Kirkpatrick Brick Yard, and granite from #Mount Airy. The 68 stained glass windows came from the German Pavilion at the World Columbian Exposition of 1893. The congregation built Greensboro's first church and established *Greensboro College in the 1830s. (See Introduction, Fig. 64.)

GF 3 U.S. Post Office and Courthouse (Federal Building)

1931–33; James A. Wetmore, supervising architect of the Treasury; 324 W. Market St.

Epitome of the Moderne classicism of the 1930s and one of the state's finest buildings from the depression years, the stone-clad

Federal building combines symmetrical classical organization with crisp Art Deco details in Mount Airy granite, limestone, marble, bronze, and polished aluminum. Its design struck a local newspaper writer in 1933 as an "extreme . . . departure from the enduring canons of the art." The contrast with "spirit-entrancing curves of the courthouse's embellishments" all too honestly expressed "our day and generation." (See Introduction, Fig. 64.)

GF 4 Southern Bell Office Building

1929; Marye Alger & Vinour (Atlanta), architects; 124 S. Eugene St.

Southern Bell Co. of Atlanta employed the Atlanta architects to plan facilities in many towns, using the Art Deco style to suggest the telephone's modernity and speed. The 6-story yellow brick building features carved stone spandrels and an ornate frame at the Eugene St. entrance.

GF 5 Masonic Temple

1928; John B. Crawford (attrib.); 426 W. Market St.

The 3-story marble and granite facade with pediment and Ionic columns above a rusticated base dignifies the large brick building. It was erected by the Masonic Temple Co., led by Jefferson Standard's Julian Price and other businessmen.

Elm St.:
Elm St. is one of the state's prime stretches of commercial architecture from the heyday of Main St. As the city blossomed as a regional retail center, leaders were so proud of their commercial street that about 1889 its namesake elm trees were "cut away to bring into full view the long lines of three-story brick stores." The northern blocks developed as a financial sector, with retail trade to the south near the railroad. Banks, drugstores, clothing stores, groceries, variety stores, restaurants, soda shops, hotels, and professional offices lined the busy street throughout the first six decades of the 20th c., before downtown gave way to the suburbs. Plain brick 3-story buildings survive from the 1880s, and more ornate iron- or stone-trimmed

ones endure from the 1890s. In the 1900s terracotta ornament was introduced, heights increased, and architect-designed buildings became more elaborate while standard commercial buildings grew plainer. Facades in round-arched Romanesque, Italianate, and Renaissance Revival styles were built to suit the princes of commerce.

GF 6 Jefferson Standard Building and Jefferson-Pilot Building

Jefferson Standard, 1923; Charles C. Hartmann, architect; 101 N. Elm St. (at Market St.); Jefferson-Pilot, 1988–90; Smallwood Reynolds Stewart & Stewart (Atlanta), architects; 100 N. Greene St.

The premier Beaux Arts skyscraper in the state, the Jefferson Standard Building still dominates the skyline, along with its tall younger companion. There were insurance companies in the city from the 1890s onward, but in 1912 the Raleigh-based Jefferson Standard Life Insurance Co. merged with Greensboro companies, moved its headquarters to the city, and emerged as a major

GF 6 *Jefferson Standard Building*

national firm. In 1922 company president Julian Price, struck by the talent of young New York architect Hartmann, who was in Greensboro to supervise construction of W. L. Stoddart's O. Henry Hotel (1918–19, razed), offered Hartmann the plum commission to design the prestigious skyscraper, on condition that he move to Greensboro. Hartmann accepted and continued work here for 40 years.

When completed in 1923, the 17-story U-shaped structure was the tallest building in the state and allegedly the South. The plan assured abundant light and air to the offices. The twin steel and brick towers mount from a shared base, their verticality elegantly expressed in alternating stout and slender piers that soar to great round arches beneath a heavy entablature. The granite and terra-cotta facades combine Gothic, Romanesque, and Renaissance detail. A bust of Thomas Jefferson crowns the entrance, and buffalo nickels adorn windows at ground level. In the 1980s the company built a second, slightly taller tower that reiterates Hartmann's themes in precast concrete.

GF 7 Elm St. Commercial Buildings

In the 100 block facing the *Jefferson Standard Building are other financial institutions, including the **American Exchange National Bank Building** (1920; 100–102 N. Elm St.), a crisply detailed 9-story classical skyscraper faced in limestone, and the **Piedmont Building** (ca. 1927; 114 N. Elm St.), 6 stories in brick with classical motifs in polychrome terra-cotta.

The **F. W. Woolworth Building** (1929; Charles C. Hartmann, architect; 132 S. Elm St.), a 2-story building faced in stone with classical–Art Deco motifs, is a landmark in the American Civil Rights movement: on Feb. 1, 1960, four students from A&T began peaceful sit-ins at the lunch counter and thus launched the national nonviolent sit-in movement for integrated lunch counters. In 1990 participants gathered to commemorate the anniversary and dedicate memorials to Franklin McCain, Ezell Blair Jr., Joseph McNeil, David Richmond, and the movement they began. In a long-standing tradition,

the adjoining side street was named February One Place. A Civil Rights museum is planned.

Among several 2-story classical facades are the **Clegg Building** (ca. 1904; Frank A. Weston, architect; 123 S. Elm St.), by an architect fresh from Denver, and **Hobbs-Mendenhall Building** (1920s; 121 S. Elm St.), with arched windows and quoins in brick and terra-cotta. Here was the drugstore where William Sidney Porter (O. Henry) worked as a young man, and later pharmacist Lunsford Richardson formulated Vick's VapoRub, the basis of a pharmaceutical empire and philanthropic foundation. The **Dixie Fire Insurance Co. Building** (1904; Frank A. Weston, architect; 125 S. Elm St.) was at 6 stories a skyscraper in its day, with a 2-story base of rough stone arches beneath brick and terra-cotta, with polygonal bay windows on the south side. The **S. H. Kress & Co. Building** (1930; Edward F. Sibbert [New York], architect; 208 S. Elm St.) is the state's premier example of the Kress architect's vibrant Art Deco style, which distinguished the firm's colorful dime stores on main streets throughout America—when chain stores were a new phenomenon. The terra-cotta ornament in citrus colors was made by the Atlantic Terra Cotta Co. of Staten Island.

The 300–600 blocks called "Old Greensborough" have many handsome facades, some uncovered in the late 20th c. The 13-story brick **Greensboro Bank & Trust Co. Building (Guilford Building)** (1927; Charles C. Hartmann, architect; 301 S. Elm St.), which extended banking into a retail block, continues the Renaissance theme in brick, stone, and terra-cotta and a great 3-story glass-framed entrance. Smaller Renaissance and Romanesque facades include the **Bain Building** (ca. 1900; W. C. Bain; 302–4 S. Elm St.), occupied by the prominent local builder; the **Newell Building** (ca. 1900; 314–16 S. Elm St.), with 4-story Romanesque Revival facade in rusticated granite; and the **Odell Hardware Co.** (ca. 1885, ca. 1901; 325–27 S. Elm St.), where brothers James A. and John M. Odell had one of the South's largest hardware businesses (*Odell-Locke-Randolph Mill, Concord).

The **Greensboro Passenger Station I** (1900; 400 S. Elm St.), of red pressed brick, once featured a corner turret and covered platforms. South of the tracks brick commercial blocks continue. **Fordham's Drug Store** (ca. 1903; 514 S. Elm St.), in continuous operation since 1903, is an Italianate building with a mortar-and-pestle finial and period interior complete with soda fountain. The **Salvation Army Building** (1928; 520 S. Elm St.) has a somewhat domestic character in Mediterranean Revival yellow brick, and the **South Greensboro National Bank** (ca. 1918; 524 S. Elm St.) features an Ionic temple front. East of Elm, the **300 block of S. Davie St.** has 2-, 3-, and 4-story brick wholesale stores and warehouses. Davie is crossed by the **Southern Railway Overpass** (ca. 1920), a decorative iron structure, the result of suggestions by city planner Charles Robinson. West of Elm, the 3-story Italianate style building—now part of a small hotel—was erected as the **Cone Export & Commission Co. (#1)** (ca. 1902; 111 W. Washington St.) for Moses and Ceasar Cone.

GF 8 Carolina Theater

1927; J. H. DeSibour (Washington, D.C.), architect; 310 S. Greene St.

Designed by a Washington architect trained at the École des Beaux Arts, the theater presents a grand facade with fluted Ionic pilasters and broad pediment rendered in illusionistic stone-colored terra-cotta, with bright colors in the capitals, frieze, and acroteria. Lauded as the largest and finest in the Carolinas, the interior continues the stage-set-like effects, with "marble" columns and "stone" walls and classical figures. It was restored in 1977.

GF 9 Cone Export & Commission Building

Ca. 1924; 330 S. Greene St.

The Tudor Revival building, in English-bond red brick adorned with carved limestone window labels and oriel window, lent a traditional English aura to the German Bavarian family's textile empire. In 1890 Bal-timore businessmen Moses and Ceasar Cone, who had traveled widely in the South, established the Cone Export & Commission Co. in New York to market southern cotton fabrics; in 1893 they opened a Greensboro office for the proximity to cotton fields and railroads, and in 1895 they founded their own factories.

GF 10 Greensboro Passenger Station II

1927; Alfred Fellheimer & Steward Wagner (New York), architects; 300 E. Washington St.

The small Beaux Arts classical train station of red brick and pale stone presents an imposing Ionic portico to the long axis of Church St. Reflecting the city's prominence on the Southern Railway, it was designed by New York specialists in depots (*Union Station, Winston-Salem). It is under development for a transport center and a stop on the Boston-Atlanta high-speed route.

GF 10 *Southern Railway Passenger Station*

GF 11 Blandwood

1844–45; Alexander Jackson Davis (New York), architect; Joseph and William Conrad (Lexington), builders; 400 W. Washington St.; open regular hours; National Historic Landmark

Embodiment of the antebellum "spirit of improvement," Blandwood was among the first of architect A. J. Davis's towered Italianate villas. Published in A. J. Downing's *Treatise on Landscape Gardening*, it popularized the center-tower villa nationwide. When Davis first visited the state in 1844 (*Old East, *Old West, University of North Carolina [UNC]), Governor John Motley Morehead carried him to Greensboro to redesign his house. Morehead was a leading proponent of internal improvements, public education, and industrial development and later became president of the NCRR. As in other N.C. projects, Davis retained (in back) the existing building, a frame house formerly owned by Henry Humphreys, founder of the Mount Hecla Mill. To create a modern but economical exemplar of Morehead's progressive ideals, Davis added a symmetrical, simply detailed stuccoed brick villa with central entrance tower and arcades to flanking wings (reconstructed 1983). The two main rooms and center passage have bold woodwork and plaster ornament, with Tuscan pilasters framing bay windows and doorways. Builders Joseph and William Conrad, father and son, were part of a family who erected several major Piedmont buildings. Blandwood has been restored as headquarters of Preservation Greensboro, Inc. (See Introduction, Fig. 33.)

GF 12 Sherwood House
Ca. 1850; 426 W. Friendly Ave.

The 2-story brick house, associated with Lyndon Swaim and Michael Sherwood, publishers of the *Greensborough Patriot*, retains much of its simple Greek Revival character behind an early 20th-c. portico.

GF 13 Former Burlington Mills Headquarters
Ca. 1935; 301 N. Eugene St.

Many textile industrialists turned to the streamlined Moderne style during the 1930s, including J. Spencer Love, who established Burlington Mills in Burlington in the 1920s. When he moved his residence and company headquarters to Greensboro in 1935, he followed an emerging pattern of traditionalism for his suburban residence (*Irving Park) and modernism for business. The rectilinear building clad in cast stone has long bands of windows, aluminum trim, and curved corners at the entrance. Love propelled the company into the largest textile manufacturing firm in the world. In 1971 Burlington Industries moved into new headquarters at 3330 W. Friendly Ave.

GF 14 Central Fire Station
1926; Charles C. Hartmann, architect; 318 N. Greene St.

As the city rebuilt its municipal facilities in the 1910s and 1920s, Hartmann designed the fire station as a Renaissance palazzo, incorporating the fire engine bays into a stone arcade. Closed in 1980, its facade was fitted into a large hotel.

GF 15 Greensboro Historical Museum (First Presbyterian Church)
1892, L. B. Volk & Son (Brooklyn, N.Y.), architect; Porter & Godwin (Goldsboro), contractor; 1903, Hook & Sawyer, Charlotte, architects; W. C. Bain, contractor; 220 Church St.; open regular hours

The complex brick church developed in two main stages, both in Romanesque Revival style with round arches, stone trim, and dramatic rooflines. After the congregation moved to *Fisher Park, in 1938 the buildings were linked and renovated for a civic library and museum; a 1990 wing expanded the museum. Grounds include the early churchyard and 19th-c. log houses, both with V-notched logs and 1-room plans: the 2-story weatherboarded **McNairy House** and the 1-story **Isley House**, restored as a memorial to Dolley Madison, born 1768 in a Guilford Co. log house.

GF 16 Lyndon St. Townhouses
Ca. 1905; 195–201 Lyndon St.

Four 2-story brick townhouse apartments, rendered in pressed brick with marble trim, bay windows, and pedimented frontispieces, are unified by a 1-story Doric porch. Built for upper-income white residents and later the home of white and black workers, this is one of the few sets of late 19th- to early 20th-c. row housing in the state.

GF 17 Green Hill Cemetery Gatekeeper's Cottage
1888–89; William G. W. Jackson; 700 Battleground Ave.

When the civic cemetery was established in 1887, chairman Judge David Schenck described the "Cottage for the Keeper of the Cemetery" as a "Gothic structure"—a mode oft chosen for picturesque 19th-c. cemeteries. The steep-gabled cross-plan house with delicate bargeboards typifies the cottages popularized in the 1840s by A. J. Davis and A. J. Downing; a Tudor arch frames angled doorways into the residence and office.

GF 18 Fisher Park

One of the state's premier streetcar suburbs, Fisher Park was envisioned ca. 1890 by entrepreneur Basil F. Fisher. Less than a mile north of the town center, the area seemed remote to some, and investment flagged after the panic of 1893. Only after the streetcar line was built in 1902 and Fisher left for New York (donating land for a city park and selling the rest) did construction begin in earnest along the curving streets. Representative of early work is the gambrel-roofed, shingled **Frank A. Weston House** (ca. 1909; 214 S. Park Dr.), home of the architect who built other homes in the neighborhood. The remarkably varied houses range from wonderfully robust Craftsman bungalows (cf. **512 Simpson St.** and **211 East Hendrix St.**) to creative renditions of Colonial Revival styles, such as **314 Isabel St.**, with a portico that outstrips the house. The **John Galloway House** (1919; Harry Barton, architect; Andrew Leopold Schlosser, stonemason; 1007 N. Elm St.), a granite building in Tudor Revival with red tile roof, was built for a tobacco broker by a noted local stonemason. Fisher Park Circle around the park has especially imposing buildings. The **James E. Latham House** (1913; Wells L. Brewer [Greensboro], architect; Andrew Leopold Schlosser, stonemason; 412 Fisher Park Cir.) is an opulent and unusual stone rendition of the Prairie style built for a financier and cotton broker instrumental in development of the neighborhood (#Tryon Palace). **Hillside** (1929; Charles C. Hartmann; 301 Fisher Park Cir.) is a Tudor Revival mansion designed for Julian Price, president of *Jefferson Standard Life Insurance Co., by the architect of the company headquarters.

Prestigious congregations enhanced the

GF 18 *First Presbyterian Church*

neighborhood and northward suburban growth. **Holy Trinity Episcopal Church** (1922, 1949; Hobart Upjohn [New York], architect; N. Greene and W. Fisher Sts.) is a small stone church in Gothic Revival style. The Greensboro Hebrew Congregation, chartered in 1909 by the Cones, Sternbergers, and others, employed the same architect for **Temple Emanuel** (1923–25; Hobart Upjohn, architect; N. Greene and Florence Sts.), Georgian Revival in red brick with marble portico.

An Upjohn masterpiece is the landmark of the neighborhood: **First Presbyterian Church** (1928–29; Hobart Upjohn, Harry Barton, architects; N. Greene and Elm Sts. at Fisher Park Cir.). The monumental edifice in Norman Revival style, inspired by Albi Cathedral, was built for a congregation founded downtown in 1824. Heightened by its site on a promontory overlooking the park, the tall, fortresslike church of brick and stone has two great rounded towers flanking an arched entrance and big rose window. The long (160 ft.), narrow nave rises to a gabled ceiling 85 feet high. In 1930 the church received a design award from the state American Institute of Architects (AIA).

GF 19 Irving Park

With the suburban ideal established, the Southern Real Estate Co. and the Irving Park Co., led by local developers A. W. McAlister, A. M. Scales, and R. G. Vaughan, developed Irving Park a mile north of Fisher

Park in 1911. For the exclusive streetcar and automobile suburb adjacent to the new country club and golf course, they employed renowned planner John Nolen (*Myers Park, Charlotte) to lay out his characteristic curvilinear streets and generous parks. Minimum house costs ranged from $3,000 to $5,000. The developers set the tone with the eclectic Renaissance-Craftsman-Prairie style **A. M. Scales House** (ca. 1913; 1511 Allendale Dr.), with wraparound bungalow style porch and green tile roof, and the expansive Colonial Revival **A. W. McAlister House** (1918; Charles Barton Keen; 700 Country Club Dr.), with long, classically detailed facade, pergolas, and tile roof typical of the Philadelphia architect of *Reynolda House. The growing business elite promptly adopted Irving Park and built in classical, colonial, Tudor, and English cottage modes. Keen also designed houses for two leaders in the Vick Chemical Co.: the **H. Smith Richardson House** (early 1920s; Charles Barton Keen, architect; 1700 Granville Rd.), with angled wings flanking a columned porch and signature green tile roof, and the **W. Y. Preyer House** (1924; Charles Barton Keen, architect; 603 Sunset Dr.) in the extended bungalow form modeled by *Reynolda. Magnates continued to build through the depression, including the conservative, red brick Georgian Revival style **J. Spencer Love House** (1936; 710 Country Club Dr.) and the eclectic French–Tudor Revival **Herman Cone House** (1936; William C. Holeyman [Greensboro], architect; 806 Country Club Dr.).

Adjoining the suburb on N. Elm St. are some of the city's most elegant apartment houses, the era's emblem of urbanity: **Irving**

Park Manor (late 1920s; 1800 N. Elm St.) has a trio of 3-story units in beautifully detailed Tudor Revival brick, stone, and half-timber. **Country Club Apartments** (1938; Charles C. Hartmann, architect; N. Elm St. and Sunset Cir.) form a well-designed "superblock" courtyard complex, with 2-story brick units combining subtle classical details with simple modernist forms.

GF 20 Summit Ave. Neighborhood

Summit Ave. from downtown to the textile mills, described in 1898 as "a magnificent boulevard," was home to the Cones, Sternbergers, and other industrialists. The chief survival is the **Sigmund Sternberger House** (1926; Harry Barton, architect; 710 Summit Ave.), an exotic Venetian Renaissance Revival house in brick, tile, and stone, built for a Sternberger son and treasurer of their *Revolution Cotton Mill. The **William Vaught House** (ca. 1906; 519 Summit Ave.) was built for a clerk at *Cone Export & Commission Co. as a turreted castle in stone-cast concrete block. The Summit Ave. neighborhood, developed as a streetcar suburb, retains a representative selection of Queen Anne, foursquare, Craftsman, Colonial Revival, and other styles. A busy architect-builder employed his free classical Colonial Revival style in his own residence, the **William P. Rose House** (ca. 1906; 517 Fifth Ave.). The frame Queen Anne style **Herman Sternberger House** (ca. 1900; 732 Park Ave.) was erected on Summit Ave. for a founder of *Revolution Cotton Mill, then moved here when his son Sigmund required the lot.

GF 21 World War Memorial Stadium
1926; Harry Barton & Leonard White, architects; NE corner Lindsay St. and Yanceyville Rd.

Built by the county on land donated by the Cones with funds raised by the American Legion, the horseshoe-shaped stadium seating over 9,000 features twin-towered concrete entrance gates in a classical-Moderne mode.

GF 19 *A. W. McAlister House*

GF 22 Cone Cotton Mills Villages

Beginning in the 1890s, Moses and Ceasar Cone developed a large area northeast of Greensboro into essentially a second city comprising their big mills and accompanying mill villages. Rail cars full of coal permitted large steam-powered operations distant from waterpower sites. The brothers, who knew the business as cotton commission merchants (*Cone Export & Commission Building), focused on filling promising gaps in southern textile production—first denim, then flannel. They started with a finishing plant in 1892, and after delays from the panic of 1893, in 1895 they bought a 2,000-acre railside tract from the N.C. Iron and Steel Co., which had failed to make Greensboro into the "little Pittsburgh of the South." Here they established Proximity Mill, which by 1896 was weaving denim for work clothes and jeans, and soon became chief supplier for Levi Strauss & Co. The Cones persuaded Emanuel and Herman Sternberger, Bavarian immigrants in South Carolina, to join in establishing the South's first flannel mill in 1899: *Revolution. In 1902–5 the Cones built White Oak Cotton Mills, soon the largest denim mill in the world, and in 1912 they added Proximity Print Works, an innovator in printing patterned fabrics. All were expanded during the 20th c., as Cone Mills became a national and international giant.

The Cones also built villages for operatives, adding sectors as the operation grew. Various sections, known as Proximity, Proximity New Town, Proximity Print Works, Revolution, White Oak, etc., form a continuous development often called simply Proximity. By the late 20th c. most of Proximity Mill (Maple St.) had been razed; Proximity Print Works (Fairview and 9th Sts.) and White Oak (Fairview and 16th Sts.) are much altered. Many mill houses, too, have been changed or razed, including the ca. 1916 East White Oak village for black workers, who unloaded bales of cotton and broke them open. Still, the Cone mill villages are among the most varied and, with *Kannapolis, *Loray Mill, and #Roanoke Rapids, among the largest in the state.

Much remains to suggest their scale and complexity.

Most intact of the factories is **Revolution Cotton Mill** (1899, 1904, 1915, 1982; sw of jct. of Yanceyville Rd. and E. 9th St.). Built by the Cones and Sternbergers and named for its intended impact on the southern textile industry, it was the first flannel mill in the region and the world's largest by the 1930s. The plant expanded to more than a million square feet and operated until 1982. The initial **Revolution Mill** (1899; 2007 Revolution Mill Dr.) is a well-preserved example of mill construction, 3 stories tall in brick with very large segmental-arched windows beneath a shallow gable roof, with standard "slow burn" construction timber posts, plank floors, and tapering brick walls. A portion has been renovated as a business center.

The Cone villages, unincorporated until 1923, were governed by the firm. The founders strove to establish a model of progressive paternalism, providing social and educational facilities seen as necessities for order and productivity: "The Cone Mills," said a 1925 anniversary booklet, "are communities not factories," their success "based upon a humanitarian policy, upon the development of character, skill and loyalty." **Proximity Methodist Church** (1924; 1200 Vine St. at 4th St.), a domed brick church with curved corner portico, was one of several company-built churches. Nearby, the **Proximity YMCA** (1921; Maple and 4th Sts.) is a 2-story Colonial Revival facility in

GF 22 *Cone Cotton Mills (village)*

red brick that originally had a gym and swimming pool. **St. Paul's Methodist Church** (ca. 1920; 2319 Yanceyville St.), frame with a corner tower, was built near the Revolution village. The company ran the schools even after incorporation, including the small, frame **East White Oak School** (1916; 1801 10th St.), in the black mill village, and the red brick Moderne-colonial **Proximity School** (1928; Charles C. Hartmann; 1401 Summit Ave.) and **Ceasar Cone School** (1935; 2501 N. Church St.) in White Oak village.

The many blocks of operatives' housing show a sequence of types. The oldest (cf. Gordon St. west of White Oak Mill) take a common regional form, 2 stories tall with low gable roofs, 6/6 sash, and 2 exterior rear chimneys. Also from the early 20th c. are 1-story frame houses with center chimneys, 2-room plans, and shed or gable porches, interspersed with 2-story 3-bay houses with shed porches. One Proximity Mill group stands on Maple and Walnut Sts., and others serving Revolution Mill stand on Maple near 12th St. White Oak New Town (north of White Oak Mill) includes bungalows and 2-story houses in stuccoed hollow tile, some with half-timbered detail, such as N. Church and Hubbard Sts., 12th to 16th Sts. Brick bungalows of Proximity New Town stand on Park and Homeland Aves. From Proximity Print Works are side-gabled frame dwellings on Bogart St., frame bungalows on Fairview St., and brick bungalows on Upland Dr.

GF 23 Buffalo Presbyterian Church
1827; NE corner 16th and Church Sts.

Built as a simple 2-story brick building with a pair of entrances in the gable front, the once rural church was one of the first brick churches in the state outside the coastal Anglican churches. A venerable center of Presbyterianism, the congregation was established ca. 1756 by minister and educator David Caldwell, who in 1767 organized "the Caldwell Log College," a classical academy where he trained many N.C. leaders. The churchyard has graves from the late 18th c. onward. Despite its 20th-c. portico and

large additions, the basic form and brick walls of the old church remain.

GF 24 East Greensboro

The large area flanking the NCRR tracks developed in the late 19th and early 20th centuries as a series of predominantly black neighborhoods near present-day *Bennett College and *A&T. The Dudley St. neighborhood north of the railroad near A&T emerged as Greensboro's premier black residential area. South of the railroad developed Nocho Park and Lincoln Grove and other neighborhoods. East Greensboro included both the small residences of working people and the substantial homes of college teachers, businessmen, and other professionals. Highways and urban renewal have altered several areas, but others retain many bungalow, foursquare, Queen Anne, Dutch Colonial, and other early 20th-c. houses. Nocho Park extended southward in the mid-20th c. and includes suburban streets distinguished by such modernist residences as the **J. Kenneth Lee House** (1960s; W. Edward Jenkins [Greensboro], architect; 1021 Broad Ave.), a sophisticated horizontal composition in brick and wood with carport and clerestory, designed by a noted black architect.

GF 25 North Carolina Agricultural & Technical State University (A&T)
N. Dudley St. betw. Bluford and Market Sts.

The Agricultural & Mechanical College for the Colored Race was authorized in 1891 as a land grant college for blacks, paralleling the North Carolina College of Agricultural & Mechanic Arts in Raleigh (NCSU) for whites and meeting the racial balance required by the federal Morrill Act. Greensboro made the winning offer of land and funds, and the college opened on this campus in 1893. Growing steadily after initial difficulties, the school became N.C. Agricultural & Technical State University in 1972. The initial eclectic buildings of student-made bricks are gone, but several classically detailed red brick structures date from state investment in higher education in the 1920s. Arranged around an open lawn and circle, these in-

GF 25 *Dudley Memorial Building*

clude **Noble Hall** (1922), **Murphy Hall** (1923), and **Morrison Hall** (1924). The most imposing is the central **Dudley Memorial Building** (1930; Charles C. Hartmann, architect), a 3-story red brick structure with contrasting quoins and entablature and a tall Ionic portico. It was named for James B. Dudley, who as president from 1896 to 1925 made the school one of regional importance. In front stands a bronze memorial (dedicated 2002; James Barnhill [A&T], sculptor) of the four A&T students who began the 1960 sit-ins at Greensboro's *Woolworth Building. **Richard B. Harrison Auditorium** (1939), a Federal works project in modern classical style, honored the A&T drama teacher who gained fame as "the Lord" in the Pulitzer Prize–winning Broadway play *Green Pastures* (1930–35).

GF 26 Bennett College
Washington and Bennett Sts.

Established in 1873 as a coeducational primary and secondary school in Warnersville, Bennett Seminary soon moved to this site and specialized in teacher training. In 1926 it was reorganized as a 4-year women's college; with Spelman College in Atlanta it was one of two colleges for black women in the nation. The formally planned campus shared in the statewide trend toward red brick Georgian Revival college architecture. From the 1920s onward these include **Jones Hall** (1922), with its tall Tuscan portico; **Kent Hall** (ca. 1930); and, especially striking, the **Annie Merner Pfeiffer Chapel** (1941; Odis Clay Poundstone [Atlanta], architect), at the head of the green, with its

GF 26 *Annie Merner Pfeiffer Chapel*

graceful arcaded and pedimented portico and tall multistage spire. The **Carnegie Negro Library** (1923–24; Washington and Macon Sts.), a small 1-story brick building with robust classical detail and large arched windows, was built by the Carnegie Foundation on land donated by the college; it opened in 1924 with 150 books as the city's first public library for black citizens and also served the college.

GF 27 L. Richardson Hospital
1927; Charles C. Hartmann, architect;
603 S. Benbow Rd.

The 3-story building of simplified Mission Revival style and fireproof construction was erected to serve black patients through the efforts of local black physicians and a gift from the family of Lunsford Richardson, inventor of Vicks VapoRub. Across the street, the Tudor Revival style **Sebastian House** (late 1920s; 1401 McConnell Rd.) was built for Dr. S. Powell Sebastian, physician at the hospital, and his wife Martha, librarian at the *Carnegie Negro Library.

GF 28 James B. Dudley High School
1929, 1959; Charles C. Hartmann,
W. Edward Jenkins, architects;
Lincoln St. S of Lee St.

Opened in 1929, part of the citywide school building campaign, the city's first public high school for black students is a large 3-story building in a Moderne-medieval blend with stylized buttresses, crenellations, and arched openings. It was named for A&T president Dudley, a state leader in education. The 1959 **Gymnasium** with an innovative roof of intersecting steel arches was an award-winning design by Jenkins, a graduate of A&T who was one of the first black architects practicing in N.C.—initially with Lowenstein & Atkinson of Greensboro, and in his own firm after 1962 (*J. Kenneth Lee House).

GF 29 South Greensboro

The suburb developed soon after the Civil War encompasses Martin Luther King Blvd. (formerly Asheboro St.) and nearby streets. The first suburb south of the city was Warnersville, a freedpeople's village begun by a Quaker, Yardley Warner, in the late 1860s near Ashe and S. Elm Sts.; it was redeveloped in the 1960s except for **Union Cemetery** (1860s; S. Elm at Whittington St.). By 1872 South Greensboro was established just to the east and in 1889 was a "beautiful suburb" offering "tasteful abodes to the businessman, comfortable houses to the artisan, and a beautiful picture to the stranger entering our gates." The area experienced losses as the city expanded but still retains houses in Italianate, Queen Anne, Colonial Revival, and Craftsman styles. A landmark is the **Southside G.F.D. Hose Co. #4** (ca. 1905–10; 414 Martin Luther King Blvd.), with a Spanish brick and tile facade. From the early years is the **William Fields House** (ca. 1875; 447 Arlington St.), the brick Gothic cottage of a tobacco manufacturer. Small industrial plants near the railroad include the **North State Milling Co.** (1910s; 816 S. Elm St.), a brick roller mill with stepped parapet gables and painted signs for its "Daily Bread Flour," and the **Cape Fear Mfg. Co.** (early

20th c.; 1311 S. Eugene St.), a simple brick structure erected for a regional construction firm of which builder-architect W. C. Bain was a vice-president.

GF 30 College Hill

Once called West End, the grid-plan neighborhood exemplifies the first years of suburban growth. It formed the western edge of the city in 1891 until present-day *UNCG opened in 1892 and encouraged development. The neighborhood took its name from **Greensboro College** (College Pl. and W. Market St.), est. 1838 and opened on this campus in 1846, one of the first women's colleges in the state and one of the few Methodist ones in the nation. The college saw its main building burn in 1863, reopen in 1873, and burn again in 1903. **Main Building** (1904; Sidney W. Foulk, architect; 1941), which incorporates elements of its predecessors, is a straightforward 3-story brick structure with central portico and projecting end pavilions, designed by the architect of *West Market St. Methodist Church; it was reworked after another fire in 1941. Other campus buildings of the 1910s and 1920s continue the red brick Neoclassical character.

The neighborhood includes a few antebellum houses, such as the **Bumpass-Troy House** (1847, ca. 1911; 114 S. Mendenhall St.), a 2-story Greek Revival brick house with later Doric portico, built for Sidney and Frances Bumpass, leading Methodists and publishers of the denominational *Weekly Message*, and the 2-story frame Italianate **Walker-Scarboro House** (ca. 1845; 911 W. McGee St.), said to have been built for Letitia and William Walker by her father,

GF 30 *College Hill*

John Motley Morehead, as a wedding gift. Predominating are late 19th- and early 20th-c. houses in diverse Queen Anne, bungalow, Colonial Revival, Shingle, and Spanish Mission styles. One of the city's liveliest Queen Anne compositions is the **Orlo Epps House** (ca. 1890; 808 Walker Ave.), which has lattice encircling the porch entrance, and a turret-balcony. Epps also designed Proximity Mill, UNCG's *Foust Building, and Moses Cone's mountain estate, #Flat Top Manor. Recalling early mixed uses in the city, **Wafco Mill** (1893–1913; 801 W. McGee St.), a roller mill complex expanded in brick and frame, operated until 1972 and is now housing.

GF 31 *Julius I. Foust Building*

GF 31 University of North Carolina at Greensboro
W. Market St.

The State Normal & Industrial School for White Girls was chartered in 1891, after Charles and Lula McIver and others campaigned long and hard for state public education and a state normal school to train teachers. Greensboro outbid Durham by offering $30,000 and a choice of four sites. The school, which educated many women for teaching and other leadership roles, was variously renamed, and in 1962–64 the "Woman's College" of UNC became the coeducational UNCG. Although many colleges of its era built grand, eclectic main buildings, most are gone. The **Julius I. Foust Building** (1891–92; Epps & Hackett, architects) is among the best examples in the state. The massive red brick and granite main building of Romanesque Revival style has a high hip roof, paired 3-story towers flanking an arcaded entrance, and a lively variety of arched window and door openings. Flanking additions continue the design. A sequence of red brick, generally classical buildings recall the state's early 20th-c. investment in higher education. Fine Georgian Revival buildings of the 1920s designed by Harry Barton include **Aycock Auditorium** (1927), 3 stories with a long 2-story portico; the gracefully composed **Chancellor's Residence** (1923); and others. Particularly striking is the **Heating Plant** (ca. 1924;

north side of Oakland Ave. betw. Forest and Highland Sts.), a big Romanesque Revival style structure of brick, terra-cotta, and concrete, with tall tower and smokestack.

GF 32 Charles D. McIver School
1922–23; Sterrett & Van Vleck (New York), architects; 605 W. Lee St.

One of the first and most imposing of Greensboro's handsome brick schools of the 1920s, the classically detailed elementary school has a central auditorium lit by tall, arched windows and flanked by classroom wings. The New York school specialists also designed Greensboro's Aycock and Caldwell elementary schools, #Goldsboro High School, and others.

GF 33 Grimsley (Greensboro) High School and Brooks Elementary School
1929; Charles C. Hartmann, architect; 801 Westover Ter.

The trio of Moderne-medieval brick buildings, called the "million dollar high school," was the capstone of the local school building campaign. Establishment of the large campus in west Greensboro, coeval with *Dudley High School in the southeast, reinforced the 20th-c. trend of middle- and upper-class white settlement to the west and north in such neighborhoods as Westerwood, Lake Daniel, and W. Market Terrace. The adjoining **Brooks Elementary School** (1950, 1952; 1215 Westover Ter.), epitomizes the post–World War II modern school with clerestory, bands of windows, horizontal forms, and simple geometric detailing influenced by Eliel Saarinen's Cranbrook School in Michigan.

GF 34 West Greensboro Suburbs

West of UNCG along W. Market St. and Friendly Ave., developers platted suburbs from the 1920s onward, building in a familiar array of revival modes: the 1000–2000 blocks of W. Market display businessmen's substantial Tudor and Georgian Revival residences. **Our Lady of Grace Catholic Church** (1950–52; Henry V. Murphy [New York], architect; W. Market St. at Chapman St.) is a late Gothic Revival style building of Salisbury granite, funded by insurance magnate Julian Price and his children in memory of his wife Ethel (d. 1943). **Hamilton Lakes** began as a separate suburban town, but little was built before the Great Depression. The **Harry Barton House** (ca. 1927; 104 Kemp Rd. W) is the architect's elegantly detailed Spanish Colonial residence. The Georgian Revival style **A. M. Scales House II** (1926; C. Gadsden Sayre [Anderson, S.C.], architect; 1207 Lakewood Dr.), with its long, towering portico, was built for the developer (*Irving Park).

GF 35 Pomona

Located on the NCRR west of town, the village of Pomona began in the mid-19th c. with Quaker entrepreneur John Van Lindley's famed horticultural nursery, named for the Roman goddess of fruit trees. In 1886 Lindley and William Boren began the Pomona Terra Cotta Co., a major producer of tile and brick, and in 1897 Lindley and others founded the *Pomona Cotton Mill and village near his nursery. The nursery and tile plant are gone, but the 2-story brick **Pomona Mill** (1897 and later; Spring Garden Rd. and Merritt Dr.) survives, along with the **Pomona Mercantile Co. Store** (ca. 1919; 802–10 Merritt Dr.), a smaller 2-story brick building, and millworkers' dwellings

that include shotgun-plan houses, gable-sided cottages, and bungalows.

GF 36 Guilford College
Est. 1834; 5800 W. Friendly Ave.

The shaded campus of the Quaker school—begun as New Garden Boarding School, the first such coeducational institution in the South—reflected the 19th-c. ideal of the rural campus, secluded from outside influences. Although the 1837 main building was rebuilt in 1980, simple red brick structures from later years include the multigabled **Archdale Hall** (1885), the columned, classically influenced **Library** (1909) and **New Garden Hall** (1912), and faculty houses. Long predating Greensboro, Quaker pioneers established a monthly meeting here in 1751 and built the first New Garden Meeting House in 1754. Near the late 20th-c. meetinghouse, **New Garden Cemetery** contains many early Quaker graves and locally carved stones.

GF 36 *Archdale Hall*

GF 37 Guilford Courthouse Battleground
Est. 1880s; Battleground Ave.

One of the state's richest commemorative landscapes, the park presents several generations of markers and interpretations of the heritage of the American Revolution. On March 15, 1781, Gen. Nathanael Greene, commander of American forces in the South, engaged the army of Lord Cornwallis near the little courthouse town of Guilford. Although the British won the battle, it cost them heavily and turned the tide of the war

GF 39 *Sedgefield Country Club*

toward the surrender at Yorktown on October 19. Local historical interest in the battleground began in the 1850s but faded during the Civil War. In the 1880s, in the wake of the 1876 centennial and amid growing enthusiasm for sectional reunion on southern terms, Judge David Schenck of Greensboro succeeded in organizing local stockholders in the Guilford Battle Ground Co. to acquire and preserve the grounds and erect memorials to commemorate the Americans' heroism. In 1917 the park was transferred to the U.S. government. Among the 29 memorials, the most imposing is the equestrian Gen. Nathanael Greene Monument (1914–15; Francis H. Packer, sculptor), a monument hoped for since 1888 and funded by Congress in 1911.

GF 38 Hoskins House and Coble Barn

19th c.; Tannenbaum Park, Battleground Ave. at Spring Garden Rd.

Restored examples of two regional log building traditions stand near the battleground. The **Hoskins House** (1857; restored 1986–87) is a 1-room 18-by-24-foot dwelling of V-notched chestnut logs. Though tree-ring dating indicates it was erected long after the 1781 battle, it represents the dwellings of many early farmers. The Hoskinses, Quakers originally from Chester Co., Pa., owned it until the 1930s. The **Coble Barn** (ca. 1830), from German territory in southeast Guilford Co., is among the finest and most accessible examples of the double-crib log barns prevalent in the 19th-c. Piedmont. Built for George Coble, a farmer of German descent, the V-notched log barn has two 15-by-22-foot cribs flanking an 18-foot wagon passage; a hollowed-log feed trough is built into the walls, and cantilevered upper logs carry a roof pent. Unusual fingernail-moon vents mark the weatherboarded gables. (See Introduction, Fig. 21.)

GF 39 Sedgefield

E side US 29/70A, at SR 1380 (Sedgefield Dr.)

In 1923 A. W. McAlister, president of Pilot Life Insurance Co., initiated development of Sedgefield, Inc., an exclusive residential area

with a country club and a Donald Ross golf course, located on the former hunting estate of tobacco magnate John Blackwell Cobb. The centerpiece is the large Tudor Revival style **Sedgefield Country Club** (1927; Harry Barton [attrib.]; Forsyth Dr. at Wayne Rd.). Secluded on curving streets are residences from the 1920s onward; one of the finest is the brick, Tudor Revival **Adamsleigh** (1931; Luther Lashmit [Northup & O'Brien]; 3210 Forsyth Dr.). Out of view are such notable modernist houses as the **E. K. Thrower House I** (1962) and **II** (1976), relatively modest, horizontally composed residences designed by George Matsumoto of the NCSU School of Design in Raleigh. The former **Pilot Life Insurance Co. Complex** (1927–28; Zantzinger, Borie & Medary [Philadelphia] and Harry Barton, architects; 1952–74 additions, McMinn, Norfleet, & Wicker; w side US 29/70A, at SR 1387) is an early suburban corporate headquarters complex, with red-brick Georgian Revival style buildings on a parklike campus planned by Philadelphia landscape architect R. B. Cridland.

GF 40 Jamestown

Flanking the old wagon road, now Main St. (US 29/70A), Jamestown contains the best collection of mid-Atlantic-influenced Quaker architecture in the state. Settled in the 18th c. principally by Quakers from Pennsylvania, the community was named for early Quaker James Mendenhall. Jamestown became a progressive intellectual center with a law school and medical school conducted by local men, a female college, and a manumission society. The 1856 arrival of the NCRR shifted the town center eastward from the old village. Though engulfed by devel-

GF 40 *Mendenhall Plantation House*

opment, much of historic Jamestown still stands.

Centerpiece of the village is the oasislike **Mendenhall Plantation** (ca. 1811; Main St.; open limited hours). It was established by James Mendenhall's descendant Richard Mendenhall, farmer, tanner, and community leader, who built his house, business, and farm beside the road. One of the most accessible examples of the region's early 19th-c. brick houses is his 2-story dwelling of Flemish-bond brick with blind segmental-arched openings, corbeled cornice, and circular gable vents flanking interior end chimneys. The hall-parlor plan interior is finished with fine, plain workmanship, including batten doors, plastered walls, and a beautiful enclosed corner stair.

Outbuildings extend down the hill. Unusual in the region is the early to mid-19th-c. **Barn**, a frame structure set into the hillside, with the upper hay storage area accessible to wagons on the hilltop, and stables sheltered beneath. The bank barn type is seen frequently in Pennsylvania but seldom in N.C. Richard Mendenhall as a youth had gone to Pennsylvania for training as a craftsman, and it is speculated that his barn reflected his experience of changing practices in the mid-Atlantic region.

Across the road in a city park are two other Quaker landmarks, open limited hours. The **Mendenhall Store** (1824) is a 2-story Flemish-bond brick building with 3 main rooms and corner fireplaces, erected for Richard Mendenhall opposite his house

and used in connection with his tanning trade. The **Jamestown Friends Meeting House** (ca. 1820s) is evidently the oldest Quaker meetinghouse in the state. The restored 1-story structure, which takes a characteristic gable-sided form with a central entrance, is built of brick laid in Flemish bond with stone foundation, segmental-arched openings, and corbeled cornice. This was an "indulged meeting," used when weather prevented the journey to Deep River Friends Meeting.

Among the other early buildings of Jamestown is the **Isaac Potter House** (ca. 1819; 211 Main St.), a modest log dwelling built in two stages. The **Shubal Coffin House I** (early 19th c., ca. 1840; Main St.) was transformed into a fine Greek Revival residence by Coffin, a physician who ran a medical school. He subsequently built the fashionable board-and-batten **Shubal Coffin House II** (ca. 1855; Main St. at Oakdale Rd.) in "New Jamestown" near the NCRR. The prime early 20th-c. edifice is the **Jamestown Public School** (1915; Brooks & Hunt [Greensboro], architects; 200 W. Main St.), a 2-story brick building with Ionic portico, now the public library.

GF 41 Oakdale Cotton Mill, Village, and School

1880s–1910s; SR 1352 and SR 1309 at Deep River

The well-preserved small textile village, located on a waterpower site, originated with an antebellum gristmill and a Civil War gun factory, with a cotton mill organized in 1865.

GF 40 *Jamestown Friends Meeting House*

In the 1880s a brick building replaced the original frame mill, and in 1896 Oakdale Mills was reorganized by Winston investors, with Joseph Ragsdale as secretary-treasurer. The number of spindles increased from 10,000 to 50,000 between 1890 and 1910. In contrast to most small mills, this has remained a family-run operation. The earliest section of the brick mill displays the characteristic Italianate tower with corbeled detail, topped by a weathervane in the form of a carp, a fish that abounded in the Deep River. The **Village** (Oakdale Mill Rd.) has some 30 houses from the early 20th c., chiefly 2-story weatherboarded frame dwellings with brick and stone chimneys, shed porches, side wings, and rear kitchen ells. A rare survival is the village **Well** in the middle of the main street. Up the hill on Oakdale Rd. are the **Superintendent's House**, a 2-story Queen Anne–Colonial Revival style frame house, and **Oakdale School** (early 20th c.), a rectangular frame structure erected by the company.

GF 42 McCulloch Gold Mill

1831; N side SR 1113, 0.4 mi. E of US 29/70; open limited hours

The imposing stone structure is the state's sole example of an antebellum gold mill engine house and one of the finest antebellum industrial structures. Here in the 1830s Charles McCulloch employed new gold processing methods—a stationary steam engine and Chilean mills—to extract gold from

GF 42 *McCulloch Gold Mill*

crushed quartz. Soon the methods became obsolete, and the mill was abandoned by 1860. In the 20th c. the engine house fell into ruin, with only two walls standing, but in 1985–87 it was rebuilt with the original stones, based on photographs, including its towering smokestack and tall Gothic-arched entrance.

High Point (GF 43–52)

Born of the NCRR and named for its peak position on the line, High Point (est. 1853) developed where the Fayetteville to Bethania plank road crossed the tracks. After the Civil War it became a major producer of textiles and wood products and gained national and international stature as a center of furniture manufacturing and home of an international furniture market. Concentrating around the crossing of Main St. and the railroad, early 20th-c. growth was so rapid that for a time the city exceeded Greensboro, and residents strove to make High Point seat of a new county. The principal landmarks date from the early 20th c., when architects including Charles C. Hartmann of Greensboro, Northup & O'Brien of Winston-Salem, Louis Voorhees of High Point, and Hobart Upjohn of New York designed mainstream Tudor, Colonial, and Neoclassical Revival style buildings.

GF 43 Downtown High Point

North and south of the railroad, Main St.'s early 20th-c. boom-era buildings range from small commercial buildings to skyscrapers. Built to accommodate visitors to the Southern Furniture Exposition, the **Sheraton Hotel** (1921; Charles C. Hartmann; 400 N. Main) is a classically detailed 10-story brick hotel. Among many handsomely detailed facades are the 3-story **High Point Enterprise Building** (1935; Tysen Ferree; 305 N. Main St.), with stylized classical and Art Deco motifs; the 3-story **Home Bank Building** (ca. 1910; 201 N. Main St.), in classically detailed brick and granite; and the 5-story **N.C. Savings Bank** (1905; Wheeler, Runge & Dickey [Charlotte], architects; 126 N. Main St.), with ornate brickwork.

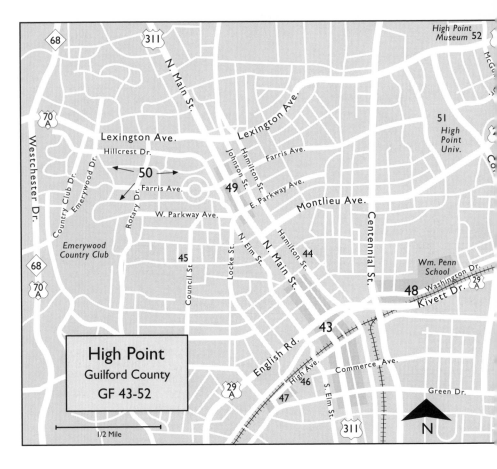

51
High
Point
Univ.

Lexington Ave.
Hillcrest Dr.
←50→
Farris Ave.

49

Farris Ave.

W. Parkway Ave.

Montlieu Ave.

45

44

Wm. Penn
School

48

43

High Point

Guilford County

GF 43-52

29
A

46

47

Green Dr.

311

N

1/2 Mile

South of the railroad, the **High Point Depot** (ca. 1905; 90 S. Main St.) is a 2-story brick building with stone base and tiled hip roof. Beside it the sunken tracks run through the center of town, with Moderne-detailed concrete walls and access upward to the depot; this was a 1937–38 public works project to eliminate grade crossings. The **Jarrell Building** (ca. 1915; 114 S. Main St.) features Doric pilasters and arched windows beneath a cornice and parapet, and **Commercial National Bank** (1924; Charles Hartmann; 164 S. Main St.) is an 8-story office building of brick and granite with classical detail. A keystone in the city's 20th-c. history is the **Southern Furniture Exposition Building** (1919–21; William P. Rose [Goldsboro, Raleigh, Greensboro], architect; later expansions; 209 S. Main St.), an enormous home furnishings showroom complex of about 2 million square feet of ex-

hibit space and the heart of the High Point furniture market; Rose's original 10-story building with Neoclassical detail is evident above street level.

Local architects' modern public architecture of the 1930s appears in the **Guilford County Office and Court Building** (1937; Eccles D. Everhart & Louis F. Voorhees; 258 S. Main St.) in brick and stone with Moderne elements. The separate county government center reflected High Point's competition with Greensboro. The **High Point Municipal Building** (1972–75; Edward Durell Stone, architect; 211 S. Hamilton St.), faced with marble with pyramidal roof and Stone's characteristic top-lighting and central spaces, showed High Point's identity in commissioning a design by the nationally known architect of the *Legislative Building. The former **U.S. Post Office** (1932; Workman, Everhart & Voorhees

GF 43 *High Point Depot*

GF 43 *Southern Furniture Exposition Building*

[High Point], architects; 100 E. Green Dr.) is a classically conceived, Art Deco detailed post office, handsomely executed inside and out.

GF 44 World's Largest Bureau
1928, ca. 1975; E side N. Hamilton St., at Westwood Ave.

Even before the famous *Thomasville Chair, the High Point chamber of commerce built its headquarters in the form of a giant bureau to symbolize the growing furniture town. The interior was finished in fine woods. When the chamber moved to larger quarters, the Jaycees bought the bureau, moved it, and ca. 1975 covered it with aluminum siding; in the late 1990s they redid it in wood-grained colonial style.

GF 45 W. K. Whitsell House
1951; W. K. Whitsell, builder; 1101 Council St.

One of several similar modest examples of the International style across the state, the rectilinear residence with flat planes, stuccoed walls, and glass brick was constructed by Whitsell, industrial arts teacher at the local high school.

GF 46 Tomlinson Furniture Co.
Ca. 1900–1920; S side High Ave. at Elm St.

The industrial complex is one of the largest and most physically dominant in the city, with well-maintained buildings from its founding by Sidney H. Tomlinson in 1900. The company was a leader in making High

Point a furniture capital. Typical of the period are the tall smokestack with brick spelling out the company name, and the brick buildings with parapets, pilasters, segmental-arched windows, and simple corbeling.

GF 47 High Ave. Residential Area

A neighborhood of substantial houses recalls the era when business leaders resided near the city center and their factories. Principally 2-story frame and a few brick houses included towered Queen Anne, porticoed and pedimented Colonial Revival, and bungalow styles. The **O. Arthur Kirkman House** (1913; 501 W. High Ave.) is part of an ensemble by the railroad, with an eclectic brick house, garage, office, and small commercial building on a landscaped lot. Kirkman had multifaceted businesses centered here, including a small High Point, Thomasville & Denton Rail Road (HPTDRR), which locals dubbed High Priced Ticket and D——d Rough Ride.

GF 48 East Washington Dr.

Washington Dr. just east of Main St. emerged in the early 20th c. as an important center of black businesses and institutions, one of many "Black Main Streets" in the South (*E. Hargett St., Raleigh). The **Kilby Hotel** (ca. 1910; NW corner Hobson St.), a 3-story, richly detailed brick commercial building, was erected by Nannie Kilby, a successful black real estate entrepreneur. Nearby are **First Baptist Church** (ca. 1907; NE corner Hobson St.) and former **St. Mark's Methodist Church** (1928; between Hobson St. and Gaylord Ct.), both red brick Gothic Revival churches, and **Odd Fellows Hall** (1907; s side w of Gaylord Ct.), a 3-story stuccoed masonry building with elaborate cornerstone and corbeled cornice. To the east is **William Penn School** (1920s; former High Point Normal & Industrial Institute; N side betw. Gaylord Ct. and Eccles Pl.), a classically detailed brick building, part of a school begun by Quakers in 1891.

GF 49 North Main St.

Once the favored address of the city's business leaders, the 1100 block of N. Main St. retains a few mansions from its early 20th-c. heyday, with Renaissance Revival themes especially popular among the princes of industry. Two of the finest were built for founders of the Adams-Millis hosiery mills: the **J. H. Adams House** (ca. 1918; 1108 N. Main St.; B&B), is an elaborate Mediterranean style 2-story house with tile roof and recessed, arcaded loggia; the **H. A. Millis House** (ca. 1920; Lorenzo S. Winslow, architect; SW corner at W. Farriss Ave.), Georgian Revival

in stucco and tile, was designed by a former employee of Harry Barton, later of Washington, D.C. Nearby are the Colonial Revival **Lee Briles House** (1907; 1103 N. Main St.), for a client who sought a "Southern Mansion"; the Mediterranean style **Hardee Apartments** (ca. 1924; 1102 N. Main St.); and others. N. Main includes residences in other classical and Colonial modes and is also site of major early 20th-c. churches, rendered in stone in Gothic Revival style. The small, picturesque **St. Mary's Episcopal Church** (1927–28; Herbert Hunter, Louis F. Voorhees & Eccles D. Everhart, architects; NW corner at W. Farriss Ave.) was designed by local architects. The much larger **First Presbyterian Church** (1928; Hobart Upjohn and Harry Barton, architects; SE corner at E. Parkway) was designed by the team who planned *First Presbyterian Church in Greensboro; built of Crab Orchard stone from Tennessee, it won a state AIA design award when that program began in 1929.

GF 50 Emerywood

The most impressive and intact architecture from the city's early 20th-c. prosperity stands in this handsome suburb, which exemplifies the emerging planning and architectural design ideas of the period. Local developer Stephen Clark, who established **Roland Park** ca. 1915, a suburb planned around a circular park, soon followed it with Emerywood, named for former landowner Emery A. Bencini. It was planned by Earle S. Draper, who had worked under John Nolen on *Myers Park in Charlotte and who applied his Olmsted-influenced principles

GF 48 *Kilby Hotel*

GF 49 *J. H. Adams House*

GF 50 *Tomlinson House*

GF 52 *Haley House*

of natural topography, curving streets, and generous parks to suburbs throughout the South. Characteristically, the ensemble of landscape and architecture is the principal attraction, but there are several excellent examples of the Colonial Revival, Tudor Revival, and French styles by noted architects. The furniture leader commissioned the especially handsome Tudor Revival style **Tomlinson House** (1924; Harry Barton; 403 Hillcrest Dr.), in brick and half-timbering with castellated porte cochere. A notable modernist composition, appropriate for a leader in modern furniture design, is the **Thayer Coggins House** (1972; Fred Babcock [Salt Lake City], architect; 1032 Rockford Rd.), a horizontally composed, 2-story residence with squared bricks, bands of windows, and period landscaping.

GF 51 High Point University

1920–24; Herbert Hunter (High Point), architect; Montlieu Ave. at E. and W. College Dr.

When the Methodist Protestant Church announced its intention of establishing a college in 1921, High Point offered land and money for a campus to enrich the city's life. In 1924 High Point College opened in its red brick, Georgian Revival style buildings on a landscaped campus. The 3-story **Roberts Hall** (1922) was the centerpiece. Despite troubles during the Great Depression, other buildings were added with Works Progress Administration assistance and private donations in the 1930s, and campus growth continued through the century.

GF 52 Haley House

1786; High Point Museum, NW corner Lexington Ave. and McGuinn Dr.; open regular hours

The oldest of several brick houses built for local Quakers, the Haley House is also one of the oldest brick dwellings in the Piedmont. It has key features in common with Moravian dwellings, but specific craftsmen and sources are not identified. The small house beside the old road sits upon a stone foundation. Interior end chimneys heat a 3-room plan with cooking fireplace in the main room. Decorative elements include the Flemish-bond brickwork with glazed headers and a circular plaque in the gable denoting the year of construction and the initials of John and Phoebe Haley. Haley was a blacksmith, farmer, and community leader. The house was extensively restored ca. 1970. Also on the grounds are two log buildings: the **Hoggett House**, from Guilford Co. (18th c.?), has V-notched logs; the other is a single-pen V-notched blacksmith shop from Davidson Co.

GF 53 Model Farm

1868; W side Brentwood St., 0.3 mi. N of Model Farm Rd.

The 2-story frame farmhouse was built by the Baltimore Association of Friends to help rebuild the South by having a Maine farmer demonstrate efficient methods on a model farm. The 5-bay I-house features interior chimneys and the Downingesque central front gable—here unusually steep—that became ubiquitous in the late 19th c.; its early use in a "model" farm building is noteworthy, as is the ongoing linkage between Downing-influenced building and scientific farming.

GF 54 Springfield Friends Meeting House
1850s; NE corner Elva Pl. and Springfield Rd.

The gable-fronted meetinghouse of brick features simple Greek Revival details. It was the third home of the Springfield Friends, whose 1927 Colonial Revival building (Herbert Hunter, architect) stands nearby; an early preservation project, it now houses a museum.

GF 55 Pennybyrne (George T. Penny House)
1926; Raleigh J. Hughes (Greensboro), architect; N side US 29/70A (Greensboro Rd.) at Penny Rd. (SR 1536)

The grandest residence in High Point is the Renaissance Revival mansion built for a native of Randleman, who with his brother Jim constituted "The World's Original Twin Auctioneers" and became a real estate entrepreneur. Since the late 1940s it has been part of Maryfield Nursing Home.

GF 56 Deep River Friends Meeting House
1875; NW corner SR 1541 (Wendover Ave.) and SR 1536 (Penny Rd.)

The brick meetinghouse, built to replace a frame structure of 1758, continued the traditional gable-fronted form and Quaker simplicity combined with such late 19th-c. details as segmental-arched windows with hoodmolds.

GF 57 Old Mill of Guilford
1820s; E side NC 68, opp. SR 2132, Oak Ridge vic.

The well-known gristmill on Beaver Creek occupies one of the county's earliest mill sites. Believed to have been built ca. 1820 to replace a 1750s mill, it was the county's first "merchant mill," grinding farmers' own grain and also selling its products. Despite

alterations, the timber framing, stone foundation, and form of the 19th-c. mill remain at one of the oldest mills in essentially continuous operation in the nation.

GF 58 Oak Ridge
Jct. NC 68, NC 150, Oak Ridge

The rural campus, now a military academy, began as a classical preparatory school, Oak Ridge Male Institute, in 1852. The stately Queen Anne–Colonial Revival style residence **Oakhurst** (1897; Frank P. Milburn) was built for Martin H. Holt, who with his brother, J. Allen Holt, served as co-principal for over 35 years; the latter's home, **Maple Glade** (1905), is a Colonial Revival dwelling. **Benbow Hall** (1905), a Mission style dormitory with arcaded galleries at both levels, was soon followed by the red brick Colonial Revival style **Alumni Building** (1914; G. Will Armfield [Greensboro]) and a temple-form **Chapel** of 1914.

GF 57 *Old Mill of Guilford*

GF 58 *Oakhurst*

Less than a mile west are the **Charles and Jesse Benbow Houses** (early, mid-19th c.; s side NC 150, 0.6 and 1 mi. w of Oak Ridge; private, visible from road). Charles Benbow built a 2-story house like those of many other local Quakers, using brick laid in Flemish bond and a 3-room plan. He was a brickmaker, tanner, textile entrepreneur, supporter of New Garden School (*Guilford College), and proponent of manumission. About 1858 his son Jesse accommodated changing styles in a broadly proportioned frame house with simple Greek Revival detail and a central-passage plan. Jesse shared his father's interests and was a founder of the Oak Ridge Institute.

GF 59 Stokesdale

The intact small-town commercial district features Italianate stores of ca. 1910: 1-, 2-, and 3-story structures with corbeled cornices, arched windows, and parapets, which housed dry goods stores, a bank, and other enterprises facing the now-vanished railroad.

GF 60 Summerfield

The crossroads village contains unusually elaborate 19th- and early 20th-c. buildings. Two brick stores at the intersection, built for two cousins by local contractor George J. Smith in the 1870s, boast unusually elaborate corbeled decoration: the **Henry Clay Brittain Store** on the northwest and the **Noah Webster Brittain Store** on the southeast. On the southwest corner stands the

GF 60 *Henry Clay Brittain Store*

substantial 2-story double-pile Greek Revival style **Alexander Strong Martin House** (ca. 1840), one of the largest brick houses of its era in the county. Nearby stands the **Henry Clay Brittain House** (ca. 1908; NE corner NC 150 and SR 2118), a full-blown Queen Anne style house highlighting the merchant's interest in current trends.

GF 61 Hillsdale Brick Store
Mid-19th c.; NW corner NC 150 and SR 2347

The rectilinear brick commercial building known as the "Old Brick Store" also housed a post office and a meeting room above. It is finished with plain Greek Revival trim and again serves as a store.

GF 62 Gibsonville

Named for Joseph Gibson, contractor to build the NCRR in the vicinity in the 1850s, the small industrial community flanking the railroad features typical turn-of-the-century housing and commercial architecture. In the 1880s, longtime millwright Berry Davidson (cf. Alamance Co.) and a nephew established the **Minneola Mill** (1880s and later; Minneola Ave.), a representative brick textile mill that became the principal industry, and clusters of mill housing served its workers. Principal rows of buildings face the railroad: on one side are simplified Italianate brick stores along Main St., and across the track on Railroad Ave. are houses including the small temple-form **Allen House** at 210 and the lavishly detailed Queen Anne–Colonial Revival style **F. Marion Smith House** at 204.

GF 63 O. W. Bright Lodge Gatehouse
Ca. 1900; NW corner US 70 and SR 2758; private, visible from road

The large Colonial Revival style house was built as the gatehouse for the hunting lodge of northerner O. W. Bright. Several lodges were built in the Piedmont in the early 20th c. by urban industrialists and financiers who came by rail for a few days of shooting quail and pheasant, but today few survive.

GF 64 Palmer Memorial Institute (Charlotte Hawkins Brown State Historic Site)
1920–30s; SW corner US 70 and SR 3054; open regular hours

The institute was founded in 1902 as an agricultural and industrial school for black students by Charlotte Hawkins Brown, who guided its transition in the 1930s into a finishing and college preparatory school. Named for her mentor, Alice Freeman Palmer of Boston, the campus includes Colonial Revival institutional buildings in a red brick, white-trimmed vocabulary, centering on **Galen Stone Hall** (1927; Harry Barton, architect), named for a Boston benefactor. **Canary Cottage** (1927), Brown's personal residence, is a frame house described in a 1935 school bulletin as "a Dutch Colonial bungalow type" furnished "to give students practical ideas on interior decoration."

GF 65 Gibson House
Early 19th c.; S side US 70, 0.9 mi. E of NC 61; private, visible from road

The 2-story frame farmhouse has a typical hall-parlor plan, heavy exterior end chimneys, vertical proportions, and Federal period details. Andrew Gibson was a Scots-born farmer, merchant, gold miner, and community leader who moved to Guilford ca. 1775; his son Joseph was namesake of Gibsonville.

GF 66 Whitsett

The community developed around the Whitsett Institute, one of many private schools of the late 19th and early 20th centuries. A public school occupies the site of the old institute, but the village retains homes of many students, teachers, and principals. Prominent are two big Queen Anne–Colonial Revival residences: **The Oaks** (ca. 1895, 1910; S side SR 3064, N of NC 61) was the residence of institute president W. T. Whitsett, and **Holly Gate** (ca. 1910; E side NC 61, N of SR 3062) was built for his brother-in-law J. Henry Joyner, a professor. **Midlawn** (ca. 1915; E side NC 61, N of SR

GF 68 *Brick Church*

3062), also a teacher's house, is a gambrel-roofed Colonial Revival house.

GF 67 Low House
1820s; W side NC 61, 1 mi. S of I-40/85; private, visible from road

The 2-story brick house was probably built for John B. Low, a planter of German descent. In contrast to the conservative Quaker brick houses, the house follows a center-passage plan and contains inventive Federal period interiors. Endangered by a water project, it was moved a short distance and restored.

GF 68 Brick Church
1839–41; N side SR 3111 at SR 3110, 0.4 mi. E of NC 61

The plain 2-story church, one of the oldest brick churches in the Piedmont, maintains its simple gable-fronted form with paired entrances in the south gable. The plainly finished sanctuary has wood sheathing, a curved ceiling, and galleries. The Reformed congregation was established in a German-settled area in the late 18th c. by George and Ludwig Clapp and was known as "the Clapp church." A log meetinghouse was succeeded in 1813 by a small brick church, for which the congregation was soon named. In 1839–41 the congregation reused its materials to erect the present 55-by-40-foot church. Repaired and coated with cement in 1946, it was restored in the late 20th c. The cemetery contains early grave markers, some in German.

Rockingham County (RK)

In 1728 William Byrd II of Virginia explored the area along the Dan River and its tributaries and subsequently acquired 26,000 acres, which he called "the Land of Eden." On the high and westwardly hillier land, settlers mainly from Virginia established farms and plantations producing tobacco, grains, and livestock. In 1785 Rockingham Co. was formed from Guilford Co., and its seat was placed at Wentworth, both named in honor of Charles Wentworth, Duke of Rockingham, supporter of American independence. Of several early 19th-c. plantation houses, *High Rock Plantation is visible from a public road. Smaller farm complexes, often with log houses, outbuildings, and tobacco barns from the 19th and early 20th centuries, are especially numerous.

To open the Dan River area to shipping, the Roanoke Navigation Co. (chartered 1812) (#Roanoke Canal) planned canals, dams, and locks from the mouth of the Roanoke to the Dan. (Remains of sluice navigation structures are still visible in the Dan.) With visions of great inland trade centers, entrepreneurs invested in Leaksville, where the Smith River meets the Dan, and at Madison, at the Mayo and Dan confluence. Land prices and buildings rose fast before the "bubble" burst with the panic of 1819. By the 1820s, however, flat-bottomed bateaux traversed the river, and in the 1830s waterpowered cotton manufacturing began at Leaksville.

In the late 19th c., industrial growth burgeoned, aided by rail lines: the Piedmont Railroad during the Civil War in eastern Rockingham, the Cape Fear & Yadkin Valley (CF&YVRR) in the western part in the 1880s, and others. Textile production expanded at Spray and later Draper near Leaksville (which all combined as Eden in the mid-20th c.), while Reidsville became a major tobacco manufacturing center.

RK 1 Wentworth

Established in 1787 and named Wentworth in 1798–99, the tiny courthouse town recalls many rural county seats of the 19th c. Even now its core consists of the courthouse and jail, an inn, and a few churches, stores, and houses by the road. When the 19th-c. courthouse burned in 1906, commissioners to build a new **Rockingham County Courthouse** (1907; Frank P. Milburn [Washington, D.C.]; B. F. Smith Construction Co. [Washington, D.C.]; s side NC 65) urged the architect to "keep the cost as near $25,000 as possible." The 3-story building of red pressed brick, including the columns at the entrance, typifies Milburn's small-town courthouses of the era, with free classical details and tile roof. Across the road is the boldly composed **Rockingham County Jail** (1910; Wheeler & Stern [Charlotte], archi-

tects; Camden Iron Works [Salem, Va.], builders), with central entrance tower, bracketed cornice, Spanish tile roof, and pressed brickwork paneling and arches.

The oldest landmark is the **Wright Tavern** (ca. 1816 and later; N side NC 65, 1 block E of courthouse; open limited hours), begun by William Wright, whose family operated it for many decades. It is one of the state's best examples of the inns essential to antebellum courthouse towns. Like others, its layout adapts a traditional 2-story house form to accommodate customers. The earliest section, on the left, has a large public room below and small but elegantly finished chambers above; the addition on the right contains 2 rooms below and 1 above. Between the two sections runs an open passage framed by an arch and finished with paneled wainscot and a handsome stair of Federal style. The nearby small, gable-fronted **Ira**

RK 1 *Wright Tavern*

RK 1 *Rockingham Co. Jail*

Humphreys Law Office (1905) was moved from the courthouse square. **Wentworth United Methodist Church** (ca. 1859; s side NC 65, w of town limit) is a simple frame church with pedimented gable end, paired entrances, and galleried interior. The similar **Wentworth Presbyterian Church** (1860; N side NC 65, E of town center) has a 60-foot steeple and entrances that flank the pulpit.

RK 2 Mulberry Island

Mid-19th c.; N side SR 2150, 0.2 mi.
W of SR 2151; private, visible from road

The big double-pile house near the Dan River was built on a plantation owned by the Scales family and later by Judge Thomas Settle II, who served as legislator, supreme court justice, minister to Peru, and Republican candidate for governor in 1876. Settle either built or greatly remodeled the double-pile house in Italianate fashion, and the

Penn family added the towering engaged porches in the 20th c.

RK 3 Madison

See Claudia P. Roberts (Brown) and Diane Lea, *An Architectural and Historical Survey of Madison, N.C.* (1979).

Located near the confluence of the Mayo and the Dan, the river town includes architecture from its early 19th-c. beginnings through its late 19th and early 20th-c. tobacco manufacturing era. During the navigation boom, Randall Duke Scales acquired a tract of family land and in 1818 auctioned off lots in a grid town. (His Federal period brick plantation house stands nearby on a secluded site.) Scales and others invested in tobacco manufacturing and various enterprises, but the panic of 1819 quelled growth, and they eventually left for Mississippi. Later in the 19th c., Madison gained a spur line from the CF&YVRR (1891) and prospered as a small tobacco sales and manufacturing town also known for its educational and cultural amenities. The commercial district near the railroad around the junction of **Murphy Street** and **Market Street** has 2- and 3-story brick stores of the late 19th and early 20th centuries, such as the **Madison Grocery** (1890s; 105 Murphy St.), which retains its bracketed wooden storefront. To the east a large brick commercial building with tower carries the **Town Clock** (1919; Dalton and Hunter Sts.) memorializing "Those Who Served Or Died For Our Flag."

Academy Street displays fine houses from various periods. There are several richly ornamented Italianate houses of the late 19th c., such as the L-plan frame **Pratt–Van Noppen House** (1890s; 101 W. Academy St.). Suggestive of early 19th-c. elegance is the **Twitchell-Galloway House** (1834; 107 W. Academy St.), a 2-story brick center-passage plan house in transitional Federal–Greek Revival style, built by Randall Duke Scales for his daughter Elizabeth on her marriage to Joseph Twitchell. After 1880 it was the home of John M. Galloway, one of the nation's largest growers of bright-leaf tobacco. The **Alfred Moore Scales Law Office** (ca. 1855; moved to Academy St. at

RK 3 *Twitchell-Galloway House*

Franklin St.) is a simple frame structure in which Scales, U.S. congressman and governor, began his career. The **Madison United Methodist Church** (1909; 112 W. Academy St.) is a small brick church with corner tower and simple Romanesque and Eastlake detail.

Streets to the north continue the variety in such houses as **Boxley** (1820s, 1840s, and later; 117 Hunter St.; B&B), a large frame Federal era house expanded in Greek Revival style, and **Rosemont** (1911; 506 W. Hunter St.), a towered brick mansion with stone trim, combining Queen Anne, classical, and Chateauesque elements. A different spirit appears in the simple pedimented Greek Revival **Madison Presbyterian Church** (1848; 204 Decatur St.). Continuing an early tradition of academies, the **Madison City School** (1920s; 306 Decatur St.) is a consolidated school in red brick with arched and square-headed openings, while the **Scott School** (1932; 410 Decatur St.) has simplified Art Deco elements.

RK 4 Mayodan

Two miles north of Madison on the Mayo River, Moravian businessman Francis H. Fries of Salem built a textile mill in 1895 and in 1899 chartered the town of Mayodan, after the Mayo and the Dan. By 1900 Fries and others had founded Avalon Mill and village farther up the Mayo. After the Avalon Mill burned in 1911, the company consolidated operations in Mayodan and moved Avalon's mill houses there. Several turn-of-the-century mill houses remain, chiefly 1-story L-plan dwellings, with a notable concentration known as **"Cotton Row"** on Washington and nearby streets; several

in the 300 block of S. 5th St. were moved from Avalon and marked with plaques accordingly.

RK 5 Kallam House

Ca. 1830; N side SR 1358, 0.2 mi. SE of Mayo River, Stoneville vic.; private, visible from road

Near an old river ford, the 1½-story log house is a prominent example of the county's strong tradition of log construction. The well-finished dwelling of V-notched logs has a hall-parlor plan plus rear shed rooms. Stone block chimneys are beautifully crafted. The story is told that when the mason completed them, he laid a board across their tops and stood on his head on the board to show his "true and level" work. The house is believed to have been built for David and Luranny Smith Kallam, who married in 1820 and reared 8 children on their small farm.

Eden (RK 6–9)

See Claudia Roberts Brown, *A Tale of Three Cities* (1986, 2000).

The city created in 1967 from Leaksville, Spray, and Draper boasts an important industrial heritage, including some of the state's largest late 19th- to early 20th-c. textile factories, an early waterpower canal, some early 19th-c. workers' housing, and planned early 20th-c. textile mill villages.

RK 6 Leaksville

Leaksville began in 1795 when John Leak platted a town on a bluff above the confluence of the Smith and the Dan rivers. He named streets for prominent national leaders and the town for himself; then he lost his property and departed by 1800. The trading community waxed in the heat of early 19th-c. speculation, then waned after the panic of 1819; it regained strength in the late 1830s when John Motley Morehead established the Leaksville Factory textile mill across the Smith River from the town. His factory (in present-day *Spray) continued through the century, while Leaksville proper developed

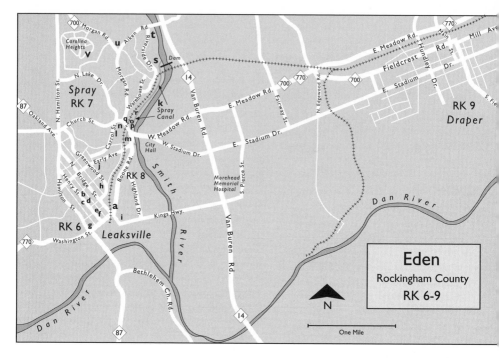

Eden
Rockingham County
RK 6-9

N

One Mile

as a small, diverse trading and manufacturing community. After the Civil War new men came to town and invested in tobacco sales and manufacturing, and prospects rose with a narrow-gauge railroad connection to Danville in 1883. Meanwhile Morehead's son, James Turner Morehead, developed around the old Leaksville Factory the separate textile town of Spray.

Leaksville's **Central Business District** (**a**) retains several late Italianate commercial buildings at **613–21 Boone Rd.** (1920s) and the **600 block of Washington St.** The Neoclassically detailed red brick **Realty Building** (1925; John Smith, contractor; 625 Washington St.) was constructed as Leaksville's "skyscraper" by a builder who came to superintend construction of a mill, stayed, and became mayor. The **Bullard-Ray House** (1830s, 1908, 1915; 650 Washington St.) began as a 2-story Greek Revival frame house built for Massachusetts mechanic John Hall Bullard, who moved here to manage Leaksville Cotton Mill and became a leading merchant; his grandson, John Bullard Ray, expanded the house at the heart of town.

The grid of streets northwest of Wash-

ington St., including Hamilton, Patrick, Henry, Monroe, and others, have small early dwellings as well as larger houses in Italianate, Queen Anne, and Colonial Revival styles. Remarkably unchanged is the **Mount Sinai Baptist Church** (1921; J. W. Hopper, architect; 512 Henry St.) (**b**), a twin-towered, late Gothic Revival brick church built for a black congregation from designs by Leaksville's leading architect; his father, James Monroe Hopper, built the church and other structures as well as several mills and mill houses in Leaksville. One of the oldest houses in town, the frame **Rogers-Martin-Taylor House** (early 19th c.; 537 Henry St.) (**c**) began as a hall-parlor plan dwelling with enclosed stair and massive brick chimney. The **Church of the Epiphany** (ca. 1844 and later; 538 Henry St.) (**d**), an antebellum Greek Revival frame building, was remodeled in the late 19th and mid-20th centuries. Architect J. W. Hopper also designed the **Leaksville Hospital** (1924; 602 Henry St.) (**e**), a red brick structure of domestic character. An early residence that grew with the town is the **Dempsey-Reynolds-Taylor House** (early 19th c. onward; 610 Henry St.) (**f**), which began as a hall-parlor plan Fed-

RK 6 *Doctor Franklin King House*

eral period dwelling, now a wing behind the ca. 1880s Italianate front block. The **J. W. Hopper House** (ca. 1920; 819 Washington St.) (**g**), a grand Tudor Revival style residence, was designed by the architect for himself.

Near the edge of town is the boldly composed **First Baptist Church** (1885–86; 533 Greenwood St.) (**h**), a brick building with a complex roof sheltering a fan-shaped sanctuary auditorium, with bands of Gothic windows, an open belfry, and Stick style trim. The most ebullient late 19th-c. house in town is the **Doctor Franklin King House** (1875; 700 block Bridge St.) (**i**), a 16-room frame residence with central entrance tower flanked by ornately decorated gabled bays. King (whose given name was Doctor) moved to town and became a leading tobacconist and banker in the post–Civil War era. Unusual is the survival of early **Workers' Housing** typically of 1-over-1 form. Especially notable is the small log house at **628 Early Ave.** (**j**); now covered with new siding, the original 16-by-15-foot dwelling has a 1-over-1 plan plus a rear shed. This form continued as later frame workers' houses were built in the area.

RK 7 Spray Industrial District

Spray contains one of the state's prime concentrations of textile factory architecture. Its main artery and raison d'être is the **Spray Power Canal** (**k**). The canal was constructed by James Barnett of Virginia, who

in 1813 purchased land for an industrial development by the Smith River. To power his large gristmill and other potential operations, he built a dam at a rapids and dug a 4,200-foot canal to Tackett Branch, which feeds back into the river. After the panic of 1819, Barnett left for Kentucky. Seeing the potential of the site, in the 1830s John Motley Morehead invested in and then acquired the property and in 1839 erected the county's first cotton mill. Construction of the big 3-story stone mill called Leaksville Factory or Morehead's Mill was superintended by mechanic John Hall Bullard of Massachusetts. There were also flour and sawmills and, beginning in the 1850s, a woolen mill near the canal. Morehead, a native of Virginia, grew up in Rockingham Co.; after moving to Greensboro (*Blandwood) and becoming governor and president of the North Carolina Railroad, he still maintained ties with Leaksville enterprises. After the old stone factory burned in 1893, a brick mill was built on its foundations; it was razed in the late 20th c., leaving only the old stone foundations. A small park encompassing the site includes a pavilion honoring banjo player and millworker Charlie Poole. The chief early landmark is the **Mill House** (early 19th c.; 118 Carroll St.) (**l**), a small 2-story brick house with a hall-parlor plan, which dates from the Barnett or early Morehead era and might have housed the mill manager during the 1840s and 1850s.

The principal focus of Spray is the series of major mills built from 1890 through the 1910s. After J. M. Morehead's death in 1866, his son James Turner Morehead, a "leading apostle of industrialization," took over and expanded the operation and developed the factory town around the mills. In 1889 he applied for a post office and suggested the name of "Splashy" for the water tossed by the mill wheel; after residents objected that it suggested a mud hole, he offered "Spray" instead, which was adopted as the name for the community that included Leaksville Factory. In the 1890s a parallel eastern branch of the canal was built, and in 1902 the old wooden and rubble dam was replaced by a granite dam.

Here in 1892 J. Turner Morehead and

Canadian chemist Thomas L. "Carbide" Willson, seeking an economical method of making aluminum, experimented with an electric arc furnace powered by the canal. In the waste products they discovered calcium carbide, a new chemical compound capable of producing acetylene gas; it was identified when J. Turner's son John Motley Morehead III, a recent graduate of the University of North Carolina (UNC), took it for analysis by his chemistry professor Francis P. Venable. J. Turner lost his fortune in 1893, then moved to New York and eventually founded the company that later became Union Carbide; he and son John, chemist and engineer with Union Carbide, made fortunes that became the source of many family benefactions to the state and the university.

After Morehead left Spray, B. Frank Mebane Jr., husband of J. T. Morehead's daughter Lily, assumed leadership of the family operation. The antebellum stone mill burned in 1893 but was soon rebuilt, and under Mebane one big mill after another was built along the canal. Around 1912, after Mebane suffered financial setbacks, the Marshall Field Co. of Chicago (a principal creditor during expansion) took control of several of the mills. In 1947 Marshall Field's textile operations became Fieldcrest Mills.

Running generally northward from the south end of the canal are key elements of the industrial district. These are imposing brick buildings of the period's standard slow-burn construction, with heavy wooden interior posts and floors, rows of large, arched windows, and stair towers. Warehouses, picker rooms, and other secondary structures are numerous, as are later expansions. The **Morehead Cotton Mill** (1902; 125 Boone Rd.) (**m**) is a prominent 3-story brick factory built to manufacture cotton yarn and warp. At Morehead's initial **Leaksville Cotton Mill** (1830s; 422 Church St.) only the stone foundations remain (**n**). The **Spray Mercantile Building** (1890; 413 Church St.) (**o**), on the canal, is an elegant 2-story brick structure with arched windows, a portion of a much longer commercial block that stood until 1983. **Spray Cotton Mills** (1896–98; 423 Church St.) (**p**), which produced cotton yarns, was the first great mill of the Mebane era; it was later owned by Dr. Karl von Ruck, a German physician resident in Asheville.

Nantucket Mills (1898, 1900; R. C. Biberstein; 100 Morgan Rd. at Church St.) (**q**) is the most striking of the mills, a large brick building 2 and 3 stories tall with arched windows and an imposing 5-story tower. Built to produce cotton fabric with power from the canal, it is the only mill at Spray for which the designer is known, a prominent Charlotte mill architect. It was

RK 7 *Nantucket Mills*

RK 7 *Rhode Island Mill*

begun by the Duke family and their associates, then acquired by the Mebane firm. The **American Warehouse Co.** (1899 and later; E side Warehouse St. N of Church St.) (**r**), the largest of the mills in Spray, was established to finish fabrics and blankets made in other mills, and its expansion continued over several years. The grandly sited **Rhode Island Mill** (1903, 1908; 540 Riverside Dr.) (**s**), on high land overlooking the dam, was the last of the Morehead family mills built by the Spray Water Power & Land Co., producing yarn and cotton blankets. The nearly contemporary **Spray Woolen Mills** (1902, 1910; 724 Riverside Dr.) (**t**) was built to manufacture woolen blankets.

Clusters of predominantly 1-story workers' houses from the turn of the century are interspersed among the factories. One section, called Flint Hill, encompassed parts of Morgan, Grove, Orchard, Riverside, and other streets. The 600 and 700 blocks of Riverside Dr. include workers' and managers' houses, with hip and gable roofs and varied plans. Along **Morgan Rd.** stood key institutions, the best preserved being **St. Luke's Episcopal Church** (1924–26; J. W. Hopper, architect; 604 Morgan Rd.) (**u**), built in simple Gothic Revival style of stones gathered by parishioners and aided by the Field company. **Carolina Heights** (1920s; North Spray) (**v**), created to meet demand for housing as Marshall Field expanded operations, was laid out with curvilinear streets lined mainly by bungalows. Several more varied clusters of mill houses stand northwest of the industrial center.

RK 8 Highlands

The hilltop area between Leaksville and Spray developed as a residential enclave for businesspeople, professionals, and upper-level mill employees from both communities. Some houses were privately built; others were erected by the companies. Especially prominent are the **John M. Morehead II House** (ca. 1900; 420 Boone Rd.), a picturesque dwelling of complex Queen Anne massing, and **Ridgecroft** (ca. 1902; 238 Highland Dr.), an early Colonial Revival residence with Dutch gambrel roof built for Spray official L. W. Clark. The simple 2-story frame **Luther Hodges House** (1920s; 233 Highland Dr.) was built by Marshall Field for the young textile executive who later became governor and U.S. secretary of commerce.

RK 9 Draper

The village, begun in 1906 under B. Frank Mebane and the Spray Water Power and Land Co. and expanded after 1911 by Marshall Field, centered on the German-American Mill (est. 1905–6; altered), which manufactured sheets and blankets and was renamed Draper-American during World War I. The large mill village south and west contains 1-story frame workers' houses, some with side-gable roofs, 1 room deep, and others with hip roofs, 2 rooms deep. The foursquare brick **Superintendent's House** (ca. 1916; 141 N. Main St.) dates from the early Field era.

RK 10 Ruffin

Mid-19th-c. Ruffin was a tobacco manufacturing center larger than Reidsville, with stores, tobacco factories, saloons, and a hotel, but as Reidsville grew, Ruffin remained a local trading village. Reminders of its heyday include several unusually elaborate 2-story frame houses with ornate millwork porches. **Worsham Mill** (1908; S side SR 1925, 1 mi. W of Ruffin), a large frame flour and gristmill, operated into the 1970s.

RK 11 Courts House

Early 19th c.; N side US 29 BUS,
2.2 mi. W of US 29 BYP

The 1½-story frame house represents the modest dwellings of all but the wealthiest early 19th-c. farmers and planters. Finished in simple Federal style, it follows a hall-parlor plan, rests on a fieldstone foundation, and has end chimneys of fieldstone with brick stacks. Located beside an old road that crossed the Dan River at Dix Ferry, the house is believed to have been built for Revolutionary War veteran George Courts, who moved to the county in 1806, or his son Robert; it may have served the miller at their nearby gristmill.

RK 12 Lick Fork
Primitive Baptist Church

19th c.; E side SR 2565, 2.1 mi. S of Ruffin

Of several Primitive Baptist churches in the county, the plain 1-story frame meetinghouse is the best preserved. Built for a congregation formed in the 18th c., it typifies the conservatism of the denomination in its straightforward form with an entrance on the long side as well as the gable end.

RK 13 High Rock Plantation House

Ca. 1830; W side SR 2614,
0.8 mi. S of SR 2619

The massive brick house stands high on a raised basement and is dominated by a pedimented portico with two plain, full-height columns of stuccoed masonry (*Dongola, Yanceyville). Brick is laid in 1:4 bond. Large front windows and central entrances at both levels have a modified Palladian treatment, each with a wide stuccoed arch with keystone and splayed ends. The center-passage plan has 2 large front rooms plus an original 2-story rear ell, all finished in elaborate late Federal style. Named for a nearby rock outcropping overlooking a ford on the Haw River, the plantation house was built for Joseph and Polly Scales McCain, who married in 1807; following his unexpected death in 1830, she offered for sale in 1836 the 1,000-acre plantation with "a large new three story BRICK HOUSE, containing ten rooms," a

RK 13 *High Rock Plantation House*

store, and a tanyard. Located beside the "main Stage Road leading from Washington City, through Salem, Salisbury, &c," the place long served as "a Public Stand, both as a Store and House of Entertainment."

RK 14 Speedwell Presbyterian Church

Ca. 1844; SE side SR 2406, opp. SR 2409

The frame church with gable front typifies many of its era and is accompanied by many early gravestones. The Presbyterian congregation, organized ca. 1759, is among the earliest in the northern Piedmont.

Reidsville (RK 15–20)

See Laura Phillips, *Reidsville, North Carolina: An Inventory of Historic and Architectural Resources* (1981).

An early 19th-c. village named for landowner Reuben Reid gained industrial strength after the Piedmont Railroad was built during the Civil War from Danville to Greensboro. Located in the heart of the Old Belt, it prospered as a center of the tobacco industry along with Danville, Va., Durham, and Winston. By 1885 the town of nearly 4,000 people had fifteen tobacco factories and ten leaf storage houses, plus a cotton mill and other factories. In the early 20th c. the F. R. Penn Tobacco Co. absorbed several small firms and became a branch of the American Tobacco Co. (ATC) in 1911, with a major Lucky Strike cigarette factory that made Reidsville the "Lucky City." Reidsville

RK 14 *Speedwell Presbyterian Church*

remained relatively small, with architecture recalling its stature as a tobacco center.

RK 15 Downtown Reidsville

On Scales St., the **Bank of Reidsville** (1894; 100 S. Scales at Morehead St.) (**a**) is the most prominent of several brick commercial buildings, with a corner tower accentuating its position at a principal intersection, which is marked by the Confederate Monument (1910; Henry Brown [Richmond]) (**b**). The eclectic Spanish–Colonial Revival style **Rockingham Theatre** (1929; Charles C. Benton [Wilson], architect; 205 Gilmer St.) (**c**) is claimed as the first theater in the state designed for talkies. Civic landmarks from the early 20th-c. stature include the Neoclassical Revival **Municipal Building** (1926; 220 W. Morehead St.) (**d**), with symmetrical massing and a Doric portico; the **U.S. Post Office** (1936; Louis K. Voorhees [High Point], architect; 230 W. Morehead St.) (**e**), in stripped Georgian Revival Moderne with Flemish-bond brickwork, which has a 1937 mural of tobacco harvesting by J. Gordon Samstang of New York. At some distance is the **Coca-Cola Bottling Plant** (1937; 697 S. Scales St.) (**f**), a fine example of the company's standard designs, an asymmetrical, streamlined composition in brick and stone with large steel windows to display the bottling process. The **Reidsville High School** (1922; 116 N. Franklin St.) (**g**), an imposing brick school with big, arched windows and Tuscan colonnades, has been renovated for housing.

RK 16 Tobacco District

North of downtown, the industrial sector along Market St. and the railroad district comprised large and small tobacco warehouses and factories, many of which were razed in the late 20th c. Still standing are the **E. M. Redd & Co. Leaf House** (late 19th c.; 129 E. Morehead St.) (**h**), a 3-story brick building with stepped gable ends, and the **J. H. Walker & Co. Flour Mill, Planing Mill, and Tobacco Box Factory** (1887; 301 SW. Market St.) (**i**), a larger 3-story brick building with segmental-arched windows and stepped gable ends. The dominant element is the huge **American Tobacco Company** (1890s–mid-20th c.; NW. Market St.) (**j**). The F. R. Penn Co. initially pulled together several small tobacco factories along the railroad. After the Penn firm was acquired by the ATC in 1911, Charles A. Penn, who became a director of the ATC in 1913 in New York, perfected the blend for the new Lucky Strike cigarette; in 1917 he succeeded in getting a Lucky Strike factory built in Reidsville. In 1939 the ATC added Pall Malls. A sequence of large industrial buildings ranges from stylized Italianate brick structures of 3 and 4 stories to the massive, streamlined Moderne buildings of the Lucky Strike and Pall Mall era. The office building on N. Scales St., by contrast, presents a genteel classical facade.

RK 17 N. Washington St.

Reidsville businessmen built scores of small houses for black and white workers in the tobacco factories. As in neighboring Caswell Co. and Virginia, many were small, vertical houses 1 or 2 stories tall, with a 1-room plan and sometimes a rear shed room. The best-kept row stands in the **300 block of N. Washington St.**, a series of small, almost saltbox-shaped frame houses with shed porches, with 1 main room per floor. These were built ca. 1915 by pharmacist Thomas Gardner as rental houses for black workers at the ATC plant and have been neatly renovated for continued use.

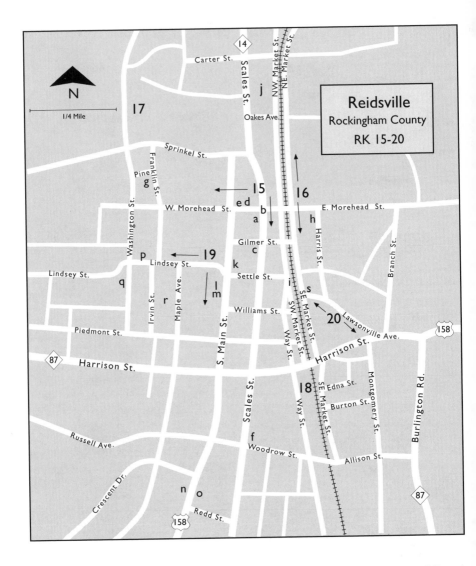

RK 18 Reidsville (Edna) Cotton Mill and Villages

South of the commercial district, business-men built the **Reidsville Cotton Mill** in 1889 to diversify the economy. The typical, Italianate brick factory was later expanded, renamed the Edna Cotton Mill, and remod-eled. Around the mill are several streets of workers' housing, mainly 2-story duplexes with 3 rooms per unit, paired central en-trances, central chimneys, and rear shed ex-tensions—essentially a doubling of the sin-gle-house type seen on *N. Washington St. The first houses were built in 1890 in the

600 block of Way St., and others followed in 1897–1900, including those in the **600 block of Landcaster Dr.** and the **100–200 blocks of Edna St.** and **Burton St.** The mill is now part of Cone Mills, and the houses have been individualized.

RK 19 S. Main St. Area

On the premier residential avenue, S. Main St., and flanking streets, industrialists and merchants built stylish houses in the Ital-ianate, Queen Anne, and Colonial Revival modes. **Main Street Methodist Church** (1890–93; W. C. Bain [Greensboro], archi-

RK 15 *Downtown Reidsville*

RK 16 *Walker Flour Mill*

RK 18 *Mill housing, Landcaster Dr.*

RK 19 *Main Street Methodist Church*

tect; Joseph McCoy, brickmason; 217 S. Main St.) (**k**) is an lively blend of Romanesque and Gothic motifs with corbeled brickwork accenting the asymmetrical towers. The brick, Italianate **William Lindsey House** (1884; 308 S. Main St.) (**l**) was built for a tobacco pioneer and gained a classical portico ca. 1908. The full-blown Queen Anne style **Tallulah A. Richardson House** (1890; Orlo Epps [Greensboro], architect; John Y. Smyth, builder; 312 S. Main St.) (**m**) was designed by a leading Greensboro archi-

tect. A grand example of the Southern Colonial Revival is the **Hugh Reid Scott House** (1909; Richard Gambier [Greensboro], architect; 802 S. Main St.) (**n**), while the **Andrew J. Boyd House** (1882; 803 S. Main St.) (**o**) is an asymmetrical towered villa. The **Womack-Stiers House** (1900; 508 Lindsey St.) (**p**) is a symmetrical, eccentrically ornate and steep-gabled Queen Anne design. (See Introduction, Fig. 63.) An architectural curiosity in its day, the **"Round House" (Chilton House)** (1960; Eddie Isaiah

RK 19 *Andrew J. Boyd House*

Chilton, builder; 3205 Washington St.) (**q**) was built for Thelma Onie Chilton, independent-spirited member of a longtime local family, who worked at the ATC. She planned the 1-story circular-plan house herself, in simple modernist style and with wedge-shaped rooms. The large **Penn House** (1932; Bryant Hurd [Danville, Va.], architect; 324 Maple Ave.) (**r**), with its Mount Vernon inspired portico, was built for Stella Penn, widow of tobacconist Charles, to replace their house that burned in 1931.

RK 20 Lawsonville Ave. Area

To the east, across the railroad, Lawsonville Ave. and nearby streets also have notable late 19th- and early 20th-c. residential architecture. A local landmark near the tracks is the **Reid House** (1881; J. M. Walker & Co., builder; Market St. at Lawsonville Ave.) (**s**), an Italianate frame house built for Thomas Reid, the son with whom the governor David S. Reid resided late in life.

RK 21 Richardson Houses
Ca. 1842, 1860s, 1912; N side Richardson Dr., W of Coach Rd.

Beyond the edge of town, Robert Paine Richardson I, farmer, merchant, and tobacco manufacturer, built a small frame farmhouse about 1842; in the 1860s he erected a larger house of Italianate style with an ornate iron porch. His son R. P. Richardson II prospered in tobacco manufacturing and in 1912 moved the two older houses down the hill and built his own columned mansion at the crest.

RK 22 *Chinqua-Penn Plantation House*

RK 22 Chinqua-Penn Plantation
Begun 1923; Harry C. Ingles (New York), architect; Gordon Hurleman (Switzerland), landscape architect; N side SR 1998, 1 mi. W of Reidsville; open limited hours

The eclectic country estate, named for the family and a local shrub, reflects the tastes of the widely traveled and sociable Thomas Jefferson "Jeff" Penn and his wife Beatrice "Betsy" Schoellkopf. Jeff Penn, a native of Virginia, grew up in Reidsville, where his father, Frank, founded the F. R. Penn Tobacco Co.; Jeff entered the business and traveled in the Far East. After the company was sold to the ATC in 1911, Penn bought a farm in Rockingham Co., where like other businessmen he engaged in dairy farming. In 1923 he married Betsy Schoellkopf (whose family developed Niagara Falls as a power source), and the couple began creating their estate. The centerpiece is the 27-room Y-shaped house (1923–25), built of oak logs and quartzite stone in a blend of the rustic and the exotic, with various rooms incorporating European and Asian elements. The ensemble includes a stone clock tower built ca. 1929 by Italian mason J. S. Skambato, gatehouses (1923–24) of rough stone and log construction, and formal gardens, greenhouses, and a pagoda. The Penns left Chinqua-Penn to UNC, complete with their diverse assemblage of furniture and artworks.

Stokes County (SK)

The Virginia border county remains one of the most rural in the Piedmont. The Dan River bisects the county diagonally, and the ancient Sauratown Mountains, named for the Saura Indians who lived along the river, tower over the landscape. The county was formed in 1789 from Surry Co. and named for Revolutionary War officer John Stokes. The strongly German southern part of the county became Forsyth Co. in 1849; the northern section (present-day Stokes) was settled primarily by English from Virginia, with a few Germans and other groups. Small farms predominated, though Peter Hairston's Sauratown Plantation on the Dan River was one of the state's largest. Railroads clipped the southern corners of the county in the late 19th c., prompting growth of *Walnut Cove, Pine Hall, King, and *Pinnacle. In the north are several communities where houses of related families cluster around a crossroads store or church and school. Log tobacco barns are still plentiful.

SK 1 Danbury

Established in 1849 on the Dan River as the centrally placed seat of the newly divided county, the town retains its small size and courthouse focus. Iron operations (*Moratock Iron Furnace) and late 19th- and early 20th-c. mineral springs resorts (*Vade Mecum) in the nearby mountains briefly boosted the economy. There are commercial buildings, houses, churches, and schools east and west along Main St. from Courthouse Square.

On the hilltop above the village, the **Former Stokes County Courthouse** (1904; Oliver Duke Wheeler [Charlotte], architect; Courthouse Square) is one of several similar courthouses by Wheeler and associates featuring porticoes and mansard cupolas, here with an Ionic portico and the least-altered interior of the group. Behind the courthouse is the Italianate **Stack-Bickett Law Office** (Town Hall) (1888), a 2-room frame building typical of 19th-c. offices. Built for Amos M. Stack, it was later shared by Thomas Bickett, governor of N.C. (1917–21).

Notable mid-19th-c. structures include the **Wilson Fulton House** (ca. 1860; N side Main St. E of courthouse), a 2-story brick house with simple Greek Revival trim, and the **McCanless Hotel** (ca. 1860, late 19th c.; N side Main St. W of courthouse), a 9-bay frame inn with 2-tier porch. Later frame buildings of simple Victorian character include the former **Danbury Presbyterian Church** (1893–94; S side Main St.), with corner belltower and wood shingles. The **Stokes County Jail** (1904; Pauly Jail Building Co. [St. Louis]; N side Old Church Rd.) is a 2-story brick building with corner tower.

SK 2 Moratock Iron Furnace

Ca. 1843; Moratock Park, E side SR 1674, 0.3 mi. E of NC 8/89, Danbury

One of the few 19th-c. iron furnaces still standing in N.C. (*Endor Iron Furnace, *Madison Iron Furnace), the trapezoidal stone structure was apparently built for Moody's Tunnel Iron Works and operated by the Moratock Mining & Mfg. Co. dur-

SK 1 *Former Stokes Co. Courthouse*

SK 2 *Moratock Iron Furnace*

ing the Civil War, when such small operations gained importance to a Confederacy cut off from outside sources of iron. It measures approximately 28 feet square at the base and is constructed of rough-quarried granite blocks, skillfully laid and unmortared on the exterior, with vaulted openings on three sides. Like others of its type, it is built against a bluff so that ore could be trundled over a bridge to the top of the furnace.

SK 3 Hartman-Priddy Store
1888; N corner SR 1670 and SR 1674, Danbury vic.

The 2-story frame country store is one of the best-preserved in the region. It was built by Raleigh Hartman and operated by the Priddy family from ca. 1930. Simply finished with shed porch and diagonal board shutters, it retains original shelving, storage drawers, and hardware.

SK 3 *Hartman-Priddy Store*

SK 4 Hanging Rock State Park Bathhouse
1939; Robert Ormand, architect; Civilian Conservation Corps (CCC), builders; SR 2015; open to public in season during park hours

The park was established in 1936 after the philanthropic Winston-Salem Foundation purchased the land in the Sauratown Mountains as a gift to the state. The CCC, which provided jobs for young men, graded roads and trails, constructed dams and built camp and picnic shelters and other facilities. The bathhouse is the largest and most distinctive facility constructed by the CCC in N.C.; it is a massive, rustic structure of random ashlar and heavy timbers that can accommodate 1,000 visitors daily at the 12-acre lake. The ground level contains dressing rooms, while the upper level is open on four sides with an enormous fireplace at one end. Architect Ormand was a Gaston Co. native working for the National Park Service. (See Introduction, Fig. 71.)

SK 5 Covington House
Ca. 1820s, ca. 1860; W side NC 89, 2.5 mi. S of NC 8/NC 89 jct., Meadows vic.; private, visible from road

The big 2½-story frame house was built in two side-by-side sections—for planter William Covington and his son James—joined by a broad, 2-tier engaged porch. Generally rare in the Piedmont, the porch form was built on several local mid-19th-c. houses.

SK 6 Pine Hall
1859; E side SR 1908, 0.7 mi. S of US 311; private, visible at a distance from road

One of the most substantial plantation houses in the northwestern Piedmont, the 2-story brick Greek Revival house was built for Leonard Anderson, a Confederate quartermaster, as the seat of his 879-acre plantation on the Dan River; it was later the home of his niece Eliza Chisman and her husband, Dr. J. L. Hanes. Outbuildings include Dr. Hanes's medical office. The nearby railroad town of Pine Hall, a brickmaking center, took its name from the plantation. (See Introduction, Fig. 31.)

SK 7 Walnut Cove

An old settlement was incorporated in 1889 after the Cape Fear & Yadkin Valley Railroad (CF&YVRR) and the Norfolk & Western Railroad made it the county's chief agricultural trading center with a hotel, wholesale businesses, tobacco warehouses, a brickyard, and a lumberyard. The principal residential avenue, **Summit St.**, retains late 19th- and early 20th-c. 2-story frame houses of Italianate, Victorian, and Colonial Revival design. The large **Capt. Robert L. Murphy House** (1890s; sw corner Summit and 4th Sts.) is a Colonial Revival dwelling with wood-shingled second story, gables, and dormers. **Christ Episcopal Church** (1886–87; N side Summit St.) is a board-and-batten Carpenter Gothic church similar to *St. Philip's Church in Germanton. **Walnut Cove Colored School** (1921; Dan River Lumber & Milling Co., builders; NW corner Brook and Dalton Sts.) is a 1-story, 5-classroom frame school building with clipped gable front. It is the county's only school built with the assistance of the Julius Rosenwald Fund, founded by Sears executive Julius Rosenwald to aid African American schools in the South. It has been restored as a community center.

SK 7 *Walnut Cove Colored School*

SK 8 Benjamin Bailey House
Mid-19th c.; NE corner jct. SR 1941 and SR 1937, Walnut Cove vic.; private, visible in winter from road

The 2-story double-pile frame house is one of the county's largest Greek Revival dwellings and one of five of similar form and detail in the locale, possibly erected by the same builder.

SK 9 Bynum-Watts House
Ca. 1870s; W side SR 1944, 0.3 mi. N of SR 1941, Germanton vic.; private, visible from road

This typical 2-story farmhouse, with 3-bay facade, gable roof, end chimneys, and rear ell, is set apart by its 2-tier front porch with fanciful lattice posts and sawn brackets. In the early 20th c. it was the seat of the William Mitchell Watts family farms.

SK 10 Leake-Browder House
Ca. 1855; E side NC 8, 0.1 mi. S of SR 1941, Germanton vic.; private, visible from road

Built for planter David Leake, the 2-story Greek Revival house of brick is akin to *Pine Hall. The wraparound classical porch came ca. 1905.

SK 11 Germanton

County seat from 1789 until Stokes was partitioned in 1849, the village was named for the German settlers, most of whom lived south in present-day Forsyth Co. The 1820s brick courthouse stood until 1957 when Main St. cut through the square. The town declined after the county seat was moved to *Danbury, then revived with the arrival of the CF&YVRR in the 1880s. Vestiges of the county seat at the square are the former **Stokes County Jail** (early 19th c.) and the **Gibson Storehouse** (1810 and later), brick buildings later altered. **Germanton Methodist Church** (1856), a simple brick Greek Revival structure with a classical belfry, features a graceful double stair and original balcony and pews. **St. Philip's Episcopal Church** (ca. 1890; NW side NC 65/8 on Forsyth Co. line) is a Gothic Revival board-and-batten church with tapered corner entrance tower and spire, probably influenced by Richard Upjohn's *Rural Architecture* (1852). Frame dwellings along Main St. include mid-19th-c. Greek Revival cottages, later 19th-c. Italianate style houses, and 20th-c. bungalows.

SK 12 *Culler-Scott House*

SK 12 Pinnacle

The village on the old CF&YVRR (1888) retains several brick and frame commercial buildings and late Victorian houses. It was first called Culler and then renamed for the view to nearby Pilot Mountain. **Culler Roller Mill** (Pinnacle Milling Co.; ca. 1900; SR 1221) is a 2-story brick building with stepped parapet gables. Proudly facing the railroad tracks, the **Culler-Scott House** (ca. 1895; NW corner SR 1148 and the RR tracks) combines Second Empire, Italianate, and Queen Anne style elements with its 3-stage mansard-roofed tower, asymmetrical massing, and sawn ornament. Built for town founder Emmanuel Culler or his son Walter, it was later the boyhood home of Ralph James Scott, a prominent mid-20th-c. congressman.

SK 13 Joseph Edwin Johnson Farm

1904, 1914; NW corner SR 2019 and SR 1998, Quaker Gap vic.; private, visible from road

One of several prosperous farms in the Quaker Gap community, the well-preserved early 20th-c. farmstead retains a smokehouse, a washhouse, a privy, a corncrib, a feed barn, a woodshed, a tobacco pack house, animal pens, and other outbuildings recalling Piedmont farm life. The 3-room house was built in 1904, and the 2-story section with simple Victorian detail was added in 1914.

SK 14 Rock House Ruin (John Martin House Ruin)

1780s; E side SR 1186 at SR 1175, Flat Rock vic.; accessible to public

Sections of 2-story stone walls with arched openings compose a dramatic architectural ruin evoking 18th-c. life in the northwestern Piedmont. The 2½-story house with raised basement was built of fieldstones stuccoed outside and plastered within, with a vista toward the Sauratown Mountains. John Martin was a lieutenant during the Revolution, county magistrate, and legislator. Subsequent occupancy of the house is shrouded in mystery, but it has been a ruin since the late 19th c. The county historical society has stabilized the walls with vertical iron pylons and cables.

SK 14 *Rock House Ruin*

SK 15 Vade Mecum Hotel

Early 20th c.; NW side SR 1001, 0.7 mi.
SW of SR 1484, Moore's Springs vic.;
private 4-H camp, access limited

Three late 19th- and early 20th-c. mineral
springs resorts—Piedmont Springs, Moore's
Springs, and Vade Mecum—operated in the
Sauratown Mountains. The only remaining
hotel is the smaller of two at Vade Mecum, a
3½-story frame structure, 9 bays long, with
2-tier wraparound porch. It was later an
Episcopal retreat and gained a stone chapel
and other buildings.

SK 16 Matthew Moore House

1786; E side SR 1484, 1.2 mi. N of
SR 1001, Moore's Springs vic.; private,
visible at a distance from road

The 18th-c. house is one of few instances
outside Salem of the mid-Atlantic architectural traditions seen in Moravian and
Quaker buildings (*John Haley House,
Guilford Co.). Altered in the 20th c., the
1½-story structure has Flemish-bond brick
walls on a raised fieldstone basement, segmental-arched openings, and interior end
chimneys serving a 3-room plan. Commanding a grand view south to Moore's
Knob in the Sauratown Mountains, it was
built for Matthew Moore, who owned over
3,000 acres in Stokes Co., and was the boyhood home of his son Gabriel, governor of
Alabama (1829–31).

SK 17 Jessup's Mill
(Stokes Co. Union Milling Co.)

1910; N side SR 1432, 1.0 mi. NE of SR 1413,
Collinstown vic.; private, visible from road

Established as a local cooperative, the complex powered by the Dan River includes the
3½-story frame turbine-powered roller mill;
a 1913 stone and concrete dam with millrace;
and the former miller's house. D. H. Jessup
ran the mill for years, and his son Porter
continued until a flood in 1979.

SK 18 R. W. George Mill

1881; S side NC 89, 0.6 mi.
NE of jct. w/NC 66, Francisco vic.;
private, visible from road

Set along a steep hillside by Big Creek, the 2-
story frame corn mill served farmers for a
half-century and then was converted to produce parachute fabric during World War II.

Forsyth County (FY)

See Gwynne S. Taylor, From Frontier to Factory (1981).

*In 1752 the Moravians, a German-speaking Protestant denomination, purchased a 98,985-acre tract on the frontier—about a third of present-day Forsyth Co.—which they called Wachovia after the Wachau valley in Austria. Settling first at *Bethabara in 1753, they established the village of *Bethania in 1759 and built *Salem as a planned congregational and trading center in 1766. Governed as a theocratic society, the Moravians made fine craftsmanship and careful stewardship part of their faith-based way of life. Their integration of material, civic, and spiritual life under strong local control persisted through the years. Rural Moravian congregations were founded at Friedland, Friedburg, and Hope. Other German and English groups settled on the edges of Wachovia, and Methodist evangelists made converts among their Moravian neighbors. Originally part of Stokes Co., in 1849 the southern part became a new county, named for Benjamin Forsythe, killed in the War of 1812. Its seat was laid out north of Salem and named for Revolutionary War officer Joseph Winston. In the late 19th c., railroad towns grew up at *Kernersville, *Rural Hall, and elsewhere, and during the 20th c. the joined city of Winston-Salem extended farther into the county.*

Winston-Salem (FY 1–64)

The architecturally diverse city, famed for Old Salem's extraordinary collection of 18th- and 19th-c. Moravian buildings, also possesses some of the state's finest early 20th-c. architecture from the tobacco, textile, and banking "age of success," when Winston-Salem was N.C.'s biggest city and by far the richest. Dramatizing the architectural landscape is the hilly topography, which offers unexpected vistas of buildings of various eras.

During the 18th and early 19th centuries, as settlement and trade grew, Salem developed from a small, isolated frontier community into a town with increasing contact with neighboring communities. In the 1830s and 1840s, some Moravians strove to maintain traditions, while other Salem leaders such as Francis Fries pressed for modernization in manufacturing, banking, transportation, and civic leadership. When the new county was formed in 1849, despite misgivings over potential disruptions, the congregation council sold the county 51 acres north of town. In 1854 the plank road called the "Appian Way of North Carolina" was completed from Fayetteville. In 1856 Salem terminated its theocratic government and incorporated as a municipality of the state, while the Moravian church continued as a Protestant denomination.

Without rails, growth was modest until the long-awaited arrival of the Northwestern N.C. Railroad (NWNCRR) from Greensboro in 1873, but then business took off. Moravians such as the Fries family expanded in textiles, railroads, banking, and electric power, and the Nissen and Spaugh families' wagonworks thrived. Newcomers, including hardworking Methodists, opened tobacco sales houses, warehouses, and factories: the Hanes brothers moved from Davie Co.; Richard J. Reynolds and his brother William came from Virginia; and James A. Gray, who came with his father from Randolph Co. at Winston's founding, joined with local men to form Wachovia Bank, which financed many industrial ventures.

By the late 1880s Winston was full of tobacco sales and storage warehouses, and more than 30 tobacco factories made it a leading producer of plug (chewing) tobacco.

FY 37 *W. 4th St.: Reynolds and Wachovia Buildings (FY 34–35) in background*

The 1887–91 Roanoke & Southern Railroad spurred further growth, including Reynolds's construction of "THE tobacco factory of the South" (plant #256). Facing Duke's American Tobacco Co. (ATC) trust, in 1899 Reynolds devised a subsidiary affiliation with American and began consolidating the plug tobacco business, including acquisition of the Hanes companies—whereupon the Haneses turned to textiles and created another economic powerhouse.

"Onward is the watchword in the Twin Cities," proclaimed the local newspaper. Between 1870 and 1880 Winston mushroomed from about 400 to 4,000 people, while the twin cities grew from 4,000 to 10,000 and by 1910 reached 22,700. In contrast to textile mills, tobacco factories employed many black as well as white men and women. As thousands of people came to work in the factories, businesses, and professions, urban middle and working classes of both races emerged and established neighborhoods, churches, and schools. Workers' housing around the factories formed a patchwork of black and white areas often differentiated by the elevation of the terrain. Executives built mansions on high ground within sight of the factories, making 5th St. a "millionaire's row."

In 1890 the city became the second in the state to gain electric streetcars and promptly inaugurated suburban development. City surveyor Jacob Lott Ludlow platted suburbs on elevated rural sites. *West End (1890), evidently the earliest curvilinear planned suburb in the state, and *Washington Park or Southside (1892) were elite white suburbs, and on the east the black suburb of *Columbian Heights (1892) centered on Slater Industrial Academy (*Winston-Salem State University [WSSU]). Architecture was mainly the work of the local Fogle Bros. and other builders, who erected eclectic Queen Anne style residences, Gothic Revival churches, and Romanesque Revival civic buildings.

Already called Winston-Salem, the two cities officially merged in 1913. The motto "50-15"—50,000 by 1915—was optimistic; but by 1920 a population of 48,000 made it the largest city in the state, and it grew to 72,000 by 1926. Although Charlotte pulled ahead in 1930 with 82,000, Winston ran a strong second with 75,000.

The city was also the richest in the state. In 1911 the Board of Trade boasted manufactures worth $8 million in textiles, tobacco, wagons, machinery, grain products, furniture, and building materials. In the follow-

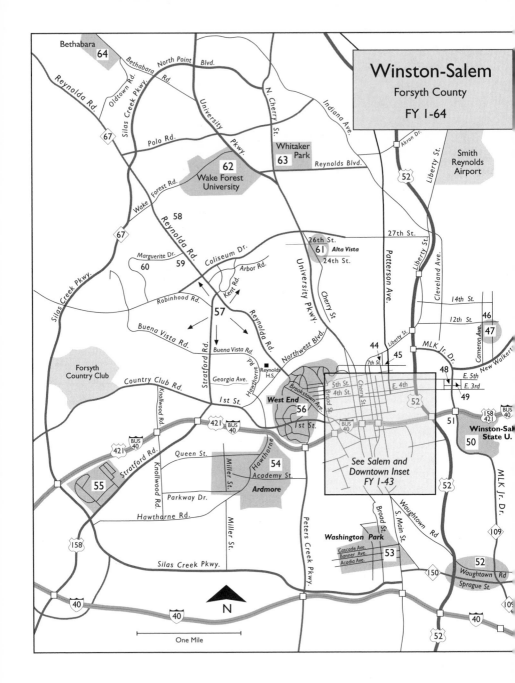

Winston-Salem
Forsyth County
FY 1-64

One Mile

N

ing decade, Wachovia Bank and Wachovia Trust Co. merged as the state's largest financial institution; Hanes factories grew into national leaders in cotton knitwear (and, later, nylon hosiery); and after the U.S. Supreme Court ruling broke up the ATC in 1911, the R. J. Reynolds Tobacco Co. (RJR)

emerged stronger than ever. In 1912 the company began an employee profit-sharing plan that spread the growing wealth locally, and in 1913 it revolutionized the cigarette business with Camels, which became the top-selling brand in the world. Local production soared to supply soldiers with tobacco, un-

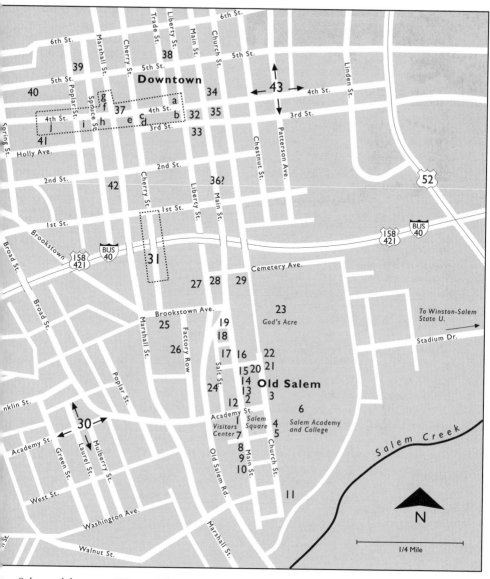

Salem and downtown Winston-Salem inset (FY 1–43)

derwear, and socks during World War I and continued to rise in the 1920s. By 1929 Winston-Salem's manufactured products were valued at over $300 million, more than twice as much as those of any other city in the state. Building permits rose in value from $500,000 in 1915 to over $8.5 million in 1928—in "The Town of a Hundred Millionaires."

A civic oligarchy including the Reynolds,

Hanes, Gray, and Fries families dominated local politics, business, philanthropy, and architecture. Between 1910 and 1930, city leaders transformed the downtown, replacing the previous generation's eclecticism with Neoclassical public and commercial buildings. Ever larger factories rose in the industrial sectors, which began to coalesce on the east, along with more workers' housing. The streetcar and the automobile, coupled with

Jim Crow practices, intensified the separation of uses and races. Sectors grew more distinct, with black and some white neighborhoods on the north and east, white working- and middle-class sections expanding south, and to the northwest, following a trail blazed by industrialists' country estates, exclusive upper- and upper middle-class white suburbs.

Winston-Salem favored the Beaux Arts tradition. Princes of industry might build Art Deco towers and streamlined factories, but generally they clothed their wealth in Colonial Revival and Neoclassical styles, along with Tudor and Norman Revival residences and Gothic Revival churches. In the early 20th c. a distinctive Moravian Revival style developed using motifs from *Home Moravian Church and other early Salem buildings. The mode was used in Moravian churches and collegiate buildings and, after World War II, for Wachovia branch banks statewide.

Local architectural firms thrived. Especially prolific was Northup & O'Brien, formed in 1916 by Willard C. Northup of Michigan, who came to Winston in 1908 (and evidently developed the Moravian Revival mode), and Leet O'Brien, a local man trained at Carnegie Tech; in 1927 Luther Lashmit, another native trained at Carnegie Tech, joined the firm. Also active were Englishmen C. G. Humphries and Harold Macklin, who came in the 1910s, and many others. Out-of-town architects gained some key commissions, including New York's Ralph Adams Cram and Mayer, Murray & Phillips, and Philadelphia country house architect Charles Barton Keen, who opened an office in the city with associate William Roy Wallace. To cap off the era, New York architects Shreve & Lamb designed the *Reynolds Building, precursor to their Empire State Building.

In the mid-20th c., growth leveled off, but though only fifth in size among the state's cities, Winston-Salem retained its stature as a corporate headquarters. RJR increased production through the Great Depression and World War II and regained a lead over the ATC in the 1950s with filter-tip Winstons and Salems. Wachovia became the

Southeast's largest bank until the early 1970s, with the tallest building in the state. Hanes maintained its leadership, and the city's Piedmont Airlines was founded in 1948. The "paternalistic oligarchy" supported undertakings that burnished the city's identity, including development of Bowman Gray Medical Center; restoration of *Old Salem (1950 onward); the move of *Wake Forest College (University) from Wake Co. (1946–56); the nation's first arts council (1949); and the state School of the Arts (1965). The city built an expressway (1954–58) through town; it was planned as a local route in 1952 and in 1957 was incorporated into the new interstate highway system. This and US 52 cut swaths through old neighborhoods, as did some of the state's earliest urban renewal projects from the 1940s onward.

In the late 20th c., global shifts in tobacco and textile markets and production cut manufacturing jobs, while corporate mergers redefined all the big firms. Hanes was acquired in 1979 by Consolidated Foods (Sara Lee); RJR acquired Nabisco and became RJR Nabisco in 1985, then underwent changes that ended with a greatly reduced RJR. USAir bought Piedmont in 1987, and Wachovia merged in 2001 with First Union of Charlotte, keeping the Wachovia name but with headquarters in Charlotte. Thus at the turn of the 21st c., the city faced a new chapter in its economic and civic life.

Salem

Salem, originally a 3,159-acre town lot within Wachovia, encompasses the restored Moravian town of *Old Salem and several blocks beyond. The Moravians are a Protestant denomination that originated in Moravia and trace from the 15th-c. martyr John Huss. After long persecution, they found sanctuary in the 1720s on Count Nicholas von Zinzendorf's estate in present-day Germany and formed a communal congregational society at Herrnhut, from which they sent out colonies. They founded Bethlehem, Pa. (1740), as their North American center, and from it in 1753 they sent pioneers to the frontier Wachovia tract. From the initial set-

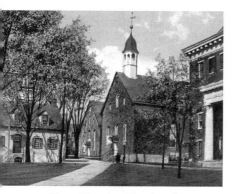

FY 3–4 *Home Moravian Church and Main Hall, Salem College*

tlement at *Bethabara they established Salem (1766).

Moravians organized the community into "choirs" according to age, sex, and marital status, which provided companionship and spiritual guidance. Governance was by congregational councils, with direction from Herrnhut and Bethlehem. In Salem the land was held in trust, with lots leased to individuals. Congregation members could build their own houses and shops, but the council administered building rules and regulated trades to control quality, costs, and discipline. The ideal was a community in which spiritual and material life were unified and consecrated. All were equal in spirit, as symbolized by Moravian graveyards, where burials are arranged by choirs, with small, flat markers.

Construction of Salem commenced January 6, 1766. Workers from *Bethabara and elsewhere built the congregation town as the "place in Wachovia for commerce and the professions." In 1772 those "destined for Salem moved thither." Positioned on a south-sloping ridge with a good water supply, the town was laid out by surveyor Christian Reuter in a grid with a central square. Around the square were sites for the church, the store, schools for boys and girls, and choir houses for single men and single women. Individual lots lined the rest of the street grid. Industries were sited at the edges—a gristmill on the south and the tannery on the west near Tanner's Run—and beyond were farms and agricultural outlots.

A key figure in planning the town and many individual buildings was Frederic William Marshall (born in Germany as Friedrich Wilhelm von Marschall), chief administrator of Wachovia.

Salem flourished as a regional trade and cultural center, known for its excellence in crafts and building. As pacifists, the Moravians did not participate in the American Revolution. In the 19th c. the town grew more exposed to outside influences, and secular concerns challenged the theocratic system. The church gradually shifted from German to English. When Salem businessmen sought to establish the *Salem Cotton Mill in 1836, and when the county wanted to purchase nearby land for Winston, conservative voices cautioned against their disruptions, but the modernizers carried the day. In 1856, after long soul-searching, the council acknowledged that changes had eroded the "original idea of a Town-Congregation" where members "unmixed by others, could build themselves up in their most holy faith." They decided to end the lease system, sell lots, and incorporate as a municipality. The Moravian church continued as an active denomination. After the Civil War, Salem leaders pioneered industrial growth and hydroelectric power production, and the community gained a rail spur and depot and a streetcar line (1890) that raised the street levels. When merger was considered in the 1870s, Winston residents feared domination by Salem; but by 1913 Winston had grown so fast that some Salemites resisted loss of town identity, and indeed Salem became a ward within the city.

Old Salem (FY 1–24)

S. Main St.; selected buildings open regular hours, others private; National Historic Landmark District

Although its Moravian heritage was revered, by the 1940s central Salem was in disrepair. The threat of a supermarket there resulted in the founding of Old Salem, Inc., in 1950. Inspired by Colonial Williamsburg—and with its architects Perry, Shaw & Hepburn (#Tryon Palace, New Bern)—restoration of Old Salem did much to define the city's post–World War II identity. Much of the handmade brick for the restoration was produced by local African American brickmaker George Black, who gained international recognition for his work. Old Salem's 1949 preservation ordinance was the first in the state. Industrial and business fortunes supported a vision to return Old Salem to its preindustrial era. Aided by the detailed records of the Moravians, late 19th- and early 20th-c. buildings were razed, some missing buildings reconstructed, and surviving early structures restored to their former appearance. In recent years the mission of Old Salem has broadened to encompass its later 19th-c. Moravian history.

The architecture represents the acculturation of Germanic traditions into the American mainstream. The initial half-timbered, log, and stone buildings were erected by European-born craftsmen who adapted Old World traditions to the scarcity of good building stone and lime. Common in the early years were tile roofs and central chimneys with cooking fireplaces and Germanic tile stoves, some made locally. After the American Revolution, and location of lime sources, native-born artisans constructed brick buildings that melded German traditions, regional elements, and in the early 19th c., stylish Federal motifs. Some buildings also show the widespread transition from combined to separate residence and workshop. Paralleling other changes, mid- and late 19th-c. Salem built Greek Revival, Gothic Revival, Romanesque, and Second Empire style structures—now the chief examples of stylish 19th-c. architecture in the city.

FY 1 Single Brothers House

1768–69, 1786; Frederic William Marshall, planner; Melchior Rasp, mason; Christian Triebel, carpenter; 600 S. Main St.; open regular hours; National Historic Landmark

One of the finest examples of *fachwerk*, or half-timber construction, in the United States, the massive building facing the square was central to Salem's initial construction campaign. The choir house for single brothers held living quarters for single men aged 14 years and older, as well as workshops. In traditional Germanic fashion the building is sited on the hillside, so that the basement is a full story at the rear. The north section was begun in August 1768 and completed in December 1769. The pegged frame of heavy timbers infilled with soft brick follows German methods wherein diagonal members do not intersect the corner posts. Other traditional elements include the tile roof and double-leaf doors. The German "kicked" eave—with a slight curve formed by a wedge tucked between the roof edge and the rafter—diverts rain from the wall below. The 1786 addition of brick in Flemish bond is similar to the *Single Sisters House. The kitchen in the basement retains

FY 1 *Single Brothers House*

its immense cooking facility. The Brothers House closed in 1823 and served various purposes before being restored in 1964. The log **Workshop** to the rear was built in 1771 and reconstructed in 1979.

FY 2 Boys School

1793–94; Johann Gottlob Krause, mason; Martin Lick, carpenter; 3 Academy St.; open regular hours

Built for boys aged 6 to 14 years, the 2-story structure displays the first local use of decoratively patterned brickwork. Apprenticed to potter Gottfried Aust, Krause became both potter and master mason. After erecting the *Single Brothers House, *Salem Tavern, and the *Single Sisters House in the 1780s, he returned to pottery and then began building again. The school, like the tavern, has a central-passage plan and tile roof but a straight (not kicked) roofline with a plastered coved cornice. The lower story is stuccoed and scored as stone blocks. Krause's new (as yet unexplained) use of English-derived motifs features lozenge patterns in the west gable, dark headers enlivening the Flemish bond, and a belt course in the east gable—elements that also appeared in the *Christoph Vogler House and farther afield.

FY 3 Home Moravian Church

1797–1800; Frederic William Marshall, designer; Johann Gottlob Krause, brickmason; William Craig (Grieg), stonemason; Johann Adam Wolff, carpenter and joiner; 1870 renovation; 1913, Willard C. Northup, architect; 529 S. Church St.

The focal point of Salem, the gable-fronted building is beautifully crafted of brick laid in Flemish bond and crowned by a cupola with weather vane from Nazareth, Pa. Administrator Marshall developed the plan after considering other Moravian churches, including that in Lititz, Pa. His graceful design shows growing Neoclassical influence in its straight roofline, belt course, and tall, arched windows, plus the introduction of the arched entrance "bonnet" (his initial drawing showed it gabled); wrought iron railings on granite steps; and painted bricks at corners, doors, and windows to resemble rubbed brick. From the cupola and balcony, the Moravian band played at deaths, on Easter morning, and for other occasions. Marshall planned the building so the "congregation might not be inconvenienced by the sun," with the pulpit on the long north side and entrances on the south and west. An 1870 remodeling oriented seating to the east, and in 1913 the sanctuary was expanded and reoriented north. The adjoining **Rondthaler Memorial Building** (1913; Willard C. Northup), named for Bishop Edward Rondthaler, shows Northup's early revival of Moravian motifs including the entrance bonnet.

FY 4 Main Hall, Girls' School (Salem College)

1854; Francis Fries, builder; Alexander Jackson Davis, architect?; 601 S. Church St.

Salem Female Academy, established in 1772 as the girls' school, became a boarding school in 1802 and grew into one of the most respected female schools in the antebellum South. In 1853 Francis Fries contracted to build the edifice; during an October visit to New York, he consulted A. J. Davis about a design for the school and paid him $25, but Davis's actual contribution is uncertain. The big Greek Revival building has a towering Doric portico across a straightforward structure of uniform brick laid in running bond without visible headers, a mid-19th-c. refinement.

FY 5 Single Sisters House

1785–86; Frederic William Marshall, supervisor; Johann Gottlob Krause, mason; Christian Triebel, Martin Lick, Johann Krause, carpenters; 627 S. Church St.; private dormitory

The long-planned building for the Single Sisters Choir was delayed by the American Revolution, and in 1784 materials for it were diverted to rebuild the *Salem Tavern, which had burned. Built February 1785–April 1786, it displayed elements introduced by Krause at the tavern, including oversized brick laid in Flemish bond and arched openings. The 2-story building with double attic and kicked eaves has its original tile roof. Dormers were added in 1812 and a south extension in 1819.

FY 6 Salem Academy and College
Early 20th c.; Willard C. Northup, Hobart Upjohn (New York), architects; E of Church St.

Attracting young women from near and far, the school established in 1772 grew eastward in the late 19th c. After the college and academy curricula were divided in the early 20th c., local architect Willard C. Northup and landscape architect Thomas Sears of Philadelphia (*Reynolda) planned a Beaux Arts campus of shaded quadrangles with gardens and buildings of Moravian-influenced "Colonial style." As Bishop Edward Rondthaler reported in 1921, they showed "an affectionate appreciation of what is best in old-time architecture with what is best in the newest interiors of college edifices." Among the first was **Clewell Hall** (1921–22; 624 S. Church St.), with Flemish-bond brickwork with dark headers and a classical doorway. Subsequent buildings developed the Moravian Revival further. Academy buildings by New York's Hobart Upjohn, including **Salem**

Academy and **Bitting Dormitory** (1930) have tall, dormered gambrel roofs inspired by European or Pennsylvania Moravian examples. Complementing Old Salem's restoration, **Mary Babcock Dormitory** (1957) and others feature Flemish-bond brick, arches over the windows, and bonnet hoods.

FY 7 T. Bagge, Merchant, Store and House
1775; 626 S. Main St.; open regular hours

Salem's first stone building was constructed as community store and storekeeper's residence, as reflected by the two entrances. Lacking good building stone or sufficient lime, the Moravians did not erect the 2-story stone buildings seen in Pennsylvania but did use stone for foundations and 1-story buildings—such as this one—covering rough stone with stucco scored to resemble stone blocks.

FY 8 John Vogler House
1819; John Vogler, plan; 700 S. Main St.; open regular hours

The symmetrical, 2-story Flemish-bond brick house with center-passage plan was planned by Salem's silversmith—who ap-

FY 9, 8 *Christoph Vogler and John Vogler Houses*

prenticed under his uncle Christoph Vogler—as his residence and shop. It illustrates transitions in style and use. Vogler combined Federal style elements, such as the fanlight in the pedimented entrance hood, with the traditional roof kick, divided Dutch door, and strap hinges. He first had his shop in a front room, then moved it to a separate structure. The rear ell held a laundry and a smithy. When Vogler's house was built, its predecessor was moved back: the **Anna Catharina House** (1771; dismantled, 1947; reassembled, 1954), a center-chimney, frame dwelling built for surveyor Christian Reuter and his wife Anna Catharina, who long survived him.

FY 10 *Salem Tavern*

FY 9 Christoph Vogler House
1797; Johann Gottlob Krause, mason;
710 S. Main St.; private

Krause's most flamboyant brickwork displays his initials in yard-high letters in dark header bricks on the south gable end and those of gunsmith Vogler on the front. He accented the Flemish-bond walls with a double-molded brick water table, rubbed brick arches over windows and doors, and herringbone patterns in the gables. The 1½-story house contained Vogler's residence to the south and workshop on the north.

FY 10 Salem Tavern
1784; Frederic William Marshall,
planner; Johann Gottlob Krause, mason;
800 S. Main St.; open regular hours;
National Historic Landmark

After the original tavern burned in January 1784, it was rebuilt on its foundations as Salem's first all-brick building. Krause introduced elements seen in the post-Revolutionary construction surge: oversized bricks laid in Flemish bond, elliptical arches over windows, a central-passage plan and symmetrical facade with end chimneys, and the town's first front porch. To accommodate "strangers" who came to trade, but to limit disruptive influences, Salem's tavern stood away from the square and had a windowless street facade. A frame building next door was added in 1816. The big barn (1830s; moved

from the *Beverly Jones Farm, Bethania) is an imposing structure with a heavy timber frame and pole rafters.

FY 11 African Moravian Church (St. Philip's)
1861; Charles Houser, bricklayer;
George Swink, carpenter;
459 S. Church St.

The brick church is believed to be the only surviving antebellum church built for blacks in N.C. As early as the 1770s Moravians had baptized African members, slave and free, into their congregation. In 1822 a separate congregation for blacks began to meet in a log structure here (reconstructed) and drew worshipers from far and wide. In 1860 Salem trustees authorized a brick church 40 by 60 feet. The gable-fronted sanctuary was built of 1:4 common bond with a steeple, tall 9/9 windows, and Greek Revival details; it was enlarged in front in 1890 and called St.

FY 11 *African Moravian Church (St. Philip's)*

Philip's after 1914. The congregation dwindled, then moved in the 1950s. Restoration began in the 1990s as part of Old Salem's interpretation of its African American history.

FY 12 Miksch House
1771; 532 S. Main St.; open regular hours

The first privately owned dwelling in Salem also held the shop of storekeepers and tobacco manufacturers Matthew and Henrietta Miksch. The weatherboarded house was built of dovetailed oak logs, with a tile roof and kicked eaves. The 3-room plan is organized around a center chimney and tile stove.

FY 13 Winkler Bakery
1800; Johann Gottlob Krause, mason;
529 S. Main St.; open regular hours

The 2-story brick building repeats Flemish-bond brickwork, steep roof with kicked eave, and stuccoed ground story. A typical domed bake oven is reconstructed. The bakery is the cultural hearth for the famous Moravian sugar cake and cookies.

FY 14 Butner House and Hat Shop
1820s; 517 S. Main St.; private

After the *Single Brothers House closed in 1823, young tradesmen often built shops in which to begin their trades, followed by nearby houses when they married. Hatmaker Adam Butner's pair of frame buildings illustrates the pattern: a small gable-fronted shop (1825) and a 3-story house (1829) with double porch over the sidewalk.

FY 15 Bank of the Cape Fear
1847; 500 S. Main St.

In 1847 the congregational council allowed the Wilmington-based Bank of the Cape Fear to open a Salem branch and even erected a 2-story brick building with separate front entrances for the bank and the residence of the cashier, Moravian Isaac Lash. The bank closed in the Civil War, but Lash founded the First National Bank of Salem in 1866, from which developed Wachovia Bank in Winston (1879).

FY 16 Belo House
1849, 1860; 455 S. Main St.; private

The big Greek Revival building dramatizes Salem's shift to nationally popular styles. It was built as a store and residence by cabinetmaker and merchant Edward Belo. In 1849 he built a long 2-story edifice of brick and frame around an existing structure, and in 1860 he added a third story and a large portico. His store occupied the first story, family quarters the second, and servants and storage the third. Ironwork may have come from Belo's foundry; the iron lion and dog figures follow popular models.

FY 17 Fourth House
1768; 438 S. Main St.; private

The 1-story center-chimney plan dwelling, the fourth to be built in Salem, used half-timbered construction infilled with brick, as

FY 14 *Butner House and Hat Shop and* FY 13 *Winkler Bakery*

FY 16 *Belo House*

did the *Single Brothers House and the neighboring (reconstructed) First, Third, and Fifth Houses. (See Introduction, Fig. 9.)

FY 18 Shaffner House

1874; Elias Vogler, architect; 428 S. Main St.; private

The finest Second Empire style building in the city, the 2½-story brick house is among the chief reminders of its era. Built for physician and industrial leader John Francis Shaffner and his wife Caroline Fries, it features stone lintels at the large windows and rounded dormers in the slate-covered mansard roof. The complex also included the doctor's pharmacy and other outbuildings.

FY 19 Coffee Pot

1858; in 400 block S. Main St.

The 7-foot tin coffee pot, fashioned by Moravian tinsmiths Julius and Samuel Mickey to advertise their shop, originally stood 2 blocks north. After the freeway cut through north Salem, their icon of enterprise was moved ca. 1960 to mark the north entrance to Old Salem.

FY 20 Salem Boys' School

1896–97; 500 S. Church St.; private

The last of Winston-Salem's late 19th-c. schoolhouses, the 2-story brick edifice has round-arched windows and corbeled brickwork akin to churches of the era. It has held Moravian offices since 1931.

FY 21 Vierling House

1802; Johann Gottlob Krause, builder; 463 S. Church St.; open regular hours

In its time the largest private house in town, the tall brick building is Krause's last work. It combines Flemish-bond brickwork, herringbone-patterned gables, and painted bricks at corners and openings. A round "bonnet" shelters the entrance into a center-passage plan 2 rooms deep. Built for Dr. Samuel Vierling and his wife Martha Miksch, it had his office in the front left room.

FY 22 Cedarhyrst

1895; Max Schroff (N.Y.), architect; Fogle Bros., builders; Peter and Paul Regennas, Nat Peterson, carvers; 459 S. Church St.; church offices, not open to the public

The picturesque Gothic Revival house was designed by a New York architect for Moravian physician Nathaniel Siewers and his wife Eleanor de Schweinitz. Built of rough blocks of Indiana limestone, it features a castellated porte cochere, Gothic arched entrance porch, and inscriptions noting the date and architect and the German phrase "Firmly Built, Having Trusted in God." Its German romanticism was probably inspired by Siewers's studies in Europe.

FY 22 *Cedarhyrst*

FY 23 God's Acre

Est. 1770; N of Church St.

A cedar-lined avenue ascends alongside the serene slope of the Moravian burial ground. Characteristic of Moravians' beliefs, graves are uniformly marked with small flat stones and placed by choir, with sections for married women and widows, single women and girls, married men and widowers, and single men and boys. An Easter sunrise service, preceded by cleaning and decorating of the cemetery, begins at Salem Square and proceeds with joyful music to God's Acre. Visible to the east is **Salem Cemetery** (est. 1857) with a curvilinear layout, individual and family plots, and diverse markers. At the northeast corner is a small Moravian graveyard (est. 1859) for African Americans.

FY 24 Lick-Boner House

1786; Martin Lick, carpenter;
512 Salt St.; private

The oldest in a row of small early dwellings, the log house was built by and for Martin Lick, with a central chimney serving the large hall-kitchen-entry room and two smaller rooms. Dovetailed logs, red painted shingle roof with kicked eaves, and herringbone Dutch door are traditional features. It was later the childhood home of poet John Henry Boner.

Salem beyond Old Salem

FY 25 Salem Cotton Mill and F. & H. Fries Arista Cotton Mill (Brookstown Inn)

1836–38, 1880s; 200 Brookstown Ave.

The best-preserved of the state's few antebellum textile mill buildings, the **Salem Cotton Mill** (1836–37) centers west Salem's 19th-c. industrial district. The 3-story structure (originally 9 bays long, 6 visible) is built of 1:5 bond with a stone foundation, corbeled cornice, and monitor roof—visible from the east courtyard. The interior retains stout, wooden posts with lamb's-tongue chamfers and heavy timber floors and roof. When Francis L. Fries and other Moravians founded the Salem Mfg. Co. spinning mill in 1836, the ambivalent congregational council sold the land but acquired controlling stock. Fries went north to study mills and obtain machinery and also supervised construction. After financial troubles, the mill closed in 1849 and was converted to a grist- and flour mill by John Motley Morehead and son-in-law Rufus Patterson; then it became Wachovia Flour Mills under the F[rancis] & H[enry] Fries Co. After the Civil War and Francis's death, his brother Henry and sons John H., Francis H., and Henry E. enlarged the flour mill and added the 4-story facade with corbeled cornice and bracketed eaves. In 1880 Francis H. Fries built on the east the **F. & H. Fries Arista Mill**, a 3-story spinning and weaving mill, 14 bays long, with bracketed eaves and 2-story stair tower, "erected on the most approved

plans of the successful New England cotton mills"; it was one of the first mills in the South with electric lights. Arista operated into the 1920s. Later endangered, it was saved as a model project with the new 1976 Preservation Tax Credits.

When Henry E. Fries developed a pioneering hydroelectric plant on the Yadkin River (*Idols Power Plant, 1897–98), the 2-story, wedge-shaped **Salem Substation** (1897; Brookstown at Marshall St.) was erected at the end of the 13¼-mile transmission line, with transformers for lines to Arista Mill and other customers. Nearby is the **Indera (Maline) Mills** (1914; 400 S. Marshall St.), a long, low brick mill for the Frieses' expansion into cotton knitwear.

FY 26 Factory Row (S. Trade St.)

1838–57; 434–48 Factory Row
(S. Trade St.); private

Three 2-story brick houses associated with *Salem Cotton Mill repeat traditional forms. The **Christian Sussdorf House** (1839; 448), with a 4-room plan, was built as a 1½-story dwelling for a Moravian horticulturalist, music teacher, manager at the cotton mill, and operator of a magic lantern show; a later owner made it 2 stories. The **Edwin Ackerman House** (1856; 440), with side-passage plan, was built for a Moravian mill supervisor. The **Rufus Lenoir Patterson House** (1850s; 434), with a 2-over-2 room plan was built for the Caldwell Co. industrialist (#Happy Valley) and his wife Marie, daughter of Governor John Motley Morehead. Patterson came to Salem in 1854 when Morehead bought him the *Salem Cotton Mill. He served as mayor and later married Mary Fries, entered business with Henry Fries, and built a big house on Cherry St.

FY 27 Winston-Salem Southbound Freight Warehouse and Office

1913; Joseph F. Leitner (Wilmington),
architect; 300 S. Liberty St.

When the Winston-Salem Southbound Railway (WSSB) was completed in 1910, it put the city on a main line at last. Led by Francis H. and Henry E. Fries, the WSSB was built in cooperation with the Atlantic Coast Line (ACL) and Norfolk & Western. Salem leaders authorized a freight spur into downtown and a freight depot on the site of old town hall. Designed by the ACL's Leitner, the brick depot, 22 bays long, angles along the former tracks, with a pent roof on brackets sheltering the freight bays.

FY 28 Salem Town Hall

1912; Willard C. Northup, architect; Fogle Bros., builders; Liberty and Cemetery Sts.

Built to accommodate the new *WSSB freight station, the eclectic brick edifice combined municipal offices and the Rough & Ready Fire Co. #4. Its generally Mediterranean character, with hefty brackets and square tower, features round entrance hoods—an early revival of the distinctive Moravian "bonnet" affirming Salem's identity on the eve of merger.

FY 28 *Salem Town Hall*

FY 29 Fogle Flats

1894; Fogle Bros.; 300–308 Cedar Ave.

A rare N.C. instance of row houses, the 5 adjoining brick dwellings, 2 stories tall with mansard roof, were erected by the local builders to accommodate growth in Salem.

FY 30 West Salem

S of I-40 betw. S. Marshall St. and Peters Creek Pkwy.

The large residential area, with buildings from the late 18th to the mid-20th c., developed on farmland west of Salem. The **Stockberger Farmhouse** (1782 and later; 510

Walnut St.) began as a log dwelling erected for farmer George Stockberger, who was to provide meat and dairy products for Salem. Later the farm was leased to the Salem gristmill and the house to the miller. After 1900 the tract was developed, and the house was raised to 2 stories. From the mid-19th c., the area filled with dwellings for workers in the *Salem Cotton Mill and other industries. The 600 block of **Poplar St.** has a concentration of mid-19th-c. houses. The **Ackerman-Reich House** (ca. 1840s; 608 Poplar St.), 2 stories with a center chimney and a brick-nogged frame, was built for Allen Ackerman, manager of the Salem Cotton Mill. The **Tesh-Butner-Bryant House** (1850s–80s; 622 Poplar St.), a plain 2-story house with 1-bay gable front to the street, likewise with brick-nogged frame, was evidently built for Samuel Butner, Salem mayor and manager at F. & H. Fries Mills; he expanded a house built ca. 1854 for Christian David Tesh. The **Pfohl House** (ca. 1870; 632 Poplar St.), a brick-nogged 1½-story frame dwelling, presents a fashionable face, with a porch with decorative millwork, a central bay, and tiny arched windows.

Franklin St. and others contain turn-of-the-century millworkers' cottages, many adorned with millwork from Fogle Bros. **Christ Moravian Church** (1895–96; Fogle Bros., builders; 919 Academy St.), begun as a chapel and Sunday school, is a Victorian Gothic Revival brick edifice. Many millworkers and others joined other denominations, as evidenced by the neoclassical **Green Street Methodist Church** (1902–21, 643 Green St.). In the 1920s and 1930s hundreds of frame bungalows rose on **Hutton St.** and elsewhere for the growing population of workers.

FY 31 South Cherry Street

Linking the twin cities, Cherry St. was one of the grand residential avenues. The once abundant Italianate style appears in the corbeled brick **Conrad House** (ca. 1880; 118 S. Cherry St.) and the eclectic **Rogers House** (1885; 102 S. Cherry St.), with Eastlake and Stick style touches. The **Blair House** (1901; Fogle Bros., builders; 210 S. Cherry St.), the residence of William A. and Mary Fries Blair, incorporates Colonial Revival details; he was a state leader in education, banking, and public welfare. The city's prime Queen Anne style house is **Hylehurst** (1884; Henry Hudson Holly [New York], architect; Fogle Bros., builders; 224 S. Cherry St.), the only known N.C. work by Holly, who promoted the "free classic" or Queen Anne style in *Harper's* magazine and *Modern Dwellings* (1878). For John W. Fries he designed an ornate frame residence with projecting gables with half-timbering, inset balconies, and a flowing plan framed by a wraparound porch—within sight of the family industries. Daughter Adelaide, who lived at Hylehurst, was historian of Forsyth Co. and the Moravians and translated and compiled 12 volumes of the *Records of the Moravians in North Carolina.* Maintained by the family until the late 20th c., the house holds offices.

FY 31 *Hylehurst*

Winston and Winston-Salem

Downtown Winston-Salem (FY 32–43)

The county seat authorized in 1849 was laid out with a grid of streets continuous with Salem's. In the 19th c., residential, commercial, and industrial uses clustered around the courthouse square. By the early 20th c. the business district covered much of the old town site, while factories extended east, and wealthy citizens were building residences chiefly to the west. Commercial architecture of the early 20th-c. rebuilding concentrates between Main and Spring Sts. from 1st to 6th Sts.

FY 33 *Wachovia Bank & Trust Co. Building* and FY 32 *Forsyth Co. Courthouse*

FY 32 Forsyth County Courthouse
1926, Northup & O'Brien, architects; 1959–60; betw. 3rd and 4th Sts., Main and Liberty

The Beaux Arts classical courthouse rose at the same time as the *City Hall, with the local architects giving both edifices a palazzo format. The courthouse, smaller of the two, is 3 stories faced in limestone, with rusticated basement and pilasters separating the windows above. (It succeeded a red brick, temple-form building of 1849–50 built by Francis Fries and an eclectic structure of 1890 by Frank Milburn.) It was expanded in 1959–60, and in 1975 a 7-story Hall of Justice rose nearby.

FY 33 Wachovia Bank & Trust Co. Building
1911, 1917; Milburn & Heister, architects; 8 W. 3rd St.

In 1911 Wachovia began a local "race to the sky"—a 7-story, metal-frame skyscraper erected by the newly merged institution formed by the Wachovia National Bank (est. 1879) and Wachovia Loan & Trust Co. (est. 1890s), which helped finance local industrial growth. Officers in 1911 included James A. Gray Sr., of the bank, and Francis H. Fries, of the trust. With its "stable financial ancestry," Wachovia emerged as the "largest and strongest bank" in the Carolinas. Before the 1911 merger was final, Frank Milburn was commissioned to design the city's first skyscraper in a classically detailed base-shaft-capital scheme. The 8-story *O'Hanlon Building spurred addition of an 8th story. After Fries's death in 1931, president Robert Hanes guided the company through the Great Depression and the post–World War II era to make it the largest bank between Philadelphia and Dallas.

FY 34 R. J. Reynolds Building
1927?–29; Shreve & Lamb (New York), architects; 401 N. Main St.

The glamorous architectural highlight of the city, the 22-story skyscraper is a soaring Art Deco monument that captures the pride and energy of the 1920s. For years its distinctive profile dominated the skyline. Opened in April 1929, it was the tallest skyscraper in the state until 1966. The steel and reinforced concrete structure, sheathed in Indiana limestone, stands 315 feet above the sidewalk, its height emphasized by slim stone strips from street to sky: 16 stories rise uninterrupted from the ground, topped by 6 stories of ziggurat setbacks. The upstreaming ziggurat tower was a bold new form on the national scene when the company commissioned the design from New York architects Shreve & Lamb. Stylized Art Deco details celebrate the golden leaf: entrances and shopfronts display tobacco motifs in Benedict metal, a gleaming alloy, and the marble lobby has tobacco designs on the elevator doors and a ceiling with gold leaf patterns suggestive of smoke rings. The skyscraper won the American Institute of Architects Building of the Year award of 1929, and the architects gained the prestigious commission for the Empire State Building.

The powerful new architectural form embodied the firm's stature and ambitions. From his first tobacco factory of 1875, Richard J. Reynolds expanded fast, acquiring Hanes (1900) and other companies, affiliating briefly with the ATC, then emerging after its breakup in 1911 as an independent firm. Reynolds had already moved into smoking tobacco, putting Prince Albert in a can in 1907, and in 1913 introduced Camel cigarettes with a revolutionary new tobacco blend and advertising campaign. RJR made Camels the most popular cigarettes in the

FY 34 *R. J. Reynolds Building*

world; they pushed the company to top position. After the founder's death in 1918, his brother William became president, followed in 1924 by Bowman Gray Sr., who with his brother James and others further expanded and modernized production and advertising. The largest taxpayer in the state and the city's largest employer, the company dominated local business, governmental, and philanthropic affairs for much of the century. Throughout corporate changes of the late 20th c., the building retained its distinction as an architectural treasure of the state. (Also see Introduction, Fig. 67.)

FY 35 Wachovia Building
1963–66; Albert B. Cameron (Charlotte), architect; C. P. Street (Charlotte), general contractors; 301 N. Main St.

When construction began in 1963 on the 30-story skyscraper, it was the city's first major downtown building since the *Reynolds Building and the first in the state to exceed its height. At 410 feet Wachovia was the tallest in the Southeast—by 1 foot above a Nashville contender—conveying its position as the largest bank in the Southeast.

The design was equally bold, for it exemplified the skyscraper mode defined by architect Mies van der Rohe and still new in the state; it was preceded only by Charlotte's 15-story *North Carolina National Bank (NCNB) of 1959–61. The clean rectangular form is built with a steel frame and concrete floors, veiled in a curtain wall of stainless steel and tinted glass. Across the top a broad band of enameled steel carried the word "WACHOVIA" and was visible for miles. The building was actually the project of a Charlotte developer, the Northwest Corp., with Wachovia the principal tenant, and was designed by a Charlotte architect, Albert B. Cameron, an early graduate of the School of Design and former Odell associate whose career was cut short by his death in 1967. Wachovia remained the state's largest bank until 1972 (*NCNB, Charlotte). The nearby **Wachovia Center** (1995; Cesar Pelli Assoc. [New Haven], architect, *Bank of America, Charlotte), stands 460 feet tall with a domed top. The company merged in 2001 with First Union, which kept the Wachovia name but has headquarters in Charlotte. (See Introduction, Fig. 67.)

FY 36 Winston-Salem City Hall

1926; Northup & O'Brien; Main St. between 1st and 2nd Sts.

As at their *Forsyth County Courthouse, Northup & O'Brien designed the 3- and 4-story city hall in a Renaissance palazzo form, with a rusticated stone base and pilasters at the upper stories, where red brick walls give a Colonial Revival character. It stands at the southern edge of Winston, near a marker (100 block, 1st St.) at the "Former Dividing Line."

FY 37 West 4th St. Area (100–600 blocks and nearby)

The main commercial street and focus of civic improvement in the 1920s, W. 4th St. was widened in 1926 from 40 to 60 feet to create "the first really modern street" in town. It was rebuilt with commercial architecture in a generally classical vocabulary, with occasional Art Deco ventures. Buildings range from 2-story terra-cotta palazzo shopfronts to skyscrapers.

Early in the local height competition, druggist E. W. O'Hanlon replaced his corner drugstore with the city's second skyscraper, the 8-story **O'Hanlon Building** (1914; Northup & O'Brien; 105–7 W. 4th), finished in "pure Greek detail" and a story taller than *Wachovia. The **Pepper Building** (1929; Northup & O'Brien; 104-6 W. 4th) was built for tobacconist Thomas Pepper as a 6-story brick structure with Art Deco touches. One of several elegant classical facades graces the **Morris Plan Industrial Bank** (1925–26; 206–8 W. 4th St.), rendered in pale terra-cotta in Renaissance palazzo form, with a first-story arcade and arched loggias above. The nearby former **Carnegie Library** (1906; Fogle Bros., builders; 411 N. Cherry St.) is a relatively small building that gains monumentality from its large-scale classical motifs, including the pedimented entrance with Doric columns.

The towering **Nissen Building** (1926; William L. Stoddart [New York], architect; 314 W. 4th St.) assured the street widening when it was announced, "Nissen to set big skyscraper back five feet." Upon the 1925 sale of his *Nissen Wagon Works, William M. Nissen began the million-dollar, 18-story office building that was briefly the tallest in the state. The twin-towered design, faced in brick and stone, follows the base-shaft-capital scheme enriched with classical details. The 11-story **Carolina Theater and Hotel** (Stevens Center) (1928; Stanhope Johnson & R. O. Brannan [Lynchburg], architects; 407 W. 4th St.) follows a similar format in red brick and rich ornament; its lavishly decorated theater claimed to be the state's first air conditioned theater. In 1983 it was rescued and renovated as a performing arts center.

Nearby, the **Winston-Salem Journal & Sentinel Building** (1926; Harold Macklin [Winston-Salem], architect; 418 N. Marshall St.) displays the Colonial Revival style of English architect Macklin, who arrived in 1919; the 3½-story red brick building blends

Philadelphia and Salem motifs, including a Moravian-inspired cupola. At the 4-story **YMCA** (1927; Harold Macklin, architect; 315 N. Spruce St.) he repeated red brick and limestone with pilasters at the twin entrances that separate the "Men" from the "Boys."

The **Sosnik-Morris-Early Block** (1929; Northup & O'Brien; 500 W. 4th St.) is a 3- and 4-story commercial block featuring a long, lively facade, with Art Deco pilasters and geometric motifs. The long, 2-story **Bolick Building** (1928; Stanhope Johnson & R. O. Brannan [Lynchburg], architects; 614–36 W. 4th St.) has one of the finest terra-cotta storefronts, with classical ornament, arches, and pilasters.

W. 5th St.

FY 38 U.S. Post Office

1914–15; Oscar Wenderoth, supervising architect of the Treasury; 101 W. 5th St.

Exemplifying the federal government's early 20th-c. emphasis on "classic style," the 2-story limestone-clad edifice (which reused elements of its predecessor) features a recessed portico of 10 full-height Corinthian columns. Pilasters, arched openings, and a roof balustrade unify the building and its addition (1936–37).

FY 39 First Baptist Church

1924–25; Dougherty & Gardner (Nashville), architects; 574 W. 5th St.

Evoking the spirit of English architect James Gibbs, the large, domed church has a commanding presence. A full-height Corinthian portico carries a 3-stage steeple enriched with quoins, pilasters, arches, and urns. The rich classical program carries around the circular, domed sanctuary—with a sweeping curve of pews facing the pulpit and a baptistry in a classical niche (#First Baptist Church, Asheville).

FY 40 Centenary Methodist Church

1930–31; Mayer, Murray & Phillips (New York), architects; 646 W. 5th St.

The imposing stone church shows the sophisticated, abstracted Gothic Revival mode

of the firm established by famed architect Bertram Goodhue. Faced in cut Indiana limestone, the cruciform church employs stylized medieval themes, including high, stepped buttresses that carry blind arches above narrow windows. The tall apse on the south reinforces the medieval character. The stunning interior has stone pillars soaring to arches 68 feet high and tile vaulting by the firm of Rafael Guastavino Jr. Erected for a congregation formed from Centenary and West End Methodist, the $1.25 million church was built early in the Great Depression with support from the Hanes family.

FY 41 Calvary Moravian Church

1923–25, Northup & O'Brien; 600 Holly Ave.

The large Flemish-bond brick church with coved plaster cornice was evidently the first in the Moravian Revival style—a suitable mode for a congregation founded in 1888 from Salem's *Home Church. Its clock came from the 1892 Winston town hall. The

FY 39 *First Baptist Church*

FY 40 *Centenary Methodist Church*

nearby **Holly Ave.** neighborhood contains a several mid- and late 19th-c. houses from the early expansion of the city.

FY 42 Shamrock Mills (Sawtooth Building)
1911; SW corner Marshall and 2nd Sts.

Surviving from the time when factories encircled the business district, the long, low brick building recalls the beginnings of the Hanes hosiery empire. Pleasant H. and John Wesley Hanes of Davie Co. became Winston's leading tobacco manufacturers, but in 1900 they sold their operations to Reynolds and switched to textiles—and made Hanes the world's largest manufacturer of women's knit hosiery. P. H. began making men's knit underwear, while J. W. founded Shamrock Mills, producing cotton socks in a former tobacco factory. In 1911 his son James G. added the sawtooth-roof facility, the first textile factory built for the Haneses. Known after 1914 as Hanes #1, the 1-story mill has 7 sections, each with a sloped roof on the south and a nearly vertical 6-foot skylight on the north. These shed north light on the exacting machine work below, where women knitted, looped, shaped, dyed, and packed Hanes hosiery. Sawtooth roofs were frequent in England and the northeastern U.S. but rare in N.C., especially after electric lighting came into use. Hanes moved to a larger plant on W. 14th St. in 1926, and the building is now an arts center.

FY 43 Central Industrial District

East of downtown, the tobacco industrial district is a dramatic sight from I-40 (BUS) or US 52. For years factories were dispersed in and around the commercial district, but in the 20th c., RJR's consolidation and growth formed an immense tobacco zone by the railroad. Despite losses, a large area along Patterson and Chestnut Sts. from 1st to 7th Sts. retains brick and concrete buildings of the late 19th and early 20th c., mainly from RJR's expansion.

The castellated, towered brick **S. J. Nissen Wagon Shop** (ca. 1895; 300 Patterson Ave.) is a rare survivor of the ornate indus-

FY 43 *S. J. Nissen Wagon Shop*

trial buildings of the late 19th c. Erected with standard mill construction, the 3½-story structure has arched windows and octagonal wood columns supporting the floors; basement furnaces ran the forges. The Nissen family of Salem began making wagons and carriages in *Waughtown before the Civil War; they grew with the tobacco industry, producing famously sturdy wagons to haul heavy hogsheads of tobacco. In the 1890s the family established the repair shop and "wagon repository" convenient to the tobacco factories.

W. F. Smith & Sons Leaf House and Brown Brothers Co. (Piedmont Leaf Tobacco Co.) (1890–95; 4th St. between Linden St. and Patterson Ave.), two prominent brick buildings, are essentially all that remain of the multitude of tobacco companies predating RJR's consolidation. The Smith & Sons building of 1890, a 4½-story structure of stuccoed brick with stepped gables and segmental-arched windows, was home of their leaf house, which bought tobacco for resale to manufacturers, and by 1895 it housed their tobacco factory. Across 4th St. is the 5½-story building with mansard roof erected ca. 1895 for Brown Brothers, which moved from Mocksville in 1877 to become one of the city's largest tobacco firms; it had grading on the first floor, redrying on the second, (de)stemming on the third, etc. Surviving while their contemporaries disappeared, they served various purposes for the ATC (1907), RJR (1912), and Piedmont (1920s–77) tobacco companies.

Although the first generations of tobacco

FY 43 *W. F. Smith & Sons Leaf Tobacco Co. and Brown Brothers Co.*

factories built by RJR have been lost (including the imposing Plant No. 256 [1892, C. R. Makepeace & Co., Providence, R.I.] and Plant No. 8 [1900]), other impressive buildings remain. Two tall **Smokestacks** emblazoned with "R J R TOB CO" spike the skyline. A burst of construction after separation from the ATC added 10 major buildings of 1913–16. Key among these was the **R. J. Reynolds Tobacco Co. Building No. 12** (1913–16; National Fireproofing Co. [Philadelphia]; 201 Chestnut St.), a 6-story concrete and steel frame building, with brick pilaster strips separating large glass block windows. RJR's first air conditioning installation, purchased from Carrier in 1916, humidified sections of No. 12. It remained the center of cigarette making until completion of the suburban *Whitaker Park plant in 1961. (See Introduction, Fig. 48.)

Other buildings, many with reinforced concrete grid walls and glass block windows, recall growth and modernization after World War I and incorporated advances in air handling, packaging, and automation, as detailed in Nannie M. Tilley's *The R. J. Reynolds Tobacco Company* (1985). Several were designed by the J. E. Sirrine Co. of Greenville, S.C. Especially striking is **Plant No. 91** (ca. 1920; Patterson and 5th St.), a glistening multistory glass brick building erected soon after World War I by the Libby-Owens Glass Co. as an experiment using glass bricks in a method developed in Germany. At first the glass bricks cracked

with expansion in heat and cold, but RJR's head brickmason James T. Solomon devised a laying technique to solve the problem.

Patterson Ave.–Liberty St. Area:
East and north of the factories, housing for their workers formed a series of black and white neighborhoods. North of the tobacco factories a social and commercial hub of African American community life developed around the intersection of Patterson Ave. (formerly Depot St.) and Liberty St., including the Depot Street School, known as one of the state's largest and best high schools for black students. As factories expanded, houses were razed to make way, and workers moved farther north and east. In the mid- and late 20th c., urban renewal leveled much of the Depot St. area, leaving a few churches as reminders of the neighborhoods and institutions that once filled the blocks.

FY 44 Lloyd Presbyterian Church
Ca. 1900; 748 Chestnut St.

Built for one of the city's oldest African American congregations, the picturesque frame church is the chief local example of the Carpenter Gothic style, with pointed-arched openings, buttresses, and a slender belfry. After worshiping in various locations in the 1870s and 1880s, the congregation obtained the Chestnut St. lot in 1889. In the 1950s and 1960s, Lloyd was a center for the city's civil rights movement.

FY 44 *Lloyd Presbyterian Church*

FY 45 Goler Memorial A.M.E. Zion Church

1917–19, 1946; 630 N. Patterson Ave.

After meeting in the courthouse, in the 1880s the Winston Tabernacle congregation settled in the Depot St. area. In 1917 they began the large Gothic Revival brick church with unequal towers, which was named for land donor and church leader Dr. W. H. Goler. After a fire in 1941, the congregation moved to present-day *Goler Metropolitan A.M.E. Zion, but some members rebuilt fire-damaged walls and stayed at "Old Goler." The nearby **A. Robinson Building** (1940–41; Lawrence Gray, brickmason; J. W. Greenwood, contractor; 715–21 N. Patterson Ave.), a 2-story, red and yellow brick structure from the once bustling commercial district, was built for Aladine Robinson and contained a funeral home and barber shop.

FY 45 *Goler Memorial A.M.E. Zion Church*

North and East Winston:
For years the area north and east of downtown encompassed alternating sectors of white and black working- and middle-class neighborhoods, with churches and small business centers. From the 1930s and especially in the 1940s and 1950s, a rapid transformation occurred: in one neighborhood after another, white families moved out and black families moved in, often redefining a street or a neighborhood within a year or two. By the mid-20th c., North and East Winston had become almost entirely African American. From the 1960s onward, hundreds of acres were cleared for highways and urban renewal. A few neighborhoods survive in North Winston, while in East Winston beyond the US 52 chasm is a large early 20th-c. residential sector, with landmark churches and schools.

FY 46 Atkins High School (Middle School)

1930–31; Harold Macklin, architect; 1200 N. Cameron Ave.

The large, classically detailed brick school was built with local funds and $50,000 from the Julius Rosenwald Fund—the first investment in a large urban school for the fund, which aided smaller rural schools for African Americans. Atkins High School also pioneered emphasis on "general education and college preparatory work" along with more usual vocational and industrial training. Located south of a strong black neighborhood around 14th St., it was named for educator Simon Green Atkins (*wssu). The 3-story main building, designed by local architect Macklin, was better equipped than most public schools for African Americans. The dedication program cited the auditorium and gym plus "such special features as principal's offices, medical rooms, teachers' room, cafeteria and kitchen, art room, library rooms, shower and locker rooms, science laboratories, and lecture rooms." Families from all over town sent their children there, and many moved to the area. After the 1954 Supreme Court ruling to end school segregation, Atkins supporters halted a proposal to make the prestigious high school into a junior high; but in 1971 it became a junior high, and since 1984 it has been Atkins Middle School.

FY 47 Reynoldstown

A rare example of tobacco workers' housing, the neighborhood known as Reynoldstown was begun in 1917 by RJR to provide employees with affordable houses to rent or buy. Located between E. 8th and E. 10th Sts., at the east end of the streetcar line, it included a section for black workers (razed) and another for whites, along B (Rich), C (Camel), and other streets, called Cameron Park. Houses range from small bungalows to 2-story Colonial Revival residences, many built by Minter Homes. When *Atkins High School was built in 1931 at 12th–14th Sts., its principal, John A. Carter, built a 2-story Colonial Revival house (1100 Rich Ave.) south of the school in Cameron Park. By the next year all the whites had left, and the neighborhood filled with black families, who bought houses or built in the established Colonial and Tudor Revival modes.

FY 48 Mars Hill Baptist Church

1914–15; Willard C. Northup, architect; 1331 E. 4th St.

When the Gothic Revival brick building was erected as Fries Memorial (East Winston) Moravian Church, it served a white neighborhood near the tobacco factories. With changing demographics in the early 1940s, the Moravians decided to move. In 1944 Mars Hill Baptist Church, formed in 1937, announced, "Our white friends, present owners, have named us a price of $30,000 and feel in doing so they have liberally contributed to our wishes." On a September Sunday in 1944, the Baptists began worship in their old sanctuary, then processed two blocks east to complete the service in their new home.

FY 49 Goler Metropolitan A.M.E. Zion Church

1924; 1435 E. 4th St.

The large brick church with Tuscan-columned portico and twin domed belfries was built as the East Fourth Street Baptist Church in a white section of East Winston. In 1941 a black man bought a house in the locale, and by 1942 nearly all the white residents had left. Members of *Goler Memorial A.M.E. Zion, which had suffered a fire in 1941, learned that the church was available and voted to move there. The name was changed to distinguish it from "Old Goler." The church became a social and religious center; a marker commemorates "Dr. M. L. K. Jr. spoke here . . . for Voter Registration Project of Winston-Salem," April 13, 1964.

FY 50 Winston-Salem State University and Columbian Heights

In 1892 African American educator Simon Green Atkins began Columbian Heights, a suburb for upper- and middle-class black families, and within it Slater Industrial Academy. Educated at *Livingstone College in Salisbury, Atkins came to Winston in 1890 as principal of the Depot St. School and worked effectively with white leaders to improve opportunities for African Americans. He proposed the suburb and academy to the local board of trade in 1891; a land company of prominent whites assembled the property; and city engineer Jacob Lott Ludlow (*West End, *Washington Park) platted the subdivision.

Atkins began Slater Industrial Academy, named for a northern benefactor, in 1892 with 25 students in a frame schoolhouse. In 1895 he left Depot St. School to direct Slater, which he led until his death in 1934. It became a state normal school in 1905 and Winston-Salem State University since 1969. The oldest buildings date from the 1920s and 1930s, chiefly red brick, Colonial Revival designs, many by Northup & O'Brien. The **Chancellor's House** (Alumni House) (1924) is a large foursquare residence with 1-story columned porch. **Colson Hall** (1921) was built as a women's dormitory. **Eller Hall** (1938–39) and **Blair Hall** (1938–39; Northup & O'Brien, architects) were part of a building campaign of 1937–39. The campus has expanded greatly in the late 20th c. The surrounding suburb of **Columbian**

Heights, evidently named after the 1893 World's Fair Columbian Exposition in Chicago, became home to the city's growing black elite. More than 25 blocks were filled with residences in popular styles of the early 20th c. In the later 20th c., the suburb was destroyed by US 52, I-40, and ironically, the growth of WSSU, leaving only a few small houses on Excelsior St. The modest frame **Simon Green Atkins House** of the founder was moved to a campus site.

FY 51 Winston-Salem Union Station (Davis Garage)
1925–26; Alfred Fellheimer & Steward Wagner (New York), architects; Northeastern Construction Co. (New York), contractors; 300 Martin Luther King Jr. Dr.

The Southern, Norfolk & Western, and Winston-Salem Southbound companies formed the Winston-Salem Terminal Corp. to build a union station to be "one of the most complete and attractive stations in the South." Railroad specialists Fellheimer & Wagner designed the Beaux Arts station of steel and concrete faced in Flemish-bond brick and limestone, with a Corinthian portico. It once served as many as twenty passenger trains a day, but service ended on June 15, 1970. In 1975 it became an automotive garage; the owner preserved it complete with marble and terrazzo, fixtures, and signs—as if the last ticket agent had simply closed the door behind him.

FY 52 Waughtown

Flanking Waughtown Rd. and Sprague St., Waughtown grew up around the *Nissen Wagon Works. A few houses date from the 19th c., such as the **Clodfelter House** (early 19th c.?; 1510 Waughtown Rd.), recognizable as a 1-story log dwelling, and others of later 19th-c. vintage. With the city's early 20th-c. growth, Waughtown became a large working- and middle-class suburb with especially strong groupings of bungalows, such as the 100–300 blocks of Sprague St. Most distinctive of several notable churches is the former **Waughtown Presbyterian Church** (1914; 1024 Waughtown Rd.) of a Tudor Revival

style. The **Nissen Wagon Works** (est. 1834, ca. 1890s, ca. 1919; 1539 Waughtown Rd.) is a large complex including a 2-story brick section built after a fire in 1919. The business was begun in 1834 by John Philip Nissen and expanded with heavy wagons for the tobacco industry. Sold by William Nissen in 1925 (*Nissen Building), the plant produced wagons into the 1940s.

The architectural marvel of the neighborhood is the **Shell Station** (ca. 1930; Peachtree and Sprague Sts.). The little shell-shaped building was constructed by the Quality Oil Co. to promote its Shell Oil products. Built around a wooden and wire frame in a patented design, the concrete structure was cast and molded on-site. Of eight built, this sole survivor has been restored by Preservation North Carolina.

FY 52 *Shell Station*

FY 53 Washington Park (Southside)

The suburb on a ridge south of Salem was begun in 1892 by the Winston-Salem Land Co. and laid out in a modified grid by civil engineer Jacob Lott Ludlow (*West End, *Columbian Heights). Initially called Southside, it was renamed after its park, which retains an arched "Washington Park" gateway of 1928. Served by the new streetcar line, the suburb attracted leading business families, many from Salem, whose houses include Queen Anne, Colonial Revival, and Tudor Revival styles and many bungalows. Stone retaining walls unify the hilly streetscape. By the 1910s Cascade Ave. was a "millionaire's row." One of the first and grandest houses was the **Henry Elias Fries House** (1914;

FY 53 *Henry Elias Fries House*   FY 54 *Ardmore Moravian Church*

Fogle Bros., builders; 104 Cascade Ave.), a massive brick residence with bracketed eaves and a tall Southern Colonial portico. Fries, who moved from Salem with his wife Rosa Mickey, was a leader in hydroelectric power, railroading, and manufacturing (*Arista Mills, *Idols Power Plant); mayor of Salem; longtime trustee of present-day *WSSU; and devoted Moravian churchman and Sunday school teacher. When he died at age 91 at his desk in the *Reynolds Building in 1949, the state legislature adjourned in his honor.

The **Cicero Lowe House** (1911; Willard C. Northup, architect; Fogle Bros.; 204 Cascade Ave.), built for a tobacco salesman with Brown & Rogers, typifies the Southern Colonial Revival style with portico overlapping a curved 1-story porch. The **A. H. Eller House** (ca. 1925; Northup & O'Brien, architects; 129 Cascade Ave.), built for a Wachovia bank officer and founder of the suburb, is a stuccoed "English bungalow" with green tile gambrel roof. The **Burton Craige House** (ca. 1850; 1929, Luther Lashmit, architect; Thomas Sears, landscape designer; 134 Cascade Ave.), home of a Salisbury lawyer who became counsel for RJR in 1911, is a rambling and luxurious Colonial Revival residence built around an earlier house.

FY 54 Ardmore

Named for the Philadelphia suburb, the development was begun in 1914 southwest of

town for middle- and upper middle-class white families. Combining grid blocks and curvilinear streets and parks, it has houses in a range from bungalows to larger Colonial Revival and Dutch Colonial residences. **Ardmore School** (1929; Northup & O'Brien, architects; 1046 Miller St.) shows a rare schoolhouse usage of Art Deco motifs. The **St. John's Lutheran Parsonage** (1939; SE corner Hawthorne Rd. and Miller St.) is an unusually fine early International style residence, attributed to the Buffalo, N.Y., sister of the minister, Richard Meibohm. **Ardmore Moravian Church** (1931; Northup & O'Brien, architects; NW corner Hawthorne Rd. and Academy St.) is an early Moravian Revival style church. **Ardmore Terrace** (ca. 1949; Queen, New, and nearby streets) is a large, well-preserved example of the mid-20th-c. "super block," with multi-unit, 2-story brick dwellings around green courtyards.

FY 55 Hanestown

The city's only textile mill village was established in 1910 and not annexed until 1957. Around the much-expanded **P. H. Hanes Knitting Mill** (1910 and later) the small grid of streets includes the **Methodist Church**, of brick with Colonial Revival details, and several blocks of millworkers' houses, mainly T-plan, 1-story frame dwellings with front ells.

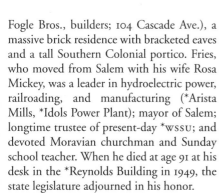

Western Suburbs:
As the city prospered, the white-collar white population moved farther west and north, continuing a pattern established by prestigious 19th-c. mansions west of the commercial section (all destroyed). First came the *West End streetcar suburb, then country estates and luxurious residential developments for many of the town's "hundred millionaires."

FY 56 West End

Evidently the state's first suburb in the curvilinear mode inspired by Frederick Law Olmsted, Winston's premier turn-of-the-century development was a project of the West End Hotel & Land Co., formed in 1890 by R. J. Reynolds, P. H. Hanes, James A. Gray, J. W. Fries, and others. They bought 180 acres from Henry Fries northwest of their homes on W. 4th and W. 5th Sts. as the site of a first-class hotel and suburb. They had Jacob Lott Ludlow, Winston's first city engineer, lay out the plan in 1890; it was a dramatic departure from the city grid, with curving streets that followed the hilly terrain and open parks in ravines and along creeks. On a ridge at 4th and Glade Sts., the company erected the Zinzendorf Hotel (1891–92), named for the early Moravian leader. It opened, then burned in 1892, but the company proceeded with the suburb; over several years, substantial houses were built on the ridges, then down the hillsides.

Most houses were planned by local architects and builders (including Fogle Bros.) in Queen Anne, Colonial Revival, and bungalow modes. The **Jacob Lott Ludlow House** (1887; Fogle Bros.; 434 Summit St.), a frame Queen Anne dwelling, was built for the engineer before the suburb began. Among the original houses is the Queen Anne style **Edgar Vaughn House** (1892; Hill Linthicum, architect; 1129 W. 4th St.), built for a "wholesale grocer and coffee roaster." There are many facets of the Colonial Revival, from the Corinthian porticoed **Rosenbacher House** (1909; 848 W. 5th St.) to the stuccoed and tile-roofed **Galloway House** (1918; Northup & O'Brien; 817 West End Blvd). The **Zevely House** (ca. 1815; 4th and Summit Sts.), a Moravian 2-story brick house, was rescued from another site in 1974 and renovated as a restaurant. The **John W. Pack House** (ca. 1948; 123 N. Sunset Dr.), built for the president of Pack Builders, is an asymmetrically composed Moderne style house with flat roof, corner windows, and curved glass block and porthole windows, evidently taken from a published design (*Lloyd House, Durham; #Benjamin Mills House, Weldon). West End's **Wachovia Branch Bank** (1949; 916 W. 4th St.), built of bricks handmade by George Black, who also supplied Old Salem, was among the first of Wachovia's Moravian Revival banks that gave a signature aura of tradition to branch banks new to residential areas.

FY 56 *Glade St., West End*

Crowning the ridge is **St. Paul's Episcopal Church** (1928–29; Cram & Ferguson, architects; Harold Macklin, associate; Jacobs & Young [New York], contractors; 520 Summit St.), an imposing Gothic Revival church designed by a national proponent of the style. The congregation began downtown in the 1870s and acquired the summit property in 1927. When architect Ralph Adams Cram saw the site, he reportedly said, "A man does not have many chances in a lifetime to build a church on a location such as this." The cruciform church with central tower, faced in Massachusetts granite and trimmed in Ohio sandstone, steps dramatically down the hillside. After a mid-20th-c. decline, from the 1970s onward West End experienced a strong revival.

FY 56 *St Paul's Episcopal Church*

FY 57 Buena Vista–West Highlands–Reynolda Park

After R. J. and Katharine Reynolds established *Reynolda in 1917, the growing business elite moved to prestigious new suburbs in the same quadrant. Encompassing most of the city's finest 1920s residences, this area is one of the state's premier ensembles of suburban landscape and architecture.

Now generally called Buena Vista, developments initially known as West Highlands, Buena Vista–Country Club, and Reynolda Park form a large zone of broad, shaded avenues and curving streets. In 1919 the West End Development Co., with P. H. Hanes as president, began an exclusive automotive suburb across the railroad from West End and called it West Highlands (now applied to a smaller area). Departing from its denser pedestrian-oriented predecessors, it set a precedent of widely spaced and luxurious

houses set back from the street on very large lots—some of 5 or more acres—screened by towering trees and lush greenery. In the 1920s the adjacent Buena Vista and Country Club areas opened, as well as the smaller Reynolda Park adjoining *Reynolda. West 1st St. was extended as Country Club Rd.

More than in the other N.C. suburbs of the era, the premier residences are like small estates. Great wealth and suburban growth combined with high-quality designs by architects including Charles Barton Keen and associate William Roy Wallace, C. Gilbert Humphries, Luther Lashmit of Northup & O'Brien, and others, with landscape designs by Thomas Sears (*Reynolda). They produced some of the state's biggest and finest period revival houses. Influences of Reynolda recur in houses with white stuccoed walls and green tile roofs, stout columns, and bungalow porches. Others display elaborate renditions of Georgian Revival and Italian Renaissance themes, as well as craggy and picturesque versions of English manorial and Tudor Revival modes.

Embowered with great trees, **North Stratford Rd.** is one of the most impressive residential avenues in the state and presents an opulent sampling: the **Thurmond Chatham House** (1925; Charles Barton Keen; 117 N. Stratford Rd.), in eclectic Georgian Revival style with stuccoed walls and tile roof; the **Womble House** (1927; Charles Barton Keen; 200 N. Stratford Rd.), with Italian Renaissance elements, balustraded terraces, and balconies, in fireproof construction; and the **Dodson House** (1926; Northup & O'Brien; 363 N. Stratford Rd.), a red brick Colonial Revival design with lavish Federal details. Nearby is the **Ferrell House** (1920; C. Gilbert Humphries; 2034 Buena Vista Rd., at Stratford Rd.), a graceful essay in the Renaissance Revival, with tile roof and arcaded loggia. On a nearby street the **P. Huber Hanes House** (1931; Charles Barton Keen; 2000 Georgia Ave.) is a red brick Georgian Revival house with full-height portico built for the textile executive and president of the development company.

Reynolda Park has especially large lots and elaborate houses and gardens, including the **Kent House** (1923; Charles Barton

FY 57 *Ferrell House*

FY 57 *R. J. Reynolds Memorial Auditorium*

Keen; 1016 Kent Rd.), built for RJR's niece Sena and her husband Charles Kent in a Reynolda-inspired form, and the **Dyer House** (1930; Mayer, Murray & Phillips [New York]; 1015 Kent Rd.), an English manor house in sophisticated cut stone simplicity by the architects of *Centenary Methodist Church. In Reynolda Park, modernism tempered by the local preference for traditionalism informs the **Howell House** (1959; Robert Myers, architect; 1100 E. Kent Rd.), aptly described as "an International style Mount Vernon." The suburbs' status and architectural quality persisted through the Great Depression and beyond, along with patronage of local architects Luther Lashmit and William Roy Wallace, who continued in revival styles.

The **Fries Memorial Moravian Church** (1944–46; William Roy Wallace, architect; 251 Hawthorne Rd.) shows the continued use of the Moravian Revival for a congregation that moved from East Winston (*Mars Hill Baptist Church). Featured in *American Colleges and Universities* (1928–29) and regarded as one of the finest public high schools in the state, **Richard J. Reynolds High School and Memorial Auditorium** (1924; Charles Barton Keen, architect; 301 Hawthorne Rd.) preside from a hilltop with a view of West End and *St. Paul's Episcopal Church. Taking inspiration from the University of Virginia, Keen designed the complex in a Palladian format, with "Georgian or Colonial style" red brick buildings, including the 2,000-seat auditorium with Corinthian portico, designed to serve school and community. Katharine Reynolds do-

nated the land and the cost of the auditorium as a memorial to her late husband.

FY 58 Reynolda

1915–17; Charles Barton Keen (Philadelphia), architect; Thomas Sears (Philadelphia), landscape architect; 2250 Reynolda Rd.; open regular hours

Built in the "informal bungalow style," the home of Katharine and Richard J. Reynolds was the center of a 1,000-acre estate with village. After tobacco magnate and longtime bachelor Reynolds married his young cousin Katharine Smith in 1905, they lived in his big Queen Anne style house on W. 5th St. Katharine, educated in Progressive Era reform values at present-day University of North Carolina at Greensboro, encouraged her husband to improve conditions for his workers; she also envisioned a healthful family home as part of a model farm to demonstrate agricultural and domestic science to

FY 58 *Reynolda*

local farm families. By 1912 the mother of four was planning Reynolda and turning for advice to experts at present-day North Carolina State University (NCSU) and to country house architect Keen of Philadelphia and landscape designer Thomas Sears.

They designed a residence that, rather than magnifying its grandeur, fitted harmoniously into the landscape and minimized the scale in a 1½-story form that actually has 4 floors within. The angled, flowing plan was originally very open to light and air: the central living room opened to porches front and back, and upper sleeping porches likewise accommodated ideas of healthful living. The white stuccoed walls, hefty stuccoed columns, and green tile roofs contrast with rusty-hued, rounded river rock foundations and retaining walls to create an aura of intentional simplicity and warmth. The interior contains Colonial Revival detailing and ironwork by Samuel Yellin of Philadelphia. The next generation added an indoor swimming pool and rooms for entertaining in the basement.

The grounds designed by Sears likewise blend formality and naturalism. Down the hill, Reynolda Village reiterates the architectural themes, with white stuccoed buildings and river rock walls emphasizing the irregular terrain. The model farm buildings and support facilities for the estate included a church, a central power plant, greenhouses, employee cottages, carriage sheds, and a blacksmith shop. The model dairy barns, built as wonders of sanitation with the latest refrigeration equipment, have gambrel roofs and big round stuccoed silos that are giant versions of the porch columns. The post office and horticulturist's cottage were designed by Willard Northup. Given to Wake Forest University in 1965, Reynolda House is a center for American art, and the village buildings hold shops and offices.

FY 59 Graylyn

1929–32; Luther Lashmit, Northup & O'Brien, architect; Thomas Sears, landscape designer; 1900 Reynolda Rd.

The opulent Norman Revival country house, a counterpoint to *Reynolda, was built for

FY 59 *Graylyn*

Nathalie and Bowman Gray. He had clerked at his father's Wachovia Bank, become a salesman for RJR in 1895, and then succeeded William Reynolds as president in 1924. In 1927 the Grays employed young Luther Lashmit to design their residence on part of the Reynolda estate. Designed in Beaux Arts fashion with private, public, and service sectors angling out from a central stair tower, the 240-foot-long mansion is built of stone from Randolph Co., home of the Gray family. Rooms from France, England, and Turkey reflect the couple's travels, and tile featuring the trademark Camel adorns a dressing room. Eccles Everhart of Northup & O'Brien designed the barn complex to resemble a Normandy farm. Owned by WFU, the estate is now a conference center.

FY 60 Hanes House (Southeastern Center for Contemporary Art)

1932; Peabody, Wilson & Brown (New York), architects; 1975 addition; Newman, Calloway, Van Etten, Winfree; 2721 Marguerite Dr.; open limited hours

One of the city's largest English manorial residences, the multigabled stone house was built for James G. Hanes, Hanes Hosiery president and mayor. Located in a parklike family enclave, in 1975 the house was adapted and expanded for the arts center.

FY 61 Alta Vista

The small development west of Cherry St. was platted in 1927 on 24½–26th Sts. specifically for black professional and management-level families. By 1930 about 25 substantial single-family residences, most with 1- and 2-car garages, stood on 24½ and 25th Sts. Bungalows and Tudor Revival and Dutch Colonial houses were home to professionals, factory workers, and others. After World War II, remaining lots filled with modest frame houses built under the GI loan program.

FY 62 Wake Forest University

1946–56 and later; Jens Larson, architect; Thomas Sears, landscape architect; Reynolda Rd. and University Pkwy.

In 1946, seeing a need for a respected liberal college to enrich the city's life, trustees of the Z. Smith Reynolds Foundation, a family philanthropy, invited the Baptist-affiliated Wake Forest College (est. 1834, *Wake Forest, Wake Co.) to move to Winston-Salem. The foundation offered substantial funding, and other donations followed. The state Baptist Convention promptly accepted the offer; Charles and Mary Reynolds Babcock gave a campus site of more than 300 acres from the Reynolda estate; city and state Baptists mounted fund-raising campaigns; and in 1951 President Harry Truman led the groundbreaking.

Meanwhile the foundation, headed by R. J. Reynolds Jr., selected New York collegiate architect Jens Larsen to plan the college in a traditional Georgian Revival style akin to the old campus. An architectural fracas ensued in 1948–49, when arch-modernist Henry Kamphoefner of the new *School of Design at NCSU in Raleigh and others publicly blasted the conservative architectural choice. Larsen and his clients proceeded undeterred. Centered on a Beaux Arts quadrangle, the fully developed red brick Georgian Revival architecture has strong forms and bold classical detailing—a theme that continued as the school has grown. The centerpiece is **Wait Chapel**, with its tall, multi-stage baroque tower, Doric portico, and 2,300-seat auditorium (scene of late 20th-c. presidential candidates' debates). A modernist exception is the **Scales Fine Arts Building** (1976; Caudill Rowlett Scott, ar-

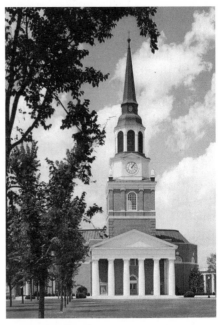

FY 62 *Wait Chapel*

chitect), with angled forms and sawtooth roof, rendered in red brick.

FY 63 R. J. Reynolds Industries Headquarters and Whitaker Park

1977; A. G. Odell & Assoc. (Charlotte), architects; Reynolds Blvd.

Extending nearly 800 feet along the boulevard, the 5-story, accordion-form office building has mirrored glass walls that rise cleanly from the ground and reflect the changing day and season. Planned by the state's leading exponent of corporate modernism, it received several design awards. Across the boulevard, the Whitaker Park research and manufacturing plant was established in 1961.

FY 63 *R. J. Reynolds Industries Headquarters*

FY 64 *Bethabara Gemeinhaus*

FY 64 Bethabara

Est. 1753; Bethabara Rd.;
National Historic Landmark District

An oasis evoking a rural past, Bethabara was the site of the Moravians' initial settlement in Wachovia. Eleven men arrived on November 17, 1753, from Bethlehem, Pa.; they occupied an abandoned cabin and called the place Bethabara, "House of Passage." Soon more settlers arrived, including married couples. The frontier congregational village operated communally, with all resources shared in "common housekeeping" and work focused on community goals: clearing land, planting crops, establishing industries, and constructing buildings—first of log, then traditional half-timbered structures. In 1756 the village was fortified against Indian conflicts, and other settlers sought refuge there. After hostilities ended, in 1766 work began on the central town of *Salem. As planned, many moved there in 1772, leaving Bethabara a country village. Although foundations remain from the early period, Bethabara's buildings date from its late 18th–early 19th-c. years.

The **Bethabara Gemeinhaus** or "congregation house" (1788; Frederic William Marshall, designer; Abraham Loesch, mason; open limited hours) is N.C.'s oldest church building west of Hillsborough. Planned by Wachovia administrator Marshall and built by Salem craftsmen, the 1½-story masonry building subtly expresses its dual purpose: it held the Saal or chapel on the east and the pastor's residence and schoolroom on the west. Marshall distinguished the Saal by its slightly higher roofline, fully arched windows, and the beautiful cupola with spire and weather vane. Craftsmen employed such traditional techniques as stuccoed brick walls above a stone foundation, asymmetrical window and door openings, and a steep roof with kicked eave. The interior, lighted by the large windows, is finished with perfect simplicity, including wide floorboards and clean, plastered walls.

Some craftsmen continued in Bethabara after 1772, occupying modest but substantial dwellings of characteristic Moravian construction. Evidently the oldest brick building in Wachovia and one of the oldest in the Piedmont, the **Schaub-Krause House** (Dyer's and Potter's House) (1782; open limited hours) is a 1-story dwelling built of brick laid in Flemish bond atop a stuccoed and scored stone basement. Reflecting the scarcity of lime, walls were laid up with clay mortar, then pointed on the outside with lime. In typical Germanic fashion, it takes advantage of the slope of the land, with a cellar entrance on the south. The Germanic hall-kitchen plan has a massive central chim-

FY 64 *Schaub-Krause House*

ney between the kitchen-entry room and a large chamber. Other traditional elements include exposed, neatly finished beams, herringbone-pattern batten doors, and fine ironwork. Built for dyer Johannes Schaub, after 1789 it was home to Johann Gottlob Krause, potter and master mason responsible for the great brick buildings of Salem.

The **Brewer's House** (1803; private) is a white-painted brick house with center-chimney plan continuing elements seen in the Dyer's and Potter's House, though here the plan includes two chambers opposite the kitchen.

FY 65 Bethania
National Historic Landmark District

The compact, tree-shaded village, now surrounded by development, is a unique survival of European town planning, with the houses hugging the road and outlots extending beyond. The second Moravian settlement in Wachovia, Bethania was laid out by surveyor Christian Gottlieb Reuter in 1759, with lots north and south of a central square (lost), and the church and graveyard east of it. Less restrictive than *Bethabara, it accommodated both Moravian families and non-Moravians who had come to Bethabara as refugees. Although the 1854 plank road from Fayetteville boosted its economy, it remained a small community and retains much of its character attained by the mid-19th c. **Bethania Moravian Church** (1806–9, 1884) repeats the gable-front form and Flemish-bond brickwork of *Home Moravian Church; gutted by fire in 1942, it was rebuilt within the walls. The quiet landscape of God's Acre lies on the hill east of the church. Twelve late 18th- or early 19th-c. residences remain, six of log construction and six of timber frame with brick nogging. Those built soon after the American Revolution typically had center chimneys, but in a flurry of modernization in the late 1840s, families tore out their old chimneys and built end chimneys. Among these is the **Reich-Strupe-Butner House** (1770), where General Cornwallis is said to have headquartered during the Revolutionary War. From a later era, the **Lehman & Butner Roller Mill** (1899) is a functional frame building with varying roof heights, representing a once common building type.

FY 65 *Bethania*

FY 66 Dr. Beverly Jones House

1846–47; Dabney Cosby, builder;
W side SR 1611 at SR 1794, N of Bethania;
private, barely visible from road

The 2-story brick plantation house is one of the few surviving N.C. works by prolific brick builder Dabney Cosby, who moved from Virginia to Raleigh in the 1840s. Built of 1:4 bond brick, it features stuccoed panels between the lower and upper windows, a motif common in Virginia but rare in N.C. (*Eaton Place, Warrenton). Several outbuildings remain, though the big frame barn was moved to the *Salem Tavern lot. Dr. Jones of Virginia married Julia Conrad and built their home on land they received from her father Abraham Conrad.

FY 67 Stauber House

1840s–50s; E and W sides SR 1611,
just S of SR 1626, Bethania vic.

The archetypal antebellum farm complex shows a Moravian family's adaptation of old and new building forms. Samuel and Sarah Shore Stauber, members of the Bethania community, had a farm of nearly 1,000 acres, where they, with a few slaves and hired workers, raised grains, flax, and livestock. In 1852 they built a frame farmhouse in simple Greek Revival style, with center-passage plan, but continued such traditional elements as brick-nogged framing and interior chimneys serving corner fireplaces. Across the road stands their imposing frame barn (1847), measuring 65 by 35 feet, complete with pents, threshing floor, and stalls. There are several other mid- to late 19th-c. outbuildings, including a slatted corncrib, a smokehouse, and small board-and-batten dwellings used for tenant and perhaps slave houses.

FY 68 Doub House and Doub's Chapel

Late 18th–early 20th c.; house S side
SR 1452, 0.1 mi. E of SR 1463; church
NW side SR 1463, 0.1 mi. E of SR 1452

The Doubs and their chapel took an important role in early Methodism. John Doub, a tanner who came from Germany via Penn-

sylvania, and his wife Mary Spainhauer, daughter of local Swiss farmers, became early converts to Methodism ca. 1780 and hosted many circuit riders and preachings. John was licensed as a preacher and began a camp meeting ground on his land by 1803. Son Michael continued the tradition, and son Peter became a prominent circuit rider and minister. Doub's chapel was considered the most important Methodist church in Wachovia, drawing many Moravian converts and producing 15 ministers. John, who operated his tannery and brick kiln on his farm, is believed to have built his 2-story brick house ca. 1780–1800. It has 1:5 bond brickwork, a hall-parlor plan, and end chimneys and was reworked in the mid-19th c. The present **Doub's Chapel** (1909) is a small Gothic Revival brick church with offset entrance tower.

FY 69 Dozier

The rural community around the junction of SR 1468 and SR 1465 was settled by the Long family who came from Germany via Pennsylvania in the 18th c. They belonged to the Hope Moravian congregation before becoming Methodists in the 19th c. J. M. Long, carpenter and storekeeper, operated the general store, now **Waller's Grocery** (ca. 1900), at the crossroads and built several family houses nearby, some with touches of Gothic Revival style. **Pleasant Hill Methodist Church** (1902; John Long & T. Houston Hunter, carpenters; E side SR 1465, 0.3 mi. S of 1468) is one of the county's best Gothic Revival country churches.

FY 70 Antioch Methodist Church

1880–82; W side SR 1635, 0.4 mi.
SW of SR 1636, Rural Hall vic.

One of several small 19th-c. brick churches in the county, the sanctuary has two arched entrances in the gable front and pilasters dividing segmental-arched windows along the sides. The congregation was founded in 1834, when Methodist evangelists were converting many Moravians and Lutherans; 20 years later the Moravian minister at *Bethania lamented "the painful experience of a good number of village people going to the camp meeting at Antioch." Church records document the 1880–82 construction of the church by members, who used brick mills borrowed from Bethania.

FY 71 Rural Hall

The small railroad town grew up in a farming area settled in the late 18th c. by German Lutherans. **Nazareth Lutheran Church** (1878; N side NC 65 at SR 1629), was built for a congregation organized by 1778 ("the Old Dutch Meeting House"). It has two entrances in the gable front and walls of 1:5 bond brick on a stone foundation. German-language stones mark the churchyard. Rural Hall developed with the 1888 arrival of the Cape Fear & Yadkin Valley Railroad (CF&YVRR) from Wilmington, soon followed by the Richmond & Danville. The **Rural Hall Depot** (1888; 8170 Depot St.), a frame station with bracketed eaves, is one of the few original CF&YVRR depots left; three sections housed waiting rooms, office, and freight warehouse. Brick stores of the railroad era include the **A. L. Payne & Sons Store** (1908; 8101 Broad St.) and the **Ledford-Styers Store** (1905; 8096 Broad St.), with ornate shopfronts. Several turn-of-the-century frame residences stand along Broad St.

FY 71 *Nazareth Lutheran Church*

FY 72 Clayton Farm
Ca. 1800, ca. 1879; NE corner NC 66 and SR 1920; private, visible from road

Built for Matthew Columbus Clayton, probably ca. 1879, the prominent 2-story brick farmhouse has broad proportions, a low gable roof, and simple Greek Revival finish. The farmstead includes several frame and log outbuildings, with a store at the intersection. The earlier house on the site, a weatherboarded log dwelling, was evidently built for John Clayton ca. 1800.

FY 73 Kernersville

Joseph Korner, a clockmaker from Germany, settled in Wachovia in 1785 and in 1817 acquired 1,000 acres and an old tavern on the road from Salem to Bethlehem. He and his sons ran the tavern and several rural industries at Korner's Crossroads. Incorporated in 1871 as Kernersville, the village thrived as a tobacco and commercial center after the arrival of the NWNCRR in 1873, and the Korner (Kerner) family multiplied and prospered.

The centerpiece is **Korner's Folly** (1878, 1886; Jule Korner; S. Main St.; open limited hours), a truly amazing and eccentric brick edifice built by and for Joseph's grandson Jule Gilmer Korner, an interior decorator and sign and portrait painter who studied art in Philadelphia and founded a company under the name Reuben Rink. In the early 1880s he concocted the advertising campaign to promote Bull Durham Tobacco for W. T. Blackwell and Julian Carr, painting realistic bulls on buildings across the nation; he also decorated tobacco tycoons' mansions. Korner began his home with a small carriage house, but after marrying Polly Masten, he enlarged it to its present form, endlessly improving and adding to it. The big brick house, with tall cross-gabled roof and Italianate corbeling, contains multiple stories of rooms of varied heights, levels, and surprises, fantastically adorned with millwork, tile, carved human and animal figures, and ceiling murals by German artist Cesar Milch. There are 22 rooms, including a third-floor theater, and 20 fireplaces, all different.

South Main St. has notable 19th-c. houses built for Kerners and others. There are several brick houses with ornate corbeling, typified by the **Theodore E. Kerner House** (1877; 620 S. Main St.), an L-plan Italianate residence. **Kernersville Moravian**

FY 73 *Korner's Folly*

Church (1867, 1892; 504 S. Main St.) was a simple brick structure remodeled by Jule Korner with Gothic Revival vestibule, steeple, and porches. Some houses feature fancy sawnwork, including the **Elias Kerner Huff House** (ca. 1880; 113 Pineview St., moved 2001 from 217 S. Main St.), an exuberant little Queen Anne style house; built for Huff, who worked for Jule Korner's decorating company, it contains motifs akin to *Korner's Folly and a connected "band-room" for Huff's Kernersville Band.

Brick commercial buildings, generally 2 stories with Italianate details, include **Bodenheimer's Store** (ca. 1900; 311 S. Main St.) and the **Bank of Kernersville** (1902; 100 S. Main St.), with bold corbeled and paneled brickwork. The big 3-story brick **Kerner & Greenfield Tobacco Factory** (1884; 402 S. Main St.) recalls the many small tobacco companies of the 19th c. Near the tracks the **Kernersville Depot** (ca. 1873; 107 Bodenheimer St.) is one of the oldest in the state and evidently the only original one from the 1873 construction of the NWNCRR. Covered in board and batten, the 1-story frame structure has wide eaves and arched and square openings. Across the tracks, the **Harmon & Reid Flour Mill** (Caudle Electric Co.) (1897; 208 Bodenheimer St.) is an imposing 2½-story industrial building with arched windows and mansard roof.

FY 74 Old Fraternity Church of the Brethren

1860; S side SR 2994, 0.15 mi. W of SR 2991, Clemmons vic.

An intact survival of the simple meeting-house form, the small frame building was built for a group of German Baptist Brethren, also known as Dunkards, who had settled near the southwest boundary of Wachovia. Tracing their origins to an adult baptism in the River Oder in Germany in 1708, they came to Pennsylvania and thence to N.C., where the Dunkards were mentioned in Moravian records from the early 1770s. They evidently met in homes until they built this church in 1860. On a hill overlooking Salem and Muddy creeks, it maintains its essential character, with the entrance on the long gable side and simple benches gathered within. In 1885 some members branched off into a congregation that worships in a later church near US 158.

FY 74 *Old Fraternity Church of the Brethren*

FY 75 Hoehns (Hanes) House

1789; W side SR 1103, 1.3 mi. S of US 158, Clemmons vic.; private, barely visible from road

One of the oldest houses in rural Forsyth Co., this is the only one constructed entirely of Flemish-bond brick with glazed headers. It features herringbone brick patterns in the gable ends, interior end chimneys, and two entrances into a 3-room plan. Philip and Johanna Frey Hoehns were members of Hope, the English-speaking Moravian congregation in Wachovia. The family name was later changed to Hanes.

FY 76 Idols (Fries) Hydroelectric Plant

1897–98; C. R. Makepeace & Co.
(Providence, R.I.), engineers;
Clemmons vic.; access restricted

Only ruins remain of the complex built by Salem's Fries Manufacturing & Power Co. as the state's first hydroelectric dam and power station to transmit electricity over a long distance. The 482-foot curved stone dam across the Yadkin adjoined a powerhouse (burned, 1996). A 13½-mile transmission line carried power to the *Salem Substation for local industries and other uses. In 1913 the company was absorbed by Southern (Duke) Power, which modernized the operation, then sold it in the mid-1990s.

FY 77 Tanglewood

1859, 1921; S side US 158, 0.3 mi. W of
SR 1101, Clemmons vic.; open regular hours

In 1921 William Neal Reynolds—brother, associate, and briefly successor of R. J. Reynolds—joined other industrial executives who became gentlemen farmers, establishing a 1,100-acre country estate where he raised and trained champion trotters. Lying outside Wachovia, the land was settled in 1757 by William Johnson, whose descendants built a 2-story brick Greek Revival house in 1859. Reynolds and his wife Kate Bitting remodeled the house and added stables, barns, and other outbuildings. He left Tanglewood to the county as a park, opened in 1954.

Also in the park is **Mount Pleasant Methodist Church** (1809; Henry Eccles, builder), a simple, timber-framed gable-fronted structure that housed an active congregation until the 1920s. One of the oldest frame churches in the region, Mount Pleasant was an important center of early Methodism; it has been restored and stands next to a graveyard with stones dating to 1756.

FY 78 Forest Hill Farm (Blumenthal Jewish Home)

1928, Charles Barton Keen, architect; Thomas Sears, landscape architect; 1933, Northup & O'Brien, architects; W side SR 1100, 0.6 mi. W of SR 1100, Clemmons vic.; access limited

Centerpiece of the Yadkin River estate is the stone, Georgian Revival style residence planned for Reynolds executive Robert E. Lasater by the designers of *Reynolda. There are several stone and stuccoed outbuildings, including Northup & O'Brien's **Lasater Mill** (1933) at Lasater Lake, a picturesque 2-story stone gristmill (later a residence).

FY 79 Pilot View

1857; E side SR 1305, 1.7 mi. N of
SR 1001; Lewisville vic.; private,
visible from road in winter

Sited near the Yadkin River and named for its view of distant Pilot Mountain, the Greek Revival frame house with 2-tier portico was built for Augustine Eugene Conrad, who ran a large farm, two gristmills, and a river ferry and served as county commissioner and justice of the peace. Other family seats nearby include the 1804 "River John" Conrad House built for his grandfather (no public visibility).

Yadkin County (YD)

See Kirk F. Mohney, Historical Architecture of Yadkin County, North Carolina *(1987).*
The county lies in the elbow of its namesake river where it bends away from the Blue Ridge and begins its long journey southward to South Carolina and the sea. Early settlers were of mostly English descent, including a number of Quakers, along with some Scotch-Irish and Germans, the latter chiefly in the northeast. A few plantations developed along the river, but it was mainly a county of small farmers who held Unionist sympathies before and during the Civil War and were primarily Republican thereafter. The rural county has high ridges with long vistas across farmland and forests, with farmsteads from the late 18th c. onward. A few early 19th-c. brick houses of Quakers stand beyond public view. More abundant are frame houses and log outbuildings, including impressive double-crib barns found around German settlements. Without a railroad, the county saw only minor industrial development, and its towns remained small trading centers.

YD 1 Yadkinville

The central county seat was established soon after Yadkin Co. was divided from Surry in 1850. The 1853 Greek Revival courthouse was replaced in 1958. The oldest public building is the former **Yadkin County Jail** (1892; E. Hemlock and Van Buren Sts.), a small brick building with hip roof and segmental-arched windows and doors, now a county museum. Less than a quarter-mile south of the courthouse is the **Mackie Farm** (E side US 601, 0.8 mi. N of US 421), homeplace of the family who sold 50 acres for the county seat. The house, a 5-bay, 1-story, weatherboarded log structure with engaged full-width porch, is said to have been built upon the 1848 marriage of Robert and Sarah Vestal Mackie. Tradition recalls that the builders of the first courthouse boarded here with the Mackies. In a grove and surrounded by boxwoods stands the early 20th-c. residence of son Miles and his wife Martha—a 2-story frame house blending Queen Anne and Colonial Revival elements. There are several barns and sheds.

YD 2 Deep Creek Friends Meetinghouse and Cemetery
Est. late 18th c.; N and S sides SR 1507, 0.4 mi. W of SR 1510

Quakers were among the earliest settlers west of the Yadkin River in present-day Yad-

kin and Davie counties. While many eventually left the Society of Friends, some in this section retained their identity; their first monthly meeting began in 1783. The cemetery retains the largest group of early markers in the county, dated 1801 onward. The brick meetinghouse is mid-20th c.

YD 3 Brickell-Shore Farm
Late 19th–early 20th c.; N and S sides SR 1506, 0.25 mi. SW of SR 1510; private, visible from road

Close to the road stand a fine double-crib log barn, a center-drive log corncrib, and a frame granary, representative of the county's traditional outbuildings. The farmhouse across the road is a frame I-house with rear ell and front porch with scrollwork trim.

YD 4 Boonville

Said to lie at the crossing of old Indian trails, the community incorporated in 1895 was named for Daniel Boone, who hunted in the area. Notable among its commercial buildings is **Day's Dry Goods Store** (ca. 1900; W side Carolina Ave.), a 2-story frame store with shed roof, bracket cornice, and intact storefront. Late 19th-c. and early 20th-c. frame houses line Main St. (NC 67) and connecting streets.

YD 5 Charity Baptist Church

Ca. 1923; NE side SR 1518, 0.4 mi. SE of NC 67, Boonville vic.

Built for a congregation founded in 1901, the prominent frame church is a late version of the gable-fronted country church with central entrance tower and belfry.

YD 6 Richmond Hill

Ca. 1860; end of SR 1530, Historic Richmond Hill Nature Park; grounds open to public

The 2-story brick house was the centerpiece of a private law school operated by jurist and legislator Richmond M. Pearson. A native of Rowan Co., he began the school in Mocksville and moved it here after 1848. He held Socratic teaching sessions in a log building that once stood near the house. Pearson is said to have trained nearly a thousand lawyers, several of whom attained state and national prominence. The austere Greek Revival–Tuscan brick structure is built on a T-plan under a low hip roof with a deep, bracketed cornice and has a transverse-passage plan and simple Greek Revival woodwork. After long neglect, it was restored by the Historic Richmond Hill Law School Commission.

YD 6 *Richmond Hill*

YD 7 Deep Creek Primitive Baptist Church

Ca. 1912; E side SR 1533, 0.7 mi. N of SR 1003, Smithtown vic.

The congregation organized by 1778 was apparently the first in the county. After worshiping in a log building near this site, members built the severely plain gable-fronted

frame building in keeping with their beliefs, with four windows on each side lighting the simply finished interior.

YD 8 Douglas-Matthews Farm

Early 20th c.; E side SR 1536, 0.6 mi. N of SR 1537, Smithtown vic.; private, visible from road

Along the county's northeastern border the land drops down to the Yadkin River, with ridges providing views across the river toward distant Pilot Mountain in Surry Co. In 1912 farmer and carpenter John W. Douglas took advantage of this dramatic setting, orienting the front porch of his simply finished frame I-house toward river and mountain instead of the road. His outbuildings across the road include a double-crib barn, a corn-crib, a smokehouse, and a tall tobacco barn.

YD 9 East Bend

When a post office was established in 1849, the trading community on an old east-west road was named for the nearby big bend in the Yadkin River. By the late 19th c. it was the county's leading manufacturing center, with buggy and tobacco factories, a roller mill, and four general stores. The industries are long gone, but two facing 2-story brick stores recall small-town business and family relationships. The **Morse-Wade Building** (ca. 1902; s side E. Main St.), with segmental-arched windows and intact wooden storefront and exterior side stair, housed enterprises of partners Thomas Morse and Otis Wade, including a hotel and a general mercantile business. Part of the second floor was the residence of Morse and his wife Anna (Wade's sister). Across the street, the similar **Davis Brothers Store** (1913; N side E. Main St.) housed a mercantile business; from 1917 to 1980 the upper floor held the office of Dr. Rosebud Morse Garriott, daughter of Thomas and Anna Morse, who was one of N.C.'s first woman dentists. Among the 1- and 2-story late Victorian frame houses along Main St. west of the commercial district are the **Jonathan Huff House** (ca. 1895; s side W. Main St.), one of

YD 12 *Glenwood*

YD 9 *Morse-Wade Building*

the county's most ambitious Queen Anne style houses, with asymmetrical massing and wraparound porch, built for a buggy manufacturer, and the **Jesse Williams House** (ca. 1890; N side W. Main St.), an I-house with sawn balustrade and brackets on its 2-story porch.

YD 10 Shore-Butner-Allgood Mill

Ca. 1850, 1900; W side SR 1562 (W fork), 0.75 mi. S of SR 1560, Flint Hill vic.; private, visible from road

The 3-story frame gristmill with overshot waterwheel, representing an important rural institution, was built on an old site ca. 1900 and operated into the 1980s; the 200-foot-wide stone dam remains in place. On the hill north of the mill, the **Miller's House** (ca. 1900) is a 1-story frame house decorated with window hoods, brackets, and scalloped eave trim.

YD 11 Henry F. Shore Farm

Late 19th c., 1914; SW corner SR 1562 and SR 1563, Flint Hill vic.; private, visible from road

One of four neighboring 19th-c. Shore family farms on the west bank of the Yadkin River, the farm encompasses a plain 2-story farmhouse and an outstanding collection of log outbuildings, including a large double-crib barn with shed additions.

YD 12 Glenwood

1851; George Carver, builder (attrib.); N side SR 1549 at SR 1566, Enon vic.; private, visible from road

Built by Tyre and Martha Bynum Glen in 1851 as the seat of their 3,500-acre plantation, the county's grandest antebellum house exemplifies the Greek Revival style, with a center-passage plan 2 rooms deep and a Doric entrance porch. An earlier 2-story frame house stands nearby. Planter Glen's associations with many state political leaders made the house a social center of the county and the state.

YD 13 Cedar Hill A.M.E. Zion Church (Enon Chapel)

Ca. 1896; NW side SR 1605, 0.6 mi. NE of SR 1571, Enon vic.

The small frame church with belfry and gabled vestibule, home of one of the county's few black congregations, was built by church members soon after they acquired the property in 1896. The small cemetery includes the grave of David Nick Glenn, a freedman who founded the church.

YD 14 Durrett-Jarrett House

Ca. 1815; NW side SR 1605, 0.3 mi. SW of SR 1571, Enon vic.; private, visible from road

The large frame house with exceptional Federal style craftsmanship was built for Davis Durrett of Virginia and owned by the Jarrett family from 1835. The north front became the rear when the road was rerouted.

YD 15 Speer-Davis Farm

Mid-, late 19th c.; N side SR 1605, 0.25 mi.
W of SR 1600; private, visible from road

John Davis's representative 2-story frame farmhouse of 1882 stands in a landscaped setting along with a fine collection of log and frame outbuildings. The imposing double-crib log barn probably predates the house. To the east is the Samuel Speer House, a hall-parlor plan log house from the 1830s or 1840s.

YD 16 Huntsville

Huntsville lies near the west bank of the Yadkin at the Shallow Ford, an ancient river crossing on the road from the Moravian settlements south to Salisbury and beyond. Settlement began in the 1740s, and a tavern opened in the mid-18th c. In 1792 Charles Hunt of Salisbury chartered Huntsville with hopes of a major trading center at the strategic spot; the 1808 Price-Strother map showed it as the only town in present-day Yadkin Co. Bypassed by later routes, Huntsville remained a village.

The chief landmark from the early years is **The White House** (late 18th–early 19th c.; NW side SR 1001 [Shallowford Rd.], 0.2 mi.

SE of SR 1747), one of the best-preserved late Georgian dwellings in the upper Yadkin valley. The 2-story, 3-room plan house is handsomely finished, including Flemish-bond chimneys with glazed header zigzag patterns. Called "the White House" after its paint color as early as 1835, it was probably built between 1795 and 1801 for Henry Young, the first postmaster, and was later owned by the Clingman family; the family was prominent in Huntsville's early years and included U.S. senator and Confederate general Thomas L. Clingman.

The village also includes two log dwellings: the **Chapman House** (ca. 1800; SE corner SR 1001 and SR 1716), a 1-room house with engaged porch and brick end chimney, and the **Walker House** (ca. 1875; S side SR 1001, 0.3 mi. W of SR 1716), with half-dovetailed notches, hip-roofed porch, and frame rear kitchen ell. **Huntsville Methodist Church** (1888; W side SR 1716, S of SR 1001) is the county's best-preserved 19th-c. church, in frame with a bracket cornice and a front entrance tower with tall, arched windows. The congregation began ca. 1808.

South of the village the **Dalton-Hunt House** (ca. 1855; E side SR 1716, 1.0 mi. S of SR 1001) is with *Glenwood one of the finest antebellum houses in the county. The 2-

YD 16 *The White House*

YD 18 *Windsor's Crossroads School*

story frame house has an austere Greek Revival exterior, with a 2-tier portico carried by big square columns. It was built for Sarah Bird Dalton, a widow in her 60s; her son-in-law, plasterer Henry S. Gorman, was in her household in 1850 and probably executed the elaborate decorative plasterwork here and in other locations (*Cedar Grove, Mecklenburg Co.). The house was later owned by Pleasant Hunt, a physician and county commissioner.

YD 17 Courtney

The settlement at the junction of two early roads began as Chinquapin Crossroads, with a Baptist church est. 1835 as Cross Roads Church. Later renamed, **Courtney Baptist Church** (1929; E side SR 1725, S of SR 1001), the congregation's third, is a Colonial Revival structure with portico and belltower, said to have been the first brick church in the county. The **Woodmen of the World Lodge** (ca. 1920; E side SR 1725, S of SR 1001) is an intact 2-story fraternal hall that housed a store at the first level, with the gable-front entrance sheltered by a shed roof on brackets; a side door leads upstairs to the meeting hall. The organization was founded in 1890 in Omaha as a fraternal insurance and relief organization and extended across rural America. In its early years the society promoted tree-stump design gravestones for members.

YD 18 Windsor's Crossroads School
Ca. 1916; SW corner SR 1100 and SR 1103

One of the state's largest and best-preserved early 20th-c. frame schoolhouses, the 2-story building has a projecting 3-bay centerpiece and hip roof capped with an open belltower. The wood-sheathed interior has two large classrooms per floor. It is maintained by the local Ruritan as a community center.

Davidson County (DV)

See Paul Baker Touart, Building the Backcountry: An Architectural History of Davidson County, North Carolina (1987).

Divided from Rowan Co. in 1822 and named for Revolutionary War general William Lee Davidson, the county on the east side of the Yadkin River shared the mid-18th-c. settlement patterns of its neighbors: German-speaking Moravian, Lutheran, and Reformed congregations dominated in the northern half, while English and Scotch-Irish groups settled to the south. The most vivid German legacy is in old Lutheran and Reformed churchyards, where carved and pierced gravestones, some with German inscriptions, compose a body of folk art unique in the nation. Double-crib log barns also distinguish German settlement areas. Moderate-sized farms produced fine crops of grain, along with tobacco, cotton, and livestock in some sections. The 1855 construction of the North Carolina Railroad (NCRR) through the county encouraged commercial agriculture and laid the foundation for industrialization in the late 19th and early 20th centuries, when textile, furniture, and other factories rose along the railroad in Lexington and Thomasville.

Lexington (DV 1–6)

By 1790 the village was known as Lexington, after the 1775 battle in Massachusetts. In 1824 it became seat of the new county for its near-central location, but it grew slowly until the NCRR sparked local ambitions, symbolized by the 1857 *Davidson Co. Courthouse. A few small industries appeared along the east-west NCRR, but "the greatest addition to the industrial life of the town" was *Wennonah Cotton Mills, established in 1886 by William E. Holt of Alamance Co., which spurred population growth from fewer than 500 in 1870 to more than 2,500 in 1900. The north-south Winston-Salem Southbound Railway (WSSB) in 1913 brought new trade links and factories along its route. Textile, furniture, mattress and upholstery, and wood products firms undergirded the economy. The era yielded numerous turn-of-the-century commercial buildings, plus early 20th-c. factories, workers' housing concentrated south of the tracks, and more elaborate residences north of downtown.

Lexington is famed as the centerpoint of Piedmont N.C. ("Lexington style") barbecue, available at Lexington BBQ #1 and many other tasty spots: pork (of course) is slow-cooked and seasoned with a tomato-in-fused sauce, representing a cultural divide from the strictly vinegar-pepper advocates in eastern N.C. (The change begins somewhere near Durham.)

DV 1 Old Davidson County Courthouse

1856–58; William Ashley & George Dudley, builders; Main St. at Center St.; open limited hours as Davidson Co. Historical Museum

Lexington's architectural centerpiece is the grandest of the state's antebellum courthouses, dramatized by its heroic Corinthian hexastyle portico and resplendently detailed with Corinthian entablature, matching pilasters, and arched windows. Stuccoed brick walls (originally scored to resemble ashlar) rise from a foundation of local granite. During a flurry of competitive courthouse building among Piedmont counties the *Greensboro Patriot* wrote in 1858 of the "beautiful and magnificent Temple of Justice" that "in point of magnificence there is nothing in the State to compare, except the Capitol at Raleigh." (The preceding 1822 courthouse was a 2-story porticoed building designed by state architect William Nichols [*Mordecai House, Raleigh] and built by Joseph Conrad.) The interior burned during Union occupation in 1865 and was rebuilt in 1867;

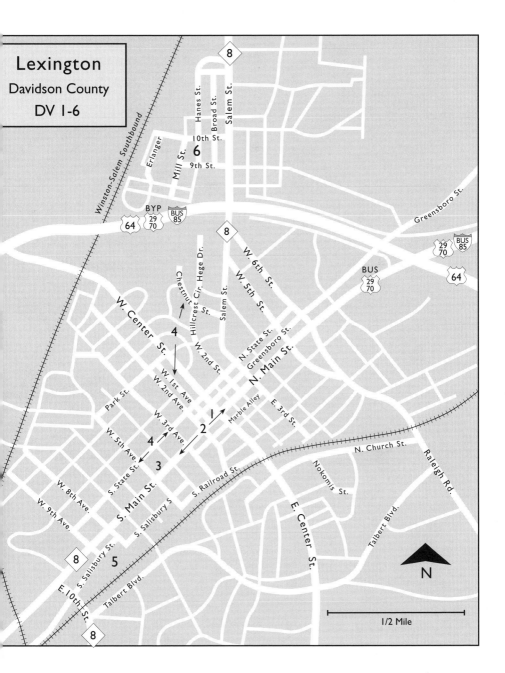

Lexington
Davidson County
DV 1-6

the cupola and other embellishments came in the early 20th c. (Also see Introduction, Fig. 35.)

DV 2 Downtown Lexington

Along S. Main St., commercial and institutional buildings reflect late 19th- and early 20th-c. industrial prosperity. Among the oldest are the brick stores at **17–21 S. Main St.** (ca. 1885), with arcaded corbeled cornices and bold arches at the windows. The **March Hotel** (ca. 1900; 100–108 S. Main St.) is a big U-shaped 3-story hostelry adorned in free classical fashion with Ionic pilasters, cornices, and keystone-topped windows.

DV 1–2 *Old Davidson Co. Courthouse with downtown streetscape*

The former **U.S. Post Office** (ca. 1912; 220 S. Main St.) shows a soberer Beaux Arts classicism in limestone with Tuscan-columned portico. **Grace Episcopal Church** (1901; 419 S. Main St.) is a small brick church in the late Gothic Revival style, with an asymmetrically placed belltower and a fine Tiffany window; in 1847 an earlier rector obtained a design from New York architect Richard Upjohn, but it was never built. **First Presbyterian Church** (ca. 1834; Joseph Conrad, supervisor; later expansions; 15 W. 3rd St.) began as a rectangular brick sanctuary that survives in part within a series of expansions and remodelings; the 3-stage late 19th-c. tower dominates the streetscape.

DV 3 *The Homestead*

DV 3 The Homestead
(Dr. William Rainey Holt House)
1834; 408 S. Main St.

Recalling early 19th-c. elegance in Lexington, the stylish frame house displays an early transition from Federal to Greek Revival Neoclassicism. Blind-arched Palladian motif windows and other Federal themes combine with Greek keys, Greek Ionic pilasters, and anthemion decorations inspired by Asher Benjamin's new *Practice of Architecture* (1833). The 1-story entrance porch, based on

the original, opens into a double-pile plan under a low hip roof. Dr. Holt, brother of Alamance Co. textile pioneer Edwin M. Holt, moved to Lexington in 1820 and led in its development and formation of the county. Typifying the venturesome client, the widely respected, Philadelphia-trained physician supported E. M.'s cotton mill in town, helped get the NCRR routed through the county, and established a famous model farm at Linwood. The designer of the house is not known, though tradition cites "a Charleston architect." After Holt's death in 1868, the house was occupied by his daughter Fannie and her husband Charles A. Hunt, founder of local mills. Among her sisters, Amelia married cousin William E. Holt (*Wennonah Cotton Mills), and Elvira married Joseph Erwin; their son William A. Erwin became a state textile leader (*Erwin Mills, *Cooleemee Cotton Mill).

DV 4 Residential Areas

In the early 20th-c. residential area north and west of downtown, a concentration of fine period revival houses appears in **"The West Avenues"** section along the first blocks of 1st, 2nd, and 3rd Aves. Handsome renditions of the Colonial Revival style range from stuccoed residences with tile roofs to frame and red brick houses with columned porticoes. The **Hillcrest** area also has a strong grouping of early 20th-c. houses along Hillcrest Cir. and nearby. **Grimes School** (1936; William Roy Wallace [Winston-Salem], architect; Hege Dr.), a 2-story brick school with Colonial Revival flourishes, was designed by an associate of architect Charles Barton Keen (*Reynolds High School) as a state-of-the-art elementary school. **S. State St.** parallel to Main St. has Queen Anne and Colonial Revival houses, with a striking contrast in the **Lloyd Rainey Hunt House** (ca. 1927; Joseph T. Levesque, architect; 417 S. State St.), a picturesque English cottage design with undulating brick studded with rough stones.

DV 5 Wennonah Cotton Mills
1886–92 and later; E. 9th Ave. at Salisbury St.

The 1-story brick mill with corbeled towers, now part of Wennonah Industrial Park, recalls a long local history of cotton manufacturing. E. M. Holt, supported by brother William R. (*The Homestead), opened a cotton mill at Lexington in the 1840s, but it burned in 1844. Further development waited until 1886, when Wennonah Mills was begun by William Edwin Holt of Alamance Co., son of E. M. and nephew of William R. In 1871 William E. married his cousin Amelia and continued management of family mills in Alamance Co., founding *Glen-

coe in 1880. In 1886, at Amelia's request, the couple moved to Lexington, where William founded the new mill, named at Amelia's suggestion for Wennonah, mother of Hiawatha in Longfellow's epic poem. Manufacturing the family's famed "Alamance Plaids," the plant gained a second factory in 1892. Charles A. Hunt, husband of Amelia's sister Fannie and briefly a partner in Wennonah, built two more Hiawatha-named mills near the tracks: Nokomis (1900) and Dacotah (1910), both gone. Scattered 1- and 2-story frame mill housing for the three mills lies south of the railroad on Dacotah and other streets.

DV 6 Erlanger Mill Neighborhood (Parkdale)

To supply cotton fabric for their "B. V. D." underwear factories in Baltimore, brothers Charles and Sydney Erlanger established beside the new WSSB tracks a mill and model mill village, complete with social and educational facilities. The grid-plan village of 200 workers' dwellings grew to 325 houses by the 1920s. Unusual are the many small shingled houses fully rendered in bungalow style, with tapered porch posts, broad eaves, and Craftsman detail (Park Circle, Olympic St.). In 1916 the engineering firm of J. E. Sirrine had made plans for 80 "bungalows," a hotel, and a school in Erlanger. Other houses follow more traditional 1- and 2-story forms. Annexed in 1941, the houses were sold to employees in the 1950s; the mill has been modernized. The **Mill Office** (ca. 1913; Mill St. at 9th Ave.) is a compact 1-story brick building with bellcast hip roof.

DV 7 Fritts Farm
Mid-19th c., ca. 1900; E side NC 8, 0.7 mi. S of NC 8/US 52 jct.; private, visible from road

The prominent farmstead north of Lexington illustrates the long development of Piedmont rural architecture. The farm began with log buildings in the mid-19th c., including a small 2-story weatherboarded log house and a big double-crib log barn. Around 1900 farmer D. T. Fritts moved the old log house down a farm lane and replaced it with the tall, weatherboarded frame house with cross-gabled roof and decorated porch. He kept the log barn, however, and built alongside it a proud frame barn and repeated the pent roof sheltering the entrance on the long side.

DV 8 Riley Everhart Farm

1885; David K. Cecil, builder; SE corner SR 1457 and SR 1468, Arnold; private, visible from road

DV 8 *Riley Everhart Farm*

The 2-story Italianate brick farmhouse, unusually ambitious for the postwar era, reflects Everhart's enterprise as manufacturer and merchant as well as farmer, evidenced by his big store and barn. The conservative I-house with ell is treated with stylish arched windows, bracket cornice, and end chimneys rising through pedimented gable ends (*Koonts House). Everhart also operated a distillery, a tobacco factory, and the gable-fronted **Arnold General Store and Post Office** adjacent to the farm. Farm buildings include a brick dairy and well house, a frame granary, and the large double-crib log barn, moved here from the nearby Shoaf farm when the brick house was built.

DV 9 Zimmerman Farm

1895; Charlie Long, carpenter; N side SR 1500, 0.3 mi. W of SR 3010, Welcome vic.

Standing under big shade trees, the 2-story frame farmhouse Charlie Long built for Joe Zimmerman's family epitomizes the classic Piedmont type at the turn of the 20th c.: an I-house form with gable-end chimneys, rear ell, and a 1-story front porch given a cheerful Victorian touch with delicate sawn brackets atop the posts. Predating the house, across the road is one of the county's best-preserved double-crib log barns; other log outbuildings include a corn crib and a smokehouse.

DV 10 Friedberg Moravian Church and Graveyard

Org. 1773; N and S sides SR 1516, 1.3 mi. W of SR 1508

In a rural setting evoking the "hill of peace" translation of "Friedberg," the cemetery recalls a long settlement history. The congregation, largest in rural Davidson Co., traces its origins to 1754, when Adam Spach and other Germans settled here on the southern edge of Wachovia tract. They sought religious instruction from the Moravians at *Bethabara, and in 1773 the Friedberg congregation was officially recognized. Spach's stone house stood nearby until the mid-20th c. Across the road from the present brick church (1970s), God's Acre is laid out in Moravian fashion with quadrants of "choirs" organized by sex and marital status; simple, uniform stone markers lie flat on the ground.

DV 11 Old Mount Vernon Church

Ca. 1900; S side SR 1700, 0.2 mi. E of Forsyth Co. line, Wallburg vic.

The utterly simple gable-end frame country church, standing in a shady grove beside its old cemetery, is among the best-preserved rural churches in the region. The site was first used by a Methodist congregation

DV 11 *Old Mount Vernon Church*

founded ca. 1830; they sold it in 1893 to the Primitive Baptists, who apparently erected the building in their typically conservative form. Graves date from the 1840s, including the Tesh family and other Methodist converts from *Friedberg.

DV 12 George W. Wall House
1896; George W. Wall, builder;
SE corner, jct. NC 109 and SR 1723,
Wallburg; private, visible from road

One of the finest Queen Anne style houses in the county, the residence dominates the village named for the Wall family, whose lumber business provided the wealth and the materials for such an elaborate structure.

DV 13 Bethany Reformed and Lutheran Cemetery and the Northern Davidson County Cemeteries
E side SR 1716, 0.4 mi. S of SR 1800,
Thomasville vic.

Davidson Co. possesses an extraordinary heritage of carved and pierced gravestones created by local artisans of German descent, some of whom were trained cabinetmakers. In these beautiful and unique markers, the craftsmen incised and pierced the soft local soapstone with woodworking as well as stonecutting tools. They combined baroque forms with Germanic folk art and *fraktur* motifs, most notably the *fylfot*, a pinwheel-like symbol of eternity. The earliest stones, by various semiskilled artisans and often inscribed in German, were followed ca. 1800–1850 by the advanced "Pierced Style," by artisans associated with local cabinetmaker John Swisegood, and the "Fraktur Style," attributed to stonecutter David Sowers. Several church cemeteries in the German-settled northern county contain such stones, which altogether number more than 300. **Bethany Church** (est. 1789) has one of the largest, most varied, and best-protected groupings. Some of its Pierced Style stones are by Joseph Clodfelter, the only positively identified carver in the style, including those of Joseph's parents, Jacob (d. 1837) and Margaret (d. 1857). Motifs include the *fylfot*, tree-of-life, tulip or starflower, sunburst, and

herringbone patterns. The stones also document the continued use and gradual deterioration of German into the 1820s. See M. Ruth Little, *Sticks and Stones: Three Centuries of North Carolina Gravemarkers* (1998).

DV 14 Brummel's Inn
1814 and later; SW side SR 1755,
0.5 mi. SE of SR 1756, Thomasville vic.

Located on the old stage road midway between Greensboro and Salisbury, Jacob Brummel's small log house was such a convenient stage stop that he added a second story and flanking rooms and marked the chimney "J. B. 1814." The inn enjoyed great popularity until the 1850s, when a larger establishment a few miles southwest supplanted it. Long a private residence, only its trio of front entrances suggests its importance as one of the region's few surviving stagecoach inns.

DV 15 Thomasville

N.C.'s "Chairtown" is a national furniture-making center, home of one of the Piedmont's main 19th- and 20th-c. industries along with textiles and tobacco. A village developed in 1852 in anticipation of the NCRR was named for John W. Thomas, a legislator who supported the railroad bill. The first chair maker was David Westmoreland, who moved his shop here from Forsyth Co. in the mid-1850s and built the state's first real chair factory in 1879. Others soon followed. Thomasville Furniture Industries began as a small chair factory on W. Main St. in 1905 and, led by the Finch family, expanded steadily into a national industry leader, with its modern factories along the railroad dominating the town. Several other furniture factories contain early 20th-c. structures amidst later buildings. The importance of the industry was symbolized by the 1922 construction of the 13½-foot-tall wooden **Thomasville Chair** by the railroad; after "The Big Chair"—the world's largest—decayed, the present 18-foot-tall steel reproduction of a Duncan Phyfe armchair was erected in 1949.

The nearby **Thomasville Depot** (1870–71; W. Main St.), a small, richly detailed

board-and-batten structure—one of the oldest depots in the state—served as a passenger station until 1912, then as a freight office and has been restored. The former **Thomasville City Hall** (ca. 1938; W. Guilford St.), now the police station, exemplifies the Art Deco style in a symmetrical stone-faced building with bold setbacks and incised ornament. The City Hall now occupies the **First National Bank of Thomasville** (ca. 1922; 10 Salem St.), a Neoclassical Revival building in limestone, with Doric columns flanking the entrance. The **Smith Clinic** (1939; Tyson T. Ferree [High Point], architect; 17 Randolph St.) is a small but striking Art Deco brick building with cast-stone frontispiece. Residential architecture near the downtown includes houses built for furniture executives of various eras, such as the Colonial Revival style **Frank S. Lambeth House** (ca. 1913; 100 Randolph St.), for a founder of the Standard Chair Co.

Southwest of downtown is the 100-acre campus of Thomasville Baptist Orphanage (Mills Home), established in 1885. **Mitchell House** (1885; 411 Biggs Ave.) is the state's oldest building constructed for the care of orphaned children—a long, 1-story brick building with inset porch with millwork trim.

DV 16 Tom's Creek Primitive Baptist Church

1903; E side SR 2383, 0.25 mi. S of NC 109, Denton vic.

In a familiar sequence the congregation, established by 1812, worshiped in a brush arbor, then built a simple wooden meetinghouse; by 1903 they had erected this modest,

neatly finished frame church with Gothic Revival touches in its pointed arched windows and paired doors in the gable front.

DV 17 Mount Ebal Methodist Protestant Church

1883; John T. Sexton & Alfred Thompson, builders; end of SR 2518, Denton vic.

The simply finished gable-fronted frame country church was erected by members Sexton and Thompson for a congregation founded about 1861. In the late 19th c. it was the site of popular annual camp meetings. The congregation has disbanded, but the building and adjacent cemetery in a pristine rural setting are maintained for homecoming. (See Introduction, Fig. 42).

DV 18 Chapel Hill Methodist Arbor

Mid- to late 19th c.; N side SR 2547, 0.4 mi. W of Randolph Co. line

A historian noted in the 1920s that "Chapel Hill is known far and near on account of the great crowds that gather here for the annual camp meetings." The congregation, founded in 1854, soon built the heavy hand-hewn, mortise-and-tenon frame arbor. After a hiatus from ca. 1860 to 1890, meetings were revived and the deep sheds on all four sides were probably added. The adjacent brick church was built in 1933.

DV 19 High Rock Dam and Power Plant

1927; N side SR 1002 on Yadkin River

The large dam, 59 feet high and 925 feet across, was constructed by the Southern Power Co. for the Alcoa Co., which had previously established a power plant and aluminum factory downstream on the Yadkin at *Badin. The immense project required fourteen months to complete, with hundreds of workers clearing the land for the large lake, erecting the dam, and rerouting several miles of the WSSB. The large High Rock Lake covers the site of the ford where the Trading Path crossed the river. Upstream, at the upper reaches of the lake, Southern Power Co. had built in 1926 the **Buck Steam Station** (end of SR 2175, Duke-ville Rd.; visible from I-85 bridge over Yadkin River, E of Spencer), a major coal-fired steam plant necessitated after droughts reduced capacity on the Catawba River, and named for James Buchanan "Buck" Duke (d. 1925). (See Introduction, Fig. 52.)

DV 20 Cotton Grove

The fertile Jersey settlement has supported productive agriculture from the 18th c., including Dr. William R. Holt's model farm called Linwood. Cotton Grove takes its name from prerailroad days when cotton growers gathered here to make a caravan of loaded wagons to Fayetteville. Two substantial brick houses recall eras of prosperity: the **Miller-Everhart House** (ca. 1860; W side NC 8, N of SR 1272), of simple 3-bay I-house form, one of the few antebellum brick houses in the county, and the **John H. Miller House** (ca. 1880; E side NC 8 opp, SR 1272), with arched windows and an early 20th-c. columned porch.

DV 21 Jersey Baptist Church
Est. ca. 1755, 1842–43, 1897–99; N side SR 1272, 0.2 mi. E of SR 1396, Linwood vic.

One of the oldest congregations in the Piedmont, the Jersey Settlement Meeting House was founded by Particular Baptists who emigrated to the Yadkin Valley from New Jersey in the early 1750s. Until after 1848 its union meetinghouse was used by Presbyterians and Episcopalians as well as Baptists, as shown by gravestones from 1772 on. The present church was erected in 1842–43 as a simple Greek Revival brick structure, then gained Gothic Revival windows and an ornate belfry in 1897–99 and a portico in the 20th c.

DV 22 Junior Order United American Mechanics National Orphans Home (American Children's Home)
1925–32; Herbert Hunter (High Point), architect; NW corner NC 47 and NC 8, Lexington vic.

The quandrangle of red brick Colonial Revival buildings centers on the Administration Building, with Flemish-bond brickwork and 2-story Ionic portico. The J.O.U.M., established in Philadelphia in 1853 to protect American labor interests, formed an N.C. chapter in 1892, which in 1924 invited the order to build one of two national orphanages here.

DV 23 Beallmont
Ca. 1800?, 1840s; S side NC 47, 1.5 mi. W of SR 1396, Linwood vic.; private, visible from road

The farm recalls the famous antebellum abundance of the fertile Jersey section. The frame house began as a small 2-story dwelling for Robert or Ebenezer Moore but gained its present form when Ebenezer's son-in-law Burgess Lamar Beall, physician and politician, transformed it with an airy lattice porch in the spirit of A. J. Downing—a mode often associated with progressive farming. Complementary landscaping includes ancient boxwood borders planted in hearts and other geometric patterns.

DV 23 *Beallmont*

DV 24 Tyro Tavern
Early to mid-19th c.; W side NC 150, 0.2 mi. N of SR 1215, Tyro; private, visible from road

The big brick building is an outstanding example of the local Greek Revival, with fine brickwork in its Flemish-bond and common-bond walls and the molded brick cornice forming pediments at the gable ends. The plan confirms traditions of its service as a tavern: a hinged, folding partition opens the 2 east rooms into 1 large space, and 4 small chambers occupy the west portion of the second story. It was built for Joseph H. Thompson, who amassed a fortune from his

DV 24 *Tyro Tavern*

Tyro Iron Works, a 19th-c. foundry that once dominated the village.

DV 25 Phillip Sowers House and Barn

Early 19th c., 1860–70; NE side SR 1162 on E. bank of Yadkin River, 3.5 mi. W of NC 150 at Churchland; private, visible from road

The unusual form of the 2-story brick house suits its commanding site above the Yadkin River. The Y-shaped triple-wing plan centers on a hexagonal stair hall—a scheme probably inspired by the cruciform plan of *Cooleemee Plantation House across the river in Davie Co. Porches were added on two facades. Likely earlier is the massive 2-story double-crib barn of half-dovetailed logs; the center wagon aisle is flanked by openings into the stables, sheltered by a

long, cantilevered pent that extends across the front.

DV 26 Koonts House

1870–80; W side SR 1186, 1.0 mi. S of US 64; private, visible from road

The farmhouse near the Yadkin River, like the *Sowers House, was evidently inspired by the cruciform plan of *Cooleemee (1855). The small but emphatically stylish 1-story frame house, built for Capt. John and Jane Koonts, follows a Y-plan with hexagonal belvedere above the center section. The entrance in the elbow of the Y is sheltered by a semicircular porch, which once had pic-

DV 25 *Sowers Barn*

DV 25 *Phillip Sowers House*

DV 27 *E. L. Greene House*

turesque lattice posts. The farmstead includes a double-crib log barn and other log outbuildings.

DV 27 Yadkin College
SR 1194, N of US 64 on
E. bank of Yadkin River

On a forested river bluff stand remnants of the once stylish village of Yadkin College, which grew up around a Methodist school, funded in 1852 by local farmer Henry Walser and opened in 1856. After the Civil War it flourished for a time, along with a small tobacco industry, but both closed in the early 20th c. The **College Building** (1856) is a 2-story 5-bay brick building stuccoed and scored to imitate stone—a treatment also seen at the contemporary *Davidson County Courthouse. When an 1881 building (lost) replaced it, it served briefly as a tobacco factory. There are houses of various Italianate styles, plus the **E. L. Greene House** (ca. 1890), a classic T-shaped Gothic cottage built for a tobacconist. **Yadkin College Methodist Church** (1886; end of SR 1436) is a gable-fronted frame church with a front tower, belfry, and spire.

Davie County (DE)

See Kirk Franklin Mohney, The Historic Architecture of Davie County, North Carolina *(1986).*

The county in the forks of the Yadkin River has some of the prettiest farmland in the western Piedmont. In 1836 the part of Rowan Co. north of the Yadkin was made a new county and named for Revolutionary leader William R. Davie. Long admired for its high and healthy land where buffalo fed, by the 1750s the county had attracted German, Scotch-Irish, and English Quaker settlers. The Bryan family settlement became a springing point for settlers of Kentucky, including Daniel Boone. In the 1770s and 1780s Baptists and Methodists formed some of their first congregations west of the Yadkin, and they grew stronger with subsequent revivals. Local leaders pressed for better river and rail links but had little success until 1891, when the N.C. Midland Railroad was built from Winston. The county remained largely rural through much of the 20th c., but in recent years it has grown increasingly urbanized, especially around Mocksville.

Mocksville (DE 1–4)

Named for a local family, the county seat has a strong collection of town architecture from the 1820s onward, concentrated along Main and Salisbury Sts. Long regarded as an especially healthful and pleasant location, the community began in the 18th c. and in 1836 became seat of the new county. Incorporated in 1839, the town was drawn as a circle with a radius of a half-mile from the courthouse, which stood in a Lancaster plan square at the meeting of four axial streets. In 1839 the Salisbury newspaper reported "very handsome private mansions" built by "industrious and enterprising citizens." These include houses of brick, frame, and log construction and a brick courthouse, jail, and academy. By the 1840s, though, Mocksville was "going down hill," and in 1855 the Salisbury paper said that "her day of prosperity was brief but an attractive one." Without a railroad until 1891, it remained a local trade and tobacco manufacturing center. In 1892 a Winston newspaper described a "quiet, benevolent little village," which "slumbers away, undisturbed by the noise, the hurry, the restlessness, the trouble and temptation of the outside world." A few years later a Mocksville paper was touting its quiet and healthy position between Winston

and Charlotte and invited "capitalists to come to our town." Rail links encouraged trade and growth, as did the juncture of major 20th-c. highways. As neighboring cities on I-40 grew, Mocksville capitalized on its small-town charm and convenience.

DE 1 Downtown Mocksville

Main St. north of Lexington Rd. epitomizes courthouse towns of the late 19th and early 20th centuries. From the early days, the former **Davie County Jail** (1839; Henry R. Austin, builder; 284 S. Main St.) is an unusually handsome rendition of the typically domestic jail form: a 2-story, late Federal style structure of brick laid in Flemish bond with interior end chimneys and a central entrance. The jailer's residence was below and cells with barred windows above. (See Introduction, Fig. 26.) To the south, on Lexington Rd., the **Woodruff House** (early 19th c.; moved, 1986; 100 Lexington Rd.), a restored log structure of modified saddlebag form, recalls the presence of log buildings in many Piedmont towns. **First Presbyterian Church** (1905; Charles C. Hook & Frank Sawyer [Charlotte], architects; 261 S. Main St.), a boldly composed Romanesque Revival church in red brick, has a corner belltower and arcaded porch across the gabled

DE 1 *Davie Co. Courthouse*

ist Church (1896; James A. Call, builder; 305 N. Main St.), a Gothic Revival brick structure with corner tower, was built for a rural congregation that moved to town in the 1830s.

DE 2 N. Main St. Residential Area

N. Main St. is lined by residences in diverse styles from the mid-19th c. onward. The **Dr. R. P. Anderson House** (ca. 1903; Barber & Kluttz [Knoxville], architects; 665 N. Main St.), one of the county's few architect-designed residences, has an asymmetrical composition with round tower and distinctive rough stonework. Fancy millwork adorns the T-shaped frame **Hugh Robertson House** (1887; 728 N. Main St.), built for a tobacco manufacturer and featuring diagonal boarding, brackets, and a 2-tier porch. Most distinctive is the boldly Gothic Revival **A. M. Nail House** (1880s; 768 N. Main St.), a 2-story brick dwelling in an exaggerated cottage style with peaked gables, windows, and shutters. The **Martin-Caudill House** (ca. 1870; 900 N. Main St.) also displays the picturesque cottage mode, with brackets at the gabled entrance porch and eaves. The **Philip Hanes House** (1902; 1085 N. Main St.) is a big Colonial Revival house with wraparound porch, built for Hanes after he sold the family tobacco company in Winston to R. J. Reynolds and retired to his native county.

front. The congregation began as the 18th-c. Joppa Church north of town and moved here ca. 1835.

The **Davie County Courthouse** (1909, 1916; 100 block S. Main St.), a typical early 20th-c. design with Corinthian-columned portico and domed cupola, was reworked after a 1916 fire. The 1839 brick courthouse stood on the square until ca. 1922. The open square is framed by brick commercial buildings, such as the prominent **Baity Store** (ca. 1905; 101 N. Main St.), with corbeled brickwork, curved parapet and pilasters. The **Gaither Tobacco Factory** (late 19th c.; 142 N. Main St.), a 2-story corbeled-brick commercial building, recalls the importance of local tobacco manufacturing. **First Method-**

DE 2 *A. M. Nail House*

DE 3 Salisbury St.

To the southwest is another notable grouping of 19th- and early 20th-c. architecture. The **Hall-Call House** (ca. 1828, ca. 1870s; 484 Salisbury St.) has small upper windows and proportions indicating its origin as a 2-story log house (home of William Hall, longtime minister at Joppa Presbyterian Church); about 1871 Samuel Call, local cabinetmaker and carpenter, gave it a stylish weatherboarded exterior with decorated porch, bracketed eaves, and curved end bay. Other 19th-c. houses include the **Harbin-Long House** (1850s; 471 Salisbury St.), brick with robust Greek Revival details, and the **Howell-Brown-Sanford-Larew House** (ca. 1850; 537 Salisbury St.), frame with decorated 2-tier entrance porch. In its yard is the 1-story brick building built as the **Mocksville Academy** (ca. 1828). The **Hugh Sanford House** (1923; 519 Salisbury St.) shows the influence of *Reynolda House in a bungalow with heavy columns, French doors, a sleeping porch over a porte cochere, and a matching servants' residence.

DE 4 Jesse Clement House

Ca. 1828; 290 E. Maple St.;
private, visible from street

The 2-story brick house in conservative Federal style exemplifies substantial local architecture of the early 19th c., with a center-passage variation of a 3-room plan. The front and west walls are laid in Flemish bond; the other two are in common bond. The house was built for Jesse Clement about the time he married Malinda Nail and began a career as a planter, tanner, merchant, politician, and Methodist leader.

DE 5 Joppa Cemetery

18th–19th c.; E side US 601,
0.4 mi. N of US 64

The graveyard associated with Joppa Presbyterian Church, formed in the 1760s, has the graves of Squire and Sarah Boone, who came to the Bryan Settlement in 1752 and died in 1765 and 1777, respectively. Their restless son Daniel married Rebecca Bryan and went to

Kentucky in 1775 with other Bryan family members.

DE 6 Center Arbor

1876; SW side US 64, 0.2 mi. NW of I-40

The capacious structure of pegged timbers under a long, broad gable roof is a late 19th-c. example of a traditional form. Rows of simple pews face the pulpit at the south end. Center Methodist Church, which emerged from a revival held in 1830, built a frame church on this site in 1872 and then constructed an arbor for revivals.

DE 6 *Center Arbor*

DE 7 Calahaln

US 64 at SR 1313

At a crossroads on an old road are three 19th-c. farmhouses built for descendants of Charles and Elizabeth Anderson, who came from Virginia in the late 18th or early 19th c. (The village was named for the Callahans, also early settlers.) The **Garland Anderson House** (ca. 1830s, late 20th c.; S side SR 1152, 0.15 SE of US 64), built for their son, is a 2-story log house with half-dovetailed notching and a central chimney rising between 2 rooms—a contrast to the usual end chimneys. There is a large addition. Nearby stand a double-crib log barn and other log outbuildings. The **Charles Anderson House** (1879; SW corner of US 64 and SR 1152), a 2-story brick house with late Greek Revival finish, was built for Garland's nephew, a partner in C. Anderson and Bros. plug tobacco factory and Anderson Bros. Store. The **Dr. John Anderson House** (ca. 1870s; W side SR 1313, NW of US 64), built for Charles's brother and partner, is a 2-story frame dwelling with a 2-tier porch. In the yard is a simple frame **Tobacco Factory** (1871).

DE 8 St. Matthews Lutheran Church
Ca. 1890; SW side SR 1143, 2.3 mi. SE of US 64, Calahaln vic.

Built for a congregation organized in 1839, the modest gable-fronted frame building with entrance tower and shingled belfry is the county's oldest church of the denomination. It recalls the county's German heritage and the ca. 1765 founding of the Heidelburg Church.

DE 9 Zion Chapel Methodist Church
1892; N side SR 1306, 0.1 mi. W of SR 1313

The frame country church takes an unusual form: 2 gabled ells join at angles to a diagonally faced vestibule, where 2 doors direct men and women into separate seating in the ells. The pulpit stands in the point opposite the entrance. The congregation traces back to Beal's Meeting House (ca. 1780), one of the first Methodist congregations in western N.C.

DE 10 Cana

The crossroads community was named in 1875 for postmaster James H. Cain, who erected the **Cana Store** (ca. 1885) as his general store and post office—a carefully preserved 2-story, gable-fronted building. With brother-in-law Ebenezer Frost he laid out a village that had several businesses and an academy in the late 19th c. Among the late 19th- and early 20th-c. frame houses is the **Cain House** (1926; Dodson Grubbs, John James, carpenters; N of Cana Store), a frame foursquare residence built for Cain's son John and his wife Ina, postmistress (1919–54).

DE 11 Eatons Baptist Church and Cemetery
18th c., 1925; E side SR 1415, opp. SR 1416

Presiding over the landscape from a hilltop, the red brick church with portico and cupola was built for a congregation that began as Dutchman Creek Baptist Church (1772), named for a stream recalling early German (Deutsch) settlers. The church was reorganized as Eatons in 1790. The churchyard across the road has gravestones from 1780 onward.

DE 12 Farmington
Jct. NC 801 and SR 1410

The crossroads on an old north-south route was known in the early 19th c. as Little Currituck for settlers fleeing coastal hurricane damage, but in 1837 it was renamed for the good farmland around it, probably by postmaster, merchant, and scientific farmer George Johnson. The **George Wesley Johnson House** (1854–55; SW corner SR 1410 and NC 801) is a 2-story Greek Revival house of brick, with 2-story entrance portico and balcony. Johnson gave land for both the Baptist and Methodist churches, which in 1881 erected gable-fronted frame buildings with belltowers. Several late 19th-c. frame houses in decorated Italianate style were built for Johnson children, also merchants.

DE 13 Win-Mock Farm
Late 1920s; N side US 158 just W of Yadkin River bridge; visible S of I-40

A landmark by I-40 at the Yadkin River, the big dairy barn with oval Quonset type roof was part of a complex including concrete silos, a bottling plant, and other buildings. One of the state's largest dairy farms, it was established by S. Clay Williams of Reynolds Tobacco Co., one of several executives who became gentlemen farmers. It was named Win-Mock for its position between towns by the Bahnson family, who acquired it in 1949.

DE 13 *Win-Mock Farm*

DE 14 Advance

The early 19th-c. community of Shady Grove was renamed in a spirit of progress and grew with the N.C. Midland Railroad after 1891. **Advance Methodist Church** (1912; E side NC 801) is a small frame church with Gothic openings and a corner tower. Successor to its earlier school is the large frame building of the **Advance Academy** (1890s). There are several late 19th- and early 20th-c. houses with sawnwork porches and center front gables.

DE 15 Fulton Methodist Church

1888; SE side NC 801, 1.6 mi. N. of US 64

The Gothic Revival brick church with central tower and Italianate brackets is unusually elaborate for a country congregation. Door and window sills are of leopardite, a patterned local stone. The tower is flanked by entrances for men and women into separate seating. Established as Hebron Church ca. 1800, the congregation takes its name from a short-lived Yadkin River town founded by Jacob Hanes in 1819 and named for Hamilton Fulton, the state engineer of the Yadkin Navigation project. Among the graves are those of Alexander and Jane March Hanes and their son Benjamin Franklin Hanes, Winston-Salem industrialist.

DE 15 *Fulton Methodist Church*

DE 16 Hodges Business College
Ca. 1894; S side SR 1819, 0.15 mi. SE of NC 801, Cooleemee vic.; private, visible from road

The 2-story brick academy building, defined by bold Gothic Revival lancet openings and steep gables, was built by county native John Hodges, who advertised his school in a "section proverbial for its health." To the west, the **John D. Hodges House** (ca. 1880s) is a 2-story T-plan frame house with decorative millwork.

DE 16 *Hodges Business College*

DE 17 Jesse Eaton House
1866; N side SR 1826, 0.1 mi. NE of US 601, Cooleemee vic.; private, visible from road

Framed by great oaks and outbuildings, the Greek Revival brick house has a 2-tier entrance portico with broad gable and square pillars. It may have been begun before the war and completed in 1866, the date on a brick.

DE 18 Cooleemee Plantation
1853–55; W. H. Ranlett; Conrad and Williams, builders; private, no public visibility or access; National Historic Landmark

Perfectly designed for its hilltop site in a bend of the Yadkin River, the classically detailed, Greek cross plan villa epitomizes antebellum planters' adoption of Romantic Revival styles. A departure from the regional traditions, it was inspired by an "Anglo-Grecian villa" in *Godey's Lady's Book* (Jan. 1850), from W. H. Ranlett's *The Architect* (1847).

Four pedimented wings extend from a polygonal center lit by a cupola, and all are unified by clustered arched windows and 1-story porches with Ionic columns. The house was built for Peter W. Hairston and his wife Columbia Stuart (sister of future general J. E. B. Stuart), who married in 1849. The Hairstons numbered among the South's largest owners of land and slaves. Peter owned over 4,000 acres and 300 slaves in Davie Co. alone; he expanded a plantation established by Gen. Jesse Pearson, who had named it for the Creek Indian "Kulami" after travels in Alabama. Like Pearson, Hair-

ston invested in Yadkin navigation projects to make the property more valuable. The builders of the house also erected other stylish edifices in the Piedmont. Woodwork and other finishing elements came from Philadelphia via water and the plank road. The plantation has remained in family stewardship.

DE 19 Cooleemee
Cotton Mill and Village
1899 and later; NC 801,
N side of South Yadkin River

The large mill community began in 1899 when the Cooleemee Water Power & Mfg. Co. established on the South Yadkin River one of the last big waterpowered textile mills in the state. An extension of the Duke family's textile investment, the company was formed by stockholders Benjamin N. Duke and William A. Erwin of Durham, along with George and B. Franklin Mebane, president of the mills at *Leaksville (Eden). With the Mebanes taking the most visible role, the company acquired several tracts, including 532 acres from Cooleemee Plantation, at the falls of the South Yadkin. The site, known as the Shoals, Pearsons Falls, and Cooleemee Falls, was a river crossing and

DE 19 *Cooleemee Cotton Mill*

waterpower source for 18th-c. mills. The company employed Ladshaw Engineers of Spartanburg, S.C., to plan the complex, extended a rail spur to the site, built workers' houses, and in 1900 completed a 477-foot stone dam for one of the state's largest mills. "Come and see what the company is doing for old Davie," invited the *Davie Record* in 1899. The mill provided jobs for local workers and a market that encouraged cotton farming. Duke and Erwin soon bought out the Mebanes and in 1901 made it Cooleemee Plant No. 3 of Erwin Mills (*Erwin Mills, Durham). Erwin, president and "the leading spirit" at Cooleemee, expanded the mill in the 1920s and later and erected more workers' and managers' houses and other facilities. Hydroelectric power soon supplemented waterpower. Erwin supported labor reforms, including reduction of working hours and child labor. By 1935 the mill employed 1,300 people with 1,250 looms and 47,000 spindles, and the village had about 360 houses, of which more than 330 survive.

The enormous, 3-story **Cooleemee Cotton Mill** (1898–99) overlooks the river, with three tall, corbeled towers breaking its long horizontal mass. From it radiate Duke, Erwin, Watts, and other streets of workers' housing on hillsides northward—one of the largest intact villages in the state. Most of the operatives' dwellings are single-family 1-story units with L- or T-plans, but some are 2 stories tall with central chimneys. Colonial Revival houses built for managers during expansion in the 1930s line Marginal St. near the edge of town. Erwin, a strong Episcopalian, built churches of various denominations, including the **Church of the Good Shepherd** (1925), a cruciform Gothic Revival building in brick and stone, which replaced a frame church of ca. 1901 (*St. Athanasius, Burlington; *St. Joseph's Episcopal Church, Durham; *Chapel of the Cross, Chapel Hill). In the 1950s the housing was sold to workers, and in the 1960s the mill was sold to Burlington Industries; downtown buildings were razed, and the mill was eventually converted to a warehouse. Although many residents work elsewhere, the community has a strong sense of identity, with a historical museum in the former superintendent's house.

DE 20 Hinton Rowan Helper House
Early 19th c.; off US 64 E of Mocksville; no public access or visibility; National Historic Landmark

Inside an early 20th-c. house is the small log home of Hinton Rowan Helper, who studied at the Mocksville Academy and tried gold mining in California before he returned home to write *The Impending Crisis of the South* (1857), a controversial attack on slavery now regarded as a contributing cause of the Civil War. In the mid-18th c. Squire and Sarah Boone and their son Daniel lived in earlier log dwellings here.

Rowan County (RW)

See Davyd Foard Hood, The Architecture of Rowan County *(1983).*

The county between the Yadkin and Catawba rivers has a rich and diverse heritage noted for its 18th- and 19th-c. Scotch-Irish and German churches and houses. When formed in 1753 from Anson Co. and named for political figure Matthew Rowan, the county encompassed the whole northwest sector of the colony and extended west indefinitely. Within Rowan's present borders, Scotch-Irish immigrants arrived from the 1740s onward and established "the Irish Settlement" in fertile western Rowan. Germans soon followed in the east, constituting as much as 40 percent of the population. Both founded congregations that became mother churches in the region. On moderate-sized farms, citizens produced abundant grains and livestock and built 1- and 2-story farmhouses of log, frame, or occasionally brick; log outbuildings; and by the 19th c., double-crib log barns. Substantial late 18th- and early 19th-c. houses show notably varied adaptations of traditional 3- and 4-room plans. In the early 19th c., soil depletion and other problems led many families to leave for "the west," while a few consolidated land and slaves into a more hierarchical plantation economy. In the 1840s, gold mining bolstered the economy, followed by the 1855 arrival of the North Carolina Railroad (NCRR) and, in the later 19th c., cotton mills and roller mills, stone quarrying, and the immense railroad repair shops at *Spencer.

Salisbury (RW 1–37)

The medium-sized county seat possesses one of the state's finest ensembles of 19th- and early 20th-c. town architecture. An unusually strong commercial district and downtown neighborhoods as well as individually distinguished landmarks make Salisbury a gem of the Piedmont. From early days, Salisbury was a regional as well as a local center, in touch with the larger world beyond. Established in 1755 as the seat of the immense new county of Rowan, it was well positioned near the Trading Ford on the Yadkin River, the crossing for the north-south Wagon Road and the east-west Trading Path. Salisbury thrived as thousands of Scotch-Irish and German settlers arrived down the Wagon Road, and travelers and traders passed through with news and goods. Daniel Boone outfitted here for treks westward. Taverns aplenty served visitors and courthouse business, and small industries sprang up. As seat of a vast and growing western zone, the town was known for its prominent attorneys and those who studied

law with them, including young Andrew Jackson. For many years the town was bilingual, but by the early 19th c. English dominated in town, while German continued in rural areas. Even after Rowan became mother and grandmother to many counties, Salisbury maintained a regional stature. Leading lawyers and political figures, merchants and artisans, ministers and schoolteachers, and tavern keepers and industrialists defined town life from the 18th c. onward, and such newspapers as the *Western Carolinian* (est. 1820) strengthened its influence.

During the out-migration of the 1830s, Salisbury leaders campaigned for railroads to "brighten the prospects." Its fortunes rebounded with the 1855 NCRR through town. Even before rails reached Salisbury, new buildings were erected and new energy infused the people, "who talk of nothing now but the rail road"; thereafter, property values jumped, and several steam-powered factories were built. The Western North Carolina Railroad (WNCRR) was begun in 1857 from Salisbury toward Asheville and beyond. By 1860 Salisbury's 2,420 people made it the

Main St.: RW 9 *Empire Hotel and* RW 5 *Grubb-Wallace Building*

fifth largest town in the state. During the Civil War it was an important rail center, and its textile mill became a Confederate prison. In 1865 Gen. George Stoneman's troops burned the prison and railroad and military facilities but spared the town.

After the war, prosperity returned slowly. During the 1870s and early 1880s, local leaders rebuffed calls for a new rail connection south, while Charlotte made itself the rail nexus of the Carolinas. In 1887 the *Charlotte Observer* commented that while Salisbury had led before the Civil War, afterward "people laid down and slept on their opportunities." The chief businesses were the railroad shops of the WNCRR, a few tobacco factories, and whiskey distilleries and saloons that made Salisbury an island within an increasingly dry region; it was called the "wettest and wickedest" town in the state until statewide prohibition in 1908.

By the end of the 1880s, new enterprise was emerging. The long delayed WNCRR finally reached through Asheville to Tennessee, and the Yadkin Railroad was completed southeast to Albemarle in 1891. Mines at *Gold Hill attracted new investors, and after a revivalist in 1887 called for a cotton mill to employ the poor, even conservative

local business leaders agreed that "next to religion Salisbury most needed a cotton factory." The population, which had grown in the 1880s from 2,723 to 6,277, slowly redoubled to 13,884 by 1920, making it ninth largest in the state. Since then, Salisbury's development has been gradual in contrast to the skyrocketing growth in cities it once equalled.

Although nothing remains of the log structures of the early town, there are notable buildings from the early to mid-19th c., including stylish Federal and Greek Revival houses and a Greek Revival courthouse. Particularly strong is the architecture from the late 19th and early 20th centuries, with nearly every nationally popular style rendered in substantial and conservative fashion. The central business district, one of the finest in the state, focuses on the intersection of Main and Innes Sts. A few antebellum brick buildings blend with 2- to 4-story structures from the late 19th and early 20th centuries, including some of local granite. Residential areas and railroad-oriented business sectors closely flank downtown. In contrast to Salisbury's booming neighbors, moderate growth and relative stability, combined with persistent preservation efforts

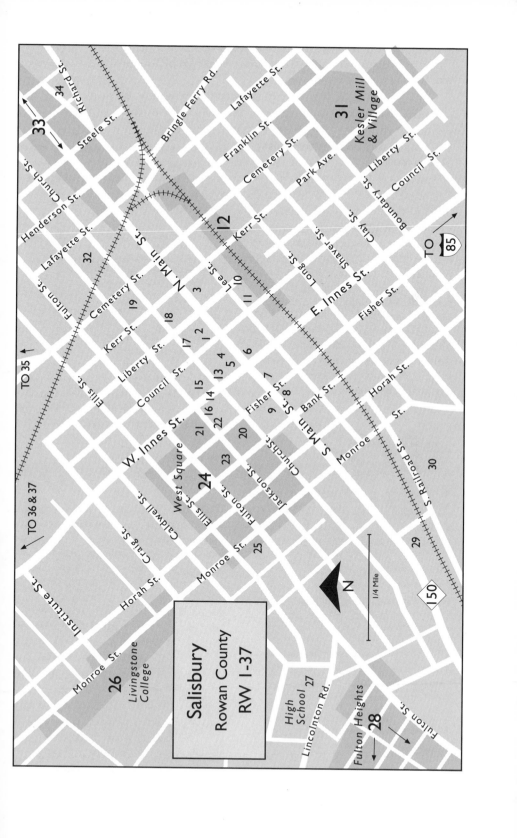

Salisbury
Rowan County
RW 1-37

Kesler Mill & Village 31

33 34
Richard St.
Steele St.
Church St.
Henderson St.
Lafayette St.
32
Cemetery St.
Kerr St.
Liberty St.
Council St.
Fulton St.
Ellis St.

Bringle Ferry Rd.
Lafayette St.
Franklin St.
Cemetery St.
Park Ave.
Liberty St.
Council St.
Boundary St.
Clay St.
Shaver St.
Long St.
Kerr St.
12
Lee St.
3 10 11
18 17 2
13 4
15 5
16 14 6
21 22 7
23 20 9 8
24
West Square
W. Innes St.
Caldwell St.
Craig St.
Institute St.
Horah St.
Monroe St.
Livingstone College 26
Monroe St. 25
Fulton St.
Jackson St.
Churchst.
S. Main St.
Bank St.
Monroe St.
Horah St.
St.
Fisher St.
Fisher St.
E. Innes St.
N. Main St.

TO 35
TO 36 & 37

TO 85

N
1/4 Mile

150

30
29
S. Railroad St.

High School 27
Lincolnton Rd.
Fulton Heights 28
Fulton St.

spearheaded by the Historic Salisbury Foundation, have maintained the town's scale and density along with its historic architecture.

Downtown Salisbury

RW 1 Old Rowan County Courthouse (Rowan Museum)

1854–57; John W. Conrad and John W. Williams (Davidson Co.); 202 N. Main St.; open regular hours

The Greek Revival "temple of justice" is dominated by a monumental Doric portico, with unusually tall columns. Large upper windows light the second-story courtroom. The courthouse, erected during the competition between Guilford, Davidson, and Rowan counties for the best facility, garnered its builders local acclaim for the "magnificent structure which when completed will be another monument of their artistic skill and ingenuity." It has been used for various community purposes.

RW 1-2 *Rowan Co. Courthouses*

RW 2 Rowan County Courthouse

1914; A. Ten Eyck Brown (Atlanta); N. Main St.

One of several imposing Neoclassical Revival courthouses from the early 20th c., the gray stone edifice with Ionic portico presents a contrasting face of classicism.

RW 3 Smith-Pearson House

Ca. 1847; 305 N. Main St.

A once common antebellum type, the 2-story brick building with stepped gable ends incorporating the chimneys is one of a few

local examples of the type (*Salisbury Female Academy).

RW 4 Washington Building

Ca. 1890; Alfred Lazenby, builder; 118–20 N. Main St.

The rough grandeur of the Romanesque Revival in local stone makes this 3-story facade especially striking: three great round-arched windows, corner bartizans, and an arched parapet give it a castle-like character. Lazenby, a native of Iredell Co., erected several local buildings.

RW 5 Grubb-Wallace Building

Ca. 1900; Frank P. Milburn; 100 N. Main St.

Salisbury's only skyscraper, the 7½-story brick building displays the Beaux Arts classical division into base, shaft, and capital; striated pilasters rise through the 5-story shaft to arched upper windows. Designed by Milburn for Henry Clay Grubb, who made his fortune as an entrepreneur and distiller, it was restored in the late 20th c.

RW 6 Kluttz Drug Store

1858; A. B. Hendren, architect; 101 N. Main St.

The intricately corbeled brick building is an early example of the commercial style that gained prominence in the mid-19th c. In 1858 the local paper said the new Purcell's drugstore building (later Kluttz's) was "more noticed and talked of than any put up in this place for some time. . . . Its most striking feature is the extraordinary beauty of the brick work"—a contrast to then-prevalent

RW 6 *Kluttz Drug Store*

stuccoed masonry. Hendren was active in Salisbury in the late 1850s.

RW 7 Bell Block

1898; David L. Gaskill, builder; 131–33 S. Main St.

Salisbury builders used local granite to create unusually fine stone commercial facades, such as this 3½-story Romanesque Revival building fronted in rough-cut ashlar with pilasters and arched windows. A (formerly turreted) rounded bay with balcony turns the corner.

RW 8 Cyrus West Building

Ca. 1839; 203 S. Main St.

Of brick laid in Flemish bond, with a corbeled, molded cornice and stepped gable ends, the 2-story building is one of the oldest downtown.

RW 9 Empire Hotel

1855; 1907; Frank P. Milburn, architect; 212–26 S. Main St.

The antebellum Boyden Hotel, deluxe in its day, was remodeled as the Empire by railroad architect Milburn, who produced a boldly modeled facade emphasized by contrasting red and cream brick, free classical details, and a name parapet.

Depot Area

RW 10 Salisbury Passenger Depot

1907–8; Frank P. Milburn; Depot St.

Southern Railway architect Milburn's dramatic Spanish Mission style station combines symmetry with romantic curvilinear gables, colorful tile roof, arched openings, and a commanding central tower. The scale and elaboration of the station, comparable to those in larger N.C. cities, asserted Salisbury's stature in the rail network; once every city prided itself on its large and elegant railroad depot, but most are lost or altered, leaving this as the chief survivor. It has been restored as community center and Amtrak stop.

RW 11 Yadkin Hotel

1912–13, Wheeler & Stern (Charlotte), architects; 1922, Louis Asbury (Charlotte), addition; Depot and Council Sts.

The big railroad hotel, built at a cost of $100,000, featured all the modern conveniences, including many rooms with private baths. The 5-story brick and steel frame building retains its colored tilework decoration complementing the neighboring depot.

RW 12 Salisbury Railroad Corridor Area

The blocks near the depot comprise many early 20th-c. brick warehouses, factories, and sales facilities that lived and died with rail traffic. **Frick & Co.** (ca. 1905; 230 E. Kerr St.), a 1-story brick building with arched windows, housed a wholesale grocer, then Frick's farm equipment. Across from the depot, the 2-story parapeted brick and stone **Cheerwine Building** (1913–14; 322 E. Council St.) was built for Mint Cola Co., creator of Salisbury's popular soft drink; it retains its big "Drink Cheerwine" sign.

RW 13 Former U.S. Post Office and Courthouse

1909–11; 130 W. Innes St.

In the early 20th c., W. Innes St. gained major institutional buildings. The large and costly Federal building in a relatively small town recalls Salisbury's powerful U.S. senator Lee S. Overman. The pale ashlar-faced structure exemplifies a popular federal Beaux Arts design, with piano nobile, lower

RW 10 *Salisbury Passenger Depot*

arched openings, and a portico at the upper
2 stories.

RW 14 Confederate Monument

*1909; Frederick Ruckstuhl, sculptor;
center median, 200 block W. Innes St.*

The dramatic monument reproduces a
Baltimore sculpture by Ruckstuhl, with a
winged victory holding a young soldier
and a laurel wreath. It was a project of Salisbury's Frances Tiernan Fisher, whose father,
Charles, had been killed in the war; as
Christian Reid she wrote works of fiction,
including *Land of the Sky* (1876), which lent
its name to western N.C. and helped fund
the monument.

RW 15 St. John's Lutheran Church

1925–26; 200 block W. Innes St.

Long after its mid-18th-c. founding as one of
the first of its denomination in N.C., the
Lutheran church was Salisbury's only house
of worship. The initial log church stood at
the site of the Old Lutheran Cemetery (N.
Lee St.), given by Lewis Beard in 1768. Early
pastors came from Germany and also served
*Zion (Organ) Church. After a decline fol-
lowing the American Revolution, the congregation was reorganized in the 1820s. A
century later they erected the large Gothic
Revival church of pressed brick, with broad
central gable flanked by large and small
crenellated towers, trimmed in stone, and
with a polychromed sanctuary. (See Introduction, Fig. 3.)

RW 16 First Presbyterian Church: Session House and Tower

*1855; 1891–93; Charles W. Bolton
(Philadelphia), architect; 225 W. Innes St.*

Although Presbyterians lived in Salisbury
from the early days and some attended
*Thyatira, not until 1821 did they organize a
town congregation, which met in the courthouse or Lutheran church until members
built a church in 1826. The **Session House**
(1855) is a small hip-roofed brick building
where deacons and elders held their meetings. In 1891–92 the first church was re-

RW 16 *First Presbyterian Church Tower*

placed by a spectacular Romanesque Revival
church with a curved sanctuary and chateauesque belltower. When it was razed in
1971, the great brick and stone belltower was
kept.

RW 17 St. Luke's Episcopal Church

*Ca. 1827–28; John Berry (Hillsborough),
builder; 220 N. Church St.*

One of the few early 19th-c. Gothic Revival
Episcopal churches in the state, the little
brick sanctuary with lancet windows was
built by brickmason John Berry, in a fashion
similar to *St. Matthew's in his native
Hillsborough. The rectangular gable-roofed
building of Flemish-bond brick has many
additions, including a baptistry and a belltower, creating a cruciform plan.

RW 18 Soldiers Memorial A.M.E. Zion Church

1910–13; 306 N. Church St.

The Gothic Revival church of pressed brick
displays a composition seen in many A.M.E.
Zion churches, with unequal entrance towers flanking a broad gable. The congregation, formed during the Civil War and
named after Union soldiers who brought
freedom, was closely associated with *Livingstone College.

RW 18 *Soldiers Memorial A.M.E. Zion Church*

RW 19 Mount Zion Baptist Church
1907, 1920s; 413 N. Church St.

The congregation was founded in 1867 by Harry Cowan, a former slave and a citizen of Salisbury known as the father of the black Baptist church in the state. A preacher from 1828 on the plantations of Thomas Cowan, after Emancipation he led in founding many churches. By 1907 the members built the broad-gabled church of frame, which was brick-veneered in the 1920s.

RW 20 Archibald Henderson Law Office
Early 19th c.; 200 S. Church St.

An early example of the tiny law offices once standard in courthouse towns, the neatly finished frame structure has a hip roof, Flemish-bond foundation, and simple Federal moldings.

West Square

RW 21 Utzman-Chambers House
Ca. 1814–19; 116 S. Jackson St. (moved 1913 from Innes and Jackson); open regular hours

The frame town house offers the only accessible example of the fine Federal style interiors of Rowan Co.; the artisan is undocumented. The 2-story dwelling has a full-width shed porch and at one end, which originally faced the street, a pedimented gable with elaborate arched window. Its unusual plan, with stair passage and large parlor in front and 2 small rooms behind, seems to be a hybrid of urban side-passage and regional 4-room plans. Locally characteristic motifs from Owen Biddle's widely used

RW 20 *Archibald Henderson Law Office*

Young Carpenter's Assistant (1805) include a beautiful curving stair adorned with delicate "bud" brackets at the tread ends; a parlor mantel with fluted colonnettes, urns, and leafy sunburst; and fancy plasterwork. The rear chambers are simply finished. The house was evidently built for Louis Utzman, a cabinetmaker, whose brother Jacob was a house carpenter; either or both may have been involved in construction. It was sold to James Martin in 1819 and acquired in 1847 by merchant Maxwell Chambers. (See Introduction, Figs. 28 and 29.)

RW 22 Salisbury Female Academy (Wrenn House)
1838–39; 115 S. Jackson St.; open as restaurant

The 2-story Flemish-bond brick building has stepped parapet gable ends and a side-passage plan with simple Federal style woodwork. The harmonizing rear ell was added in 1871.

RW 23 Dr. Josephus Hall House
Ca. 1820, 1859, ca. 1911; 226 S. Jackson St.; open limited hours

Begun as a Federal period building erected for a noted female academy, the house was expanded in several eras. The magnificent 2-tier porch of cast iron, fashioned by Salisbury metalsmith Peter Frercks, dates from a ca. 1859 remodeling for Dr. Hall, a physician from St. Louis. Remarkable interior decorative painting has been uncovered.

RW 24 West Square Residential District
W. Bank, W. Horah, S. Fulton, S. Ellis, and nearby streets

West of the business district is Salisbury's finest residential neighborhood, with 19th- and early 20th-c. architecture enhanced by nearly two decades of preservation efforts. Antebellum houses are mainly symmetrical, 2-story dwellings with Greek Revival trim. These include the frame **Andrew Murphy House** (ca. 1853; Michael Davis, builder; 229 W. Bank St.) with 2-tier porch; **Torrence House** (ca. 1838, 1899; 428 W. Bank St.), a large brick version with later Italianate brackets; and the **Pearson-Ellis House** (ca. 1850; 200 S. Ellis St.), also in brick, the home of Elizabeth Pearson and her brother John Ellis, governor early in the Civil War.

RW 24 *S. Ellis St.*

After the Civil War, L- and T-shaped Italianate houses were built for merchants and professional men. The **Murdoch-Wiley House** (ca. 1868; William Murdoch, builder; 203 W. Bank St.) is a bold Italianate house erected for and probably by the Scots-born stonemason who worked on the *State Capitol, was a contractor on the NCRR and the WNCRR, and became one of Salisbury's leading builders and manufacturers. The symmetrical brick building features granite trim and bracketed cornices on the porch, roof, and cupola. The **John Knox House** (1871–72; 303 W. Bank St.) has round-arched windows, brackets, and an L-plan. More numerous are residences from the later 19th- and early 20th-c. industrial era, especially the Queen Anne style. Epitomizing the mode is the **Gaskill House** (1898; 402 S. Ellis St.), an asymmetrical composition with sweeping roofline, gabled balcony dormer, rounded porch, and lavish millwork. The **McKenzie-Grimes House** (1902; 228 W. Bank St.) is a large Queen Anne style house with corner tower and eclectic classical motifs. There are many 1½-story Queen Anne style cottages with high hip roofs and decorated gables and porches.

The revival styles of the early 20th c. were widely popular. Among the earliest and grandest Colonial Revival residences is the **Louis H. Clement House** (1899; 302 S. Ellis

RW 24 *Murdoch-Wiley House*

St.), a 2-story frame house with high, dormered hip roof and wraparound porch, enriched with free classical motifs. The "Southern Colonial" style with giant portico and side porches defines the **Cannon-Guille House** (1906; J. M. McMichael [Charlotte], architect; Alfred Lazenby, builder; 202 S. Fulton St.). The Spanish Mission style akin to the railroad depot appears in several houses with stuccoed walls and tile roofs, including the **Franklin Smith House** (ca. 1912; 201 S. Fulton St.), with arcade and balconies, and the **Franklin Smith Jr. House** (ca. 1929; 209 S. Fulton) and others. The Tudor Revival is seen in several cottage forms and a few larger residences, such as the **Hanford House** (1937; William H. Peeps [Charlotte], architect; 712 S. Fulton), an especially fine rendition with multiple gables and chimneys in rough stone, brick, stucco, and half-timbered work. It was built for Mary and John Van Hanford, whose daughter Elizabeth Hanford Dole was elected to the U.S. Senate in 2002. The bungalow became the most universal choice for middle-class residents of the 1920s, typified by houses at 315 W. Horah St. and 434 S. Fulton St.

RW 25 Hambley-Wallace House
1902; Charles C. Hook & Frank Sawyer (Charlotte), architects; Alfred Lazenby, builder; 508 S. Fulton St.

Set apart by its scale and large lot, the mansion is among the most ambitious of its era in the Piedmont and the prime example of the Chateauesque style modeled by #Biltmore. It embodies the remarkable career and vision of Cornish civil and mining engineer Egbert Barry Cornwall Hambley. In 1881 British investors sent him briefly to mines at *Gold Hill, and he traveled the world before returning in 1887 and marrying Charlotte Coleman of Rowan Co. In the 1890s he initiated a great scheme to harness the hydroelectric power of the Yadkin River (*Badin) and began construction of the dam, using stone from *Granite Quarry. Meanwhile, he commissioned Charlotte architect Hook to design a residence suitable for entertaining potential investors. In 1902 the *Raleigh News & Observer* marveled at the 20-room house "of French architecture," with every modern convenience—"a model of perfection in res-

idential architecture." Built of warm orange brick and local granite, the house has a dramatically dormered roofline, corner tower, and a Tudor-arched stone porch. The grounds, planned (1904) by the Philadelphia firm of Thomas Meehan & Sons, have granite walls and paving. Hambley died at age 44 in a 1906 typhoid epidemic at the dam site, and the project soon ended. Since 1927 the mansion has been home of the Wallace family.

RW 26 Livingstone College
Late 19th–early 20th c.; W. W. Smith, architect; W. Monroe St.

Founded as the Zion Wesley Institute in Concord in 1879, the school was the first in the state established by the A.M.E. Zion denomination and one of the first colleges established and operated entirely by black leaders. In 1881 Bishop James W. Hood of Charlotte persuaded Joseph C. Price, a young minister and teacher, to undertake a fund-raising speaking tour of England for the school. Upon Price's return in 1882, he became president of the college, which moved to Salisbury with community support. Renamed in 1885 for the English missionary and explorer in Africa, Livingstone attracted students from many states and included theological, classical, normal, preparatory, and industrial departments. After Price's death in 1893, William Henry Goler, a native of Pennsylvania and graduate of Lincoln University, led an era of growth.

RW 25 *Hambley-Wallace House*

RW 26 *Goler Hall and Carnegie Library*

The oldest section of the campus, one of the best preserved of the state's historically black colleges, centers on a long, hedge-lined lawn. The oldest buildings, **Dodge Hall** (1886) and **Ballard Hall** (1887), are straightforward 2-story brick structures; Ballard was expanded with ornate brickwork early in the 20th c. As was typical of the era, students made bricks for construction. From the Goler era, the **Carnegie Library** (1908; Robert R. Taylor, Tuskegee architect), with its Ionic portico, introduces a classical element, and **Hood Hall** (1910), with its prominent belfry, continues the classical theme. Most distinctive is **Goler Hall** (1917; W. W. Smith [Charlotte], builder), a 3-story brick building with a center entrance tower and vivid corbeled and polychrome brickwork characteristic of its noted Charlotte builder.

The nearby residential area contains an important grouping of teachers' and other middle-class citizens' dwellings, built of brick and frame in late Queen Anne, bungalow, and Colonial Revival modes. Especially significant is the **Joseph C. Price House** (1884; 828 W. Monroe St.), a 2-story brick Victorian residence erected by students for the school president, minister, educator, and civil rights leader. A native of Elizabeth City who had lived in New Bern, Price showed such promise that Frederick Douglass envisioned him as his successor as race leader on the national scene, but his career was cut short by his death at age 39 in 1893. W. E. B. DuBois said that had he lived, Price and Livingstone College would have attained the prominence filled by Booker T. Washington and Tuskegee. The **John C. Dancy House** (1890; 814 W. Monroe St.) is a 2-story frame Victorian house built for a faculty member, minister, and publisher from Tarboro.

RW 27 Salisbury High School

1925–26; Christopher Gadsden Sayre (Anderson, S.C., and Raleigh), architect; Earle S. Draper, landscape designer; 500 Lincolnton Rd.

The 3-story Collegiate Gothic edifice of buff brick with terra-cotta trim reflected local pride in education. Salisbury leaders consulted George D. Strayer and Nickolaus Engelhardt of Columbia University on designs and employed a noted school architect of the day. Dominated by a central entrance tower, the modified H-plan has an auditorium and gymnasium projecting to form a courtyard.

RW 28 Fulton Heights

Begun in 1904 by the Southern Development Co., the grid-plan suburb in south Salisbury was served by an extension of Salisbury's streetcar line, which linked it to *Spencer on the north. Middle-class residences lining the streets include many bungalows along with Colonial Revival houses, Tudor Revival cottages, and a few apartment houses.

RW 29 Napoleon Bonaparte McCanless House

1896–97; 600 block S. Main St.

Businessman McCanless, born to a mining family in *Gold Hill, pursued opportunities in New York and the West before establishing himself in Salisbury as an entrepreneur in cotton mill development, banking, and real estate and as president of the Harris Granite Co. at *Granite Quarry, which supplied stone for the *U.S. Post Office (1877) in Raleigh. In his "handsome stone house" admired by the local newspaper in 1896, McCanless displayed his granite in a towered Second Empire design in rough stone blocks.

RW 30 National Cemetery

Est. 1865; 202 Government Rd.

Established in 1865 at the burial ground near the Confederate prison, where thousands of Union soldiers died under dreadful conditions, the cemetery also received remains of those who died in other hospitals and battlefields, along with later military burials. Three major memorials include an 1873 granite obelisk erected by the U.S. government to the 11,700 unknown dead, Maine's 1908 black- and white-granite monument with stone soldier, and the massive Pennsylvania monument of 1910, 40 feet high with a bronze soldier "to perpetuate the memory of the dead and not as a commemoration of victory."

RW 31 Kesler Mfg. Co. Mill and Village
1895–96 and later; N. B. McCanless, builder; Liberty, Kesler, Park, and Lafayette Sts.

Of the mills and villages from Salisbury's late 19th-c. cotton mill crusade, only Kesler is substantially intact. Founded in 1895 by local investors and named for stockholder Tobias Kesler, in 1899 it was sold to the J. W. Cannon Co. (*Kannapolis), which expanded the mill and its housing in 1901–6 and 1927. The 2-story brick mill with arched windows and a shallow gable roof still stands, along with warehouses and other structures. The grid-plan village contains several blocks of 1- and 2-story frame dwellings, many in rows of identical types. Side-gabled dwellings from the early years cluster near the mill, but more numerous are L-plan houses of ca. 1900–1906 and bungalows from the 1920s.

RW 32 Grimes Mill
1896–97; N. B. McCanless, builder?; 600 N. Church St.; open by appointment

Built as the North Side Roller Mill during the railroad era, the 4-story brick structure is among the state's most ornate late 19th-c. industrial buildings, rendered in Second Empire style with granite lintels, sills, and quoins and a cupola atop the mansard roof. A metal-covered addition with tower stands

beside it. Powered first by steam and later by electricity, its steel and iron rollers crushed wheat into finer flour than the stones of gristmills and served the area's wheat growers. It retains an array of original equipment. Begun by local investors, including N. B. McCanless, who probably supplied construction and materials, it was owned after 1906 by the Grimes family.

RW 33 North Main Street
1899 to early 1930s; 700–1700 N. Main St.

The most architecturally interesting route into Salisbury, this extension of Main St. began development in 1899 when *Spencer emerged as a railroad repair center. The long stretch of middle-class residential development exemplifies typical forms of the early 20th c.: late Queen Anne style, Colonial Revival, and varied Spanish Mission and bungalow examples.

RW 34 Lombardy
1799–1801; Elam Sharpe, builder; John Langdon (Philadelphia), interior carpenter; 1010 Richard St.

John Steele, local political figure who was appointed comptroller of the Treasury in 1796, modeled his plantation house on examples he had seen in Philadelphia. He built a 2-story side-passage plan house with interior chimneys, and to finish it in elegant Federal style, he employed Philadelphia house carpenter John Langdon and ordered delicate Neoclassical composition ornaments from the Wellford Co. in Philadel-

RW 32 *Grimes Mill*

RW 34 *Lombardy*

phia. Altered over the years, in the late 20th c. the house was restored to its original form.

RW 35 Walter McCanless House

1929; Benton & Benton (Wilson), architects; 204 Confederate Ave.

The county's grandest mansion was erected for Walter McCanless, son of Napoleon B., who entered the family quarrying and textile business and founded new mills. Walter's country house in Renaissance Revival style is a symmetrical composition in buff brick with a green tile roof, classical decorations in stone and tile, and a balustraded terrace.

RW 36 Catawba College

1920s and later; 2300 W. Innes St.

The centerpiece of the college, a large 3- and 4-story brick building in Tudor Gothic style with crenellated entrance tower, was begun for a short-lived military institute. It was soon acquired for a Presbyterian normal and industrial school, and in 1925 it was given to Catawba College to bring that school to Salisbury. Established in 1851 in *Newton by the Reformed Church (later the United Church of Christ), Catawba developed the campus in harmonizing red brick from 1925 onward.

RW 37 Setzer School

Early 1840s; Knox Junior High School Grounds (Catawba Rd.); open limited hours

The little building is a rare survivor of the hundreds of one-room log schools built in response to N.C.'s early public school legislation of 1839. Measuring 24 by 24 feet with its entrance in the gabled front, it was built by a committee that included Jacob Setzer; it operated until 1892.

RW 38 Spencer

The town began when the Southern Railway founded the gigantic repair facility of *Spencer Shops (1896) and developed a one-industry community for a workforce of as many as 3,000. The shops employed highly skilled, well-paid technical workers and engineers as well as laborers. In contrast to the uniform housing in mill villages, Spencer's large early 20th-c. neighborhoods possess a variety of substantial owner-occupied middle-class dwellings in Queen Anne, Colonial Revival, and bungalow forms. Prominent brick churches include N. Long St.'s **Christ Lutheran Church** (1923–24), with crenellated central tower, and **Shady Grove Baptist Church** (1913), Gothic Revival in dark red brick with two corner towers. Opposite Spencer Shops, a row of brick stores dates from the turn of the century. The town flourished with the steam age, when the repair shop activity peaked, but after World War II, as the grandson of an engineer reported, "When diesel came, the town died." The steam engine repair facility closed in 1960, and many residents left. Since then, the community has diversified its economy and maintains a strong sense of its historic identity.

RW 39 Spencer Shops
State Historic Site

1896–1935; Salisbury Ave.; open regular hours

The spectacular industrial site is one of the largest railroad shops in the nation. Famed in railroad lore, the engineer of "The Wreck of Old 97" met his death while trying to "put her into Spencer on time." The Southern Railway Co., organized from other firms in 1894 during the height of American corporate expansion, leased the NCRR route in 1895 for 99 years and decided to locate company shops (*Burlington) at a point midway between Washington and Atlanta. Salisbury leaders assisted in quietly obtaining the 168-acre tract.

Named for company official Samuel Spencer, the shops opened in 1896 with a machine shop, the first roundhouse, and offices—slate-roofed steel structures with electric lights and hot air heat. The complex grew quickly, embodying the scale and the rationalized system of the corporate rail network. The vast **Back Shop** (1904–5) is a 600-by-150-foot edifice built of steel and enclosed with brick and glass; skylights in its steel-truss gable-roofed shed illuminate the repair facility below. As in some other build-

RW 39 *Roundhouse, Spencer Shops, ca. 1970s, with Back Shop in background*

ings, floors of dense wood blocks laid like brick absorbed oil and grease to prevent slickness. Pits beneath the tracks enabled expert mechanics to repair and reassemble engines and cars. The imposing second **Roundhouse** (1924) of reinforced concrete and steel has 37 stalls facing the 100-foot turntable. In the era when the steam engine and the railroad dominated the nation's economy, Spencer became the largest heavy repair facility in the Southern system. By 1932, in a single day 75 engines were turned out for light repairs, 1 engine was completely rebuilt, and cars for as many as 21 passenger trains and 24 freight trains were serviced and reassembled into trains.

Southern's swift transition to diesel power after World War II led to the closing of the steam repair shops in 1960 and demolition of the 1896 machine shop and other early structures, though a minor diesel repair works continued in the roundhouse until 1979. (Operations were moved to Linwood Yards, between Lexington and Spencer.) Threatened with demolition, the complex was donated to the state in 1977–79 for a transportation museum.

RW 40 Alexander Long House
Ca. 1786; end of SR 1918, Spencer vic.; private, visible from road

The magnificent chimneys of the Long House, with hearts and letters outlined in glazed headers, display one of the state's finest examples of decorative brickwork, re-flecting a tradition seen elsewhere in the Piedmont in the late 18th c. At the west end of the 2-story, 4-room plan frame house rise 2 large double-shouldered Flemish-bond chimneys with glazed headers, connected by a brick pent. On each chimney, glazed headers form a heart. Beneath one are the initials of Alexander Long, and beneath the other are those of Elizabeth (Chapman) Long; they married in 1786. Hearts with a couple's initials are seen in mid-Atlantic examples, but not elsewhere in N.C. Son of John Long, who had immigrated from Lancaster County, Pa., and acquired a 500-acre tract on Grant's Creek at the Yadkin River, Alexander prospered as a farmer and ran a river ferry. (See Introduction, Fig. 27.)

RW 41 Wil-Cox Bridge
1922; US 29, Yadkin River

Eleven arches of reinforced concrete march across the river, a handsome example of the classically inspired bridges of the 1920s Good Roads movement. Nearby are the stone piers of the covered bridge erected in 1818 by engineer Ithiel Town for Salisbury's Lewis Beard. Local builder Samuel Lemly, who built the first bridge, named his son Ithiel Town Lemly.

RW 42 Granite Quarry

In 1905 the railroad village of Woodside was incorporated as Granite Quarry for the quarries developed by E. B. C. Hambley and the Whitney Co. to build a hydroelectric power dam at the narrows of the Yadkin River (cf. *Hambley-Wallace House, *Badin). Even after Hambley's death and the collapse of his project, the granite quarries continued, producing gravel, Durax paving blocks, and distinctive pink granite for monuments and buildings. Early 20th-c. buildings incorporate the stone in some small commercial buildings, pillars on porches, and retaining walls. **Wittenberg Lutheran Church** (1936; W. Bank St. at N. Oak St.) displays the stone in a Gothic Revival church with center entrance tower. The **Granite Quarry School (Colored)** (1936; SE side SR 2131) was built by volunteer African American quarry workers and aided by donations from the Slater fund and others; the stone and the land were given by the Harris quarry. Quarrying continues at several sites, including the **Harris Quarry** (off SR 2131) to the north and the **Balfour Quarry** (SR 2385) to the south.

RW 43 Michael Braun House

1766 (date stone); E side SR 2308, 0.3 mi. S of NC 52, Granite Quarry; open limited hours

The oldest German building in the state, the great stone house and the *Hezekiah Alexander House in Charlotte are among the oldest buildings in the Piedmont and the only standing examples of colonial stone structures. Michael Braun, born in Darmstadt, Germany, came as a youth to Philadelphia, prospered at the printer's and wheelwright's trades, and came to Salisbury with his wife Margareta ca. 1758. Culturally and economically bilingual, he established himself as merchant, owner of an English-German print shop, and town property owner; he then built the large stone house near Granite Ridge, where he eventually owned 15 slaves and as much as 2,000 acres. At his death at age 85 in 1807, he provided in his will for his third wife, Eleanor, and their unborn child.

Sited in a gentle slope, the 2-story stone house was, as Thomas Waterman said, "a veritable castle" among the log and frame dwellings of its era. The 3-foot-thick walls are of local granite blocks with segmental-arched openings at the first story. The massive Germanic roof frame, visible in the

upper story, has principal rafters that terminate at the collar beams and are linked by purlins. The unusual plan has four unequal first-story rooms. Corner fireplaces heat the two west rooms; a stove warms the front east room but not the little chamber behind it; and a (rebuilt) frame kitchen extends from an 8-foot cooking fireplace on the outside of the west chimney. The contrast with the traditional Germanic kitchen as a main room may reflect Braun's accommodation to British associates or to the family's use of enslaved servants. The house fell into ruin in the early 20th c. but by 1966 was restored through family and local preservation efforts. (See Introduction, Fig. 13.)

RW 44 Gold Hill

Gold mining began along the Gold Hill fault when local farmers struck a rich vein of ore in 1842. George Bernhardt, who had worked at the *Reed Gold Mine in his native Cabarrus Co. and married Reed's daughter Martha, began the first mining operation and was soon joined by other Piedmont entrepreneurs and Cornish miners. Gold Hill became one of the most productive mines in the Southeast. With New York investors came steam-powered equipment and deeper mines; some shafts ran 800 feet down. The mining village of as many as 3,000 black and white workers became a boomtown, with stores, boardinghouses, a hotel, and substantial residences. Production dwindled by 1860 and stopped during the Civil War. Late 19th-c. entrepreneurs, including engineer E. B. C. Hambley (*Granite Quarry, *Badin), had some success with various methods of extraction and processing, but in the 20th c. Gold Hill quietened to a country village. In recent years, tourism and preservation have capitalized on the gold history. SR 2352 and other roads through the village are lined by modest Italianate, Greek Revival, and Queen Anne houses. The most imposing is the big Queen Anne style frame and stone **Goodman House** (ca. 1916; SR 2350). At the center on SR 2352, two small mining-era frame stores, the **Mauney-Hedrick Store** and the facing **Montgomery Store**, have been restored. A local park nearby contains stones and equipment from mining days, as well as a big double-crib log **Barn** moved from the Bernhardt farm, home of the early mining family.

RW 45 Miller Farm

18th–19th c.; N side SR 1221,
0.6 mi. W of SR 2337, Rockwell vic.

The farmstead beside the road recalls the long use of log building among German farmers. Home of the Miller family for generations, it comprises a 2-story log house covered with weatherboards, a small log crib or granary, and a big double-crib log barn from another spot on the farm.

RW 46 Grace Evangelical and Reformed (Lower Stone) Church

1795, ca. 1880, 1901; N side SR 1221,
1.2 mi. W of SR 2337, Rockwell vic.

The monumental, superbly sited stone church is a landmark of German culture in the western Piedmont. Set in the heart of the "Dutch [Deutsch] Settlement," amidst a large churchyard with many German-language stones, it is known as Lower Stone for its relationship with its neighbor, *Zion (Organ) Lutheran Church. The German families in southern Rowan Co. shared a log

meetinghouse until the 1770s, when the Lutherans built their own meetinghouse and the Reformed members (a faith also referred to as German Presbyterian) acquired this site in 1774. In the 1790s the two congregations began construction of similar stone meetinghouses. A tablet on the south front is inscribed with German verses and the date 1795, but completion may have required a few more years. Built of rough granite with segmental-arched openings in the thick walls, the meetinghouse has the main entrance on the long south side and others in the gable ends. In the late 19th c. the interior was remodeled, and in 1901 a belfry was erected at the west gable, which became the principal entrance.

RW 47 Zion (Organ) Lutheran Church

1792–95, ca. 1900, 1929; E side SR 1006,
0.5 mi. N of SR 1221, Rockwell vic.

A minister's 1791 letter and a 1794 date stone indicate that the massive stone Lutheran church, the oldest in the state, was begun slightly before *Grace. It was completed in 1795 and dedicated in 1796. Like its neighbor, it is a 2-story meetinghouse of local granite with segmental-arched openings. Despite a tower and other early 20th-c. changes, its essential form remains, and the

RW 46 *Grace Evangelical and Reformed (Lower Stone) Church*

RW 47 *Zion (Organ) Lutheran Church*

interior has benches and a gallery facing the pulpit on the long side opposite the entrance. The popular name comes from an organ moved from the old log church and used until the late 19th c. The first pastor, Adolphus Nussman, came from Germany in 1773, when the Lutherans built their first separate meetinghouse. The stone church was built under his successor, Carl August Gottlieb Storch, a denominational leader (*Storch-Eddleman House). The nearby late 20th-c. church repeats the stone.

RW 48 John Stirewalt House
1811; no public visibility or access

The 2-story brick house is important in the regional adaptation of German traditions. A dial wall tablet dates its 1811 construction for John Stirewalt Jr., who built it on land acquired from his immigrant father. Akin to other Piedmont houses, it is built of Flemish-bond brick with lozenge patterns in dark headers on the chimney. The plan—with a wide hall on the west heated by a single large fireplace and a pair of rooms with corner fireplaces on the east—has been described as an end-chimney version of the 3-room Germanic layout.

RW 49 Storch-Eddleman House
Ca. 1805, mid-19th c.; E side SR 1002,
0.09 mi. N of SR 1221, Bostian Heights vic.

Showing two phases of German building, the house began as a 2-room dwelling built for Carl August Gottlieb Storch. Sent as a Lutheran minister from Helmstaedt, Germany, in 1788 to serve *Zion Lutheran Church, Storch led in expanding the faith, and during his pastorate the congregation built its large stone building. He lived in Salisbury before acquiring this farm in 1805, apparently to reside among fellow German-speakers. After Storch's death in 1831, farmer Daniel Eddleman enlarged the house to a 2-story structure with center-passage plan, shallow gable roof, and brick end chimneys.

RW 50 China Grove

Established as a post office by 1823 and named for its chinaberry trees, the village developed after the Civil War into a small railroad industrial center. The chief landmark is the **China Grove Roller Mill** (1903; 308 N. Main St.), a 3-story brick industrial building of simple gable-roofed form. Successor to an 1896 frame structure, it was built for steam power and converted to electricity in 1906. Active into the late 20th c., it retains its machinery and painted signs.

Boosting town growth was the 1893 founding of the **Patterson Mfg. Co.** (400 block N. Main St.), a large brick cotton mill expanded over the years. The adjoining **Patterson Mfg. Co. Store** (300 block N. Main St.) is a 2-story company store in brick with corbeled decoration. Across Main St. are several streets of well-preserved, 1-story frame mill houses, many of which follow L- or T-plans, with an especially intact group on W. Ross St. Frame houses and brick and frame churches flank N. and S. Main and adjoining streets. **St. Mark's Lutheran Church** (1917; 326 N. Main St.) is a large twin-towered church featuring the dark red brick and pale stone trim popular among Lutherans.

RW 51 Corriher School and Grange Building
Ca. 1916, 1938; E side SR 1555,
0.15 mi. S of SR 1552, Corriher Springs

Home to two important rural institutions, the 1-story frame building began ca. 1916 as a schoolhouse and served until 1935. In 1937 the Corriher Grange No. 627 made it their meeting hall. The still active agricultural and social organization was formed in 1929 when a local farmers' union allied with the state grange.

Mill Bridge Area
*In the 1740s, western Rowan's "Irish Settlement" began on the headwaters of Second Creek as one of the first Scotch-Irish settlements west of the Yadkin River. Scotch-Irish families founded farms of a few hundred acres each and soon formed Cathey's Meetinghouse (later *Thyatira) as a center of the community. In the early 19th c., a few farmers consolidated extensive holdings in land and slaves; others left for the west and south. After the Civil War a few owners sought to renew the land and introduce stock and dairy farming. The community, known for a time as "Kerrsville," was renamed in 1874 for the bridge by the mill on Kerr (Cathey's) Creek.*

RW 52 Thyatira Presbyterian Church
1858–60; William Murdoch, William Raeder, builders; W side SR 1737, just N of NC 150, Mill Bridge

The striking Gothic Revival church contrasts with the simple classicism of most antebellum Presbyterian churches. It is built of brick with corbeling accentuating the buttressed central entrance tower, sharply pointed doors and windows, and cruciform windows of the gabled front. The illustrious congregation, begun as Cathey's Meeting-

house by the early 1750s, changed its name later in the 18th c. to Thyatira (after a town and early Christian church in Asia Minor). In 1777 the church gained its first permanent minister, Dr. Samuel Eusebius McCorkle, a Princeton graduate and noted educator who established the Zion Parnassus Academy in 1794. Thyatira became a mother church to many congregations. The brick church directly reflects the antebellum railroad era, for builder Murdoch (*Murdoch-Wiley House) was a Scots stonemason and NCRR contractor, and Raeder a German civil engineer and draftsman for the NCRR. The churchyard contains numerous signed stones from Philadelphia, Charleston, Charlotte, and Salisbury.

RW 53 Kerr Mill
1822–23; S side SR 1768 at Kerr Creek, 0.6 W of NC 150, Mill Bridge vic.

The brick mill embodied the accomplishments and ambitions of Joseph Kerr and his son Samuel (*Oakland), who like many planters profited from running a gristmill. Son of Andrew, a founder of the Irish settlement, Joseph expanded his holdings to some 1,500 acres, including the Cathey farm. When Samuel returned from college in 1822, the mill on his father's land may have been one of his first projects in his career as a physician, political figure, and one of the county's wealthiest planters. In contrast to typical frame gristmills, the Kerrs built a mill comparable to fine houses and churches

RW 52 *Thyatira Presbyterian Church*

RW 53 *Kerr Mill*

of the era, of brick laid in 1:4 bond, with flat arches, molded brick cornice, and stone foundation. Timber framing has lamb's-tongue chamfering. After Kerr's death and the Civil War, the mill was run by James McCubbins and John Harrison of neighboring plantations, who updated it as a roller mill. Operated into the 1940s, the mill was restored in the late 20th c. as part of a county park.

RW 54 Oakland (Kerr House)
1822–23, 1870s; N side SR 1768, 0.8 mi. W of NC 150, Mill Bridge; private, visible from road

Joseph Kerr is believed to have erected the 2-story frame house on his 1,500-acre plantation, but it was chiefly the home of his son Samuel who returned after graduating from the University of North Carolina in 1822 and lived there long after Joseph's death in 1829. Like others in the region, the house has a center-passage adaptation of a 3-room plan, restrained Federal style finish, and Flemish-bond end chimneys (date brick, 1823). Losing his wealth with the Civil War, Kerr died in 1865. As town trade recovered, Salisbury merchant James McCubbins acquired the property in 1872 and with neighboring farmer John Harrison improved it into one of the finest stock farms in the county. McCubbins updated the house in picturesque taste with a front central gable and porch garnished with ornate millwork.

RW 55 Owen-Harrison House
1843; N side SR 1768, 1.2 mi. W of NC 150, Mill Bridge; private, visible from road in winter

The 2-story plantation house of Flemish-bond brick is one of the most imposing in the county, with pairs of tall end chimneys serving a full center-passage plan 2 rooms deep. Bold Greek Revival details derive from Asher Benjamin's *Practical House Carpenter* (1830). The house was built for planter James Owen, and from 1861 to 1910 it was the home of his daughter Frances and her husband John Harrison. In 1885 a traveler praised it as "the finest farm in Rowan if not

western North Carolina—Mr. J. M. Harrison's fine improved lands, brought up from worn out old fields," known for carefully bred pigs and cattle.

RW 56 Back Creek Presbyterian Church
1856–57; NE side SR 1763, N of SR 1765, Mt. Ulla vic.

One of several Greek Revival brick churches built for Piedmont Presbyterians (*Poplar Tent, Cabarrus Co.; *Centre Church, Iredell Co.), the simply but boldly designed church gains the appearance of an open temple. Its broad pilasters, stuccoed and scored, carry a low pediment and flank tall, oversized windows that nearly fill the bays. The congregation emerged from the Great Revival of 1802 when some members of *Thyatira Church affiliated with the evangelical minister of *Third Creek Church and founded Back Creek. They worshiped in log buildings before erecting this building. The churchyard has stones by Charlotte, Salisbury, and Concord carvers.

RW 56 *Back Creek Presbyterian Church*

RW 57 Rankin-Sherrill House
1850s; SE corner NC 801 and SR 1753, Mt. Ulla

The 2-story house with shallow hip roof and broad proportions exhibits a popular antebellum form in brick, trimmed with granite lintels and simple Greek Revival details. It continues the regional center-passage version of the 3-room plan. The house was built for Samuel and Mary Gillespie Rankin; Samuel, physician and planter, was a leader at *Back Creek and a member of its building committee of 1856–57.

RW 58 *Wood Grove*

RW 58 Wood Grove

Early 19th c.; E side SR 1743,
just S of NC 801, Bear Poplar vic.

The 2-story brick plantation house has a traditional 3-room plan and good Federal style details. Varied brick bonds include a handsome Flemish-bond chimney with concave shoulders. Although tradition claims the house was built for Thomas Cowan of Irish descent, who came as a child from Lancaster Co., Pa., it may have been built for his son Abel and his wife Maria McKenzie, who lived here for many years; their daughter Maria married Barnabus Krider of *Mount Vernon, pastor of *Thyatira Church. The place descended in the family.

RW 59 Hall Family Farmstead

1856; James G. Graham, builder (attrib.);
SE side NC 801, 0.75 mi. E of SR 1743,
Bear Poplar vic.

The farmstead by the road exemplifies one family's continuity in a changing agricultural economy. The farm was established by Newberry Franklin Hall (brother of *Josephus Hall), who came from Davie Co., married Mary Shuford, joined *Thyatira Church, and bought the land in 1856. He evidently employed local carpenter James Graham to build the 2-story frame house with center-passage 3-room plan, brick end chimneys, and Greek Revival trim. After the Civil War, sons Joseph and George established a dairy operation, which continues to the present. The many farm buildings include a 19th-c. log smokehouse, a big multi-crib log barn, and an immense frame dairy barn with gambrel roof (1925). West of the house are 3 frame tenant houses from the 1920s.

RW 60 Knox Farm

House, 1855–56; James G. Graham, carpenter;
outbuildings, late 18th c. onward; both sides
SR 1745, 0.8 mi. N of SR 1001, Cleveland vic.

The beautiful Knox lands on Third Creek have been farmed by nine generations of the family since Scotch-Irish immigrant John Knox arrived in the early 1740s; his numerous descendants included President James Knox Polk. The farm's oldest buildings, believed to date from the time of John's grandson Benjamin, include a log crib, a springhouse, and two log barns. During the antebellum era of wealth consolidation, Benjamin's son Robert purchased the 366-acre homeplace from his father's estate in 1845 and enlarged his holdings to nearly 2,000 acres, where he and several slaves raised livestock, cotton, and other crops. Carpenter James Graham built the 2-story Greek Revival frame house for Robert and his wife Catherine Clark Knox. The 2-story frame house has a 3-room plan, end chimneys, shed porch, and rear ell, detailed in simple Greek Revival style. In the 20th c. Robert Howard Knox turned to dairy and stock farming, reflected in several notable dairy and horse barns. In the late 19th c. the traditionally Presbyterian family became active in a Methodist congregation and in 1888 sold a small tract for **Knox Chapel Methodist Church** (1893; N side SR 1001 SW of SR 1745), a frame country church with customary gable-fronted form and belfry.

RW 60 *Knox Farm*

RW 61 Cleveland

Around a post office est. in 1831, the railroad community developed in the late 19th c. with a steam-powered flour mill and other mercantile interests and was named for the president in 1887. Residences from the late 19th c. onward include good examples of the Queen Anne and bungalow styles. **Cleveland Presbyterian Church** (ca. 1890; Maple and Main Sts.), a strikingly unusual frame church at a prime corner, has two gabled fronts angling back from the corner entrance tower, broad arched windows, and bracketed eaves. Pews and aisles radiate from the pulpit in the angle opposite the entrance.

RW 61 *Cleveland Presbyterian Church*

RW 62 Third Creek Presbyterian Church

1833–35; D. Lyles and H. Austin, builders; N side SR 1973, 0.2 mi. W of SR 1957, Cleveland vic.

The brick church, built for a Scotch-Irish congregation that traces its origins to the mid-18th c., exemplifies the simplicity of church building before the adoption of the Greek and Gothic Revival styles. In the early 19th c. its pastor Joseph D. Kilpatrick supported the Great Revival movement and gained many converts. In 1833 subscribers contracted for a brick church 55 by 45 feet and 16 feet high, "the house to be completed in a plain but workman-like manner, with a sufficient number of doors and windows for such a house." Henry R. Austin, a Mocks-

RW 62 *Third Creek Presbyterian Church*

ville builder (*Davie Co. Jail), and D. Lyles produced a straightforward brick building with Flemish bond at the gabled front and 1:5 bond elsewhere, stone foundations and sills, and double-hung sash windows at both stories. Entered by a pair of front doors and two others on the sides, the well-preserved sanctuary has a two-aisle plan and a gallery on square posts. The churchyard has markers from as early as 1776, many signed by regional and distant carvers.

RW 63 Mount Vernon

Early 1820s; N side SR 1003, 0.7 mi. E of SR 1972

One of the most impressive of Rowan Co.'s Federal period farmhouses, the 2-story frame house is distinguished by a pair of tall brick chimneys joined by a brick pent, which serve a center-passage variation of the 3-room plan. The house was built for Jacob and Sarah Wood Krider about 1821. Jacob, born in Pennsylvania of German stock,

RW 63 *Mount Vernon*

RW 64 *St. Andrew's Episcopal Church*

came to Salisbury as a boy ca. 1800 and learned the printing trade from his father, Barnabas. In the merging of cultures in town, he became a Presbyterian, prospered as a merchant, and founded Salisbury's *North Carolina Magazine* (1813) and *Western North Carolinian* (1820). He married Sarah Wood of Presbyterian western Rowan in 1815, and about 1821 they moved to this farm adjoining her father's grist- and sawmills, which she soon inherited. Jacob became a planter, merchant, miller, and civic and church leader at *Third Creek. The beautifully sited farmstead includes a large frame barn and other outbuildings erected by the Current family, who farmed here through most of the 20th c.

RW 64 St. Andrew's Episcopal Church
1840; Jacob Correll, contractor; SE side SR 1950, 1.1 mi. N of SR 1949, Woodleaf vic.

Set high above Fourth Creek, the utterly simple frame church epitomizes 19th-c. churches of all denominations, most of which have been changed or replaced. On

April 6, 1840, Jacob Correll, church member, planter, and mill owner, agreed to erect for $325 "on the road leading from Salisbury to Mocksville the hull of the house 44 by 34 Including the doors & windows and sash, laying two floors, and running one flight stairs and ceiling to the top of the Seats and Seat it of necessity." In May the Episcopal priest from Salisbury reported that the newly organized parish had a "plain country church . . . almost completed, sufficiently to be used for worship," and in August it was dedicated by Bishop Levi Ives. The 1-story building, covered in unpainted weatherboards and set on a dry-laid stone foundation, has simple batten doors and shutters on strap hinges and a wood-shingled gable roof. The interior has a double-aisle plan, galleries on 3 sides, plain benches, and square posts; the walls are sheathed (ceiled) only up to the gallery, above which the framing is exposed. Dry-laid stone walls enclose the small churchyard. The church hosts an annual August homecoming.

Iredell County (ID)

See Ruth Little-Stokes, An Inventory of Historic Architecture: Iredell County, North Carolina *(1978).*

Bordered by the Catawba River and traversed by the South Fork of the Yadkin, the "western district" of Rowan Co. became Iredell Co. in 1788, named to honor U.S. Supreme Court Justice James Iredell of Edenton. Scotch-Irish and other settlers arrived from the 1740s onward, and during the French and Indian War they took shelter at the British outpost at Fort Dobbs (1756; reconstructed). Most families had small and middle-sized farms, where they engaged in mixed agriculture, complemented by gristmills, tanyards, and distilleries. The county retains many modest farmsteads with traditional log and frame buildings. In the 19th c. plantation gentry emerged, and some built imposing houses that combine traditional forms with stylish patternbook details. Both large and small farms are notable for single- and double-crib log barns of the 19th c. The county possesses exceptional country churches and churchyards distinguished by locally carved gravestones, beautiful dry-laid stone walls, and iron gates. Highways, including I-40 and I-77, Lake Norman on the Catawba River, and spread from Charlotte have intensified development, but much of the county retains its rural character. The county has nine adjoining counties, supposedly more than any other in the nation.

Statesville (ID 1–13)

The county seat, established in 1788 near the old Fourth Creek (*First) Presbyterian Church, began to grow with the arrival of the Western North Carolina Railroad (WNCRR) in 1858 and developed into a regional wholesaling and shipping point for whiskey, tobacco, leather, and other goods. After the Civil War the WNCRR was completed westward; the grandly named Atlantic, Tennessee, & Ohio Railroad (AT&O), built from Charlotte to Statesville in 1862, was rebuilt in 1871; and the Statesville & Western was completed to Taylorsville in 1887. Entrepreneurs expanded into manufacturing, including cotton mills, furniture and tobacco factories, and brickmaking. Statesville also became a distilling center and a shipment point for western N.C. ginseng and other medicinal roots and herbs (*Wallace Herbarium). Statesville increased gradually to about 40,000 people in 2000. The town has preserved a strong ensemble of late 19th- and early 20th-c. town architecture in the compact downtown and surrounding residential neighborhoods.

Downtown Statesville:

Two wide streets, Broad and Center, meet at "the Square," where the first and second courthouses stood. Several blocks of substantial public and commercial architecture constitute a business district of impressive scale and quality.

ID 1 Former Iredell County Courthouse

1899–1900; Louis E. Schwend, Hayden, Wheeler & Schwend (Charlotte), architect; Nicholas Ittner (Atlanta), contractor; S. Center St. at Court St.

The Neoclassical brick edifice of complex but symmetrical form has 2- and 3-story sections mounting to a mansardlike dome and centering on a richly detailed Corinthian portico. It was the prototype for several similar courthouses in the state by the Charlotte firm in the early 20th c. The local newspaper admired its "classical style" and found the building's "architectural beauty" "far

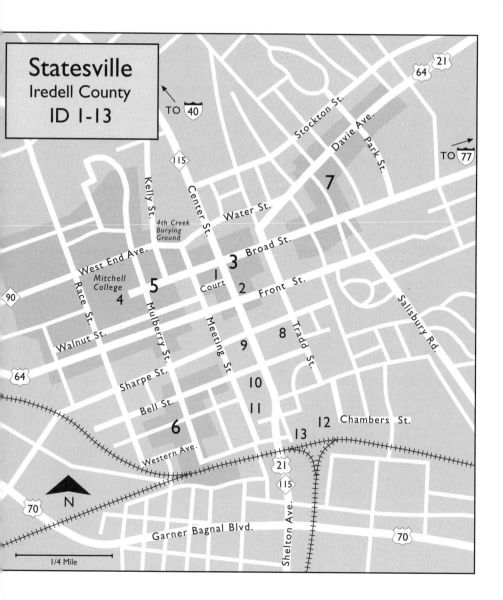

TO (40)

64   21

TO (77)

Stockton St.

Davie Ave.

Park St.

115

7

Kelly St.

Center St.

Water St.

4th Creek
Burying
Ground

West End Ave.

Broad St.

3

Mitchell
College

5

Court

2

Front St.

Race St.

4

90

Mulberry St.

Walnut St.

Meeting St.

9

8

Tradd St.

Salisbury Rd.

64

Sharpe St.

10

Bell St.

11

6

12   Chambers   St.

13

Western Ave.

21

115

N

70

Garner Bagnal Blvd.

Shelton Ave.

70

1/4 Mile

greater" than the nearby U.S. Courthouse (*Statesville City Hall), while a Charlotte newspaper said the design was "quite a credit to young Mr. Schwend, who won it in hot competition." Louis E. Schwend, an architect from Cincinnati, left the firm in 1901, but Wheeler, with various partners, retailored the design for other counties. (See Introduction, Fig. 65.) To the rear, the former **Iredell County Jail** (1909; Wheeler, Galliher & Stern [Charlotte], architects; J. A. Jones [Charlotte], builder; 122 S. Meeting St.) is unusually stylish for a jail, with twin 2-story palazzo-style pavilions of tan brick linked by an arcade.

ID 2 Statesville City Hall (Former U.S. Court House and Post Office)

1890–92; Willoughby J. Edbrooke, supervising architect of the Treasury; Peter Demens, contractor; 227 S. Center St.

Built as a Federal facility, now the city hall, the dominant building of downtown is

ID 2 *Statesville City Hall*

among the state's finest examples of the Richardsonian Romanesque style. Richly finished in red pressed brick, terra-cotta, and Wadesboro sandstone, it is one of the few survivals of several public buildings in this style. The asymmetrical design has a strong sculptural effect, with rounded tower and peaked dormers contrasting with the capacious recess of the arched entrance. Contractor Peter Demens was a Russian immigrant who founded St. Petersburg, Fla., built railroads, erected Asheville's Federal building (razed) during the city's boom (#Demens-Rumbough-Crawley House, Asheville), then left for Los Angeles, where he invested in orange groves and later covered the Russian Revolution for a Los Angeles newspaper.

ID 3 Commercial Buildings

Among many handsome buildings on Center and Broad Sts., the **Commercial National Bank** (1903; 116 S. Center St.) of tan brick matching the neighboring courthouse has a portico of Ionic order granite columns

and Ionic pilasters along the side. The 2- and 3-story **Commercial Buildings** (1895–1900) in the 100 block of S. Center St. display brick and stone facades with round arches, pilasters, and hefty cornices. At the Square is the 3-story brick **First National Bank** (ca. 1890; 101–3 S. Center St.), with the **Town Clock** on a mansard tower (ca. 1895). The **Montgomery Ward Store** (1925; 114 N. Center St.) has a glazed terra-cotta facade with flowers, urns, and a torch-bearing nymph on a globe with the logo "Spirit of Progress." The **Henkel-Craig Livestock Co.** (1895–1905; 119–25 N. Center St.) has a round-arched brick facade with parapet cornice and pilasters. The **Walton & Gage Store** (1876; 201 W. Broad St.), among the oldest intact commercial buildings, has an ornate Italianate facade in brick with Gothic Revival touches. In the back alleys and courtyards, various wagonways provide entry, and functional openings remain.

ID 4 Mitchell College Main Building

1854–57; Jacob Graves (South Carolina), architect; J. W. Conrad, builder; W end of Broad St.

The massive stuccoed brick building with broad Doric portico is one of the most imposing of the state's antebellum college buildings. It was erected for the Concord Female College, established by the Concord Presbytery as a complement to *Davidson College for men. The architect's original design for a 4-story building with Corinthian portico was nearly complete when a windstorm leveled it in June 1855. The trustees salvaged the materials and rebuilt on the foundations a plainer 3-story edifice with a Doric portico. Builder Conrad also erected other major Piedmont buildings (*Blandwood, *Rowan Co. Courthouse, *Cooleemee). In 1917 the college was renamed for Eliza Mitchell Grant and Margaret Eliot Mitchell, who ran the school for several years after the Civil War; they were daughters of state geologist Dr. Elisha Mitchell (#Mount Mitchell). The main building is now the centerpiece of a community college.

ID 4 *Mitchell College Main Building*

ID 5 Mitchell College Neighborhood

The large residential area around the college and west of downtown, the most prestigious in the late 19th and early 20th centuries, includes large and small Queen Anne style dwellings, columned Southern Colonial mansions, and simpler foursquares and other styles. The big, frame **Mills House** (1897; Louis E. Schwend [Charlotte], architect; 324 W. End Ave.) is a dramatic composition of multiple gambrel roofs with polyg-

ID 5 *West End Ave.*

onal front bay, by the architect of the courthouse. The **Shelton House** (ca. 1918; 323 Walnut St.), a big red brick house of eclectic design, combines a high hip roof, gabled ell, porch, porte cochere, and free classical and Tudor Revival motifs, all accentuated by hefty curving brackets; it has a matching servants' quarters. The **Lowenstein House** (ca. 1890; 121–31 Walnut St.; moved from Broad St.) is an exuberant towered Queen Anne style house in frame, built for Dr. Julius Lowenstein, who in 1884 founded a liquor wholesale business central to Statesville's economy before Prohibition. Thereafter he moved to Atlanta and produced Norris Candy, thus proving Ogden Nash's adage, "Candy is dandy, but liquor is quicker." **Congregation Emmanuel Synagogue** (1891; 206 Kelly St.) was built for a Jewish congregation established in 1883, the second oldest in the state (cf. #Temple of Israel, Wilmington); the eclectic gable-fronted brick building has a round-arched entrance and windows, flanked by stuccoed buttresses, with those at the corners rising to Gothic Revival pinnacles, which are topped with a Star of David motif. **Fourth Creek Burying Ground** (est. 1756) long predates the town, and within stone walls rebuilt in the 1930s are many early markers and a wrought iron gate akin to others in the county. **First Presbyterian Church** (1924–25; 125 N. Meeting St.), a yellow brick and stone church with Neoclassical detail, was built for the congregation that originated as Fourth Creek in the mid-18th c.

ID 5 *Congregation Emmanuel Synagogue*

ID 6 Academy Hill

Named after the former Statesville Male Academy on Mulberry St., the residential and industrial area south of downtown developed in the late 19th c. The 2-story brick **Mulberry St. School** (1892; 501 S. Mulberry St.), built as a public school, stands across the street from the old academy, now a residence. The **J. C. Steele House** (1878; 624 S. Mulberry St.), built for the founder of a nearby brick company, is a frame house with mansard tower, while his son's **C. M. Steele House** (1901; W. E. Poovey, probable builder; 612 S. Mulberry St.) is an ornate Queen Anne style design, executed in brick with stone trim, suitable to the owner, who with his father and brothers operated the brick business. Near the railroad is the **J. C. Steele & Sons Brick Plant** (1890 and later; 710 S. Mulberry St.), an assemblage of functional brick structures from the late 19th and early 20th centuries. It was built for Steele, who began manufacturing bricks here in the mid-1880s and soon began producing brickmaking machinery. The company still operates.

ID 7 East Broad St.–Davie Ave.

East of the commercial district, the area developed as home to manufacturers and merchants of the late 19th and early 20th centuries. Several houses show adaptations of the cottage styles promoted by A. J. Down-

ing, particularly those in the 500 and 600 blocks of Davie Ave., such as the **Robinson House** (ca. 1885; 509 Davie Ave.), with a trio of front-facade gables; the house at 624 Davie, with its lacy latticed porch posts; and the gabled and bracketed T-plan **Mott-Simons House** (ca. 1884; 619 E. Davie Ave.).

ID 8 Key Memorial Chapel (St. Philip's Catholic Church)
1898; Lazenby Bros. (Salisbury), builders; 150 E. Sharpe St.

The tiny Gothic Revival brick building with crenellated corner tower was built in memory of Philip Barton Key (grandnephew of Francis Scott Key), a native of Maryland and Confederate veteran who moved to Statesville and founded liquor wholesale (1883) and tobacco manufacturing (1892) businesses. It was renovated as offices in 1977.

ID 9 Sharpe House
1860s; 402 S. Center St.

The double-pile Greek Revival house is dominated by a graceful 2-tier porch with slender full-height columns of clustered reeds, a motif repeated at the entrance. In a treatment seen chiefly along the South Carolina border, the columns sit on bases in front of the porch floor. It was built for Silas Alexander Sharpe, an Iredell Co. native who learned the tanning trade in Laurens, S.C., then returned ca. 1853 to become a prosperous tanner and the first mayor of Statesville in the 1870s. The house, said to have been begun before the war, was evidently completed by 1866.

ID 9 *Sharpe House*

ID 10 *Mount Pleasant A.M.E. Zion Church*

ID 10 Mount Pleasant A.M.E. Zion Church
1903; 537 S. Center St.

The oldest church in town built for an African American congregation, the imposing Gothic Revival style brick building displays intricate corbeled, paneled, and molded brickwork and two unequal corner towers. The congregation was established in the late 1860s.

ID 11 Wallace Herbarium
Ca. 1920; 615 Meeting St.

Located in a once busy railroad industrial area, the plain 4-story gable-fronted frame building once housed the business described as the world's largest herbarium. The company received ginseng and herbs from western N.C., then shipped them to distant buyers for national and international markets, including Asia.

ID 12 Statesville Flour Mills
Ca. 1910 and later; near railroad at Center, Harrison, and Chambers Sts.

The towering complex, visible for some distance, is said to have been the largest flour mill in the state at one time. The oldest section is ca. 1910, a tall narrow brick building 6 stories high with arched windows and brick pilasters. Various towers and grain elevators were added over the years.

ID 13 Statesville Passenger Depot
1910–11; J. W. Elliott (Hickory), builder; Depot St., E of Center St., S of RR; open regular hours

Built for Southern Railway, the depot of pressed brick with stone trim has the broad

ID 12 *Statesville Flour Mills*

overhang and brackets typical of the era. The J. W. Elliott the newspaper reported completing it in 1911 was evidently linked with Joseph D. Elliott, the Hickory contractor who built numerous Southern depots in western N.C. (*Southern Railway Depot, Hickory; #Bryson City). Endangered on its site, it was moved across the tracks and restored as a visitors' center.

ID 14 McClelland-Davis House
Ca. 1835; N side SR 1551, 0.3 mi. W of NC 15, Statesville vic.; private, visible from road

The 2-story 5-bay frame house, built for John McClelland of a family who arrived ca. 1766, typifies the transitional Federal–Greek Revival dwellings of middling planters. It stands among large oaks and 19th-c. outbuildings, including a log smokehouse and frame granary.

ID 15 Ebenezer Academy, Bethany Presbyterian Church and Cemetery
Early 19th c., 1855; NW side US 21, 1.3 mi. NE of I-77, Statesville vic.

The half-dovetailed log building, measuring about 20 by 30 feet and containing a single room, recalls the plain log schools of the 19th c. The academy chartered in 1822 operated until 1856; the building was restored in 1913 and later. Bethany Church (est. by 1775) fostered education; its first pastor, James Hall, established two local academies, and his nephews Robert and Alexander were the first teachers at Ebenezer. The simple gable-fronted frame church was built in 1855. The large churchyard has fine, locally carved markers and dry-laid fieldstone walls with monolithic gateposts flanking wrought iron gates. "July 1825 WN" is inscribed near the front gate.

ID 16 King-Flowers-Keaton House
Early 19th c.; NE corner NC 115 and SR 1905; private, visible from road from S

Perched on a hill above the road, the 2-story frame house, 5 irregularly placed bays wide, is one of the oldest in the county; expanded from an initial 3-room plan, the relatively unpretentious dwelling typical of middling planters was probably built ca. 1800 for Samuel King, who owned about 600 acres.

ID 17 Damascus Baptist Arbor and Church
1855, 1907–9; end of SR 1582

The open timber-framed arbor, frame church, and cemetery occupy a beautiful hillside site with views of the Brushy Mountains. Built in 1855 for a congregation begun in 1839, the arbor has a hewn frame with posts set on stones and supporting a hewn and pegged gable roof surrounded by shed roof extensions. Pews sit on an earthen floor, which slopes gently uphill from the pulpit. Although numerous Methodist arbors survive, those built for Baptists are few.

ID 17 *Damascus Baptist Arbor*

ID 18 Snow Creek Methodist Church and Cemetery
1884–85; S side SR 1904, 0.3 mi. W of SR 1905

The simple gable-fronted church was erected for a congregation founded in 1801 on the eve of the Great Revival; it hosted camp meetings and became the leading antebellum church in northern Iredell Co. The large cemetery, begun in 1780 and used by both Presbyterians and Methodists, has a wall of dry-laid fieldstone (rebuilt 1954) with handwrought iron gates and stone gateposts (one dated 1879).

ID 19 Daltonia
Ca. 1858; N side SR 2115, 1.1 mi. E of US 21, Houstonville vic.; private, visible from road

The prominent plantation house combines the symmetrical form and 2-tier pedimented entrance portico of the Greek Revival with Italianate sawnwork porch posts and a floral motif at the pediment fanlight. It was built for John and Mary Houston Dalton; he was a manufacturer of plug tobacco who pioneered and promoted local tobacco cultivation in the antebellum era and continued as the county's largest tobacco producer into the late 19th c. In the yard, his first small log dwellings contrast with the big, stylish house tobacco built.

ID 20 Eccles House

Ca. 1861; NE side SR 1003, 0.1 mi. NW of US 64, Cool Springs; private, visible from road

The 2-story Greek Revival frame dwelling has a 2-tier, pedimented entrance portico and Italianate bracketed cornice. Nearby is a 2-story log barn, with half-dovetailed joints and original lean-to sheds on all 4 sides, one of the finest in the county. Tradition says that Henry Eccles, a New Yorker, built the house in connection with a Cool Springs resort hotel that closed during the Civil War.

ID 21 Waddell-Click Farm

Early to mid-19th c.; N side SR 2309, 0.5 mi. E of SR 2308; private, visible from road

The most complete antebellum farm complex in the county, the farmstead retains a remarkable ensemble of log architecture. The 2-story log farmhouse (ca. 1820–35) maintains its distinctive form beneath later covering, with end chimneys and steep gable roof and simple Federal finish. Gathered around it are a log smokehouse, a well house, and other domestic outbuildings, plus a double-crib log barn and a stable, all built with half-dovetailed notches. Representative of the middling farmers who were the backbone of the region, the house and oldest outbuildings were probably built for Greenberry and Lydia Knox Waddell, who married in 1833, or for his father, John, who obtained a 325-acre tract in 1816 from the Chambers family. It was later the home of daughter Jane and her husband Jesse Click.

ID 22 Farmville Plantation

Early 19th c.; E side SR 2362, 0.4 mi. SE of US 70, Elmwood vic.; private, visible from road

The big brick plantation house, the grandest in the county, was the center of a plantation of 2,600 acres and 23 slaves by 1837 and more by 1860. The main house was built in 1818 for merchant and planter Joseph Chambers, who inherited the land from his father, Henry. Another son, Maxwell, was a Salisbury merchant and donor to *Davidson College. A 2-story Doric entrance portico with stuccoed brick columns and plaster capitals dominates the facade; brick walls are of Flemish bond on the front and back, 1:3 on the sides. A smaller 2-story house of 1:3 common-bond brick was either built as a kitchen or built in the 18th c. for the McElwraith family.

ID 23 Mooresville

Founded in 1873, Mooresville emerged as a trading and cotton manufacturing center on the AT&O, with 1,000 people by 1900. The town limits extended a mile around the **Mooresville Depot** (1920s; Depot Square, Main St.), a brick successor to the original. The downtown has brick commercial buildings from its heyday, including the 2-story **Merchants and Farmers Bank** (1908; 188 N. Main St.), with arched windows along the front and side, and the remarkably intact **Turner Hardware Co.** (1900; 115 N. Main

ID 23 *Mooresville Depot and Main St.*

St.). A stretch of residential architecture along S. Broad St. exemplifies the railroad era in conservative versions of the Queen Anne and Italianate styles. Especially impressive, on the north side of town, is the **Espy Watts Brawley House** (1904; 601 William St.), a big frame house combining Queen Anne and Colonial Revival elements, erected for Brawley, a leading farmer, cotton and cottonseed oil manufacturer, and banker.

Southern Iredell:
Southern Iredell was part of a predominantly Presbyterian plantation neighborhood linked to Mecklenburg and Cabarrus counties and *Davidson College. Although Lake Norman and recent development have changed the landscape, early buildings survive, including plantation houses now shielded from view.

ID 24 Mount Mourne
Mid-1830s; W side NC 115 at SR 1245, Mount Mourne; private, visible from road

Overlooking an old road, Mount Mourne is one of the most visible of the area's early 19th-c. plantation houses. The large 2-story frame house, 5 bays wide with a center-passage plan 2 rooms deep, combines Federal and Greek Revival details, including a 1-story front porch with fluted Roman Doric columns and entablature. It was built for Rufus Reid and his second wife, Elizabeth Latta. An enterprising planter who named the place after the Mountains of Mourne in Ireland, Reid had a plantation of 1,800 acres plus other holdings. He operated a post office here, where students at *Davidson College received their mail. Mount Mourne was home to an extended family unusual even in an era of frequent widowhood and remarriage. Reid married three daughters of Mecklenburg planters: first, Nancy Latta, daughter of James and Jane Knox Latta (*Latta Place), with whom he had 3 daughters. After her death, he married her widowed sister, Elizabeth Latta Davidson (*Oak Lawn), who brought 6 Davidson sons to the marriage and gave birth to a daughter. After her death, Reid married Isabella Torrence Smith (*Cedar Grove), a widow with a daughter, and they had 4 more children. To

ID 24 *Mount Mourne*

manage the household, Jane Knox Latta, widowed grandmother of most of the children, moved to a cottage at Mount Mourne, where she outlived many of them.

ID 25 Centre Presbyterian Church
1854; N side SR 1245, 0.1 mi. E of SR 1246 betw. NC 115 and US 21, Mount Mourne vic.

The beautifully simple brick church was built for one of the area's most venerable congregations. Established in 1765, the congregation erected a capacious log meetinghouse on this site in 1774–75 and in 1788 hosted the formative meeting of the Presbyterian Synod of the Carolinas, followed by the first meeting of the Concord Presbytery in 1798. Like *Back Creek in Rowan Co. and *Poplar Tent in Cabarrus Co., Centre's Greek Revival brick church was built in an era of Presbyterian renewal and prosperity. Simplest of the three, Centre captures the essence of the pedimented temple form: a clean-lined brick structure opened up by generous triple-hung windows with granite sills. A smaller frame version is the **Session House**. The cemetery, enclosed by a dry-laid stone wall with wrought iron gates, contains graves from 1776 onward.

ID 26 Coddle Creek Associate Reformed Presbyterian Church
1884; E side NC 136, 0.2 mi. N of Cabarrus Co. line; Mount Mourne vic.

The congregation was founded ca. 1755 as the first in present-day Iredell Co.; its meetinghouse depicted on the 1771 Collet map of the colony was the only one shown west of

ID 25 *Centre Presbyterian Church*

ID 26 *Coddle Creek A.R.P. Church*

the Yadkin River. In 1790 Coddle Creek be-came one of the first Associate Reformed Presbyterian congregations in N.C. The As-sociate and Reformed Presbyterians, dissent-ing groups from the Church of Scotland in the mid-18th c., came to the colonies with the Scotch-Irish immigration from North-ern Ireland; the two groups joined in 1782 and in 1790 formed the Presbytery of the Carolinas and Georgia, including Coddle Creek. The frame church, built in 1884, re-peats the traditional gable-fronted form in simplified Italianate style, with arched win-dows, bracketed eaves, and a cross-gabled entrance tower. There is a simpler session house of the same era. The cemetery, dating from the mid-18th c., contains some of the county's finest 18th- and 19th-c. gravestones and stone gateposts flanking an iron gate forged by a Mr. Freeze, probably blacksmith J. L. Freeze, who may have produced other local gates.

ID 27 Lookout Shoals Dam and Power Plant

1915; SR 1006 at Catawba River

When the Southern (Duke) Power Co. began to "electrify" the Catawba River, it started in South Carolina, then built five plants in N.C. of which Lookout Shoals, with a concrete gravity dam with 933-foot spillway, was the first. It was soon followed by #Bridgewater (1923), *Mountain Island (1923), #Rhodhiss (1925), and #Oxford (1928).

Catawba County (CT)

See Sidney Halma, Project Director, Catawba County: An Architectural History *(1991)*, *and* Gary R. Freeze, The Catawbans: Crafters of a North Carolina County *(1995)*.

Lying in the great southward curve of the Catawba River and named for the native people of the region, the county was formed from Lincoln in 1842. In the mid-18th c., Scotch-Irish and English farmers settled near the river, and Germans took up lands along the South Fork Catawba, as evidenced by the many Lutheran and Reformed churches. Methodism also took hold early; the state's first congregation of that faith formed at *Terrell by 1791 and had the first of several camp meeting grounds in 1794. Early 19th-c. inhabitants raised grains and other crops traded downriver to South Carolina, and many built substantial houses. The Western North Carolina Railroad (WNCRR), which arrived in 1860, kindled new towns and industries after the Civil War. Hickory arose as a regional center for woodworking and wagonmaking, then furniture and textiles.

Two prolific local builders flourished in the railroad era. Charles Henry Lester, the county's first professional architect, came from Connecticut in 1872, settled at Sherrill's Ford, and established a regional architecture and building practice. Joseph D. Elliott of Hickory began building depots for the Southern Railway in the 1880s and in 1908 founded Elliott Building Co., which operated across the South.

CT 1 Newton

Laid out in 1845 and incorporated in 1855, the county seat was named for legislator Isaac Newton Wilson, who championed formation of the county. When the WNCRR passed north of town in 1860, a 3-mile spur was built to Newton, and the Chester & Lenoir Narrow Gauge Railway arrived in 1883. Along the rails rose textile mills and wood products factories. Lutheran, German Reformed, Methodist, and Presbyterian churches were organized by 1860, and the Reformed church's Catawba College (est. 1851) was an important local institution until it moved to Salisbury in 1923 (q.v.).

The former **Catawba County Courthouse** (1924; Willard G. Rogers [Charlotte], architect; T. R. Owens, builder), the second on the square, is a 2-story Renaissance Revival structure faced in Indiana limestone; it houses the Catawba Co. Museum. Among the 2-story brick commercial buildings around the square, the **First National Bank of Catawba** (ca. 1900; E. 1st St.) displays a Spanish Colonial Revival facade with tiled and bracketed roof.

Residential development on **N. Main Ave.** and flanking streets dates from the mid-19th c. onward, such as the **Witherspoon-Killian House** (1883, 1905; 128 W. 7th St.), a large, brick Italianate house with wraparound porch with center balcony; the Queen Anne style **Feimster House** (1908; 436 N. Main Ave.); and numerous Colonial Revival and Craftsman bungalows. Punctuating the streetscapes are **Beth-Eden Lutheran Church** (1929; 400 N. Main Ave.), a twin-towered Gothic Revival building in

CT 1 *Catawba Co. Courthouse*

brick; **First Presbyterian Church** (1878 and later; 699 N. Main Ave.), a small Romanesque Revival brick sanctuary; and the former **Newton High School** (1905, 1935; 607 N. Ashe Ave.), with porticoed frontispiece and flanking wings. The **Newton Passenger Depot** (1924; N. Main Ave. at 11th St.) is a bracketed brick station possibly by Elliott Building Co. of Hickory. It has been moved for restoration.

South of the courthouse **Grace Reformed Church** (Calvary Baptist) (1887; Charles Henry Lester, architect; S. Main Ave. at C St.), built for a congregation organized in 1849, was designed by the local architect in Gothic Revival style with unequal corner towers. Lester may also have designed the **Foil-Cline House** (1883; S. Main Ave. at E. E St.), a richly detailed Italianate style residence for John A. Foil of Catawba College. The **Self-Trott House** (1883; 331 S. College Ave.) is a simpler Italianate I-house of brick made at builder William R. Self's nearby brickyard.

CT 2 Old St. Paul's Lutheran Church and Cemetery

1818; Henry Cline, builder; NE corner SR 1149 and SR 1155, Newton vic.

The landmark church stands on an elevated site used for worship by German settlers from the mid-18th c. For the 1818 meetinghouse, one of the oldest in the region, carpenter Cline reportedly reused logs from the preceding "Dutch (Deutsch) Meeting House." The 2-story log building, covered in weatherboards, has a severely plain exterior that conceals an interior remarkable for its beauty and completeness. It follows a meetinghouse plan, with the main entrance on the long side and benches and galleries forming a U around the pulpit opposite the entrance. Walls are simply finished with wide vertical boards, but stylish touches appear in the slim fluted posts of the galleries and the extraordinary sounding board, suspended over the pulpit and adorned with stylized Adamesque motifs. Both Lutheran and German Reformed members worshiped here until the latter built their own church in 1904. There are many German-inscribed

stones in the graveyard. The congregation worships in a sanctuary across the road but maintains the old church. (See Introduction, Fig. 2.)

CT 3 St. Paul's Reformed Church

1904; E side SR 1005, 0.2 mi. N of NC 10; Startown

After sharing the union church with the Lutherans for many years, in 1904 Reformed members of *Old St. Paul's Lutheran Church completed this small Carpenter Gothic building about 3 miles south of the older church. It features lancet arch windows, kingpost gable ornaments, and an unusual tapered corner entrance tower with open belfry. Replaced in 1975, it is maintained by the congregation. Adding to the cluster of similarly named churches, across NC 10 is a second **St. Paul's Lutheran Church** (early 20th c.; w side SR 1005, s of NC 10), built for members of Old St. Paul's who in 1905 affiliated with the Tennessee rather than the N.C. Lutheran Synod.

CT 4 Conover

The town emerged after the Civil War where the spur to Newton met the WNCRR and was joined by the Chester & Lenoir Narrow Gauge Railway in 1883. A local buggy company established in 1883 by Jerome Bolick later became a major truck and bus body manufacturer; the plant and Bolick family residences lie along 1st Ave. S (NC 16) south of town. Lutherans affiliated with the Tennessee Synod founded Concordia College here in 1877 and a church of the same name. **Concordia Lutheran Church** (1957; A. G. Odell Jr. & Assoc. [Charlotte], architects; 215 5th Ave. SE) is a dramatic statement of mid-20th-c. modernism by the influential Charlotte firm and winner of an American Institute of Architects award. The broad copper roof envelopes the sanctuary and becomes taller as it narrows from the east entrance to the chancel at the west end.

CT 4 *Concordia Lutheran Church*

CT 5 Bunker Hill Covered Bridge

1895, 1900; Andrew L. Ramsour, builder; Conner Park, N side US 70, 2.1 mi. W of NC 10, Claremont vic.; National Civil Engineering Landmark

The 80-foot bridge, one of two covered bridges left in the state (*Pisgah Covered Bridge), may be the last wooden bridge in the U.S. with Haupt truss construction, patented in 1839 by military engineer Herman Haupt. Builder Ramsour operated a sawmill and a famous 1,000-foot covered toll bridge at Horseford on the Catawba (destroyed in the flood of 1916). For the small bridge on Lyle's Creek, he constructed the open span in 1895; the roof and board-and-batten walls were added by the county about 5 years later. Restored by the Catawba Co. Historical Association in 1994, it is accessible by a pedestrian trail.

CT 5 *Bunker Hill Covered Bridge*

CT 6 Perkins House

Early 19th c.; private, no public visibility or access

The 2-story house is of Flemish-bond brickwork, with lozenge patterns on the wide double-shouldered chimney. The 3-room plan interior was finished with elaborate Adamesque woodwork (1811) inspired by Owen Biddle's *Young Carpenter's Assistant* (1805), enriched with decorative painting; these elements are now in the Museum of Early Southern Decorative Arts in Winston-Salem.

CT 7 Catawba

The trading center developed where the WNCRR built a bridge over the Catawba River ca. 1859. Prominent among the brick commercial buildings on N. Main St. is the **Sherrill Tobacco Co.–Coulter & Little Store** (ca. 1895; SW corner N. Main St. and Central Ave.), a 3-story, 6-bay brick building with round-arched openings and corbeling. Behind it the **Dr. Quintus Little House** (ca. 1873; W. 1st St.), oldest in town, is a brick I-house with 2-story porch. Unusual is the **James H. Trollinger House** (ca. 1875; SE corner W. 2nd St. and S. 1st Ave.), a 5-bay frame I-house made into a Gothic Revival cottage with 5 gables across the front and triangular headed windows.

CT 8 Murray's Mill

Mill, 1913; SW side SR 1003 (Buffalo Shoals Rd.), 0.35 mi. SE of NC 10, Catawba vic.; open regular hours

Now operated by the Catawba Co. Historical Association, the picturesque mill complex on Ball's Creek illustrates a once common staple of rural life. The 2-story frame roller mill was built in 1913 by John Murray, whose father had operated a mill at the site since 1883. His son Lloyd ran the mill until 1967. The 32-acre mill pond, formed by a curved concrete dam, feeds a 28-foot overshot waterwheel. The site also includes an 1890s general store, a wheat house, and houses and outbuildings of the Murray family. (See Introduction, Fig. 43.)

CT 9 Ball's Creek Campground

Est. 1853; W side SR 1003, 2.0 mi. S of SR 1848, Bandy vic.

One of the state's largest religious campgrounds, Balls Creek has been the site of Methodist camp meetings in August almost continuously since 1853, interrupted only by war and a religious dispute in 1888. Continuing the movement begun in the 18th c., families return faithfully year after year. At the center of the 33-acre grounds is the 100-by-80-foot arbor, an open-sided, heavy-timbered structure with a low pyramidal roof protecting wooden benches. Built ca. 1930 to replace a similar older one, it shelters the annual preaching, hymn singing, and conversion experiences. Around the arbor are two concentric squares of connecting "tents" plus additional outlying rows, numbering almost 300 in all. The family-owned tents—frame structures that continue the name of earlier temporary shelters—share side walls but vary in size and form. Most follow a 2-story rectangular form with shallow gable roof and the entrance in the narrow end facing the arbor. Most have no windows but are ventilated by slats in the upper front and rear walls. All have simple shed porches, creating a continuous, irregular arcade. They were unpainted originally, but in the 20th c. owners have painted them in colors that change from year to year. The tents have

CT 9 *Ball's Creek Campground*

been repaired or rebuilt almost continuously, including over 100 rebuilt on the west side after a fire in 1956. Only a few remodelings show a break with tradition.

CT 10 Miles Alexander Sherrill House

1886; Charles Henry Lester, architect; W side SR 1849, 0.1 mi. S of SR 1848, Terrell vic.

Built for a grist- and sawmill owner, the Stick style cottage is the best-preserved house by local architect Lester. He came from Connecticut in 1872, married Susan Turner of a local family, and remodeled a plantation house near Sherrill's Ford for their home. In a long career as regional architect and contractor he worked in a variety of late Victorian styles. Here he employed horizontal and vertical banding and small side porches under a steep gable roof, an unusually faithful rendition of the Stick style.

CT 11 Terrell

NC 150 at SR 1848

Amid development from Lake Norman, Terrell remains a crossroads community from the late 19th and early 20th centuries. South of the intersection is **Rehobeth Methodist Church**, a mid-20th-c. overbuilding of an 1890 frame building designed by C. H. Lester. The Methodist congregation, believed to be the state's first west of the Catawba River, was founded in 1789 by circuit rider Daniel Asbury, who made his permanent home nearby and is buried here. The **Conner Store and Post Office** (1885), a 2-story frame store, has its original parapet storefront with recessed entrance and 1-story post office wing. Behind it, the **Gabriel Mill and Cotton Gin Complex** includes the frame mill building, gin, and cotton storage building of the early 20th c. Across the road, its owner Robert Gabriel expanded his father-in-law's 1-story house into the 2-story frame **Sherrill-Gabriel House** (1880s, 1906) with porch with turned posts and central balcony. North on SR 1848 stands the **Thomas Conner House** (1886; Charles Henry Lester, architect), the turreted Queen Anne style residence of the leading merchant and postmaster. Across SR 1848, the **Coleman-Gabriel Farm** (1854 and later) is the community's oldest house, an I-house with simple Greek Revival detail and a later porch, set amid cultivated fields and outbuildings.

CT 12 Mott's Grove Campground

Est. ca. 1870; E side SR 1848, 1.0 mi. N of NC 150

One of two African American Methodist camp meeting grounds established in the county after Emancipation, it was named for John James Mott, a physician who donated the land. The site encompasses a pyramidal-roofed pole-framed arbor about 50 feet square, a dozen frame "tents," a cemetery, and a small brick-veneered church (1960).

CT 13 Rudisill-Wilson House

Ca. 1820; W side SR 1005, 2.0 mi. S of NC 10, Startown vic.; private, visible from road

The traditional 2-story frame house, with shed porch, rear shed rooms, and simple Federal finish, was evidently built for Michael Rudisill, of a German family who came from Pennsylvania and prospered as farmers.

CT 14 Grace Union Church

1857; Joseph Irby, mason; Mr. Harrellson, carpenter; W side SR 1008, 1.7 mi. S of NC 10, Blackburn vic.

The simple Greek Revival church was built as a union church for Lutheran and Reformed congregations that formed ca. 1796 and had a log meetinghouse on the site. The early congregations were served by pioneer pastors Johannes Gottfried Arends (Lutheran) and Andrew Loretz (Reformed). In 1857 the congregations built the straightforward temple-form church with pedimented front, wide frieze, and white-stuccoed corner pilasters that contrast with the deep red brick walls. In 1940 the Lutherans built a church across the road, and after Reformed members built a new church in 1971, they sold the old building to the Lutherans, who maintain it. The churchyard has stones dated from 1822, some in a Germanic tradition.

CT 14 *Grace Union Church*

CT 15 Weidner-Wilfong Rock House

1790s, 1840s; private, no public visibility or access

According to tradition, John Wilfong built his 2-story "Rock House" in 1844 (dated stone) by dismantling and rebuilding a nearby 18th-c. house built for the German immigrant Weidner family.

CT 16 Zion Lutheran Church and Bethel United Church of Christ

Late 19th c.; W side SR 1008 at SR 1176, Brookford vic.

The two churches recall the tradition of Lutheran and German Reformed congregations settling as neighbors. Zion, established in 1790 by Johannes Gottfried Arends, was the state's first exclusively Lutheran church west of the Catawba River; the late 19th-c. brick sanctuary with round-arched windows adjoins a graveyard with stones from the 18th c. Nearby Bethel was founded in 1848 by Reformed members of *Grace Union Church seeking to worship closer to their homes. The congregation built the present simple Gothic Revival brick building about 1880 and affiliated with the United Church of Christ after union of Reformed and Congregational denominations in 1957.

CT 17 Hart's Square

In 1967 Dr. Robert Hart of Hickory purchased land in southwestern Catawba Co. as a wildlife preserve and a site for preservation of the region's endangered log building tradition. Several dozen neglected structures from Catawba and nearby counties have been moved to the site for restoration, including many 1-room houses and outbuildings, most with the regionally dominant half-dovetailed corner timbering. Their history and original sites are recorded. The site is open to the public one day a year (the last Saturday in October) through the Catawba Co. Historical Museum, Newton.

Hickory (CT 18–22)

See Kirk F. Mohney and Laura A. W. Phillips, *From Tavern to Town: The Architectural History of Hickory, North Carolina* (1988).

The county's largest town grew up at the site of a crossroads tavern. After the WNCRR arrived in 1860, businesses coalesced around the depot, and the village of Hickory Tavern was incorporated in 1869 and renamed Hickory in 1873. It became "a great campground for hundreds of mountain wagons" where farmers brought produce to ship by rail. Early industries included tobacco manufactories, architectural woodwork concerns, a tannery, and the Piedmont Wagon Co., which at one time produced 1,000 wagons per month. The Hickory Mfg. Co., established by Piedmont Wagon founder George C. Bonniwell, made woodwork for

Biltmore House in Asheville. Bonniwell, who came from Pennsylvania, established the building firm of Bonniwell & Daughter with daughter Josephine Bonniwell Lyerly. With business leaders from local families and new arrivals, the town saw rapid early 20th-c. growth in furniture and textile mills and wealth reflected in residential areas and civic landmarks. Builder, banker, and industrialist Joseph D. Elliott, also mayor and legislator, constructed numerous local buildings. His firm built the N.C. Building at the 1907 Jamestown Exposition in Virginia—a columned Southern Colonial Revival design that popularized the style. Navigating the town is complicated by a 20th-c. system of road names that repeats up to 8 variants of the same number applied to avenues (E. or W.) and streets (N. or S.) as they appear north or south of the railroad and east or west of Center St.—thus both 2nd Ave. and 2nd St. appear as SW., SE., NW., and NE.

CT 18 Downtown Hickory

Despite losses to urban renewal, several early 20th-c. brick commercial buildings stand on the north side of Union Square and on nearby streets. At town center the **Hickory Passenger Depot** (1912; Joseph D. Elliott, builder [attrib.]) is a long hip-roofed building of Flemish-bond brick with bracketed eaves and segmental-arched openings, akin to other Southern Railway depots. Contractor Elliott built depots for Southern for more than three decades, probably including this one. (See Introduction, Fig. 38.) The **U.S. Post Office** (1914; Oscar Wenderoth, supervising architect of the Treasury; Main Ave. Place SW) is a Neoclassical building of Flemish-bond brick with limestone trim and Ionic columns at the 2-story frontispiece. South of the railroad, the eclectic **Harper Ford Showroom** (ca. 1930; 219 1st Ave. SW) features a large round-arch show window rising 2 stories at the center, with classical terra-cotta and metal trim. The **First National Bank Building** (1941; SW corner 1st Ave. NW and 2nd St. NW) is a sophisticated marriage of Art Deco and streamlined classical elements in glass, marble, and ironwork. The former **Hickory Municipal**

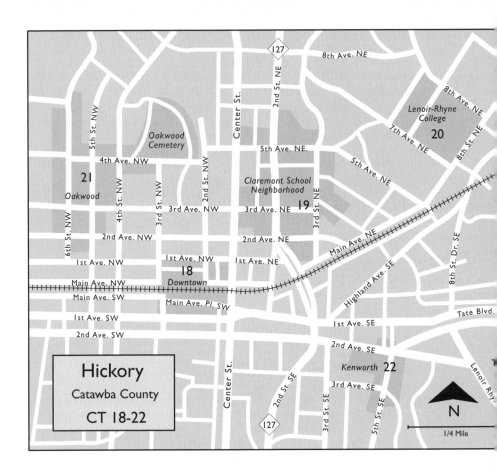

Hickory
Catawba County
CT 18-22

N

1/4 Mile

CT 18 *First National Bank*

Building (1921; Charles C. Hook [Charlotte], architect; 30 3rd St. NW), a project promoted by Mayor Joseph D. Elliott, originally housed city offices, a jail, and an auditorium. The 2-story building has massive pilasters and a 1-story Tuscan entrance portico. North of downtown, **First Presbyterian Church** (1906; Bowman Bros. [Knoxville], architects; sw corner 2nd St. NW and 3rd Ave. NW) is a solid Romanesque Revival building of rough granite, with unequal towers flanking the front gable.

CT 19 Claremont School Neighborhood

As Hickory grew, leading citizens moved to an area northeast of the commercial district near Claremont Female College (1880–1916), founded by the Reformed Church. On its site the former **Claremont High School** (1925; C. Gadsen Sayre [Raleigh and Anderson, S.C.], architect; 231 3rd Ave. NE) is one of the state's flagship high schools of the great period of school consolidation. The 3-story, H-plan red brick building features classical trim in terra-cotta, with auditorium and gymnasium wings faced with 2-story arcades. It was rescued by the community as an arts center. In the nearby neighborhood, the most elaborate Queen Anne house in town is the **Shuler-Harper**

460 CATAWBA COUNTY

CT 19 *Claremont High School*

CT 19 *Shuler-Harper House*

CT 19 *A. L. Shuford House*

House (1887; 310 N. Center St.; open as history center), with remarkable interior woodwork and decorative painting by F. A. Grace, a Frenchman whom Shuler, a banker from Michigan, is said to have enticed to Hickory. (The house may have been built by Joseph D. Elliott, whose own house [lost] was similar; he also built the Elliott Opera House [burned, 1902], backed by Shuler with interior painting by Grace.) On the north, the **Adolphus Lafayette Shuford House** (Maple Grove) (ca. 1875, 1883; 542 2nd St. NE; open by appt.) began as a farmhouse for the dairy operation of Shuford, a railroad agent and early business leader. It became the rear wing when he built the 2-story Italianate main block with 2-tier porch (1883). It is maintained by the Hickory Landmarks Society.

CT 20 Lenoir-Rhyne College

The Lutheran college, which developed from a local academy, was named in 1892 for Walter W. Lenoir, who donated land for the campus, and in 1923 added the name of benefactor Daniel Efird Rhyne, a Gaston and Lincoln Co. industrialist (*Laboratory; *Moses Rhyne House). The focal point is the **Daniel Efird Rhyne Memorial Building** (1928; Charles Hartmann [Greensboro], architect) on the original quadrangle, a 2-story brick building in Collegiate Gothic style, with flanking towers at the entrance.

CT 21 Oakwood

The neighborhood south and west of **Oakwood Cemetery** (1889) was planned by French artist F. A. Grace (*Shuler-Harper House) and contains Colonial Revival, late Queen Anne, Tudor Revival, and other period revival houses and bungalows. A delightful anomaly is the **J. Summie Propst House** (1883; 332 6th St. NW), the city's only Second Empire style house, small but grand with its mansard roof, tower, and rich detail. Propst, a carpenter and cabinetmaker,

CT 21 *Propst House*

built the house for his bride and to advertise his work. It was saved and moved by the Hickory Landmarks Society. The nearby **Abel A. Shuford II House** (ca. 1910; 534 3rd Ave. NW), built for a business and civic leader, is among the most fully realized Shingle style houses in the state, with dark shingled walls, rough stonework, and irregular gambrel and gable roof forms.

CT 22 Kenworth

The small, planned suburb, a project of the Hickory Land & Development Co. (1913)

consists chiefly of Craftsman bungalows centered on the **Kenworth Elementary School** (1913; J. S. Zimmerman [Winston-Salem], architect; 1919, 1952; 426 2nd Ave. SE), a 2-story brick school with classical details. Zimmerman collaborated with local architect C. H. Lester on the N.C. Building at the Jamestown Exposition.

Lincoln County (LN)

See Marvin A. Brown, Our Enduring Past: A Survey of 235 Years of Life and Architecture in Lincoln County, North Carolina *(1986).*

Created in 1779 from Tryon Co. during the American Revolution, the county was named for patriot Gen. Benjamin Lincoln instead of the royal governor. At first encompassing territory from the big bend of the Catawba River down to South Carolina, Lincoln shrank as Catawba, Gaston, and part of Cleveland Co. were carved from it in the 1840s.

Its farmlands were settled mostly by Scotch-Irish and English near the Catawba River, Germans along the South Fork Catawba and its tributaries in the center and west, and a few French Huguenots. In the eastern section, related planter families—Grahams, Davidsons, Forneys, and Brevards—prospered from iron mining from the late 18th c. and took leading roles in the American Revolution and state politics. The county also claims the South's first textile mill, built before 1816 by Michael Schenck and Absalom Warlick on McDaniels Creek; local mills remained small, though, until the late 19th c. A 19th-c. chronicler of the county observed, "No rural population in this country could boast of finer residences, both brick and frame." The county possesses especially fine early 19th-c. brick houses with 3-room plans and variations and Flemish-bond brickwork. Their builders remain unknown.

LN 1 Lincolnton

The county seat was established in 1785 near the South Fork Catawba River at the center of the new county. The grid of half-acre lots centers on a Lancaster plan (first used in Lancaster, Pa.) courthouse square with cut-out corners and four axial streets. As one of the state's principal towns west of the Catawba, Lincolnton flourished as an early political, social, commercial, and educational center led by a coterie of backcountry gentry. Its fortunes diminished as the county

LN 1 *Lincoln Co. Courthouse*

gave up territory in the 1840s, then improved when a plank road from Charlotte was completed in 1855 and a branch of the Wilmington, Charlotte, & Rutherford Railroad arrived in 1860. The Chester & Lenoir Narrow Gauge Railway from Gastonia added more connections in 1881, and textile mills and other industries rose along the river. Beyond the courthouse and commercial district, neighborhoods in all directions have houses from the early 19th c. onward, reflecting division of the original half-acre lots over time.

Erected to replace an 1853 Greek Revival structure, the **Lincoln County Courthouse** (1923; James A. Salter [Raleigh], architect) is a big 3-story Neoclassical Revival building faced in stone, with grand Doric porticoes east and west and wings on the north and south. Turn-of-the-century brick storefronts line the courthouse square and E. Main St., including the **Reinhardt Building** (1909; Henry A. Kistler, builder; W. Court Square) on the northwest corner, a 3-story orange brick structure with rusticated first story, heavy classical cornice, and rounded corner, built for textile mill owner Robert S. Reinhardt.

The shaded second and third blocks of **W. Main St.** retain 19th-c. houses and some of the ambience of an antebellum county seat. An important early 19th-c. town house is **Shadow Lawn** (1826; 301 W. Main St.; private), one of a regional group of 2-story Federal style brick houses with excellent craftsmanship and fashionably finished, 3-room plan interiors. The Flemish-bond brickwork is complemented by flat arches above openings, a broad water table and belt course, and a molded brick cornice. It was erected for merchant Paul Kistler and his wife Ann Smith, whose brother David built the related *Magnolia Grove a year earlier. In the 20th c. it was the home of Congressman Charles Raper Jonas. South of the square, **Aspen St.** developed in the early 20th c. with late Queen Anne and period revival houses, anchored by the 3-story, classically detailed brick **Lincolnton High School** (1923; S. Aspen St.).

North of the courthouse, the **Gen. Robert F. Hoke House** (ca. 1835; N side Chestnut St.) is an unusual 2-story frame Greek Revival style house in an H-plan, with its porch recessed between pedimented gable ends. Said to have been for Michael Hoke, lawyer and politician, at his marriage to Frances Burton in 1833—early for a fully developed Greek Revival residence—it was later the home of their son, the Confederate major general.

LN 1 *Pleasant Retreat Academy*

Pleasant Retreat Academy (1817–20; 129 E. Pine St.) is among N.C.'s prime examples of the nearly 300 private academies chartered between 1800 and 1860. The classical academy (est. 1813, opened 1820) operated for over a half-century, educating such leaders as James Pinckney Henderson (governor of Texas), William A. Graham (N.C. governor, U.S. senator, and secretary of the navy), and Robert Hoke (Confederate general). The 2-story 4-bay Federal style brick building with corbeled cornice became in 1907 N.C.'s first state-assisted historic restoration project.

Prominent brick churches include some that trace roots to "the Old White Church," built by 1788 for Lutheran and Reformed congregations as a union church called Emanuels. That church burned in 1893, but its old cemetery contains graves of many early residents, including Lutheran missionary Johann Gottfried Arends. The nearby **Emmanuel Lutheran Church** (1920; Henry A. Kistler, builder; 216 S. Aspen St.) is a Gothic Revival building with a massive central tower, its red brick walls punctuated by lancet windows, buttresses, parapets, and spires brightly capped in white stone. **First Methodist Church** (1919; C. W. Carlton [attrib.], architect; 201 E. Main St.), founded in 1824, is a Neoclassical Revival style building with a central dome and portico on a corner site with auditorium plan. **Emanuel Reformed Church** (Church of

LN 1 *Shadow Lawn*

Christ) (1913; Henry Bonitz [Wilmington], architect; 329 E. Main St.), in Gothic Revival with a corner tower, is the Wilmington architect's westernmost known building. The former **First Baptist Church** (1922; James M. McMichael [Charlotte], architect; 403 E. Main St.) is a domed, Neoclassical Revival building with Ionic portico. Farther east, **Moore's Chapel A.M.E. Zion Church** (ca. 1870, 1892, 1898, 1941; 1009 E. Main St.) grew out of a congregation of free blacks who began worshiping together in 1863. After the war it was served by A.M.E. Zion bishop John J. Moore, a Virginian who escaped slavery about 1830 and became a circuit rider in Pennsylvania and Ohio before coming to N.C. in 1868. The frame chapel of 1870 is within the 2-towered brick-veneered church.

West of the courthouse, **First Presbyterian Church** (1917; W. Main St.) is a large Gothic Revival building with an arcade linking two tall corner entrance towers. The congregation was founded in 1815 by German Reformed families who, lacking a minister after the death of Andrew Loretz in 1812, adopted the similarly Calvinist Presbyterian faith.

Northeast of the square, **St. Luke's Episcopal Church** (1886 and later; Silas McBee, architect; 303–21 N. Cedar St.) is a modest Gothic Revival church erected for a congregation est. 1842. Part of a tower survives from an 1849 church, but the main church was built in 1886 from designs by McBee, a Lincoln resident who became a noted church architect and editor of a denominational journal; he also carved much of the extraordinarily intricate rood screen and other liturgical fittings. The church was stuccoed in 1917 and brick-veneered in 1923. A frame parish hall, stuccoed rectory, and cemetery also occupy the shaded 2-acre tract. Farther east in the heart of a long-established African American neighborhood first known as Freedman, **Second Presbyterian Church** (1885; E. Pine St.), built for a congregation founded in 1880, is a gable-fronted frame chapel with a tall, thin steeple rising above a gabled vestibule.

LN 2 Woodside

Early 19th c.; S side NC 182, 0.4 mi. W of NC 27, Lincolnton vic.; private, visible from road

The well-finished house is among the oldest of the 2-story brick houses in Lincoln with 3-room plans and Federal style woodwork, here with two front doors in the 4-bay facade. It was built for Lawson Henderson, planter, county sheriff, and clerk of court, whose children raised here included Charles Cotesworth Henderson, "perhaps the principal merchant in Western Carolina," and James Pinckney Henderson, first governor (1846) of Texas.

LN 3 Henderson House

Ca. 1855; NE side SR 1008, 0.3 mi. SE of SR 1113, Lincolnton vic.; private, visible from road

The 2-story frame house with board-and-batten siding, peaked roofline, and deep porch with latticework posts typifies the stylish picturesque modeled by A. J. Downing's "Small Country House for the Southern States," in *Architecture of Country Houses* (1850). Illustrating the linkage of the modern picturesque to advocates of internal improvements and business, the house was built by Charles Cotesworth Henderson (*Woodside), merchant and plank roads advocate, for his son, Lawson.

LN 3 *Henderson House*

LN 4 *Daniels Lutheran Church*

LN 4 Daniels Lutheran Church and Daniels Evangelical and Reformed Church

1889, 1937; N side SR 1113, opp. SR 1204, Lincolnton vic.

Descending from a union church founded before 1767 to serve Lutheran and Reformed groups, these congregations are the oldest in the county and perhaps in the state west of the Catawba River. Called the Schoolhouse Church for its school, also one of the first in the region, it was renamed for early member Daniel Warlick. Itinerant Lutheran pastor Gottfried Arends and Reformed minister Andrew Loretz (*Loretz House) served this and other union churches. The congregations erected separate churches in the late 19th c. **Daniels Lutheran Church** (1889) is a small, handsome brick structure with corbeled cornice, round-arched windows, and buttresses across the gable front and sides. After the 1894 Reformed church was destroyed by lightning in 1936, the congregation built **Daniels Evangelical and Reformed Church** (1937) in Gothic Revival style faced in stone. The shared cemetery contains many early graves, including those of Andrew Loretz and Daniel Warlick.

LN 5 Andrew Loretz House

1793; E side SR 1204, 0.2 mi. S of SR 1113, Lincolnton vic.; private, visible from road

Initials, dates, and patterns executed in glazed header bricks in the gable ends of the

2-story Flemish-bond brick house show a kinship with other brick buildings in the region. Seen earlier in the 18th c. in the mid-Atlantic and eastern N.C., such brickwork appeared in the Piedmont in the late 18th c. The east wall (not visible from road) has the initials A. L., the date 1793, and lozenge, heart, cross, and chevron patterns; on the west chimney a column of lozenges extends down the center. Swiss-born Loretz, a preacher of the Reformed Church, came to N.C. via Pennsylvania and built his house within sight of the church he served from 1788 to 1812 (*Daniels Reformed Church).

LN 6 Jacob Ramseur House

Ca. 1835; W side SR 1268, opp. SR 1270; private, visible at a distance from road

Overlooking fields and pastures beside the South Fork Catawba River, the 2-story brick house was built for planter, tanner, millwright, and boot manufacturer Jacob Ramseur, whose German ancestors had owned the land since the mid-18th c. It features sturdy proportions over a raised basement, with fine Flemish-bond brickwork, a molded brick cornice, interior gable-end chimneys, and front and rear shed porches.

LN 6 *Jacob Ramseur House*

LN 7 Salem Union (Lutheran and Reformed) Church

1848, 1914, 1937; E side SR 1005, 0.9 mi. S of Catawba Co. line; Lincolnton vic.

While union churches shared by Lutheran and German Reformed congregations were once common in the region, Salem Church is believed to be the last in the state still serv-

ing that role. Erected for congregations established in the late 18th c., the gable-
fronted brick sanctuary of the present building was completed in 1848 and gained a
corner tower and lancet arch windows in
1914. The old cemetery lies adjacent.

LN 8 St. Matthew's Reformed Church (United Church of Christ) and Arbor
Arbor ca. 1845 and ca. 1990;
church 1908; W side US 321 BUS,
0.5 mi. S of Catawba Co. line

The cruciform brick building, only the second to serve the congregation (est. 1837),
features vigorous, deep red brickwork and
round-arched openings. Nearby is an open-
sided arbor of heavy timbers under a broad
pyramidal roof. After the original arbor
burned in the late 20th c., it was rebuilt by
the congregation to the original dimensions.
Lutheran and Reformed congregations did
not look favorably on the emotional camp
meetings of Methodists and Baptists, and
the structure is the state's sole example of
the meeting ground tradition among German descendants; meetings here were "remarkable for good order and religious devotion." The last recorded meeting was held in
1874.

Eastern Lincoln Iron Plantation Area:
Following legislation in 1788 to encourage
ironworks in the state, production developed
rapidly around the "Big Ore Bank" in eastern
Lincoln Co. Within a decade the related Gra-
ham, Davidson, Forney, Brevard, and other
families were operating furnaces, and they
dominated the Piedmont iron business for a
generation. Iron production created no indus-
trial cities but was integrated into the agricul-
tural economy, and many families combined
the roles of planter and ironmaster. They pro-
duced bar iron; castings in the form of skillets,
pans, and similar items; and wrought iron
products such as horseshoes and wagon wheel
rims, and they traded these in a broad regional
market. Several early houses were built from
the wealth of iron and agriculture.

LN 9 Madison-Derr Iron Furnace
Ca. 1810; off SR 1350, Pumpkin Center vic.;
under development as public park

The 35-foot trapezoid of cut stone blocks is
one of three iron furnaces surviving in the
county. It was built for Peter Forney,
Huguenot descendant, Revolutionary officer, and one of the pioneers of the industry
from the 1780s. Forney was an elector in
1808 for President James Madison, for
whom he apparently named the furnace. It
was operated by Jonas Derr between 1860
and 1878, then permanently shut down. Like
others of its type (*Moratock Furnace,
Stokes Co.; *Endor Furnace, Lee Co.), it
was built against the side of a hill, so ore
and fuel could be hauled over a bridge from
the hill to the stack, and near a stream to
provide waterpower for the bellows. Unlike
the Moratock and Endor furnaces, this
and other Lincoln Co. furnaces have triangular rather than round-arched openings
at the base. By the road leading to the furnace stands the **Jacob Forney House** (1817,
1836), home of Peter's son and brother of
Daniel Forney of *Ingleside. Long neglected
at its original site nearby, the 2-story frame
house with Flemish-bond double-shouldered chimneys was moved here in 2002 for
preservation.

LN 10 Vesuvius Furnace
Ca. 1792, ca. 1815; N side SR 1382, 1.2 mi.
W of SR 1360; private, visible from road

The big 2-story frame house of Joseph and
Isabella Davidson Graham is one of the chief
reminders of the early iron industry in Lincoln and surrounding counties. Joseph Graham, a Pennsylvania native and patriot in
the Revolution, married a daughter of John
Davidson, an ironmaster of Mecklenburg
Co., and became a leading ironmaster himself. His (now ruinous) furnace was built
about 1790 and named for the volcano that
destroyed Pompeii. His house across the
road and a post office here shared the name.
The original (E) section of the house has a 3-
room plan and a chimney of Flemish-bond
brick; it was extended to the west in Federal
style, and the full-height porch was added

ca. 1945. Joseph's son William Alexander, born here in 1804, achieved distinction as governor, U.S. senator, and secretary of the navy.

LN 11 Rock Springs Campground
Arbor, 1832; W side SR 1373, 0.5 mi. N of NC 16, Denver vic.

Along with *Ball's Creek Campground in Catawba Co., Rock Springs is one of the state's largest and most impressive camp meeting grounds. It is also the oldest, for it traces back to Methodist preacher Daniel Asbury's camp meeting begun at *Terrell in Catawba Co. in 1794, one of the first annual camp meetings in the nation. That meeting moved to this site about 1830. The open-sided, pyramidal-roofed arbor at the center of the complex, which shelters about 1,000 worshipers, was built of hand-hewn timbers in 1832 for $225. Surrounding the arbor are two complete and one partial concentric squares of "tents," small frame structures privately owned by families who occupy them during revival week in August. The intentionally simple tents, all unpainted, have common side walls, hard clay floors, sleeping lofts ventilated by slats in the upper front and rear walls, and shed front porches. The vitality of the campground endures in annual summer meetings that continue the communal religious spirit of the Great Revival. (See Introduction, Fig. 15.)

LN 12 Brevard Chapel (A.M.E. Zion)
Ca. 1890; N side SR 1373, 1.3 mi. S of Catawba Co. line, Denver vic.

The African American congregation established soon after the Civil War may have employed Catawba Co. architect Charles Henry Lester to design the well-preserved frame chapel with its elaborately cut, pierced, and incised woodwork that drapes like icing from the gable-fronted eaves, above the central entrance, and on the little mansard-roofed belltower. The building is otherwise simply finished with rectangular windows, plain weatherboards, and flush-boarded walls within.

LN 13 William A. Graham Jr. Farm
1890s; E side SR 1360, 1.2 mi. S of SR 1382, Kidville vic.

William A. Graham Jr. (son of the governor and statesman born at *Vesuvius Furnace who resided in Hillsborough) settled on family land in Lincoln Co. after the Civil War. Active in state politics and commissioner of agriculture (1908–23), at his farm he investigated the newest agricultural methods and devices. The "Round Barn," part of his innovations, is a 16-sided frame structure with polygonal roof and 8-sided cupola. His handsome farmhouse is a 2-story frame dwelling with typical late 19th-c. center roof gable, bracket cornice, and sawn and turned ornament enriching the gable and the front porch.

LN 14 Tucker's Grove
Camp Meeting Ground
Est. mid-19th c.; E corner SR 1360 and NC 73, Machpelah

Tucker's Grove was founded by Methodists before the Civil War to provide religious education for slaves; in the early years Methodist camp meetings were racially integrated, but the pattern began to change in the mid-19th c. Operated since 1876 by the A.M.E. Zion Church, it remains one of the oldest continuous black camp meeting grounds in the South. The complex has a heavy-timbered, open-sided arbor at the center, and around it are rows of small gabled "tents" of frame, owned by the families who use them during the summer revival meetings. Typically, most are 1 story tall with clay floors and adjoining side walls. Many have been

LN 12 *Brevard Chapel*

rebuilt in traditional fashion after losses to fire.

LN 15 Machpelah Presbyterian Church and Cemetery
1801, 1848; NW corner SR 1360 and SR 1511

The quiet rural site possesses great presence. Planters, ironmasters, and brothers-in-law, Joseph Graham and Alexander Brevard established a family cemetery here at the death of Graham's daughter Polly in 1801 and named it for the biblical burying place of the patriarchs. The site lay midway between Graham's *Vesuvius Furnace (N) and Brevard's plantation (S) near the road to Charlotte. Graham was a Scotch-Irish Presbyterian, and Brevard was a descendant of French Huguenots (who often became Presbyterians in America). In 1829 Brevard bequeathed funds for the church, which was completed in 1848. The magnificently austere little building is of brick laid in Flemish bond, covered with weathered white paint, with a pair of entrances at the front gable end. The interior continues the simplicity with bare plaster walls and plain wooden pews. Pastor from 1848 until services ended after the Civil War was Dr. Robert Hall Morrison, who married Graham's daughter Mary and was founding president of *Davidson College; in 1857 daughter Mary Anna married Thomas "Stonewall" Jackson. The congregation was revived in 1903, but the building is used only intermittently. A dry-laid stone wall, begun in the early 19th c., surrounds the cemetery, where Graham, Brevard, and Morrison family members lie buried.

LN 16 Ingleside
Ca. 1817; W side SR 1383, 0.1 mi. S of NC 73, Iron Station vic.; private, visible from road

Built for Daniel and Harriet Brevard Forney, both of Huguenot descent, the tall, imposing 2-story house of brick beautifully laid in Flemish bond is the grandest expression of the county's 19th-c. culture of planters and ironmasters. The full-height Ionic portico is among the earliest uses of a heroic order in the state (#First Presbyterian Church, New Bern), and the elegant Federal style finish derives from Owen Biddle's *Young Carpenter's Assistant* (1805). The plan follows a variation of the center-passage plan with 3 main rooms, plus a narrow secondary room behind the large parlor. Daniel Forney and his father, Peter, before him served in the U.S.

LN 15 *Machpelah Presbyterian Church*

LN 16 *Ingleside*

Congress. Family tradition assigns the design to architect Benjamin Latrobe (also of Huguenot descent), who was working on the Capitol during Daniel's 1815–18 tenure in Washington, but no documentation is known.

LN 17 Magnolia Grove

Ca. 1824; N corner SR 1309 and SR 1313, Iron Station vic.; private, visible from road

The 2-story brick house of fine Flemish-bond brickwork was built for David Smith, a planter of German descent, and his wife Elizabeth Arends, daughter of Lutheran minister Johann Gottfried Arends. Located on the old road between Charlotte and Lincolnton, it occupies an old tavern site and served that purpose in early days. The name comes from a rare species of big-leaf, deciduous magnolia first identified in the vicinity by botanist André Michaux in 1796. Like most of the other major early 19th-c. houses in the county, it had the 3-room plan favored by families of German, Scotch-Irish, and Huguenot origins.

LN 18 Laboratory

Early 19th-c. entrepreneurs used the South Fork Catawba River to power some of the state's pioneering cotton mills, beginning with the Lincoln Cotton Mill (ca. 1819), founded by John Hoke, James Bivens, and Michael Schenck (cofounder of the pre-1816 Schenck-Warlick Mill east of Lincolnton). Hoke and his son-in-law L. D. Childs operated the Lincoln mill until it burned ca. 1863. The community takes its name from a Confederate drug laboratory (gone) that distilled opiates from local poppies. On a hill overlooking the mill site is the **Hoke-Rhyne House** (1844; S side SR 1252 at SR 1248), a fine 2-story Greek Revival style brick house with interior end chimneys built by Hoke, probably for daughter Nancy and her husband L. D. Childs; it was later home of Daniel E. Rhyne, who with his brother-in-law J. A. Abernethy had founded the **Laboratory Cotton Mill** (1887 and later; N side SR 1252). Its brick building, visible from the roadway winding above, has a low gable roof with clerestory and louvered cupola; a stair tower with steep hip roof and gabled dormers rises on one side. The **Daniel E. Rhyne House** (ca. 1894; W side SR 1252), a frame I-house with millwork-adorned porch, was the industrialist's home before he bought the Hoke house in 1900. He was a benefactor of many charitable and Lutheran causes, including present *Lenoir-Rhyne College.

Cleveland County (CL)

Cleveland Co. was formed in 1841 from parts of Lincoln and Rutherford counties and named for Benjamin Cleveland, a hero of the Battle of Kings Mountain fought just over the state line in 1780. Watered by the Broad River and its tributaries, the county was settled in the mid-18th c. by English, Scotch-Irish, and German settlers moving in from the mid-Atlantic and South Carolina. Farms and cottage industries traded downriver to Columbia and Charleston, with first tobacco and later cotton as the major cash crops. The first cotton mills were established when railroads reached the county in the 1870s, and by the early 20th c., textile manufacturing dominated the economy.

Shelby (CL 1–2)

Shelby was established as seat of the new county in 1841 and named for Kentuckian Isaac Shelby, who fought alongside Benjamin Cleveland at Kings Mountain. The arrival of the Carolina Central Railroad (later Seaboard) in 1873 spurred growth as a cotton market and textile manufacturing center. Popular mineral springs hotels flourished in the town and county until the late 1920s, and Shelby became known as "the city of springs." In the 1920s and 1930s it was the power base of the "Shelby dynasty," a powerful group of state political leaders that included governors O. Max Gardner and Clyde R. Hoey. Architecture reflects its late 19th- and early 20th-c. growth and prosperity, with an especially fine collection of residential architecture.

CL 1 Downtown Shelby (a–f)

The town center is laid out on a grid, with broad avenues leading out from the tree-shaded courthouse square. The former **Cleveland County Courthouse** (1907; H. F. Newman, architect) (**a**) is a stone-veneered Neoclassical Revival building with porticoes on all four sides, each topped by a small ribbed dome; a massive central dome with cupola towers over the whole. It is now the county history museum. A small brick building on the east side is a springhouse converted to an office.

The nearby 4-story buff brick **Masonic**

Building (1925; Willard G. Rogers [Charlotte], architect; J. P. Little & Son, builder; 203 S. Washington St.) (**b**) is one of the state's chief examples of the Egyptian Revival style, with lotus columns flanking the entrance, a frieze of stylized wings above the first level, and piers rising 3 stories within the paneled window bays.

Of the brick commercial blocks with metal cornices and ornamental brickwork around the square, the most intact is the **Washburn Brick Block** (101–17 N. Lafayette St.) (**c**). **Rogers' Theater Block** (1930s and 1940s; 213–19 E. Marion St.) (**d**) has an Art Deco facade on a structure built in sections in the 1930s and 1940s. Key institutional buildings include **First Baptist Church** (1911; Wheeler & Stern [Charlotte], architects; 120 N. Lafayette St.) (**e**), a mas-

CL 1 *Former Cleveland Co. Courthouse*

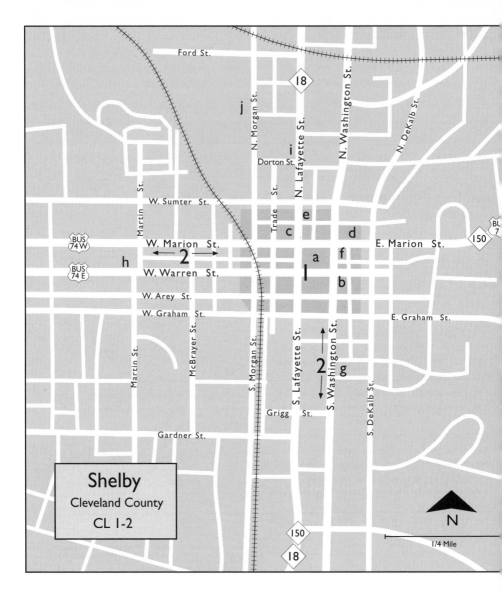

Shelby

Cleveland County

CL 1-2

N

1/4 Mile

sive Gothic Revival sanctuary in yellow brick, with three steeples and later additions, and **Central United Methodist Church** (1924; Louis Asbury [Charlotte], architect [attrib.]; 20 N. Washington St.) (**f**), a Tudor Gothic Revival design with Flemish-bond red brick and buttressed and crenellated towers.

CL 2 Residential Areas (g–j)

The principal early residential avenues extend along **S. Washington St.** and **W. Mar-** ion St. Symmetrical mid-19th-c. white frame houses survive among the later Victorian cottages, big Colonial Revival houses, and bungalows of the merchants, attorneys, physicians, and cotton brokers of the early 20th c. **Webbley** (ca. 1855, 1907; 403 S. Washington St.) (**g**) is a grand Southern Colonial overbuilding of a mid-19th-c. house, the home of Governor O. Max Gardner after 1911. West of the courthouse square is **El Nido** (1920–21; Aurelia Swanson, architect; 520 W. Warren St.) (**h**), a stuccoed Spanish Mission style bungalow of complex plan and exaggerated detail, including curved parapets, thrusting brackets, and elephantine piers. Thwarted in her dream to live in California, owner Maude Sams Gibbs and her husband E. W. created a southwestern oasis in Shelby from a plan provided by a California architect friend, complete with a yard bristling with cactus.

North of the square, the **Banker's House** (1874–75; 319 N. Lafayette St.) (**i**) is one of the state's finest Second Empire style houses and one of the few of brick. Built for Jesse Jenkins, founder of Shelby's first bank, it has since been associated with other Shelby banking families. The towered residence features a floral-patterned slate roof, ornate porch, brackets, and bold labels accenting round- and segmental-arched windows. The style suggests the hand of architect G. S. H. Appleget, specialist in the "French" style in the 1870s in Raleigh and Charlotte. The **Dr. Victor McBrayer House** (1893; 507 N. Morgan St.) (**j**) is an L-shaped house in the spirit of a late Gothic Revival cottage, lavished with mass-produced ornament: scalloped gables, kingposts, brackets, sawnwork, and blind dormers dressed with scalloped vents. Similar work appears in other Victorian cottages in the town and the county.

CL 2 *Webbley*

CL 2 *Banker's House*

CL 2 *El Nido*

CL 2 *Dr. Victor McBrayer House*

CL 3 Burwell Blanton House

1875; N side US 74, 0.1 mi. W of SR 1123, Shelby vic.; private, visible from road

A landmark on the main road west of town, the big 2-story frame Italianate house with hip roof and bracketed eaves was built for Blanton, a farmer, textile industrialist, and banker who later resided at the *Banker's House in Shelby.

CL 4 Double Shoals Mill Village

The small mill village, suggestive of the isolation of many waterpower sites, was the first (1871) textile operation in the county. Plain brick and frame industrial buildings, a company store with decorative brickwork, and cottage-style frame mill houses cling to the hillsides.

CL 5 Lawndale Mill Village

In 1888 Maj. H. F. Schenck, grandson of pioneer industrialist Michael Schenck of Lincoln Co., established Lawndale on the Broad River, which was served by a short-line railroad from Shelby. The present brick cotton mill (**Cleveland Mills Co.**) is typical of ca. 1900 construction with shallow roof and arched windows; a tower with open belfry stands near the river. The workers' houses on the hillsides include hip-roofed frame dwellings, 1-story board-and-batten houses with gable roofs, and a cluster of 2-story gabled houses whose form suggests log construction. Two-story frame houses with decorated porches near the mill probably served managers. North of the mill is the campus of the former Piedmont School, a boarding

school sponsored by Major Schenck. From the once extensive private school is the **Waters-Spangler Library** (ca. 1910; Piedmont Dr.), a brick building with mansard roof, fanlit openings, and quoined corners.

CL 6 Joshua Beam House

Early 1840s; SE side SR 1908, 1.3 mi. NE of NC 180; private, visible from road

One of the county's most prominent antebellum buildings, the traditional 2-story 5-bay center-hall plan frame farmhouse incorporates stylish Greek Revival elements in the 2-story pedimented porch, pedimented gable ends, and modillion cornice. Beam was a politician, planter, and businessman who operated an iron mine and forge nearby.

CL 7 Kings Mountain

First called White Plains, the textile town began as a post office and trading center near a 19th-c. gold mine. The 1872 arrival of the Atlanta & Charlotte Air Line Railway led to incorporation, with the name taken from the Gaston Co. peak and the Revolutionary War battle across the South Carolina line. Five decades of textile mill construction followed, led by members of the Mauney and Garrett families, who moved here from S.C. to find opportunities by the railroad. By 1930 some dozen mills and associated villages encircled the town, several named for owners' relatives—Cora, Lula, Bonnie, Pauline, and Sadie. The commercial district is oriented to the tracks and the **Kings Mountain Depot** (1925; 205 N. Battleground Ave.), a brick station with bracketed hip roof and vergeboards. The town's professional class lived northeast of the town center, chiefly along N. Piedmont, E. Ridge, and N. Battleground Aves.; standouts include the mansard-roofed **Walton Garrett House** (ca. 1890; 100 N. Piedmont Ave.) and the Queen Anne style **Rev. John D. Mauney House** (ca. 1900; 119 N. Piedmont Ave.) with corner tower. Mill housing survives in several areas.

CL 8 John Wells Log House

Late 18th c.; W side SR 2286,
0.5 mi. S of SR 2283, Grover vic.

The small house, described as the oldest in the county, is a recognizable example of the continued use and overbuilding of the region's principal early house type: the 1-room log house. Despite additions and new wall surfaces, the distinctively tall, compact form of the 1-room-with-loft structure is unmistakable, as are its windowless facade, the depth of its narrow gable-end window, and the massiveness of the chimney beneath its plaster. Family history reports it was built in 1780 for Revolutionary War veteran Wells.

CL 8 *John Wells Log House*

CL 9 Boiling Springs

The town is the home of Gardner-Webb College, a Baptist institution with a campus of conservative 20th-c. Colonial Revival brick buildings. The oldest is **E. B. Hamrick Hall** (1925, 1943, 1990), rebuilt after a late 20th-c. fire. A group of the county's distinctively decorated frame cottages lines N. Main St., including the **C. J. Hamrick House** (late 19th c.; 407 N. Main St.), with scalloped vents in the dormers (*McBrayer House, Shelby).

CL 10 Irvin-Hamrick Log House

Ca. 1794, 1860s; N side SR 1153, 0.2 mi.
NE of SR 1152, Boiling Springs vic.; private,
visible from road

The small dwelling of half-dovetailed log construction with fieldstone chimney is representative of thousands built in Piedmont and western N.C. The 2-room house was probably built by James Irvin, a veteran of

the Revolution. After 1850 it was the home of Street and Elmira Hamrick, who added the frame rear shed in the 1860s; their descendants maintain the homestead as a family shrine.

CL 11 Joseph Suttle House (Twin Chimneys)

Ca. 1840; private, no public visibility or access

The best-known antebellum residence in the county, the 2-story Federal style frame dwelling features massive gable-end chimneys and an ornamented late-19th-c. porch. Constructed for planter Minor Smith, it was owned after 1854 by Suttle, a prominent Baptist minister.

CL 12 Mooresboro

Mooresboro grew up near a junction of the Seaboard and Southern lines. From its early 20th-c. railroad era are the row of brick commercial buildings along W. Church St. and late 19th- and early 20th-c. frame residences such as the **Moorehead House** (ca. 1900; 203 W. Church St.), a 1-story Queen Anne dwelling with corner tower.

CL 13 Lattimore

Brick and frame store buildings cluster around the railroad to evoke the era when Civil War veteran Audley Martin Lattimore was the Seaboard depot agent, postmaster, and mayor, and when stores, cotton gins,

CL 11 *Joseph Suttle House*

CL 13 *Calton-Martin House*

an academy, hotels and restaurants, and William T. Calton's lumber company made the rail stop a busy center of trade from ca. 1880 to World War I. The frame **Lattimore Depot** (early 20th c.; moved to Peachtree St.) is board and batten with simple braces. There are modestly decorated cottages and numerous outbuildings. The architectural standout is the **Calton-Martin House** (1899–1900; Martin at Cherry St.) overlooking the railroad. The long, multigabled cottage doubtless served lumber manufacturer William T. Calton as an advertisement as much as a dwelling; its perfectly preserved porch of bulbous columns and rich sawnwork, swooping gables encrusted with shingles and oval vents, and fanciful "cupolas" at each end of the porch compose the county's tour-de-force example of the decorated cottage.

CL 14 Campcall General Store

Early 20th c.; NE side NC 226, opposite SR 1350, Campcall; private, visible from road

The large frame country general store is no longer in use but is well preserved, with a broad stepped-parapet front gable.

CL 15 Absolom Whisnant House

Early 19th c., ca. 1900; SW side NC 226, 0.9 mi. SE of Rutherford Co. line; private, visible from road

Showing two generations of farmhouse construction, the typical I-house, with end

CL 16 *Newton House*

chimneys and simple finish, gained a polygonal 1-story front addition, with shingled trim and turned porch posts.

CL 16 Newton House

Ca. 1885; W side NC 10, 0.2 mi. S of SR 1533, Casar vic.; private, visible from road

A distinctive element of the county's late 19th-c. rural architecture was the "kitchen flue," a small tower with pyramidal or gable roof and central chimney attached to the kitchen ells of many farmhouses. The structures housed woodstoves and expelled the heat through vents below the eaves while smoke escaped through the chimney. Some residents say the feature is of German origin and call it the "Dutch" or "Deutsch" chimney, but its source is not known. The 1-story Newton House, otherwise a typical late 19th-c. frame farmhouse, provides an excellent example of the feature close to the highway.

Gaston County (GS)

See Kim Withers Brengle, The Architectural Heritage of Gaston County, North Carolina (1982).

Known as "the combed yarn capital of the world," Gaston saw more textile mills than any other county in the nation—over 150 established between 1848 and 1950. The county was largely agricultural, however, from mid-18th-c. settlement well into the 19th c., with Scotch-Irish farmers settled along the Catawba, Germans along the South Fork and around present-day Mount Holly, and English and Africans. There were a few streamside mills and some iron, tin, and gold mining, the latter attracting Italian and Irish Catholics among the miners and leading to formation of one of the state's first Catholic churches and thence to other major Catholic institutions (*St. Joseph's, *Belmont Abbey). When the county was formed from Lincoln in 1846, it was named for William Gaston, supreme court justice from New Bern and Catholic lay leader (d. 1844).

In the mid-19th c., industrialists built the first textile mills on the great rivers, beginning with Mountain Island Mill on the Catawba (destroyed in the flood of 1916), established in 1848 as an outgrowth of Greensboro's Mount Hecla Mill. Adding good rail connections to reliable water power, enterprising descendants of Scotch-Irish and German settlers made Gaston a national textile center. When the county seat of Dallas rebuffed rail connections, Gastonia began in the 1870s on the Atlanta & Charlotte Air Line Railway, grew fast, and won county seat status in 1909. First on the Catawba and its tributaries, then beside the railroads, Gaston's mill communities constituted much of the textile "state" surrounding Charlotte, and Gaston's factories embodied early advances in technology, including electric lights at *McAden Mill and air conditioning at Chronicle Mills. In addition to those noted below, some industrial sites remain in Lowell, Bessemer City, Ranlo, and Spencer Mountain. Although many mills have been razed, important textile architecture survives, along with farmhouses and country churches from the agricultural past.

Gastonia (GS 1–7)

A national textile center known as the "City of Spindles," Gastonia has substantial architecture reflecting its early 20th-c. wealth. A stop on the 1872 Atlanta & Charlotte became a major crossing with the arrival of the Chester & Lenoir Narrow Gauge Railway a few years later, opening its future to manufacturing. The Gastonia Cotton Mfg. Co. was established in 1887 by George Gray, Robert Calvin Grier Love, and others as the first steam-powered mill in the county. (In 1924 grandson J. Spencer Love used the "old mill" machinery to begin Burlington Mills in Burlington.) Led by Gray, the Love family, and others, within 20 years Gastonia had 12 mills and became county seat in 1909. The greatest textile landmark is *Loray Mill, but a ring of other mills and villages, altered over the years, frames the city. Rapid growth and rising wealth supported commissions to architects from Charlotte, Atlanta, Columbia, and Washington, D.C. Much of the city's architectural distinction owes to architect Hugh White, who came from South Carolina in 1919 and built a legacy of Beaux Arts–influenced work.

GS 1 Downtown Gastonia

The principal public and commercial architecture concentrates along West Main Ave., South St., and Franklin Blvd. The **Former**

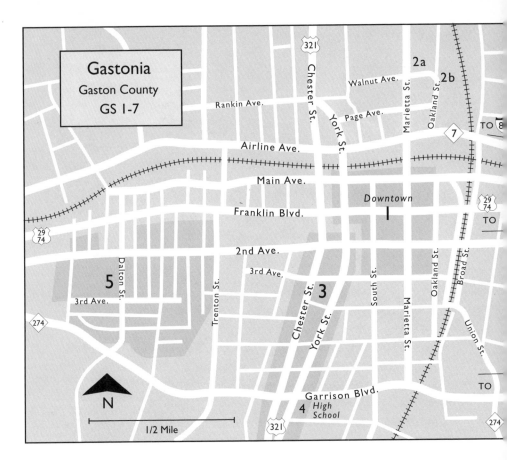

Gaston County Courthouse (1911; Milburn & Heister [Washington, D.C.], architects; 151 South St.) is a porticoed, tan brick building with Ionic-columned portico. For the **Gastonia City Hall** (1926; Hugh White, architect; 240 W. Franklin Blvd.) the resident architect provided an imposing 11-bay 2-story Renaissance Revival design with arched windows, roof balustrade, and entrance framed by four Ionic pilasters. **First Baptist Church** (1923; Willard G. Rogers [Charlotte], architect; 201 W. Franklin Blvd.), in Romanesque Revival style with Spanish Mission touches, has a green tile roof, tower, and arcaded cloister. The **First A.R.P. Church** (St. Mark's Episcopal) (1918; C. W. Spencer, builder; 258 W. Franklin Blvd.) has Doric porticoes facing two streets.

Notable commercial architecture on W. Main Ave. includes the Art Deco style **S. H. Kress Building** (1930; Edward F. Sibbert, architect; 111 W. Main Ave.), with the com-

GS 1 *Former Gaston Co. Courthouse*

pany architect's signature polychrome terra-cotta facade. Two classically detailed 7-story skyscrapers dominate the downtown: **First National Bank** (1917; Wilson & Sompayrac [Columbia, S.C.], architects; 168–70 W. Main Ave.), of tan brick with modillion cornice and roof balustrade, and **Third National Bank** (1923; Milburn & Heister; 195

GS 1 *Citizens National Bank*

W. Main Ave.), in red brick with upper and lower stories in granite. **Citizens National Bank** (1920s; Hugh White, architect; 210– 20 W. Main Ave.) is one of White's most impressive designs, a bold Neoclassical composition in stone with four Corinthian pilasters and an eagle above the entrance. The **John F. Love Building** (1904, ca. 1908; 213–23 W. Main Ave.), built for a founder of *Loray Mill, is one of the oldest commercial buildings, a 2-story stuccoed structure 11 bays long, with single and double segmental-arched windows. The **U.S. Post Office** (1935; Charles C. Hook & Walter W. Hook [Charlotte], architects; 301 W. Main Ave.), in the stripped classicism of its era, has Art Deco sunburst capitals in cast stone atop brick pilasters. The 3-story commercial buildings facing the courthouse include **Standard Hardware** (1920s; Hugh White, architect; 148–58 South St.), with triplets of windows lighting a central atrium.

Farther south, **Temple Emanuel** (1929; Hugh White, architect; 320 South St.) is a spare, temple-form Neoclassical Revival design for the city's only Jewish congregation. Nearby are **Memorial Hall** (1930; Hugh White, architect; 113 W. 2nd Ave.), a white-stuccoed auditorium with octagonal entrance tower, and **Gastonia Public Library** (1930; Hugh White; 115 W. 2nd Ave.), a simple Neoclassical building with half-round portico and authors' names over the windows. **Central School** (1914; Luther Proffitt [Spartanburg], architect; 201 E. 2nd Ave.) is an early consolidated school of red brick

with portico and flanking wings, which held all grades until *Gastonia High School was completed in 1924. The **Armstrong Hotel Apartments** (1920s; Marietta St. at E. 2nd Ave.), a complex composition of intersecting gables and porches, was built as a teacherage for Central.

GS 2 St. Stephens A.M.E. Zion Church (a) and St. Paul's Baptist Church (b)
1927; 602 N. Marietta St.;
1927; 418 N. Oakland Ave.

In the African American neighborhood that developed north of downtown, two leading denominations built similar, neighboring sanctuaries. Each is of simple Gothic Revival character with large towers flanking front gables; St. Stephens has contrasting towers, while St. Paul's has matching ones.

GS 3 York-Chester Neighborhood

The principal residential district for the white business and professional class grew along York and Chester Sts. southwest of downtown. Late 19th-c. houses include 1- or 2-story frame dwellings of traditional form with broad porches and several Queen Anne style houses. Some notable houses along the main thoroughfares were the work of Hugh White. He came to Gastonia as supervising architect for the Renaissance Revival style **Joseph Separk House** (1919; C. C. Wilson [Columbia, S.C.], architect; 209 W. 2nd Ave.) and soon established his own practice. He designed the **Beal-Ragan House** (1924; Hugh White, architect; 156 S. York St.), of "Italian renaissance type" with "mission tile roof," and many Colonial Revival residences. Bungalows and other houses line the

GS 2 *St. Paul's Baptist Church*

GS 3 *Beal-Ragan House*

intersecting numbered avenues from 2nd Ave. south to Garrison Blvd. West of the York-Chester area are millworker neighborhoods associated with *Loray and other mills.

GS 4 Former Gastonia High School

1922; Hugh White, architect; 800 S. York St.

Hailed at its completion as "one of the finest specimens of school architecture in the state" and "one of the most complete school plants in the South," the school is emblematic of the public-spiritedness of the city's business leadership. The 3-story Tudor Gothic building of dark red brick, rich with limestone moldings and ornament, presents a 4-story frontispiece with Tudor arched entrance above a grand staircase. It has been preserved and converted to apartments. (See Introduction, Fig. 57.)

GS 5 Loray Cotton Mill and Village

1900–1902, Lockwood, Greene Engineers (Boston), mill and village design; Park A. Dallis, supervisor; Flynt Construction Co. (Palmer, Mass.), builder; 1921, Robert & Co. Engineers (Atlanta); 2nd Ave. at Dalton St. and neighboring streets

Rising like a mountain above surrounding millworker neighborhoods and visible across much of the city, the 6-story Loray Cotton Mill with its 8-story tower is a prime landmark of textile history. Built of handsomely laid brick with segmental- and round-arched openings, the first immense building measures 504 by 130 feet. With its 1921 addition

of 100 by 140 feet, it was described as the largest textile mill in the South under one roof.

It was founded in 1900 by local textile leaders John F. Love, George Gray, and others, with its name formed from LOve and gRAY. Love was the son of a founder of the 1887 Gastonia Mfg. Co.; Gray, who began as a millhand as a boy and soon advanced to superintendent, was a founder of Gastonia Mfg. Co. and other mills. The company hired the prestigious Boston firm of Lockwood, Greene to plan a state-of-the-art mill and worker housing. The "Million Dollar Mill" incorporated the most advanced equipment and systems. In 1902 nearly 1,000 workers operated its 50,000 spindles and 1,600 looms. Financial problems beleaguered the enterprise, however, and management changed several times until the mill was purchased in 1920 by the Manville-Jenckes Co. of Pawtucket, R.I. The firm expanded for production of automobile tire fabrics, adding a 6-story wing and employing over 3,000 people.

Loray played a dramatic role in southern labor history. In 1928, seeking to reduce labor costs while maintaining high production levels, the company laid off hundreds of workers and reduced wages. Conditions ripened for labor confrontation. In 1929 the communist-led National Textile Workers Union targeted Loray for its southern textile organizing drive. A major strike began in April but soon weakened, and emotions flared in the divided city. The union's communist ideology blurred legitimate worker grievances, and its insistence on biracial organization eroded support among white southern millworkers. An exchange of gunfire in June between strikers and police killed Police Chief O. F. Aderholt. In September an antiunion mob fired on a truckload of strikers and killed millworker Ella Mae Wiggins, a mother of five who had composed ballads and motivated workers during the strike. National publicity focused on Loray as more violence followed. The union abandoned its efforts by late September. The failure and infamy of the strike did much to dampen organized labor in the state and region. In the 1930s Firestone pur-

GS 5 *Loray Cotton Mill and village*

chased the mill to manufacture fabric for tires. In 1998 the company donated the building to Preservation North Carolina for preservation and development.

The adjoining mill village included over 600 workers' houses and a 1929 population of 5,000. In the first decades of Loray's operation, the owners built some 30 blocks of mill housing in a then-rural outskirt. The principal house forms are a single-pile gable-end dwelling with a rear ell and small entrance porch and a double-pile variation with full-width shed porch. When Manville-Jenckes expanded, the firm spent $500,000 on the village, adding some 150 houses, most hip-roofed dwellings with offset front porches. Some were inserted between older houses; others were built on additional streets. Though altered over the years, much of the housing survives in the large village. (Also see Introduction, Fig. 49.)

GS 6 East Franklin Blvd.

Franklin Blvd. east of downtown was another focus of industrialists' houses. The **A. G. Mangum House** (1922; Hugh White, architect; 1215 E. Franklin Blvd.) shows White's Colonial Revival work in frame with hip roof and side porches. The **Robert Goldberg (Gurney) House** (1924; Joseph Neel Reid [Atlanta], architect; 1211 E. Franklin Blvd.) is one of the Atlanta Colonial Revival specialist's few works in the state: a mill owner's 7-bay Georgian Revival residence in Flemish-bond brick with pedimented entrance pavilion.

GS 7 Schiele Museum of Natural History
Est. 1961; 1500 E. Garrison Blvd.; open regular hours

The 17-acre civic museum and park encompasses a **Backcountry Farm** of moved and restored early 19th-c. buildings, including a log house from eastern Gaston, a kitchen, a barn, and other outbuildings. The **Catawba Indian Village** has reconstructions of a bark-covered house, a council house, and two log cabins representing the native people of the region.

GS 8 Lutheran Chapel Church
1923; Louis H. Asbury (Charlotte), architect; 702 N. New Hope Rd.

Built for a congregation of German descendants organized in 1828, the red brick Gothic Revival building has the cruciform plan, bold proportions, and big entrance tower with belfry favored by many Lutheran congregations.

GS 9 Dallas

The well-preserved commercial and residential buildings around the shaded courthouse square recall the scale and density once typical of county seats. The seat of the new county was established in 1846 and named for George Dallas, vice-president under James K. Polk. The **Gaston County Courthouse** (1847, 1875; now town hall) burned in 1874 but was rebuilt "on the old walls," resulting in the simple, pedimented Greek Revival style brick structure with second-story courtroom reached by a double exterior stair. Northeast is the old **Gaston County Jail** (1847; Avery or Abraham Mauney, builder; 108 E. Trade St.), a 2-story brick building of domestic scale with gable parapets, small iron-barred windows for cells above, and quarters for the sheriff and his family below.

On the southwest the **Hoffman Hotel** (1852; 131 W. Main St.) is a 3-story 7-bay brick building with 2-story porch, one of the oldest hotels in the state; it is now the Gaston County Museum of Art and History. Original woodwork and painting, including room numbers, survive on the upper floor. The **Rhyne Store** (1850; 130–32 N. Gaston St.) is a pediment-fronted brick commercial building in Greek Revival style, built for merchant and industrialist Moses Rhyne (*Moses Rhyne House). Representative of smaller 19th-c. town dwellings, the **Smyre-Pasour House** (1850, 1870; 113–15 N. Holland St.) is a 1-story house with simple Greek Revival detail. About 1880 the Chester & Lenoir Narrow Gauge Railway brought rail service, and the small, bracketed **Dallas Depot** (ca. 1900; 201 W. Main St.; moved) was built for the successor Carolina & North Western Railroad. Among many turn-of-the-century houses, the **Pinkney Summey House** (1903; 307 W. Trade St.) is a small Queen Anne dwelling rich with sawn ornament and wraparound porch with conical roof.

GS 10 Hoyle Family House

Late 18th?–early 19th c.; S side NC 275, 1.7 mi. NE of NC 279; private, visible from road

The 2-story weatherboarded house of unusual German American construction has a complex and still uncertain history. The 2-story front portion is of heavy timber frame construction with horizontal log infill—an 18th-c. method seen in mid-Atlantic German settlement areas but not otherwise in N.C. It was subsequently weatherboarded and given a "kicked" eave akin to late 18th-c. buildings in *Salem and elsewhere. The plan, altered over the years, has 4 main rooms and an interior end chimney with corner fireplaces. A rear wing came later in the 19th c. Tradition attributes its construction to German immigrant Pieter Heyl (Hoyle), granted the land in 1754, or his son Jacob. From 1794 to 1850 it was owned by Pieter's grandson "rich Andrew" Hoyle, farmer and pioneer industrialist. A dendrochronology study pointed to a surprisingly late 1820s first phase, which is still under investigation.

GS 11 Eli Hoyle House

1832; N side NC 275, 1.5 mi. NE of NC 279, Dallas vic.; private, visible from road

Built for Andrew Hoyle's son Eli, the 2-story frame house is the most sophisticated Federal style residence in the county. With its symmetrical 5-bay facade, vertical proportions, tall gable-end chimneys, and delicate Federal finish, it presents a striking contrast with the traditional house across the road.

GS 12 Andrew Carpenter House

1836–37; N side SR 1820, 2.0 mi. E of SR 1902, Lucia vic.

The 2-story 5-bay Federal style plantation house is one of the county's largest early

GS 9 *Hoffman Hotel*

19th-c. houses, 2 rooms deep with paired chimneys. It was probably built soon after Andrew's 1831 marriage to Sophia Smith, daughter of planter David Smith of nearby *Magnolia in Lincoln Co., of the close-knit society of Catawba valley planters.

GS 13 Thomas Rhyne House

1799; NW side SR 1918, 2.4 mi. E of NC 27; private, visible from road

With the date "1799" boldly laid into the brickwork of the south endwall, the house exemplifies western Piedmont decorative brickwork of the late 18th and early 19th centuries. The 2-story 5-bay house with hip roof is built of Flemish-bond brick painted white. It gained Greek Revival woodwork after an 1851 fire. Thomas Rhyne, born in Germany in 1742, settled in the area in the 1760s and amassed several thousand acres. The house and its outbuildings descended in the family.

GS 14 St. Joseph's Catholic Church

1844; SW corner NC 273 and SR 1918, Mt. Holly vic.

The small frame church with pedimented front is one of the two oldest Catholic churches in the traditionally Protestant state. St. Joseph's was established under the leadership of Father T. J. Cronin for Italian and Irish miners in the antebellum gold boom. It was dedicated in 1844 — as was #St. Paul's Catholic Church in New Bern, whose founder, William Gaston, contributed to

GS 14 *St. Joseph's Catholic Church*

St. Joseph's building fund. Father Jeremiah O'Connell, who arrived in 1871, initiated such institutions as *Belmont Abbey.

GS 15 Mountain Island Dam and Power Plant

1922–23; on Catawba River at end of SR 1933, Mount Holly vic.

Building one plant after another to maximize systematic regional use of the Catawba River's power, the Southern Power Co. chose an old waterpower site convenient to high demand in Charlotte and Gaston Co. Here Gaston's first textile mill, the Mountain Island Mill, began in 1848 as an outgrowth of Greensboro's Mount Hecla Mill; the old mill and its village were swept away in the flood of 1916. Built for Southern by the Catawba Mfg. & Electric Co., a subsidiary, the concrete gravity dam has a spillway of about 1,000 feet, and the powerhouse is a large brick and concrete structure.

GS 16 Mount Holly

The community on Dutchman's Creek began in the 18th c. as Woodlawn, evidently the first village in present-day Gaston Co. Of that old village the chief vestige is the **Johnston-Nims House** (1820, 1859; 740 Woodlawn Ave.), a 2-story frame Federal style house built for William and Mary Forney Johnston. It was enlarged with an Italianate front section for Frederick Nims, civil engineer with the Wilmington, Charlotte & Rutherford Railroad (WC&RRR), which crossed the Catawba River here by 1860 and set the stage for industrial development. In

GS 13 *Thomas Rhyne House*

1876 local men Abel P. Rhyne, Daniel E. Rhyne, and Ambrose Costner opened the **Mount Holly Mill** (N. Main St. at Alsace Ave.) on the creek, the county's fourth mill and the first built after the war; the town took its name in 1879. Akin to nearby Lowell, they named it for Mount Holly, N.J., producer of the nation's finest cotton yarns. Now the oldest in the county, the mill is a functional 2-story brick building with a 3-story addition (1916). By 1891 the town had three other mills. The **Lutheran Church of the Good Shepherd** (1903; 110 S. Main St.), built by a German-descended congregation est. 1881, is a Gothic Revival brick structure with a massive 3-stage corner entrance tower. The imposing **Augusta Rhyne Cannon House** (1894; R. F. Rankin, builder; 137 E. Charlotte Ave.), a 2-story brick Queen Anne style house with ornate porch, was a wedding gift of mill founder A. P. Rhyne to his daughter and her husband Ernest Cannon. The same builder erected the similar **Dellinger-Nantz House** (1899; R. F. Rankin, builder; 714 N. Main St.) north of town.

GS 17 Belmont

Located in the "South Point" at the confluence of the Catawba and the South Fork Catawba at the S.C. line, Belmont is one of the state's leading textile towns. Called Garibaldi after an engineer, it began as a depot on the Atlanta & Charlotte Air Line Railway when the line crossed the Catawba about 1873 and was renamed in 1886 for August Belmont of New York (*Belmont Abbey). Frame houses of business founders recall the depot village. The **Abram Stowe House** (ca. 1875; 35 E. Catawba St.) is a 2-story house of traditional form with simple late Greek Revival detail, built for the first mayor. The (first) **Robert Lee Stowe Sr. House** (1899; 32 E. Catawba St.) is a Victorian cottage with wraparound porch, first home of a young merchant and his bride and a modest beginning for a leading industrialist.

In 1901 local men Robert Lee Stowe Sr., his brother Samuel Pinckney Stowe, and Abel Caleb Lineberger founded Chronicle

Mills, beginning an association that created 20 mills in and around Belmont. (The much-altered Chronicle Mills [Chronicle St.] had a pioneering air conditioning system by Willis Carrier, who inspected it in 1906.) The mills and villages have been greatly altered, with the best preserved village at *North Belmont.

As the town grew from 145 residents in 1900 to 4,000 by 1930, textile wealth underwrote substantial commercial and residential buildings. Near the railroad is the **Stowe Brothers Co. Building** (1904; 6 N. Main St.), a 2-story brick building with segmental-arched windows and decorative brickwork, home of the mercantile business of R. L. and S. P. Stowe (est. 1889). The **Piedmont & Northern Railway Depot** (1915; Charles C. Hook [Charlotte], architect; 4 N. Main St.; railroad museum) served the state's only electrified interurban short line, operated by the Southern Power Co. between Charlotte and Gastonia via Mount Holly, with a branch to Belmont. Hook's firm had the commission for Piedmont & Northern stations, all with cheery red tile roofs and yellow brick walls above a red brick base.

GS 17 *Piedmont & Northern Depot*

Dominating the downtown is the **Bank of Belmont** (1926; Hugh White, architect; 32 N. Main St.), a 3-story building of buff brick with cast-stone Neoclassical detail. Concentrated around N. Main St. and S. Central Ave., houses of unusual distinction for a small town recall its textile wealth. The (second) **Robert L. Stowe Sr. House** (1917; 135 N. Main St.) is a big brick Colonial Revival House with elliptical arched entrance. The (first) **Abel Caleb Lineberger Sr. House** (1910; Charles C. Hook, architect; 203 N. Main St.) is a 1½-story frame house

GS 17 *(Second) A. C. Lineberger Sr. House*

blending Victorian, bungalow, and Tudor Revival motifs, while the (second) **Abel Caleb Lineberger Sr. House** (1919–21; Charles C. Hook, architect; Earle S. Draper, landscape architect; 411 N. Main St.) is among the grandest mansions in the region. Combining opulence with a Progressive Era concern for light and air, the symmetrical Renaissance Revival style residence of buff brick has a broad hip roof of green tile, which shelters 2-story porches at both ends. Arched first-floor openings with French doors open onto a terrace, and landscaping includes formal and informal gardens. Notable residences along S. Central Ave. include the **S. P. Stowe House** (ca. 1922; Hugh White, architect; 203 S. Central Ave.), a red brick Renaissance Revival house with green tile hip roof built for the third partner.

GS 18 Belmont Abbey Basilica and Belmont Abbey College

Basilica, 1892–93; Peter Dederichs (Detroit), architect (attrib.); 1900 and later, Father Michael McInerney, architect; E side SR 2093, 0.25 mi. N of I-85, Belmont vic.

Architecturally and historically, the church and associated monastery and college compose one of the most distinguished Roman Catholic institutions in the southeastern United States. (In 1998 the Abbey Cathedral was designated a basilica.) In 1871 Father Jeremiah O'Connell of *St. Joseph's acquired a farm and offered it to the abbot of St. Vincent's Archabbey in Latrobe, Pa., the first Benedictine monastery in the United States. In 1876 a group of Benedictines arrived, built a frame chapel known as Maryhelp, and opened St. Mary's college for boys. The present **Monastery**, a long, simply detailed 3-story building of brick, was erected by the monks themselves in 1880 and was later expanded. In 1884 the mission became Maryhelp Abbey, first in the Southeast. For 39 years Abbot Leo Haid led the growing institution. The brick **College Building** (Robert Lee Stowe Hall) was begun in 1886 and given a Gothic Revival tower after a 1900 fire.

On St. Benedict's Day, March 21, 1892, the monks broke ground for the **Belmont Abbey Church**, which was dedicated in

GS 18 *Belmont Abbey Basilica*

1894 by James Cardinal Gibbons. Like the town, the new name honored New York financier August P. Belmont, a friend of Abbot Haid. German-born architect Peter Dederichs of Detroit designed many Catholic buildings in Michigan. With its great spired towers of unequal size, the large church has the soaring height and rich detail of the late Gothic Revival, with dark red brick set off by stone-coped buttresses, lancet windows, and crocketed finials. The interior reflects liturgical changes of the 1960s.

Buildings erected for a half-century after 1900 embody the work of Father Michael McInerney. Son of an Irish immigrant stonemason, he apprenticed with an architectural firm in Pittsburgh before enrolling at Belmont Abbey and professing as a monk in 1903. McInerney was a master of what has been called the American Benedictine style, a Gothic Revival mode of restrained ornament and strongly vertical forms. From Belmont Abbey, for over 50 years he designed scores of Catholic buildings in at least 13 states. **St. Leo Hall** (1910), his first major work, is probably the purest expression of his style. The tall 3½-story brick building with simple Gothic detailing has buttressed corners and entrance pavilions rising into steep gabled dormers. In **The Haid** (1929) McInerney adapted the idiom for a gymnasium. He later accommodated modernist principles: **Abbot Vincent Taylor Library** is a horizontal building of rectilinear form, blending with the campus in its dark red brick and McInerney's favored long-shafted cross.

GS 19 Former Sacred Heart College

Est. 1891; 1920 and later, Father
Michael McInerney, architect;
414 N. Main St., Belmont

Following the monastery and college for men at *Belmont Abbey, Abbot Haid began a religious community and school for women (now across I-85). In 1899 **Mercedes Hall** was completed, a 2-story brick chapel and 3-story convent with cupola and gambrel-fronted pavilion. From 1922 to 1966 Father McInerney designed or supervised the

major buildings. Among these, in a quadrangle with Mercedes are the 3-story **Victory Hall** (1922) and the **Administration Building** (1928), featuring a 4-bay central tower with arcaded third stage. The school closed in 1987; the campus serves other religious and community functions.

GS 20 North Belmont Mill District

Early 20th c.; SR 2040

One of the region's most intact mill villages, North Belmont contains over 400 1-story mill houses, most with hipped roofs and front dormers, and many recently renovated. The village served four spinning mills erected in the 1910s by the Stowe-Lineberger group—Stowe, Acme, Perfection, and Linford—which continue in various states of alteration and expansion.

GS 21 Moses Rhyne House

1860–65; SE side SR 2040, 0.7 mi.
S of SR 2050, Belmont vic.

The well-preserved brick house of Italianate style was begun just before the Civil War for Moses and Margaret Hoffman Rhyne and completed afterward. Merchant and industrialist Moses founded the *Rhyne Store in Dallas and Woodlawn (Pinhook) Mill on the South Fork Catawba in 1852, the county's second textile mill. The couple's children included Susan (who married textile leader Robert Calvin Grier Love) and industrialists Abel P. and Daniel E. Rhyne (*Lenoir-Rhyne College).

GS 22 McAdenville

Surely the state's most picturesque textile mill town, and famed in recent times for its annual display of Christmas lights, McAdenville is the most intact of three nearby mill towns along the South Fork Catawba. (Upstream is Lowell, site of the 1852 Woodlawn Mill, named in 1879 for the Massachusetts textile center; downstream is *Cramerton [1906].) The community began in 1881 with construction of the Spring Shoals Mfg. Co. (named for early landowner Adam Springs), the county's sixth and then largest mill. Founder Rufus Yancey McAden of Charlotte was a Caswell Co. native and great-grandson of the pioneer Presbyterian preacher Hugh McAden. When incorporated in 1883, town and mill were named for the owner.

Two early sections of the mill survive by the river behind a later building. **McAden Mill No. 1** (1881–82) is a 1-story building with segmental-arched windows and triangular patterned brickwork. McAden Mills was first in the state if not the South to use electric lights, powered by a generator said to have been installed by Thomas Edison in 1882. McAden employed George Gray to begin the mill and install the electric lights. Formerly superintendent at Woodlawn Mill, Gray had equipped and operated the Charlotte Cotton Mill, and after McAdenville, he founded mills himself (*Loray Mill). The architecturally romantic **McAden Mill No. 2** (1885) takes a castle-like 1-story form with crenellated cornice, turreted round towers at original corners, and a 4-stage square tower over the central entrance. The **McAden Mill Office** (1906) is a 1-story 7-bay building with segmental-arched windows and parapet gables. Across the street, **McAden Mill No. 3** (1907) has apparently the state's only classically detailed mill facade, with Ionic pilasters, dentils, and egg-and-dart ornament. During the Great Depression the business was acquired by Stowe Mills of Belmont; its subsidiary, Pharr Yarns, made improvements to the mill and village.

A small commercial district of 1-story brick stores fronts Main St. **R. Y. McAden Memorial Hall** (1908; 27 Main St.) is a 2-story, frame, classically detailed library and community hall. Scattered along Main and Poplar Sts. to its south are sixteen 2-story 2-family **Mill Houses**, an unusual set of textile workers' housing in brick, which formed the original mill village when Mill #1 was completed in 1882. Later mill houses are of frame, most 1-story with gable fronts.

On hills overlooking the river and village are homes of founders and managers. The **Rufus Yancey McAden House** (1880s; N side Main St.), a gambrel-roofed Colonial Revival House built on the site of landowner Adam Springs's antebellum house, contains

GS 22 *McAden Mill No. 2*

offices for Pharr Yarns. West is the **Benjamin McAden House** (late 1880s; Hillcrest St.), the lavishly decorated Victorian cottage of the founder's son. The **W. H. Rumfelt House** (late 1880s; s side Main St. at Ford St.) is a prominent 2-story frame Italianate house with porch brackets forming graceful arches.

GS 23 Cramerton

Cramerton was long considered one of the state's model mill communities. The site where the Southern Railway crossed the South Fork Catawba offered both power and transportation for industry. In 1906 J. H. Mays of Charlotte built a spinning mill and called the place Maysworth. Stuart Cramer of Charlotte, founding director and architect of the Mays mill, acquired controlling interest in 1915 and began a major expansion. Cramer was a widely acclaimed engineer, inventor, and mill architect, described at his death in 1940 as having "stood, Saul-like, head and shoulders above the crowd" of southern textile men. First with D. A. Tompkins of Charlotte and from 1895 on his own, he is said to have designed or equipped a third of all new textile mills in the South between 1895 and 1905. His patented system of air conditioning for mills (1906) revolutionized the industry. (*Parks-Cramer Mfg. Co.; *Highland Park Mill, Charlotte).

Renaming the company and town, in the early 1920s Cramer added weaving and dying plants to the spinning operation and improved the village. The town is laid out along a high ridge above the river and is bisected by the railroad tracks. Mill houses are typically 1-story frame bungalows. Cramer provided schools, churches, recreation centers, and other amenities. Still standing are the **Cramerton Town Hall** (ca. 1907, 1920s; 155 N. Main St.), a 2-story brick building erected as offices for Mays and expanded for civic use, and two Gothic Revival brick churches of the 1920s, **Cramer Memorial Methodist Church** (154 N. Main St.) and **First Baptist Church** (235 Eighth Ave.). In 1946 Cramer heirs sold Cramerton Mills to Burlington Industries, which operated the factories into the 1970s. The mills have been demolished and their riverside site scraped clean.

GS 24 John D. B. McLean House

Ca. 1900; Lawson Henderson Stowe, builder; E side NC 279, 0.2 mi. S of NC 273; private, visible from road

The 2-story frame farmhouse is one of the most visible of several well-crafted Italianate style houses erected by builder Stowe; all are I-houses with end chimneys, low gable roofs with bracket cornices, and porches with turned and sawn ornament.

GS 25 William Joseph Wilson House

Ca. 1824; SR 1109, 0.6 mi. S of SR 1108, Crowder's Creek vic.; private, visible from road

The 2-story Flemish-bond brick house, exemplary of the region, combines mid-Atlantic traditional elements with restrained Federal style motifs. Four end chimneys serve the center-passage plan. The porch and other elements date from the later 19th c. Here in 1827 farmer Wilson hosted state geologist Dr. Elisha Mitchell (#Mt. Mitch-

GS 25 *William Joseph Wilson House*

ell), who was investigating lime and gold deposits and recorded, "He lives in a large brick house, four rooms to a floor. He is a plain man. . . . Sent word to his wife . . . that we should want some supper and nodded to her in a very kindly way when we descended into the underground room for our repast." Two years later, when gold was discovered near Kings Mountain, Wilson formed a mining company that by 1840 had produced some $60,000 worth of gold.

GS 26 Long Creek Presbyterian Church

1876; NW corner SR 1402 and 1401, Bessemer City vic.

The simple gable-fronted frame church, one of the oldest in the county, stands on a rise overlooking its ancient cemetery. The congregation was founded ca. 1780 as a center of Scotch-Irish settlement in western Gaston Co.

GS 27 Cherryville

The community in a German-settled area began as a crossroads village, which after the ca. 1862 arrival of the WC&RRR was named for a row of cherry trees along the old post road. In 1881 the *Cherryville Mfg. Co. was established, followed over the next three decades by a half-dozen other textile mills, a brick manufactory, and a foundry, which supported construction of ambitious commercial and residential buildings. A landmark in the row of 2-story brick commercial buildings is the former **Cherryville Town Hall** (Cherryville Museum) (1911; Kendrick Bros., builders; 109 E. Main St.), its tan

GS 27 *Cherryville Town Hall and Self & Hoffman Building*

brick facade a robust blend of Neoclassical and Italianate elements, with tile roof and arched bays for the fire truck, police station, and administrative offices. The **Self & Hoffman Building** (1913; 113 E. Main St.), which repeats the brick and arches below a shaped parapet, had a pharmacy below and Dr. Lucius Self's office above. The **First National Bank** (1916; Willard G. Rogers [Charlotte], architect; 100 S. Mountain St. at Main St.) is a 3-story red brick building with strong classical details. The **Cherryville Heritage Park** (Jacob St.) assembles small 19th-c. buildings from the early town, including a frame town office (1892) and log jail; a 1-room frame schoolhouse (1892) from a nearby farm; and the log **Bonded Liquor Warehouse** (1850s), a rare building from the era of small-scale government-licensed whiskey distilleries, which ended with Prohibition. Houses of various styles date from ca. 1870 to 1930. Unusual is the **N. B. Kendrick House** (1920s; Hugh White [Gastonia], architect; N. Mountain St.), a brick Neoclassical residence with arcaded brick porch, showcasing products of Kendrick's brick and tile company.

South of the town center is the **Cherryville Mfg. Co.** (1891 and later; S. Mountain St. at Academy St.), a 2-story brick building with 3-story tower, the first of several textile mills founded by local families. Later mills have been extensively altered. The **Cherry-**

ville Depot (1910s; Depot St. near E. Main St.) by the tracks is a brick station of standard form with bracketed eaves.

Beam's Shell Service Station (ca. 1930; 117 N. Mountain St.) is one of the state's best-preserved early 20th-c. gas stations, a stucco and brick building with Spanish Mission style ceramic tile roof and big round-arched windows, newly restored with antique gas pumps in front. During the depression, C. Grier Beam set up his trucking business here in his brother Guy's gas station. Starting with a used 1931 truck purchased for $360, he built the business into Carolina Freight Carriers, the nation's sixth largest trucking company, with $800 million in annual revenues at his death in 1992. Next door the **C. Grier Beam Carolina Freight Truck Museum** has a collection of antique freight trucks and tractor-trailers, most painted the company's deep red signature color of the 1930s–1950s era.

GS 28 Pasour-Black-Beam House
Ca. 1860; N side SR 1626, 0.2 mi.
E of NC 279, Cherryville vic.

On a hill overlooking the Beaverdam Creek valley, the 2-story brick Italianate house with ornate porch was built for distiller Eli Pasour and was later the home of Grier Beam.

GS 29 St. Mark's Lutheran Church
1924; E side SR 1438, 1.0 mi.
N of NC 279, Cherryville vic.

The cruciform Gothic Revival brick church, akin to the older *Bethel Lutheran Church, has buttressed central entrance tower and lancet windows. Built for a congregation founded in the 1790s, it is a landmark of German settlement in the South Fork Catawba area.

GS 30 Bethel Lutheran Church
1893; W side SR 1609, 0.8 mi.
N of NC 279, Cherryville vic.

The cruciform Gothic Revival brick church with central entrance tower is among the oldest in the area. In a familiar sequence, the congregation built an initial log church at its founding ca. 1830, built a frame church in the 1860s, then built the brick church at the end of the century.

GS 31 Lander's Chapel Methodist Church and School

Early 20th c.; W side SR 1609, 0.1 mi. N of SR 1618, High Shoals vic.

Pairing of country schools with churches was common in rural areas until public school consolidation in the 1920s. Built for a congregation founded in 1835, the brick church (1925) takes a cruciform plan with a crenellated entrance tower. The 1-story hip-roofed brick school (1912) has two classrooms and a rear auditorium-gymnasium.

Cabarrus County (CA)

See Peter R. Kaplan, The Historic Architecture of Cabarrus County, North Carolina *(1981).*

The county was formed in 1792 from northeastern Mecklenburg Co. and named for Stephen Cabarrus of Edenton, Speaker of the House of Commons. Drained by the Rocky River and its tributaries, it was settled in the mid-18th c. by Germans in the east and Scotch-Irish in the west—two principal north-south creeks are Dutch Buffalo ("Deutsch") and Irish Buffalo. A few Welsh and English settled in the center. A mixed agricultural economy was enriched by gold mining after the nation's first discovery of gold in 1799 (*Reed Gold Mine); the precious metal was extracted through the 19th c. Textile mills erected in the late 19th and early 20th centuries made Cabarrus Co. one of the state's leading producers, with the new town of *Kannapolis the state's largest one-company town. The eastern and southern sections of the county retain a rural character, while commercial and industrial development flanks the I-85 corridor in the west.

Concord (CA 1–6)

The prosperous county seat retains notable late 19th- and early 20th-c. architecture created largely by textile money: commercial district, fine residential neighborhoods along *N. and *S. Union St., and mills and their villages in satellite communities. Founded in 1796, Concord was named for the harmonious resolution of a dispute between German and Scotch-Irish inhabitants over the site of the courthouse. Its major thoroughfare, Union St., reiterated the theme. The 1856 arrival of the North Carolina Railroad (NCRR) transformed the village into a regional cotton market. Textile manufacturing began before the Civil War, and the profits of Concord's cotton buyers furnished the capital for the tremendous postwar textile boom. John Milton Odell's successful textile enterprises began in 1877 and were eventually overshadowed by those of James William Cannon. By 1900 Concord was the state's eighth largest town.

CA 1 Old Cabarrus County Courthouse
1875–76; George S. H. Appleget (Raleigh and Charlotte), architect; F. W. Ahrens (Charlotte), builder; Union St.

The towered courthouse, one of the finest Victorian public buildings in the state, is the work of New Jersey native Appleget,

who specialized in the Second Empire or "French" style (*Heck-Andrews House and *Estey Hall, Raleigh). The stuccoed building combines the mansard roof of the Second Empire style with a classical pedimented central pavilion and modillion and dentil cornices. The building was expanded to the rear and the front porch was replaced in 1914.

CA 1 *Old Cabarrus Co. Courthouse*

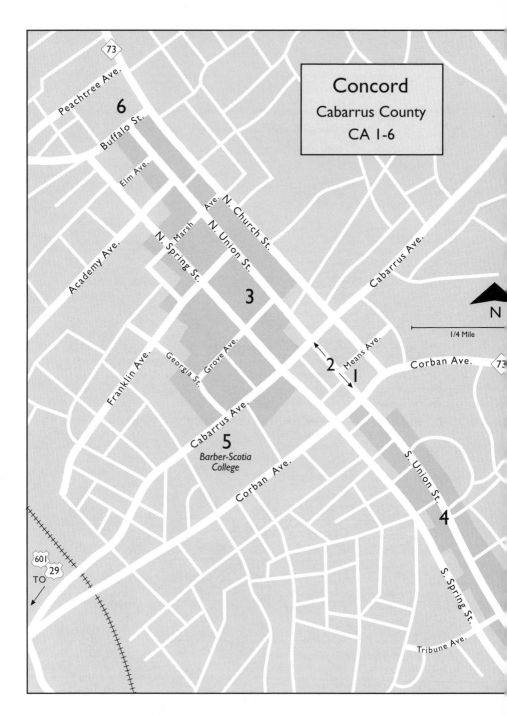

N

1/4 Mile

CA 2 Downtown Concord

Several commercial buildings retain intact upper stories, most notably the **Pythian Building** (1902; 36–40 S. Union St.), a dra- matic 3-story 5-bay facade of rusticated stone veneer. Notable from the 1920s are the **Cabarrus Bank & Trust Co.** (1923; 57 S. Union St.) and the **Concord National Bank & Hotel Concord** (1925; 2–14

N. Union St.), 6-story buildings of brick-veneered reinforced concrete with classical trim.

CA 3 North Union Street

The 25-block area was the turf of Concord's industrialists, merchants, and professionals in the late 19th and early 20th centuries and remains one of the finest neighborhoods of the period in N.C. The spine is the 6-block section of N. Union from Grove to Buffalo Aves. The full catalog of architectural fashions ranges from the traditional 3-bay houses of the early post–Civil War years to the historicism of the late 1920s, with many good examples of the Italianate, Queen Anne, Colonial Revival, and bungalow styles in between. The outstanding 19th-c. house is the resplendently bracketed **John Milton Odell House** (late 1870s, expanded 1890s; 288 N. Union St.), built for the town's leading industrialist in a Second Empire mode similar to Appleget's courthouse. (See Introduction, Fig. 61.) The Queen Anne style is exemplified in the **James William Cannon House** (ca. 1900; 65 N. Union St.), the towered home of the textile leader. Several of the finest Colonial Revival style houses are by Charlotte architect Louis H.

Asbury, including the **J. Archibald Cannon House** (1912; 108 N. Union St.), with tall hip roof and Tuscan porch. The **Charles Albert Cannon House** (1928; Charles Barton Keen [Philadelphia], architect; 94 N. Union St.), a grand 7-bay neo-Federal house with 3-bay wings, was designed by a favorite architect of Winston-Salem industrialists. Charles A. Cannon was one of the six sons of J. W. Cannon, and his wife, Ruth Coltrane Cannon, was a pioneer in the state's historic preservation movement. Another outstanding neo-Federal house is the brick **William Winslow Flowe House** (1920s; William H. Peeps [Charlotte], architect; 113 Grove Ave. NW), with Doric porch and round-arched dormer windows. Peeps also designed the elaborate Tudor Revival **E. T.**

CA 3 *James W. Cannon House*

CA 3 *North Union St.*

Cannon House (late 1920s; William H. Peeps, architect; 58 N. Union St.) in brick with stone trim and bay and oriel windows. The **First Presbyterian Church** (1927; Hobart Upjohn, architect; 70 Union St.) shows the popular architect's suave handling of the Georgian Revival, with Flemish-bond brickwork and a soaring, multistage steeple.

CA 4 South Union Street

By the late 19th c. the residential section south of the courthouse paralleled the spirit, if not the scale, of the N. Union St. neighborhood, with simplified versions of the Italianate, Second Empire, Queen Anne, Colonial Revival, and bungalow styles. The **James Dayvault House** (ca. 1901; 216 S. Union St.) is a notable Queen Anne example with arched spindle friezes dramatizing its wraparound porch. The **D. L. Bost House** (1905; Charles C. Hook & Willard G. Rogers [Charlotte], architects; 154 S. Union St.) synthesizes the Queen Anne and Colonial Revival, its second story a distinctive round tower with a conical roof. Presiding over the street is **St. James Lutheran Church** (1927–28; 100 S. Union St.), the town's most prominent late Gothic Revival sanctuary, with granite walls rising to a tall tower and nave.

CA 5 Barber-Scotia College
145 Cabarrus Ave. W

The school was founded by the Presbyterian Church in 1867 as Scotia Seminary, a boarding school for young black women, and merged with Barber Memorial College of Anniston, Ala., in 1930. **Graves Hall** (1876, 1881) and **Faith Hall** (1891) are, with the 1876 courthouse, the county's finest late 19th-c. institutional structures. Graves Hall, built by courthouse contractor F. W. Ahrens, repeats motifs from Appleget's vocabulary: a central entrance pavilion, round- and segmental-arched windows, quoins, string courses, hoodmolds, and corbeling. Faith Hall is a longer, lower building with mansard roof and tower and similar window arrangements and brickwork.

CA 6 Odell-Locke-Randolph Mill
1882, 1888, 1909; N end of N. Union St.

Occupying an elevated site at the head of N. Union St. once known as Forest Hill, this is the oldest and most prominent of Concord's several textile mills. It is preserved as one of the state's most ambitious adaptive uses of former industrial buildings. The county's first textile mill, a locally financed steam-powered plant, operated at this site from 1840 until 1873. In 1877 John Milton Odell, a Randolph Co. native who began his career with the *Cedar Falls Mfg. Co. and who had come to Concord as a cotton buyer in 1869, purchased and reopened the old mill, kindling Concord's expansion into one of the state's leading industrial towns. (Odell also had mills in *Bynum and four other Piedmont towns and a large hardware store in Greensboro [*Odell Hardware Co.].) He expanded the Concord factory four times between 1882 and 1899, and by 1888 it was the largest plaid mill in the South. In 1908 financial reversals forced Odell's sale of the mill, and fire destroyed the 1840 building and two of Odell's additions. George W. Watts of Durham, an associate of the Duke family, acquired the property, rebuilt, and founded Locke Cotton Mills, named for its manager Locke Erwin, another Duke associate. After the Locke Mill failed during the depression, Randolph Mills of *Franklinville operated the facility until it closed in 1974. In the 1980s Concord investors rehabilitated the mill for office and residential use.

The major surviving components of the mill complex are Odell's 1882 3-story addition with a corbeled 4-story tower on the

CA 5 *Graves Hall, Barber-Scotia College*

CA 6 *Odell-Locke-Randolph Mill*

southeast corner of the block, his 1-story 1899 addition with castellated 3-story tower to the north, and the largest section, a 1- and 2-story building fully 40 bays long with sawtooth skylights and 2-story tower facing Buffalo St., erected in 1909 by Watts. A few other support facilities also survive, including a 125-foot brick boiler stack of 1889. Northwest of the mill are the vestiges of the Forest Hill Mill Village, with a few dozen 1-story side-gabled mill houses erected by Odell and Locke Mills between the 1880s and 1920s.

Encircling the town are other mills, some with remnants of workers' villages, in various stages of alteration, expansion, or demolition. Several are associated with the early career of James William Cannon (*Kannapolis).

CA 7 Coleman Mill and Coleman-Franklin-Cannon Mill Village
Late 1890s–1901; expanded, 1911–21; NE side intersection of Warren Coleman Blvd. (US 601) and Old Charlotte Rd.

This was the first textile plant in the United States to be initiated, owned, and operated by blacks. Warren Clay Coleman was the son of white businessman Rufus Barringer of Concord and Roxanna Coleman, a slave. After the Civil War Coleman succeeded at several small businesses and began buying property and building rental houses. By 1895 he was one of the South's wealthiest blacks and was active in several business associations and philanthropies. Seeking to improve black economic opportunities through capitalism, in the late 1890s he sought both

black and white investors for construction of Coleman Mill, which was completed in 1901 and operated for 3 years. Market conditions and undercapitalization of the mill forced its closing in 1904, and Coleman died the same year. His short-lived venture was a source of hope for the state's black population during a time of worsening race relations, and it inspired other black enterprises. J. W. Cannon purchased the plant in 1906 and soon enlarged it to its present size. The original section is a small 3-story structure with stair tower, segmental-arched windows, and a tapered chimney stack. Coleman erected at least 5 units of employee housing that may still stand among others in the Cannon village south and east of the mill.

CA 8 Stonewall Jackson Training School
1909–40; Louis Asbury (Charlotte), architect; both sides SR 1157, 0.2 mi. N of NC 49, Concord vic.

Founded in 1907 as the state's first juvenile corrections facility, the campus of more than 30 school and farm structures was Charlotte architect Asbury's largest single project. Buildings are executed mainly in a simplified red brick Colonial Revival style and stand amid natural outcroppings of boulders. Concord became the site of the school when local citizens and the King's Daughters, a women's Masonic group, supplemented a meager legislative appropriation to purchase 300 acres south of town. The trustees hired young Asbury to design the first cottages, which began the architect's 20-

CA 8 *Stonewall Jackson Training School*

year association with the school. In time 15 cottages—actually 2-story residential buildings on raised basements—were built, some named for various donor counties; all have slate roofs, modillion cornices, Tuscan porch posts, and other Colonial Revival detail. Other structures are the porticoed Administration Building (1910), a rustic stone chapel (1913) across the road, and a stone bridge (1920) to the chapel. A school farm built in the 1920s includes gambrel- and gable-roofed barns and tiled silos.

CA 9 Kannapolis

One of the last major towns established in N.C., Kannapolis was long the state's largest unincorporated municipality and its most famous one-industry, company-controlled mill town. Industrialist J.W. Cannon began its promotion in 1907 as an expansion of his Cannon Mfg. Co. in Concord, where surrounding development and high land prices constricted growth of his business. A native of Mecklenburg Co., Cannon came to Concord in 1869, the same year as J. M. Odell (*Odell-Locke-Randolph Mill). Starting as a cotton buyer, in time he entered textile manufacturing in association with Odell and eventually overtook his mentor to head one of the largest industrial enterprises in N.C. history.

For his new town Cannon selected a site on the old NCRR (Southern Railway) at the Rowan-Cabarrus county line and engaged Charlotte mill engineer Stuart W. Cramer to lay out the town (*Cramerton, Gaston Co.), which Cannon named to suggest a Greek city of looms. The venture was an astonishing success, and Kannapolis grew rapidly between 1907 and 1920. With seven cloth mills and a full complement of finishing, sewing, packaging, storage, and distribution facilities, the complex produced more household textiles than any other mill in the world.

By 1927 Cannon and its affiliated Cabarrus Cotton Mills had erected about 1,600 workers' dwellings. Unlike most textile companies, Cannon retained ownership of the mill village into the late 20th c., making it one of the largest, best-preserved, and most uniform settlements of its type in the South. The houses are mostly detached single-family units on good-sized lots. House forms vary from the earliest 1-story side-gabled cottages through simple bungalows.

The central business district also remained in Cannon ownership. From the 1930s through the 1950s the downtown was remade in a Williamsburg image—one of the most fully realized versions of that pervasive influence (cf. *Chapel Hill). The project embodied the philosophy of J. W. Cannon's son and successor, Charles, and his wife, Ruth, an early leader in N.C. preservation; design work in the 1940s and 1950s was primarily executed by Bemis Lester of C. E. Swanson & Assoc. of Chicago. With a few exceptions in simple Art Deco style (**Gem Theatre**, 1948), the downtown buildings embody a Williamsburg colonial idiom typical of midcentury popular architecture in

6—Cannon Mills, Kannapolis, N. C.

CA 9 *Kannapolis*

the Southeast: English- and Flemish-bond brickwork, 9/9 sash, heavy moldings, paneled shutters, and gabled roofs.

In the early 1980s the town was finally incorporated, and Cannon Mills was sold to Californian David Murdoch, who instituted major changes, including sale and removal of many of the mill houses; ownership of the textile operation has since changed twice.

CA 10 Mount Pleasant

The town at the center of the county's German settlement was founded in the 18th c., incorporated in 1859, and named for its site above Dutch Buffalo Creek. It was the home of two important 19th-c. Lutheran academies, Mount Pleasant for boys and Mount Amoena for girls. The campus of the former **Mount Pleasant Collegiate Institute**, established in 1852 as Western Carolina Male Academy, occupies a hilltop above N. Main St. The centerpiece, now a local museum, is the Greek Revival **Main Building** (1854), a 3-story brick structure 7 bays wide, with pilasters and a later 19th-c. mansard roof. **Society Hall** (1858–59) is a 2-story brick Greek Revival building with pedimented gable ends and pilastered walls. The **Mathias Barrier House** (1853), home of the school's principal founder, and the side-hall plan **President's House** (1855) are conservative Greek Revival frame dwellings. The 3-story brick **New Dormitory** (1925; Louis Asbury [Charlotte], architect) was the last addition to the campus before the school closed in 1933. The board-and-batten **Lentz Hotel** (1853) is a notable antebellum example of the bracketed mode promoted by A. J. Downing; it

CA 10 *N. Main St., Mt. Pleasant*

was saved and moved from Main St. to campus in 1980.

Several residences along Main and Franklin Sts. show picturesque modes in the spirit of Downing. The **Augustus C. Barrier House** (ca. 1870; 401 S. Main St.) is a board-and-batten Gothic Revival house similar to a "symmetrical bracketed cottage" in *The Architecture of Country Houses* (1852). Sharing details with the *Lentz Hotel, the **Jeremiah Dreher House** (1858; 148 N. Main St.) is a board-and-batten house with hip roof and bowed brackets. There are a few Greek Revival houses in brick and frame and others in Queen Anne, Colonial Revival, and bungalow variations. The **Charles G. Lentz House** (1927; 123 N. Main St.) is a fine shingled bungalow with stone porch piers. The **Misenheimer-James House** (late 19th c., 1915; Charles C. Hook & Willard G. Rogers [Charlotte], architects; 311 S. Main St.) was remodeled in a bungalow mode for mill manager A. N. James; the textured stonework in the foundations, porch piers, chimneys, and outbuildings was laid by black stonemason Robert Franklin Lynn.

Key churches include the **Lutheran Church of the Holy Trinity** (1873, 1902; 202 S. Main St.), with round-arched windows and corbeled brickwork; the brick Gothic Revival **St. James Reformed Church** (1923; Louis Asbury [Charlotte], architect; N. College and Walnut Sts.); and the **First Congregational Church** (1918–21; Robert Franklin Lynn, builder; Wade St. at C St.). The latter, home of a black congregation founded in 1900, is a simple building of

CA 10 *Main Building, Mt. Pleasant Collegiate Institute*

the textured, random-course stone that was the hallmark of builder Lynn, a deacon of the church.

No railroad ever reached Mount Pleasant, but the town joined in the county's industrial boom of the late 19th and early 20th centuries with two small textile mills. **Kindley Cotton Mill** (1897 and later; Stuart Cramer, architect [attrib.]; 400 W. Franklin St.) was organized by W. R. Kindley and other local investors; Charlotte mill specialist Cramer is believed to have designed the 2-story brick mill with 3-stage tower. J. W. Cannon of Concord joined local investors in founding **Tuscarora Cotton Mill** (1901, 1919; s side E. Franklin St. at Barringer St.), which was owned by the local Foil family after 1944. The 1- and 2-story brick structure is among the least-altered mills of its period in the Piedmont, with many of the large segmental-arched windows retaining their original sash; a 2-stage tower with round-arched entrance fronts E. Franklin St. Frame 1-story mill housing remains on neighboring streets.

CA 12 *Lentz Farm and Harness Shop*

1974) carried on a trade started by his great-grandfather. The ca. 1900 dwelling typifies the familiar cross-gabled form, and there are a fine gable-roofed barn (1921) and other outbuildings. On a rise to the north is the **Victor Columbus Lentz House** (ca. 1876; w side SR 2453), home of A. C. Lentz's parents; it is a frame I-house with clipped gable ends, as seen on several houses in the area.

CA 11 St. John's Lutheran Church
Founded ca. 1750; present church 1845 and later; E side SR 2414, 0.2 mi. N of NC 73

Founded as a union church of Lutheran and German Reformed members, St. John's is one of the oldest congregations in the Piedmont. The present brick building dates from 1845, though enlargements on the gable ends have left only the 6-bay side walls of the original building intact, showing the 1:3 common-bond brickwork, slab stone foundations, and granite sills and lintels. The cemetery has gravestones dating to the 18th c.

CA 12 Adolphus Crooks Lentz Farm and Harness Shop
Early 20th c.; NE corner NC 49 and SR 2453, Mt. Pleasant vic.; private, visible from road

The rural industrial complex is a landmark along heavily traveled NC 49. The gable-fronted frame building (1914) housed the harness and horse-collar manufacturing operation of A. C. Lentz, a descendant of German settlers, who beyond his 90th year (d.

CA 13 Bost's Mill
Ca. 1900; 1.5 mi. E of US 601; private, visible from road

On the ridge overlooking the Rocky River, three generations of the Bost family operated a gristmill, a sawmill, a wool-carding operation, a cotton gin, a general store, and a post office. These enterprises have vanished, but the cluster of frame buildings evokes the rural industry and community life of the period: the 1912 steam-powered gristmill that replaced a waterpowered mill destroyed by flood, two Bost family houses, and **St. Paul's Methodist Church** (1899), a simply detailed Carpenter Gothic building.

CA 14 Boger-Hartsell Farm
Barn, 1872; house, 1881; SW corner US 601 and SR 1148

The center-passage double-crib log barn exemplifies a type characteristic of the western Piedmont; family tradition recalls that Hartsell's brother Jonah hewed and notched the logs, and that men from the surrounding community worked two days to put the logs in place. The deep frame sheds on three sides of the barn were added within a few years. The nearby farmhouse is a typical 1-story L-shaped dwelling; other farm buildings include a log corncrib, a 2-level frame granary, and a well house.

CA 15 Reed Gold Mine
State Historic Site
1799 and later; entrance E side SR 1100, 2.0 mi. S of NC 200; open regular hours

The first authenticated discovery of gold in the United States was made in 1799 by 12-year-old Conrad Reed, who while fishing in a creek on the farm of his father, John, discovered a 17-pound nugget. John Reed, born Johannes Rieth, was a Hessian mercenary during the American Revolution; after learning of a German-speaking settlement in the N.C. Piedmont, he deserted, changed his name, and acquired about 900 acres in present-day Cabarrus Co. The Reeds kept the nugget for 3 years before taking it to a Fayetteville silversmith, who identified it as gold. Reed began mining on his land, and before long the nation's first gold rush had begun. Gold mining became a major industry in the region in the 1820s, and the Reed mine alone yielded some $10 million in gold by 1843. Though overshadowed by western strikes after 1849, the N.C. mines operated into the early 20th c. The state historic site interpreting N.C.'s gold mining history includes a reopened mine tunnel, the tall stone chimney of an 1850s steam engine, and a reconstruction of the 1890s stamp mill.

CA 16 Ebenezer A.M.E.
Zion Arbor and Church
Before 1883; W side SR 1145, 0.1 mi. N of SR 1123, Cabarrus vic.

Camp meetings were a vital part of 19th-c. revivalism among blacks and whites in rural N.C., and tradition recalls that meetings took place here before the founding of the church in 1883. Log posts uphold the broad hip roof, and seating includes simple planks and pews from the ca. 1900 church building. Small cabins once clustered around the arbor. The congregation's cemetery and its third house of worship (1972) are nearby.

CA 17 Bethel Methodist
Arbor and Church
Arbor by 1866 and later; church, 1921–24; SR 1122, betw. SR 1123 and SR 1121, Cabarrus vic.

The congregation associates missionary Francis Asbury with its founding ca. 1783. The arbor's original, inner section has hewn posts; the circular-sawn outer rows of posts are later. A high, broad hip roof shelters the whole. The small cabins that housed families during meetings have been removed. The twin-towered, Gothic Revival sanctuary across the road was erected in the 1920s.

CA 17 *Bethel Methodist Arbor*

CA 18 Pioneer Mills Community

Set amid rolling fields and woodlands, the community on Caldwell Creek was settled by Scotch-Irish in the 18th c. and had a post office from 1831 until 1906. There was small-scale gold mining from the 1830s into the 1850s. At the main intersection stands the **Barnhardt-Morrison House** (mid-19th c.; SW corner SR 1135 and SR 1134), a small 2-story Greek Revival house of boxy, hip-roofed form, home to a longtime store-keeper and postmaster. To its east, the **Robert Harvey Morrison Farm** (1846–53; N side SR 1135, 0.2 mi. E of SR 1134) centers on a larger 2-story frame dwelling, also with simple Greek Revival finish. Site of the Pioneer Mills Gold Mine, the farm includes a log structure described as a miner's cabin, a double-crib log barn, a frame post office, and a reconstruction of a 2-room private schoolhouse. The **Spears Log House** (late 18th and early 19th c.; S side SR 1135, 0.8 mi. W of SR 1134), an early log house preserved on its original site, is a "dog-trot" house with passage between the two pens. The older east pen may date to the late 18th c.; the west pen and connecting passage were probably built in the early 19th c. by William Wallace Spears. Both pens have half-dovetailed notches.

CA 19 Flowe's Store Community

The community takes its name from the general store and medical office opened here by Dr. D. W. Flowe about 1880. The **Dr. Flowe Office** (mid-19th c.; W side SR 1132) is a distinctive little temple-form frame building with Greek Revival detail; Flowe reportedly moved it here from *Pioneer Mills. Nearby are the **Marshall Brown Store** (1917), with a typical false-front parapet, and the metal-clad **Brown's Cotton Gin** (ca. 1940), the last of the community's gins, once a common sight at crossroads in cotton country.

CA 20 *Rocky River Presbyterian Church*

CA 20 Rocky River Presbyterian Church
1860–61; W side SR 1139,
0.1 mi. N of SR 1136

Unusual among the Piedmont's gable-fronted brick Presbyterian churches, this late example incorporates Italianate rather than Greek Revival detail in its brick hoodmolds, round-arched windows and doors, and molded pilasters. The interior retains 19th-c. furniture and finish. The building was the fourth erected for a congregation founded by Scotch-Irish settlers in the 1750s. A stone wall encloses the cemetery, and the 1839 frame **Session House** stands nearby. To the southwest, the 2-story brick **Manse** (1873; W side SR 1158, 0.1 mi. N of SR 1139) repeats a hip-roofed double-pile Greek Revival form.

CA 21 Poplar Tent Presbyterian Church
Ca. 1850; S side SR 1394, 0.5 mi. E of I-85,
Poplar Tent vic.

Named for a tree that sheltered worshipers in the 1750s, the brick church is one of the distinctive temple-form Greek Revival churches built for antebellum Piedmont Presbyterians. Simple pilasters carry the front pediment and along the sides separate tall windows that rise through the gallery story. Despite interior remodeling, the gallery and original seating remain. A rock wall encloses a cemetery with fine 18th- and 19th-c. stones. (See Introduction, Fig. 32.)

CA 23 *Mill Hill*

CA 22 Trinity Lutheran Church
1897; W side SR 1622 at SR 1621, Kannapolis vic.

In this handsome Gothic Revival country church in brick, the intersecting pilasters and cornice of the gable front create a network of panels, all blind except the lancet-arched entrance and circular vent above it. The congregation was established in 1857 by families of German descent who came from eastern Cabarrus Co. to find more fertile croplands.

CA 23 Mill Hill
1821 and later; SE side SR 1616, 0.1 mi. N of SR 1622, Kannapolis vic.; private, visible from road

Described by Thomas Waterman as "an essay in pastoral classic beauty," the modest, beautifully finished house with an impressive Doric porch was the home of Jacob Stirewalt, a man of several trades, including miller and cabinetmaker.

Mecklenburg County (MK)

Charlotte (MK 1–55)

See Thomas Hanchett, *Sorting Out the New South City* (1998); Mary Kratt and Mary Manning Boyer, *Remembering Charlotte: Postcards from a New South City, 1905–1950* (2000); and the web page of the Charlotte-Mecklenburg Landmarks Commission.

Charlotte is the largest city in the Carolinas, with a 2000 population of more than 500,000, and center of a metropolitan region of 1.5 million. A banking, manufacturing, and distribution hub since the mid-19th c., the city epitomized the New South at the beginning of the 20th c. and is the *New* New South city at the beginning of the 21st c. Its architectural character reflects its spirit of enterprise and constant reinvention. As a 1907 publication proclaimed, "Charlotte does not hang back and wait for strangers to come in with their money and do things for it; it puts its money into things, shows the prospective investor what it is doing and bids him come in and do as well, or better, if he can." Generations of industrial plants and suburbs—including trendsetting early 20th-c. designs—spread out in chronological rings around a compact and continuously rebuilt city center that rises Oz-like above the trees.

Settled in the 1750s mainly by Scotch-Irish Presbyterians and some Germans, the county and its seat were established in the 1760s and named for Queen Charlotte of Mecklenburg, the German-born wife of England's George III. Charlotte prided itself on its early support of American independence with celebrations of the Mecklenburg Declaration of Independence, said to have been signed May 20, 1775. The trade-oriented town dealt in various crops, including grain and later cotton, and the 1799 discovery of gold in the area (*Reed Gold Mine) made it the center of the nation's first gold rush and site of a U.S. mint (1837–61).

Located on a high ridge midway between the Yadkin and Catawba rivers, Charlotte developed as a grid at the crossing of two trading paths, designated Trade and Tryon Sts. Businesses clustered at the junction, prime residences and churches went up along Trade and Tryon, and smaller houses and manufactories were concentrated on the back streets. As the 19th-c. city expanded, the grid continued along with a mix of uses and classes. In the 1850s Charlotte gained vital rail connections—the Charlotte & South Carolina Railroad (1852) from Columbia and the North Carolina Railroad (1854) across the state—that gave its cotton market competitive rates. During the Civil War, the rail town far from Union lines became the Confederate navy yard, and business rebounded after the war. By 1867 a dozen new stores and 75 new houses were cheering sights in a southern town of 4,000. In 1869 the city designated the quadrants formed by Trade and Tryon as four political wards.

Seizing the ethos of the New South, Charlotte attracted entrepreneurs who arrived from the Carolinas and elsewhere in pursuit of opportunity. New and old Charlotteans promoted business and invested in trade links—the Carolina Central Railroad to Wilmington (1872) and Atlanta & Charlotte Air Line Railway (1874)—that produced connections in six directions and the nickname "Queen City of the Piedmont." With 7,000 people in 1880, it grew to 34,000 by 1910 to overtake Wilmington as the state's largest city, ran a close second to Winston-Salem with 46,000 in 1920, then raced ahead with 82,000 residents in 1930 and 100,000 in 1940.

The 1881 Charlotte Cotton Mill opened the city's campaign to "Bring the Mills to the Cotton!" as steam, then electric power freed mills from streamside sites. From the 1890s into the 1920s, Mecklenburg ranked among the state's top three textile manufacturing counties. Some two dozen cotton mills sprang up in and around the city, each with its village. By the late 1920s more than 600 mills operated within a 100-mile radius of Charlotte, as the Carolina Piedmont sur-

Charlotte skyline

passed New England in textile production. Rather than sticking with textile production alone, Charlotteans diversified the city's economy to make it the financial, distribution, and electric power hub of the Carolinas—the "Industrial Center of the New South." They began their own good-roads movement, then led in the state campaign, developed the city as a trucking center, and in 1926 built *Wilkinson Boulevard to Gastonia, the first 4-lane highway in the state.

Downtown cotton brokers maintained offices in skylit rooms, while their goods filled long warehouses by the tracks. Industrialists built up S. Tryon St. as "the Wall Street of the South" to finance regional development. Textile machinery distributors the world over made Charlotte their southern headquarters, and it became the distribution point for everything from Coca-Cola and Lance snacks to popular music and schoolbooks. James B. Duke made Charlotte headquarters for the Southern (Duke) Power Co., established in 1905 to use the power of the Catawba River to industrialize the region, and brought Charlotte another title—"The Electric City."

The early 20th-c. city essentially rebuilt itself. As it grew, its form like that of other cities was redefined by Jim Crow segregation practices and the transforming power of the streetcar (1891) and the automobile. At the center, Trade and Tryon's business houses and mansions gave way to the flagship shops of new regional department stores and ever taller skyscrapers, competing locally and with rivals in Greensboro and Winston-Salem. In the late 19th c., Charlotte's citizens, about 60 percent white and 40 percent black, lived in dispersed patterns, with prominent white and black businessmen, doctors, lawyers, and city officials and their families residing within a few blocks of working-class citizens of both races. In the 20th c., class and racial patterns coalesced, first in a checkerboard pattern, then into larger sectors. At the city edges, textile villages grew more separate from the rest of Charlotte, especially on the north; the old wards became more predominantly black as whites moved outward; black suburbs developed mainly in the northwest; and single-class, white suburbs reached into the countryside, with the most exclusive on the south and east. The first streetcar suburb, *Dilworth (1891) repeated the mixed uses and grid plan, but soon *Myers Park (1911) and others inaugurated restricted occupancy and curvilinear designs by nationally prominent planners John Nolen and Olmsted Brothers of Boston and Earle Sumner Draper of Charlotte. By 1926 the *Charlotte Observer* declared that "the population is moving outward and taking the city with them."

The city became a regional architectural center as mill designers, engineers, and architects arrived to establish practices. D. A. Tompkins from South Carolina arrived

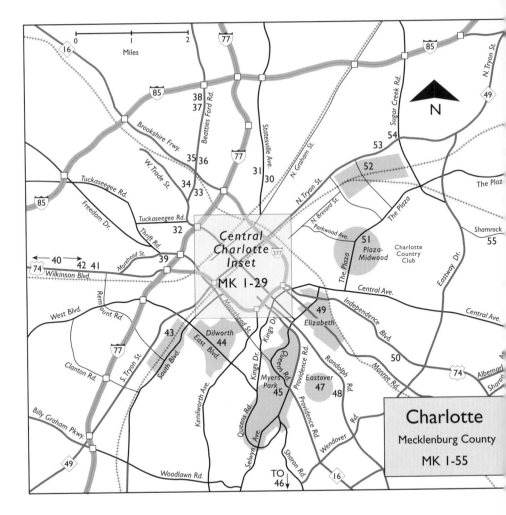

Charlotte
Mecklenburg County
MK 1-55

about 1883 and became one of the South's leading mill designers and promoters. His associate Stuart Cramer became internationally known for introducing "air conditioning" into textile mills. Mill architect R. C. Biberstein of Texas came by way of New Jersey and Indiana, and architect-engineers Lockwood, Greene & Co. of Boston established a southern office in Charlotte. Some architectural projects went to out-of-state designers, but the growing local profession took most commissions and generated regional practices. Prominent among them were Charles Christian Hook, a West Virginian by way of St. Louis (grandfather of famed postmodernist architect Charles Gwathmey); William Peeps, from London via Grand Rapids, Mich.; Oliver Wheeler,

from New York via Atlanta, and his several partners; Louis H. Asbury, a Charlotte native trained at the Massachusetts Institute of Technology who in 1908 became one of the state's first professionally trained, native architects; church specialist James M. Mc-Michael; Martin Boyer, a Virginia-born Charlottean trained at Carnegie Tech; and native builder-architect William W. Smith. Contractor James A. Jones came from nearby Anson Co. as a brickmason and established a large building firm.

Despite the Great Depression, Charlotte's diversification helped it survive downturns in cotton farming and textile manufacturing. At the end of World War II, the city stood poised for growth. Charlotte bankers strove to exceed Winston-Salem's

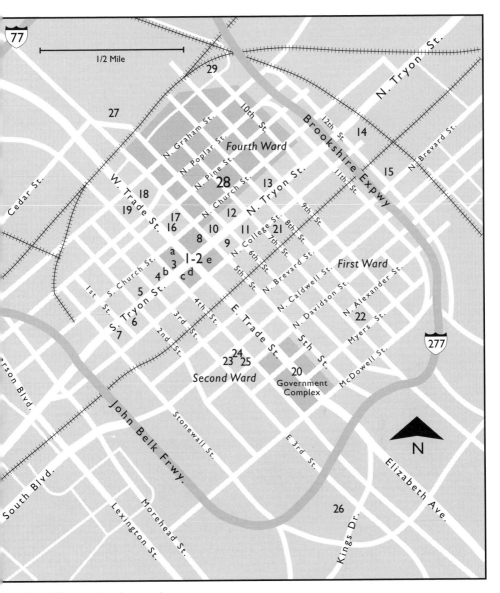

Central Charlotte inset (MK 1–29)

Wachovia as the Southeast's leading bank and built skyscrapers accordingly. National patterns of highways, shopping centers, and suburbs coupled with urban renewal shaped the city's population growth from 100,000 in 1940 to 200,000 in 1960 and more than 300,000 in 1980. The postwar city emerged as a center of corporate modernism in architecture, led by the firm of Arthur Gould (A. G.) Odell Jr. and, in time, those of J. Norman Pease; Harry Wolf; Clark, Harris, Tribble & Li; and Harvey Gantt, the first black graduate of Clemson's architecture school, mayor of Charlotte, and candidate for the U.S. Senate. Charlotte-based construction firms such as J. A. Jones, John Crosland, and Southeastern (Metric) Construction rank near the top of lists of the nation's busiest builders.

By the turn of the 21st c., the city had become a business metropolis and magnet for corporate headquarters. NationsBank, First Union (which merged in 2001 with Wachovia and consolidated its headquarters in Charlotte), and others made it a national banking center. NationsBank's 1999 merger forming Bank of America made it home of what was briefly the biggest bank in the country. In the largely post–World War II city, constant growth is yet again transforming its center as well as its edges. At the same time, a strong local preservation movement has saved many landmarks and neighborhoods in the midst of a New South City "with an unabashed love of the future."

Downtown (MK 1–29):
Bounded by I-77/277 expressway loop:
The grid of square blocks considered downtown encompasses all of pre-1900 Charlotte. Quadrants formed by Trade and Tryon Sts. constitute the four wards—First (NE), Second (SE), Third (SW), and Fourth (NW). There were both black and white residents in the four wards, with the finest houses on the main streets and smaller ones on back streets. In the 20th c., racial sectors were increasingly separated, and in the second half of the century urban renewal leveled the neighborhoods, leaving scattered institutional landmarks, chiefly churches, and part of *Fourth Ward. The central blocks of Trade and Tryon continue as the epicenter of power, with ever taller skyscrapers concentrated in a small zone, within sight of reminders of the small pre–World War II city. (Note: Bank buildings are listed under their original and current names.)

MK 1 The Square

The crossroads of Trade and Tryon was Courthouse Square until 1845, when the courthouse was shifted to another site, but it remains the central energy point, variously called Independence Square and the Square. Key businesses concentrated around it, including late 20th-c. skyscrapers set back from the street to open up the corners. In 1992–95 a private group sponsored the installation of four 25- to 30-foot bronze statues at the corners, designed by Ray Kaskey of Washington, D.C. As reported in the

local paper, the future is symbolized by a woman holding a baby; transportation, by a railroad worker; industry, by a textile worker and electric lightning bolts; and not to be missed, commerce, by a gold miner "spilling nuggets onto the head of a banker," whose face was "modeled on that of Federal Reserve Chairman Alan Greenspan."

MK 2 Mid- to Late 20th-c. Skyscrapers (a–e)

As Charlotte claimed its late 20th-c. position as a regional, then a national financial center, a cluster of competing skyscrapers proclaimed bankers' ambitions and made Charlotte a leader in corporate modernist architecture. They exemplify national trends then new to the state, as a sampling shows. The **Wachovia Building** (1956–58; A. G. Odell with Harrison & Abramovitz; 129 W. Trade St.) (**a**) began the competition when the Winston-Salem bank, largest in the state, erected the first postwar skyscraper in Charlotte, a 16-story vertical block with concrete gridded surfaces by the architects of the United Nations Building. With Wachovia under construction, Charlotte's newly formed American Commercial Bank announced plans for a competitive 18-story building, which was actually built 15 stories high and opened as **North Carolina National Bank (NCNB)** (1959–61; Walter Hook [Charlotte], architect; 200 S. Tryon St.) (**b**). The steel and concrete tower was the first in the state to display the glass and metal-mullioned curtain walls evocative of urban corporate prestige as defined by architect Mies van der Rohe. Charlotte's American Commercial Bank had been formed in 1957 by American Trust Co. (est. 1901) and Commercial National Bank (est. 1874 by the Holts of Alamance Co.). In 1960 American Commercial joined Greensboro's Security National Bank to form NCNB as a statewide bank to "chase the Wachovia." (Jefferson Standard Life Insurance Co. and other stockholders began Security National after Greensboro's banks closed in 1933.)

A modest, elegant composition appeared in the **Home Federal Savings and Loan Building** (ca. 1967; Freeman-White &

MK 2 *Downtown Charlotte, 2002*

Assoc., architects; 139 S. Tryon St.) (**c**), with 7 stories of expressed concrete structure and recessed glass bands. **NCNB (Bank of America) Plaza** (1972; A. G. Odell Jr. & Assoc. with Thompson, Venchett & Stanbach; S. Tryon St. at E. Trade St.) (**d**) began the transformation of the Square. With its angled towers and courtyard set back from the center, the darkly glittering assemblage of offices, shops, and a hotel introduced a vocabulary that dominated the late 20th-c. bumper crop of skyscrapers.

Capping off the skyline, the 60-story **NationsBank (Bank of America) Corporate Headquarters** (opened 1992; Cesar Pelli & Assoc. [New Haven], architects; N. Tryon St. at E. Trade St.) (**e**), which dominates the cityscape from distant vantages, is the tallest building in the Carolinas and between Atlanta and New York. In a familiar pattern, the skyscraper was planned by NCNB before it acquired Atlanta's C&S Sovran Corp. in 1991 to become NationsBank, the country's third largest bank. NationsBank's 1999 takeover of BankAmerica of San Francisco to form Bank of America made it for a time the nation's largest. Hugh McColl, who as chief executive of NCNB from 1983 directed its interstate mergers, also guided the creation of the signature tower. Architect Pelli's design gained praise from New York critic Paul Goldberger for its graceful resolution of "the conflict between historical form and modernist expression." With soaring setbacks recalling the classic skyscrapers of the 1920s, the walls of granite and glass rise from a rosy granite and marble base to a crown of silvery aluminum rods. The marble-clad lobby features frescoes by N.C. artist Ben Long. The complex also includes a performing arts center.

Linking many of these buildings is a less visible element of the late 20th c.: the **Overstreet Mall** (1970s–80s), a web of enclosed walkways above street level that form a pedestrian shopping arcade that runs through office buildings and over streets. The concept was published by French architectural theorist Le Corbusier as early as the 1920s, and during downtown revitalization in the 1970s, Charlotte leaders emulated Minneapolis's elevated, weatherproof mall to separate elements of downtown life.

S. Tryon St.

MK 3 First National Bank (One Tryon Center)

1926–27; Louis Asbury & Lockwood, Greene; 112 S. Tryon St.

Acclaimed in 1927 as the "tallest building in the Carolinas" and between Philadelphia and Birmingham, the classically detailed 20-

MK 3 *First National Bank*

story skyscraper captured the intercity height competition until Winston's *Reynolds Building rose in 1927–29. Under president Henry McAden (*McAdenville), the bank took prime position among the skyscrapers of S. Tryon's "Wall Street of the South." Joined to a later tower, the limestone-faced tower features a big, arched entrance carved with natural and classical motifs, including thrift-inspiring beehives and squirrels clutching acorns.

MK 4 Johnston Building
1924; William L. Stoddart (New York), architect; 212 S. Tryon St.

The classically detailed 15-story skyscraper was from 1924 to 1927 the city's tallest and is still one of the most elegant. Later in the 1920s it gained 2 more stories. Sheathed in limestone, with richly appointed lobby in marble and brass, it was built for a leading textile family (*Highland Park Mfg. Co., *Johnston Mfg. Co.).

MK 5 Latta Arcade and Brevard Court
1914; William H. Peeps, architect; 320 S. Tryon St.

One of the few commercial arcades in the state (#Grove Arcade, Asheville; #Virginia Dare Hotel Arcade, Elizabeth City), the skylit 2-story space is elegantly appointed in marble, wood, and stained glass in a stylized classical mode. It was built for small offices by Edward Dilworth Latta, who arrived in 1876 and, as founder in 1890 of the Charlotte Consolidated Construction Co. (*Dilworth), led in the city's transformation. The *Charlotte Observer* proclaimed in 1915, "The ornate quarters of steel brokers in Pittsburgh or Wall Street geniuses in New York have little to outdo the splendor of the Latta Arcade." To the rear, Brevard Court, with shops along an open walkway, was once a cotton brokers' center.

MK 6 Ratcliffe Flower Shop
1930; William H. Peeps, architect; 431 S. Tryon St.

A grace note from the early 20th c., the 2-story Mediterranean-inspired shop with stained glass and spiral-carved Corinthian colonnettes was moved in March 2000, then reinserted into the new First Union Bank (Wachovia). Founded in the 1920s, the family business—"Ratcliffe's Flowers/Brighten the Hours"—maintained its romantic ambience into the late 20th c.

MK 7 St. Peter's Catholic Church
1893; 501 S. Tryon St.

The Gothic Revival church in red brick was built for a parish est. 1851 to serve the many Irish Catholics working in local gold mines (*St. Joseph's, Gaston Co.). The frame rectory is one of the few Queen Anne houses in the central city.

N. Tryon St.

MK 8 Ivey's
1924; William H. Peeps, architect; 1995; 127 N. Tryon St.

Charlotte's great downtown department stores are gone, but a few architectural shells

MK 5 *Latta Arcade*

have been preserved. The former Ivey's, part of a chain begun in Charlotte in 1900 by J. B. Ivey and developed by David Ovens, retains its 5-story terra-cotta Gothic Revival–influenced facades and its logo script "Ivey's." Belk's was also headquartered in Charlotte.

MK 9 Montaldo's
(Mint Museum of Craft and Design)
1930 and later; Louis Asbury, architect; 220 N. Tryon St.

The prestigious women's clothing store attracted a regional clientele. Remade as a museum, it has kept its French Renaissance facade and roofline featuring classical female figures.

MK 10 Mayfair Hotel (Dunhill Hotel)
1929; Louis Asbury, architect; 237 N. Tryon St.

Outlasting most of the fifteen hotels that served Charlotte by 1929, the 10-story red brick building has Neoclassical details and a pediment over the penthouse. Originally an apartment hotel for residents and travelers, it has been rejuvenated as a downtown hotel.

MK 11 Former First Baptist Church
(Spirit Square)
1908; J. M. McMichael, architect; 318 N. Tryon St.

Characteristic of its architect, the tan brick church of "Byzantine" design features robust circular forms in its round-arched, stained glass windows and dominant domes, enriched by free classical details. The auditorium is attached to **People Place** (1980; Hardy-Holzman-Phifer, architects; 320 N. Tryon St.), an early downtown revitalization project.

MK 11 *Former First Baptist Church*

MK 12 St. Peter's Episcopal Church
1893; 339 N. Tryon St.

The stone-trimmed brick church blends Gothic and Richardsonian Romanesque elements in a compact and powerful composition, with a buttressed corner entrance tower and barrel-vaulted nave with fine stained glass.

MK 13 First Methodist Church
1927; Edwin B. Phillips (Memphis), architect; 501 N. Tryon St.

Construction of the massive limestone building in High Gothic Revival style was encouraged by James B. Duke (*Duke University), who moved to Charlotte (*Myers Park) and promised $100,000 if Trinity and Tryon St. Methodist churches would join and build a "representative stone church." The church was completed in 1927 with aid from Duke's estate.

MK 14 Charlotte Passenger Station
1896; Charles C. Hook; 1916–17, A. M. Walkup (Richmond); 1000 N. Tryon St. (access, N. College St.)

The only surviving railroad station in a railroad city, the hip-roofed 2-story Seaboard depot has restrained Neoclassical touches in its stuccoed walls and quoins.

MK 15 Alpha-Orient Cotton Mill
1888–89, 1901; 311 E. 12th St., at NW corner N. Brevard St.

The second cotton mill in the city after the *Charlotte Cotton Mill, Alpha Mill was founded by the D. A. Tompkins Co. to produce cotton yarn. It began as a 1-story brick mill at the north edge of the city but soon was part of a bustling industrial zone. In 1901 Alpha was refitted and expanded as the Orient Cotton Mill, which wove finished fabrics. The complex retains the boiler room and chimney stack of 1889 and the 1901 weaving mill, a large 2-story brick mill with low gable roof, segmental-arched windows, and ornate 3-story stair tower.

W. Trade St.

MK 16 First Presbyterian Church
1857; spire, 1883–84; sanctuary, 1895; 1917 onward; 200 W. Trade St.

The Gothic Revival style church on its large shaded lot evokes the stature of Scotch-Irish Presbyterians in the city's history. The first church in Charlotte was dedicated here in 1823 as an interdenominational town church adjoining *Settlers' Cemetery. The numerous Presbyterians acquired the property as First Presbyterian in 1835. The entrance facade survives from the 1857 church, which grew over the years. Maintaining a key green space, the church remains a vital downtown presence.

MK 17 Settlers' Cemetery
1770s–1880s; 200 W. Fifth St., between Poplar and Church Sts.

The burial ground begun soon after Charlotte's founding was designated the town cemetery in 1815 but was often called the Presbyterian Burying Ground. *Elmwood Cemetery opened in 1855, and Settlers' was essentially closed in 1867. The markers, tablets, and obelisks of many early and prominent people include the work of several local stonecutters (1770s–1810s), including J. W. McCoy (1813). Landscape architect John Nolen (*Myers Park) designed an informal planting scheme (1906).

MK 18 Union Bus Station
1940; J. A. Malcolm & E. T. Gavin (Charlotte), architects; 418 W. Trade St.

One of the few of its breed left in the state, the streamlined bus station with its curved corners and glass block windows evoked modernity and speed and was featured in *Carolina Architecture and Allied Arts* (1942). The nearby **Gateway and Century Buildings** (1924–26; Charles C. Hook, architect; J. A. Jones Co., contractor; 402–4, 408–12 W. Trade St.), with restored facades of limestone and green-and-yellow terra-cotta, were part of the westward expansion on Trade St. to create a commercial "gateway" near the railroad depot.

MK 19 United States Post Office and Courthouse (Charles Jonas Federal Building)

1915, 1934; Charles C. Hook, architect; 401 W. Trade St.

The dignified essay in conservative Neoclassicism, rendered in limestone, has a Tower of the Winds colonnade across the 7-bay facade, a marble and stone interior with matching columns, and an oak-paneled courtroom on the second floor. The U.S. Mint (*Mint Museum) was located to the west until 1934, when the Federal building was expanded.

E. Trade St. area

MK 20 Charlotte-Mecklenburg Government Complex

Charlotte City Hall (1923–25; Charles C. Hook, architect; J. A. Jones, contractor; 600 E. Trade St.); **Old Mecklenburg County Courthouse** (1926–28; Louis Asbury, architect; J. J. McDevitt, contractor; 700 E. Trade St.); **Mecklenburg County Courthouse** (1979–82; Harry Wolf, architect; 800 E. 4th St.).

Two Beaux Arts classical public buildings in a parklike plaza recall the civic vision and urban-rural tensions of the 1920s. After the city decided in 1922 to sell the 1891 city hall on N. Tryon (an eclectic brownstone marvel by Atlanta architect Gottfried L. Norman), leaders proposed a joint city-county government building. The county refused in 1923, but after the city completed its building in October 1925, in December the county decided to build next door to meet the "surge

MK 20 *Old Mecklenburg Co. Courthouse*

of present day progress and development." Both are 3-story stone edifices with long colonnades and balustraded parapets. Hook's city hall displays a light, decorative Neoclassical tone in a palazzo form, with arched windows in a rusticated basement story and a recessed Tower of the Winds portico. Asbury's courthouse has a soberer grandeur, with a towering Corinthian portico. Harry Wolff's larger courthouse, which won an American Institute of Architects (AIA) National Honor Award a half-century later, repeats the pale stone in a horizontally composed, modernist design of sheer walls and sharp angles. The obelisk memorializing the "Mecklenburg Declaration of Independence" was dedicated at the previous courthouse on May 20, 1898, and moved here.

First Ward (NE):
*For many years the ward encompassed both white and black residents. After urban renewal swept away *Brooklyn, many black residents moved here but departed when urban renewal remade this area as well.*

MK 21 First United (Seventh St.) Presbyterian Church

1894–96; 210 E. 7th St.

The prominent Gothic Revival brick church features two unequal towers, the corner one rising to a tall spire. The auditorium sanctuary soars to a vaulted ceiling. The congregation was organized in 1866 as the Colored Presbyterian Church of Charlotte after Kathleen Hayes urged her fellow black members of First Presbyterian to "come down out of the gallery and worship God on the main floor."

MK 22 Little Rock A.M.E. Zion Church (Afro-American Cultural Center)

1908–11; J. M. McMichael, architect; E. Seventh St. at N. Myers St.

The symmetrical red brick edifice with twin towers and Ionic portico displays the architect's bold classicism. The congregation was founded in the 1870s by Thomas Henry Lomax, minister at Clinton Chapel (est. 1865, the first black church in Charlotte) and later a bishop. Restored nearby are two **Shotgun Houses** (ca. 1896, moved 1986), a form now otherwise vanished from the city. These were built at 155 and 153 W. Bland St. for rental by Charles and Rosa McClure next to their home in Blandville, a black neighborhood that once existed near the edge of town.

Second Ward (SE):
In the early 20th c., the neighborhood known as Brooklyn occupied much of the Second Ward. Many black-owned businesses, formerly distributed downtown and elsewhere, coalesced here to form the principal black commercial district, complemented by leading churches, schools, and other institutions. In the 1960s most of Brooklyn fell to urban renewal.

MK 23 Mecklenburg Investment Co. Building
1921–22; William W. Smith, builder-architect; 233 S. Brevard St.

The polychromed brick building and *Grace A.M.E. Zion Church are the chief vestiges of the business and cultural focus of Brooklyn. Built to provide offices, stores, and a meeting hall, the 3-story edifice displays the brickmason's art in corbeling and lozenges in red and yellow brick (*Livingstone College, Salisbury). The Mecklenburg Investment Co. (MIC) was incorporated in

1921 by black business and professional leaders to provide high-quality quarters for black enterprises in the Jim Crow era. Founders Thaddeus Lincoln Tate (barber and developer) and Dr. John Taylor Williams (teacher, surgeon, and former consul to Sierra Leone) also led in the A.M.E. Zion church and Johnson C. Smith University and pursued the racial self-help ideals of Booker T. Washington. After World War II, MIC members worked toward desegregation and later joined the move to the suburbs.

MK 24 Grace A.M.E. Zion Church
1900–1902; Hayden, Wheeler & Schwend, architects; William W. Smith, builder; 219 S. Brevard St.

The Gothic Revival church displays the skill of church member Smith in its exuberant brickwork. Crenellated towers of unequal height flank a central gable, all enriched by corbeling and buttresses. The sanctuary has curving oak pews sloping up from the chancel. The congregation began in 1886, when members of Clinton Chapel formed Grace Chapel for "God, Religion, and Temperance." In July 1900 the *Manufacturers Record* noted that Hayden, Wheeler & Schwend had provided plans; the congregation "commenced laying brick October 22 at 11 a.m." for their "handsome brick church."

MK 25 Charlotte National Bank Facades
1918–19; Alfred Bossom (New York); 1986, Boyte-Williams (Charlotte); 428 E. 4th St.

The Doric-columned facades of N.C. granite originally graced the English-born architect's handsome bank at S. Tryon and 4th Sts. After it was razed, they became the main feature of a new building in the Second Ward area.

MK 26 Thompson Orphanage Chapel
1892; Kings Dr. and E. 3rd St.

Among the best examples of Victorian brickwork in the city, the Memorial Chapel was part of an orphanage established by the Episcopal Church in 1887.

MK 23–24 *Mecklenburg Investment Co. Building and Grace A.M.E. Zion Church*

Fourth Ward (NW)

MK 27 Elmwood-Pinewood Cemetery
Est. 1854; 700 W. 5th St.

The city cemetery contains diverse and elaborate funerary art, including Gothic, Egyptian, and Neoclassical mausoleums and the city's Confederate monument (1887). A granite log cabin honors an early history enthusiast. The Pinewood section is the city's best-preserved African American cemetery, with two polychromed brick mausoleums by William W. Smith.

MK 28 Fourth Ward Neighborhood

The Fourth Ward has the principal grouping of late 19th-c. residences in Charlotte. Sections of the ward narrowly escaped urban renewal in the 1970s and became an early model for revitalization. In the southern sector are the **Bagley-Mullen House** (ca. 1895; 123 N. Poplar St.), a Queen Anne style house in brick and one of the first stylish dwellings erected on a "back street"; the former **St. Peter's Hospital** (1907; 229 N. Poplar St.), red brick with stepped gables, which housed a facility established in the 1870s by St. Peter's Episcopal Church; and the former **North Carolina Medical College** (1907; James M. McMichael, architect; 229 N. Church St.), a bold combination of red brick and free classical detail, built for a medical school that graduated more than 300 doctors before it closed in 1914. Near the railroad, the **Charlotte Cotton Mill** (1880–81, 1890s, and later; 508 W. 5th St.), the city's first textile mill, began as a 1-story brick structure—considered innovative in 1880—and gained additions over the years, portions of which survive.

The older houses, north on Church, Poplar, and Pine Sts. from 8th to 10th, range from ornate late 19th-c. dwellings to early 20th-c. bungalows and small apartment houses. The **Liddell-McNinch House** (1890s; 511 N. Church St.; open as a restaurant), with its interpenetrating solids and voids blending the Queen Anne and Shingle styles, was home of Mayor S. S. McNinch, who hosted President William Howard Taft

here in 1909. The Spanish style **Frederick Apartments** (1931; 515 N. Church St.), 3 stories in light brick trimmed with colorful terra-cotta, are where W. J. Cash wrote part of *The Mind of the South* (1941). Other late 19th-c. highlights include the turreted Queen Anne style **Elias Overcash House** (ca. 1880; 326 W. 8th St.) and the bracketed and towered **E. W. Berryhill House** (1884; 324 W. 9th St.).

An especially fine apartment house is the Jacobethan style **Poplar Apartments** (1929–30; Lockwood, Greene & Co., architects; 301 W. 10th St.). Conceived as "the latest thing" with "ultramodern" and "magnificent" apartments of 3 to 7 rooms, the 5-story complex is garbed in Flemish-bond brickwork, half-timbering, and a porte cochere tower, akin to Tudor Revival suburban residences. The late 20th-c. infill housing designed to meet neighborhood guidelines—**Hackberry Place** (1979; James Estle Boyter [Dallas], architect; Settlers Ln.) and **Springfield Square** (1981; David Furman [Charlotte], architect; 7th-8th, Pine-Poplar Sts.)—provided early N.C. examples of neo-Victorian and other motifs that became a staple of postmodernism and neo-urbanism.

MK 28 *Poplar Apartments*

MK 29 Interstate Milling Co.
1915, 1964; 620 W. 10th St.

Built beside the railroad for a local firm begun in 1915, the immense grain elevator and storage facility attained its present form in 1964. The tall white concrete cylinders, like those in the American Midwest and plains states, have a powerful presence in the cityscape, evoking Charlotte's position as a distribution hub.

MK 30 Ford Motor Co. Plant
1925; Albert Kahn (Detroit), architect;
1804–20 Statesville Ave.

In 1915 the Ford Motor Co. selected Charlotte as a southern distribution center for parts and in 1925 opened this large plant, designed around the assembly process, to produce 300 Model-Ts per day. After making more than 110,000 Model-Ts, the plant switched to Model-A in 1927 and assembled over 105,000 before closing in 1932. It was later a military facility and assembly plant for Nike missiles. Designed by the famed industrial architect Kahn, known for his innovative and functional plans for Ford manufacture and assembly, the immense building features skylit work spaces, and its tapestry brick and tile front in stylized Art Deco style survives in good condition, including Kahn's characteristic Pewabic Pottery details.

MK 31 Double Oaks Elementary School
1952; A. G. Odell Jr., architect;
1326 Woodward St.

The horizontally composed school of brick and glass, built for black students in north Charlotte, captured widespread recognition as an advanced elementary school design, with simple rectilinear forms, abundant natural light, and a flowing plan with linked sections designed to accommodate the slope of the terrain. In 1954 it became the second N.C. building (following the *Dorton Arena) to win an AIA National Honor Award.

MK 32 Wesley Heights

The middle-class suburb was laid out between 1900 and 1910 and soon filled with brick and frame bungalows and other house types. Predominantly white at first, it became home to many black families in the diaspora after Brooklyn was razed and maintains a strong neighborhood identity. **Greater Bethel A.M.E. Zion Church** (1928; Louis Asbury, architect; 201 Grandin Rd.) is a red brick church with Florentine facade and triple-arched entrance.

MK 33 Johnson C. Smith University
100 Beatties Ford Rd.

One of the state's most important historically black colleges was founded as Biddle Institute in 1867 by white Presbyterian ministers to train "preachers and teachers." Early funding came from the Freedmen's Bureau and Mary Biddle of Philadelphia, and the hilltop site was given by William R. Myers, railroad owner, lawyer, and the city's largest landowner at the time. It continues as a 4-year liberal arts school. The imposing **Biddle Hall** (1884), 4 stories tall with a 6-story clock tower, rendered in ornate corbeled brickwork and trimmed in brownstone and stamped metal, is Charlotte's finest surviving Victorian building. Typical of the era, the students assisted in construction. It contains a stunning auditorium glowing with dark and ornate woodwork and colored glass, restored in the 1980s. (See Introduction, Fig. 54.)

Carter Hall (1895), with its wooden cupola and 4 brick turrets, was likewise built by students. The former **Carnegie Library** (1912; Hunter & Gordon [Charlotte], architects) is a Neoclassical edifice in cream brick with terra-cotta columns and pediment. Mrs. Johnson C. Smith, widow of a Pennsylvania steel executive, donated over $700,000 in 1923, which aided construction of many buildings, including the red brick Neoclassical **George E. Davis Science Hall** (1923), **University Church** (1929), and four-square **Teachers' Cottages** (125, 303, 305 Beatties Ford Rd.). Later International style buildings were constructed with the support of the Duke Endowment, including **Greenfield Hall** (1984; Odell & Assoc., architects).

MK 34 Biddleville

During the 19th c., when Biddle Institute lay at a distance from the center city, Biddleville developed across Beatties Ford Rd. to house professors and staff. The large 2-story **Dr. George E. Davis House** (1890s; brick-veneered, 1920s; 301 Campus St.) was the home of the college's first black professor in 1886 and a state public education official in the 1920s. The red brick Gothic **Old Mount Carmel Baptist Church** (1918; Louis Asbury, architect; 412 Campus St.) was built by congregation members.

MK 35 Washington Heights

By the 1910s trolley service extended up Beatties Ford Rd. from downtown, and the black streetcar suburb of Washington Heights was begun beyond Biddleville in 1913; it was advertised as a "place of tone and character," "two miles from the heart of the city, with streetcars running through it." Upper-, middle-, and working-class blacks came from all over the city to build large and small houses on the elevated site along Booker, Tate, Sanders, and other streets named for African American leaders. The most striking landmark is the **Excelsior Club** (1952; 921 Beatties Ford Rd.), designed by owner James McKee in Moderne style with stuccoed white walls, flat roof, glass brick windows, and a metal canopy to the street. Supplementing his income as a mail clerk by tending bar at local country clubs, McKee saw the need for an exclusive black club and purchased a ca. 1910 frame house for the purpose in 1944. In 1952 he remodeled it after visiting clubs elsewhere in the country. Considered the largest and most prestigious black social club in the Southeast and the only one for black professionals in the Charlotte area, the Excelsior hosted Nat "King" Cole and other major entertainers and broadcasted many on local radio, became a focus of political life, and supported many successful candidates.

MK 36 Vest Station Water Purification Plant

1922–24; William M. Platt (Durham), engineer; 1936–38, B. Atwood Skinner & T. S. Simpson, architects; George S. Rawlins, engineer; 1949; 820 Beatties Ford Rd.

In 1922–24 the growing city built a modern plant to treat 8.3 million gallons of water a day from the Catawba River; but by the mid-1930s, more was needed, and the Works Progress Administration (WPA) assisted with a project that doubled the plant's capacity and "put Charlotte in the big city class." The original red brick and concrete facility was

MK 35 *Excelsior Club*

enlarged to create a symmetrical, Moderne composition, with geometric pilasters separating large windows, unified with stuccoed walls and elegant aluminum trim.

MK 37 North Carolina National Bank Branch (Bank of America)

1970; Harry Wolf (Charlotte), architect; 2249 Beatties Ford Rd.

Winner of an AIA National Honor Award (1971) for its "attempt to create serenity in a chaotic, unstable streetscape," the beautifully simple plan has a triangle set on a square base. The geometric form rises from the ground with sheer, white-painted brick walls and clean-cut openings; inset and projecting triangles define the entrance and drive-in teller bays. Wolf was a modernist designer of national reputation. Another variation of his clean geometry appears in the stuccoed parallelogram-plan **North Carolina National Bank** (Bank of America) (1972; 4535 Park Rd.), which became another AIA National Award winner in 1974. Both banks have been carefully preserved.

MK 38 United House of Prayer For All People

1999; John Urban (Charlotte), architect; Jaco, Inc., contractors; 2321 Beatties Ford Rd.

The complex is the state's largest of new churches erected by the sect begun in Charlotte in 1926 by African American evangelist C. M. "Sweet Daddy" Grace. He was an immigrant from the Cape Verde Islands who worked as a railroad cook while spreading his message. In 1926 he held a great revival in Charlotte's Second Ward and began this congregation, the year before he chartered

MK 38 *United House of Prayer for All People*

the organization in Washington, D.C. The Charlotte mother church worshiped in Brooklyn before moving to this site in the 1960s. The new building evokes the form of a Gothic cathedral in red, blue, and gold, with triangular openings, pinnacles, and gilded spires; it has a characteristic pair of lions in front.

West of downtown

MK 39 Charlotte Coca-Cola Bottling Plant
1930; M. R. Marsh, architect; 1401–9 W. Morehead St.

The Art Deco building of red brick and cast stone, like others of its type, takes its theme from the product: large Coke bottles made by the local Ornamental Stone Co. rise at the corners, a terra-cotta script "Coca Cola" tops the entrance, and broad windows display the bottling works. J. Luther Snyder arrived in 1902 from headquarters in Atlanta to build the first Coke-bottling plant in the Carolinas; in 1930 he built his fourth plant from designs by Marsh, who came from Florida in 1916 as draftsman for J. M. McMichael and established his own practice in 1922. (See Introduction, Fig. 53.)

MK 40 Wilkinson Boulevard
1926

The state's first 4-lane highway, from Charlotte to Gastonia, was named for William C. Wilkinson, a Charlotte businessman and state highway commissioner who promoted it. The boulevard was 20 miles long, with concrete paving 40 feet wide and shoulders landscaped and planted with shrubs, "making the 60-foot-wide boulevard a show place of the South." It has a notable selection of mid-20th-c. roadside architecture, including trucking facilities and vintage drive-ins.

MK 41 Dairy Queen
1947; 2732 Wilkinson Blvd.

This compact, International style structure is said to be the first Dairy Queen in N.C., third in the Southeast, and twenty-fifth in the nation. With neon emphasizing the curved facade and a pretty Eskimo girl on its sign, it is a perfect and still-operating specimen from the post–World War II rise of drive-in culture and architecture.

MK 42 Bar-B-Q King
Ca. 1960; 2900 Wilkinson Blvd.

One of a local chain of 3 drive-ins, the tan brick building in simple modernist style still has its metal shelters and order stands with "Servus fones." Other links in the chain are the **21 South Curb Service No. 1** (1955; 3361 South Blvd.), where the sign features the "Super Boy" hamburger, and the **South 29 Drive-In** (1950s; 3101 Independence Blvd.) of similar character, opposite the *Charlotte Coliseum.

Southwest and Southeast of downtown

MK 43 South End

Promoted in 1895 as "the Manchester of Charlotte," the important industrial sector extends along the 1000–2000 blocks of South Blvd. and the Southern Railway tracks. Edward Dilworth Latta planned the city's first suburb of *Dilworth with both residential and industrial areas. Here D. A. Tompkins and Latta established key enterprises. In the late 20th c. the industrial buildings were redeveloped as "South End." **Fire Station No. 2** (1909; Wheeler, Galliher & Stern, architects; J. A. Jones, contractor; 1212 South Blvd.), built for horse-drawn equipment, is a handsomely detailed red brick building with 2-story, arched openings. The **Lance Co.** (1926 and later; 1300 South Blvd.), built for the snack food pioneer, is a large 4-story U-shaped building in red brick with stylized classical detailing in concrete. In back is part of the **Dilworth Trouser Co.** (1895), a brick building with corbeling and arched windows, where Latta (who came to Charlotte as a clothing salesman, then entered production) continued to manufacture trousers while he pursued real estate development.

Plants associated with D. A. Tompkins concentrate in the 1900–2000s blocks. Tompkins, a leading textile promoter and innovator of the 1880s and 1890s, had erected some 100 mills throughout the South by 1900. The **D. A. Tompkins Machine Shop** (1904; 1900 South Blvd.) is a long corbeled-brick structure extending back from the street. The **Leeper & Wyatt Store** (ca. 1903; 1923 South Blvd.), a 2-story Italianate building in red brick, was built for Tompkins's Atherton mill village and long served as a grocery.

Key to Charlotte's early 20th-c. diversification was the **Parks-Cramer Mfg. Co.** (1919, 1920s, and later; 2000 South Blvd.), which produced and shipped equipment for air conditioning, heating, humidifying, and ventilating factories throughout the South. It held the southern branch of a company founded in 1918 and headquartered in Massachusetts, whose innovative products had been developed and patented by Stuart Cramer, a former Tompkins associate. Cramer, who coined the term "air conditioning" in 1906, developed climate control for textile mills, including devices to remove lint and humidifiers to reduce yarn breakage. The complex consists of several 1- and 2-story brick sections; the lower buildings have central monitors with long banks of windows. Inside, timber and metal structural elements are visible along with plank ceilings and wood-block floors.

MK 43 *Parks Cramer Mfg. Co.*

To the south, the **Atherton Cotton Mill** (1892–93; D. A. Tompkins, builder; 2108 South Blvd.) was the first mill built and owned by the D. A. Tompkins Co. and the sixth mill in Charlotte. It set the standard for many others in the Piedmont, as did its (now lost) mill village. The spinning mill, which opened in 1893 with 300 workers and 10,000 spindles, follows a longitudinal plan 498 feet long, sited on a slope so that its large, arched windows light two floors of work space on the west and one on the east. The interior slow-burn mill construction has 12-by-12-inch timbers and heavy wooden floors. By the railroad track, in a train shed, is an early **Trolley** that operated in Charlotte and has been restored for short trips.

Across the tracks, the **Nebel Knitting Mill** (1927, 1929, Richard C. Biberstein [Charlotte], architect; 1946, Herman V. Biberstein, architect; 101 Worthington St. at Camden Rd.) recalls the importance of mill architects Biberstein & Biberstein. Richard, son of Texas engineer Herman R. von Biberstein, came to Charlotte in 1887, worked for Stuart Cramer around 1900, and from 1905 to 1931 had his own practice, which son Herman continued after his death. The big 2-story brick building of the 1920s frames a courtyard and has broad, double windows separated by simple pilasters, maximizing natural light to the workers at two rows of knitting equipment within. Part of a national company, the Nebel Mill was the South's first producer of fine-gauge silk hosiery and Charlotte's first maker of full-fashioned hosiery. Hosiery work required good light and paid better than many textile jobs. Postwar demand for nylon hosiery prompted the 1946 annex, with large upper windows, in Moderne style.

MK 44 Dilworth

Opened in 1891 as Charlotte's first streetcar suburb, Dilworth followed a grid plan set at an angle to the city grid. Edward Dilworth Latta began the Charlotte Consolidated Construction Co. (4Cs) to create the multi-use suburb south of the city, where the emerging urban middle class could buy a home with "rent money" payments. The 4Cs provided electricity and other services and acquired the city's horse-drawn streetcar line, converted it to electric power, and extended it from downtown. Sales were slow at first but quickened after the factory district began (*South End).

The original grid had square blocks along wide boulevards and centered on Latta Park (later reduced), designed by Joseph Forsyth Johnston, who had planned Atlanta's first streetcar suburb three years earlier. The grandest residences stood on the boulevards: Morehead St., South Blvd., and East Blvd. (the trolley route). The Atherton Cotton Mill village occupied part of the neighborhood, but only a few mill houses survive.

MK 44 *Villalonga-Alexander House*

MK 44 *E. Worthington St., Dilworth*

The diverse Queen Anne, Colonial Revival, and Craftsman houses, large and small, include several early works by Charles Christian Hook. A native of West Virginia, he came from St. Louis in 1891 and went to work for 4Cs designing houses for Dilworth, first in Queen Anne style, then as an early promoter of the Colonial Revival. A few examples represent his repertoire: the full-blown Queen Anne style defines the **Mallonee-Jones House** (1895; 400 Kingston Ave.) and the unusual Queen Anne–Craftsman blend in the 1-story **McCoy House** (1909–10; 429 E. Kingston Ave.). Freewheeling early Colonial Revival designs appear in the **Gautier-Gilchrist House** (1897; 320 Park Ave.), with its high gambrel roof and inset portico; the **Villalonga-Alexander House** (1900; 301 E. Park Ave.), with wraparound porch and eccentric classical details; and, a survivor of the great boulevard houses, the **Walter Brem House** (1902; 211 East Blvd.), a symmetrical, idiosyncratic Colonial Revival design with columned porch. The shingled, gambrel-roofed **Willard G.**

Rogers House (ca. 1907; 524 East Blvd.) was built by a Charlotte architect and Hook partner as his own residence. It is uncertain who designed the 1-story Victorian **Mayer House** (ca. 1907; 311 East Blvd.), which was home to Carson McCullers while she wrote parts of *The Heart Is a Lonely Hunter* in the 1930s.

In 1911 Latta hired Olmsted Brothers of Boston, sons of Frederick Law Olmsted, to expand Dilworth eastward in the fashionable, naturalistic mode (*Myers Park). Among many red brick Georgian Revival residences are the **Scott House** (1927; 1301 Dilworth Rd.), briefly the boyhood home of cowboy movie star Randolph Scott, and the **F. O. Sherrill House** (1928; 1401 Dilworth Rd.), built for a founder of S&W cafeterias. Especially striking among the picturesque houses is the **Ira Stone House** (1930; 1165 Linganore Pl.), a rambling English cottage in undulating brick. Landmarks along the Morehead St. thoroughfare include the **Addison Apartments** (1926; Willard G.

Rogers, architect; J. A. Jones, contractor; 831 E. Morehead St.), a 9-story apartment house with stylized classical details, a project of James Addison Jones. He came to Charlotte in 1889 as a young brickmason, founded the J. A. Jones Co. in 1894, and built many of the city's key buildings. Other facets of Neoclassicism appear in the **Charlotte Woman's Club** (1923; Charles C. Hook, architect; 1001 E. Morehead St.) and the **Coddington House** (1917–18; William H. Peeps, architect; 1122 E. Morehead St.; B&B), in white frame with a green tile roof.

MK 45 Myers Park

With its maze of curving streets, canopy of towering trees, manicured lots, and restrained but imposing Georgian and Tudor Revival residences, Myers Park epitomizes the exclusive, professionally planned New South suburb of the early 20th c. Streetcars and automobiles permitted residents to live apart from the city but convenient to it.

In 1911 Charlotte banker George Stephens began to develop the 1,200-acre suburb southeast of the city on the farmland of his father-in-law, John S. Myers. Stephens employed as planner John Nolen of Boston, whose Myers Park design, featured in his *New Towns for Old* (1927), came early in a nationally acclaimed career of more than 400 urban plans. Nolen created a state-of-the-art scheme with a main boulevard loop called Queens Rd., spacious parks, curved streets shaded by hundreds of transplanted trees, and custom landscape designs for homeowners. Stone gateways and trolley stations marked key entries. Supervising construction was Earle Sumner Draper, who stayed to become the South's first professionally trained resident landscape architect. Hailed as the "finest unified suburban development south of Baltimore," Myers Park inspired a wave of designs, including Nolen's *Irving Park in Greensboro and #Asheville city plan, and Draper's *Forest Hills in Durham, *Hayes Barton in Raleigh, *Emerywood in High Point, *Eastover in Charlotte, and others.

As intended, the exclusivity and high design quality of the suburb attracted leading business and professional people, including textile and electric power executives. The first residences cluster in the north near J. S. Myers Park at Hermitage and Ardsley Rds. The largest is the **James B. Duke Mansion** (1915, 1919; Charles C. Hook, architect; 400 Hermitage Rd.), a columned, white frame Colonial Revival residence that the tobacco and electric power magnate acquired in 1919, tripled in size, and enhanced with a "Wonder Fountain" (gone) that spouted 150 feet high. When the first saplings were trans-

MK 45 *Queens Rd., Myers Park*

MK 45 *James B. Duke Mansion*

MK 45 *Earle S. Draper House*

planted to Myers Park, Duke replaced them with mature trees at his own expense.

Beyond the Duke mansion, Myers Park boasts no palatial estates but substantial, relatively restrained houses designed by various architects with the harmonious proportions and careful detailing of the era. Georgian and Tudor Revival residences predominate, but there are many bungalows, foursquare houses, and Dutch Colonial dwellings. Charles Barton Keen (*Reynolda House) designed the white-stuccoed French Renaissance style **Charles Lambeth House** (1927; 435 Hermitage Rd.) and the red brick Georgian Revival **H. M. Wade House** (1928–31; 530 Hermitage Rd.). The **J. L. Snyder House** (1920; Martin E. Boyer Jr., architect; 1901 Queens Rd.), for the Carolinas Coca-Cola leader, is among the grandest of many red brick Georgian Revival houses. Other leading businessmen erected simpler but substantial foursquare houses, such as the red brick **David Ovens House** (1916; 825 Ardsley Rd.), home of the Ivey's Stores developer, and the stuccoed tile-roofed **David Clark House** (1914; 100 Hermitage Rd.), for the publisher of the *Southern Textile Bulletin*. Among several fine Tudor Revival residences are the **E. C. Marshall House** (1915; Franklin Gordon [Charlotte], architect; 500 Hermitage Rd.), with its steep gables and half-timbered upper story, and the **Earle S. Draper House** (1923; Franklin Gordon, architect; 1621 Queens Rd.), the home of the landscape architect. Whimsical variations on English cottage and Tudor themes include the **Ross House** (1925; Martin Boyer, architect; 2001 Sherwood Rd.); the **Mary H. Lethco House** (1928; William H. Peeps, architect; 2038 Roswell Ave.); and the

Gresham House (1926; 724 Edgehill Rd.), a stone cottage-bungalow with "thatched" roof.

Queens College (1916; Charles C. Hook, architect; 1900 Selwyn Ave.) occupies a campus laid out by John Nolen in an H-plan of two quadrangles (*University of North Carolina [UNC], Chapel Hill). Stephens persuaded the Presbyterian women's college to move from downtown, and Charles C. Hook designed the initial buildings in red tapestry brick and limestone with free classical details. The **Myers Park Elementary School** (1928; Charles C. Hook, architect; 2132 Radcliffe Ave.) is a handsome public school in brick with Italianate arcaded loggias. Adjoining Myers Park, developer Floyd M. Simmons created in 1912 the smaller **Hermitage Court**, with houses that range from his big Southern Colonial style **Simmons House** (1913; 625 Hermitage Ct.), with semicircular portico, to the **Nesbit Cottage** (1921; Martin E. Boyer Jr., architect; 522 Hermitage Ct.), a picturesque English concoction shown in *Architecture* magazine.

MK 46 Morrocroft

1927; Harrie T. Lindeberg (New York), architect; 2525 Richardson Dr. (near 3700 Sharon Rd.)

The once rural Tudor Revival mansion was built for "Good Roads Governor" Cameron Morrison and his wife Sara Watts Morrison, a wealthy widow. After his term (1921–25), they established a 3,000-acre model farm south of town, with manorial residence designed by a country house architect who published it in his *Domestic Architecture* (1940). Amid development, the rambling brick house retains its picturesque grandeur: multigabled forms and complex chimney stacks rendered in rough brickwork with steep roofs of mossy red tile, and matching outbuildings.

MK 47 Eastover

Designed by Earle S. Draper in 1927 in the curvilinear mode of Myers Park, Eastover lay beyond the streetcar line and was strictly an automobile suburb for the elite. The architectural palette had few deviations from the Colonial-Tudor norm. Fine examples by Charlotte architect Martin Boyer include the white frame **E. C. Griffith House** (1928; 301 Eastover Rd.), in a New England Colonial mode, and the stone Tudor Revival style **Hamilton C. Jones House** (1929–31; 201 Cherokee Rd.). A spectacular exception is the flamboyant Tuscan Revival **Gourmajenko House** (Villa Square) (1920s; William Bottomley [New York], architect; 715 Providence Rd.), designed for "world traveler and independent spirit" Blanche Reynolds Gourmajenko by an architect best known for Georgian Revival mansions (*Tatton Hall). A highlight of the neighborhood is the **Charlotte Fire Station No. 6** (1929; Charles C. Hook, architect; 249 Laurel Ave.), in rustic brick and stone with arched engine bays, arched windows, and green tile roof giving a domestic aura.

MK 47 *Charlotte Fire Station No. 6*

MK 48 Mint Museum of Art

1934–36, Martin E. Boyer Jr., architect; original, 1837, William Strickland, architect; 1985, expansion and reorientation, Clark, Tribble, Harris & Li; 2730 Randolph Rd. near Eastover Rd.

When the U.S. Mint in downtown Charlotte was razed in 1934, "the women of Charlotte" rescued the materials to reconstruct it on a new site as an art museum, assisted by WPA funds and architect Boyer. The original brick building with pedimented frontispiece, the only N.C. work by Philadelphia architect Strickland, was the U.S. Mint (1837–61) after the early 19th-c. gold boom.

East of downtown

MK 49 Elizabeth

Platted as a series of small suburban developments beginning in the 1890s and annexed in 1907, Elizabeth has especially fine examples of the Shingle style, Craftsman bungalows, and other informal modes along with Colonial Revival work. The **John B. Alexander House** (1912–13; 509 Clement Ave.), built for a developer, is a big, robust composition with multiple gables and dormers, wide eaves and Craftsman brackets, shingled walls, and granite block stonework. The **William Henry Belk House** (1924; Charles C. Hook, architect; 200 Hawthorne Ln.), a mammoth Colonial Revival house in cream brick with tile roof, was built for the founder of the South's largest department store chain (*Monroe). In 1911 one developer advertised his "Bungalowland" under construction along E. 8th St. and Hawthorne Ln., including the **Cocke-Golden House** (1910; 1701 E. 8th St.), one of several Tudoresque bungalows, with rough stuccoed walls and dark wood trim. Once owned by power company official Norman Cocke, in 1973–81 it was the home of humorist and journalist Harry Golden, author of *Only in America*. Among several handsome apartment houses is the **Rutzler Apartments** (ca. 1929; 712 Louise Ave.), in red brick with classical details. **Independence Park** (1904; John Nolen; Hawthorne

MK 49 *John B. Alexander House, Clement Ave.*

Ln., near 7th St.) was Charlotte's first public park and the first civic commission for Nolen, then a graduate student at Harvard. Helen Hodge, one of the South's first woman landscape architects, designed the stone pool and pavilion of the Arhelger Memorial (1931).

MK 50 Old Charlotte Coliseum and Ovens Auditorium

1953–56; A. G. Odell Jr. & Assoc., architects; 2700 E. Independence Blvd.

When built, the Coliseum was the world's largest unsupported domed structure. Featured in *Look* magazine and *Progressive Architecture*, it became one of the South's most publicized examples of 1950s modern architecture, symbol of a southern city focused on progress. The idea of a municipal coliseum and auditorium emerged immediately after World War II; a committee led by Ivey's executive David Ovens selected architect Odell in 1950. Delayed in part by Korean War materials restrictions, construction was completed in 1956. Son of a Concord, N.C., textile family (*Concord), A. G. Odell Jr. studied at Cornell and the École des Beaux Arts and worked for New York's Wallace Harrison and Raymond Loewy before establishing an office in Charlotte in 1939. After serving in World War II, he made his firm into a state and regional leader in corporate modernism and a "graduate school" for

young architects and engineers. The project won the firm its first state design award and wide attention for innovative design and "simple expression of structural forms."

Conceived as an automobile-oriented regional center on the new Independence Blvd., both the 13,500-seat Coliseum for sports events and the 2,500-seat Auditorium for concerts and theater are built of steel and reinforced and cast concrete. The Coliseum's slanting columns carry a circular dome of steel construction, 332 feet in diameter, roofed in aluminum—publicized by Bethlehem Steel and Alcoa, including the "Alcoa Hour" on TV in 1956. Bands of seating are visible through the glass between the columns. The smaller Auditorium has a fan-shaped theater behind a glass-enclosed lobby and automobile portico. Still in use, these exemplars of mid-20th-c. modernism retain their architectural character, from the carefully detailed terrazzo, metal railings, and concrete surfaces to the smoothly landscaped setting. (See Introduction, Fig. 73.)

MK 51 Plaza-Midwood

Contemporary with *Myers Park and the extension of *Dilworth to the south, in 1910 Paul Chatham, Elkin textile manufacturer, and others established a northeastern suburb called Chatham Estates near the Charlotte Country Club. Local designer Leigh Colyer laid it out along a broad boulevard, The

Plaza. Among the first residences was the **VanLandingham House** (1913; Charles C. Hook & Willard G. Rogers, architects; 2010 The Plaza), a big shingled house with Craftsman detail and rough stonework and a garden designed by Colyer. Ralph VanLandingham was a cotton broker and, with his wife Susie, a civic leader. After a bright start, the development sputtered while the southern suburbs flourished. Gradually large and small houses, including many notable bungalows, were built in a larger area that became known as Plaza-Midwood. **Victoria** (1890–91; 1600 The Plaza), moved from N. Tryon St. in 1915, is the only survivor of the Queen Anne residences that once graced Tryon St. The **Charlotte Country Club** (1931; Aymar Embury II [New York], architect; 2465 Mecklenburg Dr.; private) centers on a clubhouse with a white-columned "Old South" facade and eclectic rooms within. Country house architect Embury (*Southern Pines, *Pinehurst) influenced the development of the American country club with its formal clubhouse and professionally designed golf course.

MK 51 *Victoria*

Northeast of downtown

MK 52 North Charlotte Textile Area
1880s–1930s

The city's prime collection of textile architecture illustrates the era when the region around Charlotte surpassed New England in textile production. Along the Southern Rail-

way route and Davidson St. north from downtown are three related mills, storage and manufacturing buildings, a small commercial district, and several areas of housing, which constitute the largest assemblage of mill houses in the city. Reuse and renovation of mills began ca. 2000.

Development began in 1903 when the Highland Park Mfg. Co. (est. 1892 by D. A. Tompkins and others) acquired 103 acres of farmland 2 miles north of the city center and 1 mile north of the *Alpha Mill, for the site for Highland Park No. 3 Mill. By 1903 the company was led by William E. Holt (president from 1895) of the Alamance Co. textile family and Charlotte businessmen Jesse Spencer and Charles Worth Johnston. They employed leading mill designer Stuart Cramer to plan Highland No. 3 and its village as a state-of-the-art model.

Highland Park No. 3 Mill (1903–4; Stuart W. Cramer; 2901 N. Davidson St., at 32nd St.) was the state's largest cotton mill when it opened. Oriented to the railroad track, the L-shaped building covers more than 100,000 square feet. It stands 2 stories tall with segmental-arched windows and multiple ornate towers, including a 4-story brick stair tower with corbeled and pillared cap that carries the water tank. Cramer, who designed as many as a third of the mills built in the South between 1895 and 1915, featured the mill in his book, *Useful Information for Cotton Manufacturers* (1906). He planned it for efficient and integrated flow of work, from the unloading of cotton at trackside (which was pneumatically blown from the warehouse to the mill) to finished cotton gingham. It was one of the first designed specifically for electric power, with its own generating plant (demolished). When completed, the mill had 30,000 spindles, 1,000 looms, and more than 800 employees.

Although many mill owners provided social facilities for their workers, relatively few N.C. examples survive. Built by a family involved in several mills, the **Johnston Family Memorial YMCA** (ca. 1951; 3025 N. Davidson St., at 33rd St.), a red brick building in domestic Colonial Revival style, shows the continuation of the practice even after World War II. The large and intact mill vil-

MK 52 *Highland Park No. 3 Mill*

lage of 1-story frame houses extends along N. Davidson St. between 32nd and 36th Sts. and several blocks eastward. Cramer planned his model village with a hotel, a school, churches, and stores around a "village square." The plan was not fully realized, but the **Highland Inn** (1903; 3020 N. Alexander St.) was built, a 2-story frame structure of simple Colonial Revival character. Spaced in even rows in the grid of streets, most of the houses are side-gabled 1-story single-family dwellings, with a living room and bedroom in front and a rear dining-kitchen ell. There are also a few duplexes and shotgun-plan houses.

On Davidson St. near 36th St. at a rail crossing is the commercial district of **North Charlotte**, with brick stores, a movie theater, and other facilities for the mill communities. The **Charlotte Fire Station No. 7** (1936; 3210 N. Davidson St.), a handsome little civic building in red brick, has a fire engine portal in front, jail cells in back, and firemen's quarters above with a loggia and a pediment. The **Grinnell Mfg. Co.** (ca. 1910, ca. 1950; 430 E. 36th St.), which made sprinkler fire extinguisher systems used in southern mills, includes a brick building with a low gable roof and large windows, and a smaller but striking office building with Moderne curved corners and glass block.

North of the commercial center, the **Johnston Mill** (1916, 1926, and later; 3301 N. Davidson St.) follows a relatively simple design, in brick with cast-concrete details, 2-story pilasters, and a plain stair tower. It was established by C. W. Johnston, president of the Highland Park Mfg. Co., to meet wartime European demand for cotton, which as the local paper reported in 1915, brought "Amazing Activity Among the Mills" and $3 million in mill expansion.

Farther north, **Mecklenburg Mill** (1903–4; 3401 N. Davidson St.) is a 2-story brick building with arched windows and a central stair tower, contemporary with Highland Park No. 3. It was built by Charlotte investors and the Duke family. Housing for the Mecklenburg Mill is well preserved, both the original section along Mercury and nearby streets and an additional group on Warp and Card Sts. The 1-story frame dwellings include L-plans and several in a T-plan depicted as a "Three-room Gable House" in Tompkins's *Cotton Mill: Commercial Features*. In 1919 the local *Southern Textile Bulletin* lauded the village of 175 workers, where each "cottage" had a large garden and employees showed "considerable civic pride in keeping their village and their homes neat and clean"; plans were under way for "a host of new and modern cottages" on Patterson, Warp, and Card Sts.

MK 53 *Rosedale*

MK 53 Rosedale

Ca. 1815; 3421 N. Tryon St.;
open limited hours

The stylish Federal period plantation house was built for Archibald Frew, but in 1819 it was acquired by planter William Davidson, in whose family it descended. The tripartite configuration has a 2½-story main block with 1½-story flanking wings. The interior has an unexpected combination of stylish Adamesque decorations with an unusual hall-parlor-like plan, with the front entrance opening into the main room. Smaller rooms occupy the wings, two on the left, one on the right. Lavish trim adapted from Owen Biddle's *Young Carpenter's Assistant* features carved urns and swags and foliate ornament in the main room. Endangered in the mid-20th c., the house and garden have been restored.

MK 54 Sugaw Creek Presbyterian Church and Academy

Est. 1750s; NW corner Sugar Creek Rd. and NC 49 (N. Tryon St.)

A pioneer congregation of Scotch-Irish Presbyterians began gathering here for worship in brush arbors by the mid-1750s and gained its first pastor, Alexander Craighead, in 1758. Mother church to many in the region, the congregation also shared the denomination's concern for education, establishing an academy in the 1760s. The brick church has been changed over the years. The Sugaw Creek Academy (ca. 1837) is a simple 1-story building of brick laid in Flemish bond. The large churchyard includes markers from the 18th c. onward, including those of notable Revolutionary War–era figures.

MK 55 Hezekiah Alexander House

1774; restored 1950, 1970s; 3500 Shamrock Dr.;
open regular hours

The unique and massive stone house is one of only two intact 18th-c. stone dwellings in the state (*Michael Braun House), and one of the few colonial buildings associated with a Scotch-Irish settler. It was built for Hezekiah Alexander and his wife Mary Sample, natives of Cecil County, Md., and parents of 10 children. Alexander was a blacksmith and farmer in Pennsylvania before moving to Mecklenburg in the 1760s with other Scotch-Irish Presbyterians. He continued his trade and became one of the wealthiest and most influential men in the county: a planter with as many as 13 slaves, an elder at *Sugaw Creek Presbyterian Church, and like other local Presbyterians, a leader during the American Revolution, as a member of the Committee of Safety and a framer of the state's first constitution.

The well-crafted stone house resembles many in Maryland and Pennsylvania. The only adornments to the thick stone walls are arches with keystones over the asymmetrically placed doors and windows. The 4-room plan has the entrance into the right-

MK 55 *Hezekiah Alexander House*

hand room, which contains a corner stair. Rooms are finished with smoothly plastered walls, planed board partitions, and beaded ceiling joists. Heat was scarce, for corner fireplaces serve only the first-floor rooms. In contrast to Germans' preference for sloping sites, the Alexanders placed their house on a level site, with few openings to the full cellar. A stone springhouse survives, a rare example of its type.

Huntersville area:
The area around Huntersville in northern Mecklenburg Co. supported a plantation society of predominantly Presbyterian families who arrived in the county in the 18th c. and acquired good, well-watered farmland. In the early 19th c. they built handsome plantation houses with stylish details and conservative forms and plans, some of which survive amid the suburban development that arrived in the late 20th c.

MK 56 Hopewell Presbyterian Church
1833–35, H. Hoover, builder;
1859–60, Thomas Rice, builder; 1928;
10500 Beatties Ford Rd., Huntersville vic.

One of the earliest of the Presbyterian congregations whose members dominated the county, Hopewell was founded ca. 1762 with pastor Alexander Craighead. Part of a thriving Presbyterian plantation settlement, the congregation included many of the local planter elite, such as the Davidson, Alexander, Latta, Torrence, and Knox families. In the 1830s the congregation replaced a wooden meetinghouse with a brick one; the oldest section of the church is a plain, rectangular, gable-fronted structure of brick laid in Flemish bond. They subsequently expanded it in Greek Revival style, with tall triple-hung windows with granite sills along the sides and arched openings at the gable front, which was extended forward about 12 feet for a vestibule. The interior is remarkably intact, with Greek Revival and Federal style detailing. The substantial Sunday school building of 1928 continues the red brick and basic design. The large churchyard contains fine grave markers from the 1770s onward, including box and chest tombs from Charleston carvers, indicative of the congregation's wealth and trade connections.

MK 57 Latta Plantation
Early 19th c.; end of SR 2125;
open regular hours

A distinctive blend of stylish and regional elements, the 2-story frame plantation house shows an unusual adaptation of a side-passage plan. The entrance, located at the south gable end beside the heavy Flemish-bond chimney, opens into a passage that runs along the west side and serves two rooms along the east, with a window from the passage into the parlor. Ornate Georgian-Federal detailing includes crossetted door and window frames and elaborate mantels and overmantels. Like other local houses, doors have traditional chevron boarding on the backs and six flush panels on the fronts. Log and frame outbuildings, including a slave house, have been moved here.

The plantation was established by James Latta, who came from Ireland to America in 1785, "a traveling merchant and a planter with a mind set chiefly on gold in the accumulation of which he was singularly successful," according to local historian Chalmers Davidson. In 1795 he married Jane Knox, of a strong Presbyterian family. They soon built the plantation house for their family of daughters, who were educated at *Salem Academy and became mistresses of leading plantations: Mary at *Cedar Grove, Nancy

MK 57 *Latta Plantation House*

at *Mount Mourne in nearby Iredell Co., and Elizabeth at *Oak Lawn and later *Mount Mourne. When Latta's plantation was sold after his death in 1837, it boasted "a good two story Dwelling House, with all necessary out-buildings, unusually well built, and arranged more conveniently than on most places in this county." The widow Jane moved to *Mount Mourne to look after her many grandchildren.

MK 58 Holly Bend

Early 19th c.; N side SR 2074, 2.75 mi. W of SR 2128; private, visible from road

Located in a bend of the Catawba River, the 2-story frame house was the home of Robert and Margaret Osborne Davidson, who married in 1801. Robert received the land in 1795 from his father, John, and became one of the county's wealthiest planters. The relatively modest house follows a center-passage plan, 1 room deep, with Flemish-bond end chimneys and early Federal style details akin to his brother's *Oak Lawn.

MK 59 Oak Lawn

Ca. 1820; W side SR 2138, 0.6 mi. N of SR 2130; private, visible from road

Benjamin Davidson and Elizabeth Latta (*Latta House) married in 1818 and built a house on land received from his father, John. Accounts of 1821 show purchases of construction items in Charleston. The 2-story frame house with Flemish-bond chimneys has an off-center passage dividing a large room on the left and two small rooms on the

MK 60 *Cedar Grove*

right. Georgian-Federal style detail similar to *Holly Bend may be drawn from builders' guides by William Pain. Widowed in 1829, Elizabeth in 1835 married Rufus Reid of nearby *Mount Mourne, Iredell Co.

MK 60 Cedar Grove

1830–33; David Hampton and Jacob Shuman, builders; H. S. Gorman, plasterer; N side 2136, 1.0 mi. W of SR 2138; private, visible from road

The massive brick house proclaimed the success of entrepreneurial merchant and planter James G. Torrence. Son of Irish immigrant planter Hugh Torance, in 1805 James opened a store on his father's plantation, and in 1816 he inherited over 1,400 acres. (The frame **Torrence House and Store**, encompassing an initial log structure, stands nearby.) Expanding his corn and cotton plantation to more than 3,000 acres, James also operated a gold mine and a saw- and gristmill. In 1830 he began one of the most ambitious plantation houses in the Piedmont, for which he ordered hardware, finish items, and furniture from New York, Philadelphia, and Charleston. The 5-bay house of Flemish-bond brick, some 60 by 40 feet, with a center-passage plan stands 2 stories above a high basement, its impact heightened by tall stepped gables with end chimneys. Bold Greek Revival details from

MK 59 *Oak Lawn*

Asher Benjamin's *Practical House Carpenter* (1830) are some of the earliest in the state.

MK 61 Davidson

The pleasant college town maintains much of its late 19th- to early 20th-c. scale and its focus on the school that gave it life. In 1835, when the Concord Presbytery sought a site for a Presbyterian men's college, churchman and planter William Davidson offered 469 acres on a high and healthy ridge between the Catawba and Yadkin rivers, "at a distance from all haunts of dissipation." Presbyterians from many congregations came to help clear the land and haul bricks for the initial eight buildings. He later donated funds for **Davidson College**, which was named for his father and earned a lasting reputation for its academic excellence.

MK 61 *Chambers Hall, Davidson College*

MK 61 *Elm Row, Davidson College*

On the spacious, shaded campus two buildings still stand from the original eight attributed to builder Samuel Lemly—**Oak Row** and **Elm Row**, which were ready for the opening of the college in 1837. Both are 1-story gabled dormitories of brick laid in common bond and contain 4 rooms each, all with outside entrances. Two little classical temples, **Eumenean Hall and Philanthropic Hall** (1848–50; Lewis Dinkins and Daniel Alexander, plasterer and carpenter), recall that at Davidson, as at *UNC in Chapel Hill, antebellum student life centered on two debating clubs. In November 1842, "Eu" decided to erect a hall, followed by "Phi" in January 1843. The usually competitive societies agreed to build a pair of structures "alike in size, material, and magnificence" and to cost $1,500 apiece. Eu was dedicated in 1849, and Phi in 1850. With pedimented porticoes facing each other, both are 2-story structures with the main room in the second story. (See Introduction, Fig. 19.) In the 1850s, after a bequest from Maxwell Chambers of Salisbury made the school one of the wealthiest in the nation, work began on a massive, columned Main Building in Tuscan style, designed by leading American architect Alexander Jackson Davis as part of an immense campus quadrangle scheme. Only the central portion was completed before the Civil War halted con-

struction. Known as Chambers Hall, it burned in 1921.

In the early 20th c., especially after James B. Duke provided a substantial endowment, the college began a program of expansion, commissioning a campus plan and several handsome Neoclassical buildings in a red brick Georgian Revival vocabulary, designed by Nashville college designer Henry C. Hibbs. **Chambers Hall** (1924), the main building erected to replace its antebellum predecessor, is a massive and symmetrical building with monumental portico and dome, the latter apparently designed in part by Rafael Guastavino. Other Hibbs designs included a dormitory, a science building, and a library in 1939–40. There is a small brick business district opposite campus on Main St., including **The Inn** (1848; Lewis Dinkins, builder; Main St.), a 2-story brick building with 2-tier porch, pilasters, and simple Greek Revival detail; Dinkins built the "brick store house" in a style similar to that of the society halls. In the 1850s it was enlarged to become a hotel; later it was a boarding and rooming house for college visitors. The many faculty houses of the late

19th and early 20th centuries are typically of frame with capacious porches.

MK 62 Beaver Dam

1829 (date brick); E side NC 73,
0.6 mi. S of SR 2420, Davidson vic.;
private, visible from road

Presbyterian planter William Lee Davidson (*Davidson College donor) bought the plantation in 1808 and built a log house, which he replaced with a larger log dwelling in 1829. Covered in weatherboards and re-modeled over the years, the house has the appearance of an asymmetrical frame I-house. In the 20th c. it was the home of Chalmers Davidson, history professor at the college and early preservation leader.

MK 63 Ramah Presbyterian Church

1881; W side SR 2427, 0.9 mi.
S of NC 73, Huntersville vic.

The picturesque frame church combines a traditional gable-fronted form with stylish Italianate touches in the segmental-arched openings at both levels and heavy molding over the central, arched entrance. The churchyard has notable markers from ca. 1800 onward. The congregation was orga-nized ca. 1783 to serve the Huntersville farm-ing community.

MK 64 Croft

NC 115 and SR 2483

The most intact of several railroad trading villages in the county, Croft maintains its identity despite development of its sur-rounding farmland. It is located north of Charlotte beside the Southern Railway and the old Statesville road. The **S. W. & C. S. Davis General Store** (1908), a 2-story brick store complete with painted signs and deco-rative brickwork and original interior, was built by the Davis brothers, Silas and Charles, local farmers who began to buy land flanking the railroad in 1903. They built the 2-story Queen Anne style **Davis House** (ca. 1903) facing the tracks, adorned with fancy millwork and a wraparound porch; outbuildings include a brick flower house, a frame smokehouse and a corncrib, and various barns. Their store offered rail-delivered goods from ribbons to fertilizer to nearby farmers in exchange for cotton and other produce. The Davises also operated a cotton gin and had other stores. They sup-ported the **Croft School** (ca. 1890, 1924), and Silas, who had 10 children, is recalled as paying for the 1924 expansion of the 2-story frame building to its present form. After Silas died in 1925, Charles married Nena Faye Thomasson, a teacher at the school, and moved into a smaller house nearby.

MK 63 *Ramah Presbyterian Church*

MK 65 White Oak

*Late 18th c.; W side SR 2826, 0.3 mi.
N of SR 2822; private, visible from road*

Planter and Revolutionary War veteran William Johnston is said to have built the house ca. 1792, one of several Piedmont houses with 3-room plan, Flemish-bond brickwork, and Georgian-Federal detail. The tall porch is 20th c. Early outbuildings include two of brick and one of stone.

MK 66 Providence Presbyterian Church

1858; 10140 Providence Rd., Matthews vic.

The antebellum frame church beside the road is among the most striking renditions of the simplified Greek Revival style popular among Piedmont Presbyterians: the straightforward gable-fronted form gains drama from the great triple-hung windows—16/16/16—that rise nearly from floor level to second-story ceiling height and flood the sanctuary with light. The congregation was organized in 1767 and perhaps met earlier; it was one of the "seven sister" colonial Presbyterian churches of the area where early settlers and leading citizens were predominantly Scotch-Irish Presbyterians. Providence ministers were leaders in the denomination and its educational efforts, and pastor Robert Hall Morrison became founding president of *Davidson College. The present church was built during the pastorate of Jethro Rumple, later minister and historian in Salisbury. Across the road the large churchyard includes many early graves and fine markers.

MK 67 Steele Creek Presbyterian Church

*1889; H. J. Norris, builder; E side NC 160,
3.5 mi. SW of US 521, Charlotte vic.*

The gable-fronted brick church features Gothic Revival pointed-arched openings flanked by pilasters, decorative corbeling, and small crenellated entrance towers at the gable front. Built to replace an 1858 church that burned, it is the sixth house of worship of a Scotch-Irish congregation founded in the mid-18th c.—by 1760 and perhaps as early as the 1740s. A landmark in a county renowned for its Presbyterian heritage, Steele Creek was one of the "seven sisters" or "Pleiades" colonial churches, which also included *Providence, *Sugaw Creek, *Hopewell, *Centre (Iredell Co.), and *Rocky River and *Poplar Tent (Cabarrus Co.). Especially notable is the collection of gravestones from the 1760s to ca. 1820, several by the local Bigham family of carvers, who were members; a handsome 19th-c. stone wall retains early wrought iron gates.

Glossary

This glossary has been adapted from lists of architectural terms that have appeared in survey publications on historic architecture in N.C., including especially Dru Gatewood Haley and Raymond A. Winslow, *The Historic Architecture of Perquimans County, North Carolina* (1982); Davyd Foard Hood, *The Architecture of Rowan County* (1983); Peter B. Sandbeck, *The Historic Architecture of New Bern and Craven County, North Carolina* (1988); and Kelly Lally, *The Historic Architecture of Wake County, North Carolina* (1994). For analysis of period usages of early architectural terms, including many N.C. references, see Carl R. Lounsbury, *An Illustrated Glossary of Early Southern Architecture and Landscape* (1994).

Adam or Adamesque: See *Federal style*.

Akron plan: A design for Sunday schools developed by an Akron businessman and Sunday school teacher in the 19th c. for maximum efficiency in use of space. A central room for general teaching was surrounded by smaller rooms, opening from it, for smaller class groups. Often an Akron-plan Sunday school was attached to a church with an *auditorium plan*, and in some examples the two could be combined by opening a partition to provide a larger auditorium for large services.

anta, antae (in antis): *Pilasters* or piers at the corners of a building. Typically these are used at the ends of a colonnade (pair or row of columns) as part of a *portico* set into (rather than projecting from) the building, so that the antae flank the colonnade. This is described as a portico "in antis." Usually the antae are simpler than the columns they flank.

apse: A semicircular or polygonal portion of a building, such as a church or a courthouse.

arcade: A row of arches supported on piers or columns, attached to or detached from a wall.

architrave: The lowest part of a 3-part classical *entablature* (architrave, frieze, cornice). Often used by itself as a casing for a window, door, etc. A single architrave consists of an inner *bead*, a broad band, and an outer raised molding; a double architrave has two bands separated by a molding.

Art Deco: A style of decorative arts and architecture popular in the 1920s and 1930s, characterized by geometric forms and exotic motifs. So called by later era historians from the popularization of the style at the

Exposition Internationale des Arts Décoratifs et Industriels Modernes, held in 1925 in Paris.

Arts and Crafts: An approach to decorative arts and architecture in late 19th- and early 20th-c. Britain and America that emphasized handicrafts and direct expression of materials and construction. One of many movements that developed in reaction to the Industrial Revolution, it took its name from the Arts and Crafts Exhibition Society (est. 1888). In N.C. the Arts and Crafts movement influenced the revival of traditional crafts such as pottery and weaving; in architecture it encouraged the use of native materials and the revival—and continuation—of rough stonework and rustic log construction. See *Craftsman* style.

ashlar: Stonework consisting of individual stones that are shaped and tooled to have even faces and square edges.

auditorium plan: A plan employed in late 19th- and early 20th-c. church architecture, in which the *sanctuary* is treated like the auditorium of a theater, to maximize sight and hearing of the word preached from the pulpit. Often the floor slopes down toward the pulpit, which may be in front or in a corner, and pews are curved or angled concentrically from the pulpit. Sometimes confused with the *Akron plan* for Sunday schools often joined with auditorium plan sanctuaries.

balustrade (baluster): A series of regularly spaced uprights (balusters) topped by a railing to provide an ornamental and protective barrier along the edge of a stair, roof, balcony, porch, etc. Balusters (and railings) were typically heavy and *turned* in the 18th c. as part of the *Georgian style*, became simpler and more delicate in the *Federal style* in the early 19th c., grew heavier again in the mid-19th c. with the *Greek Revival* and *Italianate* styles, and gained heft and ornateness with the *eclecticism* of the late 19th c.

bargeboard: A board attached to and covering the sloping edge of a *gable roof* or *dormer*. Often sawn in a decorative, curvilinear design when used in the picturesque styles of the mid-19th c., especially the *Gothic Revival*. Also called vergeboard.

bartizan: A small, overhanging turret projecting from a tower, often rounded, sometimes polygonal; a feature of chateauesque, *Gothic Revival*, and *Romanesque Revival* styles, especially on church towers.

bay: (1) An opening or division along a face of a building; for example, a wall with a door flanked by two windows is three bays wide. (2) The space between principal structural members, as in a timber frame, the space between posts. (3) A projection from the *façade* of a building, in particular a polygonal or semicircular projection with windows, called a bay window.

bead: A rounded molding semicircular in section, often used to finish an edge or corner of a wooden element, such as a *weatherboard* or *flush sheathing* board. A bead provides a neat appearance and protects against splitting and wear.

Beaux Arts: A style or school of design characterized by the academic and *eclectic* use of historical—typically *classical*—architectural elements, usually on a monumental scale, as promulgated by the École des Beaux Arts in Paris in the 19th c. The Beaux Arts style attained great popularity in American architecture from the 1890s through the 1920s, especially in public architecture, banks, and mansions. Beaux Arts design stressed rational and hierarchical planning in form, layout, and detail. Beaux Arts classicism produced monumental architecture—epitomized and popularized by the World's Columbian Exposition of 1893 in Chicago—that employed Roman and Renaissance *orders* and forms on a grand scale, with imposing formality and dignity. Through commissions to nationally and regionally active architects, and through the federal government's supervising architect of the Treasury, N.C. towns gained public buildings in Beaux Arts–influenced styles in the early 20th c.

belt course: A projecting horizontal course of brick, stone, or wood used on exterior walls, usually to delineate the line between stories, also called a string course.

board and batten: A method of covering a wall using vertical boards, with narrow strips of wood (battens) covering the joints between the boards. Popularized in the mid-19th c. for modest wooden buildings in the picturesque movement, especially cottages and Gothic churches. The *Carpenter Gothic* style typically employs board-and-batten walls and *bargeboards*.

bond: The pattern in which masonry, particularly brickwork, is laid to tie together the thickness of the wall; specifically, the pattern of the *headers* and *stretchers* seen on the outer face of the masonry. A header is a brick laid through the wall so that only its short end is visible. A stretcher is a brick laid along the wall so that its long side is visible. The principal bonds used in N.C. were *English bond*, *Flemish bond*, and *common bond*.

In English bond, a row of headers alternates with a row of stretchers, creating a very strong wall. English bond was used from the 17th c. well into the 18th c. but became rare by the end of the 18th c.

In Flemish bond, stretchers and headers alternate in each row and are staggered vertically, with each header centered over the stretcher below, creating a decorative checkerboard effect. Especially in the 18th c. the use of all *glazed headers* emphasized this pattern. (Glazed headers attained a vitrified, dark, shiny surface during firing by being placed toward the heat in the brick kiln.) Flemish bond was used from the 17th c. into the early 19th c. and occasionally into the mid-19th c. It was the predominant bond in the 18th c. Often 18th-c. brick buildings displayed English bond up to the water table and Flemish bond above it.

Common bond (1:3, also called American bond) has 1 row of headers to 3, 5, or 7 rows of stretchers. Until the late 18th c., 1:3

bond predominated; 1:5 and 1:7 ratios grew more frequent in the 19th c. Common bond was more economical than Flemish bond, and in some early and mid-19th-c. buildings the principal *facades* were of Flemish bond; the others, of common bond. In the mid-19th c., stretcher or all-stretcher bond came into use, with the outer banks bonded to interior ones with concealed diagonal bricks. Flemish bond, either as a solid wall or veneer, saw renewed use in *Colonial Revival* architecture.

bracket: A device—ornamental, structural, or both—set under an overhanging element, such as the *eave* of a building. Brackets are especially characteristic of the *Italianate* style. Also, the decorative element attached to the ends of steps in a staircase.

bungalow: A house type and architectural style popular in the early 20th c. Typically defined as a relatively modest, 1½-story dwelling of informal character, the bungalow traced its origins to British colonial dwellings in India, as well as to the *Arts and Crafts* movement of the 19th c. Popularized through magazines and plan books, the bungalow was promoted as a wholesome, natural, inexpensive, modern, and convenient house. It saw its greatest development in California, which lent sunny associations of an ideal home. Its basic characteristics include a low-slung silhouette with a dominant roof form, usually a *gable* or *clipped gable* roof; 1½-story height even in larger examples; deep overhanging *eaves*; broad porches—*engaged* or attached—with square, squat brick piers supporting wood posts, which are often tapered; and informal plans emphasizing open spaces and deemphasizing *passages*. Decorative elements, particularly in bungalows rendered in the characteristic *Craftsman* style, stressed straightforward expression of construction elements, such as exposed *rafter* ends, triangular *brackets* beneath the roof, and natural shingles. Some bungalows incorporated Japanese and other Oriental motifs; a few featured Tudor or Spanish motifs; and in N.C. simplified *Colonial Revival* detailing was also popular. In N.C. bungalows began to appear in the mid-1910s, became widely popular in the 1920s,

persisted through the 1930s, but were seldom built after World War II, when the ranch house dominated the market for unpretentious, modern, convenient houses. The Aladdin Company, which had a factory in Wilmington, N.C., produced thousands of prefab bungalows, many of which were delivered by railroad to N.C. towns and counties.

buttress: A vertical mass of masonry projecting from or built against a wall to give additional strength at the point of maximum stress. Sometimes wooden buttresses are added to frame *Gothic Revival* style buildings as decorative features.

capital: The topmost member, usually decorated or molded, of a column or *pilaster*. Each classical *order—Doric, Ionic, Corinthian, Composite,* etc.—has its characteristic capital.

Carpenter Gothic: A popular term referring to the mid-19th-c. adaptation of the *Gothic Revival* style to wooden buildings produced by carpenters, typified by *board-and-batten* walls and decorative *bargeboards* and porch trim.

castellated: Featuring elements associated with castles, such as *crenellation* and turrets.

center-passage plan (center-hall plan): A plan in which the hall or passage extends through the center of a house and is flanked by one or more pairs of rooms. A center-passage plan two rooms deep—with four main rooms divided by the passage—became especially popular among large houses in the Georgian period and is sometimes referred to as a Georgian plan (also as a *double-pile* plan). This plan continued in widespread use long past the Georgian period, especially from the mid-19th c. onward.

chair rail: A horizontal board or molding fixed on a wall at or about the height of the top of a chair; often the topmost member or cap of *wainscoting*. Until the mid-19th c. this feature was called a chair board.

chamfer: A traditional method of finishing a post, beam, *joist*, or other element, in which the square corners are beveled (cut away at an oblique angle). Often the chamfer ends in a decorative terminus or chamfer stop, the most common in N.C. being the curved lamb's-tongue chamfer stop.

chancel: The end of a church containing the altar and often set apart for the use of clergy by a railing or screen. A chancel may be extended as a distinct architectural unit projecting from the main body of the church.

classical: Embodying or based on the principles and forms of ancient Greek and Roman architecture.

Classical Revival: A general term referring to styles that reuse the principles and forms of ancient Greek and Roman architecture. See *Greek Revival, Beaux Arts, Colonial Revival, Neoclassical.*

clipped gable: A *gable* where the peak is truncated for decorative effect; often seen in *bungalows.*

coastal cottage, coastal plain cottage: A recent, general term for 1½-story dwellings characterized by *engaged* or inset porches, so called because of their predominance in the coastal plain and tidewater areas of N.C. Not a standard architectural term, but useful locally as a shorthand word for a common form.

Colonial Revival: A late 19th- and early 20th-c. American architectural style that drew freely on architectural motifs associated with the American past, including not only elements of the colonial period but also those of the early national era and even the *Greek Revival* and a host of *classical* designs. The *Southern Colonial Revival* and the *Georgian Revival* were developments of the broader Colonial Revival movement. The popularity of the Colonial Revival, chiefly in residential architecture, paralleled the closely kin *Beaux Arts* classicism in public and institutional architecture. In N.C. the Colonial Revival saw occasional use as early as the 1880s, grew in popularity in the mid- and late 1890s—often mixed with the late *Queen Anne* style—and became a dominant residential style in the early 20th c. Its popularity has continued in various guises to the present.

colonnette: A small column, generally employed as a decorative element on mantels, overmantels, and *porticoes.*

common bond: See *bond.*

common rafter, common-rafter roof: One of a series of rafters of uniform size, spaced evenly along a roof. In a common-rafter roof, the roof is made entirely of pairs of common rafters, which may join at the apex in a ridgepole or be joined in opposing pairs by a lapped joint without a ridgepole. This type of roof was extremely common in N.C. from the earliest buildings on. See also *principal rafter.*

Composite order: A classical order characterized by a column whose *capital* combines *Ionic* volutes and *Corinthian* acanthus leaves.

corbel: A projecting brick or stone, used for supporting or decorative purposes in masonry construction. In a corbeled *cornice,* each row projects farther out than those below it.

Corinthian order: One of the five classical architectural orders, developed in the 5th c. B.C. The most ornate of the orders, its column is characterized by a *capital* with acanthus leaves and curled ferns.

corncrib: A building, usually small, for storing shelled corn or ears of corn. Usually a separate structure, sometimes attached to a barn; sometimes built with solid walls, sometimes with spaces between logs or slats for ventilation. A common outbuilding on N.C. farms from the 17th c. into the mid-20th c.

cornerblock: A square element, either plain or decorated with a circular or other design, usually marking the upper corner of a window or door *surround.* Typical of the *Greek Revival* style during the mid-19th c.; also widely employed ca. 1890–1910.

cornerboard: A vertical board applied to an external corner of a frame building to finish the *facades* and cover the ends of the *weatherboards.* Often treated with a *capital* and base to form a corner *pilaster.*

cornice: The uppermost part of a 3-part classical *entablature* (architrave, frieze, cornice); also, a horizontal molded element used to crown the wall of a building, *portico,* or doorway. The term is loosely applied to almost any horizontal molding forming a main decorative feature, such as a molding (nowadays often called a crown molding) at the junction of walls and ceiling in a room. When enriched with *dentils* or *modillions,* it is called a dentil cornice or a modillion cornice. A raking cornice extends along a slanting (raking) side of a *gable* or *pediment*. A boxed cornice is a simple treatment with a vertical fascia board and a horizontal soffit board enclosing the ends of the ceiling *joists* where they project at the *eaves*.

Craftsman: A style of furniture and architectural design promoted by Gustav Stickley's magazine *The Craftsman* as an American interpretation of the *Arts and Crafts* movement. The style emphasized informal plans and forms, natural materials, and direct expression (or suggestion) of construction. Stickley's magazine and those influenced by it promoted various house types, including English cottage forms and, most popular, the *bungalow*. Typical Craftsman details include heavy, tapered porch posts, exposed *rafter* and purlin ends beneath broad eaves, and exaggerated angular eave *brackets* and other carpentry features; interiors often feature simple, naturally finished woodwork, built-in cabinetry, and heavily crafted hardware.

crenellation, crenellated: Alternating indentations and raised sections (embrasures and merlons) of a *parapet*, creating a toothlike profile sometimes known as a battlement. In the medieval period these were defensive features of castles. Crenellated rooflines, especially on towers, are most often used in the *Gothic Revival* style.

cresting: Ornamental ironwork used to embellish the ridge of a *gable roof* or the curb or upper *cornice* of a mansard roof.

crib: A corncrib; also, a log structural unit of a barn or other farm building, making up double-crib barns and other forms.

crossette: A lateral projection of the head of the molded frame (architrave) of a door, window, mantel, or panel; also known as an "ear." The motif is characteristically used in the *Georgian style* but also appears in *Greek Revival* and *Italianate* and occasionally in *Colonial Revival* work (esp. *Georgian Revival*).

cupola: A small structure, usually polygonal, built on top of a roof or tower, mostly for ornamental purposes, sometimes as an observation point.

dentils: Small, closely placed blocks set in a horizontal row (like little teeth, dim. of *dens*: dentil), used as an ornamental element of a classical *cornice*. Distinguished from *modillions*, which are spaced farther apart. Cornices might have courses of both dentils and modillions.

distyle: Having two columns, typically in a portico *in antis*.

dogtrot: A plan seen principally in log houses in which two *pens* (log-walled units) are separated by an open *passage*. Relatively rare in N.C. today.

Doric order: A classical order characterized by heavy columns with simple, unadorned *capitals* supporting a *frieze* of vertically grooved tablets or triglyphs set at intervals. Renaissance architectural authorities classified the order into the Greek Doric, in which the column has no base, and the Roman Doric, in which the column stands on a base. The Doric order, often greatly simplified, was popularly used in N.C., especially in *Greek Revival* buildings during the antebellum period.

dormer, dormer window: An upright window, set in a sloping roof, with vertical sides and front, usually with a *gable, shed,* or *hip roof*. Used to light rooms in a half-story.

double-pen: See *pen*.

double-pile: A plan two rooms deep, most often used to refer to a *center-passage plan* house that is two rooms deep on either side of the passage.

double-shouldered chimney: An exterior chimney the sides of which angle inward to form shoulders twice as it ascends from the base to the cap, accommodating a fireplace in each of two stories. Typically in N.C. double-shouldered chimneys were employed through the 18th c. and into the 19th c. but were gradually supplanted by single-shouldered chimneys in the early 19th c. See *shoulder*.

dovetail: A joint in woodworking, commonly used in furniture and in plank or log building, wherein a piece of timber is cut (like a dove's tail) with two outward flaring sides meant to fit into correspondingly shaped spaces in adjoining members. A half-dovetail has only one edge flared; the other is straight. Various framing members might be dovetailed together. The most frequently noted usage is in construction of hewn or sawn plank (and sometimes log) structures with full- or half-dovetailed corner notches. In N.C. this method continued to be used in small outbuildings, from the 18th c. through much of the 19th c.

eave: The edge of a roof, usually above a *cornice*, often overhanging to shed water beyond the face of the wall. Eaves were often flush with the wall at the *gable* ends of 18th- and early 19th-c. buildings. Mid- and late 19th-c. eaves normally extended beyond the walls.

eclectic, eclecticism: An approach to design, including architecture, in which elements are selected from a variety of sources—historical, stylistic—and combined. Often applied to mid- and, especially, late 19th-c. architecture such as the *Queen Anne* style.

ell: A wing or extension of a building, often a rear addition, positioned at right angles to the principal mass.

engaged porch: A porch whose roof is continuous structurally with that of the main roof of the building. Typically in eastern N.C., a double-slope roof shelters an engaged porch. Partial *rafters* are attached to the main rafters of a *gable-roofed* house at a point partway down the gable slope, so that the roof breaks to a gentler slope within the block of the house and continues outward over the porch. *Shed rooms* to the rear may be treated in the same fashion. In an inset porch, the porch is set entirely within the block of the house, under a gable roof composed of a single set of rafters.

English bond: See *bond.*

entablature: The upper horizontal part of a classical *order* of architecture, usually positioned above columns or *pilasters*. It consists of three parts: the lowest molded portion is the *architrave*; the middle band (plain or decorated) is the *frieze*; the uppermost molded element is the *cornice*. Variously adapted and simplified entablatures are incorporated into doorways, windows, mantels, and the like.

exposed face chimney: In a frame house, an *interior end chimney* built so that the outside face or "back" of the chimney is exposed

rather than covered with *weatherboards*. It may be exposed as far up as the *eave* line or only in the first story. This feature is most common in N.C. in the New Bern area.

exterior end chimney: A chimney located outside the wall of a building, usually rising at the *gable* end.

facade: The face or front of a building.

fanlight: A semicircular window, usually above a door or window, with radiating *muntins* suggesting a fan.

Federal style: A style of *Neoclassical* architecture popular in America in the late 18th and early 19th centuries, reflecting the influence of the *Adam* style, the Roman-inspired mode of Scots architects Robert and James Adam, which emphasized delicate, linear forms, attenuated proportions, and curved forms and spaces. In N.C. the Federal style began to appear along with the continuing *Georgian style* about 1800, and many buildings into the 1810s and even the 1820s show elements of both styles. The Federal style became widely popular in the 1810s and 1820s and continued into the 1830s and, in some areas, the 1840s, despite the growing influence of the *Greek Revival* style. The style is characterized by the use of delicate Neoclassical ornament such as fans, garlands, and sunbursts and by attenuation of such elements as *balusters*, window *muntins*, columns, and *pilasters*. Popularized by English and American builders' guides, it lent itself to individualized interpretation, particularly in lavish *reeding* and gougework, by local artisans.

fenestration: The arrangement of windows on a building.

finial: A vertical ornament placed on the apex of an architectural feature such as a *gable*, turret, or *pediment.*

Flemish bond: See *bond.*

flume: A channel or chute to carry water, as at a gristmill or sawmill.

flush sheathing: A wall treatment consisting of closely fitted boards with tight joints, all laid in the same plane to give a uniform, flat appearance. Boards may be finished with a *bead* on the edge. Used in N.C. in interior finishes but also on the portion of an exterior wall sheltered by a porch, where it gives a smoother, more interior-like character than would lapped *weatherboards*.

flutes, fluted, fluting: Shallow, concave grooves running vertically on the shaft of a column, *pilaster*, or other surface.

foursquare, American foursquare: A popular house form 2 stories tall with a *hip roof*, taking a straightforwardly square shape and generally without elaborate decoration. The type was quite popular in the late 19th and especially the early 20th centuries, amid the Progressive Era's emphasis on simplicity and practicality, but the terms "foursquare" or "American foursquare" are recent coinages, not period names.

frieze: The middle portion of a classical *entablature*, located above the *architrave* and below the *cornice*. It may be plain or ornamented. By extension, the term is often used to describe the flat, vertical board used beneath a cornice and above the *weatherboards* of a frame building, and also for the flat board between the *pilasters* and shelf (cornice) of a mantel.

gable: The triangular portion of a wall formed or defined by the two sloping sides of a ridged roof.

gable roof: A roof formed with two opposing planes sloping to a common ridge, forming triangular *gables* at the ends. Sometimes called a pitched roof or A-roof. Gable roofs were the most common roof form in N.C. buildings.

gambrel roof: A roof with two pitches rising to a ridge, the upper slope being markedly flatter than the lower one. In central N.C., gambrel-roofed houses were built in the 18th c. and continued into the early 19th c. The form was revived and sometimes called "Dutch" or "Dutch colonial" in the early 20th-c. *Colonial Revival* era.

Georgian plan: See *center-passage plan*.

Georgian Revival: A revival of Georgian architectural forms, both in England and America, and as part of the larger *Colonial Revival* style in America. In N.C. the style became especially popular after about 1910 and often took the form of symmetrical, restrained designs with rich *classical* detail, quite frequently in a Virginia vocabulary. The Georgian Revival was particularly popular for public buildings, churches, and residences, often executed in red brick with contrasting white.

Georgian style: The prevailing architectural style of the 18th c. in Great Britain and the North American colonies. Popularly called Georgian style (not a term at the time) after the monarchs who reigned during its heyday, George I, George II, and George III. It is derived from *classical* Renaissance and Baroque forms and was shaped in Britain by architects such as Christopher Wren and James Gibbs. Builders' guides published in England, such as those of Batty Langley, Abraham Swan, James Gibbs, William Salmon, William Pain, and others, made the elements of the style available to craftsmen and clients. As expressed in relatively simple form in N.C., the Georgian style is characterized by symmetrical forms and plans, relatively heavy classical moldings, raised *panels*, robust classically derived ornament, and such motifs as *pediments*, *modillion cornices*, *turned balustrades*, and *crossetted surrounds* on doorways, windows, and mantels. Georgian motifs appeared in a few N.C. buildings in the 1750s, but fully realized examples of the style came only in the late 1760s and thereafter. Use of the Georgian style continued into the early 19th c., often in transitional combinations with the *Federal style*.

glazed header: A brick having a glossy dark surface on one end, ranging in color from gray green to almost black, formed through direct exposure to flame and intense heat in the firing process. In Flemish-bond brickwork (see *bond*), this glazed surface is often used for decorative effect by laying the bricks so that the glazed ends of headers emphasize the checkerboard pattern in the wall or, in some cases, delineate letters, numerals, or other designs. Such work appeared in the mid-18th c. in northeastern N.C. and in the late 18th and early 19th centuries in the Piedmont.

Gothic Revival: The revival of the forms and ornament of medieval Gothic architecture, characterized by the use of the pointed arch, *buttresses*, pinnacles, and other Gothic details. Begun in Europe in the late 18th c., the Gothic Revival came into N.C. use in the mid-19th c. (though there were a few early gestures in the style in the 1810s and 1820s, chiefly in work by architect William Nichols). The Gothic Revival style appeared occasionally in residential architecture in picturesque cottages (a few in the 1850s, more in the post–Civil War era) influenced by the publications of Andrew Jackson Downing, but it was vastly more popular in religious architecture. Introduced in the state by the Episcopal Church in the 1830s and 1840s, the Gothic Revival flourished from the 1850s onward as a predominant religious style and continued in use in church architecture through the 20th c.

graining: A decorative painted treatment on wood, usually used to simulate exotic or costly woods, sometimes stylized to the point of abstraction.

Greek Revival: The mid-19th-c. revival of the forms and ornamentation of the architecture of ancient Greece. The Greek Revival, often much simplified, was the most popular style in N.C. from the 1830s until the Civil War. A few early motifs appear in the 1810s and 1820s in work by architect William Nichols, and in some areas elements of the style persist into the 1870s. Builders' guides by Asher Benjamin and Minard Lafever were widely used sources. The Greek Revival dominated fashionable architecture and was translated by local carpenters into greatly simplified versions. It is characterized by broad, rectilinear, usually symmetrical forms; wide *friezes* and *pilasters*; flat surfaces; doors and window frames marked by *cornerblocks*, and heavy mantels featuring columns and *entablature*, or a plain pilaster and frieze format. Porches are often treated as *porticoes*, with the *Doric order* frequently employed—and simplifications thereof often with squared *pillars*. Courthouses and churches were often rendered as gable-fronted temple forms with projecting or recessed porticoes, but this treatment was rare in residential architecture.

hall-parlor plan: A traditional plan consisting of two principal rooms: a larger "hall," often nearly square, and an adjoining smaller "parlor." In most instances the hall

was entered directly from the outside and had a fireplace centered on the end wall. It was the room where most domestic activities took place and from which doors led to other rooms and to the stairs. The smaller parlor was often used for sleeping. This plan was used from the late 17th c. through the 18th c. in top-quality houses in N.C. and continued into the mid-19th c. in middling and small houses.

header: A brick placed in a wall so that the short end faces outward. See *bond*.

hexastyle: Having six columns, usually referring to a portico.

hip roof: A roof that slopes back equally from each side (usually four) of a building. A hip roof may have a pyramidal form or have a slight ridge. A hip roof on a porch usually has three slopes, the center one being widest.

I-house: A term coined by geographer Fred Kniffen to describe a certain house type commonly seen in states beginning with the letter *I*, but also seen frequently elsewhere, including N.C. Kniffen applied the term to 2-story houses one room deep and two or more rooms wide. The tall, thin profile also suited the term "I-house." The term is employed as a convenient shorthand for a common form but has no basis in traditional architectural language.

inset porch: See *engaged porch*.

interior end chimney: A chimney positioned inside the end wall of a house.

International style: A term first used by Henry-Russell Hitchcock and Philip Johnson in 1932 to describe the nontraditional architecture that had begun in the 1920s in Europe and was appearing in the United States. Simplified, abstracted forms, rejection of historical allusions, and direct expression of volume and materials were among its characteristics. Before World War II the style was most popular in advanced urban settings and among especially progressive clients. It became more generally used after World War II and continued into the 1970s. The Bauhaus and Miesian styles are related developments.

Ionic order: One of the five *orders* of classical architecture, which was associated with the

Ionian Greeks and was used by the Greeks and the Romans. The order is characterized by a column whose *capital* features large volutes (spirals), sometimes enriched with other decoration. The Ionic order was considered to be between the plain *Doric* and the elaborate *Corinthian.*

Italianate: A revival of elements of Italian Renaissance architecture popular during the mid- and late 19th c., influenced by both villas and palazzos. Characterized by the presence of deep overhanging *eaves* and *cornices* supported by ornate *brackets,* arched windows often with heavy hoodmolds, and, less often, square towers placed centrally or asymmetrically. In antebellum N.C., where examples appeared by the 1840s and 1850s, the style was restricted to large towns and progressive rural areas and found favor among elite, relatively cosmopolitan clients. Later in the 19th c. the style found widespread use in commercial and industrial as well as residential architecture.

joist: One of a series of parallel timbers or beams, usually set on edge, that span a room from wall to wall to support a floor or ceiling; a beam to which floorboards, ceiling boards, or plaster laths are nailed. In the 18th c., ceiling joists meant to be left exposed in a neatly finished house were often finished with a *bead* or *chamfer.*

keystone: The central, wedge-shaped stone at the crown of an arch or in the center of a *lintel.*

kitchen: A room or building used for cooking and sometimes eating. In the 17th, 18th, and much of the 19th c., common practice in N.C., especially in the countryside but also in towns, was the use of a freestanding kitchen as one of the domestic outbuildings. This was regarded as a specifically southern practice, variously attributed to keeping the heat, smells, and threat of fire separated from the dwelling house. Kitchens commonly had large chimneys with cooking fireplaces until the late 19th c. Some had one room, some two, with a separate dining room, and many had upper chambers for servants. In the late 19th and

early 20th centuries kitchens became more frequently attached to the main house by a breezeway or *passage,* and in more and more cases were incorporated into the main block of the house as cooking technology changed from open fireplaces to cookstoves.

lintel: A horizontal element of wood or stone that spans an opening. In masonry construction it frequently supports the masonry above the opening.

marbling: Painted treatment on wood simulating the color and pattern of marble. Now often called marbleizing, but the 18th- and 19th-c. term was "marbling."

medallion: A large, typically circular or oval ornament that adorns the center of a ceiling.

meetinghouse: A place of worship or public gathering, often preferred by dissenting denominations and sects over the word "church" when describing a building. Meetinghouses were typically plain rather than elaborated. They were planned to focus on the word, with emphasis on the pulpit rather than the altar. In a meetinghouse plan, typically benches or pews were arranged around the pulpit, which was often on the long side (often the north) rather than in the *gabled* end. In many cases the main entrance was on the long side opposite the pulpit, and secondary entrances opened on the two gable ends.

Moderne: A general architectural term applied to designs from the 1920s through the 1940s and sometimes the 1950s, defined by stylized forms, often streamlined with smooth curves and flat planes.

modillion: A horizontal *bracket,* often in the form of a plain block, supporting the underside of a *cornice.* Undercut modillions, with an S-curved bottom outline, were used in classically detailed buildings.

mortise and tenon: A joint made by one member having its end cut as a projecting tongue (tenon) that fits exactly into a groove or hole (mortise) in the other member. Once joined in this fashion, the two pieces are often secured by a peg. In traditional framed buildings, many elements are so joined.

muntin: The strip of wood separating the panes of a window *sash*, often molded.

Neoclassical: A general term for an approach to design drawing inspiration from ancient Greek and Roman precedents. It is often used in reference to the revival of Roman, then Greek classical forms in the late 18th and early 19th centuries (the *Federal* and *Greek Revival* styles), and also to the renewed interest in classicism around the turn of the 20th c., though the latter is frequently called Neoclassical Revival or *Beaux Arts* classicism.

newel, newel post: The principal post used to terminate the railing or *balustrade* of a flight of stairs.

order: In *classical* and *Neoclassical* architecture, the basic unit of design, composed of a column with base, shaft, *capital*, and *entablature*, proportioned and detailed according to certain rules codified in the Renaissance and based on observation of ancient Roman examples. Each order—Tuscan, *Doric, Ionic, Corinthian*—had its own distinctive features and proportions. In N.C. some architects and builders used British, then American books that explained these rules and illustrated both the elements and how to work out the proportions. Often the motifs of the orders were freely adapted in actual use.

Palladian: An approach to design associated with the buildings and books of the 16th-c. Italian architect Andrea Palladio and popularized by British architectural books of the 18th c. The term is often used to describe buildings with a symmetrical three- or five-part composition, usually consisting of a large central block flanked by (usually smaller) wings. It is also applied to buildings with a central pedimented *pavilion* projecting from the *facade.*

Palladian window: A window design featuring a symmetrical, three-part arrangement with a central arched opening flanked by lower, square-headed openings and separated from them by columns, *pilasters*, piers, or narrow vertical *panels*. Inspired by the work

of Renaissance architect Andrea Palladio, who like many of his contemporaries, often used this motif. The period term was "Venetian window."

panel: A portion of flat surface set off by molding or some other decorative device. Generally, *raised panels* were used as well as flat panels in the 18th and early 19th centuries as part of the *Georgian style*. Flat panels became popular with the *Federal style* in the early 19th c. and continued in use throughout most of the century, though slightly raised panels came back into use late in the 19th c. and were reiterated in the *Georgian Revival* style.

parapet: A low wall along a roof or terrace, used as decoration or protection.

passage: An enclosed space leading between rooms, today usually called a "hall" or "hallway." In the 17th, 18th, and much of the 19th c. the term "passage" was employed, and "hall" more often referred to a principal room.

paved shoulder: In a brick chimney, the treatment of the sloped transition from the wider base to the narrower shaft by a smooth diagonal surface topped with bricks laid flat like pavers on the slope. This treatment was generally used in the 18th c. but was superseded in the early 19th c. by the *stepped shoulder.*

pavilion: A portion of a building's *facade* that projects forward slightly to give architectural emphasis, sometimes accentuated by a *pediment.*

pediment: A crowning element of *porticoes, pavilions*, doorways, and other architectural features, usually of low triangular form, with a *cornice* extending across its base and carried up the raking sides. Sometimes broken in the center as if to accommodate an ornament; sometimes open at the bottom; sometimes of segmental, elliptical, or serpentine form.

pen: A rectangular or square structural unit. The term is usually used when referring to log buildings and specifies a structure enclosed by log walls. Most single-pen log houses had only one room in the space enclosed by the logs, but within a single pen there may be partitions dividing the space into smaller rooms, such as a *hall-parlor plan*. Many dwellings in N.C. were single-pen structures. Often these were expanded into two-pen houses following the double-pen, *saddlebag*, or *dogtrot* plans.

penstock: Pipe or other conduit to carry water to a turbine or waterwheel; a sluice to control the flow of water.

pent: A single-sloped lean-to or *shed*, typically small, attached to a building, or, such a roof.

piano nobile: The principal story in a building; the term is usually employed when the main story is above the ground story and is taller and more elaborately treated than the story beneath. Characteristic of Renaissance palaces, the treatment appears in N.C. chiefly in public buildings such as courthouses where the courtroom is in the second story.

piazza: An Italian term for a plaza. Used in the 18th, 19th, and 20th centuries in N.C. for a covered porch, pronounced with a short *a*, and usually for a porch large enough to accommodate seating.

pilaster: A shallow pier or rectangular column projecting only slightly from or attached to a wall. Pilasters are usually decorated like columns with a base, shaft, and *capital*.

pillar: A general term for a vertical supporting member, often used interchangeably with "pier," "post," and "column." Commonly used for fairly massive examples, often square in section, as opposed to columns that take a particular *order* and are circular in section.

porte cochere: A projecting porch that provides protection for vehicles and passengers. A common feature of the *Queen Anne*, *Colonial Revival*, and *bungalow* houses of the late 19th and early 20th centuries. Predecessor of the carport.

portico: A roofed space, open or partly enclosed, often with columns and a *pediment*, usually employed as centerpiece of the *facade* of a building and to shelter the main entrance. Typically treated in *classical* fashion.

principal rafter, principal-rafter roof: A member of a pair of large, diagonal framing members composing a truss roof. In a prin-

cipal-rafter roof, the large principal rafters support horizontal purlins, upon which rest secondary *common rafters*. This roof type was unusual in N.C. except in especially large or heavily built structures and in Germanic framed buildings in the Piedmont.

Queen Anne: A popular late 19th-c. revival of early 18th-c. English architecture, characterized by irregularity of plan and massing and a variety of textures. In N.C. the style was frequently rendered in wood in residential architecture, with asymmetrical plans, high *hip roofs* with projecting *gables* and *dormers*, and abundant mass-produced, *eclectic* ornament. The style continued into the early 20th c. and was frequently executed with *Colonial Revival*, classically inspired detail.

quoins: Ornamental blocks of wood, stone, brick, or stucco placed at the corners of a building and projecting slightly.

rafter: A structural timber rising from the plate at the top of a wall to the ridge of the roof and supporting the roof covering.

raised panel: A portion of a flat surface, as in the panel of a door or *wainscot*, that is set off from the surrounding area by a molding or other device and is raised above the surrounding area. Raised panels were especially typical of *Georgian* architecture and appeared in N.C. from the 18th c. into the early 19th c.

reed, reeding: Decoration consisting of parallel convex moldings, often vertically applied to a column or *pilaster*, derived from a bundle of reeds.

return: A horizontal portion of a *cornice* that extends part of the way across the *gable* end of a structure at *eave* level.

Romanesque Revival: A 19th-c. revival of pre-Gothic medieval architecture, characterized by round-headed arches, often with heavy stone-faced stone or brick walls, sometimes with foliated *terra-cotta* ornament.

rosehead nail: A handmade, wrought iron nail having a broad, conical head. Often the heads of such nails have four or five faces or facets formed by the hand hammering process.

saddlebag: A plan in which two single-pen rooms flank a single interior chimney. Especially common in log houses but also applied to small frame houses. The form was common in slave houses.

sanctuary: (1) A term used generally for a church, a holy place, or the main worship space within a church. (2) The portion of the church containing the principal altar, within the *chancel* and east of the choir.

sash: The frame, usually of wood, that holds the pane(s) of glass in a window. It may be movable or fixed. It may slide in a vertical plane or may pivot. Windows with double-hung sash are sometimes described by the number of panes in the upper and lower sash, such as 9/6 (9 over 6), etc. In period documents, however, they were described by the total number of panes (lights), e.g., 15 lights of sash.

Second Empire: An *eclectic* style derived from the grandiose architecture of the French Second Empire of Napoleon III, popularly used in America from the 1860s to the 1880s, especially for public buildings, and characterized by heavy ornament and high mansard roofs with *dormers*. At the time it was frequently called the "French" style. In N.C. the Second Empire style was relatively rare and mainly urban, appearing in residences and a few public and commercial buildings associated with the recovery of wealth after the Civil War.

segmental arch: An arch formed on a segment of a circle or an ellipse.

shed, shed room: (1) A 1-story appendage to a larger structure, covered by a single-slope roof that "leans" (as in "lean-to") against the principal building mass. A shed porch is one with such a single-slope roof. Often a rear shed or shed rooms may be built as a rear, balancing pendant to a front porch of similar form, or as a pendant to an *engaged porch*, in which case the double-slope roof form is usually repeated. (2) A simple, general-purpose outbuilding, often used for storage.

shotgun: A house or house plan one room wide and two or more rooms deep, with the narrow, usually gable-fronted end toward the street. The entrance opens directly into the front room, and doors lead directly into each successive room proceeding to the rear. This narrow house form was built most often in African American neighborhoods, though not exclusively so, and some writers argue that it had its origins in New Orleans, the West Indies, and ultimately African precedents. In N.C. the form was built most in the rapid urbanization of the early 20th c.

shoulder: The sloping shelf or ledge created on the side of a masonry chimney where the width of the chimney changes. Sometimes called "weathering."

sidelight: A framed area of fixed glass of one or more panes located to either side of a door or window opening.

side-passage, side-hall plan: A plan with an unheated (no chimney) passage along one side and one or (usually) two heated rooms on the other, with the main entrances at the front and rear of the passage. Side-passage plans were especially common in late 18th- and early 19th-c. town houses, particularly in New Bern, but the plan was also used in rural dwellings, especially in plantation areas. In the late 19th and early 20th centuries, many towns and cities throughout Piedmont and eastern N.C. saw construction of hundreds of side-passage plan houses 2 stories tall with *gable* fronts, especially as working- and middle-class dwellings on narrow lots.

sill: A heavy horizontal timber, positioned at the bottom of the frame of a wood structure, that rests on top of the foundation; also, the horizontal bottom member of a door or window frame.

smokehouse: A small building where meat (mainly pork) is cured by smoking, and subsequently stored, usually hanging from *joists* or *rafters*. A common outbuilding type in N.C., typically built of frame or log without windows and of tight construction.

Southern Colonial Revival: A primarily residential style within the broader *Colonial Revival*, which drew upon themes popularly associated with the antebellum plantation house but included under the broader term "colonial." The typical "Southern Colonial" residence featured a massive, full-height *portico* that overlapped a 1-story porch or terrace that extended across the front *facade* and in some cases around the side(s) of the house. Houses were fairly symmetrical, with broad center *passages*, and some retained vestiges of *Queen Anne* massing. The style was very popular from the 1890s to the 1910s in N.C. in work by local and regional architects.

Spanish Colonial Revival, Spanish Revival, Spanish Mission Revival: The revival of designs associated with the Spanish colonial missions in the American Southwest and in Mexico and translated loosely in popular architecture into stuccoed buildings with red tile roofs and a variety of motifs such as arched openings, exposed timbers, and towers. In N.C. the style appeared occasionally in the 1910s–1930s in houses and especially in buildings associated with rail or auto travel or with festive and marketing pursuits.

spindle frieze: A row of lathe-turned members (spindles), usually as a decorative feature of a porch below the *cornice*.

stepped shoulder: On a brick chimney, a sloping ledge formed by the successively stepped course of bricks to make the transition from the lower, wider base to the narrower stack. Generally in N.C. stepped shoulders appear in the early 19th c., superseding the *paved shoulders* typical of the 18th c.

stretcher: The long face of a brick when laid horizontally. (See *bond*.)

surround: The border or casing of a window or door opening, sometimes molded.

terra-cotta: A ceramic material, molded decoratively and often glazed, used for facings for buildings or as inset ornament. Tobacco farmers experimented with terra-cotta blocks for their curing barns in the 1920s and 1930s.

tobacco barn: A building in which tobacco is cured. Typically in eastern and Piedmont N.C. these are flue-cure tobacco barns, built specifically for the purpose of curing bright-leaf tobacco through a carefully regulated process of heating the barn full of tobacco. In the mountains of N.C., farmers raise burley tobacco and air cure it by hanging it in well-ventilated barns.

Tower of the Winds: The Horologium of Andronikos Cyrrhestes in Athens, which has columns showing a distinctive variation of the *Corinthian order*, with the *capitals* lacking volutes and having a row of palmlike leaves. The motif was used occasionally in the antebellum era and often in the early 20th c.

transom: A horizontal window unit above a door.

tripartite: Having three parts. Often applied to symmetrical buildings with a principal central feature or block and subsidiary flanking elements.

triple-A: A locally used, nonstandard colloquialism for the roof form especially popular after the Civil War, where a center front *gable* (often a cross-gable, sometimes simply a gabled wall *dormer*) rises from the *facade* roofline. Coined in the mid-1970s by Franklin County health inspector Thilbert Pearce during an architectural survey of Franklin County conducted with the authors of this guidebook, the term is now widely used as a shorthand reference to a common form.

Tudor Revival: A popular style, primarily residential, in the early 20th c., characterized by motifs associated with Tudor and Jacobean English architecture, particularly half-timbered walls (often applied rather than structural), diamond-paned casement windows, steep *gables*, irregular plans, and chimneys with multiple stacks or chimney pots. Rather rarely used in N.C., except among expensive houses, typically interspersed among the more popular *Colonial Revival*, especially *Georgian Revival* styles.

turned: Fashioned on a lathe, as in a *baluster*, *newel*, or porch post.

Venetian window: See *Palladian window*.

Victorian: A general term for a period, the reign of Queen Victoria (1837–1901), and often used broadly to describe the wide variety of *eclectic* revival styles that were introduced in British and American architecture during that era.

wainscot: A decorative or protective facing applied to the lower portion of an interior wall or partition.

weatherboards, weatherboarding: Wood siding consisting of overlapping horizontal boards usually thicker at one edge than the other. More commonly used in N.C. than the term "clapboard." The usual method of covering a frame building in N.C.

Bibliography and Sources of Information

SELECTED BIBLIOGRAPHY

Note: The bibliography encompasses surveys and other studies of local architecture in the region, plus selected general works. Not included here for reasons of space are dozens of fine town and county histories and studies of individual buildings or districts.

Alexander, Ann C. *Perspective on a Resort Community: Historic Buildings Inventory of Southern Pines, North Carolina.* Southern Pines: Town of Southern Pines, 1981.

Allcott, John V. *The Campus at Chapel Hill: Two Hundred Years of Architecture.* Chapel Hill: Chapel Hill Historical Society, 1986.

Anderson, Jean Bradley, *Durham County: A History of Durham County, North Carolina.* Durham: Duke University Press, 1990.

Arsenault, Raymond. "The End of the Long Hot Summer: The Air Conditioner and Southern Culture." *Journal of Southern History* 50, no. 4 (Nov. 1984): 597–628.

Badger, Anthony J. *North Carolina and the New Deal.* Raleigh: Division of Archives and History, 1981.

Bell, John L., Jr. *Hard Times: Beginnings of the Great Depression in North Carolina, 1929–1933.* Raleigh: Division of Archives and History, 1982.

Bishir, Catherine W. "Jacob W. Holt, an American Builder." *Winterthur Portfolio* (Spring 1981). Reprinted in *Common Places: Readings in American Vernacular Architecture*, edited by Dell Upton and John Michael Vlach. Athens: University of Georgia Press, 1986.

———. *North Carolina Architecture.* Photographs by Tim Buchman. Chapel Hill: University of North Carolina Press, 1990.

Bishir, Catherine W., Charlotte V. Brown, Carl R. Lounsbury, and Ernest H. Wood III. *Architects and Builders in North Carolina: A History of the Practice of Building.* Chapel Hill: University of North Carolina Press, 1990.

Bishir, Catherine W., and Lawrence S. Earley,

eds. *Early Twentieth-Century Suburbs in North Carolina.* Raleigh: Archaeology and Historic Preservation Section, Division of Archives and History, 1985.

Black, Allison Harris. *An Architectural History of Burlington, North Carolina.* Burlington: Burlington Historic District Commission, 1987.

Bouldin, Edwin E., Jr. *Architectural Guide to Winston-Salem and Forsyth County.* Winston-Salem: North Carolina Chapter of the American Institute of Architects, Winston-Salem Section, 1978.

Brengle, Kim Withers. *The Architectural Heritage of Gaston County, North Carolina.* Gastonia: Gaston County, 1982.

Brooks, Jerome E. *Green Leaf and Gold: Tobacco in North Carolina.* Raleigh: State Department of Archives and History, 1962.

Brown, Claudia Roberts. *A Tale of Three Cities: Eden's Heritage, a Pictorial Survey.* Edited by M. Ruth Little. Eden: Eden Historic Properties Commission, 1986, 2000.

Brown, Claudia Roberts, Burgess McSwain, and John Florin. *Carrboro, North Carolina: An Architectural and Historic Inventory.* Carrboro: Carrboro Appearance Commission, 1983.

Brown, Marvin A. *Greensboro: An Architectural Record.* Greensboro: Preservation Greensboro, 1995.

———. *Our Enduring Past: A Survey of 235 Years of Life and Architecture in Lincoln County, North Carolina.* Lincolnton: Lincoln County Historic Properties Commission, 1986.

Brown, Marvin A., and Andrew J. Carlson. *Heritage and Homesteads: The History and Architecture of Granville County, North Carolina.* Oxford: Granville Historical Society, 1988.

Crow, Jeffrey J., Paul D. Escott, and Flora J. Hatley. *A History of African Americans in North Carolina.* Raleigh: Division of Archives and History, 1992.

Davis, Edward T., and John L. Sanders. *A*

Romantic Architect in Antebellum North Carolina: The Works of Alexander Jackson Davis. Raleigh: Historic Preservation Foundation of North Carolina and The State Capitol Foundation, 2000.

Dodenhoff, Donna. *Stanly County: The Architectural Legacy of a Rural North Carolina County.* Albemarle: Albemarle-Stanly County Historic Preservation Commission, 1992.

Dreyer, Martha A. *The Spencer Architectural and Historic Inventory.* Spencer: Town of Spencer, 1984.

Durden, Robert F. *The Dukes of Durham, 1865–1929.* Durham: Duke University Press, 1975.

Escott, Paul D. *Many Excellent People: Power and Privilege in North Carolina, 1850–1900.* Chapel Hill: University of North Carolina Press, 1985.

Federal Writers' Project, WPA of North Carolina. *North Carolina: A Guide to the Old North State.* Chapel Hill: University of North Carolina Press, 1939.

Glass, Brent D. *North Carolina: An Inventory of Historic Engineering and Industrial Sites.* Washington, D.C.: Historic American Engineering Record, National Park Service, U.S. Department of the Interior, 1975.

———. "Southern Mill Hills." In *Carolina Dwelling,* edited by Douglas Swaim, 138–49. Raleigh: North Carolina State University School of Design Student Publication, 1978.

———. *The Textile Industry in North Carolina: A History.* Raleigh: Division of Archives and History, 1992.

Glass, Brent D., and Pat Dickinson. *Badin: A Town at the Narrows, an Historical and Architectural Survey.* Albemarle: Stanly County Historical Properties Commission, 1982.

Goldfield, David R. *Cotton Fields and Skyscrapers: Southern City and Region, 1607–1980.* Baton Rouge: Louisiana State University Press, 1982.

Hall, Jacquelyn Dowd, James Leloudis, Robert Korstad, Mary Murphy, Lu Ann Jones, and Christopher B. Daly. *Like a Family: The Making of a Southern Cotton Mill World.* Chapel Hill: University of North Carolina Press, 1987.

Halma, Sidney, ed. *Catawba County: An Architectural History.* Hickory: Catawba County Historical Association, 1991.

Hanchett, Thomas W. *Sorting Out the New South City: Race, Class, and Urban Development in Charlotte, 1875–1975.* Chapel Hill: University of North Carolina Press, 1998.

Harris, Linda. *Early Raleigh Neighborhoods and Buildings.* Raleigh: City of Raleigh, 1983.

Harris, Linda, and Mary Ann Lee. *The Raleigh Historic Inventory.* Raleigh: Raleigh Historic Properties Commission, 1978.

Hill, Michael, ed. *Guide to North Carolina Highway Historical Markers.* 9th ed. Raleigh: Division of Archives and History, 2001.

Hobbs, Samuel Huntington, Jr. *North Carolina: An Economic and Social Profile.* Chapel Hill: University of North Carolina Press, 1958.

———. *North Carolina: Economic and Social.* Chapel Hill: University of North Carolina Press, 1930.

Hood, Davyd Foard. *The Architecture of Rowan County: A Catalogue and History of Surviving 18th, 19th, and Early 20th Century Structures.* Salisbury: Rowan County Historic Properties Commission, 1983; 2nd ed., 2001.

Hutchinson, John. *No Ordinary Lives: A History of Richmond County, North Carolina, 1750–1900.* Rockingham: Richmond County Historical Society, 1998.

Jackson, C. David, and Charlotte V. Brown. *History of the North Carolina Chapter of the American Institute of Architects, 1913–1998.* Raleigh: North Carolina Chapter of the American Institute of Architects, 1998.

Johnson, Guion Griffis. *Ante-Bellum North Carolina: A Social History.* Chapel Hill: University of North Carolina Press, 1937.

Johnston, Frances Benjamin, and Thomas Tileston Waterman. *The Early Architecture of North Carolina.* Chapel Hill: University of North Carolina Press, 1941.

Jones, H. G. *North Carolina Illustrated, 1524–1984.* Chapel Hill: University of North Carolina Press, 1983.

Kaplan, Peter R. *The Historic Architecture of Cabarrus County, North Carolina.* Concord: City of Concord and Historic Cabarrus, 1981.

Lally, Kelly. *The Historic Architecture of Wake County, North Carolina.* Raleigh: Wake County, 1994.

Lane, Mills. *The Architecture of the Old South: North Carolina.* Savannah: Beehive Press, 1985.

Lee, Mary Ann. *An Inventory of Historic Architecture: Monroe, North Carolina.* Monroe: City of Monroe, 1978.

Leyburn, James G. *The Scotch-Irish: A Social History.* Chapel Hill: University of North Carolina Press, 1962.

Little, M. Ruth. *Sticks and Stones: Three Centuries of North Carolina Gravemarkers.* Chapel Hill: University of North Carolina Press, 1998.

Little-Stokes, Ruth. *An Inventory of Historic Architecture: Caswell County, North Carolina.* Yanceyville: Caswell County Historical Association, 1979.

————. *An Inventory of Historic Architecture: Greensboro, North Carolina.* Greensboro: City of Greensboro, 1976.

————. *An Inventory of Historic Architecture: Iredell County, North Carolina.* Statesville: Iredell County, City of Statesville, Town of Mooresville, and Iredell County Historic Properties Commission, 1978.

Lounsbury, Carl R. *Alamance County Architectural Heritage.* Graham: Alamance County Historic Properties Commission, 1980.

————. *An Illustrated Glossary of Early Southern Architecture and Landscape.* New York: Oxford University Press, 1994.

Mason, Vickie E. *The Historic District of Louisburg, North Carolina: A Catalog and History of Surviving 18th, 19th, and Early 20th Century Structures.* Louisburg: Town of Louisburg, 1990.

McFarland, Kenneth. *The Architecture of Warren County, North Carolina, 1770s to 1860s.* Warrenton: Warren County Historical Association, 2001.

Mohney, Kirk Franklin. *The Historic Architecture of Davie County, North Carolina: An Inventory Analysis and Documentary Catalogue.* Mocksville: Davie County Historical and Genealogical Society, 1986.

————. *Historical Architecture of Yadkin County, North Carolina.* Edited by Lewis Brumfield. Yadkinville: Yadkin County Historical Society, 1987.

Mohney, Kirk Franklin, and Laura A. W. Phillips. *From Tavern to Town: The Architectural History of Hickory, North Carolina.* Hickory: Hickory Historic Properties Commission and the Hickory Landmarks Society, 1988.

Murphy, Ann Melanie. *An Inventory of Historic Architecture: Henderson, North Carolina.* Henderson: City of Henderson, 1979.

Murray, Elizabeth Reid. *Wake: Capital County of North Carolina.* Raleigh: privately published, 1983.

National Register of Historic Places Nomination Forms, Archaeology and Historic Preservation Section, and Archives and Records Section, Division of Archives and History, Department of Cultural Resources, Raleigh (originals at National Park Service, Washington, D.C.).

Osborn, Rachel, and Ruth Selden-Sturgill. *The Architectural Heritage of Chatham County, North Carolina.* Pittsboro: Chatham County Historical Association, 1991.

Pearce, T. H. *Early Architecture of Franklin County.* Rev. ed. Louisburg: Franklin County Historical Society, 1988.

Pezzoni, J. Daniel. *The History and Architecture of Lee County, North Carolina.* Sanford: Railroad House Historical Association, 1995.

Phillips, Laura A. W. *Reidsville, North Carolina: An Inventory of Historic and Architectural Resources.* Reidsville: Reidsville Historic Properties Commission, 1981.

Pickens, Suzanne S. *Sweet Union: An Architectural and Historical Survey of Union County, North Carolina.* Monroe: Union County Board of Commissioners, Monroe-Union County Historical Properties Commission, and Union County Historical Society, 1990.

Powell, William S. *Dictionary of North Carolina Biography.* 6 vols. Chapel Hill:

University of North Carolina Press, 1979–96.

———. *The North Carolina Gazetteer*. Chapel Hill: University of North Carolina Press, 1968.

———. *North Carolina through Four Centuries*. Chapel Hill: University of North Carolina Press, 1989.

Roberts, Claudia P. (Brown), and Diane Lea. *An Architectural and Historical Survey of Madison, N.C.* Madison: Town of Madison, 1979.

———. *The Durham Architectural and Historic Inventory*. Durham: City of Durham, 1982.

Robinson, Blackwell P. *The North Carolina Guide*. Chapel Hill: University of North Carolina Press, 1955.

Sharpe, Bill. *A New Geography of North Carolina*. Vols. 1–4. Raleigh: Sharpe, 1954–65.

Simmons-Henry, Linda, and Linda Harris Edmisten. *Culture Town: Life in Raleigh's African American Communities*. Raleigh: Raleigh Historic Districts Commission, 1993.

Smith, H. McKelden. *Architectural Resources: An Inventory of Historic Architecture (High Point, Jamestown, Gibsonville, Guilford County)*. Raleigh: Division of Archives and History, 1979.

Southern, Michael T. "The I-House as a Carrier of Style in Three Counties of the Northeastern Piedmont." In *Carolina Dwelling*, edited by Douglas Swaim. Raleigh: North Carolina State University School of Design Student Publication, 1978.

State Board of Agriculture. *North Carolina and Its Resources*. Raleigh: M. I. and J. C. Stewart, 1896.

Swaim, Douglas, ed. *Carolina Dwelling*. Raleigh: North Carolina State University School of Design Student Publication, 1978.

Taylor, Gwynne Stephens. *From Frontier to Factory: An Architectural History of Forsyth County*. Winston-Salem: Winston-Salem and Forsyth County Historic Properties Commission and the City-County Planning Board, 1981.

Tilley, Nannie May. *The Bright Tobacco Industry, 1860–1929*. Chapel Hill: University of North Carolina Press, 1948.

Touart, Paul Baker. *Building the Backcountry: An Architectural History of Davidson County, North Carolina*. Lexington: Davidson County Historical Association, 1987.

Tullos, Allen. *Habits of Industry: White Culture and the Transformation of the Carolina Piedmont*. Chapel Hill: University of North Carolina Press, 1989.

Ward, H. Trawick, and R. P. Stephen Davis Jr. *Time before History: The Archaeology of North Carolina*. Chapel Hill: University of North Carolina Press, 1999.

Waugh, Elizabeth. *North Carolina's Capital, Raleigh*. Chapel Hill: University of North Carolina Press for the Junior League of Raleigh, 1967.

Wells, John E., and Robert E. Dalton. *The South Carolina Architects, 1835–1935: A Biographical Dictionary*. Richmond: New South Architectural Press, 1992.

———. *The Virginia Architects, 1835–1955: A Biographical Dictionary*. Richmond: New South Architectural Press, 1997.

Whatley, Lowell MacKay, Jr. *Architectural History of Randolph County, North Carolina*. Asheboro: City of Asheboro and County of Randolph, 1985.

SOURCES OF INFORMATION

Division of Travel and Tourism
N.C. Department of Commerce
Mail Service Center 4324, Raleigh NC 27699
919-733-4171, or
1-800-VISIT NC (1-800-847-4862)

County Map Section
N.C. Department of Transportation
1535 Mail Service Center, Raleigh NC 27699
919-733-3250

State Historic Preservation Office
Division of Archives and History
N.C. Department of Cultural Resources
4617 Mail Service Center, Raleigh NC 27699
919-733-4763

State Historic Sites
Division of Archives and History
N.C. Department of Cultural Resources
4620 Mail Service Center, Raleigh NC 27699
919-733-7862

Preservation North Carolina
P.O. Box 27644
Raleigh NC 27611-7644
919-832-3652

Photography Credits

Most of the photographs used in this volume are from the North Carolina Division of Archives and History. The following photographs from other sources are used with permission and acknowledged with thanks.

Blue Cross Blue Shield, Chapel Hill: Blue Cross Blue Shield Service Center, Orange County (OR 53).

Division of Travel and Tourism, North Carolina Department of Commerce, Raleigh: St. John's Episcopal Church, Vance County (Fig. 11); Legislative Building, Raleigh (WK 7); Executive Mansion, Raleigh (WK 32); Latta Place, Mecklenburg Co. (MK 57).

Duke University Rare Book, Manuscript, and Special Collections Library, Durham: Elm St., Greensboro (Fig. 66); R. J. Reynolds Building and Wachovia Building, Winston-Salem (Fig. 67); North Elm St., Greensboro (Fig. 68); Mechanics & Farmers Bank, Durham (DH 14); R. J. Reynolds Building, Winston-Salem (FY 34); First Baptist Church, Winston-Salem (FY 39); Centenary Methodist Church, Winston-Salem (FY 40); Mooresville streetscape, Iredell Co. (ID 23).

GlaxoSmithKline, Research Triangle Park: Burroughs-Wellcome Building, Research Triangle Park (Fig. 74).

Levine Museum of the New South, Charlotte: Charlotte skyline (beginning of Mecklenburg County section; photograph by John Hilarides).

North Carolina Collection, Wilson Library, University of North Carolina, Chapel Hill: Innes St., Salisbury (Fig. 3); University of N.C. campus, ca. 1892 (Fig. 14); Hickory Passenger Depot (Fig. 38); Overby Farm, Stokes Co. (Fig. 44); R. J. Reynolds Tobacco Co. factory, Winston-Salem (Fig. 48); Loray Mill, Gastonia (Fig. 49); High Rock Dam and Power Station, Davidson Co. (Fig. 52); Duke Chapel, Durham (Fig. 55); Louis Round Wilson Library, Chapel Hill (Fig. 56); Gastonia High School, Gaston Co. (Fig. 57);

bird's-eye view of Winston-Salem, 1891 (Fig. 60); Charlotte Coliseum (Fig. 73); Insurance Building, Raleigh (WK 16); Durham County Courthouse (DH 1); Baldwin Auditorium, Duke University, Durham (DH 49); Dormitory Quadrangle, Duke University (DH 49); South Building with Old Well, Chapel Hill (OR 45); Wilrick Hotel, Sanford (LE 1); Southern Railway Passenger Station, Greensboro (GF 10); Sedgefield, Guilford Co. (GF 39); Southern Furniture Exposition Building, High Point (GF 43); Home Moravian Church and Main Hall, Salem College, Winston-Salem (FY 3 and FY 4); John Vogler House and Christoph Vogler House, Winston-Salem (FY 8 and FY 9); Wait Chapel, Wake Forest University, Winston-Salem (FY 62); Kannapolis, Cabarrus Co. (CA 9).

Odell Associates, Inc., Charlotte: Blue Cross Blue Shield Service Center (OR 53)

Sarah Pope Postcard Collection, private: W. T. Blackwell and Co., Durham (Fig. 47); Coca-Cola Bottling Plant, Charlotte (Fig. 53); Biddle Hall, Johnson C. Smith University, Charlotte (Fig. 54); Downtown Graham (Fig. 58); West Market St. Methodist Church and U.S. Post Office and Courthouse, Greensboro (Fig. 64); Ruffin Building, Raleigh (WK 6); Broughton High School, Raleigh (WK 51); Louisburg College Main Building, Louisburg (FN 1); Henderson Fire Station (VN 1); U.S. Post Office, Henderson (VN 1); First National Bank, Roxboro (PR 1); Duke Memorial United Methodist Church, Durham (DH 26); Heartsease, Hillsborough (OR 30); Smith Hall (Playmakers Theater), Chapel Hill (OR 45); Burlington Passenger Station (AM 2); Atlantic Bank & Trust Co. Building, Burlington (AM 3); White Furniture Co., Mebane (AM 22); Lee County Courthouse, Sanford (LE 3); Carolina Hotel, Pinehurst (MR 15); Richmond County Courthouse, Rockingham

(RH 1); Union County Courthouse, Monroe (UN 1); Elm St., Greensboro (GF 7); Guilford County Courthouse, Greensboro (GF 1); First Presbyterian Church, Greensboro (GF 18); High Point Depot (GF 43); St. Paul's Episcopal Church, Winston-Salem (FY 56); R. J. Reynolds Memorial Auditorium, Winston-Salem (FY 57); Catawba County Courthouse, Newton (CT 1); Belmont Abbey and College, Belmont (GS 17); Stonewall Jackson Training School, Cabarrus Co. (CA 8); First National Bank, Charlotte (MK 3); First Baptist Church, Charlotte (MK 11); Old Mecklenburg Co. Courthouse (MK 20); Chambers Hall; Davidson College (MK 61).

Preservation North Carolina, Raleigh: Oakley Hall, Warren Co. (WR 52).

Anne Raines Postcard Collection, private: Jefferson Standard Building, Greensboro (GF 6); Downtown Reidsville, Rockingham Co. (RK 15).

Tufts Archive, Given Memorial Library, Pinehurst: Pinehurst Country Club (Fig. 59); Pinehurst Country Club Arcade (beginning of catalog).

Index

Page numbers in **boldface** represent the main entry for a subject; *italic* page numbers represent illustrations.

Bagley-Daniels-Pegues House (Raleigh), **122**
Bagley-Mullen House (Charlotte), **513**
Bahama (Durham Co.), **214**
Bailey, Benjamin, House (Stokes Co.), **363**
Bain, Grady L. (engineer), 320
Bain, W. C. (contractor), 67, 278, 325, 328, 330, 336, 358
Bain Building (Greensboro), **328**
Baity Store (Mocksville), **417**
Baker Farm (Franklin Co.), **144**
Baldwin Auditorium (Duke University, Durham), **210–11**, *211*
Baldwin's Mill (Chatham Co.), **257–58**
Balfour Quarry (Rowan Co.), 436
Ball's Creek Campground (Catawba Co.), **457**, *457*
Banker's House (Shelby), **473**, *473*
Bank of America, 239, 253, 506, 507; Corporate Headquarters (Charlotte), *503*, **507**, *507*; Branch Bank (NCNB) (Charlotte), **515**
Banks Presbyterian Church (Union Co.), **310**
Barbecue, Lexington style, 406
Bar-B-Q King (Charlotte), **516**
Barber, George F. (architect), 66, 68, 145, 246
Barber, O. Z. (builder), 265
Barber & Kluttz (architects), 417
Barber-Scotia College (Concord), **494**, *494*
Barnhardt-Morrison House (Cabarrus Co.), **500**
Barns, tobacco, 43, 182–83, 176, 214, 215
—accessible example: Duke Homestead (Durham), 212
Barns and outbuildings, 27, 43
—accessible examples: Oak View (Wake Co.), 136; Duke Homestead (Durham Co.), 212; Horton Grove (Durham Co.), 214–15; Cedarock Park (Alamance Co.), 251; Malcolm Blue Farm (Moore Co.), 276; Coble Barn (Guilford Co.), 27, 339; Mendenhall Barn (Jamestown), 340; Jones Barn (Old Salem), 375; Bernhardt Barn (Rowan Co.), 436–37; Schiele Museum (Gaston Co.), 481; Latta Plantation (Mecklenburg Co.), 526–27
Barrett, Charles W. (architect), 106, 120, 125, 135, 139, 151, 248, 249; *Colonial Southern Homes*, 135, 139; *Plans for Public Schoolhouses*, 248, 249
Barrett & Thompson (architects), 128, 139, 248, 249, 272
Barrier, Augustus C., House (Mount Pleasant), **497**

Barringer, Mathias, House (Mount Pleasant), **497**
Barton, Harry (architect), 63, 69, 239, 261, 313, 325, 326, 331, 332, 337, *338*, 339, 344, 345, 348; House (Greensboro), **338**
Bassett, John Spencer, House (Durham), **204**
Battle, Judge William Horn, 235, 237
Battle-Malone-Bass House (Franklin Co.), **140**
Battle Park (Chapel Hill), **236**
Battle-Vance-Pettigrew Building (UNC–Chapel Hill), **233**
Bauer, Adolphus Gustavus (architect), 68, 106, 109, 110, 118, 119, 121, 128
Baynes House (Person Co.), **177**, *177*
Beallmont (Davidson Co.), **413**, *413*
Beal-Ragan House (Gastonia), **479**, *480*
Beam, C. Grier, Carolina Freight Truck Museum (Cherryville), **489**
Beam, Joshua, House (Cleveland Co.), **474**
Beamon, J. R. (contractor), 242
Beam's Shell Service Station (Cherryville), **489**
Beane-Cox Mill (Randolph Co.), **319**
Beaux Arts classicism, 69–70
—selected examples: Capitol Square government buildings (Raleigh), 110; Duke University (Durham), 210–11; University of North Carolina (Chapel Hill), 229–35; Carolina Theater (Greensboro), 319; Jefferson Standard Building (Greensboro), 327; First Baptist Church (Winston-Salem), 383; R. J. Reynolds High School and Auditorium (Winston-Salem), 392; Chambers Hall, Davidson College (Mecklenburg Co.), 451. *See also various county courthouses, banks, post offices, and colleges*
Beaver Dam (Knightdale vic.), **137**
Beaver Dam (Mecklenburg Co.), **529**
Becket, Welton, & Assoc. (architects), 201
Beckwith-Goodwin Farm (Chatham Co.), **259**, *259*
Belk, Dr. John M., House (Monroe), **305–6**, *305*, 308
Belk, R. J., Store (Union Co.), **309**
Belk, William Henry, House (Charlotte), **521**
Belk Buildings (Monroe), **305**
Bell, Richard C. (landscape architect), 110
Bell Block (Salisbury), **427**
Bellemont Mill Village (Alamance Co.), *54*, **253**
Bellevue Mfg. Co. (Hillsborough), **226**

Cooleemee Plantation House (Davie Co.), 414, **420–21**, *421*
Cooper, Thomas (architect), 106
Cordova (Richmond Co.), **293–94**
Correll, Jacob (contractor), 443
Corriher School and Grange Building (Rowan Co.), **438–39**
Cosby, Dabney (builder), 39, 118, 180, 181, 231, 237, 397
Cosby, John (architect), 180
Cotton gins, 137, 144
Cotton Grove (Davidson Co.), **413**
Cotton mills. *See* Textile manufacturing
Cotton production, 42
Country Club Apartments (Greensboro), **332**
Courtney (Yadkin Co.), **405**; Baptist Church, **405**
Courtney, William, House (Hillsborough), **224**
Courts House (Rockingham Co.), **356**
Covered Bridges. *See* Bridges
Covington House (Stokes Co.), **362**
Covington Rosenwald School (Richmond Co.) **296**
Cox House (Randolph Co.), **317**
Cox-Pope-Tippett House (Durham Co.), **213**
Craig (Greig), William (stonemason), 373
Craige, Burton, House (Winston-Salem), **389**
Cram, Goodhue & Ferguson (architects), 194
Cram, Ralph Adams (architect), 68, 192, 193, 194, 223, 370, 391
Cram & Ferguson (architects), 391
Cramer Memorial Methodist Church (Gaston Co.), **488**
Cramer, Stuart W. (mill designer-industrialist), 53, 57, 487–88, 496, 504, 517, 523–24
Cramerton (Gaston Co.), **487–88**; Town Hall, **488**
Craven, Braxton, 210, 321
Crawford, John B. (architect), 327
Credle, C. G., School (Oxford), **169**
Creedmore (Granville Co.), **174**
Creel, T. B. (builder), 275
Croft (Mecklenburg Co.), **529**; School, **529**
Crosby-Garfield Elementary School (Raleigh), **123**
Crosland, John (contractor), 505
Crossroads Community (Alamance Co.), **248**
Crow, Edward, House (Union Co.), **306**
Crowell House (Durham), **204**

Crow's Nest (Union Co.), **306**
Crudup, Josiah, House (Vance Co.), **165**
Culler Roller Mill and Culler-Scott House (Stokes Co.), **364**
Culp, Henry W., Sr., House (Stanly Co.), *73*, **285**
Cumnock (Lee Co.), **266**
Curtis, D. A. (carpenter), 318
Curtis, N. C. (architect-stonemason), 236
Curtis-Blue House (Randolph Co.), **318**
Cypress Hall (Archibald Davis) Plantation (Franklin Co.), **142–43**

Dairy Queen (Charlotte), **516**
Dalkeith (Warren Co.), **157**
Dallas (Gaston Co.), **481–82**; Depot, **482**
Dalton-Hunt House (Yadkin Co.), **404–5**
Daltonia (Iredell Co.), **450–51**
Damascus Baptist Arbor and Church (Iredell Co.), **450**, *450*
Dams. *See* Hydroelectric power
Danbury (Stokes Co.), **361**; Presbyterian Church, **361**
Dancy, John C., House (Salisbury), **432**
Daniels, Josephus, 122; House (Raleigh), **130–31**
Daniels Evangelical and Reformed Church (Lincoln Co.), **466**
Daniels Lutheran Church (Lincoln Co.), **466**, *466*
Danielson, John (contractor), 131
Dan River Lumber & Milling Co. (builders), 363
Darling, Timothy, Presbyterian Church (Oxford), **169–70**
Davidson (Mecklenburg Co.), **528–29**
Davidson, Berry (millwright), 54, 239, 250, 251, 252, 347
Davidson, James A. (builder-architect), 106, 131
Davidson College (Mecklenburg Co.), 25, 59, 451, 452, 469, **528**, *528*, 530
Davidson County, 96 (map), 406–15
Davidson Co. Courthouse, Old (Lexington), *37*, **406–7**, *408*
Davie, Governor William R., 229, 231
Davie County, 96 (map), 416–22
Davie Co. Courthouse (Mocksville), **417**, *417*
Davie Co. Jail, former (Mocksville), *31*, **416**, 442
Davie Street Presbyterian Church (Raleigh), **122**

Dudley Memorial Building (Greensboro), **335**, *335*

Duke, Benjamin N., 138, 171, 190, 192, 194, 198, 201, 203, 208, 212, 246, 421, 422

Duke, Brodie L., 190, 198, 204, 212; Warehouse (Durham), **199**

Duke, Green, House (Warren Co.), **157**

Duke, James Buchanan "Buck," 41, 51, 59, 148, 190, 192, 198, 211, 212, 246, 503, 510, 519; Mansion, (Charlotte), **519**, *520*

Duke, Sarah P., Memorial Gardens (Duke University, Durham), **211**

Duke, W., Sons & Co., 190, 192; Tobacco Factory, **198**

Duke, Washington, 59, 138, 190, 198, 199, 200, 202, 210, 212, 321

Duke Chapel (Duke University, Durham), *59*, **211**

Duke Endowment, 59, 210, 313

Duke family, 48, 50, 56, 191, 208, 367

Duke Homestead (Durham Co.), **212**, *212*

Duke Memorial United Methodist Church (Durham), **200**, *200*

Duke Park (Durham), **204-5**

Duke Power Co. *See* Southern (Duke) Power Co.

Duke University (Durham), 60, 76, 192, **210-11**, 216, 321, 510

Dunhill Hotel (Charlotte), **509**

Dunkards (German Baptists), 13, 399

Dunstan neighborhood (Durham), **206**

Durham (Durham Co.), 65, **189-211**, *190-91* (maps)

Durham Athletic Park, **200**

Durham Auditorium, **196-97**

Durham Cotton Mfg. Co., **202**

Durham County, 89 (map), 189-217

Durham Co. Courthouse (Durham), **193**, *193*

Durham Co. Public Library, former, **193**, *193*

Durham High School, **200**

Durham Hosiery Mills, **201**, *202*

Durham Water Works, 210

Durrett-Jarrett House (Yadkin Co.), **403**

Dyer House (Winston-Salem), **392**

Eagle Lodge (Hillsborough), **220-21**, *221*

East Bend (Yadkin Co.), **402-3**

East Fourth Street Baptist Church (Winston-Salem), **387**

Eastover (Charlotte), 519, **521**

Eaton, Jesse, House (Davie Co.), 420

Eaton Place (Warrenton), **149**, *150*, 397

Eatons Baptist Church and Cemetery (Davie Co.), **419**

Ebenezer A.M.E. Zion Church and Arbor (Cabarrus Co.), **499**

Ebenezer Academy (Iredell Co.), **450**

Ebenezer Methodist Church (Chatham Co.), **259**

Eccles, Henry (builder), 400

Eccles House (Iredell Co.), **451**

Edbrooke, Willoughby J. (architect), 445

Eden (Rockingham Co.), **351**, *352*

Education, 57-62. *See also* Academies; Public schools; Colleges and universities

Education Building (Raleigh), **110**

Edwards, G. A. (architect-builder), 114, 122

Efird Mfg. Co. & village (Albemarle), **284**

Efird's (Burlington), **242**

Egerton-Brown House (Warren Co.), **158**

Eggers & Higgins (architects), 233

Egypt. *See* Cumnock

Electric power. *See* Hydroelectric power; Southern (Duke) Power Co.

Elgin (Warren Co.), **154-55**, *154*

Elizabeth (Charlotte), 73, **521-22**, *522*

Eller, A. H., House (Winston-Salem), **389**

Ellerbe Springs Hotel (Richmond Co.), **296**, *296*

Ellington, George (carpenter), 256

Elliott, J. W. (builder), 449, 450

Elliott, Joseph D. (builder), 40, 450, 454, 459, 460, 461

Ellis, Governor John, 430

Ellis House (Orange Co.), **227**

Ellison, Stewart (builder), 117

Elmhurst (Graham), **240**, *240*

Elm Street (Greensboro), *70*, *323*, **327-29**

Elm Street, North (Greensboro), *72*

Elmwood (Raleigh), **124**

Elmwood-Pinewood Cemetery (Charlotte), **513**

El Nido (Shelby), **472**, *473*

Elon University (Alamance Co.), **254**

Emanuel Reformed Church (Lincolnton), **464-65**

Embury, Aymar, II (architect), 68, 273, 277, 279, 523

Emerywood (High Point), 72, **344-45**

Emmanuel A.M.E. Church (Durham), **207**

Emmanuel Episcopal Church (Warrenton), **149**, *149*

Emmanuel Lutheran Church (Lincolnton), **464**

Empire Hotel (Salisbury), *424*, **427**
Endor Iron Furnace (Lee Co.), **266–67**, *267*, 467
Engleside (Warrenton), *38*, **153**
Eno Cotton Mill (Hillsborough), **226**
Eno Presbyterian Church (Orange Co.), **227**
Enterprise Mfg. Co. (Randolph Co.), **320**
Entwistle House (Rockingham), **292**
Epps, Orlo (architect), 68, 325, 359; House (Greensboro), **337**
Epps & Hackett (architects), 337
Erlanger Mill Village (Lexington), **409**
Erwin, William Allen, 48, 208, 209, 236, 243, 409, 421, 422
Erwin Cotton Mills No. 1 & Erwin Mills Village (Durham), *40*, **208–9**, 204, *208*, 409
Estey Hall (Shaw University, Raleigh), **114**, *115*, 491
Ethnic groups. *See* Settlement patterns and ethnic groups
Eumenean Hall (Davidson College, Mecklenburg Co.), *25*, **528**
Euphronia Presbyterian Church (Lee Co.), **268**
Evans, Eli N., House (Durham), **207**
Evergreen Academy (Randolph Co.), **320**
Everhart, Eccles D. (architect), 342, 344, 393
Everhart, Riley, Farm (Davidson Co.), **410**, *410*
Excelsior Club (Charlotte), **515**, *515*
Executive Mansion (Raleigh), 106, **118**, *118*, 120
Export Leaf Tobacco Co. Building (Oxford), **170**

Factory Row (S. Trade St.) (Winston-Salem), **378**
Fadum House (Raleigh), **132**
Fain-Frederick House (Warrenton), **148**
Fain-Ivey House (Vance Co.), **163**
Fair Grove Methodist Church (Randolph Co.), **320**
Fairmount (Warren Co.), **156**
Fairntosh (Durham Co.), **215–16**, *216*
Fair Promise A.M.E. Zion Church (Sanford), **264**
Faith Presbyterian Church (Aberdeen), **275**
Falls of the Neuse Mill (Wake Co.), **134**
Farm and plantation complexes
—selected accessible examples: Oak View (Wake Co.), 136; Duke Homestead (Durham Co.) 212; Horton Grove (Durham

Co.) 214–15; Leigh Farm (Durham Co.), 216; Cedarock Park (Alamance Co.), 251; Malcolm Blue Farm (Moore Co.), 276; Mendenhall Plantation (Guilford Co.) 340; Schiele Museum (Gaston Co.), 481, Latta Plantation (Mecklenburg Co.), 526–27
Farmers' Alliance, 44
Farmers' Union Stores (Chatham Co.), **260**, *260*
Farmington (Davie Co.), **419**
Farmville Plantation (Iredell Co.), **451**
Farrell's Store (Chatham Co.), **258**, *258*
Farrish-Lambeth House (Lee Co.), **267**
Faucette House (Orange Co.), **227**
Federal style and Federal period architecture, 32–34
—selected examples open to public: Union Tavern (Milton), 21, 184; Person Place (Louisburg), 28, 139; Utzman-Chambers House (Salisbury), 32–33, 429; Mordecai House (Raleigh), 34, 121; State Bank (Raleigh), 111; Haywood Hall (Raleigh), 111–12; Calvin Jones House (Wake Forest), 135; Stagville (Durham Co.), 214–15; Ayr Mount (Hillsborough), 226; Ruffin-Roulhac House (Hillsborough), 223–24; Moorefields (Hillsborough vic.), 227; James Bryant House (Moore Co.), 270–71; Shaw House (Moore Co.), 274; Boggan-Hammond House and Alexander Little Wing (Wadesboro), 299; Mendenhall Plantation House (Jamestown), 340; Haley House (Guilford Co.), 345; Wright Tavern (Rockingham Co.), 350; Old Salem, 372–78; Bethabara, 395–96, Josephus Hall House (Salisbury), 429; Kerr Mill (Rowan Co.), 439; Rosedale (Charlotte), 525; Latta Plantation (Mecklenburg Co.), 526
Feimster House (Newton), **454**
Fellheimer, Alfred (architect), 329, 388
Ferguson, Wade Hampton, House (Chatham Co.), **262**
Ferree, Tyson T. (architect), 341, 412
Ferrell House (Winston-Salem), **391**, *392*
Few, William P., 210
Fields, William, House (Greensboro), **336**
Findlater, Robert (mason), 108
First A.R.P. Church (Gastonia), **478**
First Baptist Church (Burlington), **243**
First Baptist Church (Charlotte), **509**, *509*
First Baptist Church (Cramerton), **488**
First Baptist Church (Durham), **196**

Foust, Julius I., Building (UNC Greensboro), **337**, *337*
Franklin Academy (Louisburg), **138**
Franklin Blvd., East (Gastonia), **481**
Franklin County, 86 (map), 138–45
Franklin Co. Courthouse (Louisburg), **138**
Franklin Street, East (Chapel Hill), **236–38**
Franklinton (Franklin Co.), **144–45**; Depot, **144–45**, *145*; Methodist Church, **145**
Franklinville (Randolph Co.), 311, **317–18**; Methodist Church, **318**; Mfg. Co., **317**
Fraternal order buildings: Masonic Temple Buildings (Raleigh), 112–13, 122; Adoniram Lodge (Granville Co.), 172; Eagle Lodge (Hillsborough), 220–21; Pittsboro Masonic Lodge, 256; Hank's Lodge (Franklinville), 318; Masonic Temple (Greensboro), 327; Woodmen of the World Lodge (Yadkin Co.), 405; Masonic Building (Shelby), 471
Frederick Apartments (Charlotte), **513**
Freedmen's Bureau, 119
Freedmen's villages, 65; Oberlin (Raleigh), 126–27; Method (Raleigh), 128–29
Freeman, Lewis, House (Pittsboro), **257**
Freeman, Ralf, 300
Freeman House and Cotton Gin (Franklin Co.), **144**
Freeman-White & Assoc. (architects), 506–7
Freeze, J. L. (blacksmith), 453
Frick & Co. (Salisbury), **427**
Friedberg Moravian Church (Davidson Co.), **410**
Fries, Adelaide, 380
Fries, Francis H., 351, 378, 380
Fries, Francis L., 252, 373, 378
Fries, Henry Elias, 378, 388–89, 390; House (Winston-Salem), **388–89**, *389*
Fries, John H., 378
Fries, John W., 380, 390
Fries family, 48, 56, 366, 369, 378
Fries Manufacturing & Power Co., 400
Fries Memorial (East Winston) Moravian Church (Winston-Salem), 387, **392**
Fritts Farm (Davidson Co.), **409**
Fuller, Buckminster (architect), 106
Fuller, George A., Co. (builder), 193
Fuller House (Louisburg), **139**
Fulton, Hamilton (engineer), 420
Fulton, Wilson, House (Danbury), **361**
Fulton Heights (Salisbury), **432**
Fulton Methodist Church (Davie Co.), **420**
Fuquay Mineral Spring (Wake Co.), **134**

Fuquay-Varina (Wake Co.), **134**
Furman, David (architect), 513
Furniture production, 55, 77, 459

Gabriel Mill and Cotton Gin Complex (Catawba Co.), **458**
Gaither Tobacco Factory (Mocksville), **417**
Galloway, John, House (Greensboro), **331**
Gambier, Richard (architect), 359
Gamble House (Durham), **204–5**, *205*
Gant, Allen, House (Burlington), **244**
Gantt, Harvey (architect), 505
Gardner, Governor O. Max, 471, 472
Gardner Baptist Church (Warren Co.), 159
Gardner-Webb College (Cleveland Co.), **475**
Garland-Buford House (Caswell Co.), **186**, *186*
Garner (Wake Co.), **137**; Depot, **137**; High School, **137**
Garrett, Walton, House (Kings Mountain), **474**
Garrett Farmstead (Alamance Co.), **251**
Gaskill, David L. (builder), 427
Gaskill House (Salisbury), **430**
Gaston, Judge William, 124, 477, 483
Gaston County, 99 (map), 477–90
Gaston Co. Courthouse, former (Dallas), **482**
Gaston Co. Courthouse, former (Gastonia), **478**, *478*
Gaston Co. Jail, old (Dallas), **482**
Gastonia (Gaston Co.), **477–81**, *478* (map); City Hall, **478**; Public Library, **479**; High School, *61*, 479, **480**
Gastonia Cotton Mfg. Co., 477
Gateway Building (Charlotte), **510**
Gattis, Samuel, House (Hillsborough), **221**
Gautier-Gilchrist House (Charlotte), **518**
Gavin, E. T. (architect), 510
Gem Theatre (Kannapolis), **496**
George, R. W., Mill (Stokes Co.), **365**
Georgian style, 34. *See also* Colonial period architecture; Federal style and Federal period architecture
Gerard Hall (UNC–Chapel Hill), **232**
Germanic building traditions, 14, 17–18; selected accessible examples: Old St. Paul's Lutheran Church (Catawba Co.), *4*, 455; Fourth House (Old Salem), *14*, 376–77; Michael Braun House (Rowan Co.), *17*, 436; Coble Barn (Guilford Co.), *27*, 339; Old Salem, 371–78; Bethabara (Forsyth Co.), 395–96; Bethania (Forsyth Co.),

Holt-Frost House (Burlington), **243–44**
Holt-McEwen House (Burlington), **244**
Holy Innocents Episcopal Church (Henderson), **162**
Holy Trinity Episcopal Church (Greensboro), **331**
Home Acres (Wake Co.), **134–35**, *135*
Home Bank Building (High Point), **341**
Home Federal Savings and Loan Building (Charlotte), **506–7**
Home Federal Savings Bank (Durham), **196**
Home Moravian Church (Winston-Salem), **373**, *371*, 383, 396
Home Security Life Insurance Building (Durham), **200–201**
Homestead, the (Lexington), **408**, *408*
Hood, Bishop James W., 122, 431
Hook, Charles C. & Frank Sawyer (architects), 330, 416, 431
Hook, Charles Christian (architect), 69, 192, 194, 202, 210, 275, 291, 304, 305, 306, 330, 416, 431, 460, 479, 484, 485, 494, 497, 504, 510, 511, 518, 519, 520, 521, 523
Hook, Walter W. (architect), 479, 506
Hook & Rogers (architects), 494, 497, 523
Hooper, William, 218, 222
Hooper-Kyser House (Chapel Hill), **237**
Hoover, H. (builder), 526
Hope Valley (Durham), **212**
Hopewell Presbyterian Church (Mecklenburg Co.), **526**, 530
Hopkins, Samuel (builder), 231
Hopper, J. W. (architect), 355
Horton Grove (Durham Co.), **214–15**, *215*
Hoskins House (Guilford Co.), **339**
Hotel Hadley (Siler City), **260–61**
Houck, M. Frank (builder), 140
House in the Horseshoe (Moore Co.), *16*, **271–72**
Houser, Charles (bricklayer), 375
Houston, William, House (Union Co.), **310**
Houston-Redfearn House (Monroe), **306**
Howell-Brown-Sanford-Larew House (Mocksville), **418**
Howell House (Winston-Salem), **392**
Hoyle, Eli, House (Gaston Co.), **482**
Hoyle Family House (Gaston Co.), **482**
Huff, Elias Kerner, House (Kernersville), **399**
Huff, Jonathan, House (Yadkin Co.), **402–3**
Hughes, Raleigh J. (architect), 346
Hughes Academy (Hillsborough), **224**

Humphreys, Ira, Law Office (Wentworth), **350**
Humphries, C. Gilbert (architect), 370, 392
Hunt, Lloyd Rainey, House (Lexington), **409**
Hunt, Reuben Harrison (architect), 196
Hunter, Herbert B. (architect), 243, 254, 344, 345, 413
Hunter, T. Houston (carpenter), 397
Hunter & Gordon (architects), 514
Hunting lodges, 347
Huntsville (Yadkin Co.), **404–5**; Methodist Church, **404**
Hurd, Bryant (architect), 360
Hurd, Thad (architect), 127
Hurleman, Gordon (landscape architect), 360
Huston & McKnight (builders), 243
Hydroelectric power, 56–57
—selected dams and power plants: Lake Tillery, (Montgomery Co.), 282; Narrows (Stanly Co.), 287; Blewett Falls (Anson Co.), 301; Idols (Forsyth Co.), 400; High Rock (Davidson Co.), 412–13; Lookout Shoals (Iredell Co.), 453; Mountain Island (Gaston Co.), 483
Hylehurst (Winston-Salem), **380**, *380*

Iceman House (Monroe), **306**
Idlewild (Raleigh), **121**
Idols (Fries) Hydroelectric Plant (Forsyth Co.), 56, 378, **400**
Imperial Tobacco Co. (Durham), **199**, *200*
Imperial Tobacco Co. (Oxford), **170**
Independence Park (Charlotte), **521–22**
Indera (Maline) Mills (Winston-Salem), **378**
Industrial production, 24, 48–50, *49*, 77
Ingles, Harry C. (architect), 360
Ingleside (Lincoln Co.), **469–70**, *470*
Ingram, Benjamin, House (Anson Co.), **301**
Inns and taverns: Union Tavern (Milton), 21, 184; Colonial Inn (Hillsborough), 221; Yellow House (Pittsboro), 256–57; Ellerbe Springs Hotel (Richmond Co.), 296; Burns Inn (Wadesboro), 298; Wright Tavern, (Wentworth), 349–50; Salem Tavern (Winston-Salem), 375; Brummel's Inn (Davidson Co.), 411; Tyro Tavern (Davidson Co.), 413–14; The Inn (Davidson), 528
Insurance Building (Wake Co. Office Building), **113**, *114*
Internal improvements, 20
International style, 71
—selected examples: Wachovia Building

St. Stephen's Episcopal Church (Oxford), **168**, 169

St. Theresa neighborhood (Durham), **206**

St. Thomas's Episcopal Church (Sanford), **265**

Salem (Forsyth Co.), 366, **370–79**; Town Hall, **379**, *379*

Salem Academy and College (Winston-Salem), 59, 60, 373, **374**; Main Hall, Girls' School, **373**, *371*, 526

Salem Boys' School (Winston-Salem), **377**

Salem Cemetery (Winston-Salem), **377**

Salem Cotton Mill (Winston-Salem), 24, **378**

Salem Methodist Church (Granville Co.), **172–73**, *173*

Salem Tavern (Winston-Salem), 373, **375**, *375*

Salem Union Church (Lincoln Co.), **466–67**

Salisbury (Rowan Co.), 10, **423–34**, 425 (map); Passenger Depot, **427**, *427*; Female Academy, **429**; High School, **432**

Salter, James A. (architect), 106, 114, 116, 118, 126, 463

Salvation Army Building (Greensboro), **329**

Sandy Creek Baptist Meeting House (Randolph Co.), 280, **316**, *316*

Sandy Plain (Wake Co.), **134**

Sanford (Lee Co.), **263–65**; Town Hall, **263**, *263*; Passenger Depot, **264**; High School, **265**

Sanford, Hugh, House (Mocksville), **418**

San Souci (Hillsborough), **225**

Sapona Mfg. Co. (Randolph Co.), **317**

Satterfield, Howard (builder-architect), 106, 131, 153

Saunders, Romulus, 124, 184

Savannah Methodist Church (Anson Co.), **300–301**

Sawtooth Building (Winston-Salem), **384**

Sawyer, Frank (architect), 330, 416, 431

Saxapahaw Mill and Village (Alamance Co.), **250**

Sayre, Christopher Gadsden (architect), 123, 150, 264, 269, 338, 432

Scales, A. M., Houses (Greensboro), **332, 338**

Scales, Governor Alfred Moore, Law Office (Madison), **350–51**

Scales Fine Arts Building (WFU, Winston-Salem), **394**

Scarborough, J. C., House (Durham), **206**

Schaub-Krause House (Bethabara), **395–96**, *396*

Schenck, Judge David, 330–31, 339

Schenck-Warlick Mill (Lincoln Co.), 463, 470

Schiele Museum of Natural History (Gastonia), **481**

Schlosser, Leopold (stonemason), 331

School of Design (NCSU, Raleigh), 77, 78, 106, 129, 131

Schools. *See* Academies; Colleges and universities; Public Schools; Rosenwald, Julius, Fund

Schroff, Max (architect), 377

Schwend, Louis (architect), 69, 444, 445, 447

Scott, Caudill Rowlett (architect), 394

Scott, Henry, and sons (builders), 271

Scott, Hugh Reid, House (Reidsville), **359**

Scott, Governor Kerr, Farm (Alamance Co.), **249–50**

Scott, Governor Robert, 250

Scott House (Charlotte), **518**

Scott-Mebane Mfg. Co. (Graham), **240**

Scott School (Madison), **351**

Seaboard (Raleigh & Gaston) Building (Raleigh), **118**

Seaboard Freight Depot (Sanford), **264**

Seaboard Railroad Depot (Raleigh), **120**

Sears, Thomas (landscape designer), 389, 391, 392, 393, 394, 400

Sears & Roebuck Co., 295

Sebastian House (Greensboro), **335**

Second Empire style, 66–67

—selected accessible examples: U.S. (Century) Post Office (Raleigh), 113; Heck-Andrews House (Raleigh), 118–19; Dodd-Hinsdale House (Raleigh), 116–17; Page-Walker Hotel (Cary), 133; Union Co. Courthouse (Monroe), 304–5; Cabarrus Co. Courthouse (Concord), 491

Second Presbyterian Church (Lincolnton), **465**

Sedgefield (Guilford Co.), **339**; Country Club, **339**, *339*

Self & Hoffman Building (Cherryville), **489**, *489*

Self-Trott House (Newton), **455**

Senlac (Chapel Hill), **235–36**

Separk, Joseph, House (Gastonia), **479**

Set-Back Room (Anson Co.), **302**

Settle, Judge Thomas, II, 350

Settlement patterns and ethnic groups, 4, 9–13, 17; Maps depicting, 11–12; *See also individual counties*

Settlers' Cemetery (Charlotte), **510**

Setzer School (Salisbury), 434

Seven Hearths (Hillsborough), **224**